Beginning Java 8 Language Features

Lambda Expressions, Inner Classes, Threads, I/O, Collections, and Streams

Kishori Sharan

Beginning Java 8 Language Features: Lambda Expressions, Inner Classes, Threads, I/O, Collections, and Streams

ISBN-13 (pbk): 978-1-4302-6658-7

ISBN-13 (electronic): 978-1-4302-6659-4

Publisher: Heinz Weinheimer
Lead Editor: Steve Anglin
Development Editor: Matthew Moodie
Technical Reviewers: Jeff Friesen, John Zukowski
Editorial Board: Steve Anglin, Mark Beckner, Ewan Buckingham, Gary Cornell, Louise Corrigan, James T. DeWolf, Jonathan Gennick, Jonathan Hassell, Robert Hutchinson, Michelle Lowman, James Markham, Matthew Moodie, Jeff Olson, Jeffrey Pepper, Douglas Pundick, Ben Renow-Clarke, Dominic Shakeshaft, Gwenan Spearing, Matt Wade, Steve Weiss
Coordinating Editors: Anamika Panchoo
Copy Editor: Mary Behr
Compositor: SPi Global
Indexer: SPi Global
Artist: SPi Global
Cover Designer: Anna Ishchenko

Distributed to the book trade worldwide by Springer Science+Business Media New York, 233 Spring Street, 6th Floor, New York, NY 10013. Phone 1-800-SPRINGER, fax (201) 348-4505, e-mail orders-ny@springer-sbm.com, or visit www.springeronline.com. Apress Media, LLC is a California LLC and the sole member (owner) is Springer Science + Business Media Finance Inc (SSBM Finance Inc). SSBM Finance Inc is a Delaware corporation.

For information on translations, please e-mail rights@apress.com, or visit www.apress.com.

Apress and friends of ED books may be purchased in bulk for academic, corporate, or promotional use. eBook versions and licenses are also available for most titles. For more information, reference our Special Bulk Sales–eBook Licensing web page at www.apress.com/bulk-sales.

Any source code or other supplementary materials referenced by the author in this text is available to readers at www.apress.com. For detailed information about how to locate your book's source code, go to www.apress.com/source-code/.

To My parents, Ram Vinod Singh and Pratibha Devi

Contents at a Glance

Contents

About the Author

Kishori Sharan is a senior software consultant at Doozer, Inc. He holds a Master of Science in Computer Information Systems from Troy State University in Montgomery, Alabama. He is a Sun Certified Java Programmer and Sybase Certified PowerBuilder Developer Professional. He specializes in developing enterprise application using Java SE, Java EE, PowerBuilder, and Oracle database. He has been working in the software industry for over 16 years. He has helped several clients to migrate legacy applications to the Web. He loves writing technical books in his free time. He maintains his web site at www.jdojo.com where he posts blogs on Java and JavaFX.

About the Technical Reviewers

Jeff Friesen is a freelance tutor, author, and software developer with an emphasis on Java, Android, and HTML5. In addition to writing several books for Apress and serving as a technical reviewer for other Apress books, Jeff has written numerous articles on Java and other technologies for JavaWorld (`www.javaworld.com`), informIT (`www.informit.com`), java.net, SitePoint (`www.sitepoint.com`), and others. Jeff can be contacted via his website at tutortutor.ca.

John Zukowski is currently a software engineer with TripAdvisor, the world's largest travel site (`www.tripadvisor.com`). He has been playing with Java technologies for 20 years now and is the author of 10 Java-related books. His books cover Java 6, Java Swing, Java Collections, and JBuilder from Apress, Java AWT from O'Reilly, and introductory Java from Sybex. He lives outside Boston, Massachusetts and has a Master's degree in Software Engineering from The Johns Hopkins University. You can follow him on Twitter at `http://twitter.com/javajohnz`.

Acknowledgments

My heartfelt thanks are due to my father-in-law, Mr. Jim Baker, for displaying extraordinary patience in reading the initial draft of the book. I am very grateful to him for spending so much of his valuable time teaching me quite a bit of English grammar that helped me produce better material.

I would like to thank my friend Richard Castillo for his hard work in reading my initial draft of the book and weeding out several mistakes. Richard was instrumental in running all examples and pointing out errors.

My wife, Ellen, was always patient when I spent long hours at my computer desk working on this book. She would happily bring me snacks, fruit, and a glass of water every 30 minutes or so to sustain me during that period. I want to thank her for all of her support in writing this book. She also deserves my sincere thanks for letting me sometimes seclude myself on weekends so I could focus on this book.

I would like to thank my family members and friends for their encouragement and support for writing this book: my elder brothers, Janki Sharan and Dr. Sita Sharan; my sister and brother-in-law, Ratna and Abhay; my nephews Babalu, Dabalu, Gaurav, Saurav, and Chitranjan; my friends Shivashankar Ravindranath, Kannan Somasekar, Mahbub Choudhury, Biju Nair, Srinivas Kakkera, Anil Kumar Singh, Chris Coley, Willie Baptiste, Rahul Jain, Larry Brewster, Greg Langham, Ram Atmakuri, LaTondra Okeke, Rahul Nagpal, Ravi Datla, Prakash Chandra, and many more friends not mentioned here.

My sincere thanks are due to the wonderful team at Apress for their support during the publication of this book. Thanks to Anamika Panchoo, the Senior Coordinating Editor, for providing excellent support and for being exceptionally patient with me when I asked her so many questions in the beginning, Thanks to Matthew Moodie, Jeff Friesen, and John Zukowski for their technical insights and feedback during the editing process. My special thanks to Kevin Shea, the coordinating editor who filled in for Anamika for a few months and brought in Jeff as an additional technical reviewer to expedite the technical reviews. Last but not least, my sincere thanks to Steve Anglin, the Lead Editor at Apress, for taking the initiative for the publication of this book.

Foreword

The evolving Java language has much to offer, and its wealth of features can overwhelm even advanced Java developers. Oracle's recent Java 8 release has increased this wealth by offering exciting new features such as lambdas and the Streams API.

Perhaps you already know the basics of this language (e.g., types, operators, statements, and a few assorted APIs) and want to learn more about Java without becoming too overwhelmed. If so, I heartily recommend that you check out this book by author Kishori Sharan.

Kishori provides a solid introduction to annotations, inner classes, reflection, generics, lambdas, threads, I/O, archive files, New I/O, New I/O 2, garbage collection, the Collections Framework, and the Streams API. You'll discover many aspects of the Java language that may be new to you (e.g., intersection types and how the compiler implements inner classes), and you will definitely want to augment your basic Java knowledge with these more advanced language/API topics to increase your desirability as a Java developer. *Beginning Java 8 Language Features* is one book that definitely deserves a place on your bookshelf.

—Jeff Friesen
June, 2014

Introduction

How This Book Came About

My first encounter with the Java programming language was during a one-week Java training session in 1997. I did not get a chance to use Java in a project until 1999. I read two Java books and took a Java 2 Programmer certification examination. I did very well on the test, scoring 95 percent. The three questions that I missed on the test made me realize that the books I read did not adequately cover all of the details on all of the necessary Java topics. I made up my mind to write a book on the Java programming language. So, I formulated a plan to cover most of the topics that a Java developer needs understand to use the Java programming language effectively in a project, as well as to get a certification. I initially planned to cover all essential topics in Java in 700 to 800 pages.

As I progressed, I realized that a book covering most of the Java topics in detail could not be written in 700 to 800 hundred pages. One chapter that covered data types, operators, and statements spanned 90 pages. I was then faced with the question, "Should I shorten the content of the book or include all the details that I think a Java developer needs?" I opted for including all the details in the book, rather than shortening the content to keep the number of pages low. It has never been my intent to make lots of money from this book. I was never in a hurry to finish this book because that rush could have compromised the quality and the coverage of its contents. In short, I wrote this book to help the Java community understand and use the Java programming language effectively, without having to read many books on the same subject. I wrote this book with the plan that it would be a comprehensive one-stop reference for everyone who wants to learn and grasp the intricacies of the Java programming language.

One of my high school teachers used to tell us that if one wanted to understand a building, one must first understand the bricks, steel, and mortar that make up the building. The same logic applies to most of the things that we want to understand in our lives. It certainly applies to an understanding of the Java programming language. If you want to master the Java programming language, you must start by understanding its basic building blocks. I have used this approach throughout this book, endeavoring to build each topic by describing the basics first. In the book, you will rarely find a topic described without first learning its background. Wherever possible, I have tried to correlate the programming practices with activities in our daily life. Most books about the Java programming language either do not include any pictures at all or have only a few. I believe in the adage, "A picture is worth a thousand words." To a reader, a picture makes a topic easier to understand and remember. I have included plenty of illustrations in this book to aid readers in understanding and visualizing the contents. Developers who have little or no programming experience can have difficulty putting things together to make a complete program. Keeping them in mind, the book contains over 290 complete Java programs that are ready to be compiled and run.

I spent countless hours doing research for writing this book. My main sources of research were the Java Language Specification, white papers and articles on Java topics, and Java Specification Requests (JSRs). I also spent quite a bit of time reading the Java source code to learn more about some of the Java topics. Sometimes it took a few months to research a topic before I could write the first sentence on it. It was always fun to play with Java programs, sometimes for hours, to add them to the book.

Structure of the Book

This is the second book in the three-book Beginning Java series. This book contains 13 chapters. The chapters contain language-level topics of Java such as annotations, generics, lambda expressions, threads, I/O, collections, streams, etc. Chapters introduce Java topics in an increasing order of complexity. The new features of Java 8 are included wherever they fit in the chapter. The lambda expressions and Streams API, which were added in Java 8, are covered in depth.

After finishing this book, take your Java knowledge to the next level by learning the Java APIs, extensions, and libraries; all of this is covered in the last book in this series, *Beginning Java 8 APIs, Extensions, and Libraries* (ISBN 978-1-4302-6661-7).

Audience

This book is designed to be useful for anyone who wants to learn the Java programming language. If you are a beginner, with little or no programming background in Java, you are advised to read the companion book *Beginning Java 8 Fundamentals* before reading this book. This book contains topics of various degrees of complexity. As a beginner, if you find yourself overwhelmed while reading a section in a chapter, you can skip to the next section or the next chapter, and revisit it later when you gain more experience.

If you are a Java developer with an intermediate or advanced level of experience, you can jump to a chapter or to a section in a chapter directly. If a section uses an unfamiliar topic, you need to visit that topic before continuing the current one.

If you are reading this book to get a certification in the Java programming language, you need to read almost all of the chapters, paying attention to all of the detailed descriptions and rules. Most of the certification programs test your fundamental knowledge of the language, not the advanced knowledge. You need to read only those topics that are part of your certification test. Compiling and running over 290 complete Java programs will help you prepare for your certification.

If you are a student who is attending a class in the Java programming language, you should read the chapters of this book selectively. Some topics such as lambda expressions, collections, and streams are used extensively in developing Java applications, whereas some topics such as threads and archive files are infrequently used. You need to read only those chapters that are covered in your class syllabus. I am sure that you, as a Java student, do not need to read the entire book page by page.

How to Use This Book

This book is the beginning, not the end, of gaining the knowledge of the Java programming language. If you are reading this book, it means you are heading in the right direction to learn the Java programming language, which will enable you to excel in your academic and professional career. However, there is always a higher goal for you to achieve and you must constantly work hard to achieve it. The following quotations from some great thinkers may help you understand the importance of working hard and constantly looking for knowledge with both your eyes and mind open.

The learning and knowledge that we have, is, at the most, but little compared with that of which we are ignorant.

—Plato

True knowledge exists in knowing that you know nothing. And in knowing that you know nothing, that makes you the smartest of all.

—Socrates

Readers are advised to use the API documentation for the Java programming language as much as possible while using this book. The Java API documentation is where you will find a complete list of everything available in the Java class library. You can download (or view) the Java API documentation from the official web site of Oracle Corporation at www.oracle.com. While you read this book, you need to practice writing Java programs yourself. You can also practice by tweaking the programs provided in the book. It does not help much in your learning process if you just read this book and do not practice by writing your own programs. Remember that "practice makes perfect," which is also true in learning how to program in Java.

Source Code and Errata

Source code and errata for this book may be downloaded from www.apress.com/source-code.

Questions and Comments

Please direct all your questions and comments for the author to ksharan@jdojo.com.

■ ■ ■

CHAPTER 1

Annotations

In this chapter, you will learn

- What annotations are

- How to declare annotations

- How to use annotations

- What meta-annotations are and how to use them

- Commonly used annotations

- How to access annotations at runtime

- How to process annotations in source code

What Are Annotations?

Annotations were introduced in Java 5. Before I define annotations and discuss their importance in programming, let's discuss a simple example. Suppose you have an Employee class, which has a method called setSalary() that sets the salary of an employee. The method accepts a parameter of the type double. The following snippet of code shows a trivial implementation for the Employee class:

```
public class Employee {
        public void setSalary(double salary) {
                System.out.println("Employee.setSalary():" + salary);
        }
}
```

A Manager class inherits from the Employee class. You want to set the salary for managers differently. You decide to override the setSalary() method in the Manager class. The code for the Manager class is as follows:

```
public class Manager extends Employee {
        // Override setSalary() in the Employee class
        public void setSalary(int salary) {
                System.out.println("Manager.setSalary():" + salary);
        }
}
```

Note that there is a mistake in the above code for the Manager class, when you attempt to override the setSalary() method. (You'll correct the mistake shortly.) You have used the int data type as the parameter type for the incorrectly overridden method. It is time to set the salary for a manager. The following code is used to accomplish this:

```
Employee ken = new Manager();
int salary = 200;
ken.setSalary(salary);
```

```
Employee.setSalary():200.0
```

This snippet of code was expected to call the setSalary() method of the Manager class but the output does not show the expected result.

What went wrong in your code? The intention of defining the setSalary() method in the Manager class was to override the setSalary() method of the Employee class, not to overload it. You made a mistake. You used the type int as the parameter type in the setSalary() method, instead of the type double, in the Manager class. You put comments indicating your intention to override the method in the Manager class. However, comments do not stop you from making logical mistakes. You might spend, as every programmer does, hours and hours debugging errors resulting from this kind of logical mistake. Who can help you in such situations? Annotations might help you in a few situations like this. Let's rewrite your Manager class using an annotation. You do not need to know anything about annotations at this point. All you are going to do is add one word to your program. The following code is the modified version of the Manager class:

```
public class Manager extends Employee {
        @Override
        public void setSalary(int salary) {
                System.out.println("Manager.setSalary():" + salary);
        }
}
```

All you have added is a @Override annotation to the Manager class and removed the "dumb" comments. Trying to compile the revised Manager class results in a compile-time error that points to the use of the @Override annotation for the setSalary() method of the Manager class:

```
Manager.java:2: error: method does not override or implement a method from a supertype
        @Override
        ^
1 error
```

The use of the @Override annotation did the trick. The @Override annotation is used with a non-static method to indicate the programmer's intention to override the method in the superclass. At source code level, it serves the purpose of documentation. When the compiler comes across the @Override annotation, it makes sure that the method really overrides the method in the superclass. If the method annotated does not override a method in the superclass, the compiler generates an error. In your case, the setSalary(int salary) method in the Manager class does not override any method in the superclass Employee. This is the reason that you got the error. You may realize that using an annotation is as simple as documenting the source code. However, they have compiler support. You can use them to instruct the compiler to enforce some rules. Annotations provide benefits much more than you have seen in this example.

Let's go back to the compile-time error. You can fix the error by doing one of the following two things:

- You can remove the @Override annotation from the setSalary(int salary) method in the Manager class. It will make the method an overloaded method, not a method that overrides its superclass method.

- You can change the method signature from setSalary(int salary) to setSalary(double salary).

Since you want to override the setSalary() method in the Manager class, use the second option and modify the Manager class as follows:

```java
public class Manager extends Employee {
        @Override
        public void setSalary(double salary) {
                System.out.println("Manager.setSalary():" + salary);
        }
}
```

Now the following code will work as expected:

```java
Employee ken = new Manager();
int salary = 200;
ken.setSalary(salary);
```

```
Manager.setSalary():200.0
```

Note that the @Override annotation in the setSalary() method of the Manager class saves you debugging time. Suppose you change the method signature in the Employee class. If the changes in the Employee class make this method no longer overridden in the Manager class, you will get the same error when you compile the Manager class again. Are you starting to understand the power of annotations? With this background in mind, let's start digging deep into annotations.

According to the Merriam Webster dictionary, the meaning of annotation is

"A note added by way of comment or explanation".

This is exactly what an annotation is in Java. It lets you associate (or annotate) metadata (or notes) to the program elements in a Java program. The program elements may be a package, a class, an interface, a field of a class, a local variable, a method, a parameter of a method, an enum, an annotation, a type parameter in a generic type/method declaration, a type use, etc. In other words, you can annotate any declaration or type use in a Java program. An annotation is used as a modifier in a declaration of a program element like any other modifiers (public, private, final, static, etc.). Unlike a modifier, an annotation does not modify the meaning of the program elements. It acts like a decoration or a note for the program element that it annotates.

An annotation differs from regular documentation in many ways. A regular documentation is only for humans to read and it is "dumb." It has no intelligence associated with it. If you misspell a word, or state something in the documentation and do just the opposite in the code, you are on your own. It is very difficult and impractical to read the elements of documentation programmatically at runtime. Java lets you generate Javadocs from your documentation and that's it for regular documentation. This does not mean that you do not need to document your programs. You do need regular documentation. At the same time, you need a way to enforce your intent using a documentation-like mechanism. Your documentation should be available to the compiler and the runtime. An annotation serves this purpose. It is human readable, which serves as documentation. It is compiler readable, which lets the compiler verify the intention of the programmer; for example, the compiler makes sure that the programmer has really overridden the method if it comes across a @Override annotation for a method. Annotations are also available at runtime so that a program can read and use it for any purpose it wants. For example, a tool can read annotations and generate boilerplate code. If you have worked with Enterprise JavaBeans (EJB), you know the pain of keeping all the interfaces and classes in sync and adding entries to XML configuration files. EJB 3.0 uses annotations to generate the boilerplate code, which makes EJB development painless for programmers. Another example of an annotation being used in a framework/tool is JUnit version 4.0. JUnit is a unit test framework for Java programs. It uses annotations to mark methods that are test cases. Before that, you had to follow a naming convention for the test case methods. Annotations have a variety of uses, which are documentation, verification, and enforcement by the compiler, the runtime validation, code generation by frameworks/tools, etc.

To make an annotation available to the compiler and the runtime, an annotation has to follow rules. In fact, an annotation is another type like a class and an interface. As you have to declare a class type or an interface type before you can use it, you must also declare an annotation type.

An annotation does not change the semantics (or meaning) of the program element that it annotates. In that sense, an annotation is like a comment, which does not affect the way the annotated program element works. For example, the @Override annotation for the setSalary() method did not change the way the method works. You (or a tool/framework) can change the behavior of a program based on an annotation. In such cases, you make use of the annotation rather than the annotation doing anything on its own. The point is that an annotation by itself is always passive.

Declaring an Annotation Type

Declaring an annotation type is similar to declaring an interface type, except for some restrictions. According to Java specification, an annotation type declaration is a special kind of interface type declaration. You use the interface keyword, which is preceded by the @ sign (at sign) to declare an annotation type. The following is the general syntax for declaring an annotation type:

```
<modifiers> @ interface <annotation-type-name> {
        // Annotation type body goes here
}
```

The <modifiers> for an annotation declaration is the same as for an interface declaration. For example, you can declare an annotation type as public or package level. The @ sign and the interface keyword may be separated by whitespaces or they can be placed together. By convention, they are placed together as @interface. The interface keyword is followed by an annotation type name. It should be a valid Java identifier. The annotation type body is placed within braces.

Suppose you want to annotate your program elements with the version information, so you can prepare a report about new program elements added in a specific release of your product. To use a custom annotation type (as opposed to built-in annotation, such as @Override), you must declare it first. You want to include the major and the minor versions of the release in the version information. Listing 1-1 has the complete code for your first annotation declaration.

Listing 1-1. The Declaration of an Annotation Type Named Version

```
// Version.java
package com.jdojo.annotation;

public @interface Version {
        int major();
        int minor();
}
```

Compare the declaration of the Version annotation with the declaration of an interface. It differs from an interface definition only in one aspect: it uses the @ sign before its name. You have declared two abstract methods in the Version annotation type: major() and minor(). Abstract methods in an annotation type are known as its *elements*. You can think about it in another way: an annotation can declare zero or more elements, and they are declared as abstract methods. The abstract method names are the names of the elements of the annotation type. You have declared two elements, major and minor, for the Version annotation type. The data types of both elements are int.

▨ **Note**   Although it is allowed to declare static and default methods in interface types, they are not allowed in annotation types.

You need to compile the annotation type. When Version.java file is compiled, it will produce a Version.class file. The simple name of your annotation type is Version and its fully qualified name is com.jdojo.annotation.Version. Using the simple name of an annotation type follows the rules of any other types (e.g. classes, interfaces, etc.). You will need to import an annotation type the same way you import any other types.

How do you use an annotation type? You might be thinking that you will declare a new class that will implement the Version annotation type, and you will create an object of that class. You might be relieved to know that you do not need to take any additional steps to use the Version annotation type. An annotation type is ready to be used as soon as it is declared and compiled. To create an instance of an annotation type and use it to annotate a program element, you need to use the following syntax:

```
@annotationType(name1=value1, name2=value2, names3=values3...)
```

The annotation type is preceded by an @ sign. It is followed by a list of comma-separated name=value pairs enclosed in parentheses. The name in a name=value pair is the name of the element declared in the annotation type and the value is the user supplied value for that element. The name=value pairs do not have to appear in the same order as they are declared in the annotation type, although by convention name=value pairs are used in the same order as the declaration of the elements in the annotation type.

Let's use an annotation of the Version type, which has the major element value as 1 and the minor element value as 0. The following is an instance of your Version annotation type:

```
@Version(major=1, minor=0)
```

You can rewrite the above annotation as @Version(minor=0, major=1) without changing its meaning. You can also use the annotation type's fully qualified name as

```
@com.jdojo.annotation.Version(major=0, minor=1)
```

You use as many instances of the Version annotation type in your program as you want. For example, you have a VersionTest class, which was added to your application since release 1.0. You have added some methods and instance variables in release 1.1. You can use your Version annotation to document additions to the VersionTest class in different releases. You can annotate your class declaration as

```
@Version(major=1, minor=0)
public class VersionTest {
        // Code goes here
}
```

An annotation is added in the same way you add a modifier for a program element. You can mix the annotation for a program element with its other modifiers. You can place annotations in the same line as other modifiers or in a separate line. It is a personal choice whether you use a separate line to place the annotations or you mix them with other modifiers. By convention, annotations for a program element are placed before all other modifiers. Let's follow this convention and place the annotation in a separate line by itself, as shown above. Both of the following declarations are technically the same:

```
// Style #1
@Version(major=1, minor=0) public class VersionTest {
        // Code goes here
}

// Style #2
public @Version(major=1, minor=0) class VersionTest {
        // Code goes here
}
```

Listing 1-2 shows the sample code for the VersionTest class.

Listing 1-2. A VersionTest Class with Annotated Elements

```
// VersionTest.java
package com.jdojo.annotation;

// Annotation for class VersionTest
@Version(major = 1, minor = 0)
public class VersionTest {
        // Annotation for instance variable xyz
        @Version(major = 1, minor = 1)
        private int xyz = 110;

        // Annotation for constructor VersionTest()
        @Version(major = 1, minor = 0)
        public VersionTest() {
        }

        // Annotation for constructor VersionTest(int xyz)
        @Version(major = 1, minor = 1)
        public VersionTest(int xyz) {
                this.xyz = xyz;
        }

        // Annotation for the printData() method
        @Version(major = 1, minor = 0)
        public void printData() {
        }

        // Annotation for the setXyz() method
        @Version(major = 1, minor = 1)
        public void setXyz(int xyz) {
```

```
                        // Annotation for local variable newValue
                        @Version(major = 1, minor = 2)
                        int newValue = xyz;

                        this.xyz = xyz;
            }
}
```

In Listing 1-2, you use @Version annotation to annotate the class declaration, class field, constructors, and methods. There is nothing extraordinary in the code for the VersionTest class. You just added the @Version annotation to various elements of the class. The VersionTest class would work the same, even if you remove all @Version annotations. It is to be emphasized that using annotations in your program does not change the behavior of the program at all. The real benefit of annotations comes from reading it during compilation and runtime.

What do you do next with the Version annotation type? You have declared it as a type. You have used it in your VersionTest class. Your next step is to read it at runtime. Let's defer this step for now; I will cover it in detail in a later section.

Restrictions on Annotation Types

An annotation type is a special type of interface with some restrictions. I will cover some of the restrictions in the sections to follow.

Restriction #1

An annotation type cannot inherit from another annotation type. That is, you cannot use the extends clause in an annotation type declaration. The following declaration will not compile because you have used the extends clause to declare WrongVersion annotation type:

```
// Won't compile
public @interface WrongVersion extends BasicVersion {
        int extended();
}
```

Every annotation type implicitly inherits the java.lang.annotation.Annotation interface, which is declared as follows:

```
package java.lang.annotation;

public interface Annotation {
        boolean equals(Object obj);
        int hashCode();
        String toString();
        Class<? extends Annotation> annotationType();
}
```

This implies that all of the four methods declared in the Annotation interface are available in all annotation types. A word of caution needs to be mentioned here. You declare elements for an annotation type using abstract method declarations. The methods declared in the Annotation interface do not declare elements in an annotation type. Your Version annotation type has only two elements, major and minor, which are declared in the Version

type itself. You cannot use the annotation type Version as @Version(major=1, minor=2, toString="Hello").
The Version annotation type does not declare toString as an element. It inherits the toString() method from the
Annotation interface.

Restriction #2

Method declarations in an annotation type cannot specify any parameters. A method declares an element for the
annotation type. An element in an annotation type lets you associate a data value to an annotation's instance.
A method declaration in an annotation is not called to perform any kind of processing. Think of an element as an
instance variable in a class having two methods, a setter and a getter, for that instance variable. For an annotation,
the Java runtime creates a proxy class that implements the annotation type (which is an interface). Each annotation
instance is an object of that proxy class. The method you declare in your annotation type becomes the getter method
for the value of that element you specify in the annotation. The Java runtime will take care of setting the specified
value for the annotation elements. Since the goal of declaring a method in an annotation type is to work with a data
element, you do not need to (and are not allowed to) specify any parameters in a method declaration. The following
declaration of an annotation type would not compile because it declares a concatenate() method, which accepts
two parameters:

```
// Won't compile
public @interface WrongVersion {
        // Cannot have parameters
        String concatenate(int major, int minor);
}
```

Restriction #3

Method declarations in an annotation type cannot have a throws clause. A method in an annotation type is defined
to represent a data element. Throwing an exception to represent a data value does not make sense. The following
declaration of an annotation type would not compile because the major() method has a throws clause:

```
// Won't compile
public @interface WrongVersion {
        int major() throws Exception; // Cannot have a throws clause
        int minor(); // OK
}
```

Restriction #4

The return type of a method declared in an annotation type must be one of the following types:

- Any primitive type: byte, short, int, long, float, double, boolean, and char

- java.lang.String

- java.lang.Class

- An enum type

- An annotation type

- An array of any of the above mentioned type, for example, String[], int[], etc. The return
  type cannot be a nested array. For example, you cannot have a return type of String[][] or
  int[][].

The return type of Class needs a little explanation. Instead of the Class type, you can use a generic return type that will return a user-defined class type. Suppose you have a Test class and you want to declare the return type of a method in an annotation type of type Test. You can declare the annotation method as shown:

```
public @interface GoodOne {
        Class element1(); // Any Class type
        Class<Test> element2(); // Only Test class type
        Class<? extends Test> element3(); // Test or its subclass type
}
```

Restriction #5

An annotation type cannot declare a method, which would be equivalent to overriding a method in the Object class or the Annotation interface.

Restriction #6

An annotation type cannot be generic.

Default Value of an Annotation Element

The syntax for an annotation type declaration lets you specify a default value for its elements. You are not required to specify a value for an annotation element that has a default value specified in its declaration. The default value for an element can be specified using the following general syntax:

```
<modifiers> @interface <annotation type name> {
        <data-type> <element-name>() default <default-value>;
}
```

The keyword default is used to specify the default value. The default value must be of the type compatible to the data type for the element.

Suppose you have a product that is not frequently released, so it is less likely that it will have a minor version other than zero. You can simplify your Version annotation type by specifying a default value for its minor element as zero, as shown:

```
public @interface Version {
        int major();
        int minor() default 0; // Set zero as default value for minor
}
```

Once you set the default value for an element, you do not have to pass its value when you use an annotation of this type. Java will use the default value for the missing value of the element.

```
@Version(major=1) // minor is zero, which is its default value
@Version(major=2) // minor is zero, which is its default value
@Version(major=2, minor=1) // minor is 1, which is the specified value
```

All default values must be compile-time constants. How do you specify the default value for an array type? You need to use the array initializer syntax. The following snippet of code shows how to specify default values for an array and other data types:

```
// Shows how to assign default values to elements of different types
public @interface DefaultTest {
        double d() default 12.89;
        int num() default 12;
        int[] x() default {1, 2};
        String s() default "Hello";
        String[] s2() default {"abc", "xyz"};
        Class c() default Exception.class;
        Class[] c2() default {Exception.class, java.io.IOException.class};
}
```

The default value for an element is not compiled with the annotation. It is read from the annotation type definition when a program attempts to read the value of an element at runtime. For example, when you use @Version(major=2), this annotation instance is compiled as is. It does not add minor element with its default value as zero. In other words, this annotation is not modified to @Version(major=2, minor=0) at the time of compilation. However, when you read the value of the minor element for this annotation at runtime, Java will detect that the value for the minor element was not specified. It will consult the Version annotation type definition for its default value and return the default value. The implication of this mechanism is that if you change the default value of an element, the changed default value will be read whenever a program attempts to read it, even if the annotated program was compiled before you changed the default value.

Annotation Type and Its Instances

I use the terms "annotation type" and "annotation" frequently. *Annotation type* is a type like an interface. Theoretically, you can use annotation type wherever you can use an interface type. Practically, we limit its use only to annotate program elements. You can declare a variable of an annotation type as shown:

```
Version v = null; // Here, Version is an annotation type
```

Like an interface, you can also implement an annotation type in a class. However, you are never supposed to do that, as it will defeat the purpose of having an annotation type as a new construct. You should always implement an interface in a class, not an annotation type. Technically, the code in Listing 1-3 for the DoNotUseIt class is valid. This is just for the purpose of demonstration. Do not implement an annotation in a class even if it works.

Listing 1-3. A Class Implementing an Annotation Type

```
// DoNotUseIt.java
package com.jdojo.annotation;

import java.lang.annotation.Annotation;

public class DoNotUseIt implements Version {
        // Implemented method from the Version annotation type
        @Override
        public int major() {
                return 0;
        }
```

```
        // Implemented method from the Version annotation type
        @Override
        public int minor() {
                return 0;
        }

        // Implemented method from the Annotation annotation type,
        // which is the supertype of the Version annotation type
        @Override
        public Class<? extends Annotation> annotationType() {
                return null;
        }
}
```

The Java runtime implements the annotation type to a proxy class. It provides you with an object of a class that implements your annotation type for each annotation you use in your program. You must distinguish between an annotation type and instances (or objects) of that annotation type. In your example, Version is an annotation type. Whenever you use it as @Version(major=2, minor=4), you are creating an instance of the Version annotation type. An instance of an annotation type is simply referred to as an *annotation*. For example, we say that @Version(major=2, minor=4) is an annotation or an instance of the Version annotation type. An annotation should be easy to use in a program. The syntax @Version(...) is shorthand for creating a class, creating an object of that class, and setting the values for its elements. I will cover how to get to the object of an annotation type at runtime later in this chapter.

Using Annotations

In this section, I will discuss the details of using different types of elements while declaring annotation types. Remember that the supplied value for elements of an annotation must be a compile-time constant expression and you cannot use null as the value for any type of element in an annotation.

Primitive Types

The data type of an element in an annotation type could be any of the primitive data types: byte, short, int, long, float, double, boolean, and char. The Version annotation type declares two elements, major and minor, and both are of int data type. The following code snippet declares an annotation type called PrimitiveAnnTest:

```
public @interface PrimitiveAnnTest {
        byte a();
        short b();
        int c();
        long d();
        float e();
        double f();
        boolean g();
        char h();
}
```

You can use an instance of the PrimitiveAnnTest type as

```
@PrimitiveAnnTest(a=1, b=2, c=3, d=4, e=12.34F, f=1.89, g=true, h='Y')
```

You can use a compile-time constant expression to specify the value for an element of an annotation. The following two instances of the Version annotation are valid, and have the same values for their elements:

```
@Version(major=2+1, minor=(int)13.2)
@Version(major=3, minor=13)
```

String Types

You can use an element of the String type in an annotation type. Listing 1-4 contains the code for an annotation type called Name. It has two elements, first and last, which are of the String type.

Listing 1-4. Name Annotation Type, Which Has Two Elements, first and last, of the String Type

```
package com.jdojo.annotation;

public @interface Name {
        String first();
        String last();
}
```

The following snippet of code shows how to use the Name annotation type in a program:

```
@Name(first="John", last="Jacobs")
public class NameTest {
        @Name(first="Wally", last="Inman")
        public void aMethod() {
                // More code goes here...
        }
}
```

It is valid to use the string concatenation operator (+) in the value expression for an element of a String type. The following two annotations are equivalent:

```
@Name(first="Jo" + "hn", last="Ja" + "cobs")
@Name(first="John", last="Jacobs")
```

The following use of the @Name annotation is not valid because the expression new String("John") is not a compile-time constant expression:

```
@Name(first=new String("John"), last="Jacobs")
```

Class Types

The benefits of using the Class type as an element in an annotation type are not obvious. Typically, it is used where a tool/framework reads the annotations with elements of a class type and performs some specialized processing on the element's value or generates code. Let's go through a simple example of using a class type element. Suppose you are writing a test runner tool for running test cases for a Java program. Your annotation will be used in writing test cases. If your test case must throw an exception when it is invoked by the test runner, you need to use an annotation to indicate that. Let's create a DefaultException class as shown in Listing 1-5.

Listing 1-5. A DefaultException Class That Is Inherited from the Throwable Exception Class

```
// DefaultException.java
package com.jdojo.annotation;

public class DefaultException extends java.lang.Throwable {
        public DefaultException() {
        }

        public DefaultException(String msg) {
                super(msg);
        }
}
```

Listing 1-6 shows the code for a TestCase annotation type.

Listing 1-6. A TestCase Annotation Type Whose Instances Are Used to Annotate Test Case Methods

```
// TestCase.java
package com.jdojo.annotation;

import java.lang.annotation.ElementType;
import java.lang.annotation.Retention;
import java.lang.annotation.RetentionPolicy;
import java.lang.annotation.Target;

@Retention(RetentionPolicy.RUNTIME)
@Target(ElementType.METHOD)
public @interface TestCase {
        Class<? extends Throwable> willThrow() default DefaultException.class;
}
```

The return type of the willThrow element is defined as the wild card of the Throwable class, so that the user will specify only the Throwable class or its subclasses as the element's value. You could have used the Class type as the type of your willThrow element. However, that would have allowed the users of this annotation type to pass any class type as its value. Note that you have used two annotations, @Retention and @Target, for the TestCase annotation type. The @Retention annotation type specified that the @TestCase annotation would be available at runtime. It is necessary to use the retention policy of RUNTIME for your TestCase annotation type because it is meant for the test runner tool to read it at runtime. The @Target annotation states that the TestCase annotation can be used only to annotate methods. I will cover the @Retention and @Target annotation types in detail in later sections when I discuss meta-annotations. Listing 1-7 shows the use of your TestCase annotation type.

Listing 1-7. A Test Case That Uses the TestCase Annotations

```
// PolicyTestCases.java
package com.jdojo.annotation;

import java.io.IOException;

public class PolicyTestCases {
        // Must throw IOExceptionn
        @TestCase(willThrow=IOException.class)
        public static void testCase1(){
```

```
        // Code goes here
    }

    // We are not expecting any exception
    @TestCase()
    public static void testCase2(){
        // Code goes here
    }
}
```

The testCase1() method specifies, using the @TestCase annotation, that it will throw an IOException. The test runner tool will make sure that when it invokes this method, the method does throw an IOException. Otherwise, it will fail the test case. The testCase2() method does not specify that it will throw an exception. If it throws an exception when the test is run, the tool should fail this test case.

Enum Type

An annotation can have elements of an enum type. Suppose you want to declare an annotation type called Review that can describe the code review status of a program element. Let's assume that it has a status element and it can have one of the four values: PENDING, FAILED, PASSED, and PASSEDWITHCHANGES. You can declare an enum as an annotation type member. Listing 1-8 shows the code for a Review annotation type.

Listing 1-8. An Annotation Type, Which Uses an enum Type Element

```
// Review.java
package com.jdojo.annotation;

public @interface Review {
    ReviewStatus status() default ReviewStatus.PENDING;
    String comments() default "";

    // ReviewStatus enum is a member of the Review annotation type
    public enum ReviewStatus {PENDING, FAILED, PASSED, PASSEDWITHCHANGES};
}
```

The Review annotation type declares a ReviewStatus enum type and the four review statuses are the elements of the enum. It has two elements, status and comments. The type of status element is the enum type ReviewStatus. The default value for the status element is ReviewStatus.PENDING. You have an empty string as the default value for the comments element.

Here are some of the instances of the Review annotation type. You will need to import the com.jdojo.annotation.Review.ReviewStatus enum in your program to use the simple name of the ReviewStatus enum type.

```
// Have default for status and comments. Maybe code is new
@Review()

// Leave status as Pending, but add some comments
@Review(comments="Have scheduled code review on June 3 2014")

// Fail the review with comments
@Review(status=ReviewStatus.FAILED, comments="Need to handle errors")
```

```
// Pass the review without changes
@Review(status=ReviewStatus.PASSED)
```

Here is the sample code that annotates a Test class indicating that it passed the code review:

```
import com.jdojo.annotation.Review.ReviewStatus;
import com.jdojo.annotation.Review;

@Review(status=ReviewStatus.PASSED)
public class Test {
        // Code goes here
}
```

Annotation Type

An annotation type can be used anywhere a type can be used in a Java program. For example, you can use an annotation type as the return type for a method. You can also use an annotation type as the type of an element inside another annotation type's declaration. Suppose you want to have a new annotation type called Description, which will include the name of the author, version, and comments for a program element. You can reuse your Name and Version annotation types as its name and version elements type. Listing 1-9 has code the for Description annotation type.

Listing 1-9. An Annotation Type Using Other Annotation Types as Data Type of Its Elements

```
// Description.java
package com.jdojo.annotation;

public @interface Description {
        Name name();
        Version version();
        String comments() default "";
}
```

To provide a value for an element of an annotation type, you need to use the syntax that is used to create an annotation type instance. For example, @Version(major=1, minor=2) creates an instance of the Version annotation. Note the nesting of an annotation inside another annotation in the following snippet of code:

```
@Description(name=@Name(first="John", last="Jacobs"),
             version=@Version(major=1, minor=2),
             comments="Just a test class")
public class Test {
        // Code goes here
}
```

Array Type Annotation Element

An annotation can have elements of an array type. The array type could be of one of the following types:

- A primitive type
- java.lang.String type
- java.lang.Class type
- An enum type
- An annotation type

You need to specify the value for an array element inside braces. Elements of the array are separated by a comma. Suppose you want to annotate your program elements with a short description of a list of things that you need to work on. Listing 1-10 creates a ToDo annotation type for this purpose.

Listing 1-10. *ToDo Annotation Type with String[ ] as Its Sole Element*

```
// ToDo.java
package com.jdojo.annotation;

public @interface ToDo {
        String[] items();
}
```

The following snippet of code shows how to use a @ToDo annotation:

```
@ToDo(items={"Add readFile method", "Add error handling"})
public class Test {
        // Code goes here
}
```

If you have only one element in the array, it is allowed to omit the braces. The following two annotation instances of the ToDo annotation type are equivalent:

```
@ToDo(items={"Add error handling"})
@ToDo(items="Add error handling")
```

■ **Tip**   If you do not have valid values to pass to an element of an array type, you can use an empty array. For example, @ToDo(items={}) is a valid annotation where the items element has been assigned an empty array.

No Null Value in an Annotation

You cannot use a null reference as a value for an element in an annotation. Note that it is allowed to use an empty string for the String type element and empty array for an array type element. Using the following annotations will result in compile-time errors:

```
@ToDo(items=null)
@Name(first=null, last="Jacobs")
```

Shorthand Annotation Syntax

The shorthand annotation syntax is little easier to use in a few circumstances. Suppose you have an annotation type Enabled with an element having a default value, as shown:

```
public @interface Enabled {
        boolean status() default true;
}
```

If you want to annotate a program element with the Enabled annotation type using the default value for its element, you can use the @Enabled() syntax. You do not need to specify the values for the status element because it has a default value. You can use shorthand in this situation, which allows you to omit the parentheses. You can just use @Enabled instead of using @Enabled(). The Enabled annotation can be used in either of the following two forms:

```
@Enabled
public class Test {
        // Code goes here
}

@Enabled()
public class Test {
        // Code goes here
}
```

An annotation type with only one element also has a shorthand syntax. You can use this shorthand as long as you adhere to a naming rule for the sole element in the annotation type. The name of the element must be value. If an annotation type has only one element that is named value, you can omit the name from name=value pair from your annotation. The following snippet of code declares a Company annotation type, which has only one element named value:

```
public @interface Company {
        String value(); // the element name is value
}
```

You can omit the name from name=value pair when you use the Company annotation, as shown below. If you want to use the element name with the Company annotation, you can always do so as @Company(value="Abc Inc.").

```
@Company("Abc Inc.")
public class Test {
        // Code goes here
}
```

You can use this shorthand of omitting the name of the element from annotations, even if the element data type is an array. Let's consider the following annotation type called Reviewers:

```
public @interface Reviewers {
        String[] value(); // the element name is value
}
```

Since the Reviewers annotation type has only one element, which is named value, you can omit the element name when you are using it.

```
// No need to specify name of the element
@Reviewers({"John Jacobs", "Wally Inman"})
public class Test {
        // Code goes here
}
```

You can also omit the braces if you specify only one element in the array for the value element of the Reviewers annotation type.

```
@Reviewers("John Jacobs")
public class Test {
        // Code goes here
}
```

You just saw several examples using the name of the element as value. Here is the general rule of omitting the name of the element in an annotation: if you supply only one value when using an annotation, the name of the element is assumed value. This means that you are not required to have only one element in the annotation type, which is named value, to omit its name in the annotations. If you have an annotation type, which has an element named value (with or without a default value) and all other elements have default values, you can still omit the name of the element in annotation instances of this type. Here are some examples to illustrate this rule:

```
public @interface A {
        String value();
        int id() default 10;
}

// Same as @A(value="Hello", id=10)
@A("Hello")
public class Test {
        // Code goes here
}

// Won't compile. Must use only one value to omit the element name
@A("Hello", id=16)
public class WontCompile {
        // Code goes here
}

// OK. Must use name=value pair when passing more than one value
@A(value="Hello", id=16)
public class Test {
        // Code goes here
}
```

Marker Annotation Types

A marker annotation type is an annotation type that does not declare any elements, not even one with a default value. Typically, a marker annotation is used by the annotation processing tools, which generate boilerplate code based on the marker annotation type.

```
public @interface Marker {
        // No element declarations
}
```

```
@Marker
public class Test {
        // Code goes here
}
```

Meta-Annotation Types

Meta-annotations types are annotation types, which are used to annotate other annotation types. The following annotation types are meta-annotation types:

- Target
- Retention
- Inherited
- Documented
- Repeatable
- Native

Meta-annotation types are part of the Java class library. They are declared in the package java.lang.annotation.

The Target Annotation Type

The Target annotation type is used to annotate an annotation type to specify the context in which the annotation type can be used. It has only one element named value. Its value element is an array of java.lang.annotation. ElementType enum type. Table 1-1 lists all constants in the ElementType enum.

Table 1-1. *List of Constants in the java.lang.annotation.ElementType enum*

Constant Name	Description
ANNOTATION_TYPE	The annotation can be used to annotate another annotation type declaration. This makes the annotation type a meta-annotation.
CONSTRUCTOR	The annotation can be used to annotate constructors.
FIELD	The annotation can be used to annotate fields and enum constants.
LOCAL_VARIABLE	The annotation can be used to annotate local variables.
METHOD	The annotation can be used to annotate methods.
PACKAGE	The annotation can be used to annotate package declarations.
PARAMETER	The annotation can be used to annotate parameters.
TYPE	The annotation can be used to annotate class, interface (including annotation type), or enum declarations.
TYPE_PARAMETER	The annotation can be used to annotate type parameters in generic classes, interfaces, methods, etc. It was added in Java 8.
TYPE_USE	The annotation can be used to annotate all uses of types. It was added in Java 8. The annotation can also be used where an annotation with ElementType.TYPE and ElementType.TYPE_PARAMETER can be used. It can also be used before constructors in which case it represents the objects created by the constructor.

The following declaration of the Version annotation type annotates the annotation type declaration with the Target meta-annotation, which specifies that the Version annotation type can be used with program elements of only three types: any type (class, interface, enum, and annotation types), a constructors, and methods.

```java
// Version.java
package com.jdojo.annotation;

import java.lang.annotation.Target;
import java.lang.annotation.ElementType;

@Target({ElementType.TYPE, ElementType.CONSTRUCTOR, ElementType.METHOD})
public @interface Version {
        int major();
        int minor();
}
```

The Version annotation cannot be used on any program elements other than the three types specified in its Target annotation. The following use of the Version annotation is incorrect because it is being used on an instance variable (a field):

```java
public class WontCompile {
        // A compile-time error. Version annotation cannot be used on a field.
        @Version(major = 1, minor = 1)
        int id = 110;
}
```

The following uses of the Version annotation are valid:

```java
// OK. A class type declaration
@Version(major = 1, minor = 0)
public class VersionTest {
        // OK. A constructor declaration
        @Version(major = 1, minor = 0)
        public VersionTest() {
                // Code goes here
        }

        // OK. A method declaration
        @Version(major = 1, minor = 1)
        public void doSomething() {
                // Code goes here
        }
}
```

Prior to Java 8, annotation were allowed on formal parameters of methods and declarations of packages, classes, methods, fields, and local variables. Java 8 added support for using annotations on any use of a type and on type parameter declaration. The phrase "any use of a type" needs little explanation. A type is used in many contexts, for example, after the extends clause as a supertype, in an object creation expression after the new operator, in a cast, in a throws clause, etc. From Java 8, annotations may appear before the simple name of the types wherever a type is used. Note that the simple name of the type may be just used as a name, not as a type, for example in an import statement. Consider the declarations of the Fatal and NonZero annotation types in Listing 1-11 and Listing 1-12.

Listing 1-11. A Fatal Annotation Type That Can Be Used with Any Type Use

```
// Fatal.java
package com.jdojo.annotation;

import java.lang.annotation.ElementType;
import java.lang.annotation.Target;

@Target({ElementType.TYPE_USE})
public @interface Fatal {
}
```

Listing 1-12. A NonZero Annotation Type That Can Be Used with Any Type Use

```
// NonZero.java
package com.jdojo.annotation;

import java.lang.annotation.ElementType;
import java.lang.annotation.Target;

@Target({ElementType.TYPE_USE})
public @interface NonZero {
}
```

The Fatal and NonZero annotation types can be used wherever a type is used. Their uses in the following contexts are valid:

```
public class Test {
        public void processData() throws @Fatal Exception {
                double value = getValue();
                int roundedValue = (@NonZero int) value;

                Test t = new @Fatal Test();
                // More code goes here
        }

        public double getValue() {
                double value = 189.98;
                // More code goes here
                return value;
        }
}
```

Tip   If you do not annotate an annotation type with the Target annotation type, the annotation type can be used as a modifier for any declaration, except a type parameter declaration.

The Retention Annotation

You can use annotations for different purposes. You may want to use them solely for documentation purposes, to be processed by the compiler, and/or to use them at runtime. An annotation can be retained at three levels.

- Source code only

- Class file only (the default)

- Class file and the runtime

The Retention meta-annotation type is used to specify how an annotation instance of an annotation type should be retained by Java. This is also known as the *retention policy* of an annotation type. If an annotation type has a "source code only" retention policy, instances of its type are removed when compiled into a class file. If the retention policy is "class file only," annotation instances are retained in the class file, but they cannot be read at runtime. If the retention policy is "class file and runtime" (simply known as runtime), the annotation instances are retained in the class file and they are available for reading at runtime.

The Retention meta-annotation type declares one element, named value, which is of the java.lang.annotation.RetentionPolicy enum type. The RetentionPolicy enum has three constants, SOURCE, CLASS, and RUNTIME, which are used to specify the retention policy of source only, class only, and class-and-runtime, respectively. The following code uses the Retention meta-annotation on the Version annotation type. It specifies that the Version annotations should be available at runtime. Note the use of two meta-annotations on the Version annotation type: Target and Retention.

```
// Version.java
package com.jdojo.annotation;

import java.lang.annotation.Target;
import java.lang.annotation.ElementType;
import java.lang.annotation.Retention;
import java.lang.annotation.RetentionPolicy;

@Target({ElementType.TYPE, ElementType.CONSTRUCTOR,
         ElementType.METHOD})
@Retention(RetentionPolicy.RUNTIME)
public @interface Version {
    int major();
    int minor();
}
```

■ **Tip** If you do not use the Retention meta-annotation on an annotation type, its retention policy defaults to class file only. This implies that you will not be able to read those annotations at runtime. You will make this common mistake in the beginning. You would try to read annotations and the runtime will not return any values. Make sure that your annotation type has been annotated with the Retention meta-annotation with the retention policy of RetentionPolicy.RUNTIME before you attempt to read them at runtime. An annotation on a local variable declaration is never available in the class file or at runtime irrespective of the retention policy of the annotation type. The reason for this restriction is that the Java runtime does not let you access the local variables using reflection at runtime, and unless you have access to the local variables at runtime, you cannot read annotations for them.

The Inherited Annotation Type

The Inherited annotation type is a marker meta-annotation type. If an annotation type is annotated with an Inherited meta-annotation, its instances are inherited by a subclass declaration. It has no effect if an annotation type is used to annotate any program elements other than a class declaration. Let's consider two annotation type declarations: Ann2 and Ann3. Note that Ann2 is not annotated with an Inherited meta-annotation, whereas Ann3 is annotated with an Inherited meta-annotation.

```
public @interface Ann2 {
        int id();
}

@Inherited
public @interface Ann3 {
        int id();
}
```

Let's declare two classes, A and B, as follows. Note that class B inherits class A.

```
@Ann2(id=505)
@Ann3(id=707)
public class A {
        // Code for class A goes here
}

// Class B inherits Ann3(id=707) annotation from the class A
public class B extends A {
        // Code for class B goes here
}
```

In the above snippet of code, class B inherits the @Ann3(id=707) annotation from class A because the Ann3 annotation type has been annotated with an Inherited meta-annotation. Class B does not inherit the @Ann2(id=505) annotation because the Ann2 annotation type is not annotated with an Inherited meta-annotation.

The Documented Annotation

The Documented annotation type is a marker meta-annotation type. If an annotation type is annotated with a Documented annotation, the Javadoc tool will generate documentation for all of its instances. Listing 1-13 has the code for the final version of the Version annotation type, which has been annotated with a Documented meta-annotation.

Listing 1-13. The Final Version of the Version Annotation Type

```
// Version.java
package com.jdojo.annotation;

import java.lang.annotation.Documented;
import java.lang.annotation.Target;
import java.lang.annotation.ElementType;
import java.lang.annotation.Retention;
import java.lang.annotation.RetentionPolicy;
```

```
@Target({ElementType.TYPE, ElementType.CONSTRUCTOR, ElementType.METHOD,
        ElementType.PACKAGE, ElementType.LOCAL_VARIABLE, ElementType.TYPE_USE})
@Retention(RetentionPolicy.RUNTIME)
@Documented
public @interface Version {
        int major();
        int minor();
}
```

Suppose you annotate a Test class with your Version annotation type as follows:

```
package com.jdojo.annotation;

@Version(major=1, minor=0)
public class Test {
        // Code for Test class goes here
}
```

When you generate documentation for the Test class using the Javadoc tool, the Version annotation on the Test class declaration is also generated as part of the documentation. If you remove the Documented annotation from the Version annotation type declaration, the Test class documentation would not contain information about its Version annotation.

The Repeatable Annotation

Prior to Java 8, it was not allowed to repeat an annotation in the same context. For example, the following repeated use of the Version annotation would generate a compile-time error:

```
@Version(major=1, minor=1)
@Version(major=1, minor=2)
public class Test {
        // Code goes here
}
```

Java 8 added a Repeatable meta-annotation type. An annotation type declaration must be annotated with a @Repeatable annotation if its repeated use is to be allowed. The Repeatable annotation type has only one element named value whose type is a class type of another annotation type.

Creating a repeatable annotation type is a two-step process:

- Declare an annotation type (say T) and annotate it with the Repeatable meta-annotation. Specify the value for the annotation as another annotation that is known as containing annotation for the repeatable annotation type being declared.

- Declare the containing annotation type with one element that is an array of the repeatable annotation.

Listing 1-14 and Listing 1-15 contain declarations for ChangeLog and ChangeLogs annotation types. ChangeLog is annotated with the @Repeatable(ChangeLogs.class) annotation, which means that it is a repeatable annotation type and its containing annotation type is ChangeLogs.

Listing 1-14. A Repeatable Annotation Type That Uses the ChangeLogs as the Containing Annotation Type

```
// ChangeLog.java
package com.jdojo.annotation;

import java.lang.annotation.Repeatable;
import java.lang.annotation.Retention;
import java.lang.annotation.RetentionPolicy;

@Retention(RetentionPolicy.RUNTIME)
@Repeatable(ChangeLogs.class)
public @interface ChangeLog {
        String date();
        String comments();
}
```

Listing 1-15. A Contaning Annotation Type for the ChangeLog Repeatable Annotation Type

```
// ChangeLogs.java
package com.jdojo.annotation;

import java.lang.annotation.Retention;
import java.lang.annotation.RetentionPolicy;

@Retention(RetentionPolicy.RUNTIME)
public @interface ChangeLogs {
        ChangeLog[] value();
}
```

You can use the ChangeLog annotation to log change history for the Test class, as shown:

```
@ChangeLog(date="02/01/2014", comments="Declared the class")
@ChangeLog(date="02/21/2014", comments="Added the process() method")
public class Test {
        public static void process() {
                // Code goes here
        }
}
```

The Native Annotation

The Native annotation type is a meta-annotation that is used to annotate fields. It indicates that the annotated field may be referenced from native code. It is a marker annotation. Typically, it is used by tools that generate some code based on this annotation.

Commonly Used Standard Annotations

Java API defines many standard annotation types. This section discusses four of the most commonly used standard annotations. They are defined in the java.lang package. They are

- Deprecated
- Override
- SuppressWarnings
- FunctionalInterface

The Deprecated Annotation Type

The deprecated annotation type is a marker annotation type. Developers are discouraged from using a program element annotated with a Deprecated annotation because it is not safe to use the program element anymore or a better alternative exists. If you use a deprecated program element in a non-deprecated code, the compiler will generate a warning. Suppose you have a DeprecatedTest class as follows. Note the annotation of the class with a @Deprecated annotation. Its getInstance() method uses the class type as its return type, which will not generate a compiler warning because it is inside the deprecated class.

Listing 1-16. An Example of Deprecating a Class Named DeprecatedTest

```java
// DeprecatedTest.java
package com.jdojo.annotation;

@Deprecated
public class DeprecatedTest {
        private DeprecatedTest() {
        }

        public static DeprecatedTest getInstance() {
                // Using the deprecated class inside its own body
                DeprecatedTest dt = new DeprecatedTest();
                return dt;
        }
}
```

Let's attempt to use the DeprecatedTest class inside a new class called Test, as follows. When you compile the Test class, it will generate a compiler note stating that the deprecated DeprecatedTest class should not be used.

```java
package com.jdojo.annotation;

public class Test {
        public static void main(String[] args) {
                DeprecatedTest dt; // Generates a compile-time note
        }
}
```

```
Note  Test.java uses or overrides a deprecated API.
Note  Recompile with -Xlint:deprecation for details.
```

The Override Annotation Type

The override annotation type is a marker annotation type. It can only be used on methods. It indicates that a method annotated with this annotation overrides a method declared in its supertype. In Java 5, it could be used only in class methods. From Java 6, it can be used for methods of any types. This is very helpful for developers to avoid types that lead to logical errors in the program. If you mean to override a method in a supertype, it is recommended to annotate the overridden method with a @Override annotation. The compiler will make sure that the annotated method really overrides a method in the supertype. If the annotated method does not override a method in the supertype, the compiler will generate an error.

Consider two classes, A and B. Class B inherits from class A. The m1() method in the class B overrides the m1() method in its superclass A. The annotation @Override on the m1() method in class B just makes a statement about this intention. The compiler verifies this statement and finds it to be true in this case.

```
public class A {
        public void m1() {
        }
}

public class B extends A {
        @Override
        public void m1() {
        }
}
```

Let's consider class C.

```
// Won't compile because m2() does not override any method
public class C extends A {
        @Override
        public void m2() {
        }
}
```

The method m2() in class C has a @Override annotation. However, there is no m2() method in its superclass A. The method m2() is a new method declaration in class C. The compiler finds out that method m2() in class C does not override any superclass method, even though its developer has indicated so. The compiler generates an error in this case.

The SuppressWarnings Annotation Type

The SuppressWarnings is used to suppress named compiler warnings. It declares one element named value whose data type is an array of String. Let's consider the code for the SuppressWarningsTest class, which uses the raw type for the ArrayList<T> in the test() method. The compiler generates an unchecked named warning when you use a raw type.

```
// SuppressWarningsTest.java
package com.jdojo.annotation;

import java.util.ArrayList;
```

```
public class SuppressWarningsTest {
        public void test() {
                ArrayList list = new ArrayList();
                list.add("Hello"); // The compiler issues an unchecked warning
        }
}
```

Compile the SuppressWarningsTest class with an option to generate an unchecked warning using the command

```
javac -Xlint:unchecked SuppressWarningsTest.java
```

```
com\jdojo\annotation\SuppressWarningsTest.java:10: warning: [unchecked] unchecked call to add(E)
as a member of the raw type ArrayList
                list.add("Hello"); // The compiler issues an unchecked warning
                         ^
  where E is a type-variable
    E extends Object declared in class ArrayList
1 warning
```

As a developer, sometimes you are aware of such compiler warnings and you want to suppress them when your code is compiled. You can do so by using a @SuppressWarnings annotation on your program element by supplying a list of the names of the warnings to be suppressed. For example, if you use it on a class declaration, all specified warnings will be suppressed from all methods inside that class declaration. It is recommended that you use this annotation on the innermost program element on which you want to suppress the warnings.

The following snippet of code uses a SuppressWarnings annotation on the test() method. It specifies two named warnings: unchecked and deprecated. The test() method does not contain code that will generate a deprecated warning. It was included here to show you that you could suppress multiple named warnings using a SuppressWarnings annotation. If you recompile the SuppressWarningsTest class with the same options as shown above, it will not generate any compiler warnings.

```
// SuppressWarningsTest.java
package com.jdojo.annotation;

import java.util.ArrayList;

public class SuppressWarningsTest {
        @SuppressWarnings({"unchecked", "deprecation"})
        public void test() {
                ArrayList list = new ArrayList();
                list.add("Hello"); // The compiler does not issue an unchecked warning
        }
}
```

The FunctionalInterface Annotation Type

An interface with one abstract method declaration is known as a functional interface. Previously, a functional interface was known as SAM (Single Abstract Method) type. The compiler verifies all interfaces annotated with a @FunctionalInterface that the interfaces really contain one and only one abstract method. A compile-time error is generated if the interfaces annotated with this annotation are not functional interfaces. It is also a compile-time error to use this annotation on classes, annotation types, and enums. The FunctionalInterface annotation type is a marker interface.

The following declaration of the Runner interface uses a @FunctionalInterface annotation. The interface declaration will compile fine.

```
@FunctionalInterface
public interface Runner {
        void run();
}
```

The following declaration of the Job interface uses a @FunctionalInterface annotation, which will generate a compile-time error because the Job interface declares two abstract methods, and therefore it is not a functional interface.

```
@FunctionalInterface
public interface Job {
        void run();
        void abort();
}
```

The following declaration of the Test class uses a @FunctionalInterface annotation, which will generate a compile-time error because a @FunctionalInterface annotation can only be used on interfaces.

```
@FunctionalInterface
public class Test {
        public void test() {
                // Code goes here
        }
}
```

▒ **Tip** An interface with only one abstract method is always a functional interface whether it is annotated with a @FunctionalInterface annotation or not. Use of the annotation instructs the compiler to verify the fact that the interface is really a functional interface.

Annotating a Java Package

Annotating program elements such as classes and fields are intuitive, as you annotate them when they are declared. How do you annotate a package? A package declaration appears as part of a top-level type declaration. Further, the same package declaration occurs multiple times at different places. The question arises: how and where do you annotate a package declaration?

You need to create a file, which should be named package-info.java, and place the annotated package declaration in it. Listing 1-17 shows the contents of the package-info.java file. When you compile the package-info.java file, a class file will be created.

Listing 1-17. Contents of a package-info.java File

```
// package-info.java
@Version(major=1, minor=0)
package com.jdojo.annotation;
```

You may need some import statement to import annotation types or you can use the fully qualified names of the annotation types in the package-info.java file. Even though the import statement appears after the package declaration, it should be okay to use the imported types. You can have contents like the following in a package-info.java file:

```
// package-info.java
@com.jdojo.myannotations.Author("John Jacobs")
@Reviewer("Wally Inman")
package com.jdojo.annotation;

import com.jdojo.myannotations.Reviewer;
```

Accessing Annotations at Runtime

Accessing annotation on a program element is easy. Annotations on a program element are Java objects. All you need to know is how to get the reference of objects of an annotation type at runtime. Program elements that let you access their annotations implement the java.lang.reflect.AnnotatedElement interface. There are several methods in the AnnotatedElement interface that let you access annotations of a program element. The methods in this interface let you retrieve all annotations on a program element, all declared annotations on a program element, and annotations on a program element of a specified type. I will show some examples of using those methods shortly. The following classes implement the AnnotatedElement interface:

- java.lang.Class
- java.lang.reflect.Executable
- java.lang.reflect.Constructor
- java.lang.reflect.Field
- java.lang.reflect.Method
- java.lang.reflect.Parameter
- java.lang.Package
- java.lang.reflect.AccessibleObject

Methods of the AnnotatedElement interface are used to access annotation on the above-listed types of objects.

■ **Caution**   It is very important to note that an annotation type must be annotated with the Retention meta-annotation with the retention policy of runtime to access it at runtime. If a program element has multiple annotations, you would be able to access only annotations, which have runtime as their retention policy.

Suppose you have a Test class and you want to print all its annotations. The following snippet of code will print all annotations on the class declaration of the Test class:

```
// Get the class object reference
Class<Test> c = Test.class;
```

```
// Get all annotations on the class declaration
Annotation[] allAnns = c.getAnnotations();
System.out.println("Annotation count: " + allAnns.length);

// Print all annotations
for (Annotation ann : allAnns) {
        System.out.println(ann);
}
```

The toString() method of the Annotation interface returns the string representation of an annotation. Suppose you want to print the Version annotation on the Test class. You can do so as follows. The following code shows that you can use the major() and minor() methods. It also shows that you can declare a variable of an annotation type (e.g. Version v), which can refer to an instance of that annotation type. The instances of an annotation type are created by the Java runtime. You never create an instance of an annotation type using the new operator.

```
Class<Test> c = Test.class;

// Get the instance of the Version annotation of Test class
Version v = c.getAnnotation(Version.class);
if (v == null) {
        System.out.println("Version annotation is not present.");
}
else {
        int major = v.major();
        int minor = v.minor();
        System.out.println("Version: major=" + major + ", minor=" + minor);
}
```

You will use the Version and Deprecated annotation types to annotate your program elements, and access those annotations at runtime. You will also annotate a package declaration and a method declaration. You will use the code for the Version annotation type as listed in Listing 1-18. Note that it uses the @Retention(RetentionPolicy.RUNTIME) annotation, which is needed to read its instances at runtime.

Listing 1-18. A Version Annotation Type

```
// Version.java
package com.jdojo.annotation;

import java.lang.annotation.Documented;
import java.lang.annotation.Target;
import java.lang.annotation.ElementType;
import java.lang.annotation.Retention;
import java.lang.annotation.RetentionPolicy;

@Target({ElementType.TYPE, ElementType.CONSTRUCTOR, ElementType.METHOD, ElementType.PACKAGE})
@Retention(RetentionPolicy.RUNTIME)
@Documented
public @interface Version {
        int major();
        int minor();
}
```

Listing 1-19 shows the code that you need to save in a `package-info.java` file and compile it along with other programs. It annotates the `com.jdojo.annotation` package. Listing 1-20 has the code for a class for demonstration purpose that has some annotations. Listing 1-21 is the program that demonstrates how to access annotations at runtime. Its output shows that you are able to read all annotations used in the `AccessAnnotation` class successfully. The `printAnnotations()` method accesses the annotations. It accepts a parameter of the `AnnotatedElement` type and prints all annotations of its parameter. If the annotation is of the `Version` annotation type, it prints the values for its major and minor versions.

Listing 1-19. Contents of package-info.java File

```
// package-info.java
@Version(major=1, minor=0)
package com.jdojo.annotation;
```

Listing 1-20. AccessAnnotation Class Has Some Annotations, Which Will Be Accessed at Runtime

```
// AccessAnnotation.java
package com.jdojo.annotation;

@Version(major=1, minor=0)
public class AccessAnnotation {
        @Version(major=1, minor=1)
        public void testMethod1() {
                // Code goes here
        }

        @Version(major=1, minor=2)
        @Deprecated
        public void testMethod2() {
                // Code goes here
        }
}
```

Listing 1-21. Using the AccessAnnotationTest Class to Access Annotations

```
// AccessAnnotationTest.java
package com.jdojo.annotation;

import java.lang.annotation.Annotation;
import java.lang.reflect.AnnotatedElement;
import java.lang.reflect.Method;

public class AccessAnnotationTest {
        public static void main(String[] args) {
                // Read annotation of class declaration
                Class<AccessAnnotation> c = AccessAnnotation.class;
                System.out.println("Annotations for class:" + c.getName());
                printAnnotations(c);

                // Read annotation of package declaration
                Package p = c.getPackage();
                System.out.println("Annotations for package:" + p.getName());
                printAnnotations(p);
```

```
                // Read annotation of method declaration
                System.out.println("Method annotations:");
                Method[] m = c.getDeclaredMethods();
                for (int i = 0; i < m.length; i++) {
                        System.out.println("Annotations for method:" + m[i].getName());
                        printAnnotations(m[i]);
                }
        }

        public static void printAnnotations(AnnotatedElement programElement) {
                Annotation[] annList = programElement.getAnnotations();
                for (int i = 0; i < annList.length; i++) {
                        System.out.println(annList[i]);
                        if (annList[i] instanceof Version) {
                                Version v = (Version)annList[i];
                                int major = v.major();
                                int minor = v.minor();
                                System.out.println("Found Version annotation: " +
                                        "major =" + major + ", minor=" + minor);
                        }
                }
                System.out.println();
        }
}
```

```
Annotations for class:com.jdojo.annotation.AccessAnnotation
@com.jdojo.annotation.Version(major=1, minor=0)
Found Version annotation: major =1, minor=0

Annotations for package:com.jdojo.annotation
@com.jdojo.annotation.Version(major=1, minor=0)
Found Version annotation: major =1, minor=0

Method annotations:
Annotations for method:testMethod1
@com.jdojo.annotation.Version(major=1, minor=1)
Found Version annotation: major =1, minor=1

Annotations for method:testMethod2
@com.jdojo.annotation.Version(major=1, minor=2)
Found Version annotation: major =1, minor=2
@java.lang.Deprecated()
```

Accessing instances of a repeatable annotation is a little different. Recall that a repeatable annotation has a companion containing an annotation type. For example, you declared a ChangeLogs annotation type that is a containing annotation type for the ChangeLog repeatable annotation type. You can access repeated annotations using either the annotation type or the containing annotation type. Use the getAnnotationsByType() method passing it the class reference of the repeatable annotation type to get the instances of the repeatable annotation in an array. Use the getAnnotation() method passing it the class reference of the containing annotation type to get the instances of the repeatable annotation as an instance of its containing annotation type.

Listing 1-22 contains the code for a RepeatableAnnTest class. The class declaration has been annotated with the ChangeLog annotation twice. The main() method accesses the repeated annotations on the class declaration using the above discussed both methods.

Listing 1-22. Accessing Instances of Repeatable Annotations at Runtime

```java
// RepeatableAnnTest.java
package com.jdojo.annotation;

@ChangeLog(date = "02/01/2014", comments = "Declared the class")
@ChangeLog(date = "02/22/2014", comments = "Added the main() method")
public class RepeatableAnnTest {
        public static void main(String[] args) {
                Class<RepeatableAnnTest> mainClass = RepeatableAnnTest.class;
                Class<ChangeLog> annClass = ChangeLog.class;

                // Access annotations using the ChangeLog type
                System.out.println("Using the ChangeLog type...");
                ChangeLog[] annList = mainClass.getAnnotationsByType(ChangeLog.class);
                for (ChangeLog log : annList) {
                        System.out.println("Date=" + log.date() +
                                        ", Comments=" + log.comments());
                }

                // Access annotations using the ChangeLogs containing annotation type
                System.out.println("\nUsing the ChangeLogs type...");
                Class<ChangeLogs> containingAnnClass = ChangeLogs.class;
                ChangeLogs logs = mainClass.getAnnotation(containingAnnClass);
                for (ChangeLog log : logs.value()) {
                        System.out.println("Date=" + log.date() +
                                        ", Comments=" + log.comments());
                }
        }
}
```

```
Using the ChangeLog type...
Date=02/01/2014, Comments=Declared the class
Date=02/22/2014, Comments=Added the main() method

Using the ChangeLogs type...
Date=02/01/2014, Comments=Declared the class
Date=02/22/2014, Comments=Added the main() method
```

Evolving Annotation Types

An annotation type can evolve without breaking the existing code that uses it. If you add a new element to an annotation type, you need supply its default value. All existing instances of the annotation will use the default value for the new elements. If you add a new element to an existing annotation type without specifying a default value for the element, the code that uses the annotation will break.

Annotation Processing at Source Code Level

This section is for experienced programmers. You may skip this section if you are learning Java for the first time.

This section discusses in detail how to develop annotation processors to process annotation at the source code level when you compile Java programs. The University of Washington has developed a Checker Framework that contains a lot of annotations to be used in programs. It also ships with many annotation processors. You can download the Checker Framework from `http://types.cs.washington.edu/checker-framework`. It contains a tutorial for using different types of processors and a tutorial on how to create your own processor.

Java lets you process annotations at runtime as well as at compile time. You have already seen how to process annotations at runtime. Now, I will discuss, in brief, how to process annotations at compile time (or at source code level).

Why would you want to process annotations at compile time? Processing annotations at compile time opens up a wide variety of possibilities that can help Java programmers in during development of applications. It also helps developers of Java tools immensely. For example, boilerplate code and configuration files can be generated based on annotations in the source code; custom annotation-based rules can be validated at compile time, etc.

Annotation processing at compile time is a two-step process. First, you need to write a custom annotation processor. Second, you need to use the `javac` command line utility tool. You need to pass your custom annotation processor to the `javac` compiler using the `–processor` option. You can pass multiple custom annotation processors to `javac,` separating them by a comma. The following command compiles the Java source file, `MySourceFile.java`, and passes two custom annotation processors, `MyProcessor1` and `MyProcessor2`:

```
javac -processor MyProcessor1,MyProcessor2 MySourceFile.java
```

Using `–proc` option, the `javac` command-line utility lets you specify if you want to process annotation and/or compile the source files. You can use `–proc` option as `–proc:none` or `–proc:only`. The `–proc:none` option does not perform annotation processing. It only compiles source files. The `–proc:only` option performs only annotation processing and skips the source files compilation. If the `–proc:none` and the `–processor` options are specified in the same command, the `–processor` option is ignored. The following command processes annotations in the source file `MySourceFile.java` using custom processors: `MyProcessor1` and `MyProcessor2`. It does not compile the source code in the `MySourceFile.java` file.

```
javac -proc:only -processor MyProcessor1,MyProcessor2 MySourceFile.java
```

To see the compile-time annotation processing in action, you must write an annotation processor using the classes in the `javax.annotation.processing` package.

While writing a custom annotation processor, you often need to access the elements from the source code, for example, the name of a class and its modifiers, the name of a method and its return type, etc. You will need to use classes in the `javax.lang.model` package and its subpackages to work with the elements of the source code. In your example, you will write an annotation processor for your `@Version` annotation. It will validate all `@Version` annotations that are used in the source code to make sure the `major` and `minor` values for a `Version` are always zero or greater than zero. For example, if `@Version(major=-1, minor=0)` is used in source code, your annotation processor will print an error message because the `major` value for the version is negative.

An annotation processor is an object of a class, which implements the `Processor` interface. The `AbstractProcessor` class is an abstract annotation processor, which provides a default implementation for all methods of the `Processor` interface, except an implementation for the `process()` method. The default implementation in the `AbstractProcessor` class is fine in most of the circumstances. To create your own processor, you need to inherit your processor class from the `AbstractProcessor` class and provide an implementation for the `process()` method. If the `AbstractProcessor` class does not suit your need, you can create your own processor class, which implements the `Processor` interface. Let's call your processor class `VersionProcessor`, which inherits the `AbstractProcessor` class, as shown:

```
public class VersionProcessor extends AbstractProcessor {
      // Code goes here
}
```

The annotation processor object is instantiated by the compiler using a no-args constructor. You must have a no-args constructor for your processor class, so that the compiler can instantiate it. The default constructor for your VersionProcessor class will meet this requirement.

The next step is to add two pieces of information to the processor class. The first one is about what kind of annotations processing are supported by this processor. You can specify the supported annotation type using @SupportedAnnotationTypes annotation at class level. The following snippet of code shows that the VersionProcessor supports processing of com.jdojo.annotation.Version annotation type:

```
@SupportedAnnotationTypes({"com.jdojo.annotation.Version"})
public class VersionProcessor extends AbstractProcessor {
        // Code goes here
}
```

You can use an asterisk (*) by itself or as part of the annotation name of the supported annotation types. The asterisk works as a wild card. For example, "com.jdojo.*" means any annotation types whose names start with "com.jdojo.". An asterisk only ("*") means all annotation types. Note that when an asterisk is used as part of the name, the name must be of the form PartialName.*. For example, "com*" and "com.*jdojo" are invalid uses of an asterisk in the supported annotation types. You can pass multiple supported annotation types using the SupportedAnnotationTypes annotation. The following snippet of code shows that the processor supports processing for the com.jdojo.Ann1 annotation and any annotations whose name begins with com.jdojo.annotation:

```
@SupportedAnnotationTypes({"com.jdojo.Ann1", "com.jdojo.annotation.*"})
```

You need to specify the latest source code version that is supported by your processor using a @SupportedSourceVersion annotation. The following snippet of code specifies the source code version 8 as the supported source code version for the VersionProcessor class:

```
@SupportedAnnotationTypes({"com.jdojo.annotation.Version"})
@SupportedSourceVersion(SourceVersion.RELEASE_8)
public class VersionProcessor extends AbstractProcessor {
        // Code goes here
}
```

The next step is to provide the implementation for the process() method in the processor class. Annotation processing is performed in rounds. An instance of the RoundEnvironment interface represents a round. The javac compiler calls the process() method of your processor by passing all annotations that the processor declares to support and a RoundEnvironment object. The return type of the process() method is boolean. If it returns true, the annotations passed to it are considered to be claimed by the processor. The claimed annotations are not passed to other processors. If it returns false, the annotations passed to it are considered as not claimed and other processor will be asked to process them. The following snippet of code shows the skeleton of the process() method:

```
public boolean process(Set<? extends TypeElement> annotations, RoundEnvironment roundEnv) {
        // The processor code goes here
}
```

The code you write inside the process() method depends on your requirements. In your case, you want to look at the major and minor values for each @Version annotation in the source code. If either of them is less than zero, you want to print an error message. To process each Version annotation, you will iterate through all Version annotation instances passed to the process() method as

```
for (TypeElement currentAnnotation : annotations) {
        // Code to validate each Version annotation goes here
}
```

You can get the fully qualified name of an annotation using the getQualifiedName() method of the TypeElement interface.

```
Name qualifiedName = currentAnnotation.getQualifiedName();

// Check if it is a Version annotation
if (qualifiedName.contentEquals("com.jdojo.annotation.Version")) {
        // Get Version annotation values to validate
}
```

Once you are sure that you have a Version annotation, you need to get all its instances from the source code. To get information from the source code, you need to use the RoundEnvironment object. The following snippet of code will get all elements of the source code (e.g. classes, methods, constructors, etc.) that are annotated with a Version annotation:

```
Set<? extends Element> annotatedElements = roundEnv.getElementsAnnotatedWith(currentAnnotation);
```

At this point, you need to iterate through all elements that are annotated with a Version annotation; get the instance of the Version annotation present on them; and validate the values of the major and minor elements. You can perform this logic as follows:

```
for (Element element : annotatedElements) {
        Version v = element.getAnnotation(Version.class);
        int major = v.major();
        int minor = v.minor();
        if (major < 0 || minor < 0) {
                // Print the error message here
        }
}
```

You can print the error message using the printMessage() method of the Messager object. The processingEnv is an instance variable defined in the AbstractProcessor class that you can use inside your processor to get the Messager object reference, as shown below. If you pass the source code element's reference to the printMessage() method, your message will be formatted to include the source code file name and the line number in the source code for that element. The first argument to the printMessage() method indicates the type of the message. You can use Kind.NOTE and Kind.WARNING as the first argument to print a note and warning, respectively.

```
String errorMsg = "Version cannot be negative. " +
                  "major=" + major + " minor=" + minor;
Messager messager = this.processingEnv.getMessager();
messager.printMessage(Kind.ERROR, errorMsg, element);
```

Finally, you need to return true or false from the process() method. If a processor returns true, it means it claimed all the annotations that were passed to it. Otherwise, those annotations are considered unclaimed and they will be passed to other processors. Listing 1-23 has the complete code for the VersionProcessor class.

Listing 1-23. An Annotation Processor to Process Version Annotations

```java
// VersionProcessor.java
package com.jdojo.annotation;

import java.util.Set;
import javax.annotation.processing.AbstractProcessor;
import javax.annotation.processing.Messager;
import javax.annotation.processing.RoundEnvironment;
import javax.annotation.processing.SupportedAnnotationTypes;
import javax.annotation.processing.SupportedSourceVersion;
import javax.lang.model.SourceVersion;
import javax.lang.model.element.Element;
import javax.lang.model.element.Name;
import javax.lang.model.element.TypeElement;
import javax.tools.Diagnostic.Kind;

@SupportedAnnotationTypes({"com.jdojo.annotation.Version"})
@SupportedSourceVersion(SourceVersion.RELEASE_8)
public class VersionProcessor extends AbstractProcessor {
        // A no-args constructor is required for an annotation processor
        public VersionProcessor() {
        }

        public boolean process(Set<? extends TypeElement> annotations,
                        RoundEnvironment roundEnv) {

                // Process all annotations
                for (TypeElement currentAnnotation: annotations) {
                        Name qualifiedName = currentAnnotation.getQualifiedName();

                        // check if it is a Version annotation
                        if (qualifiedName.contentEquals("com.jdojo.annotation.Version" )) {
                                // Look at all elements that have Version annotations
                                Set<? extends Element> annotatedElements;
                                annotatedElements = roundEnv.getElementsAnnotatedWith(
                                                        currentAnnotation);
                                for (Element element: annotatedElements) {
                                        Version v = element.getAnnotation(Version.class);
                                        int major = v.major();
                                        int minor = v.minor();
                                        if (major < 0 || minor < 0) {
                                                // Print the error message
                                                String errorMsg = "Version cannot" +
                                                                " be negative." +
                                                                " major=" + major +
                                                                " minor=" + minor;

                                                Messager messager =
                                                        this.processingEnv.getMessager();
```

```
                                  messager.printMessage(Kind.ERROR,
                                          errorMsg, element);
                            }
                     }
              }
       }

       return true;
    }
}
```

Now you have an annotation processor. It is time to see it in action. You need to have a source code that uses invalid values for the major and minor elements in the Version annotation. The VersionProcessorTest class in Listing 1-24 uses the Version annotation three times. It uses negative values for major and minor elements for the class itself and for the method m2(). The processor should catch these two errors when you compile the source code for the VersionProcessorTest class.

Listing 1-24. A Test Class to Test VersionProcessor

```java
// VersionProcessorTest.java
package com.jdojo.annotation;

import java.lang.annotation.Annotation;

@Version(major = -1, minor = 2)
public class VersionProcessorTest {
       @Version(major = 1, minor = 1)
       public void m1() {
       }

       @Version(major = -2, minor = 1)
       public void m2() {
       }
}
```

To see the processor in action, you need to run the following command. Make sure the VersionProcessor class is available in the CLASSPATH.

```
javac -processor com.jdojo.annotation.VersionProcessor VersionProcessorTest.java
```

The output of the above command is as follows. The output displays two errors with the source file name and the line number at which errors were found in the source file.

```
VersionProcessorTest.java:5: error: Version cannot be negative. major=-1 minor=2
public class VersionProcessorTest {
       ^
VersionProcessorTest.java:11: error: Version cannot be negative. major=-2 minor=1
       public void m2() {
                ^
2 errors
```

Summary

Annotations are types in Java. They are used to associate information to the declarations of program elements or type uses in a Java program. Using annotations does not change the semantics of the program.

Annotations can be available in the source code only, in the class files, or at runtime. Their availability is controlled by the retention policy that is specified when the annotation types are declared.

There are two types of annotations: regular annotation or simply annotations, and meta-annotations. Annotations are used to annotate program elements whereas meta-annotations are used to annotate other annotations. When you declare an annotation, you can specify its targets that are the types of program elements that it can annotate. Prior to Java 8, annotations were not allowed to be repeated on the same element. Java 8 lets you create a repeatable annotation.

Java library contains many annotation types that you can use in your Java programs; `Deprecated`, `Override`, `SuppressWarnings`, `FunctionalInterface`, etc. are a few of the commonly used annotation types. They have compiler support, which means that the compiler generates errors if the program elements annotated with these annotations do not adhere to specific rules.

Java lets you write annotation processors that can be plugged into the Java compiler to process annotations when Java programs are compiled. You can write processors to enforce custom rules based on annotation.

CHAPTER 2

■ ■ ■

Inner Classes

In this chapter, you will learn

- What inner classes are
- How to declare inner classes
- How to declare member, local, and anonymous inner classes
- How to create objects of inner classes

What Is an Inner Class?

You have worked with classes that are members of a package. A class, which is a member of a package, is known as a top-level class. For example, Listing 2-1 shows a top-level class named TopLevel.

Listing 2-1. An Example of a Top-Level Class

```
// TopLevel.java
package com.jdojo.innerclasses;

public class TopLevel {
    private int value = 101;

    public int getValue() {
        return value;
    }

    public void setValue (int value) {
        this.value = value;
    }
}
```

The TopLevel class is a member of the package com.jdojo.innerclasses. The class has three members:

- One instance variable: value
- Two methods: getValue() and setValue()

A class can also be declared within another class. This type of class is called an *inner* class. If the class declared within another class is explicitly or implicitly declared static, it is called a nested class, not an inner class. The class that contains the inner class is called an *enclosing* class or an *outer* class. Consider the following snippet of code:

```
package com.jdojo.innerclasses;

public class Outer {
        public class Inner {
                // Members of the Inner class go here
        }
        // Other members of the Outer class go here
}
```

The Outer class is a top-level class. It is a member of the com.jdojo.innerclasses package. The Inner class is an inner class. It is a member of the Outer class. The Outer class is the enclosing (or outer) class for the Inner class. An inner class can be the enclosing class for another inner class. There are no limits on the levels of nesting of inner classes.

An instance of an inner class can only exist within an instance of its enclosing class. That is, you must have an instance of the enclosing class before you can create an instance of an inner class. This is useful in enforcing the rule that one object cannot exist without the other. For example, a computer must exist before a processor can exist; an organization must exist before a president for that organization exists. In such cases, Processor and President can be defined as inner classes whereas Computer and Organization are their enclosing classes, respectively. An inner class has full access to all the members, including private members, of its enclosing class.

Java 1.0 did not support inner classes. They were added to Java 1.1 without any changes in the way the JVM used to handle the class files. How was it possible to add a new construct like an inner class without affecting the JVM? Inner classes have been implemented fully with the help of the compiler. The compiler generates a separate class file for each inner class in the compilation unit. The class files for inner classes have the same format as the class files for the top-level classes. Therefore, the JVM treats the class files for an inner and top-level classes the same. However, the compiler has to do a lot of behind-the-scenes work to implement inner classes. I will discuss some of the work done by the compiler to implement inner classes.

You may ask whether it is possible to achieve everything in Java that is facilitated by inner classes without using them. To some extent, the answer is yes. You can implement most of the functionalities, if not all, provided by inner classes without using the inner classes. The compiler generates additional code for an inner class. Instead of using inner class constructs and letting the compiler generate the additional code for you, you can write the same code yourself. This idea sounds easy. However, who wants to reinvent the wheel?

Advantages of Using Inner Classes

The following are some of the advantages of inner classes. Subsequent sections in this chapter explain all of the advantages of inner classes with examples.

- They let you define classes near other classes that will use them. For example, a computer will use a processor, so it is better to define a Processor class as an inner class of the Computer class.

- They provide an additional namespace to manage class structures. For example, before the introduction of inner classes, a class can only be a member of a package. With the introduction of inner classes, top-level classes, which can contain inner classes, provide an additional namespace.

- Some design patterns are easier to implement using inner classes. For example, the adaptor pattern, enumeration pattern, and state pattern can be easily implemented using inner classes.

- Implementing a callback mechanism is elegant and convenient using inner classes. Lambda expressions in Java 8 offer a better and more concise way of implementing callbacks in Java. I will discuss lambda expressions in Chapter 5.

- It helps implement closures in Java.

- Programmers can have a flavor of multiple inheritance of classes using inner classes. An inner class can inherit another class. Thus, the inner class has access to its enclosing class members as well as members of its superclass. Note that accessing members of two or more classes is one of the aims of multiple inheritance, which can be achieved using inner classes. However, just having access to members of two classes is not multiple inheritance in a true sense.

Types of Inner Classes

You can define an inner class anywhere inside a class where you can write a Java statement. There are three types of inner classes. The type of inner class depends on the location and the way it is declared.

- Member inner class
- Local inner class
- Anonymous inner class

Member Inner Class

A member inner class is declared inside a class the same way a member field or a member method for the class is declared. It can be declared as `public`, `private`, `protected`, or package-level. The instance of a member inner class may exist only within the instance of its enclosing class. Let's consider an example of a member inner class shown in Listing 2-2.

Listing 2-2. Tire Is a Member Inner Class of the Car Class

```
// Car.java
package com.jdojo.innerclasses;

public class Car {
        // A member variable for the Car class
        private int year;

        // A member inner class named Tire
        public class Tire {
                // A member variable for the Tire class
                private double radius;

                // Constructor for the Tire class
                public Tire (double radius) {
                        this.radius = radius;
                }
```

```
                // A member method for the Tire class
                public double getRadius() {
                        return radius;
                }
        } // Member inner class declaration ends here

        // A constructor for the Car class
        public Car(int year) {
                this.year = year;
        }

        // A member method for the Car class
        public int getYear() {
                return year;
        }
}
```

In Listing 2-2, Car is a top-level class and Tire is a member inner class of the Car class. The fully qualified name for the Car class is com.jdojo.innerclasses.Car. The fully qualified name of the Tire class is com.jdojo.innerclasses. Car.Tire. The Tire inner class has been declared public. That is, its name can be used outside the Car class. The constructor for the Tire class is also declared public. This means you can create an object of the Tire class outside the Car class. Since Tire is a member inner class of the Car class, you must have an object of the Car class before you can create an object of the Tire class. The new operator is used differently to create an object of a member inner class. The "Creating Objects of Inner Class" section in this chapter explains how to create objects of an inner member class.

Local Inner Class

A local inner class is declared inside a block. Its scope is limited to the block in which it is declared. Since its scope is always limited to its enclosing block, its declaration cannot use any access modifiers such as public, private, or protected. Typically, a local inner class is defined inside a method. However, it can also be defined inside static initializers, non-static initializers, and constructors. Listing 2-3 shows an example of a local inner class.

Listing 2-3. An Example of a Local Inner Class

```
// TitleList.java
package com.jdojo.innerclasses;

import java.util.ArrayList;
import java.util.Iterator;

public class TitleList {
        private ArrayList<String> titleList = new ArrayList<>();

        public void addTitle (String title) {
                titleList.add(title);
        }

        public void removeTitle(String title) {
                titleList.remove(title);
        }
```

```java
        public Iterator<String> titleIterator() {
                // A local inner class - TitleIterator
                class TitleIterator implements Iterator<String> {
                        int count = 0;

                        @Override
                        public boolean hasNext() {
                                return (count < titleList.size());
                        }

                        @Override
                        public String next() {
                                return titleList.get(count++);
                        }
                } // Local Inner Class TitleIterator ends here

                // Create an object of the local inner class and return the reference
                TitleIterator titleIterator = new TitleIterator();
                return titleIterator;
        }
}
```

A TitleList object can hold a list of book titles. The addTitle() method is used to add a title to the list. The removeTitle() method is used to remove a title from the list. The titleIterator() method returns an Iterator for the title list. The titleIterator() method defines a local inner class called TitleIterator, which implements the Iterator interface. Note that the TitleIterator class uses the private instance variable titleList of its enclosing class. At the end, the titleIterator() method creates an object of the TitleIterator class and returns the object's reference. Listing 2-4 shows how to use the titleIterator() method of the TitleList class.

Listing 2-4. Using a Local Inner Class

```java
// TitleListTest.java
package com.jdojo.innerclasses;

import java.util.Iterator;

public class TitleListTest {
        public static void main(String[] args) {
                TitleList tl = new TitleList();

                // Add two titles
                tl.addTitle("Beginning Java 8");
                tl.addTitle("Scripting in Java");

                // Get the iterator
                Iterator iterator = tl.titleIterator();

                // Print all titles using the iterator
                while (iterator.hasNext()) {
                        System.out.println(iterator.next());
                }
        }
}
```

The fact that the scope of a local inner class is limited to its enclosing block has some implications on how to declare a local inner class. Consider the following class declaration:

```
package com.jdojo.innerclasses;

public class SomeTopLevelClass {
        // Some code for SomeTopLevelClass goes here

        public void someMethod() {
                class SomeLocalInnerClass {
                        // Some code for SomeLocalInnerClass goes here
                }

                // SomeLocalInnerClass can only be used here
        }
}
```

SomeTopLevelClass is a top-level class. The someMethod() method of SomeTopLevelClass declares the SomeLocalInnerClass local inner class. Note that the name of the local inner class, SomeLocalInnerClass, can only be used inside the someMethod() method. This implies that objects of the SomeLocalInnerClass can only be created and used inside the someMethod() method. This limits the use of a local inner class to only being used inside its enclosing block—in your case the someMethod() method. At this point, it may seem that a local inner class is not very useful. However, Listing 2-4 demonstrated that the code for the local inner class TitleIterator can be called from another class, TitleListTest. This was possible because the local inner class TitleIterator implemented the Iterator interface.

To use a local inner class outside its enclosing block, the local inner class must do one or both of the following:

- Implement a public interface
- Inherit from another public class and override some of its superclass methods

The name of the interface or another class must be available outside the enclosing block that defines the local inner class. Listing 2-3 and Listing 2-4 illustrate the first case where a local inner class implements an interface. Listing 2-5 and Listing 2-6 illustrate the second case, where a local inner class inherits from another public class. Listing 2-7 provides a test class to test a local inner class. The example is trivial. However, it illustrates the concept of how to use a local inner class by inheriting it from another class. Note that you may get a different output when you run the program in Listing 2-7.

Listing 2-5. Declaring a Top-Level Class, Which Is Used as the Superclass for a Local Class

```
// RandomInteger.java
package com.jdojo.innerclasses;

import java.util.Random;

public class RandomInteger {
        protected Random rand = new Random();
```

```java
        public int getValue() {
                return rand.nextInt();
        }
}
```

Listing 2-6. *A Local Inner Class That Inherits from Another Class*

```java
// RandomLocal.java
package com.jdojo.innerclasses;

public class RandomLocal {
        public RandomInteger getRandomInteger() {
                // Local inner class that inherits RandomInteger class
                class RandomIntegerLocal extends RandomInteger {
                        @Override
                        public int getValue() {
                                // Get two random integers and return the average
                                // ignoring the fraction part
                                long n1 = rand.nextInt();
                                long n2 = rand.nextInt();

                                int value = (int) ((n1 + n2)/2);
                                return value;
                        }
                }

                return new RandomIntegerLocal();
        } // End of getRandomInteger() method
}
```

Listing 2-7. *Testing a Local Inner Class*

```java
// LocalInnerTest.java
package com.jdojo.innerclasses;

public class LocalInnerTest {
        public static void main(String[] args) {
                // Generate random integers using the RandomInteger class
                RandomInteger rTop = new RandomInteger();
                System.out.println("Random integers using Top-level class:");
                System.out.println(rTop.getValue());
                System.out.println(rTop.getValue());
                System.out.println(rTop.getValue());

                // Generate random integers using the RandomIntegerLocal class
                RandomLocal local = new RandomLocal();
                RandomInteger rLocal = local.getRandomInteger();
```

```
                    System.out.println("\nRandom integers using local inner class:");
                    System.out.println(rLocal.getValue());
                    System.out.println(rLocal.getValue());
                    System.out.println(rLocal.getValue());
            }
    }
```

```
Random integers using Top-level class:
13145674
-152214550
2023137461

Random integers using local inner class:
984022582
-948114876
1226102834
```

The RandomInteger class contains a getValue() method. The only purpose of the RandomInteger class is to get a random integer using its getValue() method. The RandomLocal class is another class, which has a getRandomInteger() method, which declares a local inner class called RandomIntegerLocal, which inherits the RandomInteger class. The RandomIntegerLocal class overrides its ancestor's getValue() method. The overridden version of the getValue() method generates two random integers. It returns the average of the two integers. The LocalInnerTest class illustrates the use of the two classes. The name RandomIntegerLocal is not available outside the method in which it is declared because it is a local inner class. Two things are worth noting.

- The getRandomInteger() method of the RandomLocal class declares that it returns an object of the RandomInteger class, not the RandomIntegerLocal class. Inside the method it is allowed to return an object of the RandomIntegerLocal class because the RandomIntegerLocal local inner class inherits from the RandomInteger class.

- In the LocalInnerTest class, you declared the rLocal reference variable of the RandomInteger type.

```
// Generate random integers using RandomIntegerLocal class
RandomLocal local = new RandomLocal();
RandomInteger rLocal = local.getRandomInteger();
```

However, at runtime, rLocal will receive a reference of the RandomIntegerLocal class. Since getValue() method is overridden in the local inner class, the rLocal object will generate random integers differently.

Anonymous Inner Class

An anonymous inner class is the same as a local inner class with one difference: it does not have a name. Since it does not have a name, it cannot have a constructor. Recall that a constructor name is the same as the class name. You may wonder how you can create objects of an anonymous class if it does not have a constructor. An anonymous class is a one-time class. You define an anonymous class and create its object at the same time. You cannot create more than one object of an anonymous class. Since anonymous class declaration and its object creation are interlaced, an anonymous class is always created using the new operator as part of an expression. The general syntax for creating an anonymous class and its object is as follows:

```
new <interface-name or class-name> (<argument-list>) {
        // Anonymous class body goes here
}
```

The new operator is used to create an instance of the anonymous class. It is followed by either an existing interface name or an existing class name. Note that the interface name or class name is not the name for the newly created anonymous class. Rather, it is an existing interface/class name. If an interface name is used, the anonymous class implements the interface. If a class name is used, the anonymous class inherits from the class.

The <argument-list> is used only if the new operator is followed by a class name. It is left empty if the new operator is followed by an interface name. If <argument-list> is present, it contains the actual parameter list for a constructor of the existing class to be invoked. The anonymous class body is written as usual inside braces. The above syntax can be broken into two for simplicity: the first syntax is used when the anonymous class implements an interface and the second one is used when it inherits a class.

```
new Interface() {
        // Anonymous class body goes here
}
```

and

```
new Superclass(<argument-list-for-a-superclass-constructor>) {
        // Anonymous class body goes here
}
```

Anonymous classes are very powerful. However, its syntax is not easy to read and is somewhat unintuitive. The anonymous class body should be short for better readability. Let's start with a simple example of an anonymous class. You will inherit your anonymous class from the Object class, as shown:

```
new Object() {
        // Anonymous class body goes here
}
```

This is the simplest anonymous class you can have in Java. It is created and it dies anonymously without making any noise!

Now you want to print a message when an object of an anonymous class is created. An anonymous class does not have a constructor. Where do you place the code to print the message? Recall that all instance initializers of a class are invoked when an object of the class is created. Therefore, you can use an instance initializer to print the message in your case. The following snippet of code shows your anonymous class with an instance initializer:

```
new Object() {
        // An instance initializer
        {
                System.out.println ("Hello from an anonymous class.");
        }
}
```

Listing 2-8 contains the complete code for a simple anonymous class, which prints a message on the standard output.

Listing 2-8. An Anonymous Class Example

```java
// HelloAnonymous.java
package com.jdojo.innerclasses;

public class HelloAnonymous {
    public static void main(String[] args) {
        new Object() {
            // An instance initializer
            {
                System.out.println ("Hello from an anonymous class.");
            }
        }; // A semi-colon is necessary to end the statement
    }
}
```

```
Hello from an anonymous class.
```

Since an anonymous inner class is the same as a local class without a class name, you can also implement the examples in Listing 2-3 and Listing 2-4 by replacing the local inner classes with anonymous inner classes. Listing 2-9 rewrites the code for the TitleList class to use an anonymous class. You will notice the difference in the syntax inside the titleIterator() method shown in Listing 2-3 and Listing 2-9. When using an anonymous class, it is important to indent the code properly for better readability. You can test the TitleListWithInnerClass by replacing TitleList with TitleListWithInnerClass in Listing 2-4 and you will get the same output.

Listing 2-9. The TitleList Class Rewritten Using an Anonymous Class as TitleListWithInnerClass

```java
// TitleListWithInnerClass.java
package com.jdojo.innerclasses;

import java.util.ArrayList;
import java.util.Iterator;

public class TitleListWithInnerClass {
    private ArrayList<String> titleList = new ArrayList<>();

    public void addTitle (String title) {
        titleList.add(title);
    }

    public void removeTitle(String title) {
        titleList.remove(title);
    }

    public Iterator<String> titleIterator() {
        // An anonymous class
        Iterator<String> iterator =
                new Iterator<String> () {
                    int count = 0;
```

```
                @Override
                public boolean hasNext() {
                        return (count < titleList.size());
                }

                @Override
                public String next() {
                        return titleList.get(count++);
                }
        }; // Anonymous inner class ends here

        return iterator;
    }
}
```

The titleIterator() method of TitleListWithInnerClass has two statements. The first statement creates an object of an anonymous class and stores the object's reference in the iterator variable. The second statement returns the object reference stored in the iterator variable. In such cases, you can combine the two statements into one statement. The getRandomInteger() method shown in Listing 2-5 can be rewritten using an anonymous class as follows:

```
public RandomInteger getRandomInteger() {
        // Anonymous inner class that inherits the RandomInteger class
        return new RandomInteger() {
                public int getValue() {
                        // Get two random integers and return
                        // the average ignoring the fraction part
                        long n1 = rand.nextInt();
                        long n2 = rand.nextInt();

                        int value = (int)((n1 + n2)/2);
                        return value;
                }
        };
}
```

A static Member Class Is Not an Inner Class

A member class defined within the body of another class may be declared static. The following snippet of code declares a top-level class A and a static member class B:

```
package com.jdojo.innerclasses;

public class A {
        // Static member class
        public static class B {
                // Body for class B goes here
        }
}
```

A static member class is not an inner class. It is considered a top-level class. It is also called a nested top-level class. Since it is a top-level class, you do not need an instance of its enclosing class to create its object. An instance of class A and an instance of class B can exist independently because both are top-level classes. A static member class can be declared public, protected, package-level, or private to restrict its accessibility outside its enclosing class.

What is the use of a static member class if it is nothing but another top-level class? There are two advantages of using a static member class:

- A static member class can access the static members of its enclosing class including the private static members. In your example, if class A has any static members, those static members can be accessed inside class B. However, class B cannot access any instance members of class A because an instance of class B can exist without an instance of class A.

- A package acts like a container for top-level classes by providing a namespace. Within a namespace, all entities must have unique names. Top-level classes having static member classes provide an additional layer of namespaces. A static member class is the direct member of its enclosing top-level class, not a member of the package in which it is declared. In your example, class A is a member of the package com.jdojo.innerclasses, whereas class B is a member of class A. The fully qualified name of class A is com.jdojo.innerclasses.A. The fully qualified name of class B is com.jdojo.innerclasses.A.B. This way, a top-level class can be used to group together related classes defined as its static member classes.

An object of a static member class is created the same way as you create an object of a top-level class using the new operator. To create an object of class B, you write

```
A.B bReference = new A.B();
```

Since the simple name of class B is in the scope inside class A, you can use its simple name to create its object inside class A as

```
B bReference2 = new B(); // This statement appears inside class A code
```

You can also use the simple name B outside class A by importing the com.jdojo.innerclasses.A.B class. However, using the simple name B outside class A is not intuitive. It gives an impression to the reader that class B is a top-level class, not a nested top-level class. You should use A.B for class B outside class A for better readability. Listing 2-10 declares two static member classes, Monitor and Keyboard, which have ComputerAccessory as their enclosing class. Listing 2-11 shows how to create objects of these static member classes.

Listing 2-10. An Example of Declaring Static Member Classes

```
// ComputerAccessory.java
package com.jdojo.innerclasses;

public class ComputerAccessory {
        // Static member class - Monitor
        public static class Monitor {
                private int size;

                public Monitor(int size) {
                        this.size = size;
                }
```

```java
        public String toString() {
                return "Monitor - Size:" + this.size + " inch";
        }
    }

    // Static member class - Keyboard
    public static class Keyboard {
            private int keys;

            public Keyboard(int keys) {
                    this.keys = keys;
            }

            public String toString() {
                    return "Keyboard - Keys:" + this.keys;
            }
    }
}
```

Listing 2-11. An Example of Using Static Member Classes

```java
// ComputerAccessoryTest.java
package com.jdojo.innerclasses;

public class ComputerAccessoryTest {
        public static void main(String[] args) {
                // Create two monitors
                ComputerAccessory.Monitor m17 = new ComputerAccessory.Monitor(17);
                ComputerAccessory.Monitor m19 = new ComputerAccessory.Monitor(19);

                // Create two Keyboards
                ComputerAccessory.Keyboard k122 = new ComputerAccessory.Keyboard(122);
                ComputerAccessory.Keyboard k142 = new ComputerAccessory.Keyboard(142);

                System.out.println(m17);
                System.out.println(m19);
                System.out.println(k122);
                System.out.println(k142);
        }
}
```

```
Monitor - Size:17 inch
Monitor - Size:19 inch
Keyboard - Keys:122
Keyboard - Keys:142
```

Creating Objects of Inner Classes

Creating objects of a local inner class, an anonymous class, and a static member class is straightforward. Objects of a local inner class are created using the new operator inside the block, which declares the class. An object of an anonymous class is created at the same time the class is declared. A static member class is another type of top-level class. You create objects of a static member class the same way you create objects of a top-level class.

Note that to have an object of a member inner class, a local inner class, and an anonymous class, you must have an object of the enclosing class. In the previous examples of local inner classes and anonymous inner classes, you had placed these classes inside instance methods. You had an instance of the enclosing class on which you called those instance methods. Therefore, instances of those local inner classes and anonymous inner classes had the instance of their enclosing classes on which those methods were called. For example, in Listing 2-4, first you created an instance of TitleList class and you stored its reference in t1 as shown:

```
TitleList tl = new TitleList();
```

To get the iterator of t1, you called the titleIterator() method:

```
Iterator iterator = tl.titleIterator();
```

The method call t1.titleIterator() creates an instance of the TitleIterator local inner class inside the titleIterator() method as

```
TitleIterator titleIterator = new TitleIterator();
```

Here, titleIterator is an instance of the local inner class and it exists within t1, which is an instance of its enclosing class. This relationship exists for all inner classes as depicted in Figure 2-1.

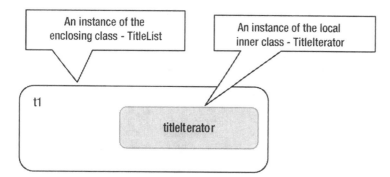

Figure 2-1. *The relationship between an instance of an inner class and an instance of its enclosing class*

■ **Note**   There are situations where an instance of the enclosing class is not required for the existence of an instance of a local inner class or an anonymous inner class. This happens when local inner classes or anonymous inner classes are defined inside a static-context, for example, inside a static method or a static initializer. I will discuss these cases later in this chapter.

An instance of a member inner class always exists within an instance of its enclosing class. The new operator is used to create the instance of the member inner class with a slightly different syntax. The general syntax to create an instance of a member inner class is as follows:

```
OuterClassReference.new MemberInnerClassConstructor()
```

Here, OuterClassReference is the reference of the enclosing class followed by a dot that is followed by the new operator. The member inner class's constructor call follows the new operator. Let's revisit the first example of the member inner class, which is

```
package com.jdojo.innerclasses;

public class Outer {
    public class Inner {
    }
}
```

To create an instance of the Inner member inner class, you must first create an instance of its enclosing class Outer.

```
Outer out = new Outer();
```

Now, you need to use the new operator on the out reference variable to create an object of the Inner class.

```
out.new Inner();
```

To store the reference of the instance of the Inner member inner class in a reference variable, you can write the following statement:

```
Outer.Inner in = out.new Inner();
```

After the new operator, you always use the constructor name, which is the same as the simple class name for the member inner class. Since the new operator is already qualified with the enclosing instance reference (as in out.new), the Java compiler figures out the fully qualified name of the enclosing class name automatically. It is a compile-time error to qualify the inner class constructor with its outer class name while creating an instance of an inner class. The following statement will result in a compile-time error:

```
Outer.Inner in = out.new Outer.Inner(); // A compile-time error
```

Consider the following class declaration with inner classes nested at multiple levels:

```
package com.jdojo.innerclasses;

public class OuterA {
    public class InnerA {
        public class InnerAA {
            public class InnerAAA {
            }
        }
    }
}
```

To create an instance of InnerAAA, you must have an instance of InnerAA. To create an instance of InnerAA, you must have an instance of InnerA. To create an instance of InnerA, you must have an instance of OuterA. Therefore, to create an instance of InnerAAA, you must start by creating an instance of OuterA. The important point is that to create an instance of a member inner class, you must have an instance of its immediate enclosing class. The following snippet of code illustrates how to create an instance of InnerAAA:

```
OuterA outa = new OuterA();
OuterA.InnerA ina = outa.new InnerA();
OuterA.InnerA.InnerAA inaa = ina.new InnerAA();
OuterA.InnerA.InnerAA.InnerAAA inaaa = inaa.new InnerAAA();
```

Listing 2-12 uses the member inner class called Car.Tire from Listing 2-2 to illustrate the steps needed to create an instance of a member inner class.

Listing 2-12. Creating Objects of a Member Inner Class

```java
// CarTest.java
package com.jdojo.innerclasses;

public class CarTest {
    public static void main(String[] args) {
        // Create an instance of Car with year as 2015
        Car c = new Car(2015);

        // Create a Tire for that car of 9.0 inch radius
        Car.Tire t = c.new Tire(9.0);

        System.out.println("Car's year:" + c.getYear());
        System.out.println("Car's tire radius:" + t.getRadius());
    }
}
```

```
Car's year:2015
Car's tire radius:9.0
```

Accessing Enclosing Class Members

An inner class has access to all instance members, instance fields, and instance methods of its enclosing class. Listing 2-13 declares a class called Outer and a member inner class called Inner.

Listing 2-13. Accessing Instance Members of the Enclosing Class from an Inner Class

```java
// Outer.java
package com.jdojo.innerclasses;

public class Outer {
    private int value = 1116;
```

```
        // Inner class starts here
        public class Inner {
                public void printValue() {
                        System.out.println("Inner: Value = " + value);
                }
        } // Inner class ends here

        // Instance method for the Outer class
        public void printValue() {
                System.out.println("Outer: Value = " + value);
        }

        // Another instance method for the Outer class
        public void setValue(int newValue) {
                this.value = newValue;
        }
}
```

The Outer class has a private instance variable called value, which is initialized to 1116. It also defines two instance methods: printValue() and setValue(). The Inner class defines an instance method called printValue(), which prints the value of the value instance variable of its enclosing class Outer.

Listing 2-14 creates an instance of the Inner class and invokes its printValue() method. The output shows that the inner class instance can access the instance variable value of its enclosing instance out.

Listing 2-14. Testing an Inner Class That Accesses the Instance Members of its Enclosing Class

```
// OuterTest.java
package com.jdojo.innerclasses;

public class OuterTest {
        public static void main(String[] args) {
                Outer out = new Outer();
                Outer.Inner in = out.new Inner();

                // Print the value
                out.printValue();
                in.printValue();

                // Set a new value
                out.setValue(828);

                // Print the value
                out.printValue();
                in.printValue();
        }
}
```

```
Outer: Value = 1116
Inner: Value = 1116
Outer: Value = 828
Inner: Value = 828
```

Let's make things a little complex by adding an instance variable named value to the inner class. Call the classes Outer2 and Inner2, as shown in Listing 2-15. Note that the instance variables for both Outer2 and Inner2 classes have the same name as value.

Listing 2-15. A Member Inner Class Having the Same Instance Variable Name as Its Enclosing Class

```java
// Outer2.java
package com.jdojo.innerclasses;

public class Outer2 {
        // Instance variable for Outer2 class
        private int value = 1116;

        // Inner2 class starts here
        public class Inner2 {
                // Instance variable for Inner2 class
                private int value = 1720;

                public void printValue() {
                        System.out.println("Inner2: Value = " + value);
                }
        } // Inner2 class ends here

        // Instance method for Outer class
        public void printValue() {
                System.out.println("Outer2: Value = " + value);
        }

        // Another instance method for Outer2 class
        public void setValue(int newValue) {
                this.value = newValue;
        }
}
```

If you run the Outer2Test class shown in Listing 2-16, the output is different from the output when you ran the OuterTest class in Listing 2-14.

Listing 2-16. Testing an Inner Class That Accesses the Instance Members of Its Enclosing Class

```java
// Outer2Test.java
package com.jdojo.innerclasses;

public class Outer2Test {
        public static void main(String[] args) {
                Outer2 out = new Outer2();
                Outer2.Inner2 in = out.new Inner2();

                // Print the value
                out.printValue();
                in.printValue();
```

```
                // Set a new value
                out.setValue(828);

                // Print the value
                out.printValue();
                in.printValue();
        }
}
```

```
Outer: Value = 1116
Inner: Value = 1720
Outer: Value = 828
Inner: Value = 1720
```

Note that the output has changed. When printing the value for the first time, the Outer2 class's instance prints 1116, whereas the Inner2 class's instance prints 1720. After you set the new value using out.setValue(828), the Outer2 class's instance prints the new value of 828, whereas Inner2 class's instance still prints 1720. Why does the output differ?

To fully understand the above output, you need to understand the concept of the current instance and the keyword this. So far, you understand that the keyword this refers to the current instance of the class. For example, inside the setValue() instance method of the Outer2 class, this.value refers to the value field of the current instance of the Outer class.

You need to revise the meaning of the keyword this with respect to the instance of a class. The meaning of the keyword this that it refers to the current instance is sufficient as long as you deal with only instances of top-level classes. In dealing with only top-level classes, there is only one current instance in context when a piece of code is executed. In such cases, you can use the keyword this to qualify the instance member names to refer to the instance members of the class. You can also qualify the keyword this with the class name to refer to the instance of the class in context. For example, inside the setValue() method of the Outer2 class, instead of writing this.value, you can also write Outer2.this.value. If the name of a variable used inside a class in a non-static context is an instance variable name, the use of the keyword this is implicit. That is, the use of the simple name of a variable inside a class in a non-static context refers to the instance variable of that class unless that variable hides the name of an instance variable with the same name in its superclass. The use of the keyword this alone and its use qualified with class name is illustrated in Listing 2-17. The program in Listing 2-18 tests the uses of the keyword this concept.

Listing 2-17. Use of the Keyword this Qualified with the Class Name

```java
// QualifiedThis.java
package com.jdojo.innerclasses;

public class QualifiedThis {
        // Instance variable - value
        private int value = 828;

        public void printValue() {
                // Print value using simple name of instance variable
                System.out.println("value=" + value);

                // Print value using keyword this
                System.out.println("this.value=" + this.value);

                // Print value using keyword this qualified with the class name
                System.out.println("QualifiedThis.this.value=" + QualifiedThis.this.value);
        }
```

```
        public void printHiddenValue() {
                // Declare a local variable value, which hides the value instance variable
                int value = 131;

                // Print value using simple name, which refers to the local variable - 131
                System.out.println("value=" + value);

                // Print value using keyword this, which refers to the instance
                // variable value with value 828
                System.out.println("this.value=" + this.value);

                // Print value using keyword this qualified with the class name,
                // which refers to instance variable value as 828
                System.out.println("QualifiedThis.this.value=" + QualifiedThis.this.value);
        }
}
```

Listing 2-18. Testing the Use of the Keyword this Qualified with the Class Name

```java
// QualifiedThisTest.java
package com.jdojo.innerclasses;

public class QualifiedThisTest {
        public static void main(String[] args) {
                QualifiedThis qt = new QualifiedThis();
                System.out.println("printValue():");
                qt.printValue();

                System.out.println("\nprintHiddenValue():");
                qt.printHiddenValue();
        }
}
```

```
printValue():
value=828
this.value=828
QualifiedThis.this.value=828

printHiddenValue():
value=131
this.value=828
QualifiedThis.this.value=828
```

You can refer to an instance variable in any of the following three ways, if its name is not hidden:

- Using the simple name, such as value

- Using the simple name qualified with the keyword this, such as this.value

- Using the simple name qualified with the class name and the keyword this, such as QualifiedThis.this.value

If the instance variable name is hidden, you must qualify its name with the keyword this or the class name as well as the keyword this. The code inside an inner class always executes in the context of more than one current instance. The number of current instances depends on the level of nesting of the inner class. Consider the following class declaration:

```java
public class TopLevelOuter {
        private int v1 = 100;

        // Here, only v1 is in scope

        public class InnerLevelOne {
                private int v2 = 200;

                // Here, only v1 and v2 are in scope

                public class InnerLevelTwo {
                        private int v3 = 300;

                        // Here, only v1, v2, and v3 are in scope

                        public class InnerLevelThree {
                                private int v4 = 400;

                                // Here, all v1, v2, v3, and v4 are in scope

                        }
                }
        }
}
```

When the code for the InnerLevelThree class is executed, there are four current instances: one for the InnerLevelThree class and one for each of its three enclosing classes. When the code for the InnerLevelTwo class is executed, there are three current instances: one for the InnerLevelTwo class and one for each of its two enclosing classes. When the code for the TopLevelOuter class is executed, there is only one current instance because it is a top-level class. When the code for an inner class is executed, all instance members, instance variables, and methods of all current instances are in scope unless hidden by local variable declarations.

The above example has comments indicating which instance variables are in the scope in an inner class. When an instance member is hidden inside an inner class, you can always refer to the hidden member by using the keyword this qualified with the class name. Listing 2-19 is the modified version of Listing 2-15. It illustrates the use of the class name with the keyword this to refer to the instance member of the enclosing class of an inner class. Listing 2-20 contains the code to test the ModifiedOuter2 class.

Listing 2-19. Using the Keyword this Qualified with the Class Name

```java
// ModifiedOuter2.java
package com.jdojo.innerclasses;

public class ModifiedOuter2 {
        // Instance variable for ModifiedOuter2 class
        private int value = 1116;
```

```
        // Inner class starts here
        public class Inner {
                // Instance variable for Inner class
                private int value = 1720;

                public void printValue() {
                        System.out.println("\nInner - printValue()...");
                        System.out.println("Inner: Value = " + value);
                        System.out.println("Outer: Value = " + ModifiedOuter2.this.value);
                }
        } // Inner class ends here

        // Instance method for ModifiedOuter2 class
        public void printValue() {
                System.out.println("\nOuter - printValue()...");
                System.out.println("Outer: Value = " + value);
        }

        // Another instance method for the ModifiedOuter2 class
        public void setValue(int newValue) {
                System.out.println("\nSetting Outer's value to " + newValue);
                this.value = newValue;
        }
}
```

Listing 2-20. Testing the ModifiedOuter2 Class

```
// ModifiedOuter2Test.java
package com.jdojo.innerclasses;

public class ModifiedOuter2Test {
        public static void main(String[] args) {
                ModifiedOuter2 out = new ModifiedOuter2();
                ModifiedOuter2.Inner in = out.new Inner();

                // Print the value
                out.printValue();
                in.printValue();

                // Set a new value
                out.setValue(828);

                // Print the value
                out.printValue();
                in.printValue();
        }
}
```

```
Outer - printValue()...
Outer: Value = 1116

Inner - printValue()...
Inner: Value = 1720
Outer: Value = 1116

Setting Outer's value to 828

Outer - printValue()...
Outer: Value = 828

Inner - printValue()...
Inner: Value = 1720
Outer: Value = 828
```

■ **Note**   Java restricts programmers from naming the inner class the same as its enclosing class. This is needed for the inner classes to access the hidden members of their enclosing classes using the enclosing class name with the keyword this.

Restrictions on Accessing Local Variables

A local inner class is declared inside a block—typically inside a method of a class. A local inner class can access the instance variables of its enclosing class as well as the local variables, which are in scope. The instance of an inner class exists within an instance of its enclosing class. Therefore, accessing the instance variables of the enclosing class inside a local inner class is not a problem because they exist throughout the life cycle of the instance of the local inner class. However, the local variables in a method exist only during the execution of that method. All local variables become inaccessible when method execution is over. Java makes a copy of the local variables that are used inside a local inner class and stores that copy along with the inner class object. However, to guarantee that the values of the local variables can be reproduced when accessed inside the local inner class code after the method call is over, Java puts a restriction that the local variables must be *effectively final*. An effectively final variable is a variable whose value does not change after it is initialized. One way to have an effectively final variable is to declare the variable final. Another way is not to change its value after it is initialized. Therefore, a local variable or an argument to a method must be effectively final if it is used inside a local inner class. This restriction also applies to an anonymous inner class declared inside a method.

■ **Tip**   Prior to Java 8, a local variable must be declared final if it is accessed inside a local inner class or an anonymous class. Java 8 changed this rule: the local variable need not be declared final, but it should be effectively final.

The program in Listing 2-21 demonstrates the rules for accessing local variables inside a local inner class. The main() method declares two local variables called x and y. Both variables are effectively final. The variable x is never changed after it is initialized and the variable y cannot be changed because it is declared as final.

Listing 2-21. Accessing Local Variables Inside localclasses

```
// AccessingLocalVariables.javapackage com.jdojo.innerclasses;

public class AccessingLocalVariables {
        public static void main(String... args) {
                int x = 100;
                final int y = 200;

                class LocalInner {
                        void print() {
                                // Accessing the local varibale x is fine as
                                // it is effectively final.
                                System.out.println("x = " + x);

                                // The local variable y is effectively final as
                                // it has been declared final.
                                System.out.println("y = " + y);
                        }
                }

                /* Uncommenting the following statement will make the variable x no longer
                   an effectively final variable and the LocalIneer class wil not compile.
                */
                // x = 100;

                LocalInner li = new LocalInner();
                li.print();
        }
}
```

```
x = 100
y = 200
```

Inner Class and Inheritance

An inner class can inherit from another inner class, a top-level class, or its enclosing class. For example, in the following snippet of code, inner class C inherits from inner class B; inner class D inherits from its enclosing top-level class A, and inner class F inherits from inner class A.B:

```
public class A {
        public class B {
        }

        public class C extends B {
        }
```

```
        public class D extends A {
        }
}

public class E extends A {
        public class F extends B {
        }
}
```

The situation becomes trickier when you want to inherit a top-level class from an inner class:

```
public class G extends A.B {
        // This code won't compile
}
```

Before I discuss why the above code would not compile, recall that you must have an instance of the enclosing class before you can create an instance of an inner class. In the above case, if you want to create an instance of class G (using new G()), you must also create (indirectly though) an instance of A.B, because A.B is its ancestor class. Here, A.B is an inner class. Therefore, in order to create an instance of the inner class A.B, you must have an instance of its enclosing class A. Therefore, you must create an instance of class A before you can create an instance of class G. You must also make the instance of class A available to class G so that it can be used as the enclosing instance when A.B instance is created while creating an instance of its subclass G. The Java compiler enforces this rule. In this case, you must declare a constructor for class G, which accepts an instance of class A and calls the ancestor's constructor on that instance. The above class declaration for class G must be changed to the following:

```
public class G extends A.B {
        public G(A a) {
                a.super(); // Must be the first statement
        }
}
```

In order to create an instance of class G, you should follow two steps:

```
// Create an instance of class A first
A a = new A();

// Pass class A's instance to G's constructor
G g = new G(a);
```

You can combine the above two statements into one statement:

```
G g = new G(new A());
```

Note that inside G's constructor you have added one statement: a.super(). The compiler requires this to be the first statement inside the constructor. At the time of compilation, the compiler modifies a.super() to super(a). Here, super(a) means call the constructor of its ancestor, which is class B, passing the reference of class A. In other words, with the above coding rule, the Java compiler ensures that the constructor of class B gets a reference to its enclosing class A when the instance of class B is created.

Let's change the declaration of the class E in the above examples to the following:

```
// The following code won't compile
public class E {
        public class F extends A.B {
        }
}
```

This code will not compile. In order to create an instance of the inner class F, you need an instance of A.B, which in turn requires an instance of class A. In the earlier case, E was inherited from A. Therefore, it was guaranteed that an instance of A exists when an instance of E is created. An instance of F can only be created when you have an instance of its ancestor's A.B's enclosing class A. When E inherited from A, it was guaranteed, when an instance of F is created, you always have an instance of class A. In order to make the above code work, you need to apply the same logic as you did for class G. You need to declare a constructor for class F that takes an instance of class A as its parameter, like so:

```
// The following code will compile
public class E {
        public class F extends A.B {
                public F(A a) {
                        a.super(); // Must be the first statement
                }
        }
}
```

No static Members in an Inner Class

The keyword static in Java makes a construct a top-level construct. Therefore, you cannot declare any static members (fields, methods, or initializers) for an inner class. The following code will not compile because inner class B declares a static field DAYS_IN_A_WEEK:

```
public class A {
        public class B {
                // Cannot have the following declaration
                public static int DAYS_IN_A_WEEK = 7; // A compile-time error
        }
}
```

However, it is allowed to have static fields in an inner class that are compile-time constants.

```
public class A {
        public class B {
                // Can have a compile-time static constant field
                public final static int DAYS_IN_A_WEEK = 7; // OK

                // Cannot have the following declaration, because it is not a compile-time
                // constant, even though it is final
                public final String str = new String("Hello");
        }
}
```

■ **Tip**   A member interface and a member enum are implicitly static and therefore they cannot be declared inside an inner class.

Generated Class Files for Inner Classes

Each inner class is compiled into a separate class file. The names of the generated class files follow a naming convention. The class file name format for a member inner class and a static inner class is as follows:

```
<outer-class-name>$<member-or-static-inner-class-name>
```

The format for the class file name for a local inner class is as follows:

```
<outer-class-name>$<a-number><local-inner-class-name>
```

The format for the class file name for an anonymous class is as follows:

```
<outer-class-name>$<a-number>
```

`<a-number>` in a class file name is a number that is generated sequentially starting from 1 to avoid any name conflicts. The following nine class files, one for the top-level and eight for inner classes, are generated when you compile the source code in Listing 2-22:

```
InnerClassFile.class
InnerClassFile$MemberInnerClass.class
InnerClassFile$StaticInnerClass.class
InnerClassFile$1$LocalInnerClass.class
InnerClassFile$1$LocalInnerClass$LocalInnerClass2.class
InnerClassFile$1$AnotherLocalInnerClass.class
InnerClassFile$1.class
InnerClassFile$2$AnotherLocalInnerClass.class
InnerClassFile$1$TestLocalClass.class
```

Listing 2-22. An Example for Generating File Names for Inner Classes

```java
// InnerClassFile.java
package com.jdojo.innerclasses;

public class InnerClassFile {
    public class MemberInnerClass {
    }

    public static class StaticInnerClass {
    }

    public void testMethod1() {
        // A local class
        class LocalInnerClass {
            // A local class
            class LocalInnerClass2 {
            }
        }
```

```
            // A local class
            class AnotherLocalInnerClass {
            }

            // Anonymous Inner class
            new Object() {
            };
        }

    public void testMethod2() {
            // A local class. Its name is the same as a local class in testMethod1() method
            class AnotherLocalInnerClass {
            }

            // Another local class
            class TestLocalClass {
            }
        }
    }
}
```

Inner Classes and the Compiler Magic

Inner classes are implemented with the help of the compiler. The compiler does all the magic behind the scenes for the features provided by inner classes. It alters your code and adds new code to implement inner classes. Here is the simplest example of an inner class:

```
public class Outer {
    public class Inner {
    }
}
```

When the Outer class is compiled, two class files are generated: Outer.class and Outer$Inner.class. If you decompile these two class files, you get the following output. You can use any available decompilers for class files. Some Java class file decompilers are available free on the Internet. You can also use the javap tool, which ships with the JDK, to decompile class files. The javap utility is located on your machine in JAVA_HOME\bin folder, where JAVA_HOME is the JDK installation folder.

```
// Decompiled code from Outer.class file
public class Outer {
    public Outer() {
    }
}

// Decompiled code from Outer$Inner.class file
public class Outer$Inner {
    final Outer this$0;
    public Outer$Inner(Outer outer) {
        this$0 = outer;
        super();
    }
}
```

The following points may be observed in the above decompiled code:

- As usual, the compiler provided a default constructor for the Outer class because you did not provide one in your source code.

- The Inner class definition is entirely taken out from the body of the Outer class. Therefore, the Inner class becomes a class that stands by itself in its compiled form. Its class name is changed to Outer$Inner according to the rules discussed earlier in this chapter. By just looking at the definition of only the Outer$Inner class, no one can notice that Outer$Inner is the code for an inner class.

- In the Inner class definition (the Outer$Inner class in the decompiled code), the compiler added an instance variable named this$0, which is of its enclosing class type Outer (see the declaration "final Outer this$0;" in the decompiled code).

- Since you did not include any constructors for the Inner class, you were expecting that the compiler would add a default constructor. However, that is not the case. In the case of an inner class, if you do not provide a constructor, the compiler includes a constructor, which has one argument. The argument type is the same as its enclosing class. If you include a constructor for an inner class, the compiler adds one argument to all the constructors you have included. The argument is added in the beginning of the constructor's arguments list. The argument type is the same as the enclosing class type. Consider the following declaration of the Inner class:

```
public class Outer {
      public class Inner {
            public Inner(int a) {
            }
      }
}
```

Now the compiler will add an extra argument to its constructor, as shown:

```
public class Outer$Inner {
    final Outer this$0;
        public Outer$Inner(Outer outer, int i) {
        this$0 = outer;
        super();
        }
}
```

- The constructor's body for the Inner class is

```
this$0 = outer;
super();
```

The first statement assigns the constructor's argument, which is the reference to its enclosed class instance, to the instance variable. The second statement calls the default constructor of the ancestor of the Inner class, which is the Object class in this case. Recall that if there is a call to the ancestor's constructor inside a constructor of a class, it must be the first statement inside the constructor. However, it is the second statement for the synthesized inner class as shown above. Can you think of a reason why the call to the ancestor's constructor is placed as the second statement as opposed to the first statement?

Let's add an instance variable to the outer class and access that instance variable inside the inner class. To keep the example simple, you have added a new getValue() method to the Inner class in order to access the Outer class's instance variable called dummy. The modified code is as follows:

```
public class Outer {
        int dummy = 101;
        public class Inner {
                public int getValue() {
                        // Access Outer's class dummy field
                        int x = dummy + 200;
                        return x;
                }
        }
}
```

The decompiled code for Outer.class and Outer$Inner.class files are as follows:

```
// Decompiled code from Outer.class file
public class Outer {
        int dummy = 0;
        public Outer() {
                dummy = 101;
        }
}
```

```
// The decompiled code from Outer$Inner.class file
public class Outer$Inner {
        final Outer this$0;
        public Outer$Inner(Outer outer) {
                this$0 = outer;
                super();
        }

        public int getValue() {
                int x = this$0.dummy + 200;
                return x;
        }
}
```

Note the use of this$0.dummy to access the instance variable of the Outer class inside the getValue() method of the Inner class. The dummy instance variable in the Outer class has a package-level access. Since an inner class is always the part of the same package as its enclosing class, this method of referring to the instance variable of the Outer class from outside works fine. However, if the instance variable dummy is declared private, the Outer$Inner class code cannot refer to it directly as it did in the previous example. The compiler uses a different way to access the private instance variable of the outer class from an inner class. The following is the modified code and the corresponding decompiled code for the Outer and Inner classes:

```
// Modified Outer class code with dummy as private instance variable
public class Outer {
        private int dummy = 101; // Declare dummy as private
```

```
        public class Inner {
                public int getValue() {
                        int x = dummy + 200; // Access Outer's dummy field
                        return x;
                }
        }
}

// Decompiled code from Outer.class file
public class Outer {
        private int dummy = 0;
        public Outer() {
                dummy = 101;
        }

        // Method added by the compiler to access the dummy private field
        static int access$000(Outer outer) {
                return outer.dummy;
        }
}

// Decompiled code from Outer$Inner.class file
public class Outer$Inner {
        final Outer this$0;
        public Outer$Inner(Outer outer) {
                this$0 = outer;
                super();
        }

        public int getValue() {
                int x = Outer.access$000(this$0) + 200;
                return x;
        }
}
```

Note that the compiler has added a new static method to the Outer class, which is declared as

```
static int access$000(Outer outer)
```

The compiler adds a new method to the enclosing class for each of its private instance variables accessed inside the inner class. The method, access$000(), is known as a synthetic method because it is synthesized by the compiler. The compiler sets a flag for each synthetic method in order to prevent direct access to these methods from the source code. Another difference for you to note is that inside the getValue() method of the Inner class the compiler has used the synthetic method Outer.access$000(this$0) to access the Outer class's dummy instance variable.

The compiler does many things to implement inner classes. To learn more about the implementation details of inner classes, you can write inner classes; compile the code to generate class files; and then, decompile the generated class files to see the work done by the compiler.

Closures and Callbacks

In functional programming, a higher order function is an anonymous function that can be treated as a data object. That is, it can be stored in a variable and passed around from one context to another. It might be invoked in a context that did not necessarily define it. Note that a higher order function is an anonymous function, so the invoking context does not have to know its name. A closure is a higher order function packaged with its defining environment. A closure carries with it the variables in scope when it was defined, and it can access those variables even when it is invoked in a context other than the context in which it was defined.

In object-oriented programming, a function is called a method and it is always part of a class. An anonymous class in Java allows a method to be packaged in an object that can be treated much as a higher order function. The object can be stored in a variable and passed around from one method to another. The method defined in an anonymous class can be invoked in a context other than the one in which was defined. However, one important difference between a higher order function and a method defined in an anonymous class is that a higher order function is anonymous, whereas a method in an anonymous class is named. The invoker of the anonymous class method must know the method name. An anonymous class carries with it its environment. An anonymous class can use the local variables and the parameters of a method inside which it is defined. However, Java places a restriction that local variables and parameters to the method must be effectively final if they are accessed inside an anonymous class.

The callback mechanism can be implemented using anonymous classes and interfaces. In the simplest form, you register an object, which implements an interface. A particular method is called (back) on the registered object later. Let's define an interface named Callable with one method of call(), as shown in Listing 2-23.

Listing 2-23. A Callable Interface to Implement a Callback Mechanism

```
// Callable.java
package com.jdojo.innerclasses;

public interface Callable {
    void call();
}
```

The CallbackTest class illustrates the implementation details of the callback mechanism. The generateCallable() method is used to generate the object that implements the Callable interface. You also pass an integer to that method in order to recognize the object that it creates. The register() method registers a Callable object and it stores the object's reference in an ArrayList so that these object's call() method can be executed later. The callback() method calls back all registered objects by invoking their call() methods. See Listing 2-24.

Listing 2-24. Implementing Callback Mechanism

```
// CallbackTest.java
package com.jdojo.innerclasses;

import java.util.ArrayList;

public class CallbackTest {
    // To hold all registered Callable objects
    private ArrayList<Callable> callableList = new ArrayList<>();

    public static void main(String[] args) {
        CallbackTest cbt = new CallbackTest();
```

```java
            // Create three Callable objects and register them
            Callable c1 = cbt.generateCallable(1);
            cbt.register(c1);

            Callable c2 = cbt.generateCallable(2);
            cbt.register(c2);

            Callable c3 = cbt.generateCallable(3);
            cbt.register(c3);

            // Callback all the registered Callable objects
            cbt.callback();
    }

    private void callback() {
            int count = this.callableList.size();

            // Callback all the registered Callable objects
            for(int i = 0; i < count ; i++) {
                    Callable c = this.callableList.get(i);
                    c.call();
            }
    }

    public void register(Callable c) {
            this.callableList.add(c);
    }

    public Callable generateCallable(int no) {
            // Note that this object is created here, but it's call() method is
            // used later. It is also capturing the method parameter no which
            // will be used in printing a message later.
            Callable c = new Callable() {
                    public void call() {
                            System.out.println("Called #" + no);
                    }
            };

            return c;
    }
}
```

```
Called #1
Called #2
Called #3
```

The callback mechanism described in this section is used extensively in Java when working with GUI applications developed using Swing and JavaFX.

■ **Note** Java 8 introduced lambda expressions that make working with callbacks more concise. I will discuss lambda expressions in Chapter 5.

Defining Inner Classes in Static Contexts

You can also define an inner class in a static context such as inside a static method or a static initializer. There is no current instance of the outer class present in a static context, and therefore such an inner class cannot access instance fields of the outer class. However, all static field members are accessible to such an inner class.

```
public class Outer {
        static int k = 1001;
        int m = 9008;

        public static void staticMethod() {
                // Class Inner is defined in a static context
                class Inner {
                        int j = k; // OK. Referencing static field k
                        int n = m; // An error. Referencing non-static field m
                }
        }
}
```

Summary

Classes declared inside the body of another class are called inner classes. The class within which the inner class is declared is known as the enclosing class. Inner classes have direct access to all members of their enclosing class. Instances of inner classes exist only within an instance of the enclosing class, except when they are declared in a static context, for example, inside a static method.

There are three types of inner classes: member inner class, local inner class, and anonymous inner class. Inner classes are declared in non-static contexts. A member inner class is declared inside a class the same way a member field or a member method for the class is declared. It can be declared as public, private, protected, or package-level. A local inner class is declared inside a block. Its scope is limited to the block in which it is declared. An anonymous inner class is the same as a local inner class with one difference: it does not have a name. An anonymous class is a one-shot class; it is declared and an object of the class is created at the same time.

A class declared inside another class in a static member class is simply called a static nested class. A static nested class has access to the static members of the enclosing class.

Inside an inner class, the keyword this refers to the current instance of the inner class. To refer to the current instance of the enclosing class, you need to qualify the keyword this with the class name of the enclosing class.

You cannot declare a static member for inner classes. This implies that interfaces and enums cannot be declared as members for inner classes.

CHAPTER 3

███

Reflection

In this chapter, you will learn

- What reflection is

- How to use reflection to get information about classes, constructors, methods, etc. at runtime

- How to access fields of an object and a class using reflection

- How to create objects of a class using reflection

- How to invoke methods of a class using reflection

- How to create arrays using reflection

What Is Reflection?

Reflection is the ability of a program to query and modify its state "as data" during the execution of the program.
The ability of a program to query or obtain information about itself is known as *introspection*. The ability of a program
to modify its execution state, modify its own interpretation or its meaning, or add new behaviors to the program as it is
executing is called *intercession*.

Reflection is further divided into two categories:

- Structural reflection

- Behavioral reflection

The ability of a program to query about the implementation of its data and code is called structural introspection,
whereas its ability to modify or create new data structure and code is called structural intercession.

The ability of a program to obtain information about its runtime environment is called behavioral introspection,
whereas its ability to modify the runtime environment is called behavioral intercession.

Providing the ability to a program to query or modify its state requires a mechanism for encoding the execution
state as data. In other words, the program should be able to represent its execution state as data elements (as objects
in objected-oriented languages such as Java) so that it can be queried and modified. The process of encoding the
execution state into data is called *reification*. A programming language is called reflective if it provides the programs
with reflection capability.

Reflection in Java

The support for reflection in Java is mostly limited to introspection. It supports intercession in a very limited form.
The introspection features provided by Java let you obtain class information about an object at runtime. They also let
you obtain information about the fields, methods, modifiers, and the superclass of a class at runtime.

The intercession features provided by Java lets you create an instance of a class whose name is not known until runtime, invoke methods on such instances, and get/set its fields. However, Java does not allow you to change the data structure at runtime. For example, you cannot add a new field or a method to an object at runtime. All fields of an object are always determined at compile time. Examples of behavioral intercession are the ability to change the method execution at runtime or add a new method to a class at runtime. Java does not provide any of these intercession features. That is, you cannot change a class's method code at runtime to change its execution behavior; neither can you add a new method to a class at runtime.

Java provides reification by providing an object representation for a class and its methods, constructors, fields, etc. at runtime. In most cases, Java does not support reification for generic types. Java 5 added support for generic types. Please refer to Chapter 4 for more details on generic types. A program can work on the reified objects in order to get information about the runtime execution. For example, you have been using the object of java.lang.Class class to get the information about the class of an object. A Class object is the reification of the bytecode for the class of an object. When you want to gather information about the class of an object, you do not have to worry about the bytecode of the class from which the object was instantiated. Rather, Java provides the reification of the bytecode as an object of the Class class.

The reflection facility in Java is provided through the reflection API. Most of the reflection API classes and interfaces are in the java.lang.reflect package. The Class class which is central to the reflection in Java, is in the java.lang package. Some of the frequently used classes in reflection are listed in Table 3-1.

Table 3-1. *Commonly Used Classes in Reflection*

Class Name	Description
java.lang.Class	An object of this class represents a single class loaded by a class loader in the JVM.
java.lang.reflect.Field	An object of this class represents a single field of a class or an interface. The field represented by this object may be a static field or an instance field.
java.lang.reflect.Constructor	An object of this class represents a single constructor of a class.
java.lang.reflect.Method	An object of this class represents a method of a class or an interface. The method represented by this object may be a class method or an instance method.
java.lang.reflect.Modifier	This class has static methods that are used to decode the access modifiers for a class and its members.
java.lang.reflect.Array	This class provides static methods that are used to create arrays at runtime.

Some of the things you can do using the reflection features in Java are as follows:

- If you have an object reference, you can find out the class name of the object.

- If you have a class name, you can know its full description, for example, its package name, its access modifiers, etc.

- If you have a class name, you can find out the methods defined in the class, their return type, access modifiers, parameters type, parameter names, etc. The support for parameter names was added in Java 8.

- If you have a class name, you can find out all field descriptions of the class.

- If you have a class name, you can find out all constructors defined in the class.

- If you have a class name, you can create an object of the class using one of its constructors.

- If you have an object reference, you can invoke its method knowing just the method's name and method's parameter types.

- You can get or set the state of an object at runtime.

- You can create an array of a type dynamically at runtime and manipulate its elements.

The java.lang.Class Class

The java.lang.Class class is central to reflection in Java. The Class class is a generic class. It takes a type parameter, which is the type of the class represented by the Class object. For example, Class<String> represents the class object for the String class. Class<?> represents a class type whose class is unknown.

The Class class lets you discover everything about a class at runtime. An object of the Class class represents a class in a program at runtime. When you create an object in your program, Java loads the class's byte code and creates an object of the Class class to represent the byte code. Java uses that Class object to create any object of that class. No matter how many objects of a class you create in your program, Java creates only one Class object for each class loaded by a class loader in a JVM. Each class is also loaded only once by a particular class loader. In a JVM, a class is uniquely identified by its fully qualified name and its class loader. If two different class loaders load the same class, the two loaded classes are considered two different classes and their objects are not compatible with each other.

You can get the reference to the Class object of a class in one of the followings ways:

- Using class literal

- Using the getClass() method of the Object class

- Using the forName() method of the Class class

A class literal is the class name followed by a dot and the word "class." For example, if you have a class Test, its class literal is Test.class and you can write

```
Class<Test> testClass = Test.class;
```

Note that the class literal is always used with a class name, not with an object reference. The following statement to get the class reference is invalid:

```
Test test = new Test();
Class<Test> testClass = test.class; // A compile-time error. Must use Test.class
```

You can also get the class object for primitive data types and the keyword void using class literals as boolean.class, byte.class, char.class, short.class, int.class, long.class, float.class, double.class, and void.class. Each wrapper class for these primitive data types has a static field named TYPE, which has the reference to the class object of the primitive data type it represents. Therefore, int.class and Integer.TYPE refer to the same class object and the expression int.class == Integer.TYPE evaluates to true. Table 3-2 shows the class literals for all primitive data types and the void keyword.

Table 3-2. *Class Literals for Primitive Data Types and the void Keyword*

Data Type	Primitive Class Literal	Wrapper Class Static Field
boolean	boolean.class	Boolean.TYPE
byte	byte.class	Byte.TYPE
char	char.class	Character.TYPE
short	short.class	Short.TYPE
int	int.class	Integer.TYPE
long	long.class	Long.TYPE
float	float.class	Float.TYPE
double	double.class	Double.TYPE
void	void.class	Void.TYPE

The Object class has a getClass() method, which returns the reference to the Class object of the class of the object. This method is available in every class in Java because every class in Java, explicitly or implicitly, inherits Object class. The method is declared final, so no descendant class can override it. For example, if you have testRef as a reference to an object of class Test, you can get the reference to the Class object of the Test class as follows:

```
Test testRef = new Test();
Class<Test> testClass = testRef.getClass();
```

The Class class has a forName() static method which returns a reference to a Class object. It is an overloaded method The declarations of the two overloaded versions of this method are

- Class<?> forName(String className)

- Class<?> forName(String name, boolean initialize, ClassLoader loader)

The first version of the forName() method takes an argument, which is the fully qualified name of the class to be loaded. It loads the class, initializes it, and returns the reference to its Class object. If the class is already loaded, it simply returns the reference to the Class object of that class. The second version of this method gives you the option to initialize or not to initialize the class when it is loaded, and which class loader should load the class. Both methods throw a ClassNotFoundException if the class could not be loaded. To load a class named pkg1.Test, you would write

```
Class testClass = Class.forName("pkg1.Test");
```

To get a Class object reference using the Class.forName() method, you do not have to know the name of the class until runtime. The forName(String className) method initializes the class if it is not already initialized, whereas the use of a class literal does not initialize the class. Prior to Java 5, a class was initialized when you used its class literal. Java 5 does not initialize the class when you use its class literal. When a class is initialized, all its static initializers are executed and all static fields are initialized. Listing 3-1 lists a Bulb class with only one static initializer, which prints a message on the console. Listing 3-2 uses various methods to load and initialize the Bulb class.

Listing 3-1. A Bulb Class to Demonstrate Initialization of a Class

```java
// Bulb.java
package com.jdojo.reflection;

public class Bulb {
        static {
                // This will execute when this class is loaded and initialized
                System.out.println("Loading class Bulb...");
        }
}
```

Listing 3-2. Testing Class Loading and Initialization

```java
// BulbTest.java
package com.jdojo.reflection;

public class BulbTest {
        public static void main(String[] args) {
                /* Uncomment only one of the following statements at a time.
                   Observe the output to see the difference in the way the Bulb class
                   is loaded and initialized.
                */

                BulbTest.createObject();
                // BulbTest.forName();
                // BulbTest.forNameVersion2();
                // BulbTest.classLiteral();
        }

        public static void classLiteral() {
                // Will load the class, but won't initialize in Java 5 and later.
                // Prior version of Java will initialize the class too.
                Class<Bulb> c = Bulb.class;
        }

        public static void forNameVersion2() {
                try {
                        String className = "com.jdojo.reflection.Bulb";
                        boolean initialize = false;

                        // Get the classloader for the current class
                        ClassLoader cLoader = BulbTest.class.getClassLoader();

                        // Will load, but not initialize the class, because we have
                        // set the initialize variable to false
                        Class c = Class.forName(className, initialize, cLoader);
                }
                catch (ClassNotFoundException e) {
                        System.out.println(e.getMessage());
                }
        }
```

```java
        public static void forName() {
                try {
                        String className = "com.jdojo.reflection.Bulb";

                        // Will load and initialize the class
                        Class c = Class.forName(className);
                }
                catch (ClassNotFoundException e) {
                        System.out.println(e.getMessage());
                }
        }

        public static void createObject() {
                // Will load and initialize the Bulb class
                new Bulb();
        }
}
```

```
Loading class Bulb...
```

Reflecting on a Class

This section will demonstrate the features of Java reflection that enable you to get the description of a class, such as its package name, its access modifiers, etc. You will use a Person class as listed in Listing 3-3 to demonstrate the reflection features. It is a simple class with two instance fields, two constructors, some methods, and it implements two interfaces.

Listing 3-3. A Person Class Used to Demonstrate Reflection

```java
// Person.java
package com.jdojo.reflection;

import java.io.Serializable;

public class Person implements Cloneable, Serializable {
        private int id = -1;
        private String name = "Unknown";

        public Person() {
        }

        public Person(int id, String name) {
                this.id = id;
                this.name = name;
        }

        public int getId() {
                return id;
        }
```

```
        public String getName() {
                return name;
        }

        public void setName(String name) {
                this.name = name;
        }

        public Object clone() {
                try {
                        return super.clone();
                }
                catch (CloneNotSupportedException e) {
                        throw new RuntimeException(e.getMessage());
                }
        }

        public String toString() {
                return "Person: id=" + this.id + ", name=" + this.name;
        }
}
```

Listing 3-4 illustrates how to get the description of a class. It lists the class access modifiers, its name, its superclass name, and all interfaces implemented by it.

Listing 3-4. Reflecting on a Class

```
// ClassReflection.java
package com.jdojo.reflection;

import java.lang.reflect.Modifier;
import java.lang.reflect.TypeVariable;

public class ClassReflection {
        public static void main(String[] args) {
                // Print the class declaration for the Person class
                String classDesciption = getClassDescription(Person.class);
                System.out.println(classDesciption);
        }

        public static String getClassDescription(Class c) {
                StringBuilder classDesc = new StringBuilder();

                // Prepare the modifiers and construct keyword (class, enum, interface etc.)
                int modifierBits = 0;
                String keyword = "";

                // Add keyword @interface, interface or class
                if (c.isPrimitive()) {
                        // We do not want to add anything
                }
```

```
        else if (c.isInterface()) {
                modifierBits = c.getModifiers() & Modifier.interfaceModifiers();

                // AN annotation is an interface
                if (c.isAnnotation()) {
                    keyword = "@interface";
                }
                else {
                    keyword = "interface";
                }
        }
        else if (c.isEnum()) {
                modifierBits = c.getModifiers() & Modifier.classModifiers();
                keyword = "enum";
        }
        else {
                modifierBits = c.getModifiers() & Modifier.classModifiers();
                keyword = "class";
        }

        // Convert modifiers to their string represenation
        String modifiers = Modifier.toString(modifierBits);

        // Append modifiers
        classDesc.append(modifiers);

        // Append the construct keyword
        classDesc.append(" " + keyword);

        // Append simple name
        String simpleName = c.getSimpleName();
        classDesc.append(" " + simpleName);

        // Append generic parameters
        String genericParms = getGenericTypeParams(c);
        classDesc.append(genericParms);

        // Append super class
        Class superClass = c.getSuperclass();
        if (superClass != null) {
                String superClassSimpleName = superClass.getSimpleName();
                classDesc.append(" extends " + superClassSimpleName);
        }

        // Append Interfaces
        String interfaces = ClassReflection.getClassInterfaces(c);
        if (interfaces != null) {
                classDesc.append(" implements " + interfaces);
        }

        return classDesc.toString();
    }
```

```
public static String getClassInterfaces(Class c) {
        // Get a comma-separated list of interfaces implemented by the class
        Class[] interfaces = c.getInterfaces();
        String interfacesList = null;
        if (interfaces.length > 0) {
                String[] interfaceNames = new String[interfaces.length];
                for(int i = 0; i < interfaces.length; i++) {
                        interfaceNames[i] = interfaces[i].getSimpleName();
                }
                interfacesList = String.join(", ", interfaceNames);
        }
        return interfacesList;
}

public static String getGenericTypeParams(Class c) {
    StringBuilder sb = new StringBuilder();
    TypeVariable<?>[] typeParms = c.getTypeParameters();

    if (typeParms.length > 0) {
        String[] paramNames = new String[typeParms.length];
        for(int i = 0; i < typeParms.length; i++) {
            paramNames[i] = typeParms[i].getTypeName();
        }

        sb.append('<');
        String parmsList = String.join(",", paramNames);
        sb.append(parmsList);
        sb.append('>');
    }
    return sb.toString();
}
}
```

```
public class Person extends Object implements Cloneable, Serializable
```

To get the simple class name, use the getSimpleName() method of the Class class, like so:

```
String simpleName = c.getSimpleName();
```

The modifiers of a class are the keywords that appear before the keyword class in the class declaration. In the following example, public and abstract are the modifiers for the MyClass class:

```
public abstract class MyClass {
    // Code goes here
}
```

The getModifiers() method of the Class class returns all modifiers for the class. Note that the getModifiers() method returns an integer. To get the textual form of the modifiers, you need to call the toString(int modifiers) static method of the java.lang.reflect.Modifier class passing the modifiers value in an integer form. Assuming c is the reference of a Class object, you get the modifiers of the class as shown:

```
// You need to AND the returned value from the getModifiers() method with
// appropriate value returned from xxxModifiers() method of the Modifiers class
int mod = c.getModifiers() & Modifier.classModifiers();
String modifiers = Modifier.toString(mod);
```

It is straightforward to get the name of the superclass of a class. Use the getSuperclass() method of the Class class to get the reference of the superclass. Note that every class in Java has a superclass except the Object class. If the getSuperclass() method is invoked on the Object class, it returns null. Therefore, it is important that you check the returned value of the getSuperclass() method for null reference before you try to use it to get its name. This check is removed below for clarity. However, the code for the ClassReflection class has this check:

```
Class superClass = c.getSuperclass();
if (superClass != null) {
        String superClassName = superClass.getSimpleName();
}
```

▓ **Tip** The getSuperclass() method of the Class class returns null when it represents the Object class, a class for an interface such as List.class, and a class for a primitive type such as int.class, void.class, etc.

To get the names of all interfaces implemented by a class, you use the getInterfaces() method of the Class class. It returns an array of Class object. Each element in the array represents an interface implemented by the class. To get the list of all interfaces, you need to loop through all the elements of this array. The ClassReflection class has a getClassInterfaces() method that returns all interfaces implemented by a Class object separated by a comma.

```
// Get all interfaces implemented by c
Class[] interfaces = c.getInterfaces();
```

The getClassDescription() method of the ClassReflection class puts all parts of a class declaration into a string and returns that string. The main() method of this class demonstrates how to use this class.

▓ **Note** Java 8 added a method called toGenericString() to the Class class that returns a string describing the class. The string contains the modifiers and type parameters for the class. The call Person.class.toGenericString() will return public class com.jdojo.reflection.Person.

Reflecting on Fields

A field of a class is represented by an object of the java.lang.reflect.Field class. The following four methods in the Class class can be used to get information about the fields of a class:

- Field[] getFields()
- Field[] getDeclaredFields()
- Field getField(String name)
- Field getDeclaredField(String name)

The getFields() method returns all the accessible public fields of the class or interface. The accessible public fields include public fields declared in the class or inherited from the superclass. The getDeclaredFields() method returns all the fields that appear in the declaration of the class. It does not include inherited fields. The other two methods, getField() and getDeclaredField(), are used to get the Field object if you know the name of the field. Let's consider the following declarations of classes A and B, and an interface IConstants:

```
interface IConstants {
        int DAYS_IN_WEEK = 7;
}

class A implements IConstants {
        private int aPrivate;
        public int aPublic;
        protected int aProtected;
}

class B extends A {
        private int bPrivate;
        public int bPublic;
        protected int bProtected;
}
```

If bClass is the reference of the Class object for class B, the expression bClass.getFields()will return the following three fields that are accessible and public:

- public int B.bPublic

- public int A.aPublic

- public static final int IConstants.DAYS_IN_WEEK

However, bClass.getDeclaredFields() will return all three fields that are declared in class B.

- private int B.bPrivate

- public int B.bPublic

- protected int B.bProtected

To get all the fields of a class and its superclass, you must get the reference of the superclass using the getSuperclass() method and use the combinations of these methods. Listing 3-5 illustrates how to get the information about the fields of a class. Note that you do not get anything when you call the getFields() method on the Class object of the Person class because there are no public fields that are accessible through the Person class.

Listing 3-5. Reflecting on Fields of a Class

```
// FieldReflection.java
package com.jdojo.reflection;

import java.lang.reflect.Field;
import java.lang.reflect.Modifier;
import java.util.ArrayList;

public class FieldReflection {
    public static void main(String[] args) {
        Class<Person> c = Person.class;
```

```java
        // Print declared fields
        ArrayList<String> fieldsDesciption = getDeclaredFieldsList(c);

        System.out.println("Declared Fields for " + c.getName());
        for (String desc : fieldsDesciption) {
            System.out.println(desc);
        }

        // Get the accessible public fields
        fieldsDesciption = getFieldsList(c);

        System.out.println("\nAccessible Fields for " + c.getName());
        for (String desc : fieldsDesciption) {
            System.out.println(desc);
        }

    }

    public static ArrayList<String> getFieldsList(Class c) {
        Field[] fields = c.getFields();
        ArrayList<String> fieldsList = getFieldsDesciption(fields);
        return fieldsList;
    }

    public static ArrayList<String> getDeclaredFieldsList(Class c) {
        Field[] fields = c.getDeclaredFields();
        ArrayList<String> fieldsList = getFieldsDesciption(fields);
        return fieldsList;
    }

    public static ArrayList<String> getFieldsDesciption(Field[] fields) {
        ArrayList<String> fieldList = new ArrayList<>();

        for (Field f : fields) {
            // Get the modifiers for the field
            int mod = f.getModifiers() & Modifier.fieldModifiers();
            String modifiers = Modifier.toString(mod);

            // Get the simple name of the field type
            Class<?> type = f.getType();
            String typeName = type.getSimpleName();

            // Get the name of the field
            String fieldName = f.getName();

            fieldList.add(modifiers + " " + typeName + " " + fieldName);
        }

        return fieldList;
    }
}
```

```
Declared Fields for com.jdojo.reflection.Person
private int id
private String name

Accessible Fields for com.jdojo.reflection.Person
```

■ **Tip** You cannot use this technique to describe the length field of an array object. Each array type has a corresponding class. When you try to get the fields of an array class using the getFields() method, you get an array of Field objects of zero length. The array length is not part of the array's class definition. Rather, it is stored as part of the array object in the object header. For more information on array's length field, please refer to Chapter 11.

Reflecting on an Executable

An instance of the Method class represents a method. An instance of the Constructor class represents a constructor. Structurally, methods and constructors have few things in common. Both use modifiers, parameters, and throws clause. Java 8 refactored these classes to inherit them from a common abstract superclass, Executable. Methods to retrieve information common to both have been added/moved to the Executable class.

A parameter in an Executable is represented by an object of the Parameter class, which was added in Java 8. The getParameters() method in the Executable class returns all parameters of an Executable as an array of Parameter. By default, the formal parameter names are not stored in the class files to keep the file size smaller. The getName() method of the Parameter class returns synthesized parameter names like arg0, arg1, etc. unless the actual parameter names are retained. If you want to retain the actual parameter names in class files, you need to compile the source code using the -parameters option with the javac compiler.

The getExceptionTypes() method of the Executable class returns an array of Class objects, which describes the exceptions thrown by the Executable. If no exceptions are listed in the throws clause, it returns an array of length zero.

The getModifiers() method of the Executable class returns the modifiers as an int.

The getTypeParameters() method of the Executable class returns an array of TypeVariable that represents the type parameters for generic methods/constructors. The examples in this chapter will not include the generic type variable declarations in method/constructors.

Listing 3-6 contains a utility class that consists of static methods to get information about an Executable such as the list of modifiers, parameters, and exception. I will use the class when I discuss methods and constructors in the subsequent sections.

Listing 3-6. A Utility Class to Get Information for an Executable

```java
// ExecutableUtil.java
package com.jdojo.reflection;

import java.lang.reflect.Constructor;
import java.lang.reflect.Executable;
import java.lang.reflect.Method;
import java.lang.reflect.Modifier;
import java.lang.reflect.Parameter;
import java.util.ArrayList;
```

```java
public class ExecutableUtil {
        public static ArrayList<String> getParameters(Executable exec) {
                Parameter[] parms = exec.getParameters();
                ArrayList<String> parmList = new ArrayList<>();
                for (int i = 0; i < parms.length; i++) {
                        // Get modifiers, type, and name of teh parameter
                        int mod = parms[i].getModifiers() & Modifier.parameterModifiers();
                        String modifiers = Modifier.toString(mod);
                        String parmType = parms[i].getType().getSimpleName();
                        String parmName = parms[i].getName();
                        String temp = modifiers + " " + parmType + " " + parmName;

                        // Trim it as it may have leading spaces when modifiers are absent
                        parmList.add(temp.trim());
                }
                return parmList;
        }

        public static ArrayList<String> getExceptionList(Executable exec) {
                ArrayList<String> exceptionList = new ArrayList<>();
                for (Class<?> c : exec.getExceptionTypes()) {
                        exceptionList.add(c.getSimpleName());
                }
                return exceptionList;
        }

        public static String getThrowsClause(Executable exec) {
                ArrayList<String> exceptionList = getExceptionList(exec);
                String exceptions = ExecutableUtil.arrayListToString(exceptionList, ",");
                String throwsClause = "";
                if (exceptionList.size() > 0) {
                        throwsClause = "throws " + exceptions;
                }

                return throwsClause;
        }

        public static String getModifiers(Executable exec) {
                // Get the modifiers for the class
                int mod = exec.getModifiers();
                if (exec instanceof Method) {
                        mod = mod & Modifier.methodModifiers();
                }
                else if (exec instanceof Constructor) {
                        mod = mod & Modifier.constructorModifiers();
                }
                return Modifier.toString(mod);
        }
```

```
        public static String arrayListToString(ArrayList<String> list, String saparator) {
                String[] tempArray = new String[list.size()];
                tempArray = list.toArray(tempArray);
                String str = String.join(saparator, tempArray);
                return str;
        }
}
```

Reflecting on Methods

The following four methods in the Class class can be used to get information about the methods of a class:

- Method[] getMethods()

- Method[] getDeclaredMethods()

- Method getMethod(String name, Class... parameterTypes)

- Method getDeclaredMethod(String name, Class... parameterTypes)

The getMethods() method returns all the accessible public methods of the class. The accessible public methods include any public method declared in the class or inherited from the superclass. The getDeclaredMethods() method returns all the methods declared only in the class. It does not return any methods that are inherited from the superclass. The other two methods, getMethod() and getDeclaredMethod(), are used to get the Method object if you know the name of the method and its parameter types.

The getReturnType() method of the Method class returns the Class object, which contains information about the return type of the method.

Listing 3-7 illustrates how to get information about the methods of a class. You can uncomment the code in the main() method to print all methods in the Person class—declared in the Person class and inherited from the Object class.

Listing 3-7. Reflecting on Methods of a Class

```java
// MethodReflection.java
package com.jdojo.reflection;

import java.lang.reflect.Method;
import java.util.ArrayList;

public class MethodReflection {
    public static void main(String[] args) {
        Class<Person> c = Person.class;

        // Get the declared methods
        ArrayList<String> methodsDesciption = getDeclaredMethodsList(c);
        System.out.println("Declared Methods for " + c.getName());
        for (String desc : methodsDesciption) {
            System.out.println(desc);
        }
```

```
        /* Uncomment the following code to print all methods in the Person class
        // Get the accessible public methods
        methodsDesciption = getMethodsList(c);
        System.out.println("\nMethods for " + c.getName());
        for (String desc : methodsDesciption) {
                System.out.println(desc);
        }
        */
    }

    public static ArrayList<String> getMethodsList(Class c) {
        Method[] methods = c.getMethods();
        ArrayList<String> methodsList = getMethodsDesciption(methods);
        return methodsList;
    }

    public static ArrayList<String> getDeclaredMethodsList(Class c) {
        Method[] methods = c.getDeclaredMethods();
        ArrayList<String> methodsList = getMethodsDesciption(methods);
        return methodsList;
    }

    public static ArrayList<String> getMethodsDesciption(Method[] methods) {
        ArrayList<String> methodList = new ArrayList<>();

        for (Method m : methods) {
            String modifiers = ExecutableUtil.getModifiers(m);

            // Get the method return type
            Class returnType = m.getReturnType();
            String returnTypeName = returnType.getSimpleName();

            // Get the name of the method
            String methodName = m.getName();

            // Get the parameters of the method
            ArrayList<String> paramsList = ExecutableUtil.getParameters(m);
            String params = ExecutableUtil.arrayListToString(paramsList, ",");

            // Get the Exceptions thrown by method
            String throwsClause = ExecutableUtil.getThrowsClause(m);

            methodList.add(modifiers + " " + returnTypeName + " " +
                        methodName + "(" + params + ") " + throwsClause);
        }

        return methodList;
    }
}
```

```
Declared Methods for com.jdojo.reflection.Person
public String toString()
public Object clone()
public String getName()
public int getId()
public void setName(String arg0)
```

Reflecting on Constructors

Getting information about constructors of a class is similar to getting information about a method of a class. The following four methods in the Class class can be used to get information about the constructors represented by a Class object:

- Constructor[] getConstructors()

- Constructor[] getDeclaredConstructors()

- Constructor<T> getConstructor(Class... parameterTypes)

- Constructor<T> getDeclaredConstructor(Class... parameterTypes)

The getConstructors() method returns all public constructors. The getDeclaredConstructors() method returns all declared constructors. The other two methods, the getConstructor() and getDeclaredConstructor(), are used to get the Constructor object if you know the parameter types of the constructor. Listing 3-8 illustrates how to get information for the constructors represented by a Class object.

Listing 3-8. Reflecting on Constructors of a Class

```java
// ConstructorReflection.java
package com.jdojo.reflection;

import java.lang.reflect.Constructor;
import java.util.ArrayList;

public class ConstructorReflection {
        public static void main(String[] args) {
                Class<Person> c = Person.class;

                // Get the declared constructors
                System.out.println("Constructors for " + c.getName());
                Constructor[] constructors = c.getConstructors();
                ArrayList<String> constructDescList = getConstructorsDesciption(constructors);
                for (String desc : constructDescList) {
                        System.out.println(desc);
                }
        }

        public static ArrayList<String> getConstructorsDesciption(Constructor[] constructors) {
                ArrayList<String> constructorList = new ArrayList<>();
                for (Constructor constructor : constructors) {
                        String modifiers = ExecutableUtil.getModifiers(constructor);
```

```
                   // Get the name of the constructor
                   String constructorName = constructor.getName();

                   // Get the parameters of the constructor
                   ArrayList<String> paramsList =
                                   ExecutableUtil.getParameters(constructor);
                   String params = ExecutableUtil.arrayListToString(paramsList, ",");

                   // Get the Exceptions thrown by the constructor
                   String throwsClause = ExecutableUtil.getThrowsClause(constructor);

                   constructorList.add(modifiers + " " + constructorName
                                   + "(" + params + ") " + throwsClause);
           }
           return constructorList;
      }
}
```

```
Constructors for com.jdojo.reflection.Person
public com.jdojo.reflection.Person()
public com.jdojo.reflection.Person(int arg0,String arg1)
```

Creating Objects

Java lets you use reflection to create objects of a class. The class name needed not be known until runtime. You can create the object by invoking one of the constructors of the class. You can also access the values of fields of objects, set their values, and invoke their methods. The following sections explain these features in detail. There are two ways to create objects:

- Using the no-args constructor of the class
- Using any constructor of the class

If you have the reference of a Class object, you can create an object of the class using the newInstance() method on the Class class. This method takes no parameter. It is equivalent to using the new operator on the no-args constructor of the class. If personClass is the reference to the class object of the Person class, you can create a Person object as shown:

```
Person p = personClass.newInstance();
```

Note that the return type of the newInstance() method is the same as the type parameter T of the Class<T> class. The above statement has the same effect as the following statement:

```
Person p = new Person();
```

Listing 3-9 illustrates how to use the newInstance() method of the Class object to create an object of the Person class.

Listing 3-9. Creating an Object Using newInstance( ) Method of a Class Object

```java
// NewInstanceTest.java
package com.jdojo.reflection;

public class NewInstanceTest {
        public static void main(String[] args) throws InstantiationException {
                Class<Person> personClass = Person.class;
                try {
                        // Create new instance of Person class
                        Person p = personClass.newInstance();
                        System.out.println(p);
                }
                catch (InstantiationException | IllegalAccessException e) {
                        System.out.println(e.getMessage());
                }
        }
}
```

```
Person: id=-1, name=Unknown
```

Note that there are two exceptions listed in the catch block in the main() method. The InstantiationException is thrown if there was any problem in creating the object, for example, attempting to create an object of an abstract class, an interface type, primitive types, or the void type. This exception may also be thrown if the class does not have a no-args constructor. The IllegalAccessException may be thrown if the class itself is not accessible or the no-args constructor is not accessible. For example, if there is a no-args constructor and it is declared private. In this case, this exception will be thrown.

You can create an object using reflection by invoking a constructor of your choice. In this case, you must get the reference to the constructor you want to invoke and invoke the newInstance() method on that constructor reference. The Person class has a constructor with a signature Person(int id, String name). You can get the reference of this constructor as shown:

```java
Constructor<Person> cons = personClass.getConstructor(int.class, String.class);
```

After you get the reference to the desired constructor, you need to call the newInstance() method on that constructor passing the arguments to the constructor to create an object.

Listing 3-10 illustrates how to use a constructor of your choice to create an object using reflection. The catch block lists a generic exception to catch all exceptions for brevity. Note that the Constructor<T> class is a generic type. Its type parameter is the class type that declares the constructor, for example, Constructor<Person> type represents a constructor for the Person class.

Listing 3-10. Using a Specific Constructor to Create a New Object

```java
// InvokeConstructorTest.java
package com.jdojo.reflection;

import java.lang.reflect.Constructor;
import java.lang.reflect.InvocationTargetException;

public class InvokeConstructorTest {
        public static void main(String[] args) {
                Class<Person> personClass = Person.class;
```

```
            try {
                    // Get the constructor "Person(int, String)"
                    Constructor<Person> cons =
                                personClass.getConstructor(int.class, String.class);

                    // Invoke the constructor with values for id and name
                    Person chris = cons.newInstance(1994, "Chris");
                    System.out.println(chris);
            }
            catch (NoSuchMethodException | SecurityException |
                    InstantiationException | IllegalAccessException |
                    IllegalArgumentException | InvocationTargetException e) {
                    System.out.println(e.getMessage());
            }
        }
}
```

```
Person: id=1994, name=Chris
```

Invoking Methods

You can invoke methods of an object using reflection. You need to get the reference to the method that you want to invoke. Suppose you want to invoke the setName() method of the Person class. You can get the reference to the setName() method as

```
Class<Person> personClass = Person.class;
Method setName = personClass.getMethod("setName", String.class);
```

To invoke this method, call the invoke() method on the method's reference. The first parameter of the invoke() method is the object on which you want to invoke the method and the second parameter is a varargs arguments parameter in which you pass all the argument values in the same order as declared in the method's declaration. Since the setName() method takes a String argument, you need to pass a String object as the second argument to the invoke() method.

The same invoke() method is used to invoke static methods as well. In case of a static method, the first argument is ignored; you may specify null for the first argument.

Listing 3-11 illustrates how to invoke a method using reflection.

Listing 3-11. Invoking a Method on an Object Reference Using Reflection

```
// InvokeMethodTest.java
package com.jdojo.reflection;

import java.lang.reflect.InvocationTargetException;
import java.lang.reflect.Method;

public class InvokeMethodTest {
        public static void main(String[] args) {
                Class<Person> personClass = Person.class;
                try {
                        // Create an object of Person class
                        Person p = personClass.newInstance();
```

```
                   System.out.println(p);

                   // Get the reference of teh setName() method
                   Method setName = personClass.getMethod("setName", String.class);

                   // Invoke the setName() method on p passing
                   // a new value for name as "Ann"
                   setName.invoke(p, "Ann");
                   System.out.println(p);
            }
            catch (InstantiationException | IllegalAccessException |
                   NoSuchMethodException | SecurityException |
                   IllegalArgumentException | InvocationTargetException e) {
                   System.out.println(e.getMessage());
            }
        }
    }
}
```

```
Person: id=-1, name=Unknown
Person: id=-1, name=Ann
```

Accessing Fields

You can read or set the value of a field of an object using reflection. First, you need get the reference of the field you want to work with. To read the field's value, you need to call the getXxx() method on the field, where Xxx is the data type of the field. For example, to read a boolean field value, you would call the getBoolean() method, and to read an int field you would call the getInt() method. To set the value of a field, you call the corresponding setXxx() method.

▓ **Tip**   Static and instance fields are accessed the same way.

Note that you can access fields only that have been declared as accessible such as public field. In the Person class, all fields are declared private. Therefore, you cannot access any of these fields using normal Java programming language rules. To access a field that is not normally accessible, for example, if it is declared private, please refer to the "Bypassing Accessibility Check" section later in this chapter.

You will use the PublicPerson class listed in Listing 3-12 to learn the technique to access the fields. Listing 3-13 demonstrates how to get the reference of a field of an object and how to read and set its value.

Listing 3-12. A PublicPerson Class with a Public Name Field

```
// PublicPerson.java
package com.jdojo.reflection;

public class PublicPerson {
        private int id = -1;
        public String name = "Unknown";
```

```
        public PublicPerson() {
        }

        public String toString() {
                return "Person: id=" + this.id + ", name=" + this.name;
        }
}
```

Listing 3-13. Accessing Fields Using Reflection

```
// FieldAccessTest.java
package com.jdojo.reflection;

import java.lang.reflect.Field;

public class FieldAccessTest {
        public static void main(String[] args) {
                Class<PublicPerson> ppClass = PublicPerson.class;
                try {
                        // Create an object of PublicPerson class
                        PublicPerson p = ppClass.newInstance();

                        // Get the reference of name field
                        Field name = ppClass.getField("name");

                        // Get the current value of name field
                        String nameValue = (String) name.get(p);
                        System.out.println("Current name is " + nameValue);

                        // Set the value of name to Ann
                        name.set(p, "Ann");

                        // Get the new value of name field
                        nameValue = (String) name.get(p);
                        System.out.println("New name is " + nameValue);
                }
                catch (InstantiationException | IllegalAccessException |
                        NoSuchFieldException | SecurityException |
                        IllegalArgumentException e) {
                        System.out.println(e.getMessage());
                }
        }
}
```

```
Current name is Unknown
New name is Ann
```

Bypassing Accessibility Check

You can access even non-accessible fields, methods, and constructors of a class using reflection if the security manager permits you to do so. You need to get the reference of the desired field, method, and constructor using the getDeclaredXxx() method of the Class object. Note that using the getXxx() method to get the reference of an inaccessible field, method, or constructor will throw an exception. The Field, Method, and Constructor classes have the AccessibleObject class as their ancestor. The AccessibleObject class has a setAccessible(boolean flag) method. You need to call this method on a field, method, and constructor reference with a true argument to make that field, method, and constructor accessible to your program.

Listing 3-14 illustrates how to get access to a private field of the Person class, read its value, and set its new value. You can use the same technique to access inaccessible methods and constructors.

Listing 3-14. Accessing Normally Inaccessible Class Member Using Reflection

```java
// AccessPrivateField.java
package com.jdojo.reflection;

import java.lang.reflect.Field;

public class AccessPrivateField {
        public static void main(String[] args) {
                Class<Person> personClass= Person.class;
                try {
                        // Create an object of the Person class
                        Person p = personClass.newInstance();

                        // Get the reference to name field
                        Field nameField = personClass.getDeclaredField("name");

                        // Make the private name field accessible
                        nameField.setAccessible(true);

                        // Get the current value of name field
                        String nameValue = (String) nameField.get(p);
                        System.out.println("Current name is " + nameValue);

                        // Set a new value for name
                        nameField.set(p, "Sherry");

                        // Read the new value of name
                        nameValue = (String) nameField.get(p);
                        System.out.println("New name is " + nameValue);
                }
                catch(InstantiationException | IllegalAccessException |
                        NoSuchFieldException | SecurityException |
                        IllegalArgumentException e) {
                        System.out.println(e.getMessage());
                }
        }
}
```

```
Current name is Unknown
New name is Sherry
```

So far, everything looks fine. You might think that if you cannot access a private member of a class, you can always use reflection to access them. However, this is not always true. Access to otherwise inaccessible members of a class is handled through the Java security manager. By default, when you run your application on your computer, the security manager is not installed for your application. The absence of the security manager for your application lets you access all fields, methods, and constructors of a class using the setAccessible(true) method. However, if a security manager is installed for your application, whether you can access an inaccessible class member depends on the permission granted to your application to access such members. You can check if the security manager is installed for your application or not by using the following piece of code:

```
SecurityManager securityMgr = System.getSecurityManager();
if (securityMgr == null) {
        System.out.println("Security manager is not installed");
}
```

You can install a default security manager by passing the –Djava.security.manager option on the command line when you run the Java application. The security manager uses a Java security policy file to enforce the rules specified in that policy file. The Java security policy file is specified using the –Djava.security.policy command line option. If you want to run the com.jdojo.reflection.AccessPrivateField class with the Java security manager with the Java policy file stored in the c:\myjava.policy file, you would use the following command:

```
java –Djava.security.manager –Djava.security.policy=c:\myjava.policy
com.jdojo.reflection.AccessPrivateField
```

If you want to allow your program to access an inaccessible field of a class using reflection, the contents of the myjava.policy file would look as follows:

```
grant {
        // Grant permission to all programs to access inaccessible class members
        permission java.lang.reflect.ReflectPermission "suppressAccessChecks";
};
```

If you want to stop the Java program from accessing inaccessible members of a class using reflection, either you remove or comment out the following line in your Java security policy file, and run your application using a security manager with a Java security file:

```
permission java.lang.reflect.ReflectPermission "suppressAccessChecks";
```

If you run the program listed in Listing 3-14 without the above permission, the setAccessible(true) method call will throw a security exception.

You can check if your program can access normally inaccessible class members. The check is performed using the ReflectPermission class in the java.lang.reflect package. You can create an object of the class with the name of the permission. The permission name to use is "suppressAccessChecks". You can call the checkGuard() method on this object. If this method returns true, it means your program has access to those normally inaccessible class members. If this method throws a SecurityException, "it means you do not have permission to access the normally inaccessible class members. The checkGuard() method takes an object as an argument. Currently, this argument is ignored.

Listing 3-15 illustrates how to check if your program can access normally inaccessible class members using reflection. You can run the ReflectPermissionTest class by installing the Java security manager and a Java security policy file. The output of this program will be different depending on the reflect permission grant in your Java security policy file. If you run this class without a Java security manager, the output will always indicate that the reflect permission is granted to your program.

Listing 3-15. Checking for Reflect Permission in a Program

```java
// ReflectPermissionTest.java
package com.jdojo.reflection;

import java.lang.reflect.ReflectPermission;

public class ReflectPermissionTest {
        public static void main(String[] args) {
                try {
                        // Create a permission object
                        ReflectPermission rp = new ReflectPermission("suppressAccessChecks");

                        // check for permission
                        rp.checkGuard(null);
                        System.out.println("Reflect permission is granted");
                }
                catch (SecurityException e) {
                        System.out.println("Reflect permission is not granted");
                }
        }
}
```

Reflecting on Arrays

Java provides special APIs to work with arrays. The Class class lets you find out if a Class reference represents an array by using its isArray() method. You can also create an array, and read and modify its element's values using reflection. The java.lang.reflect.Array class is used to dynamically create an array and to manipulate its elements. As stated before, you cannot reflect on the length field of an array using normal reflection procedure. However, the Array class provides you the getLength() method to get the length value of an array. Note that all methods in the Array class are static and most of them have the first argument as the array object's reference on which they operate.

To create an array, use the newInstance() static method of the Array class. The method is overloaded and it has two versions.

- Object newInstance(Class<?> componentType, int arrayLength)
- Object newInstance(Class<?> componentType, int... dimensions)

One version of the method creates an array of the specified component type and the array length. The other version creates an array of the specified component type and dimensions. Note that the return type of the newInstance() method is Object. You will need to use an appropriate cast to assign it to the actual array type.

If you want to create an array of int of length 5, you would write

```java
int[] ids = (int[])Array.newInstance(int.class, 5);
```

The above statement is the same as

```java
Object ids = new int[5];
```

If you want to create an array of int of dimension 5 X 8, you would write

```java
int[][] matrix = (int[][])Array.newInstance(int.class, 5, 8);
```

Listing 3-16 illustrates how to create an array dynamically and manipulate its elements.

Listing 3-16. Reflecting on Arrays

```java
// ArrayReflection.java
package com.jdojo.reflection;

import java.lang.reflect.Array;

public class ArrayReflection {
        public static void main(String[] args) {
                try {
                        // Create the array of int of length 2
                        Object arrayObject = Array.newInstance(int.class, 2);

                        // Print the values in array element. Default values will be zero
                        int n1 = Array.getInt(arrayObject, 0);
                        int n2 = Array.getInt(arrayObject, 1);
                        System.out.println("n1 = " + n1 + ", n2=" + n2);

                        // Set the values
                        Array.set(arrayObject, 0, 101);
                        Array.set(arrayObject, 1, 102);

                        // Print the values in array element again
                        n1 = Array.getInt(arrayObject, 0);
                        n2 = Array.getInt(arrayObject, 1);
                        System.out.println("n1 = " + n1 + ", n2=" + n2);
                }
                catch (NegativeArraySizeException | IllegalArgumentException |
                        ArrayIndexOutOfBoundsException e) {
                        System.out.println(e.getMessage());
                }
        }
}
```

```
n1 = 0, n2=0
n1 = 101, n2=102
```

Java does not support a truly multi-dimensional array. Rather, it supports an array of arrays. The Class class has a method called getComponentType(), which returns the Class object for an array's element type. Listing 3-17 illustrates how to get the dimension of an array.

Listing 3-17. Getting the Dimension of an Array

```java
// ArrayDimension.java
package com.jdojo.reflection;

public class ArrayDimension {
        public static void main(String[] args) {
                int[][][] intArray = new int[6][3][4];
```

```
            System.out.println("int[][][] dimension is " + getArrayDimension(intArray));
    }

    public static int getArrayDimension(Object array) {
            int dimension = 0;
            Class c = array.getClass();

            // Perform a check that the object is really an array
            if (!c.isArray()) {
                    throw new IllegalArgumentException("Object is not an array");
            }

            while (c.isArray()) {
                    dimension++;
                    c = c.getComponentType();
            }
            return dimension;
    }
}
```

```
int[][][] dimension is 3
```

Expanding an Array

An array in Java is a fixed-length data structure. That is, once you create an array, its length is fixed. The statement "An array in Java is a fixed length data structure" is always true. You can create an array of a bigger size and copy the old array elements to the new one at runtime. The Java collection classes such as ArrayList apply this technique to let you add elements to the collection without worrying about its length. You can use the combination of the getComponentType() method of the Class class and the newInstance() method of the Array class to create a new array of a type. When you have the new array created, you can use the arraycopy() static method of the System class to copy the old array elements to the new array. Listing 3-18 illustrates how to create an array of a particular type using reflection. All runtime checks have been left out of the code for clarity.

Listing 3-18. Expanding an Array Using Reflection

```java
// ExpandingArray.java
package com.jdojo.reflection;

import java.lang.reflect.Array;
import java.util.Arrays;

public class ExpandingArray {
        public static void main(String[] args) {
                // Create an array of length 2
                int[] ids = {101, 102};

                System.out.println("Old array length: " + ids.length);
                System.out.println("Old array elements:" + Arrays.toString(ids));

                // Expand the array by 1
                ids = (int[]) expandBy(ids, 1);
```

```
                      // Set the third element to 103
                      ids[2] = 103; // This is newly added element
                      System.out.println("New array length: " + ids.length);
                      System.out.println("New array elements:" + Arrays.toString(ids));
              }

       public static Object expandBy(Object oldArray, int increment) {
                      Object newArray = null;

                      // Get the length of old array using reflection
                      int oldLength = Array.getLength(oldArray);
                      int newLength = oldLength + increment;

                      // Get the class of the old array
                      Class<?> c = oldArray.getClass();

                      // Create a new array of the new length
                      newArray = Array.newInstance(c.getComponentType(), newLength);

                      // Copy the old array elements to new array
                      System.arraycopy(oldArray, 0, newArray, 0, oldLength);

                      return newArray;
              }
}
```

```
Old array length: 2
Old array elements:[101, 102]
New array length: 3
New array elements:[101, 102, 103]
```

Who Should Use Reflection?

If you have used any integrated development environment (IDE) to develop a GUI application using drag-and-drop features, you have already used an application that uses reflection in one form or another. All GUI tools that let you set the properties of a control, say a button, at design time uses reflection to get the list of the properties for that control. Other tools such as class browsers and debuggers also use reflection. As an application programmer, you will not use reflection much in your programs unless you are developing advanced applications that make use of dynamism provided by the reflection API. It should be noted that using too much reflection slows down the performance of your application.

Summary

Reflection is the ability of a program to query and modify its state "as data" during the execution of the program. Java represents the byte code of a class as an object of the Class class to facilitate reflection. The class fields, constructors, and methods can be accessed as an object of the Field, Constructor, and Method classes, respectively. Using a Field object, you can access and change the value of the field. Using a Method object, you can invoke the method. Using a Constructor object, you can invoke the constructor. Using the Array class, you can also create arrays of a specified type and dimension using reflection and manipulate the elements of the arrays.

CHAPTER 4

■ ■ ■

Generics

In this chapter, you will learn

- What generics are

- How to define generic types, methods, and constructors

- How to define bounds for type parameters

- How to use wildcards as the actual type parameters

- How the compiler infers the actual type parameters for generic type uses

- Generics and their limitations in array creations

- How the incorrect use of generics may lead to heap pollution

What Are Generics?

Generics let you write true polymorphic code, which is code that works with any type. Please refer to Chapter 1 in the book *Beginning Java Fundamentals* (ISBN 978-1-4302-6652-5) for more details on polymorphism and writing polymorphic code.

Let's discuss a simple example before I define what generics are and what they do for us. Suppose you want to create a new class whose sole job is to store a reference to any type, where "any type" means any reference type. Let's call this class ObjectWrapper, as shown in Listing 4-1.

Listing 4-1. A Wrapper Class to Store a Reference of Any Type

```java
// ObjectWrapper.java
package com.jdojo.generics;

public class ObjectWrapper {
        private Object ref;

        public ObjectWrapper(Object ref) {
                this.ref = ref;
        }

        public Object get() {
                return ref;
        }
```

```
        public void set(Object reference) {
               this.ref = ref;
        }
}
```

As a Java developer, you would agree that we write this kind of code when we do not know the type of the objects that we have to deal with. The ObjectWrapper class can store a reference of any type in Java, such as String, Integer, Person, etc. How do you use the ObjectWrapper class? The following is one of the ways to use your Wrapper class:

```
ObjectWrapper stringWrapper = new ObjectWrapper("Hello");
stringWrapper.set("another string");
String myString =(String)stringWrapper.get();
```

There's one problem in the above code. Even though you knew that you stored (and wanted to) a String in the stringWrapper object, you had to cast the return value of the get() method to a String type in (String) stringWrapper.get(). Consider writing the following snippet of code:

```
ObjectWrapper stringWrapper = new ObjectWrapper("Hello");
stringWrapper.set(new Integer(101));
String myString =(String)stringWrapper.get();
```

The above snippet of code compiles fine. However, you get a runtime ClassCastException in the third statement because you stored an Integer in the second statement and attempted to cast an Integer to String in the third statement. First, it allowed you to store an Integer in stringWrapper. Second, it did not complain about the code in the third statement because it had no knowledge of your intent that you only wanted to use a String with stringWrapper.

Java has made some progress with the way it helps developers write type-safe programs. Wouldn't it be nice if the ObjectWrapper class had some way of letting you tell it that you want to use it only for a specific type, say, String this time and Integer the next? Your wish is fulfilled by generics in Java. It lets you specify a *type parameter* with a type (class or interface). Such a type is called a generic type (more specifically generic class or generic interface). The *type parameter value* could be specified when you declare a variable of the generic type and create an object of your generic type. Let's rewrite the ObjectWrapper class to use generics. Call the new class simply Wrapper.

If a type accepts a parameter, you need to specify the parameter name (a valid identifier) in angle brackets (< >) after the name of the type. You will use T as the parameter name.

```
public class Wrapper<T> {
}
```

It is an unwritten convention that parameter names are one character, and to use T to indicate that the parameter is a type, E to indicate that the parameter is an element, K to indicate that the parameter is a key, and V to indicate that the parameter is a value. In the previous example, you could have used any name for the type parameter, like so:

```
public class Wrapper<Hello> {
}
```

```
public class Wrapper<MyType> {
}
```

If you want to use more than one parameter for a type, they must be separated by a comma. The following declaration for MyClass takes four parameters named T, U, V, and W:

```
public class MyClass<T, U, V, W> {
}
```

You will be using your type parameter named T inside the class code in instance variable declarations, constructors, the get() method, and the set() method. Right now, T means any type for you, which will be known when you use this class. Listing 4-2 has the complete code for the Wrapper class.

Listing 4-2. Using a Type Parameter to Define a Generic Class

```java
// Wrapper.java
package com.jdojo.generics;

public class Wrapper<T> {
        private T ref;

        public Wrapper(T ref) {
                this.ref = ref;
        }

        public T get() {
                return ref;
        }

        public void set(T a) {
                this.ref = ref;
        }
}
```

Are you still confused about using T in Listing 4-2? Here, T means any class type or interface type. It could be String, Object, com.jdojo.generics.Person, etc. If you replace T with Object everywhere in this program and remove <T> from the class name, it is the same code that you had for the ObjectWrapper class.

How do you use the Wrapper class? Since its class name is not just Wrapper, rather it is Wrapper<T>, you may specify (but do not have to) the value for T. To store a String reference in the Wrapper object, you would create it as follows:

```java
Wrapper<String> greetingWrapper = new Wrapper<String>("Hello");
```

How do you use the set() and get() methods of the Wrapper class? Since you have specified the type of the parameter for the class Wrapper<T> to be String, the set() and get() method will work only with String types. This is because you have used T as an argument type in the set() method and T as the return type in the get() method declarations. Imagine replacing T in the class definition with String and you should have no problem in understanding the following code:

```java
greetingWrapper.set("Hi"); // OK to pass a String
String greeting = greetingWrapper.get(); // No need to cast
```

This time, you did not have to cast the return value of the get() method. The compiler knows that greetingWrapper has been declared of type String and its get() method returns a String. Let's try to store an Integer object in greetingWrapper.

```java
// A compile-time error. You can use greetingWrapper only to store a String.
greetingWrapper.set(new Integer(101));
```

The statement will generate the following compile-time error:

```
error: incompatible types: Integer cannot be converted to String
                greetingWrapper.set(new Integer(101));
```

You cannot pass an Integer to the set() method. The compiler will generate an error. If you want to use the Wrapper class to store an Integer, your code will be as follows:

```
Wrapper<Integer> idWrapper = new Wrapper<Integer>(new Integer(101));
idWrapper.set(new Integer(897)); // OK to pass an Integer
Integer id = idWrapper.get();

// A compile-time error. You can use idWrapper only wth an Integer.
idWrapper.set("hello");
```

Assuming that a Person class exists that contains a constructor with two parameters, you store a Person object in Wrapper as follows:

```
Wrapper<Person> personWrapper = new Wrapper<Person>(new Person(1, "Chris"));
personWrapper.set(new Person(2, "Laynie"));
Person laynie = personWrapper.get();
```

The parameter that is specified in the type declaration is called a *formal type parameter*; for example, T is a formal type parameter in the Wrapper<T> class declaration. When you replace the formal type parameter with the actual type (e.g. in Wrapper<String> you replace the formal type parameter T with String), it is called a *parameterized type*. A reference type in Java, which accepts one or more type parameters, is called a generic type. A generic type is mostly implemented in the compiler. The JVM has no knowledge of a generic type. All actual type parameters are erased during compile time using a process known as *erasure*. Compile-time type-safety is the benefit that you get when you use a parameterized generic type in your code without the need to use casts.

Supertype-Subtype Relationship

Now, let's play a trick. The following code creates two parameterized instances of the Wrapper<T> class, one for the String type and one for the Object type:

```
Wrapper<String> stringWrapper = new Wrapper<String>("Hello");
stringWrapper.set("a string");

Wrapper<Object> objectWrapper = new Wrapper<Object>(new Object());
objectWrapper.set(new Object()); // set another object

// Use a String object with objectWrapper
objectWrapper.set("a string"); // ok
```

It is fine to store a String object in objectWrapper. After all, if you intended to store an Object in objectWrapper, a String is also an Object.

Is the following assignment allowed?

```
objectWrapper = stringWrapper;
```

No, the above assignment is not allowed. That is, Wrapper<String> is not assignment compatible to Wrapper<Object>. To understand why this assignment is not allowed, let's assume for a moment that it was allowed. You would be able to write code like the following:

```
// Now objectWrapper points to stringWrapper
objectWrapper = stringWrapper;
```

```
// We could store an Object in stringWrapper using objectWrapper
objectWrapper.set(new Object());

// The following statement will throw a runtime ClassCastException
String s = sgw.get();
```

Do you see the danger of allowing an assignment like objectWrapper = stringWrapper? The compiler cannot make sure that stringWrapper will store only a reference of String type if this assignment was allowed.

Remember that a String is an Object because String is a subclass of Object. However, Wrapper<String> is not a Wrapper<Object>. The normal supertype/subtype rules do not apply with parameterized types. Don't worry about memorizing this rule if you do not understand it. If you attempt to make an assignment like the one shown above, the compiler will tell you that you can't.

Raw Type

Implementation of generic types in Java is backward compatible. If an existing non-generic class is rewritten to take advantage of generics, the existing code that uses the non-generic version of the class should keep working. The code may use (though it is not recommended) a non-generic version of a generic class by just omitting references to the generic type parameters. The non-generic version of a generic type is called a raw type. Using raw types is discouraged. If you use raw types in your code, the compiler will generate unchecked warnings, as shown in the following snippet of code:

```
Wrapper rawType = new Wrapper("Hello"); // An unchecked warning
Wrapper<String> genericType = new Wrapper<String>("Hello");
genericType = rawType; // An unchecked warning
rawType = genericType;
```

The compiler generates the following warnings when the above snippet of code is compiled:

```
warning: [unchecked] unchecked call to Wrapper(T) as a member of the raw type Wrapper
                Wrapper rawType = new Wrapper("Hello"); // An unchecked warning
                                  ^
  where T is a type-variable:
    T extends Object declared in class Wrapper

warning: [unchecked] unchecked conversion
                genericType = rawType; // An unchecked warning
                              ^
  required: Wrapper<String>
  found:    Wrapper
2 warnings
```

Unbounded Wildcards

As usual, let's start with an example. It will help you understand the need for as well as the use of wildcards in generic types. Let's build a utility class for the Wrapper class. Call it WrapperUtil. Add a utility method called printDetails() to this class, which will take an object of the Wrapper<T> class. How should you define the argument of this method? The following is the first attempt:

```
public class WrapperUtil {
        public static void printDetails(Wrapper<Object> wrapper){
                // More code goes here
        }
}
```

Since your printDetails() method is supposed to print details about a Wrapper of any type, Object as parameter type seemed to be more suitable. Let's use your new printDetails() method, as shown:

```
Wrapper<Object> objectWrapper = new Wrapper<Object>(new Object());
WrapperUtil.printDetails(objectWrapper); // OK

Wrapper<String> stringWrapper = new Wrapper<String>("Hello");
WrapperUtil.printDetails(stringWrapper); // A compile-time error
```

The compile-time error is as follows:

```
error: method printDetails in class WrapperUtil cannot be applied to given types;
                WrapperUtil.printDetails(stringWrapper); // A compile-time error
                            ^
  required: Wrapper<Object>
  found: Wrapper<String>
  reason: argument mismatch; Wrapper<String> cannot be converted to Wrapper<Object>
1 error
```

You are able to call the printDetails() method with the Wrapper<Object> type, but not with the Wrapper<String> type because they are not assignment compatible, which is contradictory to what your intuition tells you. To understand it fully, you need to know about the *wildcard type* in generics. A wildcard type is denoted by a question mark, as in <?>. For a generic type, a wildcard type is what an Object type is for a raw type. You can assign a generic of known type to a generic of wildcard type. Here is the sample code:

```
// Wrapper of String type
Wrapper<String> stringWrapper = new Wrapper<String>("Hi");

// You can assign a Wrapper<String> to Wrapper<?> type
Wrapper<?> wildCardWrapper = stringWrapper;
```

The question mark in a wildcard generic type (e.g., <?>) denotes an *unknown* type. When you declare a parameterized type using a wildcard (means unknown) as a parameter type, it means that it does not know about its type.

```
// wildCardWrapper has unknown type
Wrapper<?> wildCardWrapper;

// Better to name it as an unknownWrapper
Wrapper<?> unknownWrapper;
```

Can you create a Wrapper<T> object of an unknown type? Let's assume that John cooks something for you. He packs the food in a packet and hands it over to you. You hand over the packet to Donna. Donna asks you what is inside the packet. Your answer is that you do not know. Can John answer the same way you did? No. He must know what he cooked because he was the person who cooked the food. Even if you did not know what was inside the packet, you had no problem in carrying it and giving it to Donna. What would be your answer if Donna asked you to give her vegetable from the packet? You would say that you do not know if a vegetable is inside the packet.

Here are the rules for using a wildcard (unknown) generic type. Since it does not know its type, you cannot use it to create an object of its unknown type. The following code is illegal:

```
// Cannot use <?> with new operator. It is a compile-time error.
new Wrapper<?>("");
```

It generates the following error:

```
error: unexpected type
              new Wrapper<?>("");
                        ^
  required: class or interface without bounds
  found:    ?
1 error
```

As you were holding the packet of unknown food type (John knew the type of food when he cooked the food), a wildcard generic type can refer to a known generic type object, as shown:

```
Wrapper<?> unknownWrapper = new Wrapper<String>("Hello");
```

There is a complicated list of rules as to what a wildcard generic type reference can do with the object. However, there is a simple rule of thumb to remember. The purpose of using generics is to have compile-time type-safety in Java programs. As long as the compiler is satisfied that the operation will not produce any surprising results at runtime, it will allow the operation on the wildcard generic type reference.

Let's apply the rule of thumb to your unknownWrapper reference variable. One thing that this unknownWrapper variable is sure about is that it refers to an object of the Wrapper<T> class of a known type. However, it does not know what that known type is. Can you use the following get() method?

```
String str = unknownWrapper.get(); // A compile-time error
```

The above statement will not compile. The compiler generates the following error:

```
error: incompatible types: CAP#1 cannot be converted to String
              String str = unknownWrapper.get(); // A compile -time error
                                        ^
  where CAP#1 is a fresh type-variable:
    CAP#1 extends Object from capture of ?
1 error
```

The compiler knows that the get() method of the Wrapper<T> class returns an object of type T. However, for the unknownWrapper variable, type T is unknown. Therefore, the compiler cannot make sure that the method call, unknownWrapper.get(), will return a String and its assignment to str variable is fine at runtime. All you have to do is convince the compiler that the assignment will not throw a ClassCastException at runtime. Will the following line of code compile?

```
Object obj = unknownWrapper.get(); // OK
```

The above code will compile because the compiler is convinced that this statement will not throw a ClassCastException at runtime. It knows that the get() method returns an object of a type, which is not known to the unknownWrapper variable. No matter what type of object the get() method returns, it will always be assignment-compatible with the Object type. After all, all reference types in Java are subtypes of the Object type.

Will the following snippet of code compile?

```
unknownWrapper.set("Hello");          // A compile-time error
unknownWrapper.set(new Integer());    // A compile-time error
unknownWrapper.set(new Object());     // A compile-time error
unknownWrapper.set(null);             // OK
```

Were you surprised by the above snippet of code? You will find out that it is not as surprising as it seems. The set(T a) method accepts the generic type argument. This type, T, is not known to unknownWrapper, and therefore the compiler cannot make sure that the unknown type is a String type, an Integer type, or an Object type. This is the reason that the first three calls to set() are rejected by the compiler. Why is the fourth call to the set() method correct? A null is assignment-compatible to any reference type in Java. The compiler thought that no matter what type T would be in the set(T a) method for the object to which unknownWrapper reference variable is pointing to, a null can always be safe to use. The following is your printDetails() method code. If you pass a null Wrapper object to this method, it will throw a NullPointerException.

```
public class WrapperUtil {
        public static void printDetails(Wrapper<?> wrapper) {
                // Can assign get() return value to Object
                Object value = wrapper.get();
                String className = null;

                if (value != null) {
                        className = value.getClass().getName();
                }

                System.out.println("Class: " + className);
                System.out.println("Value: " + value);
        }
}
```

■ **Tip** Using only a question mark as a parameter type (<?>) is known as an *unbounded wildcard*. It places no bounds as to what type it can refer. You can also place an upper bound or a lower bound with a wildcard. I will discuss bounded wildcards in the next two sections.

Upper-Bounded Wildcards

Suppose you want to add a method to your WrapperUtil class. The method should accept two numbers that are wrapped in your Wrapper objects and it will return their sum. The wrapped objects may be an Integer, Long, Byte, Short, Double, or Float. Your first attempt is to write the sum() method as shown:

```
public static double sum(Wrapper<?> n1, Wrapper<?> n2) {
        //Code goes here
}
```

There are some obvious problems with the method signature. The parameters n1 and n2 could be of any parameterized type of Wrapper<T> class. For example, the following call would be a valid call for the sum() method:

```
// Try adding an Integer and a String
sum(new Wrapper<Integer>(new Integer(125)), new Wrapper<String>("Hello"));
```

Computing the sum of an Integer and a String does not make sense. However, the code will compile and you should be ready to get some runtime exceptions depending on the implementation of the sum() method. You must restrict this kind of code from compiling. It should accept two Wrapper objects of type Number or its subclasses, not just anything. Therefore, you do know the upper bound of the type of the actual parameter that the Wrapper object should have. The upper bound is the Number type. If you pass any other type, which is a subclass of the Number type, it is fine. However, anything that is not a Number type or its subclass type should be rejected at compile time. You express the upper bound of a wildcard as

```
<? extends T>
```

Here, T is a type. <? extends T> means anything that is of type T or its subclass is acceptable. Using your upper bound as Number, you can define your method as

```
public static double sum(Wrapper<? extends Number> n1, Wrapper<? extends Number> n2){
        Number num1 = n1.get();
        Number num2 = n2.get();
        double sum = num1.doubleValue() + num2.doubleValue();
        return sum;
}
```

The following snippet of code inside the method compiles fine:

```
Number num1 = n1.get();
Number num2 = n2.get();
```

No matter what you pass for n1 and n2, they will always be assignment-compatible with Number because the compiler will make sure that the parameters passed to the sum() method follow the rules specified in its declaration of <? extends Number>. The attempt to compute the sum of an Integer and a String will be rejected by the compiler.

Consider the following snippet of code:

```
Wrapper<Integer> intWrapper = new Wrapper<Integer>(new Integer(10));
Wrapper<? extends Number> numberWrapper = intWrapper; // Ok
numberWrapper.set(new Integer(1220)); // A compile-time error
numberWrapper.set(new Double(12.20)); // A compile-time error
```

Can you figure out the problem with this snippet of code? The type of numberWrapper is <? extends Number>, which means it can refer to (or it is assignment-compatible with) anything that is a subtype of the Number class. Since Integer is a subclass of Number, the assignment of intWrapper to numberWrapper is allowed. When you try to use the set() method on numberWrapper, the compiler starts complaining because it cannot make sure at compile time that numberWrapper is a type of Integer or Double, which are subtypes of a Number. Be careful with this kind of compiler error when working with generics. On the surface, it might look obvious to you and you would think that code should compile and run fine. Unless the compiler makes sure that the operation is type-safe, it will not allow you to proceed. After all, compile-time and runtime type-safety is the primary goal of generics!

Lower-Bounded Wildcards

Specifying a lower-bound wildcard is the opposite of specifying an upper-bound wildcard. The syntax for using a lower-bound wildcard is `<? super T>`, which means "anything that is a supertype of T." Let's add another method to the WrapperUtil class. You will call the new method copy() and it will copy the value from a source wrapper object to a destination wrapper object. Here is the first attempt. The `<T>` is the formal type parameter for the copy() method. It specifies that the source and dest parameters must be of the same type.

```
public class WrapperUtil {
        public static <T> void copy(Wrapper<T> source, Wrapper<T> dest) {
                T value = source.get();
                dest.set(value);
        }
}
```

Copying the content of a Wrapper<String> to a Wrapper<Object> using your copy() method will not work.

```
Wrapper<Object> objectWrapper = new Wrapper<Object>(new Object());
Wrapper<String> stringWrapper = new Wrapper<String>("Hello");
WrapperUtil.copy(stringWrapper, objectWrapper); // A compile-time error
```

The above code will generate a compile-time error because the copy() method requires the source and the dest arguments be of the same type. However, for all practical purposes a String is always an Object. Here, you need to use a lower-bounded wildcard, as shown:

```
public class WrapperUtil {
        // New definition of the copy() method
        public static <T> void copy(Wrapper<T> source, Wrapper<? super T> dest){
                T value = source.get();
                dest.set(value);
        }
}
```

Now you are saying that the dest argument of the copy() method could be either T, same as source, or any of its supertype. You can use the copy() method to copy the contents of a Wrapper<String> to a Wrapper<Object> as shown below. Since Object is the supertype of String, the new copy() method will work. However, you cannot use it to copy from an Object type wrapper to a String type wrapper, as an Object is a String is not always true.

```
Wrapper<Object> objectWrapper = new Wrapper<Object>(new Object());
Wrapper<String> stringWrapper = new Wrapper<String>("Hello");
WrapperUtil.copy(stringWrapper, objectWrapper); // OK with the new copy() method
```

Listing 4-3 shows the complete code for the WrapperUtil class.

Listing 4-3. A WrapperUtil Utility Class That Works with Wrapper Objects

```
// WrapperUtil.java
package com.jdojo.generics;

public class WrapperUtil {
        public static void printDetails(Wrapper<?> gw) {
                // Can assign get() return value to Object
```

```
                Object value = gw.get();
                String className = null;

                if (value != null) {
                        className = value.getClass().getName();
                }

                System.out.println("Class: " + className);
                System.out.println("Value: " + value);
        }

        public static double sum(Wrapper<? extends Number> n1,
                                 Wrapper<? extends Number> n2) {
                Number num1 = n1.get();
                Number num2 = n2.get();
                double sum = num1.doubleValue() + num2.doubleValue();
                return sum;
        }

        public static <T> void copy(Wrapper<T> source, Wrapper<? super T> dest) {
                T value = source.get();
                dest.set(value);
        }
}
```

Generic Methods and Constructors

You can define type parameters in a method declaration. They are specified in angle brackets before the return type of the method. The type that contains the generic method declaration does not have to be a generic type. You can use the type parameter specified for the generic type inside the non-static method declaration. In your Wrapper class, you have used the type parameter T in the get() and set() methods. You can also define new type parameters for methods. The snippet of code shown below defines a new type parameter V for method m1(). The new type parameter V forces the first and the second arguments of method m1() to be of the same type. The third argument must be of the same type T, which is the type of the class instantiation.

```
public class Test<T> {
        public <V> void m1(Wrapper<V> a, Wrapper<V> b, T c) {
                // Do something
        }
}
```

How do you specify the generic type for a method when you want to call the method? Usually, you do not need to specify the actual type parameter when you call the method. The compiler figures it out for you using the value you pass to the method. However, if you ever need to pass the actual type parameter for the method's formal type parameter, you must specify it in angle brackets (< >) between the dot and the method name in the method call, as shown:

```
Test<String> t = new Test<String>();
Wrapper<Integer> iw1 = new Wrapper<Integer>(new Integer(201));
Wrapper<Integer> iw2 = new Wrapper<Integer>(new Integer(202));
```

```
// Specify that Integer is the actual type for the type parameter for m1()
t.<Integer>m1(iw1, iw2, "hello");

// Let the compiler figure out the actual type parameter for the m1() call
// using types for iw1 and iw2
t.m1(iw1, iw2, "hello"); // OK
```

Listing 4-3 demonstrated how to declare a generic static method. You cannot refer to the type parameters of the containing class inside the static method. A static method can refer only to its own declared type parameters. Below is the copy of your copy() static method from the WrapperUtil class. It defines a type parameter T, which is used to constrain the type of arguments source and dest.

```
public static <T> void copy(Wrapper<T> source, Wrapper<? super T> dest) {
        T value = source.get();
        dest.set(value);
}
```

The compiler will figure out the actual type parameter for a method whether the method is non-static or static. However, if you want to specify the actual type parameter for a static method call, you can do so as follows:

```
WrapperUtil.<Integer>copy(iw1, iw2);
```

You can also define type parameters for constructors the same way as you do for a method. The following code defines a type parameter U for the constructor of class Test. It places a constraint that the constructor's type parameter U must be the same or a subtype of the actual type of its class type parameter T.

```
public class Test<T> {
        public <U extends T> Test(U k) {
                // Do something
        }
}
```

The compiler will figure out the actual type parameter passed to the constructor with the value you pass. If you want to specify the actual type parameter value for the constructor, you can specify it in angle brackets between the new operator and the name of the constructor, as shown in the following snippet of code:

```
// Specify the actual type parameter for the constructor as Double
Test<Number> t1 = new <Double>Test<Number>(new Double(12.89));

// Let the compiler figure out that we are using Integer as
// the actual type parameter for the constructor
Test<Number> t2 = new Test<Number>(new Integer(123));
```

Type Inference in Generic Object Creation

Java 7 added limited support for type inference in an object-creation expression for generic types. Note that the type inference support in the object-creation expression is limited to the situations where the type is obvious. Consider the following statement:

```
List<String> list = new ArrayList<String>();
```

With the declaration of list as List<String>, it is obvious that you want to create an ArrayList with type parameter as <String>. However, you needed to specify the <String> type parameter with ArrayList in the above statement before Java 7. In Java 7, you can specify empty angle brackets, <> (known as the diamond operator or simply the diamond), as the type parameter for ArrayList in the above statement. You can rewrite the above statement in Java 7 and later as shown:

```
List<String> list = new ArrayList<>(); // Works in Java 7 and later
```

Note that if you do not specify a type parameter for a generic type in an object-creation expression, the type is the raw type and the compiler generates unchecked warnings. For example, the following statement will compile with unchecked warnings:

```
// Using ArrayList as a raw type, not a generic type
List<String> list = new ArrayList(); // Generates an unchecked warning
```

The compiler warning will be as follows:

```
warning: [unchecked] unchecked conversion
                List<String> list = new ArrayList(); // Generates an unchecked warning
                                    ^
   required: List<String>
   found:    ArrayList
1 warning
```

Sometimes it is not possible for the compiler to infer correctly the parameter type of a type in an object-creation expression. In those cases, you need to specify the parameter type instead of using the diamond operator (<>). Otherwise, the compiler will infer a wrong type, which will generate an error.

When the diamond operator is used in an object creation expression, the compiler uses a four-step process to infer the parameter type for the parameterized type. Let's consider a typical object-creation expression:

```
T1<T2> var = new T3<>(constructor-arguments);
```

1. First, it tries to infer the type from the static type of the constructor-arguments. Note that constructor-arguments may be empty, for example, new ArrayList<>().

2. If it cannot infer the type from the static type of the constructor-arguments, it uses the left-hand side of the assignment operator to infer the type. In the above statement, it will infer T2 as the type if the constructor-arguments are empty. Note that an object-creation expression may not be part of an assignment statement. In such cases, it will use the third step.

3. This rule applies to Java 8 and later. If you are using Java 7, skip to the next rule. If the object-creation expression is used as an actual parameter for a method call, the compiler tries to infer the type by looking at the type of the formal parameter for the method being called.

4. If all else fails and it cannot infer the type using the above steps, it infers Object as the type.

Let's discuss a few examples that involve all steps in the type inference process. Create the two lists, list1 of List<String> type and list2 of List<Integer> type.

```
import java.util.Arrays;
import java.util.List;

// Other code goes here

List<String> list1 = Arrays.asList("A", "B");
List<Integer> list2 = Arrays.asList(9, 19, 1969);
```

Consider the following statement that uses the diamond operator:

```
List<String> list3 = new ArrayList<>(list1); // Inferred type is String
```

The compiler used the constructor argument list1 to infer the type. The static type of list1 is List<String>, so the type String was inferred by the compiler. The above statement compiles fine. The compiler did not use the left-hand side of the assignment operator, List<String> list3, during the inference process. You may not trust this argument. Consider the following statement to prove this:

```
List<String> list4 = new ArrayList<>(list2); // A compile-time error
```

Compiling the above statement generates the following error:

```
required: List<String>
found:    ArrayList<Integer>
1 error
```

Do you believe it now? The constructor argument is list2 whose static type is List<Integer>. The compiler inferred the type as Integer and replaced ArrayList<> by ArrayList<Integer>. The type of list4 is List<String>, which is not assignment-compatible with the ArrayList<Integer>, which resulted in the compile-time error.
Consider the following statement:

```
List<String> list5 = new ArrayList<>(); // Inferred type is String
```

This time, there is no constructor argument. The compiler uses the second step to look at the left-hand side of the assignment operator to infer the type. On the left-hand side, it finds List<String> and it correctly infers the type as String. Consider a process() method that is declared as follows:

```
public static void process(List<String> list) {
      // Code goes here
}
```

The following statement makes a call to the process() method, which might generate a compile-time error:

```
// The inferred type is Object in Java 7, and String in Java 8 and later
process(new ArrayList<>());
```

The above statement generates the following compile-time error in Java 7. It will compile fine in Java 8 as Java designers have been trying to make the compiler smarter a little bit at time!

```
required: List<String>
found: ArrayList<Object>
1 error
```

In Java 7, the compiler attempts to infer the type in the object creation expression, new ArrayList<>(). The expression does not have any constructor argument. It does not include a left-hand side expression. Therefore, the compiler uses the fourth step in its inference process. It infers the type as Object. It replaces the call to the process() method by the following call, which results in the argument type mismatch for the method call. Note that the compiler does not look at the method's signature (process() method in your case) to infer the type in the object-creation expression.

```
process(new ArrayList<Object>());
```

In Java 8, the compiler looks at the type of the formal parameter of the process() method and it finds List<String> and it infers the type as String.

■ **Tip**   Using the diamond operator saves some typing. Use it when the type inference is obvious. However, it is better, for readability, to specify the type, instead of the diamond operator, in a complex object-creation expression. Always prefer readability over brevity.

No Generic Exception Classes

Exceptions are thrown at runtime. The compiler cannot ensure the type-safety of exceptions at runtime if you use a generic exception class in a catch clause to catch an exception, because the erasure process erases the mention of any type parameter during compilation. This is the reason that it is a compile-time error to attempt to define a generic class, which is a direct or indirect subclass of java.lang.Throwable.

No Generic Anonymous Classes

An anonymous class is a one-time class. You need a class name to specify the actual type parameter. An anonymous class does not have a name. Therefore, you cannot have a generic anonymous class. However, you can have generic methods inside an anonymous class. Your anonymous class can inherit a generic class. An anonymous class can implement a generic interface. Any class, except an exception type, enums, and anonymous inner classes, can have type parameters.

Generics and Arrays

Let's look at the following code for a class called GenericArrayTest:

```
public class GenericArrayTest<T> {
        private T[] elements;

        public GenericArrayTest(int howMany) {
                elements = new T[howMany]; // A compile-time error
        }
        // More code goes here
}
```

The GenericArrayClass declares a type parameter T. In the constructor, it attempts to create an array of the generic type. You cannot compile the above code. The compiler will complain about the following statement:

```
elements = new T[howMany]; // A compile-time error
```

Recall that all references to the generic type are erased from the code when a generic class or code using it is compiled. An array needs to know its type when it is created, so that it can perform a check at runtime when an element is stored in it to make sure that the element is assignment-compatible with its type. An array's type information will not be available at runtime if you use a type parameter to create it. This is the reason that the above statement is not allowed.

You cannot create an array of generic type because the compiler cannot ensure the type-safety of the assignment to the array element. You cannot write the following code:

```
Wrapper<String>[] gsArray = null;

// Cannot create an array of generic type
gsArray = new Wrapper<String>[10]; // A compile-time error
```

It is allowed to create an array of unbounded wildcard generic types, as shown:

```
Wrapper<?>[] anotherArray = new Wrapper<?>[10]; // Ok
```

Suppose you want to use an array of a generic type. You can do so by using the newInstance() method of the java.lang.reflect.Array class as follows. You will have to deal with the unchecked warnings at compile time because of the cast used in the array creation statement. The following snippet of code shows that you can still bypass the compile-time type-safety check when you try to sneak in an Object into an array of Wrapper<String>. However, this is the consequence you have to live with when using generics, which does not carry its type information at runtime. Java generics are as skin deep as you can imagine.

```
Wrapper<String>[] a = (Wrapper<String>[])Array.newInstance(Wrapper.class, 10);

Object[] objArray = (Object[])a;
objArray[0] = new Object();  // Will throw a java.lang.ArrayStoreExceptionxception
a[0] = new Wrapper<String>("Hello"); // OK. Checked by compiler
```

Runtime Class Type of Generic Objects

What is the class type of the object for a parameterized type? Consider the program in Listing 4-4.

Listing 4-4. All Objects of a Parameterized Type Share the Same Class at Runtime

```
// GenericsRuntimeClassTest.java
package com.jdojo.generics;

public class GenericsRuntimeClassTest {
        public static void main(String[] args) {
                Wrapper<String> a = new Wrapper<String>("Hello");
                Wrapper<Integer> b = new Wrapper<Integer>(new Integer(123));
                Class aClass = a.getClass();
                Class bClass = b.getClass();
                System.out.println("Class for a: " + aClass.getName());
```

```
            System.out.println("Class for b: " + bClass.getName());
            System.out.println("aClass == bClass: " + (aClass == bClass));
        }
    }
}
```

```
Class for a: com.jdojo.generics.Wrapper
Class for b: com.jdojo.generics.Wrapper
aClass == bClass: true
```

The program creates objects of the Wrapper class by using String and Integer as type parameters. It prints the class names for both objects and they are the same. The output shows that all parameterized objects of the same generic type share the same class object at runtime. As mentioned earlier, the type information you supply to the generic type is removed from the code during compilation. The compiler changes the Wrapper<String> a; statement to Wrapper a;. For the JVM, its business as usual (before pre-generics)!

Heap Pollution

Representing a type at runtime is called *reification*. A type that can be represented at runtime is called a reifiable type. A type that is not completely represented at runtime is called a non-reifiable type. Most generic types are non-reifiable because generics are implemented using erasure, which removes the type's parameters information at compile time. For example, when you write Wrapper<String>, the compiler removes the type parameter <String> and the runtime sees only Wrapper instead of Wrapper<String>.

Heap pollution is a situation that occurs when a variable of a parameterized type refers to an object not of the same parameterized type. The compiler issues an unchecked warning if it detects possible heap pollution. If your program compiles without any unchecked warnings, heap pollution will not occur. Consider the following snippet of code:

```
Wrapper nWrapper = new Wrapper<Integer>(101);          // #1

// Unchecked warning at compile-time and heap pollution at runtime
Wrapper<String> sWrapper = nWrapper;                    // #2
String str = sWrapper.get();                            // #3 - ClassCastException
```

The first statement (labeled #1) compiles fine. The second statement (labeled #2) generates an unchecked warning because the compiler cannot determine if nWrapper is of the type Wrapper<String>. Since parameter type information is erased at compile-time, the runtime has no way of detecting this type mismatch. The heap pollution in the second statement makes it possible to get a ClassCastException in the third statement (labeled #3) at runtime. If the second statement was not allowed, the third statement will not cause a ClassCastException.

Heap pollution may also occur because of an unchecked cast operation. Consider the following snippet of code:

```
Wrapper<? extends Number> nW = new Wrapper<Long>(1L); // #1

// Unchecked cast and unchecked warning occurs when the following
// statement #2 is compiled. Heap pollution occurs, when it is executed.
Wrapper<Short> sw = (Wrapper<Short>)nW; // #2
short s = sw.get(); //#3 ClassCastException
```

The statement labeled #2 uses an unchecked cast. The compiler issues an unchecked warning. At runtime, it leads to heap pollution. As a result, the statement labeled #3 generates a runtime ClassCastException.

Varargs Methods and Heap Pollution Warnings

Java 7 has improved warnings for a varargs method with a non-reifiable type parameter. Java implements the varargs parameter of a varargs method by converting the varargs parameter into an array. If a varargs method uses a generic type varargs parameter, Java cannot guarantee the type-safety. A non-reifiable generic type varargs parameter may possibly lead to heap pollution.

Consider the following snippet of code that declares a process() method with a parameterized type parameter nums. The comments in the method's body indicate the heap pollution and other types of problems.

```
// A unchecked and varargs warnings in Java 7
public static void process(Wrapper<Long>…nums) {
        Object[] obj = nums; // Heap pollution
        obj[0] = new Wrapper<String>("Hello"); // Array corruption
        Long lv = nums[0].get(); // A ClassCastException
        // Other code goes here
}
```

When the process() method is compiled, the compiler removes the type information <Long> from its parameterized type parameter and changes its signature to process(Wrapper[] nums). When you compile the above declaration of the process() method, you will get the following unchecked warning:

```
warning: [unchecked] Possible heap pollution from parameterized vararg type Wrapper<Long>
        public static void process(Wrapper<Long>...nums) {
                                                   ^
1 warning
```

Consider the following snippet of code that calls the process() method:

```
Wrapper<Long> v1 = new Wrapper<Long>(10L);
Wrapper<Long> v2 = new Wrapper<Long>(11L);
process(v1, v2); // An unchecked warning in Java 5, 6, 7
```

When the above snippet of code is compiled, it generates the following compiler unchecked warning:

```
warning: [unchecked] unchecked generic array creation for varargs parameter of type Wrapper<Long>[]
                process(v1, v2);
                ^
1 warning
```

Until Java 6, the compiler generated a warning at the location where the varargs method with a non-reifiable generic varargs type parameter was called. The possible heap pollution problem may exist inside the method. Java 7 has improved the warning by generating a warning at the method declaration as well as at the location of the method call. If you create such a method, it is your responsibility to ensure that heap pollution does not occur inside your method's body.

If you create a varargs method with a non-reifiable type parameter, you can suppress the unchecked warnings at the location of the method's declaration as well as the method's call by using @java.lang.SafeVarargs annotation. By using the @SafeVarargs annotation, you are asserting that your varargs method with non-reifiable type parameter is safe to use. The following snippet of code uses @SafeVarargs annotation with the process() method:

```
@java.lang.SafeVarargs
public static void process(Wrapper<Long>...nums) {
        Object[] obj = nums; // Heap pollution
```

```
        obj[0] = new Wrapper<String>("Hello"); // Array corruption
        Long lv = nums[0].get(); // A ClassCastException
        // Other code goes here
}
```

When you compile the above declaration of the process() method, you do not get an *unchecked* warning. However, you get the following *varargs* warning because the compiler sees possible heap pollution when the varargs parameter nums is assigned to the Object array obj:

```
warning: [varargs] Varargs method could cause heap pollution from non-reifiable varargs parameter
nums
                Object[] obj = nums; // Heap pollution
                    ^
1 warning
```

You can suppress the *unchecked* and *varargs* warnings for a varargs method with a non-reifiable type parameter by using @java.lang.SuppressWarnings annotation as follows:

```
@SuppressWarnings({"unchecked", "varargs"})
public static void process(Wrapper<Long>...nums) {
        // Code goes here
}
```

Note that when you use the @SuppressWarnings annotation with a varargs method, it suppresses warnings only at the location of the method's declaration, not at the locations where the method is called.

Summary

Generics are the Java language features that allow you to declare types (classes and interfaces) that use type parameters. Type parameters are specified when the generic type is used. The type when used with the actual type parameter is known a parameterized type. When a generic type is used without specifying its type parameters, it is called a raw type. For example, if Wrapper<T> is a generic class, Wrapper<String> is a parameterized type with String as the actual type parameter and Wrapper as the raw type. Type parameters can also be specified for constructors and methods. Generics allow you to write true polymorphic code in Java—code using a type parameter that works for all types.

By default, a type parameter is unbounded, meaning that you can specify any type for the type parameter. For example, if a class is declared with a type parameter <T>, you can specify any type available in Java, such as <String>, <Object>, <Person>, <Employee>, <Integer>, etc., as the actual type for T. Type parameters in a type declaration can also be specified as having upper bounds or lower bounds. The declaration Wrapper<U extends Person> is an example of specifying an upper bound for the type parameter U that specifies that U can be of a type that is Person or a subtype of Person. The declaration Wrapper<? super Person> is an example of specifying a lower bound; it specifies that the type parameter is the type Person type of a supertype of Person.

Java also lets you specify the wildcard, which is a question mark, as the actual type parameter. A wildcard as the actual parameter means the actual type parameter is unknown; for example, Wrapper<?> means that the type parameter T for the generic type Wrapper<T> is unknown.

The Java compiler attempts to infer the type of an expression using generics, depending on the context in which the expression is used. If the compiler cannot infer the type, it generates a compile-time error and you will need to specify the type explicitly.

The supertype–subtype relationship does not exist with parameterized types. For example, `Wrapper<Long>` is not a subtype of `Wrapper<Number>`.

The generic type parameters are erased by the compiler using a process called type erasure. Therefore, the generic type parameters are not available at runtime. For example, the runtime type of `Wrapper<Long>` and `Wrapper<String>` are the same, which is `Wrapper`.

▨ ▨ ▨

CHAPTER 5

Lambda Expressions

In this chapter, you will learn

- What lambda expressions are
- Why we need lambda expressions
- The syntax for defining lambda expressions
- Target typing for lambda expressions
- Commonly used built-in functional interfaces
- Method and Constructor references
- Lexical scoping of lambda expressions

What Is a Lambda Expression?

A lambda expression is an unnamed block of code (or an unnamed function) with a list of formal parameters and a body. Sometimes a lambda expression is simply called a *lambda*. The body of a lambda expression can be a block statement or an expression. An arrow (->) is used to separate the list of parameters and the body. The term "lambda" in "lambda expression" has its origin in Lambda calculus that uses the Greek letter lambda (λ) to denote a function abstraction. The following are some examples of lambda expressions in Java:

```
// Takes an int parameter and returns the parameter value incremented by 1
(int x) -> x + 1

// Takes two int parameters and returns their sum
(int x, int y) -> x + y

// Takes two int parameters and returns the maximum of the two
(int x, int y) -> { int max = x > y ? x : y;
                    return max;
                  }

// Takes no parameters and returns void
() -> { }
```

```
// Takes no parameters and returns a string "OK"
() -> "OK"

// Takes a String parameter and prints it on the standard output
(String msg) -> { System.out.println(msg); }

// Takes a parameter and prints it on the standard output
msg -> System.out.println(msg)

// Takes a String parameter and returns its length
(String str) -> str.length()
```

At this point, you will not be able to understand the syntax of lambda expressions completely. I will cover the syntax in detail shortly. For now, just get the feel of it, keeping in mind that the syntax for lambda expressions is similar to the syntax for declaring methods.

■ **Tip** A lambda expression is not a method, although its declaration looks similar to a method. As the name suggests, a lambda expression is an expression that represents an instance of a functional interface.

Every expression in Java has a type; so does a lambda expression. The type of a lambda expression is a functional interface type. When the abstract method of the functional interface is called, the body of the lambda expression is executed.

Consider the lambda expression that takes a String parameter and returns its length:

```
(String str) -> str.length()
```

What is the type of this lambda expression? The answer is that we do not know. By looking at the lambda expression, all you can say is that it takes a String parameter and returns an int, which is the length of the String. Its type can be any functional interface type with an abstract method that takes a String as a parameter and returns an int. The following is an example of such a functional interface:

```
@FunctionalInterface
interface StringToIntMapper {
        int map(String str);
}
```

The lambda expression represents an instance of the StringToIntMapper functional interface when it appears in the assignment statement, like so:

```
StringToIntMapper mapper = (String str) -> str.length();
```

In this statement, the compiler finds that the right-hand side of the assignment operator is a lambda expression. To infer its type, it looks at the left-hand side of the assignment operator that expects an instance of the StringToIntMapper interface; it verifies that the lambda expression conforms to the declaration of the map() method in the `StringToIntMapper` interface; finally, it infers that the type of the lambda expression is the `StringToIntMapper` interface type. When you call the `map()` method on the `mapper` variable passing a `String`, the body of the lambda expression is executed as shown in the following snippet of code:

```
StringToIntMapper mapper = (String str) -> str.length();
String name = "Kristy";
int mappedValue = mapper.map(name);
System.out.println("name=" + name + ", mapped value=" + mappedValue);
```

```
name=Kristy, mapped value=6
```

So far, you have not seen anything that you could not do in Java without using lambda expressions. The following snippet of code uses an anonymous class to achieve the same result as the lambda expression used in the previous example:

```
StringToIntMapper mapper = new StringToIntMapper() {
        @Override
        public int map(String str) {
                return str.length();
        }
};
String name = "Kristy";
int mappedValue = mapper.map(name);
System.out.println("name=" + name + ", mapped value=" + mappedValue);
```

```
name=Kristy, mapped value=6
```

At this point, a lambda expression may seem to be a concise way of writing an anonymous class, which is true as far as the syntax goes. There are some subtle differences in semantics between the two. I will discuss the differences between a lambda expressions and anonymous classes as I discuss more details later.

■ **Tip**   Java is a strongly-typed language, which means that the compiler must know the type of all expressions used in a Java program. A lambda expression by itself does not have a type, and therefore, it cannot be used as a standalone expression. The type of a lambda expression is always inferred by the compiler by the context in which it is used.

Why Do We Need Lambda Expressions?

Java has supported object-oriented programming since the beginning. In object-oriented programming, the program logic is based on mutable objects. Methods of classes contain the logic. Methods are invoked on objects, which typically modify their states. In object-oriented programming, the order of method invocation matters as each method invocation may potentially modify the state of the object, thus producing side effects. Static analysis of the program logic is difficult as the program state depends on the order in which the code will be executed. Programming with mutating objects also poses a challenge in concurrent programming in which multiple parts of the program may attempt to modify the state of the same object concurrently. As the processing power of computers has increased in recent years, so has the amount of data to be processed. Nowadays, it is not uncommon to process data as big as terabytes in size, requiring the need for parallel programming. Now it is common for computers to have a multi-core processor that give users the opportunity to run software programs faster; at the same time, this poses a challenge to programmers to write more parallel programs, taking advantage of all the available cores in the processor. Java has supported concurrent programming since the beginning. It added support for parallel programming in Java 7 through the fork/join framework, which was not easy to use.

Functional programming, which is based on Lambda calculus, existed long before object-oriented programming. It is based on the concept of functions, a block of code that accepts values, known as parameters, and the block of code is executed to compute a result. A function represents a functionality or operation. Functions do not modify data, including its input, thus producing no side-effects; for this reason, the order of the execution of functions does not matter in functional programming. In functional programming, a higher order function is an anonymous function that can be treated as a data object. That is, it can be stored in a variable and passed around from one context to another. It might be invoked in a context that did not necessarily define it. Note that a higher order function is an anonymous function, so the invoking context does not have to know its name. A closure is a higher order function packaged with its defining environment. A closure carries with it the variables in scope when it was defined, and it can access those variables even when it is invoked in a context other than the context in which those variables were defined.

In recent years, functional programming has become popular because of its suitability in concurrent, parallel, and event-driven programming. Modern programming languages such as C#, Groovy, Python, and Scala support functional programming. Java did not want to be left behind, and hence, it introduced lambda expressions to support functional programming, which can be mixed with its already popular object-oriented features to develop robust, concurrent, parallel programs. Java adopted the syntax for lambda expressions that is very similar to the syntax used in other programming languages such as C# and Scala.

In object-oriented programming, a function is called a method and it is always part of a class. If you wanted to pass functionality around in Java, you needed to create an object, add a method to the object to represent the functionality, and pass the object around. A lambda expression in Java is like a higher-order function in functional programming, which is an unnamed block of code representing a functionality that can be passed around like data. A lambda expression may capture the variables in its defining scope and it may access those variables later in a context that did not define the captured variable. This features let you use lambda expressions to implement closures in Java.

Java 8 introduced lambda expressions that represent an instance of a functional interface. You were able to do everything prior to Java 8 using anonymous classes what you can do with lambda expressions. Functional interfaces are not a new addition in Java 8; they have existed since the beginning.

So why and where do we need lambda expressions? Anonymous classes use a bulky syntax. Lambda expressions use a very concise syntax to achieve the same result. Lambda expressions are not a complete replacement for anonymous classes. You will still need to use anonymous classes in a few situations. Just to appreciate the conciseness of the lambda expressions, compare the following two statements from the previous section that create an instance of the StringToIntMapper interface; one uses an anonymous class, taking six lines of code, and another uses a lambda expression, taking just one line of code:

```
// Using an anonymous class
StringToIntMapper mapper = new StringToIntMapper() {
        @Override
        public int map(String str) {
                return str.length();
        }
};

// Using a lambda expression
StringToIntMapper mapper = (String str) -> str.length();
```

Syntax for Lambda Expressions

A lambda expression describes an anonymous function. The general syntax for using lambda expressions is very similar to declaring a method. The general syntax is

```
(<LambdaParametersList>) -> { <LambdaBody> }
```

A lambda expression consists of a list of parameters and a body that are separated by an arrow (->). The list of parameters is declared the same way as the list of parameters for methods. The list of parameters is enclosed in parentheses, as is done for methods. The body of a lambda expression is a block of code enclosed in braces. Like a method's body, the body of a lambda expression may declare local variables; use statements including break, continue, and return; throw exceptions, etc. Unlike a method, a lambda expression does not have four parts.

- A lambda expression does not have a name.

- A lambda expression does not have a return type. It is inferred by the compiler from the context of its use and from its body.

- A lambda expression does not have a throws clause. It is inferred from the context of its use and its body.

- A lambda expression cannot declare type parameters. That is, a lambda expression cannot be generic.

Table 5-1 contains some examples of lambda expressions and equivalent methods. I have given a suitable name to methods as you cannot have a method without a name in Java. The compiler infers the return type of lambda expressions.

Table 5-1. *Examples of Lambda Expressions and Equivalent Methods*

Lambda Expression	Equivalent Method

`(int x, int y) -> {`
`    return x + y;`
`}`
	`int sum(int x, int y) {`
	`    return x + y;`
	`}`

`(Object x) -> {`
`    return x;`
`}`
	`Object identity(Object x)  {`
	`    return x;`
	`}`

`(int x, int y) -> {`
`    if ( x > y) {`
`        return x;`
`    }`
`    else {`
`        return y;`
`    }`
`}`
	`int getMax(int x, int y) {`
	`    if ( x > y) {`
	`        return x;`
	`    }`
	`    else {`
	`        return y;`
	`    }`
	`}`

`(String msg) -> {`
`    System.out.println(msg);`
`}`
	`void print(String msg) {`
	`    System.out.println(msg);`
	`}`

`() -> {`
`    System.out.println(LocalDate.now());`
`}`
	`void printCurrentDate() {`
	`    System.out.println(LocalDate.now());`
	`}`

`() -> {`
`    // No code goes here`
`}`
	`void doNothing() {`
	`    // No code goes here`
	`}`

One of the goals of the lambda expression was to keep its syntax concise and let the compiler infer the details. The following sections discuss the shorthand syntax for declaring lambda expressions.

Omitting Parameter Types

You can omit the declared type of the parameters. The compiler will infer the types of parameters from the context in which the lambda expression is used.

```
// Types of parameters are declared
(int x, int y) -> { return x + y; }

// Types of parameters are omitted
(x, y) -> { return x + y; }
```

If you omit the types of parameters, you must omit it for all parameters or for none. You cannot omit for some and not for others. The following lambda expression will not compile because it declares the type of one parameter and omits for the other:

```
// A compile-time error
(int x, y) -> { return x + y; }
```

■ **Tip** A lambda expression that does not declare the types of its parameters is known as an implicit lambda expression or an implicitly-typed lambda expression. A lambda expression that declares the types of its parameters is known as an explicit lambda expression or an explicitly-typed lambda expression.

Declaring a Single Parameter

Sometimes a lambda expression takes only one parameter. You can omit the parameter type for a single parameter lambda expression as you can do for a lambda expression with multiple parameters. You can also omit the parentheses if you omit the parameter type in a single parameter lambda expression. The following are three ways to declare a lambda expression with a single parameter:

```
// Declares the parameter type
(String msg) -> { System.out.println(msg); }

// Omits the parameter type
(msg) -> { System.out.println(msg); }

// Omits the parameter type and parentheses
msg -> { System.out.println(msg); }
```

The parentheses can be omitted only if the single parameter also omits its type. The following lambda expression will not compile:

```
// Omits parentheses, but not the parameter type, which is not allowed.
String msg -> { System.out.println(msg); }
```

Declaring No Parameters

If a lambda expression does not take any parameters, you need to use empty parentheses.

```
// Takes no parameters
() -> { System.out.println("Hello"); }
```

It is not allowed to omit the parentheses when the lambda expression takes no parameter. The following declaration will not compile:

```
-> { System.out.println("Hello"); }
```

Parameters with Modifiers

You can use modifiers, such as final, in the parameter declaration for explicit lambda expressions. The following two lambda expressions are valid:

```
(final int x, final int y) -> { return x + y; }
```

```
(int x, final int y) -> { return x + y; }
```

The following lambda expression will not compile because it uses the final modifier in parameter declarations, but omits the parameter type:

```
(final x, final y) -> { return x + y; }
```

Declaring Body of Lambda Expressions

The body of a lambda expression can be a block statement or a single expression. A block statement is enclosed in braces; a single expression is not enclosed in braces.

When a block statement is executed the same way as a method's body. A return statement or the end of the body returns the control to the caller of the lambda expression.

When an expression is used as the body, it is evaluated and returned to the caller. If the expression evaluates to void, nothing is returned to the caller. The following two lambda expressions are the same; one uses a block statement and the other an expression:

```
// Uses a block statement. Takes two int parameters and returns their sum.
(int x, int y) -> { return x + y; }

// Uses an expression. Takes a two int parameters and returns their sum.
(int x, int y) -> x + y
```

The following two lambda expressions are the same; one uses a block statement as the body and the other an expression that evaluates to void:

```
// Uses a block statement
(String msg) -> { System.out.println(msg); }

// Uses an expression
(String msg) -> System.out.println(msg)
```

Target Typing

Every lambda expression has a type, which is a functional interface type. In other words, a lambda expression represents an instance of a functional interface. Consider the following lambda expression:

```
(x, y) -> x + y
```

What is the type of this lambda expression? In other words, an instance of which functional interface does this lambda expression represent? We do not know the type of this lambda expression at this point. All we can say about this lambda expression with confidence is that it takes two parameters named x and y. We cannot tell its return type as the expression x + y, depending on the type of x and y, may evaluate to a number (int, long, float, or double) or a String. This is an implicit lambda expression, and therefore, the compiler will have to infer the types of two parameters using the context in which the expression is used. This lambda expression may be of different functional interface types depending on the context in which it is used.

There are two types of expressions in Java:

- Standalone Expressions

- Poly Expressions

A standalone expression is an expression whose type can be determined by the expression without knowing the context of its use. The following are examples of standalone expressions:

```
// The type of expression is String
new String("Hello")

// The type of expression is String (a String literal is also an expression)
"Hello"

// The type of expression is ArrayList<String>
new ArrayList<String>()
```

A poly expression is an expression that has different types in different contexts. The compiler determines the type of the expression. The contexts that allow the use of poly expressions are known as *poly contexts*. All lambda expressions in Java are poly expressions. You must use it in a context to know its type. Poly expressions existed in Java prior to Java 8 and lambda expressions. For example, the expression new ArrayList<>() is a poly expression. You cannot tell its type unless you provide the context of its use. This expression is used in the following two contexts to represent two different types:

```
// The type of new ArrayList<>() is ArrayList<Long>
ArrayList<Long> idList = new ArrayList<>();

ArrayList<String> nameList = new ArrayList<>();
```

The compiler infers the type of a lambda expression. The context in which a lambda expression is used expects a type, which is called the *target type*. The process of inferring the type of a lambda expression from the context is known as *target typing*. Consider the following pseudo code for an assignment statement where a variable of type T is assigned a lambda expression:

```
T t = <LambdaExpression>;
```

The target type of the lambda expression in this context is T. The compiler uses the following rules to determine whether the <LambdaExpression> is assignment compatible with its target type T:

- T must be a functional interface type.

- The lambda expression has the same number and type of parameters as the abstract method of T. For an implicit lambda expression, the compiler will infer the types of parameters from the abstract method of T.

- The type of the returned value from the body of the lambda expression is assignment compatible to the return type of the abstract method of T.

- If the body of the lambda expression throws any checked exceptions, those exceptions must be compatible with the declared throws clause of the abstract method of T. It is a compile-time error to throw checked exceptions from the body of a lambda expression, if its target type's method does not contain a throws clause.

Let's look at few examples of target typing. Consider two functional interfaces, Adder and Joiner, as shown in Listing 5-1 and Listing 5-2, respectively.

Listing 5-1. A Functional Interface Named Adder

```
// Adder.java
package com.jdojo.lambda;

@FunctionalInterface
public interface Adder {
        double add(double n1, double n2);
}
```

Listing 5-2. A Functional Interface Named Joiner

```
// Joiner.java
package com.jdojo.lambda;

@FunctionalInterface
public interface Joiner {
        String join(String s1, String s2);
}
```

The add() method of the Adder interface adds two numbers. The join() method of the Joiner interface concatenates two strings. Both interfaces are used for trivial purposes; however, they will serve the purpose of demonstrating the target typing for lambda expressions very well.

Consider the following assignment statement:

```
Adder adder = (x, y) -> x + y;
```

The type of the adder variable is Adder. The lambda expression is assigned to the variable adder, and therefore, the target type of the lambda expression is Adder. The compiler verifies that Adder is a functional interface. The lambda expression is an implicit lambda expression. The compiler finds that the Adder interface contains a double add(double, double) abstract method. It infers the types for x and y parameters as double and double, respectively. At this point, the compiler treats the statement as shown:

```
Adder adder = (double x, double y) -> x + y;
```

The compiler now verifies the compatibility of the returned value from the lambda expression and the return type of the add() method. The return type of the add() method is double. The lambda expression returns x + y, which would be of a double as the compiler already knows that the types of x and y are double. The lambda expression does not throw any checked exceptions. Therefore, the compiler does not have to verify anything for that. At this point, the compiler infers that the type of the lambda expression is the type Adder.

Apply the rules of target typing for the following assignment statement:

```java
Joiner joiner = (x, y) -> x + y;
```

This time, the compiler infers the type for the lambda expression as Joiner. Do you see an example of a poly expression where the same lambda expression (x, y) -> x + y is of the type Adder in one context and of the type Joiner in another.

Listing 5-3 shows how to use these lambda expressions in a program. Note that it's business as usual after you use a lambda expression to create an instance of a functional interface. That is, after you create an instance of a functional interface, you use the instance as you used before Java 8. The lambda expression does not change the way the instance of a functional interface is used to invoke its method.

Listing 5-3. Examples of Using Lambda Expressions

```java
// TargetTypeTest.java
package com.jdojo.lambda;

public class TargetTypeTest {
        public static void main(String[] args)  {
                // Creates an Adder using a lambda expression
                Adder adder = (x, y) -> x + y;

                // Creates a Joiner using a lambda expression
                Joiner joiner = (x, y) -> x + y;

                // Adds two doubles
                double sum1 = adder.add(10.34, 89.11);

                // Adds two ints
                double sum2 = adder.add(10, 89);

                // Joins two strings
                String str = joiner.join("Hello", " lambda");

                System.out.println("sum1 = " + sum1);
                System.out.println("sum2 = " + sum2);
                System.out.println("str = " + str);
        }
}
```

```
sum1 = 99.45
sum2 = 99.0
str = Hello lambda
```

I will now discuss the target typing in the context of method calls. You can pass lambda expressions as arguments to methods. Consider the code for class LambdaUtil shown in Listing 5-4.

Listing 5-4. A LambdaUtil Class That Uses Functional Interfaces as an Argument in Methods

```java
// LambdaUtil.java
package com.jdojo.lambda;

public class LambdaUtil {
        public void testAdder(Adder adder) {
                double x = 190.90;
                double y = 8.50;
                double sum = adder.add(x, y);
                System.out.print("Using an Adder:");
                System.out.println(x + " + " + y + " = " + sum);
        }

        public void testJoiner(Joiner joiner) {
                String s1 = "Hello";
                String s2 = "World";
                String s3 = joiner.join(s1,s2);
                System.out.print("Using a Joiner:");
                System.out.println("\"" + s1 + "\" + \"" + s2 + "\" = \"" + s3 + "\"");;
        }
}
```

The LambdaUtil class contains two methods: testAdder() and testJoiner(). One method takes an Adder as an argument and another Joiner as an argument. Both methods have simple implementations. Consider the following snippet of code:

```java
LambdaUtil util = new LambdaUtil();
util.testAdder((x, y) -> x + y);
```

The first statement creates an object of the LambdaUtil class. The second statement calls the testAdder() method on the object, passing a lambda expression of (x, y) -> x + y. The compiler must infer the type of the lambda expression. The target type of the lambda expression is the type Adder because the argument type of the testAdder(Adder adder) is Adder. The rest of the target typing process is the same as you saw in the assignment statement before. Finally, the compiler infers that the type of the lambda expression is Adder.

The program in Listing 5-5 creates an object of the LambdaUtil class and calls the testAdder() and testJoiner() methods.

Listing 5-5. Using Lambda Expressions as Method Arguments

```java
// LambdaUtilTest.java
package com.jdojo.lambda;

public class LambdaUtilTest {
        public static void main(String[] args)  {
                LambdaUtil util = new LambdaUtil();

                // Call the testAdder() method
                util.testAdder((x, y) -> x + y);

                // Call the testJoiner() method
                util.testJoiner((x, y) -> x + y);
```

```java
        // Call the testJoiner() method. The Joiner will
        // add a space between the two strings
        util.testJoiner((x, y) -> x + " " + y);

        // Call the testJoiner() method. The Joiner will
        // reverse the strings and join resulting strings in
        // reverse order adding a comma in between
        util.testJoiner((x, y) -> {
                StringBuilder sbx = new StringBuilder(x);
                StringBuilder sby = new StringBuilder(y);
                sby.reverse().append(",").append(sbx.reverse());
                return sby.toString();
        });
    }
}
```

```
Using an Adder:190.9 + 8.5 = 199.4
Using a Joiner:"Hello" + "World" = "HelloWorld"
Using a Joiner:"Hello" + "World" = "Hello World"
Using a Joiner:"Hello" + "World" = "dlroW,olleH"
```

Notice the output of the LambdaUtilTest class. The testJoiner() method was called three times, and every time it printed a different result of joining the two strings "Hello" and "World". This is possible because different lambda expressions were passed to this method. At this point, you can say that you have parameterized the behavior of the testJoiner() method. That is, how the testJoiner() method behaves depends on its parameter. Changing the behavior of a method through its parameters is known as *behavior parameterization*. This is also known as passing code as data because you pass code (logic, functionality, or behavior) encapsulated in lambda expressions to methods as if it is data.

It is not always possible for the compiler to infer the type of a lambda expression. In some contexts, there is no way the compiler can infer the type of a lambda expression; those contexts do not allow the use of lambda expressions. Some contexts may allow using lambda expressions, but the use itself may be ambiguous to the compiler; one such case is passing lambda expressions to overloaded methods.

Consider the code for the class LambdaUtil2 shown in Listing 5-6. The code for this class is the same as for the LambdaUtil class in Listing 5-4, except that this class changed the names of the two methods to the same name of test(), making it an overloaded method.

Listing 5-6. A LambdaUtil2 Class That Uses Functional Interfaces as an Argument in Methods

```java
// LambdaUtil2.java
package com.jdojo.lambda;

public class LambdaUtil2 {
        public void test(Adder adder) {
                double x = 190.90;
                double y = 8.50;
                double sum = adder.add(x, y);
                System.out.print("Using an Adder:");
                System.out.println(x + " + " + y + " = " + sum);
        }
```

```
        public void test(Joiner joiner) {
                String s1 = "Hello";
                String s2 = "World";
                String s3 = joiner.join(s1,s2);
                System.out.print("Using a Joiner:");
                System.out.println("\"" + s1 + "\" + \"" + s2 + "\" = \"" + s3 + "\"");;
        }
}
```

Consider the following snippet of code:

```
LambdaUtil2 util = new LambdaUtil2();
util.test((x, y) -> x + y); // A compile-time error
```

The second statement results in the following compile-time error:

```
Reference to test is ambiguous. Both method test(Adder) in LambdaUtil2 and method test(Joiner) in
LambdaUtil2 match.
```

The call to the test() method fails because the lambda expression is implicit and it matches both versions of the test() method. The compiler does not know which method to use: test(Adder adder) or test(Joiner joiner). In such circumstances, you need to help the compiler by providing some more information. The following are the some of the ways to help the compiler resolve the ambiguity:

- If the lambda expression is implicit, make it explicit by specifying the type of the parameters.

- Use a cast.

- Do not use the lambda expression directly as the method argument. First, assign it to a variable of the desired type, and then, pass the variable to the method.

Let's discuss all three methods to resolve the compile-time error. The following snippet of code changes the lambda expression to an explicit lambda expression:

```
LambdaUtil2 util = new LambdaUtil2();
util.test((double x, double y) -> x + y); // OK. Will call test(Adder adder)
```

Specifying the type of parameters in the lambda expression resolved the issue. The compiler has two candidate methods: test(Adder adder) and test(Joiner joiner). With the (double x, double y) parameter information, only the test(Adder adder) method matches.

The following snippet of code uses a cast to cast the lambda expression to the type Adder:

```
LambdaUtil2 util = new LambdaUtil2();
util.test((Adder)(x, y) -> x + y); // OK. Will call test(Adder adder)
```

Using a cast tells the compiler that the type of the lambda expression is Adder, and therefore, helps it choose the test(Adder adder) method.

Consider the following snippet of code that breaks down the method call into two statements:

```
LambdaUtil2 util = new LambdaUtil2();
Adder adder = (x, y) -> x + y;
util.test(adder); // OK. Will call test(Adder adder)
```

The lambda expression is assigned to a variable of type Adder and the variable is passed to the test() method. Again, it helps the compiler choose the test(Adder adder) method based on the compile-time type of the adder variable.

The program in Listing 5-7 is similar to the one shown in Listing 5-5, except that it uses the LambdaUtil2 class. It uses explicit lambda expressions and a cast to resolve the ambiguous match for lambda expressions.

Listing 5-7. Resolving Ambiguity During Target Typing

```java
// LambdaUtil2Test.java
package com.jdojo.lambda;

public class LambdaUtil2Test {
    public static void main(String[] args) {
        LambdaUtil2 util = new LambdaUtil2();

        // Calls the testAdder() method
        util.test((double x, double y) -> x + y);

        // Calls the testJoiner() method
        util.test((String x, String y) -> x + y);

        // Calls the testJoiner() method. The Joiner will
        // add a space between the two strings
        util.test((Joiner)(x, y) -> x + " " + y);

        // Calls the testJoiner() method. The Joiner will
        // reverse the strings and join resulting strings in
        // reverse order adding a comma in between
        util.test((Joiner)(x, y) -> {
            StringBuilder sbx = new StringBuilder(x);
            StringBuilder sby = new StringBuilder(y);
            sby.reverse().append(",").append(sbx.reverse());
            return sby.toString();
        });
    }
}
```

```
Using an Adder:190.9 + 8.5 = 199.4
Using a Joiner:"Hello" + "World" = "HelloWorld"
Using a Joiner:"Hello" + "World" = "Hello World"
Using a Joiner:"Hello" + "World" = "dlroW,olleH"
```

Lambda expressions can be used only in the following contexts:

- *Assignment Context*: A lambda expression may appear to the right-hand side of the assignment operator in an assignment statement. For example,

  ```java
  ReferenceType variable1 = LambdaExpression;
  ```

- *Method Invocation Context*: A lambda expression may appear as an argument to a method or constructor call. For example,

  ```java
  util.testJoiner(LambdaExpression);
  ```

- *Return Context*: A lambda expression may appear in a return statement inside a method, as its target type is the declared return type of the method. For example,

```
return LambdaExpression;
```

- *Cast Context*: A lambda expression may be used if it is preceded by a cast. The type specified in the cast is its target type. For example,

```
(Joiner) LambdaExpression;
```

Functional Interfaces

A functional interface is simply an interface that has exactly one abstract method. The following types of methods in an interface do not count for defining a functional interface:

- Default methods
- Static methods
- Public methods inherited from the Object class

Note that an interface may have more than one abstract method, and can still be a functional interface if all but one of them is a redeclaration of the methods in the Object class. Consider the declaration of the Comparator class that is in the java.util package, as shown:

```
package java.util;

@FunctionalInterface
public interface Comparator<T> {
        // An abstract method declared in the interface
        int compare(T o1, T o2);

        // Re-declaration of the equals() method in the Object class
        boolean equals(Object obj);

        /* Many static and default methods that are not shown here. */
}
```

The Comparator interface contains two abstract methods: compare() and equals(). The equals() method in the Comparator interface is a redeclaration of the equals() method of the Object class, and therefore it does not count against the one abstract method requirement for it to be a functional interface. The Comparator interface contains several default and static method that are not shown here.

A lambda expression is used to represent an unnamed function as used in functional programming. A functional interface represents one type of functionality/operation in terms of its lone abstract method. This commonality is the reason why the target type of a lambda expression is always a functional interface.

Using the @FunctionalInterface Annotation

The declaration of a functional interface may optionally be annotated with the annotation @FunctionalInterface, which is in the java.lang package. So far, all functional interfaces declared in this chapter, such as Adder and Joiner, have been annotated with @FunctionalInterface. The presence of this annotation tells the compiler to make sure that the declared type is a functional interface. If the annotation @FunctionalInterface is used on a non-functional interface or other types such as classes, a compile-time error occurs. If you do not use the annotation @FunctionalInterface on an interface with one abstract method, the interface is still a functional interface and it can be the target type for lambda expressions. Using this annotation gives you an additional assurance from the compiler. The presence of the annotation also protects you from inadvertently changing a functional interface into a non-functional interface, as the compiler will catch it.

The following declaration for an Operations interface will not compile, as the interface declaration uses the @FunctionalInterface annotation and it is not a functional interface (defines two abstract methods):

```
@FunctionalInterface
public interface Operations {
        double add(double n1, double n2);
        double subtract(double n1, double n2);
}
```

To compile the Operations interface, either remove one of the two abstract methods or remove the @FunctionalInterface annotation.

The following declaration for a Test class will not compile, as @FunctionalInterface cannot be used on a type other than a functional interface:

```
@FunctionalInterface
public class Test {
        // Code goes here
}
```

Generic Functional Interface

It is allowed for a functional interface to have type parameters. That is, a functional interface can be generic. An example of a generic functional parameter is the Comparator interface with one type parameter T.

```
@FunctionalInterface
public interface Comparator<T> {
        int compare(T o1, T o2);
}
```

A functional interface may have a generic abstract method. That is, the abstract method may declare type parameters. The following is an example of a non-generic functional interface called Processor whose abstract method process() is generic:

```
@FunctionalInterface
public interface Processor {
        <T> void process(T[] list);
}
```

A lambda expression cannot declare type parameters, and therefore, it cannot have a target type whose abstract method is generic. For example, you cannot represent the Processor interface using a lambda expression. In such cases, you need to use a method reference, which I discuss in the next section, or an anonymous class.

Let's have a short example of a generic functional interface and instantiating it using lambda expressions. Listing 5-8 shows the code for a functional interface named Mapper.

Listing 5-8. A Mapper Functional Interface

```java
// Mapper.java
package com.jdojo.lambda;

@FunctionalInterface
public interface Mapper<T> {
        // An abstract method
        int map(T source);

        // A generic static method
        public static <U> int[] mapToInt(U[] list, Mapper<? super U> mapper) {
                int[] mappedValues = new int[list.length];

                for (int i = 0; i < list.length; i++) {
                        // Map the object to an int
                        mappedValues[i] = mapper.map(list[i]);
                }

                return mappedValues;
        }
}
```

Mapper is a generic functional interface with a type parameter T. Its abstract method map() takes an object of type T as a parameter and returns an int. The mapToInt() method is a generic static method that accepts an array of type U and a Mapper of a type that is U itself or a supertype of U. The method returns an int array whose elements contain the mapped value for the corresponding elements passed as an array.

The program in Listing 5-9 shows how to use lambda expressions to instantiate the Mapper<T> interface. The program maps a String array and an Integer array to int arrays.

Listing 5-9. Using the Mapper Functional Interface

```java
// MapperTest.java
package com.jdojo.lambda;

public class MapperTest {
        public static void main(String[] args) {
                // Map names using their length
                System.out.println("Mapping names to their lengths:");
                String[] names = {"David", "Li", "Doug"};
                int[] lengthMapping = Mapper.mapToInt(names, (String name) -> name.length());
                printMapping(names, lengthMapping);

                System.out.println("\nMapping integers to their squares:");
                Integer[] numbers = {7, 3, 67};
                int[] countMapping = Mapper.mapToInt(numbers, (Integer n) -> n * n);
                printMapping(numbers, countMapping);
        }
```

```
        public static void printMapping(Object[] from, int[] to) {
            for(int i = 0; i < from.length; i++) {
                System.out.println(from[i] + " mapped to " + to[i]);
            }
        }
    }
}
```

```
Mapping names to their lengths:
David mapped to 5
Li mapped to 2
Doug mapped to 4

Mapping integers to their squares:
7 mapped to 49
3 mapped to 9
67 mapped to 4489
```

Intersection Type and Lambda Expressions

Java 8 introduced a new type called an *intersection type* that is an intersection (or subtype) of multiple types. An intersection type may appear as the target type in a cast. An ampersand is used between two types, such as (Type1 & Type2 & Type3), represents a new type that is an intersection of Type1, Type2, and Type3. Consider a marker interface called Sensitive, shown in Listing 5-10.

Listing 5-10. A Marker Interface Named Sensitive

```
// Sensitive.java
package com.jdojo.lambda;

public interface Sensitive {
    // It ia a marker interface. So, no methods exist.
}
```

Suppose you have a lambda expression assigned to a variable of the Sensitive type.

```
Sensitive sen = (x, y) -> x + y; // A compile-time error
```

This statement does not compile. The target type of a lambda expression must be a functional interface; Sensitive is not a functional interface. You should be able to make such assignment, as a marker interface does not contain any methods. In such cases, you need to use a cast with an intersection type that creates a new synthetic type that is a subtype of all types. The following statement will compile:

```
Sensitive sen = (Sensitive & Adder) (x, y) -> x + y; // OK
```

The intersection type Sensitive & Adder is still a functional interface, and therefore, the target type of the lambda expression is a functional interface with one method from the Adder interface.

In Java, you can convert an object to a stream of bytes and restore the object back later. This is called *serialization*. A class must implement the java.io.Serializable marker interface for its objects to be serialized. If you want a lambda expression to be serialized, you will need to use a cast with an intersection type. The following statement assigns a lambda expression to a variable of the Serializable interface:

```
Serializable ser = (Serializable & Adder) (x, y) -> x + y;
```

■ **Tip** I will cover the Serializable interface and serialization of objects in Chapter 7.

Commonly Used Functional Interfaces

Java 8 has added many frequently used functional interfaces in the package java.util.function. They are listed in Table 5-2.

Table 5-2. *List of Functional Interfaces Declared in the Package java.util.function*

Interface Name	Method	Description
Function<T,R>	R apply(T t)	Represents a function that takes an argument of type T and returns a result of type R.
BiFunction<T,U,R>	R apply(T t, U u)	Represents a function that takes two arguments of types T and U, and returns a result of type R.
Predicate<T>	boolean test(T t)	In mathematics, a predicate is a boolean-valued function that takes an argument and returns true or false. The function represents a condition that returns true or false for the specified argument.
BiPredicate<T,U>	boolean test(T t, U u)	Represents a predicate with two arguments.
Consumer<T>	void accept(T t)	Represents an operation that takes an argument, operates on it to produce some side effects, and returns no result.
BiConsumer<T,U>	void accept(T t, U u)	Represents an operation that takes two arguments, operates on them to produce some side effects, and returns no result.
Supplier<T>	T get()	Represents a supplier that returns a value.
UnaryOperator<T>	T apply(T t)	Inherits from Function<T,T>. Represents a function that takes an argument and returns a result of the same type.
BinaryOperator<T>	T apply(T t1, T t2)	Inherits from BiFunction<T,T,T>. Represents a function that takes two arguments of the same type and returns a result of the same.

Table 5-2 shows only the generic versions of the functional interfaces. Several specialized versions of these interfaces exist. They have been specialized for frequently used primitive data types; for example, IntConsumer is a specialized version of Consumer<T>. Some interfaces in the table contain convenience default and static methods. The table lists only the abstract method, not the default and static methods.

Using the Function<T,R> Interface

Six specializations of the Function<T, R> interface exist:

- IntFunction<R>

- LongFunction<R>

- DoubleFunction<R>

- ToIntFunction<T>

- ToLongFunction<T>

- ToDoubleFunction<T>

IntFunction<R>, LongFunction<R>, and DoubleFunction<R> take an int, a long, and a double as an argument, respectively, and return a value of type R. ToIntFunction<T>, ToLongFunction<T>, and ToDoubleFunction<T> take an argument of type T and return an int, a long, and a double, respectively. Similar specialized functions exist for other types of generic functions listed in the table.

■ **Tip**   The Mapper<T> interface in Listing 5-8 represents the same function type as ToIntFunction<T> in the java.util.function package. You created the Mapper<T> interface to learn how to create and use a generic functional interface. From now on, please look at built-in functional interfaces before creating your own; use them if they meet your needs.

The following snippet of code shows how to use the same lambda expression to represent a function that accepts an int and returns its square, using four variants of the Function<T, R> function type:

```
// Takes an int and returns its square
Function<Integer, Integer> square1 = x -> x * x;
IntFunction<Integer> square2 = x -> x * x;
ToIntFunction<Integer> square3 = x -> x * x;
UnaryOperator<Integer> square4 = x -> x * x;

System.out.println(square1.apply(5));
System.out.println(square2.apply(5));
System.out.println(square3.applyAsInt(5));
System.out.println(square4.apply(5));
```

```
25
25
25
25
```

The Function interface contains the following default and static methods:

- default <V> Function<T,V> andThen(Function<? super R,? extends V> after)

- default <V> Function<V,R> compose(Function<? super V,? extends T> before)

- static <T> Function<T,T> identity()

The andThen() method returns a composed Function that applies this function to the argument, and then applies the specified after function to the result. The compose() function returns a composed function that applies the specified before function to the argument, and then applies this function to the result. The identify() method returns a function that always returns its argument.

The following snippet of code demonstrates how to use default and static methods of the Function interface to compose new functions:

```
// Create two functions
Function<Long, Long> square = x -> x * x;
Function<Long, Long> addOne = x -> x + 1;

// Compose functions from the two functions
Function<Long, Long> squareAddOne = square.andThen(addOne);
Function<Long, Long> addOneSquare = square.compose(addOne);

// Get an identity function
Function<Long, Long> identity = Function.<Long>identity();

// Test the functions
long num = 5L;
System.out.println("Number : " + num);
System.out.println("Square and then add one: " + squareAddOne.apply(num));
System.out.println("Add one and then square: " + addOneSquare.apply(num));
System.out.println("Identity: " + identity.apply(num));
```

```
Number: 5
Square and then add one: 26
Add one and then square: 36
Identity: 5
```

You are not limited to composing a function that consists of two functions that are executed in a specific order. A function may be composed of as many functions as you want. You can chain lambda expressions to create a composed function in one expression. Note that when you chain lambda expressions, you may need to provide hints to the compiler to resolve the target type ambiguity that may arise. The following is an example of a composed function by chaining three functions. A cast is provided to help the compiler. Without the cast, the compiler will not be able to infer the target type.

```
// Square the input, add one to the result, and square the result
Function<Long, Long> chainedFunction = ((Function<Long, Long>)(x -> x * x))
                                       .andThen(x -> x + 1)
                                       .andThen(x -> x * x);
System.out.println(chainedFunction.apply(3L));
```

```
100
```

Using the Predicate<T> Interface

A predicate represents a condition that is either true or false for a given input. The Predicate interface contains the following default and static methods that let you compose a predicate based on other predicates using logical NOT, AND, and OR.

- default Predicate<T> negate()

- default Predicate<T> and(Predicate<? super T> other)

- default Predicate<T> or(Predicate<? super T> other)

- static <T> Predicate<T> isEqual(Object targetRef)

The negate() method returns a Predicate that is a logical negation of the original predicate. The and() method returns a short-circuiting logical AND predicate of this predicate and the specified predicate. The or() method returns a short-circuiting logical OR predicate of this predicate and the specified predicate. The isEqual() method returns a predicate that tests if the specified targetRef is equal to the specified argument for the predicate according to Objects.equals(Object o1, Object o2); if two inputs are null, this predicate evaluates to true. You can chain the calls to these methods to create complex predicates. The following snippet of code shows some examples of creating and using predicates:

```
// Create some predicates
Predicate<Integer> greaterThanTen = x -> x > 10;
Predicate<Integer> divisibleByThree = x -> x % 3 == 0;
Predicate<Integer> divisibleByFive = x -> x % 5 == 0;
Predicate<Integer> equalToTen = Predicate.isEqual(null);

// Create predicates using NOT, AND, and OR on other predciates
Predicate<Integer> lessThanOrEqualToTen = greaterThanTen.negate();
Predicate<Integer> divisibleByThreeAndFive = divisibleByThree.and(divisibleByFive);
Predicate<Integer> divisibleByThreeOrFive = divisibleByThree.or(divisibleByFive);

// Test the predicates
int num = 10;
System.out.println("Number: " + num);
System.out.println("greaterThanTen: " + greaterThanTen.test(num));
System.out.println("divisibleByThree: " + divisibleByThree.test(num));
System.out.println("divisibleByFive: " + divisibleByFive.test(num));
System.out.println("lessThanOrEqualToTen: " + lessThanOrEqualToTen.test(num));
System.out.println("divisibleByThreeAndFive: " + divisibleByThreeAndFive.test(num));
System.out.println("divisibleByThreeOrFive: " + divisibleByThreeOrFive.test(num));
System.out.println("equalsToTen: " + equalToTen.test(num));
```

```
Number: 10
greaterThanTen: false
divisibleByThree: false
divisibleByFive: true
lessThanOrEqualToTen: true
divisibleByThreeAndFive: false
divisibleByThreeOrFive: true
equalsToTen: false
```

Using Functional Interfaces

Functional interfaces are used in two contexts by two different types of users:

- By the library designers for designing APIs

- By library users for using the APIs

Functional interfaces are used to design APIs by library designers. They are used to declare a parameter's type and return type in method declarations. They are used the same way non-functional interfaces are used. Functional interfaces existed in Java since the beginning, and Java 8 has not changed the way they are used in designing the APIs.

In Java 8, library users use functional interfaces as target types for lambda expressions. That is, when a method in the API takes a functional interface as an argument, the user of the API should use a lambda expression to pass the argument. Using lambda expressions has the benefit of making the code concise and more readable.

In this section, I will show you how to design APIs using functional interfaces and how to use lambda expressions to use the APIs. Functional interfaces have been used heavily in designing the Java library for Collection and Stream APIs that I will cover in Chapter 13 and 14.

I will use one enum and two classes in subsequent examples. The Gender enum, shown in Listing 5-11, contains two constants to represent the gender of a person. The Person class, shown in Listing 5-12, represents a person; it contains, apart from other methods, a getPersons() method that returns a list of persons.

Listing 5-11. A Gender enum

```
// Gender.java
package com.jdojo.lambda;

public enum Gender {
    MALE, FEMALE
}
```

Listing 5-12. A Person Class

```
// Person.java
package com.jdojo.lambda;

import java.time.LocalDate;
import java.util.ArrayList;
import java.util.List;
import static com.jdojo.lambda.Gender.MALE;
import static com.jdojo.lambda.Gender.FEMALE;

public class Person {
        private String firstName;
        private String lastName;
        private LocalDate dob;
        private Gender gender;

        public Person(String firstName, String lastName, LocalDate dob, Gender gender) {
                this.firstName = firstName;
                this.lastName = lastName;
                this.dob = dob;
                this.gender = gender;
        }
```

```java
        public String getFirstName() {
                return firstName;
        }

        public void setFirstName(String firstName) {
                this.firstName = firstName;
        }

        public String getLastName() {
                return lastName;
        }

        public void setLastName(String lastName) {
                this.lastName = lastName;
        }

        public LocalDate getDob() {
                return dob;
        }

        public void setDob(LocalDate dob) {
                this.dob = dob;
        }

        public Gender getGender() {
                return gender;
        }

        public void setGender(Gender gender) {
                this.gender = gender;
        }

        @Override
        public String toString() {
                return firstName + " " + lastName + ", " + gender + ", " + dob;
        }

        // A utility method
        public static List<Person> getPersons() {
                ArrayList<Person> list = new ArrayList<>();
                list.add(new Person("John", "Jacobs", LocalDate.of(1975, 1, 20), MALE));
                list.add(new Person("Wally", "Inman", LocalDate.of(1965, 9, 12), MALE));
                list.add(new Person("Donna", "Jacobs", LocalDate.of(1970, 9, 12), FEMALE));
                return list;
        }
}
```

The FunctionUtil class in Listing 5-13 is a utility class. Its methods apply a function on a List. List is an interface that is implemented by the ArrayList class. The forEach() method applies an action on each item in the list, typically producing side effects; the action is represented by a Consumer. The filter() method filters a list based on a specified Predicate. The map() method maps each item in the list to a value using a Function. As a library designer, you will design these methods using functional interfaces. Note that the FunctionUtil class contains no mention of lambda expressions. You could have designed this class the same way even before Java 8.

Listing 5-13. A FunctionUtil Class

```
// FunctionUtil.java
package com.jdojo.lambda;

import java.util.ArrayList;
import java.util.List;
import java.util.function.Consumer;
import java.util.function.Function;
import java.util.function.Predicate;

public class FunctionUtil {
        // Applies an action on each item in a list
        public static <T> void forEach(List<T> list, Consumer<? super T> action) {
                for(T item : list) {
                        action.accept(item);
                }
        }

        // Applies a filter to a list and returned the filtered list items
        public static <T> List<T> filter(List<T> list, Predicate<? super T> predicate) {
                List<T> filteredList = new ArrayList<>();
                for(T item : list) {
                        if (predicate.test(item)) {
                                filteredList.add(item);
                        }
                }
                return filteredList;
        }

        // Maps each item in a list to a value
        public static <T, R> List<R> map(List<T> list, Function<? super T, R> mapper) {
                List<R> mappedList = new ArrayList<>();
                for(T item : list) {
                        mappedList.add(mapper.apply(item));

                }
                return mappedList;
        }
}
```

You will now use the FunctionUtil class as a library user and use the functional interfaces as target types of lambda expressions. Listing 5-14 shows how to use the FunctionUtil class.

Listing 5-14. Using Functional Interfaces as Target Types of Lambda Expressions as Library Users

```
// FunctionUtilTest.java
package com.jdojo.lambda;

import static com.jdojo.lambda.Gender.MALE;
import java.util.List;
```

```java
public class FunctionUtilTest {
        public static void main(String[] args) {
                List<Person> list = Person.getPersons();

                // Use the forEach() method to print each person in the list
                System.out.println("Original list of persons:");
                FunctionUtil.forEach(list, p -> System.out.println(p));

                // Filter only males
                List<Person> maleList = FunctionUtil.filter(list, p -> p.getGender() == MALE);

                System.out.println("\nMales only:");
                FunctionUtil.forEach(maleList, p -> System.out.println(p));

                // Map each person to his/her year of birth
                List<Integer> dobYearList = FunctionUtil.map(list, p -> p.getDob().getYear());

                System.out.println("\nPersons mapped to year of their birth:");
                FunctionUtil.forEach(dobYearList, year -> System.out.println(year));

                // Apply an action to each person in the list
                // Add one year to each male's dob
                FunctionUtil.forEach(maleList, p -> p.setDob(p.getDob().plusYears(1)));

                System.out.println("\nMales only after ading 1 year to DOB:");
                FunctionUtil.forEach(maleList, p -> System.out.println(p));
        }
}
```

```
Original list of persons:
John Jacobs, MALE, 1975-01-20
Wally Inman, MALE, 1965-09-12
Donna Jacobs, FEMALE, 1970-09-12

Males only:
John Jacobs, MALE, 1975-01-20
Wally Inman, MALE, 1965-09-12

Persons mapped to year of their birth:
1975
1965
1970

Males only after ading 1 year to DOB:
John Jacobs, MALE, 1976-01-20
Wally Inman, MALE, 1966-09-12
```

The program gets a list of persons, applies a filter to the list to get a list of only males, maps persons to the year of their birth, and adds one year to each male's date of birth. It performs each of these actions using lambda expressions. Note the conciseness of the code; it uses only one line of code to perform each action. Most notable is the use of the forEach() method. This method takes a Consumer function. Then each item is passed to this function. The function can take any action on the item. You passed a Consumer that prints the item on the standard output as shown:

```
FunctionUtil.forEach(list, p -> System.out.println(p));
```

Typically, a Consumer applies an action on the item it receives to produce side effects. In this case, it simply prints the item, without producing any side effects.

Method References

A lambda expression represents an anonymous function that is treated as an instance of a functional interface. A method reference is shorthand to create a lambda expression using an existing method. Using method references makes your lambda expressions more readable and concise; it also lets you use the existing methods. If a lambda expression contains a body that is an expression using a method call, you can use a method reference in place of that lambda expression.

▪ **Tip** A method reference is not a new type in Java. It is not a function pointer as used in some other programming languages. It is simply shorthand for writing a lambda expression using an existing method. It can only be used where a lambda expression can be used.

Let's consider an example before I explain the syntax for method references. Consider the following snippet of code:

```
import java.util.function.ToIntFunction;
...
ToIntFunction<String> lengthFunction = str -> str.length();
String name = "Ellen";
int len = lengthFunction.applyAsInt(name);
System.out.println("Name = " + name + ", length = " + len);
```

```
Name = Ellen, length = 5
```

The code uses a lambda expression to define an anonymous function that takes a String as an argument and returns its length. The body of the lambda expression consists of only one method call that is the length() method of the String class. You can rewrite the above lambda expression using a method reference to the length() method of the String class, as shown:

```
import java.util.function.ToIntFunction;
...
ToIntFunction<String> lengthFunction = String::length;
String name = "Ellen";
int len = lengthFunction.applyAsInt(name);
System.out.println("Name = " + name + ", length = " + len);
```

```
Name = Ellen, length = 5
```

The general syntax for a method reference is

`<Qualifier>::<MethodName>`

The `<Qualifier>` depends on the type of the method reference. Two consecutive colons act as a separator. The `<MethodName>` is the name of the method. For example, in the method reference `String::length`, `String` is the qualifier and `length` is the method name.

■ **Tip** A method reference does not call the method when it is declared. The method is called later when the method of its target type is called.

The syntax for method references allows specifying only the method name. You cannot specify the parameter types and return type of the method. Recall that a method reference is shorthand for a lambda expression. The target type, which is always a functional interface, determines the method's details. If the method is an overloaded method, the compiler will choose the most specific method based on the context. See Table 5-3.

Table 5-3. *Types of Method References*

Syntax	Description
`TypeName::staticMethod`	A method reference to a static method of a class, an interface, or an enum
`objectRef::instanceMethod`	A method reference to an instance method of the specified object
`ClassName::instanceMethod`	A method reference to an instance method of an arbitrary object of the specified class
`TypeName.super::instanceMethod`	A method reference to an instance method of the supertype of a particular object
`ClassName::new`	A constructor reference to the constructor of the specified class
`ArrayTypeName::new`	An array constructor reference to the constructor of the specified array type

Using method references may be a little confusing in the beginning. The main point of confusion is the process of mapping the number and type of arguments in the actual method to the method reference. To help understand the syntax, I will use a method reference and its equivalent lambda expression in all examples.

Static Method References

A static method reference is used to use a static method of a type as a lambda expression. The type could be a class, an interface, or an enum. Consider the following static method of the `Integer` class:

- `static String toBinaryString(int i)`

The toBinaryString() method represents a function that takes an int as an argument and returns a String. You can use it in a lambda expression as shown:

```
// Using a lambda expression
Function<Integer, String> func1 = x -> Integer.toBinaryString(x);
System.out.println(func1.apply(17));
```

```
10001
```

The compiler infers the type of x as Integer and the return type of the lambda expression as String, by using the target type Function<Integer, String>. You can rewrite this statement using a static method reference, as shown:

```
// Using a method reference
Function<Integer, String> func2 = Integer::toBinaryString;
System.out.println(func2.apply(17));
```

```
10001
```

The compiler finds a static method reference to the toBinaryString() method of the Integer class on the right-hand side of the assignment operator. The toBinaryString() method takes an int as an argument and returns a String. The target type of the method reference is a function that takes an Integer as an argument and returns a String. The compiler verifies that after unboxing the Integer argument type of the target type to int, the method reference and target type are assignment compatible.

Consider another static method sum() in the Integer class:

```
static int sum(int a, int b)
```

The method reference would be Integer::sum. Let's use it in the same way you used the toBinaryString() method in the above example.

```
Function<Integer, Integer> func2 = Integer::sum; // A compile-time error
```

The compiler generates the following error message when you compile this code:

```
Error: incompatible types: invalid method reference
                Function<Integer, Integer> func2 = Integer::sum;
method sum in class Integer cannot be applied to given types
required: int,int
found: Integer
reason: actual and formal argument lists differ in length
```

The error message is stating that the method reference Integer::sum is not assignment compatible with the target type Function<Integer, Integer>. The sum(int, int) method takes two int arguments whereas the target type takes only one Integer argument. The mismatch in the number of arguments caused the compile-time error.

To fix the error, the target type of the method reference `Integer::sum` should be a functional interface whose abstract method takes two int arguments and returns an int. Using a `BiFunction<Integer, Integer, Integer>` as the target type will work. The following snippet of code shows how to use a method reference `Integer::sum` as well as the equivalent lambda expression:

```
// Uses a lambda expression
BiFunction<Integer, Integer, Integer> func1 = (x, y) -> Integer.sum(x, y);
System.out.println(func1.apply(17, 15));

// Uses a method reference
BiFunction<Integer, Integer, Integer> func2 = Integer::sum;
System.out.println(func2.apply(17, 15));
```

```
32
32
```

Let's try using a method reference of the overloaded static method `valueOf()` of the Integer class. The method has three versions:

- `static Integer valueOf(int i)`

- `static Integer valueOf(String s)`

- `static Integer valueOf(String s, int radix)`

The following snippet of code shows how different target types will use the three different versions of the `Integer.valueOf()` static method. It is left as an exercise for readers to write the following snippet of code using lambda expressions:

```
// Uses Integer.valueOf(int)
Function<Integer, Integer> func1 = Integer::valueOf;

// Uses Integer.valueOf(String)
Function<String, Integer> func2 = Integer::valueOf;

// Uses Integer.valueOf(String, int)
BiFunction<String, Integer, Integer> func3 = Integer::valueOf;

System.out.println(func1.apply(17));
System.out.println(func2.apply("17"));
System.out.println(func3.apply("10001", 2));
```

```
17
17
17
```

The following is the last example in this category. The `Person` class, shown in Listing 5-12, contains a `getPersons()` static method that has a declaration as shown:

- `static List<Person> getPersons()`

The method takes no argument and returns a List<Person>. A Supplier<T> represents a function that takes no argument and returns a result of type T. The following snippet of code uses the method reference Person::getPersons as a Supplier<List<Person>>:

```
Supplier<List<Person>>supplier = Person::getPersons;
List<Person> personList = supplier.get();
FunctionUtil.forEach(personList, p -> System.out.println(p));
```

```
John Jacobs, MALE, 1975-01-20
Wally Inman, MALE, 1965-09-12
Donna Duncan, FEMALE, 1970-09-12
```

Instance Method References

An instance method is invoked on an object's reference. The object reference on which an instance method is invoked is known as the *receiver* of the method invocation. The receiver of a method invocation can be an object reference or an expression that evaluates to an object's reference. The following snippet of code shows the receiver of the length() instance method of the String class:

```
String name = "Kannan";

// name is the receiver of the length() method
int len1 = name.length();

// "Hello" is the receiver of the length() method
int len2 = "Hello".length();

// (new String("Kannan")) is the receiver of the length() method
int len3 = (new String("Kannan")).length();
```

In a method reference for an instance method, you can specify the receiver of the method invocation explicitly or you can provide it implicitly when the method is invoked. The former is called a *bound receiver* and the latter is called an *unbound receiver*. The syntax for an instance method reference supports two variants:

- objectRef::instanceMethod
- ClassName::instanceMethod

Bound Receiver

For a bound receiver, use the objectRef.instanceMethod syntax. Consider the following snippet of code:

```
Supplier<Integer> supplier = () -> "Ellen".length();
System.out.println(supplier.get());
```

5

This statement uses a lambda expression that represents a function that takes no argument and returns an int. The body of the expression uses a String object called "Ellen" to invoke the length() instance method of the String class. You can rewrite this statement using an instance method reference with the "Ellen" object as the bound receiver using a Supplier<Integer> as the target type as shown:

```
Supplier<Integer> supplier = "Ellen"::length;
System.out.println(supplier.get());
```

```
5
```

Consider the following snippet of code to represent a Consumer<String> that takes a String as an argument and returns void:

```
Consumer<String> consumer = str -> System.out.println(str);
consumer.accept("Hello");
```

```
Hello
```

This lambda expression invokes the println() method on the System.out object. This can be rewritten using a method reference with System.out as the bound receiver, as shown:

```
Consumer<String> consumer = System.out::println;
consumer.accept("Hello");
```

```
Hello
```

When the method reference System.out::println is used, the compiler looks at its target type, which is Consumer<String> that represents a function type that takes a String as an argument and returns void. The compiler finds a println(String) method in the PrintStream class of the System.out object and uses that method for the method reference.

As the last example in this category, you will use the method reference System.out::println to print the list of persons, as shown:

```
List<Person> list = Person.getPersons();
FunctionUtil.forEach(list, System.out::println);
```

```
John Jacobs, MALE, 1975-01-20
Wally Inman, MALE, 1965-09-12
Donna Jacobs, FEMALE, 1970-09-12
```

Unbound Receiver

For an unbound receiver, use the ClassName::instanceMethod syntax. Consider the following statement in which the lambda expression takes a Person as an argument and returns a String:

```
Function<Person, String> fNameFunc = (Person p) -> p.getFirstName();
```

This statement can be rewritten using the instance method reference, as shown:

```
Function<Person, String> fNameFunc = Person::getFirstName;
```

In the beginning, this is confusing for two reasons:

- The syntax is the same as the syntax for a method reference to a static method.

- It raises a question: which object is the receiver of the instance method invocation?

The first confusion can be cleared by looking at the method name and checking whether it is a static or instance method. If the method is an instance method, the method reference represents an instance method reference.

The second confusion can be cleared by keeping a rule in mind that the first argument to the function represented by the target type is the receiver of the method invocation. Consider an instance method reference called String::length that uses an unbound receiver. The receiver is supplied as the first argument to the apply() method, as shown:

```
Function<String, Integer> strLengthFunc = String::length;

String name ="Ellen";

// name is the receiver of String::length
int len = strLengthFunc.apply(name);
System.out.println("name = " + name + ", length = " + len);
```

```
name = Ellen, length = 5
```

The instance method concat() of the String class has the following declaration:

```
String concat(String str)
```

The method reference String::concat represents an instance method reference for a target type whose function takes two String arguments and returns a String. The first argument will be the receiver of the concat() method and the second argument will be passed to the concat() method. The following snippet of code shows an example:

```
String greeting = "Hello";
String name = " Laynie";

// Uses a lambda expression
BiFunction<String, String, String> func1 = (s1, s2) -> s1.concat(s2);
System.out.println(func1.apply(greeting, name));

// Uses an instance method reference on an unbound receiver
BiFunction<String, String, String> func2 = String::concat;
System.out.println(func2.apply(greeting, name));
```

```
Hello Laynie
Hello Laynie
```

As the last example in this category, you will use the method reference `Person::getFirstName` that is an instance method reference on an unbound receiver, as shown:

```
List<Person> personList = Person.getPersons();

// Maps each Person object to its first name
List<String> firstNameList = FunctionUtil.map(personList, Person::getFirstName);

// Prints the first name list
FunctionUtil.forEach(firstNameList, System.out::println);
```

```
John
Wally
Donna
```

Supertype Instance Method References

The keyword `super` is used as a qualifier to invoke the overridden method in a class or an interface. The keyword is available only in an instance context. Use the following syntax to construct a method reference that refers to the instance method in the supertype and the method that's invoked on the current instance:

```
TypeName.super::instanceMethod
```

Consider the `Priced` interface and the `Item` class in Listing 5-15 and Listing 5-16. The `Priced` interface contains a default method that returns 1.0. The `Item` class implements the `Priced` interface. It overrides the `toString()` method of the `Object` class and the `getPrice()` method of the `Priced` interface. I have added three constructors to the `Item` class that display a message on the standard output. I will use them in examples in the next section.

Listing 5-15. A Priced Interface with a Default Method of getPrice()

```
// Priced.java
package com.jdojo.lambda;

public interface Priced {
        default double getPrice() {
                return 1.0;
        }
}
```

Listing 5-16. An Item Class That Implements the Priced Interface

```
// Item.java
package com.jdojo.lambda;

import java.util.function.Supplier;

public class Item implements Priced {
        private String name = "Unknown";
        private double price = 0.0;
```

```java
public Item() {
        System.out.println("Constructor Item() called.");
}

public Item(String name) {
        this.name = name;
        System.out.println("Constructor Item(String) called.");
}

public Item(String name, double price) {
        this.name = name;
        this.price = price;
        System.out.println("Constructor Item(String, double) called.");
}

public String getName() {
        return name;
}

public void setName(String name) {
        this.name = name;
}

public void setPrice(double price) {
        this.price = price;
}

@Override
public double getPrice() {
        return price;
}

@Override
public String toString() {
        return "name = " + getName() + ", price = " + getPrice();
}

public void test() {
        // Uses the Item.toString() method
        Supplier<String> s1 = this::toString;

        // Uses Object.toString() method
        Supplier<String> s2 = Item.super::toString;

        // Uses Item.getPrice() method
        Supplier<Double> s3 = this::getPrice;

        // Uses Priced.getPrice() method
        Supplier<Double> s4 = Priced.super::getPrice;
```

```
                // Uses all method references and prints the results
                System.out.println("this::toString: " + s1.get());
                System.out.println("Item.super::toString: " + s2.get());
                System.out.println("this::getPrice: " + s3.get());
                System.out.println("Priced.super::getPrice: " + s4.get());
        }
}
```

The test() method in the Item class uses four method references with a bound receiver. The receiver is the Item object on which the test() method is called.

- The method reference this::toString refers to the toString() method of the Item class.

- The method reference Item.super::toString refers to the toString() method of the Object class, which is the superclass of the Item class.

- The method reference this::getPrice refers to the getPrice() method of the Item class.

- The method reference Priced.super::getPrice refers to the getPrice() method of the Priced interface, which is the superinterface of the Item class.

The program in Listing 5-17 creates an object of the Item class and calls its test() method. The output shows the method being used by the four method references.

Listing 5-17. Testing the Item Class

```
// ItemTest.java
package com.jdojo.lambda;

public class ItemTest {
        public static void main(String[] args) {
                Item apple = new Item("Apple", 0.75);
                apple.test();
        }
}
```

```
Constructor Item(String, double) called.
this::toString: name = Apple, price = 0.75
Item.super::toString: com.jdojo.lambda.Item@24d46ca6
this::getPrice: 0.75
Priced.super::getPrice: 1.0
```

Constructor References

Sometimes the body of a lambda expression may be just an object creation expression. Consider the following two statements that use a String object creation expression as the body for lambda expressions:

```
Supplier<String> func1 = () -> new String();
Function<String,String> func2 = str -> new String(str);
```

You can rewrite these statements by replacing the lambda expressions with constructor references as shown:

```
Supplier<String> func1 = String::new;
Function<String,String> func2 = String::new;
```

The syntax for using a constructor is

```
ClassName::new
```

```
ArrayTypeName::new
```

The ClassName in ClassName::new is the name of the class that can be instantiated; it cannot be the name of an abstract class. The keyword new refers to the constructor of the class. A class may have multiple constructors. The syntax does not provide a way to refer to a specific constructor. The compiler selects a specific constructor based on the context. It looks at the target type and the number of arguments in the abstract method of the target type. The constructor whose number of arguments matches with the number of arguments in the abstract method of the target type is chosen. Consider the following snippet of code that uses three constructors of the Item class, shown in Listing 5-16, in lambda expressions:

```
Supplier<Item> func1 = () -> new Item();
Function<String,Item> func2 = name -> new Item(name);
BiFunction<String,Double, Item> func3 = (name, price) -> new Item(name, price);

System.out.println(func1.get());
System.out.println(func2.apply("Apple"));
System.out.println(func3.apply("Apple", 0.75));
```

```
Constructor Item() called.
name = Unknown, price = 0.0
Constructor Item(String) called.
name = Apple, price = 0.0
Constructor Item(String, double) called.
name = Apple, price = 0.75
```

The following snippet of code replaces the lambda expressions with a constructor reference Item::new. The output shows the same constructors are used as before.

```
Supplier<Item> func1 = Item::new;
Function<String,Item> func2 = Item::new;
BiFunction<String,Double, Item> func3 = Item::new;

System.out.println(func1.get());
System.out.println(func2.apply("Apple"));
System.out.println(func3.apply("Apple", 0.75));
```

```
Constructor Item() called.
name = Unknown, price = 0.0
Constructor Item(String) called.
name = Apple, price = 0.0
Constructor Item(String, double) called.
name = Apple, price = 0.75
```

When the statement Supplier<Item> func1 = Item::new; is executed, the compiler finds that the target type Supplier<String> does not accept any argument. Therefore, it uses the no-args constructor of the Item class.

When the statement Function<String,Item> func2 = Item::new; is executed, the compiler finds that the target type Function<String,Item> takes a String argument. Therefore, it uses the constructor of the Item class that takes a String argument.

When the statement BiFunction<String,Double,Item> func3 = Item::new; is executed, the compiler finds that the target type BiFunction<String,Double,Item> takes two arguments: a String and a Double. Therefore, it uses the constructor of the Item class that takes a String and a double argument.

The following statement generates a compile-time error, as the compiler does not find a constructor in the Item class that accepts a Double argument:

```
Function<Double,Item> func4 = Item::new; // A compile-time error
```

Arrays in Java do not have constructors. There is a special syntax to use constructor references for arrays. Array constructors are treated to have one argument of int type that is the size of the array. The following snippet of code shows the lambda expression and its equivalent constructor reference for an int array:

```
// Uses a lambda expression
IntFunction<int[]> arrayCreator1 = size -> new int[size];
int[] empIds1 = arrayCreator1.apply(5); // Creates an int array of five elements

// Uses an array constructor reference
IntFunction<int[]> arrayCreator2 = int[]::new;
int[] empIds2 = arrayCreator2.apply(5); // Creates an int array of five elements
```

You can also use a Function<Integer,R> type to use an array constructor reference, where R is the array type.

```
// Uses an array constructor reference
Function<Integer,int[]> arrayCreator3 = int[]::new;
int[] empIds3 = arrayCreator3.apply(5); // Creates an int array of five elements
```

The syntax for the constructor reference for arrays supports creating an array of multiple dimensions. However, you can specify the length for only the first dimension. The following statement creates a two-dimensional int array with the first dimension having the length of 5:

```
// Uses an array constructor reference
IntFunction<int[][]> TwoDimArrayCreator = int[][]::new;
int[][] matrix = TwoDimArrayCreator.apply(5); // Creates an int[5][] array
```

You might be tempted to use a BiFunction<Integer,Integer,int[][]> to use a constructor reference for a two-dimensional array to supply the length for both dimensions. However, the syntax is not supported. Array constructors are supposed to accept only one parameter that is the length of the first dimension. The following statement generates a compile-time error:

```
BiFunction<Integer,Integer,int[][]> arrayCreator = int[][]::new;
```

Generic Method References

Typically, the compiler figures out the actual type for generic type parameters when a method reference refers to a generic method. Consider the following generic method in the Arrays class in the java.util package:

- static <T> List<T> asList(T... a)

The asList() method takes a varargs argument of type T and returns a List<T>. You can use Arrays::asList as the method reference for this method. The syntax for the method reference allows you to specify the actual type parameter for the method just after the two consecutive colons. For example, if you are passing String objects to the asList() method, its method reference can be written as Arrays::<String>asList.

■ **Tip** The syntax for a method reference also supports specifying the actual type parameters for generic types. The actual type parameters are specified just before the two consecutive colons. For example, the constructor reference ArrayList<Long>::new specifies Long as the actual type parameter for the generic ArrayList<T> class.

The following snippet of code contains an example of specifying the actual type parameter for the generic method Arrays.asList(). In the code, Arrays::asList will work the same as the compiler will infer String as the type parameter for the asList() method by examining the target type.

```java
import java.util.Arrays;
import java.util.List;
import java.util.function.Function;
...
Function<String[],List<String>>asList = Arrays::<String>asList;

String[] namesArray = {"Jim", "Ken", "Li"};
List<String> namesList = asList.apply(namesArray);
for(String name : namesList) {
        System.out.println(name);
}
```

```
Jim
Ken
Li
```

Lexical Scoping

A scope is the part of a Java program within which a name can be referred to without using a qualifier. Classes and methods define their own scope. Scopes may be nested. For example, a method scope does not exist independently as a method is always part of another construct, for example a class; an inner class appears inside the scope of another class; a local or anonymous class appears inside the scope of a method.

Even though a lambda expression looks like a method declaration, it does not define a scope of its own. It exists in its enclosing scope. This is known as *lexical scoping* for lambda expressions. For example, when a lambda expression is used inside a method, the lambda expression exists in the scope of the method.

The meanings of the keywords this and super are the same inside the lambda expression and its enclosing method. Note that this is different from the meanings of these keywords inside a local and anonymous inner class in which the keyword this refers to the current instance of the local and anonymous inner class, not its enclosing class.

Listing 5-18 contains code for a functional interface named Printer that you will use to print messages in examples in this section.

Listing 5-18. A Printer Functional Interface

```java
// Printer.java
package com.jdojo.lambda;

@FunctionalInterface
public interface Printer {
        void print(String msg);
}
```

The program in Listing 5-19 creates two instances of the Printer interface: one using a lambda expression in the getLambdaPrinter() method and one using an anonymous inner class in the getAnonymousPrinter() method. Both instances use the keyword this inside the print() method. Both methods print the class name that the keyword this refers to. The output shows that the keyword this has the same meaning inside the getLambdaPrinter() method and the lambda expression.

Listing 5-19. Testing Scope of a Lambda Expression and an Anonymous Class

```java
// ScopeTest.java
package com.jdojo.lambda;

public class ScopeTest {
        public static void main(String[] args) {
                ScopeTest test - new ScopeTest();
                Printer lambdaPrinter = test.getLambdaPrinter();
                lambdaPrinter.print("Lambda Expressions");

                Printer anonymousPrinter = test.getAnonymousPrinter();
                anonymousPrinter.print("Anonymous Class");
        }

        public Printer getLambdaPrinter() {
                System.out.println("getLambdaPrinter(): " + this.getClass());

                // Uses a lmabda expression
                Printer printer = msg -> {
                        // Here, this refers to the current object of the
                        // ScopeTest class
                        System.out.println(msg + ": " + this.getClass());
                };

                return printer;
        }

        public Printer getAnonymousPrinter() {
                System.out.println("getAnonymousPrinter(): " + this.getClass());

                // Uses an anonymous class
                Printer printer = new Printer() {
                        @Override
                        public void print(String msg) {
```

```
                            // Here, this refers to the current object of the
                            // anonymous class
                            System.out.println(msg + ": " + this.getClass());
                    }
            };

            return printer;
        }
}
```

```
getLambdaPrinter(): class com.jdojo.lambda.ScopeTest
Lambda Expressions: class com.jdojo.lambda.ScopeTest
getAnonymousPrinter(): class com.jdojo.lambda.ScopeTest
Anonymous Class: class com.jdojo.lambda.ScopeTest$1
```

Lexical scoping of a lambda expression means that variables declared in the lambda expression, including its parameters, exist in the enclosing scope. Simple names in a scope must be unique. It means that a lambda expression cannot redefine variables with the same name that already exist in the enclosing scope.

The following code for a lambda expression inside a method generates a compile-time error as its parameter name msg is already defined in the method's scope:

```
public class Test {
        public static void main(String[] args) {
                String msg = "Hello";

                // A compile-time error. The msg variable is already defined and
                // the lambda parameter is attempting to redefine it.
                Printer printer = msg -> System.out.println(msg);
        }
}
```

The following code generates a compile-time error for the same reason that the local variable name msg is in scope inside the body of the lambda expression and the lambda expression is attempting to declare a local variable with the same name msg:

```
public class Test {
        public static void main(String[] args) {
                String msg = "Hello";

                Printer printer = msg1 -> {
                        String msg = "Hi"; // A compile-time error
                        System.out.println(msg1);
                };
        }
}
```

Variable Capture

Like a local and anonymous inner class, a lambda expression can access *effectively final* local variables. A local variable is effectively final in the following two cases:

- It is declared final.

- It is not declared final, but initialized only once.

In the following snippet of code, the msg variable is effectively final, as it has been declared final. The lambda expression accesses the variable inside its body.

```
public Printer test() {
        final String msg = "Hello"; // msg is effectively final

        Printer printer = msg1 -> System.out.println(msg + " " + msg1);
        return printer;
}
```

In the following snippet of code, the msg variable is effectively final, as it is initialized once. The lambda expression accesses the variables inside its body.

```
public Printer test() {
        String msg = "Hello"; // msg is effectively final

        Printer printer = msg1 -> System.out.println(msg + " " + msg1);
        return printer;
}
```

The following snippet of code is a slight variation of the above example. The msg variable is effectively final, as it has been initialized only once.

```
public Printer test() {
        String msg;
        msg = "Hello"; // msg is effectively final

        Printer printer = msg1 -> System.out.println(msg + " " + msg1);
        return printer;
}
```

In the following snippet of code, the msg variable is not effectively final as it is assigned a value twice. The lambda expression is accessing the msg variable that generates a compile-time error.

```
public Printer test() {
        // msg is not effectively final as it is changed later
        String msg = "Hello";

        // A compile-time error as a lambda expression can access only
        // effectively final local variables and the msg variable is not
        // effectively final as it is changed afterwards.
```

```
    Printer printer = msg1 -> System.out.println(msg + " " + msg1);

    msg = "Hi"; // msg is changed

    return printer;
}
```

The following snippet of code generates a compile-time error because the lambda expression accesses the msg variable that is declared lexically after its use. In Java, forward referencing of variable names in method's scope is not allowed. Note that the msg variable is effectively final.

```
public Printer test() {
    // A compile-time error. The msg variable is not declared yet.
    Printer printer = msg1 -> System.out.println(msg + " " + msg1);

    String msg = "Hello"; // msg is effectively final

    return printer;
}
```

Can you guess why the following snippet of code generates a compile-time error?

```
public Printer test() {
    String msg = "Hello";

    Printer printer = msg1 -> {
        msg = "Hi " + msg1; // A compile-time error. Attempting to modify msg.
        System.out.println(msg);
    };

    return printer;
}
```

The lambda expression accesses the local variable msg. Any local variable accessed inside a lambda expression must be effectively final. The lambda expression attempts to modify the msg variable inside its body that causes the compile-time error.

▓ **Tip** A lambda expression can access instance and class variables of a class whether they are effectively final or not. If instance and class variables are not final, they can be modified inside the body of the lambda expressions. A lambda expression keeps a copy of the local variables used in its body. If the local variables are reference variables, a copy of the references is kept, not a copy of the objects.

The program in Listing 5-20 demonstrates how to access the local and instance variables inside lambda expressions.

Listing 5-20. Accessing Local and Instance Variables Inside Lambda Expressions

```java
// VariableCapture.java
package com.jdojo.lambda;

public class VariableCapture {
        private int counter = 0;

        public static void main(String[] args) {
                VariableCapture vc1 = new VariableCapture();
                VariableCapture vc2 = new VariableCapture();

                // Create lambdas
                Printer p1 = vc1.createLambda(1);
                Printer p2 = vc2.createLambda(100);

                // Execute the lambda bodies
                p1.print("Lambda #1");
                p2.print("Lambda #2");
                p1.print("Lambda #1");
                p2.print("Lambda #2");
                p1.print("Lambda #1");
                p2.print("Lambda #2");
        }

        public Printer createLambda(int incrementBy) {
                Printer printer = msg -> {
                        // Accesses instance and local variables
                        counter += incrementBy;
                        System.out.println(msg + ": counter = " + counter);
                };

                return printer;
        }
}
```

```
Lambda #1: counter = 1
Lambda #2: counter = 100
Lambda #1: counter = 2
Lambda #2: counter = 200
Lambda #1: counter = 3
Lambda #2: counter = 300
```

The createLambda() method uses a lambda expressions to create an instance of the Printer functional interface. The lambda expression uses the method's parameter incrementBy. Inside the body, it increments the instance variable counter and prints its value. The main() method creates two instances of the VariableCapture class and calls the createLambda() method on those instances by passing 1 and 100 as incrementBy values. The print() method of the Printer objects are called three times for both instances. The output shows that the lambda expression captures the incrementBy value and it increments the counter instance variable every time it is called.

Jumps and Exits

Statements such as break, continue, return, and throw are allowed inside the body of a lambda expression. These statements indicate jumps inside a method and exits from a method. Inside a lambda expression, they indicate jumps inside the body of the lambda expression and exits from the body of the lambda expressions. They indicate local jumps and exits in the lambda expressions. Non-local jumps and exits in lambda expressions are not allowed.

The program in Listing 5-21 demonstrates the valid use of the break and continue statements inside the body of a lambda expressions.

Listing 5-21. Using Break and Continue Statements Inside the Body of a Lambda Expression

```java
// LambdaJumps.java
package com.jdojo.lambda;

import java.util.function.Consumer;

public class LambdaJumps {
    public static void main(String[] args) {
        Consumer<int[]> printer = ids -> {
            int printedCount = 0;
            for (int id : ids) {
                if (id % 2 != 0) {
                    continue;
                }

                System.out.println(id);
                printedCount++;

                // Break out of the loop after printing 3 ids
                if (printedCount == 3) {
                    break;
                }
            }
        };

        // Print an array of 8 integers
        printer.accept(new int[]{1, 2, 3, 4, 5, 6, 7, 8});
    }
}
```

```
2
4
6
```

In the following snippet of code, the break statement is inside a for-loop statement and it is also inside the body of a lambda statement. If this break statement is allowed, it will jump out of the body of the lambda expression. This is the reason that the code generates a compile-time error.

```java
public void test() {
        for(int i = 0; i < 5; i++) {
                Consumer<Integer> evenIdPrinter = id -> {
                        if (id < 0) {
                                // A compile-time error
                                // Attempting to break out of the lambda body
                                break;
                        }
                };
        }
}
```

Recursive Lambda Expressions

Sometimes a function may invoke itself from its body. Such a function is called a *recursive function*. A lambda expression represents a function. However, a lambda expression does not support recursive invocations. If you need a recursive function, you need to use a method reference or an anonymous inner class.

The program in Listing 5-22 shows how to use a method reference when a recursive lambda expression is needed. It defines a recursive method called factorial() that computes the factorial of an integer. In the main() method, it uses the method reference RecursiveTest::factorial in place of a lambda expression.

Listing 5-22. Using a Method Reference When a Recursive Lambda Expressions Is Needed

```java
// RecursiveTest.java
package com.jdojo.lambda;

import java.util.function.IntFunction;

public class RecursiveTest {
        public static void main(String[] args) {
                IntFunction<Long> factorialCalc = RecursiveTest::factorial;

                int n = 5;
                long fact = factorialCalc.apply(n);
                System.out.println("Factorial of " + n + " is " + fact);
        }

        public static long factorial(int n) {
                if (n < 0) {
                        String msg = "Number must not be negative.";
                        throw new IllegalArgumentException(msg);
                }

                if (n == 0) {
                        return 1;
                }
```

```
        else {
                return n * factorial(n - 1);
        }
    }
}
```

---

factorial of 5 is 120

You can achieve the same results using an anonymous inner class as shown:

```
IntFunction<Long> factorialCalc = new IntFunction<Long>() {
        @Override
        public Long apply(int n) {
                if (n < 0) {
                        String msg = "Number must not be negative.";
                        throw new IllegalArgumentException(msg);
                }

                if (n == 0) {
                        return 1L;
                }
                else {
                        return n * this.apply(n - 1);
                }
        }
};
```

Comparing Objects

The Comparator interface is a functional interface with the following declaration:

```
package java.util;

@FunctionalInterface
public interface Comparator<T> {
        int compare(T o1, T o2);

        /* Other methods are not shown. */
}
```

The Comparator interface contains many default and static methods that can be used along with lambda expressions to create its instances. It is worth exploring the API documentation for the interface. In this section, I will discuss the following two methods of the Comparator interface:

- static <T,U extends Comparable<? super U>>Comparator<T> comparing(Function<? super T,? extends U> keyExtractor)

- default <U extends Comparable<? super U>>Comparator<T> thenComparing(Function<? super T,? extends U> keyExtractor)

The comparing() method takes a Function and returns a Comparator. The Function should return a Comparable that is used to compare two objects. You can create a Comparator object to compare Person objects based on their first name, as shown:

```
Comparator<Person> firstNameComp = Comparator.comparing(Person::getFirstName);
```

The thenComparing() method is a default method. It is used to specify a secondary comparison if two objects are the same in sorting order based on the primary comparison. The following statement creates a Comparator<Person> that sorts Person objects based on their last names, first names, and DOBs:

```
Comparator<Person> lastFirstDobComp =
        Comparator.comparing(Person::getLastName)
                .thenComparing(Person::getFirstName)
                .thenComparing(Person::getDob);
```

The program in Listing 5-23 shows how to use the method references to create a Comparator objects to sort Person objects. It uses the sort() default method of the List interface to sort the list of persons. The sort() method takes a Comparator as an argument. Thanks to lambda expressions and default methods in interfaces for making the sorting task so easy!

Listing 5-23. Sorting a List of Person Objects

```java
// ComparingObjects.java
package com.jdojo.lambda;

import java.util.Comparator;
import java.util.List;

public class ComparingObjects {
        public static void main(String[] args) {
                List<Person> persons = Person.getPersons();

                // Sort using the first name
                persons.sort(Comparator.comparing(Person::getFirstName));

                // Print the sorted list
                System.out.println("Sorted by the first name:");
                FunctionUtil.forEach(persons, System.out::println);

                // Sort using the last name, first name, and then DOB
                persons.sort(Comparator.comparing(Person::getLastName)
                                .thenComparing(Person::getFirstName)
                                .thenComparing(Person::getDob));

                // Print the sorted list
                System.out.println("\nSorted by the last name, first name, and dob:");
                FunctionUtil.forEach(persons, System.out::println);
        }
}
```

```
Sorted by the first name:
Donna Jacobs, FEMALE, 1970-09-12
John Jacobs, MALE, 1975-01-20
Wally Inman, MALE, 1965-09-12

Sorted by the last name, first name, and dob:
Wally Inman, MALE, 1965-09-12
Donna Jacobs, FEMALE, 1970-09-12
John Jacobs, MALE, 1975-01-20
```

Summary

A lambda expression is an unnamed block of code (or an unnamed function) with a list of formal parameters and a body. A lambda expression provides a concise way, as compared with anonymous inner classes, to create an instance of functional interfaces. Lambda expressions and default methods in interfaces have given new life to the Java programming languages as far as expressiveness and fluency in Java programming goes. The Java collection library has benefited the most from lambda expressions.

The syntax for defining lambda expressions is similar to declaring a method. A lambda expression may have a list of formal parameters and a body. A lambda expression is evaluated to an instance of a functional interface. The body of the lambda expression is not executed when the expression is evaluated. The body of the lambda expression is executed when the method of the functional interface is invoked.

One of the design goals of lambda expressions was to keep it concise and readable. The lambda expression syntax supports shorthand for common use cases. Method references are shorthand to specify lambda expressions that use existing methods.

A poly expression is an expression whose type depends on the context of its use. A lambda expression is always a poly expression. A lambda expression cannot be used by itself. Its type is inferred by the compiler from the context. A lambda expression can be used in assignments, method invocations, returns, and casts.

When a lambda expression occurs inside a method, it is lexically scoped. That is, a lambda expression does not define a scope of its own; rather, it occurs in a method's scope. A lambda expression may use the effectively final local variables of a method. A lambda expression may use the statements such as break, continue, return, and throw. The break and continue statements specify local jumps inside the body of the lambda expression. Attempting to jump outside the body of the lambda expression generates a compile-time error. The return and throw statements exit the body of the lambda expression.

CHAPTER 6

■ ■ ■

Threads

In this chapter, you will learn

- What threads are
- How to create threads in Java
- How to execute your code in separate threads
- What the Java Memory Model is
- The life cycle of threads
- How to use object monitors to synchronize access to a critical section by threads
- How to interrupt, stop, suspend, and resume threads
- Atomic variables, explicit locks, synchronizer, executor framework, fork/join framework, and thread-local variables

What Is a Thread?

Threads are a vast topic. They deserve an entire book. This chapter does not discuss the concept of threads in detail. Rather, it discusses how to work with threads using Java constructs. Before I define the term *thread*, it is necessary to understand the meaning of some related terms, such as program, process, multitasking, sequential programming, concurrent programming, etc.

A *program* is an algorithm expressed in a programming language. A *process* is a running instance of a program with all system resources allocated by the operating system to that instance of the program. Typically, a process consists of a unique identifier, a program counter, executable code, an address space, open handles to system resources, a security context, and many other things. A *program counter*, also called an instruction pointer, is a value maintained in the CPU register that keeps track of the instruction being executed by the CPU. It is automatically incremented at the end of the execution of an instruction. You can also think of a process as a unit of activity (or a unit of work, or a unit of execution, or a path of execution) within an operating system. The concept of process allows one computer system to support multiple units of executions.

Multitasking is the ability of an operating system to execute multiple tasks (or processes) at once. On a single CPU machine, multitasking is not possible in a true sense because one CPU can execute instructions for only one process at a time. In such a case, the operating system achieves multitasking by dividing the single CPU time among all running processes and switching between processes quickly enough to give an impression that all processes are running simultaneously. The switching of the CPU among processes is called a *context switch*. In a context switch, the running process is stopped, its state is saved, the state of the process that is going to get the CPU is restored, and the new process is run. It is necessary to save the state of the running process before the CPU is allocated to another process, so when this process gets the CPU again, it can start its execution from the same point where it left. Typically, a process state consists of a program counter, register values used by the process, and any other pieces of information that are necessary to restore the process later. An operating system stores a process state in a data structure, which is called a *process control block* or a *switchframe*. A context switch is rather an expensive task.

There are two types of multitaskin: cooperative and preemptive. In cooperative multitasking, the running process decides when to release the CPU so that other processes can use it. In preemptive multitasking, the operating system allocates a time slice to each process. Once a process has used up its time slice, it is preempted, and the operating system assigns the CPU to another process. In cooperative multitasking, a process may monopolize the CPU for a long time and other processes may not get a chance to run. In preemptive multitasking, the operating system makes sure all processes get CPU time. UNIX, OS/2, and Windows (except Windows 3.x) use preemptive multitasking. Windows 3.x used cooperative multitasking.

Multiprocessing is the ability of a computer to use more than one processor simultaneously. *Parallel processing* is the ability of a system to simultaneously execute the same task on multiple processors. You may note that, for parallel processing, the task must be split up into subtasks, so that the subtasks can be executed on multiple processors simultaneously. Let's consider a program that consists of six instructions:

```
Instruction-1
Instruction-2
Instruction-3
Instruction-4
Instruction-5
Instruction-6
```

To execute this program completely, the CPU has to execute all six instructions. Suppose the first three instructions depend on each other. Assume that Instruction-2 uses the result of Instruction-1; Instruction-3 uses the result of Instruction-2. Assume that the last three instructions also depend on each other the same way the first three depend on each other. Suppose the first three and the last three instructions, as two groups, do not depend on each other. How would you like to execute these six instructions to get the best result? One of the ways to execute them is sequentially as they appear in the program. This gives you one sequence of execution in your program. Another way of executing them is to have two sequences of executions. One sequence of execution will execute Instruction-1, Instruction-2, and Instruction-3, and at the same time, another sequence of execution will execute Instruction-4, Instruction-5, and Instruction-6. The phrases "unit of execution" and "sequence of execution" mean the same; I will use them interchangeably. These two scenarios are depicted in Figure 6-1.

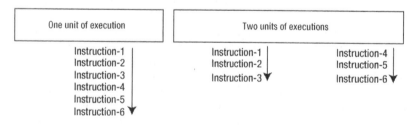

Figure 6-1. *Dividing a program into multiple units of execution*

Note that a process is also a unit of execution. Therefore, the two sets of instructions can be run as two processes to achieve concurrency in their execution. So far, we have assumed that the two sets of instructions are independent of each other. Suppose this assumption still holds true. What if the two sets of instructions access a shared memory; or, when both sets of instructions finish running, you need to combine the results from both to compute the final result? Processes are generally not allowed to access another process's address space. They must communicate using inter-process communication facilities such as sockets, pipes, etc. The very nature of a process—that it runs independent of another process—may pose problems when multiple processes need to communicate or share resources. All modern operating systems let you solve this problem by allowing you to create multiple units of execution within a process, where all units of execution can share address space and resources allocated to the process. Each unit of execution within a process is called a *thread*.

Every process has at least one thread. A process can create multiple threads, if needed. The resources available to the operating system and its implementation determine the maximum number of threads a process can create. All threads within a process share all resources including the address space; they can also communicate with each other easily because they operate within the same process and they share the same memory. Each thread within a process operates independent of the other threads within the same process.

A thread maintains two things: a program counter and a stack. The program counter lets a thread keep track of the instruction that is currently executed by it. It is necessary to maintain a separate program counter for each thread because each thread within a process may be executing different instructions at the same time. Each thread maintains its own stack to store the values of the local variables. A thread can also maintain its private memory, which cannot be shared with other threads, even if they are in the same process. The private memory maintained by a thread is called *thread-local storage (TLS)*. Figure 6-2 depicts threads represented within a process.

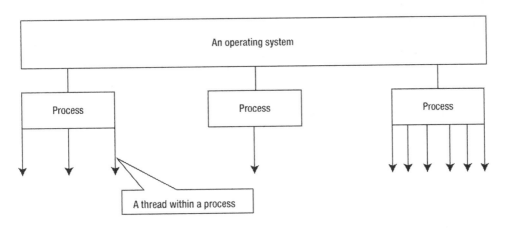

Figure 6-2. *Processes and threads*

In all modern operating systems, threads are scheduled on the CPU for execution, not the processes. Therefore, the CPU context switch occurs between the threads. The context switch between threads is less expensive compared to the context switch between processes. Because of the ease of communication, sharing resources among threads within a process, and a cheaper context switch, it is preferred to split a program into multiple threads, rather than multiple processes. Sometimes a thread is also called a *lightweight process*. The program with six instructions as discussed above can also be split into two threads within a process as depicted in Figure 6-3. On a multi-processor machine, multiple threads of a process may be scheduled on different processors, thus providing true concurrent executions of a program. A program that uses multiple threads is called a *multi-threaded program*.

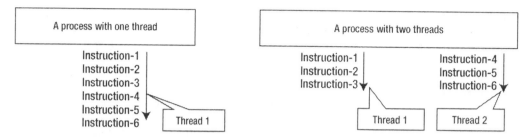

Figure 6-3. *Dividing the program logic to use two threads within a process*

You can think of the relationship between a process and threads as

```
Process = address space + resources + threads
```

where threads are units of execution within the process; they maintain their own unique program counter and stack; they share the process address space and resources; they are scheduled on a CPU independently and may execute on different CPUs, if available.

Creating a Thread in Java

The Java API makes it easy to work with threads. It lets you represent a thread as an object. An object of the `java.lang.Thread` class represents a thread. Creating and using a thread in Java is as simple as creating an object of the Thread class and using that object in a program. Let's start with the simplest example of creating a thread in Java. There are at least two steps involved in working with a thread:

- Creating an object of the Thread class
- Invoking the `start()` method of the Thread class to start the thread

Creating an object of the Thread class is the same as creating an object of any other classes in Java. In its simplest form, you can use the default constructor of the Thread class to create a Thread object.

```
// Creates a thread object
Thread simplestThread = new Thread();
```

Creating an object of the Thread class allocates memory for that object on the heap. It does not start or run the thread.

After you have created an object of the Thread class, you must call its `start()` method to start the thread represented by that object.

```
// Starts the thread
simplestThread.start();
```

The `start()` method returns after doing some housekeeping work. It puts the thread in the runnable state. In this state, the thread is ready to receive the CPU time. Note that invoking the `start()` method of a Thread object does not guarantee "when" this thread will start getting the CPU time. That is, it does not guarantee when the thread will start running. It just schedules the thread to receive the CPU time.

Let's write a simple Java program with the above two statements as shown in Listing 6-1. The program will not do anything useful. However, it will get you started using threads.

Listing 6-1. The Simplest Thread in Java

```java
// SimplestThread.java
package com.jdojo.threads;

public class SimplestThread {
    public static void main(String[] args) {
        // Creates a thread object
        Thread simplestThread = new Thread();

        // Starts the thread
        simplestThread.start();
    }
}
```

When you run the SimplestThread class, you do not see any output. The program will start and finish silently. Even though you did not see any output, here are few things the JVM did when the two statements in the main() method were executed:

- When the second statement, simplestThread.start(), is executed, the JVM scheduled this thread for execution.

- At some point in time, this thread got the CPU time and started executing. What code does a thread in Java start executing when it gets the CPU time?

- A thread in Java always starts its execution in a run() method. You can define the run() method to be executed by a thread when you create an object of the Thread class. In your case, you created an object of the Thread class using its default constructor. When you use the default constructor of the Thread class to create its object (as in new Thread()), the run() method of the Thread class is called when the thread starts its execution. The following sections in this chapter will explain how to define your own run() method for a thread.

- The run() method of the Thread class checks how the object of the Thread class was created. If the thread object was created using the default constructor of the Thread class, it does not do anything, and immediately returns. Therefore, in your program, when the thread got the CPU time, it called the run() method of the Thread class, which did not execute any meaningful code, and returned.

- When the CPU finishes executing the run() method, the thread is dead, which means the thread will not get the CPU time again.

Figure 6-4 depicts how the simplest thread example works.

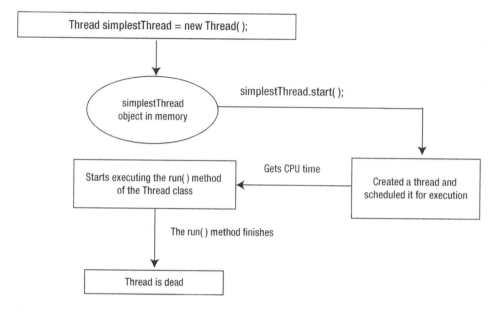

Figure 6-4. *The simplest thread execution*

There are two important points to add to the current discussion.

- When a thread is dead, it does not mean the thread object is garbage collected. Note that a thread is a unit of execution. "A thread is dead" means that the unit of execution that the thread represented has finished its work. However, the thread object representing the unit of execution still exists in memory. After the thread is dead, the object will be garbage collected based on the same garbage collection rules that are used for any other Java objects. Some restrictions exist that dictate the methods you can call on a dead thread. For example, you cannot call its start() method again. That is, a thread object can be started only once. However, you can still check if the thread is dead by calling the isAlive() method of the thread object.

- The thread does not get the CPU time to execute run() method in one go. Rather, the operating system decides the amount of time to allocate and when to allocate that time to the thread.

Specifying Your Code for a Thread

There are three ways you can specify your code to be executed by a thread:

- By inheriting your class from the Thread class

- By implementing the Runnable interface in your class

- By using the method reference to a method that takes no parameters and returns void

> ■ **Tip** Inheriting your class from the Thread class may not be possible if your class already inherits from another class. In that case, you will need to use the second method. You can use the third method from Java 8. Before Java 8, it was common to use an anonymous class to define a thread object where the anonymous class would either inherit from the Thread class or implement the Runnable interface.

Inheriting Your Class from the Thread Class

When you inherit your class from the Thread class, you should override the run() method and provide the code to be executed by the thread.

```java
public class MyThreadClass extends Thread {
    @Override
    public void run() {
        System.out.println("Hello Java thread!");
    }
    // More code goes here
}
```

The steps to create a thread object and start the thread are the same.

```java
MyThreadClass myThread = new MyThreadClass();
myThread.start();
```

The thread will execute the run() method of the MyThreadClass class.

Implementing the Runnable Interface

You can create a class that implements the java.lang.Runnable interface. Runnable is a functional interface and it is declared as follows:

```java
@FunctionalInterface
public interface Runnable {
    void run();
}
```

From Java 8, you can use a lambda expression to create an instance of the Runnable interface.

```java
Runnable aRunnableObject = () -> System.out.println("Hello Java thread!");
```

Create an object of the Thread class using the constructor that accepts a Runnable object.

```java
Thread myThread = new Thread(aRunnableObject);
```

Start the thread by calling the start() method of the thread object.

```java
myThread.start();
```

The thread will execute the code contained in the body of the lambda expressions.

Using a Method Reference

From Java 8, you can use the method reference of a method of any class that takes no parameters and returns void as the code to be executed by a thread. The following code declares a ThreadTest class that contains an execute() method. The method contains the code to be executed in a thread.

```java
public class ThreadTest {
        public static void execute() {
                System.out.println("Hello Java thread!");
        }
}
```

The following snippet of code uses the method reference of the execute() method of the ThreadTest class to create a Runnable object:

```java
Thread myThread = new Thread(ThreadTest::execute);
myThread.start();
```

The thread will execute the code contained in the execute() method of the ThreadTest class.

A Quick Example

Let's look at a simple example to print integers from 1 to 500 in a new thread. Listing 6-2 lists the code for the PrinterThread class that performs the job. When the class is run, it prints integers from 1 to 500 on the standard output.

Listing 6-2. Printing Integers from 1 to 500 in a New Thread

```java
// PrinterThread.java
package com.jdojo.threads;

public class PrinterThread {
        public static void main(String[] args) {
                // Create a Thread object
                Thread t = new Thread(PrinterThread::print);

                // Start the thread
                t.start();
        }

        public static void print() {
                for (int i = 1; i <= 500; i++) {
                        System.out.print(i + " ");
                }
        }
}
```

```
1 2 3 4 5 6 7 8 9 10 11 12 13 14   ... 497 498 499 500
```

I used a method reference to create the thread object in the example. You can use any of the other ways discussed earlier to create a thread object.

Using Multiple Threads in a Program

Using multiple threads in a Java program is as simple as creating multiple Thread objects and starting them. Java does not have any upper limit on the number of threads that can be used in a program. It is limited by the operating system and the memory available to the program. Listing 6-3 uses two threads. Both threads print integers from 1 to 500. The code prints a newline after each integer. However, the output shows a space after each integer to keep the output short. Only partial output is shown.

Listing 6-3. Running Multiple Threads in a Program

```java
// MultiPrinterThread.java
package com.jdojo.threads;

public class MultiPrinterThread {
        public static void main(String[] args) {
                // Create two Thread objects
                Thread t1 = new Thread(MultiPrinterThread::print);
                Thread t2 = new Thread(MultiPrinterThread::print);

                // Start both threads
                t1.start();
                t2.start();
        }

        public static void print() {
                for (int i = 1; i <= 500; i++) {
                        System.out.println(i);
                }
        }
}
```

```
1   2   3   4   5   1   2   3   4   5   6   7   8   9   10   11   12   13   14   15   16   17   18   19   20   21   22   23
24   25   26   6   7   27   28   8   9   10   11   12   29   30   31   13   14   32   15   16   17   ...   496   497   498
499   500   424   425   ...   492   493   494   495   496   497   498   499   500
```

You will find some interesting things in the output. Every time you run this program, you may get a different output. However, the nature of the output on your computer can be compared to the output shown above. Note that in a very fast machine the output may print 1 to 500 and 1 to 500. However, let's focus the discussion assuming that your output is like the one shown.

The program created two threads. Each thread prints integers from 1 to 500. It starts the thread t1 first and the thread t2 second. You might expect that the thread t1 will start first to print integers from 1 to 500, and then the thread t2 will start to print integers from 1 to 500. However, it is obvious from the output that the program did not run the way you might have expected.

The start() method of the Thread class returns immediately. That is, when you call the start() method of a thread, the JVM takes note of your instruction to start the thread. However, it does not start the thread right away. It has to do some housekeeping before it can really start a thread. When a thread starts, it is up to the operating system to decide when and how much CPU time is given to that thread to execute its code. Therefore, as soon as the t1.start() and t2.start() methods return, your program enters the indeterminate realm. That is, both threads will start running; however, you do not know when they will start running and in what sequence they will run to execute their code. When you start multiple threads, you do not even know which thread will start running first. Looking at the output, you can observe that one of the threads started and it got enough CPU time to print integers from 1 to 5 before it was preempted.

Another thread got CPU time to print from 1 to 26 before it was preempted. The second time, the first thread (the thread that started printing integers first) got the CPU time and it printed only two integers, 6 and 7, and so on. You can see that both threads got CPU time. However, the amount of CPU time and the sequence in which they got the CPU time are unpredictable. Each time you run this program, you may get a different output. The only guarantee that you get from this program is that all integers between 1 and 500 will be printed twice in some order.

Issues in Using Multiple Threads

Some issues are involved when you use multiple threads in a program. You need to consider these issues only if multiple threads have to coordinate based on some conditions or some shared resources.

In the previous sections, the examples involving threads were trivial. They simply printed some integers on the standard output. Let's have a different kind of example that uses multiple threads, which access and modify the value of a variable. Listing 6-4 has the code for a BalanceUpdate class. Note that all methods defined in the BalanceUpdate class are static.

Listing 6-4. Multiple Threads Modifying the Same Variable

```java
// BalanceUpdate.java
package com.jdojo.threads;

public class BalanceUpdate {
        // Initialize balance to 100
        private static int balance = 100;

        public static void main(String[] args) {
                startBalanceUpdateThread();  // Thread to update the balance value
                startBalanceMonitorThread(); // Thread to monitor the balance value
        }

        public static void updateBalance() {
                // Add 10 to balance and subtract 10 from balance
                balance = balance + 10;
                balance = balance - 10;
        }

        public static void monitorBalance() {
                int b = balance;
                if (b != 100) {
                        System.out.println("Balance changed: " + b);
                        System.exit(1); // Exit the program
                }
        }

        public static void startBalanceUpdateThread() {
                // Start a new thread that calls the updateBalance() method in an infinite loop
                Thread t = new Thread(() -> {
                        while (true) {
                                updateBalance();
                        }
                });
                t.start();
        }
```

```
        public static void startBalanceMonitorThread() {
                // Start a thread that monitors the balance value
                Thread t = new Thread(() -> {
                        while (true) {
                                monitorBalance();
                        }
                });
                t.start();
        }
}
```

Balance changed: 110

A brief description of each component of this class is as follows:

- balance: It is a static variable of type int. It is initialized to 100.

- updateBalance(): It is a static method that adds 10 to the static variable balance and subtracts 10 from it. Upon completion of this method, the value of the static variable balance is expected to remain the same as 100.

- startBalanceUpdateThread(): It starts a new thread that keeps calling the updateBalance() method in an infinite loop. That is, once you call this method, a thread keeps adding 10 to the balance variable and subtracting 10 from it.

- startBalanceMonitorThread(): It starts a new thread that monitors the value of the balance static variable. When the thread detects that the value of the balance variable is other than 100, it prints the current value and exits the program.

- main(): This method is used to run the program. It starts a thread that updates the balance class variable in a loop using the updateBalance() method. It also starts another thread that monitors the value of the balance class variable.

The program consists of two threads. One thread calls the updateBalance() method, which adds 10 to balance and subtracts 10 from it. That is, after this method finishes executing, the value of the balance variable is expected to remain unchanged. Another thread monitors the value of the balance variable. When it detects that the value of the balance variable is anything other than 100, it prints the new value and exits the program.

Intuitively, the balance monitor thread should not print anything because the balance should always be 100 and the program should never end because both threads are using infinite loops. However, that is not the case. If you run this program, you will find, in a short time, the program prints the balance value other than 100 and exits.

Suppose on a particular machine the statement "balance = balance + 10;" is implemented as the following machine instructions assuming register-1 as a CPU register:

```
register-1 = balance;
register-1 = register-1 + 10;
balance = register-1;
```

Similarly, assume that the statement "balance = balance - 10;" is implemented as the following machine instructions assuming register-2 as another CPU register:

```
register-2 = balance;
register-2 = register-2 - 10;
balance = register-2;
```

When the updateBalance() method is invoked, the CPU has to execute six instructions to add 10 to and subtract 10 from the balance variable. When the balance update thread is in the middle of executing any of the first three instructions, the balance monitor thread will read the balance value as 100. When the balance update thread has finished executing the third instruction, the balance monitor thread will read its value as 110. The value 110 for the balance variable will be restored to 100 only when the balance update thread executes the sixth instruction. Note that if the balance monitor thread reads the value of the balance variable any time after the execution of the third instruction and before the execution of the sixth instruction by the balance update thread, it will read a value that is not the same as the value that existed at the start of the updateBalance() method execution. Table 6-1 shows how the value of the balance variable will be modified and read by the two threads.

Table 6-1. *Instruction Executions for Multiple Threads*

Statement (Suppose Balance Value is 100 to Start With)	Instructions Being Executed by the Balance Update Thread	The Value of Balance Read by the Balance Monitor Thread
balance = balance + 10;	register-1 = balance;	100
	register-1 = register-1 + 10;	100
	balance = register-1;	Before execution: 100 After execution: 110
balance = balance - 10;	register-2 = balance;	110
	register-2 = register-2 - 10;	110
	balance = register-2;	Before execution: 110 After execution: 100

In your program, the monitor thread was able to read the value of the balance variable as 110 because you allowed two threads to modify and read the value of the balance variable concurrently. If you allowed only one thread at a time to work with (modify or read) the balance variable, the balance monitor thread would never read the value of the balance variable other than 100.

The situation where multiple threads manipulate and access a shared data concurrently and the outcome depends on the order in which the execution of threads take place is known as a *race condition*. A race condition in a program may lead to unpredictable results. Listing 6-4 is an example of a race condition where the program output depends on the sequence of execution of the two threads.

To avoid a race condition in a program, you need to make sure that only one of the racing threads works with the shared data at a time. To solve this problem, you need to synchronize the access to the two methods updateBalance() and monitorBalance() of the BalanceUpdate class. That is, only one thread should access one of these two methods at a time. In other words, if one thread is executing the updateBalance() method, another thread that wants to execute the monitorBalance() method must wait until the thread executing the updateBalance() method is finished. Similarly, if one thread is executing the monitorBalance() method, another thread that wants to execute the updateBalance() method must wait until the thread executing the monitorBalance() method is finished. This will ensure that when a thread is in the process of updating the balance variable, no other threads will read the inconsistent value of the balance variable and vice versa.

This kind of problem that needs synchronizing the access of multiple threads to a section of code in a Java program can be solved using the synchronized keyword. To understand the use of the synchronized keyword, I need to discuss the Java Memory Model in brief, and the lock and wait sets of an object.

Java Memory Model (JMM)

All program variables (instance fields, static fields, and array elements) in a program are allocated memory on the main memory of a computer. Each thread has a working memory (processor cache or registers). JMM describes how, when and in what order program variables are stored to, and read from, the main memory. JMM is described in the Java Language Specification in detail. You may visualize JMM as depicted in Figure 6-5.

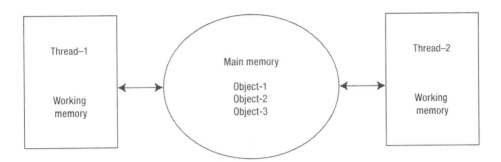

Figure 6-5. *Java Memory model*

Figure 6-5 shows two threads sharing the main memory. Let's assume that you have a Java program that is running two threads, thread-1 and thread-2, and each thread is running on different processors. Suppose thread-1 reads the value of an instance variable of object-1 in its working memory, updates the value, and does not write the updated value back to the main memory. Let's run through some possible scenarios.

- What happens if thread-2 tries to read the value of the same instance variable of object-1 from the main memory? Would thread-2 read the old value from the main memory, or would it be able to read the updated value from the working memory of thread-2?

- Suppose thread-1 is in the middle of writing the updated value to the main memory, and at the same time, thread-2 is trying to read the same value from the main memory. Would thread-2 read the old value or some garbage value from the main memory because the value is not written back to the main memory completely?

JMM answers all such questions. In essence, JMM describes three important aspects of the execution of instructions in a Java program. They are as follows:

- Atomicity

- Visibility

- Ordering

Atomicity

JMM describes actions that should be executed atomically. It describes atomicity rules about read and write actions on instance variables, static variables, and array elements. It guarantees that read and write on an object's field of any type, except long and double, are always atomic. However, if a field of type long or double is declared volatile (I will discuss the volatile keyword in detail later in this chapter), read and write on that field are also guaranteed to be atomic.

Visibility

JMM describes the conditions under which the effects produced by actions in one thread are visible to another thread. Mainly, it describes, when a thread writes a value to a field, at what point that new value of that field can be visible to another thread. I will discuss more about the visibility aspect of JMM when I discuss locks, synchronization, and volatile variables later in this chapter. For completeness, the following are some of the visibility rules:

- When a thread reads the value of a field for the first time, it will read either the initial value of the field or some value that was written to that field by some other thread.

- A write to a volatile variable is always written to the main memory. A read on a volatile variable is always read from the main memory. That is, a volatile variable is never cached in the working memory of a thread. In effect, any write to a volatile variable is flushed to the main memory, immediately making the new value visible to other threads.

- When a thread terminates, the working memory of the thread is written to the main memory immediately. That is, after a thread terminates, all variables values visible only to the terminated thread are made visible to all threads.

- When a thread enters a synchronized block, that thread reloads the values of all variables in its working memory. When a thread leaves a synchronized block, it writes all variables values from its working memory to the main memory.

Ordering

JMM describes in what order actions are performed within a thread and among threads. It guarantees that all actions performed within a thread are ordered. Actions in different threads are not guaranteed to be performed in any order. You may achieve some ordering while working with multiple threads by using the synchronization technique described later in this chapter.

■ **Tip** Each thread in a Java program uses two kinds of memory: working memory and main memory. A thread cannot access the working memory of another thread. Main memory is shared among the threads. Threads communicate with each other using the main memory. Every thread has its own stack, which is used to store local variables.

Object's Monitor and Threads Synchronization

In a multi-threaded program, a section of code that may have undesirable effects on the outcome of the program if executed by multiple threads concurrently is called a *critical section*. Often, the undesirable effects result from the concurrent use of a resource by multiple threads in the critical section. It is necessary to control the access to a critical section in a program so only one thread can execute the critical section at a time.

In a Java program, a critical section can be a block of statements or a method. Java has no built-in mechanism to identify a critical section in a program. However, Java has many built-in constructs that allow programmers to declare a critical section, and to control and coordinate access to it. It is the programmer's responsibility to identify critical sections in a program and control the access to that critical section by multiple threads. Controlling and coordinating the access to a critical section by multiple threads is known as *threads synchronization*. Threads synchronization is always a challenging task when writing a multi-threaded program. In Listing 6-4, the updateBalance() and monitorBalance() methods are critical sections and you must synchronize the threads' access to these two methods to get a consistent output.

Two kinds of threads synchronizations are built into the Java programming language:

- Mutual exclusion synchronization

- Conditional synchronization

In mutual exclusion synchronization, only one thread is allowed to have access to a section of code at a point in time. Listing 6-4 is an example of a program where mutual exclusion synchronization is needed so that only one thread can execute updateBalance() and monitorBalance() at a point in time. In this case, you can think of the mutual exclusion as an exclusive access to the balance variable by a thread.

The conditional synchronization allows multiple threads to work together to achieve a result. For example, consider a multi-threaded program to solve a *producer/consumer* problem. There are two threads in a program: one thread produces data (the producer thread) and another thread consumes the data (the consumer thread). The consumer thread must wait until the producer thread produces data and makes it available for consuming. The producer thread must notify the consumer thread when it produces data so the consumer thread can consume it. In other words, producer and consumer threads must coordinate/cooperate with each other to accomplish the task. During conditional synchronization, mutual exclusion synchronization may also be needed. Suppose the producer thread produces data one byte at a time and puts the data into a buffer whose capacity is also one byte. The consumer thread consumes data from the same buffer. In this case, only one of the threads should have access to the buffer at a time (a mutual exclusion). If the buffer is full, the producer thread must wait for the consumer thread to empty the buffer; if the buffer is empty, the consumer thread must wait for the producer thread to produce a byte of data and put it into the buffer (a conditional synchronization).

The mutual exclusion synchronization is achieved through a lock. A lock supports two operations: acquire and release. A thread that wants exclusive access to a resource must acquire the lock associated with that resource. As long as a thread possesses the lock to a resource, other threads cannot acquire the same lock. Once the thread that possesses the lock is finished with the resource, it releases the lock so another thread can acquire it.

The conditional synchronization is achieved through condition variables and three operations: wait, signal, and broadcast. Condition variables define the conditions on which threads are synchronized. The wait operation makes a thread wait on a condition to become true so it can proceed. The signal operation wakes up one of the threads that was waiting on the condition variables. The broadcast operation wakes up all threads that were waiting on the condition variables. Note that the difference between the signal operation and broadcast operation is that the former wakes up only one waiting thread, whereas the latter wakes up all waiting threads.

A *monitor* is a programming construct that has a lock, condition variables, and associated operations on them. Threads synchronization in a Java program is achieved using monitors. Every object in a Java program has an associated monitor.

A critical section in a Java program is defined with respect to an object's monitor. A thread must acquire the object's monitor before it can start executing the piece of code declared as a critical section. The synchronized keyword is used to declare a critical section. There are two ways to use the synchronized keyword:

- To declare a method as a critical section

- To declare a block of statements as a critical section

You can declare a method as a critical section by using the keyword synchronized before the method's return type, as shown:

```
public class CriticalSection {
        public synchronized void someMethod_1() {
                // Method code goes here
        }

        public static synchronized void someMethod_2() {
                // Method code goes here
        }
}
```

▨ **Tip** You can declare both an instance method and a `static` method as `synchronized`. A constructor cannot be declared as `synchronized`.

In the case of a `synchronized` instance method, the entire method is a critical section and it is associated with the monitor of the object for which this method is executed. That is, a thread must acquire the object's monitor lock before executing the code inside a synchronized instance method of that object. For example,

```
// Create an object called cs_1
CriticalSection cs_1 = new CriticalSection();

// Execute the synchronized instance method. Before this method execution
// starts, the thread that is executing this statement must acquire the
// monitor lock of the cs_1 object
cs_1.someMethod_1();
```

In case of a `synchronized` `static` method, the entire method is a critical section and it is associated with the class object that represents that class in memory. That is, a thread must acquire the class object's monitor lock before executing the code inside a synchronized `static` method of that class. For example,

```
// Execute the synchronized static method. Before this method execution starts,
// the thread that is executing this statement must acquire the monitor lock of
// the CriticalSection.class object
CriticalSection.someMethod_2();
```

The syntax for declaring a block of code as critical section is

```
synchronized(<objectReference>) {
        // one or more statements of the critical section
}
```

The `<objectReference>` is the reference of the object whose monitor lock will be used to synchronize the access to the critical section. The above syntax is used to define part of a method body as a critical section. This way, a thread needs to acquire the object's monitor lock only, while executing a smaller part of the method code, which is declared as a critical section. Other threads can still execute other parts of the body of the method concurrently. Additionally, this method of declaring a critical section lets you declare a part or whole of a constructor as a critical section. Recall that you cannot use the keyword synchronized in the declaration part of a constructor. However, you can use it inside a constructor's body to declare a block of code synchronized. The following snippet of code illustrates the use of the keyword synchronized:

```
public class CriticalSection2 {
        public synchronized void someMethod_1() {
                // method code goes here
                // only one thread can execute here at a time
        }
```

```
    public void someMethod_11() {
        synchronized(this) {
            // method code goes here
            // only one thread can execute here at a time
        }
    }

    public void someMethod_12() {
        // some statements go here
        // multiple threads can execute here at a time

        synchronized(this) {
            // some statements go here
            // only one thread can execute here at a time
        }

        // some statements go here
        // multiple threads can execute here at a time
    }

    public static synchronized void someMethod_2() {
        // method code goes here
        // only one thread can execute here at a time
    }

    public static void someMethod_21() {
        synchronized(CriticalSection2.class) {
            // method code goes here
            // only one thread can execute here at a time
        }
    }

    public static void someMethod_22() {
        // some statements go here: section_1
        // multiple threads can execute here at a time

        synchronized(CriticalSection2.class) {
            // some statements go here: section_2
            // only one thread can execute here at a time
        }

        // some statements go here: section_3
        // multiple threads can execute here at a time
    }
}
```

The CriticalSection2 class has six methods: three instance methods and three class methods. The someMethod_1() method is synchronized as the synchronized keyword is used in the method declaration. The someMethod_11() method differs from the someMethod_1() method only in the way it uses the synchronized keyword. It puts the entire method body inside the synchronized keyword as a block, which has the same effect as declaring the method synchronized. The method someMethod_12() is different. It declares only part of the method's body as a synchronized block. There can be more than one thread that can execute someMethod_12() concurrently. However, only one of them can be executing inside the synchronized block at one point in time. Other sets of methods, someMethod_2(), someMethod_21() and someMethod_22(), are class methods, and they will behave the same way, except that class's object monitor will be used to achieve the synchronization.

The process of acquiring and releasing an object's monitor lock is handled by the JVM. The only thing you need to do is to declare a method (or a block) synchronized. Before entering a synchronized method or block, the thread acquires the monitor lock of the object. On exiting the synchronized method or block, it releases the object's monitor lock. A thread that has acquired an object's monitor lock can acquire it again as many times as it wants. However, it must release the object's monitor lock as many times as it had acquired it in order for another thread to acquire the same object's monitor lock. Let's consider the following code for a MultiLocks class:

```
public class MultiLocks {
        public synchronized void method_1() {
                // some statements go here

                this.method_2();

                // some statements go here
        }

        public synchronized void method_2() {
                // some statements go here
        }

        public static synchronized void method_3() {
                // some statements go here

                MultiLocks.method_4();

                // some statements go here
        }

        public static synchronized void method_4() {
                // some statements go here
        }
}
```

The MultiLocks class has four methods and all of them are synchronized. Two of them are instance methods, which are synchronized using the reference of the object on which the method call will be made. Two of them are class methods, which are synchronized using the reference of the class object of the MultiLocks class. If a thread wants to execute method_1() or method_2(), it must first acquire the monitor lock of the object on which the method is called. You are calling method_2() from inside the method method_1(). Since a thread that is executing method_1() must already have acquired the object's monitor lock and a call to method_2() requires the acquisition of the same lock, that thread will reacquire the same object's monitor lock automatically when it executes method_2() from inside method_1() without competing with other threads to acquire the object's monitor lock. Therefore, when a thread executes method_2() from inside method_1(), it will have acquired the object's monitor lock twice. When it exits method_2(), it will release the lock once; when it exits method_1(), it will release the lock the second time; and then the object's monitor lock will be available for other threads for acquisition. The same argument applies to the call to method_4() from inside method_3() except that, in this case, the MultiLocks class object's monitor lock is involved in the synchronization. Consider calling method_3() from method_1(), like so:

```
public class MultiLocks {
        public synchronized void method_1() {
                // some statements go here

                this.method_2();
                MultiLocks.method_3();

                // some statements go here
        }
        // rest of the code remains the same as shown before
}
```

Suppose you call method_1(), like so:

```
MultiLocks ml = new MultiLocks();
ml.method_1();
```

When ml.method_1() is executed, the executing thread must acquire the monitor lock of the object ml. However, the executing thread must acquire the monitor lock of the MultiLocks.class object to execute the MultiLocks.method_3() method. Note that ml and MultiLocks.class are two different objects. The thread that wants to execute the MultiLocks.method_3() method from the method_1() method must possess both objects' monitor locks at the same time.

You can apply the same arguments to work with synchronized blocks. For example, you can have a snippet of code like

```
synchronized (objectReference) {
        // trying to synchronize again on the same object is ok
        synchronized(objectReference) {
                // some statements go here
        }
}
```

It is time to take a deeper look into the workings of threads synchronization using an object's monitor. Figure 6-6 depicts how multiple threads can use an object's monitor.

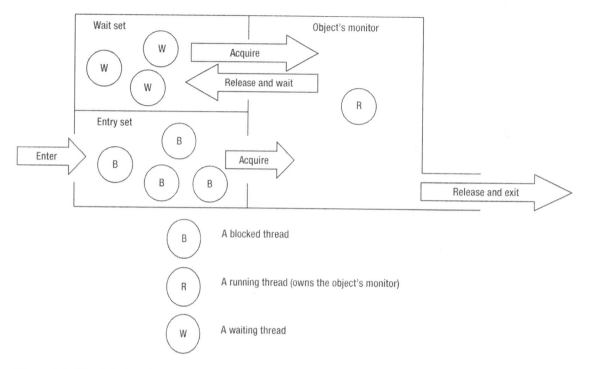

Figure 6-6. *Multiple threads using an object's monitor*

I will use a doctor-patients analogy while discussing threads synchronization. Suppose a doctor has a clinic to treat patients. We know that it is very important to allow only one patient access to the doctor at a time. Otherwise, the doctor may mix up one patient's symptoms with another patient's symptom; a patient with fever may get a prescription for headache! Therefore, we will assume that only one patient can have access to the doctor at any point in time. It is the same assumption that only one thread (patient) can have access to an object's monitor (doctor) at a time.

Any patient who wants an access to the doctor must sign in and wait in the waiting room. Similarly, each object monitor has an *entry set* (waiting room for newcomers) and any thread that wants to acquire the object's monitor lock must enter the entry set first. If the patient signs in, he may get access to the doctor immediately, if the doctor is not treating a patient and there were no patients waiting for his turn in the waiting room. Similarly, if the entry set of an object's monitor is empty and there is no other thread that possesses the object's monitor lock, the thread entering the entry set acquires the object's monitor lock immediately. However, if there were patients waiting in the waiting room or one being treated by the doctor, the patient who signs in is blocked and he must wait for the doctor to become available again. Similarly, if a thread enters the entry set, and other threads are already blocked in the entry set, or another thread already possesses the object's monitor lock, the thread that just signed in is said to be blocked and must wait in the entry set.

A thread entering the entry set is shown by the arrow labelled Enter. A thread itself is shown in the figure using a circle. A circle with the text B shows a thread that is blocked in the entry set. A circle with the text R shows a thread that has acquired the object's monitor.

What happens to the threads that are blocked in the entry set? When do they get a chance to acquire the object's monitor? You can think about the patients blocked in the waiting room and getting their turn to be treated by the doctor. Many factors decide which patient will be treated next. First, the patient being treated must free the doctor before another patient can have access to the doctor. In Java, the thread that has the ownership of the object's monitor must release the object's monitor before any threads that are blocked in the entry set can have the ownership of the object's monitor. A patient may free the doctor for one of two reasons:

- The patient is done with his treatment and he is ready to go home. This is a straightforward case of a patient freeing the doctor after his treatment is over.

- A patient is in the middle of his treatment. However, he must wait for some time in order for the doctor to resume his treatment. Let's assume that the clinic has a special waiting room (separate from the one where patients who just signed in wait) for those patients who are in the middle of their treatment. This case needs some explanation. Let's say that the doctor is an eye specialist and he has some patients in his clinic. The patient who is being treated needs an eye examination for which his pupils must be dilated first. It takes about 30 minutes after the patient receives eye drops for full pupil dilation, which is required for the examination. Should the doctor be waiting for 30 minutes for the patient's pupils to dilate? Should this patient release the doctor for 30 minutes and let other patient have access to the doctor? You would agree that if doctor's time can be used to treat other patients while this patient's pupils are being dilated, it is fine for this patient to release the doctor. What should happen when once this patient's pupils are dilated, however, and the doctor is still busy treating another patient? The doctor cannot leave any patient in the middle of treatment. Therefore, the patient who released the doctor and waited for some condition to be true (here dilation process to complete) must wait until doctor is free again. I will have more explanations on this issue later in this chapter and I will try to correlate this situation with threads and the object's monitor lock.

I must discuss another issue in the context of the doctor-patients example before I can compare this with monitor-threads case. When the doctor is free and only one patient is waiting to get access to him, there is no problem. The sole patient waiting for the doctor will get access to him immediately. However, what happens when the doctor becomes available and there is more than one patient waiting to get access to him? Which one of the waiting patients should get access to the doctor first? Should it be the patient who came first (First In, First Out or FIFO)? Should it be the patient who came in last (Last In, First Out or LIFO)? Should it be the patient who needs the least (or the most) amount of time for his treatment? Should it be the patient who is in the most serious condition? The answer is that it depends on the policy followed by the clinic management.

Similar to a patient in the doctor-patients example, a thread can also release an object's monitor lock for two reasons:

- At this time, the thread has completed the work for which it had acquired the object's monitor lock. The arrow "Release and exit" indicates this scenario in the diagram. When a thread simply exits a synchronized method/block, it releases the object's monitor lock it had acquired.

- The thread is in the middle of a task and it needs to wait for some condition to be true to complete its remaining task. Let's consider the producer/consumer problem. Suppose the producer acquires the buffer object's monitor lock and wants to write some data into the buffer. However, it finds that the buffer is full and the consumer must consume the data and make the buffer empty before it can write to it. In this case, the producer must release the buffer object's monitor lock and wait until the consumer acquires the lock and empties the buffer. The same logic applies for the consumer when it acquires the buffer's monitor lock and finds that buffer is empty. At that time, the consumer must release the lock and wait until the producer produces some data. This kind of temporarily releasing of the object's monitor lock and waiting for some condition to occur is shown in the diagram as the "Release and wait" arrow. An object can have multiple threads that can be in "Release and wait" state at the same time. All threads that have released the object's monitor lock and are waiting for some conditions to occur are put in a set called a *wait set*.

How is a thread placed in the wait set? Note that a thread can be placed in the wait set of an object monitor only if it once acquired the object's monitor lock. Once a thread has acquired the object's monitor lock, it must call the wait() method of the object in order to place itself into the wait set. This means a thread must always call the wait() method from inside a synchronized method or a block. The wait() method is defined in the java.lang.Object class and it is declared final; that is, no other class in Java can override this method. You must consider the following two rules before you call the wait() method of an object.

Rule #1

The call to the wait() method must be placed inside a synchronized method (static or non-static) or a synchronized block.

Rule #2

The wait() method must be called on the object whose monitor the current thread has acquired. It throws a java.lang.InterruptedException. The code that calls this method must handle this exception. The wait() method throws an IllegalMonitorStateException when the current thread is not the owner of the object's monitor. The following snippet of code does not place the wait() method call inside a try-catch to keep the code simple and readable. For example, inside a synchronized non-static method, the call to the wait() method may look like the following:

```
public class WaitMethodCall {
        // Object that is used to synchronize a block
        private Object objectRef = new Object();

        public synchronized void someMethod_1() {
                // The thread running here has already acquired the monitor lock on
                // the object represented by the reference this because it is a
                // synchronized and non-static method

                // other statements go here

                while (some condition is true) {
                        // It is ok to call the wait() method on this, because the
                        // current thread possesses monitor lock on this
                        this.wait();
                }
                // other statements go here
        }

        public static synchronized void someMethod_2() {
                // The thread executing here has already acquired the monitor lock on
                // the class object represented by the WaitMethodCall.class reference
                // because it is a synchronized and static method

                while (some condition is true) {
                        // It is ok to call the wait() method on WaitMethodCall.class
                        // because the current thread possesses monitor lock on
                        // WaitMethodCall.class object
                        WaitMethodCall.class.wait();
                }
                // other statements go here
        }
```

```
        public void someMethod_3() {
                // other statements go here

                synchronized(objectRef) {
                        // Current thread possesses monitor lock of objectRef

                        while (some condition is true) {
                                // It is ok to call the wait() method on objectRef because
                                // the current thread possesses monitor lock on objectRef
                                objectRef.wait();
                        }
                }
                // other statements go here
        }
}
```

Note that objectRef is an instance variable and it is of the type java.lang.Object. Its only use is to synchronize threads' access to a block inside the someMethod_3() method. Since it is declared an instance variable, all threads calling someMethod_3() will use its monitor to execute the synchronized block. A common mistake made by beginners is to declare objectRef as a local variable inside a method and use it to in a synchronized block. The following snippet of code shows such a mistake:

```
public void wrongSynchronizationMethod {
        // This objectRef is created every time a thread calls this method
        Object objectRef = new Object();

        // It is a blunder to use objectRef for synchronization below
        synchronized(objectRef) {
                // In fact, this block works as if there is no synchronization, because every
                // thread  creates a new objectRef and acquires its monitor lock immediately
        }
}
```

With the above snippet of code in mind, you must use an object reference that is common to all threads to synchronize access to a block.

Let's get back to the question of which patient will get access to the doctor when he becomes available again. Will it be a patient from the waiting room who is waiting after signing in or a patient from another waiting room who was waiting in the middle of his treatment? Before you answer this question, let's make it clear that there is a difference between the patients in the waiting room who are waiting after signing in and the patients waiting for some condition (e.g. dilation to complete) to occur in another waiting room. After signing in, patients wait on the availability of the doctor, whereas patients in the middle of their treatments wait on a particular condition to occur. For patients in the second category, a particular condition must hold before they can seek access to the doctor, whereas patients in the first category are ready to grab access to the doctor as soon as possible. Therefore, someone must notify a patient in the second category that a particular condition has occurred and it is time for him to seek access to the doctor again to continue his treatment. Let's assume that this notification must come from a patient being currently treated by the doctor. That is, the patient who currently has access to the doctor notifies the patients waiting in the middle of their treatments to get ready to gain access to the doctor again. Note that it is just a notification that some condition has occurred and it is delivered only to the patients waiting in the middle of their treatments. Whether the patient in the middle of his treatment will get access to the doctor right after the current patient is done with the doctor is not guaranteed. It only guarantees that the condition on which a patient was waiting holds at the time of notification and the waiting patient may try to get access to the doctor to continue his treatment. Let's correlate this example to monitor-threads example.

The threads in the entry set are blocked and they are ready to grab access to the monitor as soon as possible. The threads in the wait set are waiting for some condition to occur. A thread that has ownership of the monitor must notify the threads waiting in the wait set about the fulfillment of the conditions on which they are waiting. In Java, the notification is made by calling the notify() and notifyAll()methods of the java.lang.Object class. Like the wait() method, the notify()and notifyAll() methods are also declared final. Like the wait() method, these two methods must be called by a thread using an object whose monitor has already been acquired by the thread. If a thread calls these methods on an object before acquiring the object's monitor, a java.lang.IllegalMonitorStateException is thrown. The call to the notify() method wakes up one thread from the wait set, whereas the call to the notifyAll() method wakes up all threads in the wait set. In case of the notify() method call, the thread that is woken up is chosen arbitrarily. Note that when a thread calls the notify() or notifyAll() method, it still holds the lock on the object's monitor. Threads in the wait set are only woken up by the notify() or notifyAll() call. They do not acquire the object's monitor lock immediately. When the thread that called the notify() or notifyAll() method releases the object's monitor lock by "Release and exit" or "Release and wait," the woken up threads in the wait set competes with the threads in the entry set to acquire the object's monitor again. Therefore, a call to the notify() and notifyAll() serves only as a wake-up call for threads in the wait set and it does not guarantee access to the object's monitor.

■ **Tip**　There is no way to wake up a specific thread in the wait set. The call to notify() chooses a thread arbitrarily, whereas the call to notifyAll() wakes up all threads. Use notifyAll() when you are in doubt about which method to use.

The following snippet of code shows a pseudo code for using the notifyAll() method along with the wait() method. You may observe that the call to the wait() and notify() methods are made on the same object, because if objectRef.wait() puts a thread in the wait set of the objectRef object, the objectRef.notify() or objectRef.notifyAll() method will wake that thread from the wait set of the objectRef object.

```java
public class WaitAndNotifyMethodCall {
        private Object objectRef = new Object();

        public synchronized void someMethod_1() {
                while (some condition is true) {
                        this.wait();
                }

                if (some other condition is true) {
                        // Notify all waiting threads
                        this.notifyAll();
                }
        }

        public static synchronized void someMethod_2() {
                while (some condition is true) {
                        WaitAndNotifyMethodCall.class.wait();
                }

                if (some other condition is true) {
                        // Notify all waiting threads
                        WaitAndNotifyMethodCall.class.notifyAll();
                }
        }
```

```
        public void someMethod_3() {
                synchronized(objectRef) {
                        while (some condition is true) {
                                objectRef.wait();
                        }

                        if (some other condition is true) {
                                // Notify all waiting threads
                                objectRef.notifyAll();
                        }
                }
        }
}
```

Once a thread is woken up in the wait set, it has to compete with the threads in the entry set to acquire the monitor lock of the object. After a thread is woken up in the wait set and acquires the object's monitor lock, it has choices: to do some work and release the lock by invoking the wait() method (release and wait) again, or release the lock by exiting the synchronized section (release and exit). One important point to remember about the call to the wait() method is that, typically, a call to the wait() method is placed inside a loop. Here is the reason why it is necessary to do so. A thread looks for a condition to hold. It waits by calling the wait() method and placing itself in the wait set if that condition does not hold. The thread wakes up when it is notified by another thread, which calls the notify() or notifyAll() method. When the thread that woke up acquires the lock, the condition that held at the time of notification may not still hold. Therefore, it is necessary to check for the condition again, when the thread wakes up and acquires the lock, to make sure the condition it was looking for is true, and it can continue its work. For example, consider the producer/consumer problem. Suppose there is one producer and many consumers. Suppose a consumer calls the wait() method as

```
if (buffer is empty) {
        buffer.wait();
}

buffer.consume();
```

Suppose the buffer is empty and all consumers are waiting in the wait set. The producer produces some data and it calls the buffer.notifyAll() method to wake up all consumer threads in the wait set. All consumer threads wake up; however, only one will get a chance to acquire the monitor lock next. The first one acquires the lock and executes the buffer.consume() method to empty the buffer. When the next consumer acquires the monitor lock, it will also execute the buffer.consume() statement. However, the consumer that woke up and acquired the lock before this one had already emptied the buffer. The logical mistake in the above snippet of code is that the call to the wait() method is placed inside an if statement instead of inside a loop. That is, after a thread wakes up, it is not checking if the buffer contains some data or not, before trying to consume the data. The corrected snippet of code is the following:

```
while (buffer is empty) {
        buffer.wait();
}

buffer.consume();
```

I will answer one more question before you can see this big discussion about thread synchronization in action. The question is, "Which thread gets a chance to acquire the object's monitor lock when there are some blocked threads in the entry set and some woken up threads in the wait set?" Note that the threads that are in the wait set do not compete for the object's monitor until they are woken up by the notify() or notifyAll() call. The answer to this question is that it depends on the scheduler's algorithm of the operating system.

Listing 6-5 has the code for the BalanceUpdateSynchronized class, which is a modified version of the BalanceUpdate class listed in Listing 6-4. The only difference between the two classes is the use of the keyword synchronized to declare the updateBalance() and monitorBalance() methods in the new class, so only one thread can enter one of the methods at a time. When you run the new class, you will not see any output because the monitorBalance() method will never see the value of the balance variable other than 100.

Listing 6-5. Synchronized Balance Update

```java
// BalanceUpdateSynchronized.java
package com.jdojo.threads;

public class BalanceUpdateSynchronized {
        // Initialize balance to 100
        private static int balance = 100;

        public static void main(String[] args) {
                startBalanceUpdateThread();  // Thread to update the balance value
                startBalanceMonitorThread(); // Thread to monitor the balance value
        }

        public static synchronized void updateBalance() {
                // Add 10 to balance and subtract 10 from balance
                balance = balance + 10;
                balance = balance - 10;
        }

        public static synchronized void monitorBalance() {
                int b = balance;
                if (b != 100) {
                        System.out.println("Balance changed: " + b);
                        System.exit(1); // Exit the program
                }
        }

        public static void startBalanceUpdateThread() {
                // Start a new thread that calls the updateBalance() method in an infinite loop
                Thread t = new Thread(() -> {
                        while (true) {
                                updateBalance();
                        }
                });
                t.start();
        }
```

```
        public static void startBalanceMonitorThread() {
                // Start a thread that monitors the balance value
                Thread t = new Thread(() -> {
                        while (true) {
                                monitorBalance();
                        }
                });
                t.start();
        }
}
```

I will show examples of using the wait() and notify() methods in the next section, which discusses the producer/consumer problem.

The wait() method in the java.lang.Object class is overloaded and it has three versions:

- wait(): The thread waits in the object's wait set until another thread calls the notify() or notifyAll() method on the same object.

- wait(long timeinMillis): The thread waits in the object's wait set until another thread calls the notify() or notifyAll() method on the same object or the specified amount of timeinMillis time has elapsed.

- wait(long timeinMillis, long timeinNanos): This version lets you specify time in milliseconds and nanoseconds.

The Producer/Consumer Synchronization Problem

The producer/consumer is a typical thread synchronization problem that uses the wait() and notify() methods. I will keep it simple. The problem statement goes like this:

> There are four classes: Buffer, Producer, Consumer, and ProducerConsumerTest. An object of the Buffer class will have an integer data element that will be produced by the producer and consumed by the consumer. Therefore, in this example, a Buffer object can hold only one integer at a point in time. Your goal is to synchronize the access to the buffer, so the Producer produces a new data element only when the Buffer is empty and the Consumer consumes the buffer's data only when it is available. The ProducerConsumerTest class is used to test the program.

Listing 6-6, Listing 6-7, Listing 6-8, and Listing 6-9 contain the code for the four classes.

Listing 6-6. A Buffer Class for Producer/Consumer Synchronization

```
// Buffer.java
package com.jdojo.threads;

public class Buffer {
        private int data;
        private boolean empty;

        public Buffer() {
                this.empty = true;
        }
```

```java
        public synchronized void produce(int newData) {
                // Wait until the buffer is empty
                while(!this.empty) {
                        try {
                                this.wait();
                        }
                        catch(InterruptedException e) {
                                e.printStackTrace();
                        }
                }

                // Store the new data produced by the producer
                this.data = newData;

                // Set the empty flag to false, so the consumer may consume the data
                this.empty = false;

                // Notify the waiting consumer in the wait set
                this.notify();

                System.out.println("Produced:" + newData);
        }

        public synchronized int consume() {
                // Wait until the buffer gets some data
                while(this.empty) {
                        try {
                                this.wait();
                        }
                        catch(InterruptedException e) {
                                e.printStackTrace();
                        }
                }

                // Set the empty flag to true, so that the producer can store new data
                this.empty = true;

                // Notify the waiting producer in the wait set
                this.notify();

                System.out.println("Consumed:" + data);

                return data;
        }
}
```

Listing 6-7. A Producer Class for Producer/Consumer Synchronization

```java
// Producer.java
package com.jdojo.threads;

import java.util.Random;

public class Producer extends Thread {
        private Buffer buffer;

        public Producer(Buffer buffer) {
                this.buffer = buffer;
        }

        public void run() {
                Random rand = new Random();
                while(true) {
                        // Generate a random integer and store it in the buffer
                        int n = rand.nextInt();
                        buffer.produce(n);
                }
        }
}
```

Listing 6-8. A Consumer Class for Producer/Consumer Synchronization

```java
// Consumer.java
package com.jdojo.threads;

public class Consumer extends Thread {
        private Buffer buffer;

        public Consumer(Buffer buffer) {
                this.buffer = buffer;
        }

        public void run() {
                int data;
                while(true) {
                        // Consume the data from the buffer. We are not using the consumed
                        // data for any other puporse here
                        data = buffer.consume();
                }
        }
}
```

201

Listing 6-9. A ProducerConsumerTest Class to Test the Producer/Consumer Synchronization

```java
// ProducerConsumerTest.java
package com.jdojo.threads;

public class ProducerConsumerTest {
        public static void main(String[] args) {
                // Create Buffer, Producer and Consumer objects
                Buffer buffer = new Buffer();
                Producer p = new Producer(buffer);
                Consumer c = new Consumer(buffer);

                // Start the producer and consumer threads
                p.start();
                c.start();
        }
}
```

```
Produced:1872733184
Consumed:1872733184
...
```

When you run the `ProducerConsumerTest` class, you may get a different output. However, your output will look similar in the sense that two lines printed will be always of the following form, where XXX indicate an integer:

```
Produced:XXX
Consumed:XXX
```

In this example, the `Buffer` class needs some explanation. It has two instance variables:

- private int data

- private boolean empty

The producer uses the `data` instance variable to store the new data. The consumer uses it to read the data. The `empty` instance variable is used as an indicator whether the buffer is empty or not. In the constructor, it is initialized to true indicating that the new buffer is empty.

It has two synchronized methods: `produce()` and `consume()`. Both methods are declared `synchronized` because the goal is to protect the `Buffer` object to be used by multiple threads concurrently. If the producer is producing new data by calling the `produce()` method, the consumer must wait to consume the data until the producer is done and vice versa. The producer thread calls the `produce()` method, passing the newly generated data to it. However, before the new data is stored in the `data` instance variable, the producer makes sure that the buffer is empty. If the buffer is not empty, it calls the `this.wait()` method to place itself in the wait set of the buffer object until the consumer notifies it using the `this.notify()` method inside the `consume()` method.

Once the producer thread detects that the buffer is empty, it stores the new data in the `data` instance variable, sets the empty flag to `false`, and calls `this.notify()` to wake up the consumer thread in the wait set to consume the data. At the end, it also prints a message on the console that data has been produced.

The `consume()` method of the `Buffer` class is similar to its counterpart, the `produce()` method. The only difference is that the consumer-thread calls it and it performs a logic just opposite to the `produce()` method. For example, it checks if buffer is not empty and consumes the data.

The Producer and Consumer classes inherit the Thread class. They override the run() method of the Thread class. Both of them accept an object of the Buffer class in their constructors to use it in their run() method. The Producer class generates a random integer in its run() method inside an infinite loop and keeps writing it to the buffer. The Consumer class keeps consuming data from the buffer in an infinite loop.

The ProducerConsumerTest class creates all three objects (a buffer, a producer, and a consumer) and starts the producer and consumer threads. Since both classes (Producer and Consumer) use infinite loops inside the run() method, you will have to terminate the program forcibly, such as by pressing Ctrl + C, if you are running this program from a Windows command prompt.

Which Thread Is Executing?

The Thread class has some useful static methods; one of them is the method currentThread(). It returns the reference of the Thread object that calls this method. Consider the following statement:

```
Thread t = Thread.currentThread();
```

The statement will assign the reference of the thread object that executes the above statement to the variable t. Note that a statement in Java can be executed by different threads at different points in time during the execution of a program. Therefore, t may be assigned the reference of a different Thread object when the statement is executed at different times in the same program. Listing 6-10 demonstrates the use of the currentThread() method.

Listing 6-10. Using the Thread.currentThread() Method

```
// CurrentThread.java
package com.jdojo.threads;

public class CurrentThread extends Thread {
        public CurrentThread(String name) {
                super(name);
        }

        @Override
        public void run() {
                Thread t = Thread.currentThread();
                String threadName = t.getName();
                System.out.println("Inside run() method: " + threadName);
        }

        public static void main(String[] args) {
                CurrentThread ct1 = new CurrentThread("First Thread");
                CurrentThread ct2 = new CurrentThread("Second Thread");
                ct1.start();
                ct2.start();

                // Let's see which thread is executing the following statement
                Thread t = Thread.currentThread();
                String threadName = t.getName();
                System.out.println("Inside main() method: " + threadName);
        }
}
```

(Your output may be in a different order.)
Inside main() method: main
Inside run() method: First Thread
Inside run() method: Second Thread

Two different threads call the Thread.currentThread() method inside the run() method of the CurrentThread class. The method returns the reference of the thread executing the call. The program simply prints the name of the thread that is executing. It is interesting to note that when you called the Thread.currentThread() method inside the main() method, a thread named main executed the code. When you run a class, the JVM starts a thread named main, which is responsible for executing the main() method.

Letting a Thread Sleep

The Thread class contains a static sleep() method, which makes a thread sleep for a specified duration. It accepts a timeout as an argument. You can specify the timeout in milliseconds, or milliseconds and nanoseconds. The thread that executes this method sleeps for the specified amount of time. A sleeping thread is not scheduled by the operating system scheduler to receive the CPU time. If a thread has the ownership of an object's monitor lock before it goes to sleep, it continues to hold those monitor locks. The sleep() method throws a java.lang.InterruptedException and your code should be ready to handle it. Listing 6-11 demonstrates the use of the Thread.sleep() method.

Listing 6-11. A Sleeping Thread

```java
// LetMeSleep.java
package com.jdojo.threads;

public class LetMeSleep {
        public static void main(String[] args) {
                try {
                        System.out.println("I am going to sleep for 5 seconds.");
                        Thread.sleep(5000); // The "main" thread will sleep
                        System.out.println("I woke up.");
                }
                catch(InterruptedException e) {
                        System.out.println("Someone interrupted me in my sleep.");
                }
                System.out.println("I am done.");
        }
}
```

```
I am going to sleep for 5 seconds.
I woke up.
I am done.
```

> ■ **Tip** The TimeUnit enum in the java.util.concurrent package represents a measurement of time in various units such as milliseconds, seconds, minutes, hours, days, etc. It has some convenience methods. One of them is the sleep() method. The Thread.sleep() method accepts time in milliseconds. If you want a thread to sleep for five seconds, you need to call this method as Thread.sleep(5000) by converting the seconds into milliseconds. You can use the sleep() method of TimeUnit instead to avoid the time duration conversion, like so:
>
> TimeUnit.SECONDS.sleep(5); // Same as Thread.sleep(5000);

I will Join You in Heaven

I can rephrase this section heading as "I will wait until you die." That's right. A thread can wait for another thread to die (or terminate). Suppose there are two threads, t1 and t2. If the thread t1 executes t2.join(), thread t1 starts waiting until thread t2 is terminated. In other words, the call t2.join() blocks until t2 terminates. Using the join() method in a program is useful if one of the threads cannot proceed until another thread has finished executing.

Listing 6-12 has an example where you want to print a message on the standard output when the program has finished executing. The message to print is "We are done."

Listing 6-12. An Incorrect Way of Waiting for a Thread to Terminate

```java
// JoinWrong.java
package com.jdojo.threads;

public class JoinWrong {
    public static void main(String[] args) {
        Thread t1 = new Thread(JoinWrong::print);
        t1.start();
        System.out.println("We are done.");
    }

    public static void print() {
        for (int i = 1; i <= 5; i++) {
            try {
                System.out.println("Counter: " + i);
                Thread.sleep(1000);
            }
            catch (InterruptedException e) {
                e.printStackTrace();
            }
        }
    }
}
```

```
We are done.
Counter: 1
Counter: 2
Counter: 3
Counter: 4
Counter: 5
```

In the main() method, a thread is created and started. The thread prints integers from 1 to 5. It sleeps for one second after printing an integer. In the end, the main() method prints a message. It seems that this program should print the numbers from 1 to 5, followed by your last message. However, if you look at the output, it is in the reverse order. What is wrong with this program?

The JVM starts a new thread called main that is responsible for executing the main() method of the class that you run. In your case, the main() method of the JoinWrong class is executed by the main thread. This thread will execute the following statements:

```
Thread t1 =  new Thread(JoinWrong::print);
t1.start();
System.out.println("We are done.");
```

When the t1.start() method call returns, you have one more thread running in your program (thread t1) in addition to the main thread. The t1 thread is responsible for printing the integers from 1 to 5, whereas the main thread is responsible for printing the message "We are done." Since there are two threads responsible for two different tasks, it is not guaranteed which task will finish first. What is the solution? You must make your main thread wait on the thread t1 to terminate. This can be achieved by calling the t1.join() method inside the main() method.

Listing 6-13 lists the correct version of Listing 6-12 by using the t1.join() method call, before printing the final message. When the main thread executes the join() method call, it waits until the t1 thread is terminated. The join() method of the Thread class throws a java.lang.InterruptedException, and your code should be ready to handle it.

Listing 6-13. A Correct Way of Waiting for a Thread to Terminate

```java
// JoinRight.java
package com.jdojo.threads;

public class JoinRight {
        public static void main(String[] args) {
                Thread t1 = new Thread(JoinRight::print);
                t1.start();

                try {
                        t1.join(); // "main" thread waits until t1 is terminated
                }
                catch (InterruptedException e) {
                        e.printStackTrace();
                }

                System.out.println("We are done.");
        }

        public static void print() {
                for (int i = 1; i <= 5; i++) {
                        try {
                                System.out.println("Counter: " + i);
                                Thread.sleep(1000);
                        }
                        catch (InterruptedException e) {
                                e.printStackTrace();
                        }
                }
        }
}
```

```
Counter: 1
Counter: 2
Counter: 3
Counter: 4
Counter: 5
We are done.
```

The join() method of the Thread class is overloaded. Its other two versions accept a timeout argument. If you use the join() method with a timeout, the caller thread will wait until the thread on which it is called is terminated or the timeout has elapsed. If you replace the t1.join() statement in the JoinRight class with t1.join(1000), you will find that the output is not in the same order because the main thread will wait only for a second for the t1 thread to terminate before it prints the final message.

Can a thread join multiple threads? The answer is yes. A thread can join multiple threads like so:

```
t1.join(); // Join t1
t2.join(); // Join t2
t3.join(); // Join t3
```

You should call the join() method of a thread after it has been started. If you call the join() method on a thread that has not been started, it returns immediately. Similarly, if you invoke the join() method on a thread that is already terminated, it returns immediately.

Can a thread join itself? The answer is yes and no. Technically, it is allowed for a thread to join itself. However, a thread should not join itself in most circumstances. In such a case, a thread waits to terminate itself. In other words, the thread waits forever.

```
// "Bad" call (not if you know what you are doing) to join. It waits forever
// until another thread interrupts it.
Thread.currentThread().join();
```

If you write the statement, make sure that your program interrupts the waiting thread using some other threads. In such a case, the waiting thread will return from the join() method call by throwing an InterruptedException.

Be Considerate to Others and Yield

A thread may voluntarily give up the CPU by calling the static yield() method of the Thread class. The call to the yield() method is a hint to the scheduler that it may pause the running thread and give the CPU to other threads. A thread may want to call this method only if it executes in a long loop without waiting or blocking. If a thread frequently waits or blocks, the yield() method call is not very useful because this thread does not monopolize the CPU and other threads will get the CPU time when this thread is blocked or waiting. It is advisable not to depend on the yield() method because it is just a hint to the scheduler. It is not guaranteed to give a consistent result across different platforms. A thread that calls the yield() method continues to hold the monitor locks. Note that there is no guarantee as to when the thread that yields will get the CPU time again. You may use it like so:

```
// The run() method of a thread class
public void run() {
        while(true) {
                // do some processing here...
                Thread.yield(); // Let's yield to other threads
        }
}
```

Life Cycle of a Thread

A thread is always in one of the following six states:

- New
- Runnable
- Blocked
- Waiting
- Timed-waiting
- Terminated

All these states of a thread are JVM states. They do not represent the states assigned to a thread by an operating system.

When a thread is created and its start() method is not yet called, it is in the new state.

```
Thread t = new SomeThreadClass(); // t is in the new state
```

A thread that is ready to run or running is in the runnable state. In other words, a thread that is eligible for getting the CPU time is in a runnable state.

▦ **Tip**   The JVM combines two OS-level thread states: ready-to-run and running into a state called the runnable state. A thread in the ready-to-run OS state means it is waiting for its turn to get the CPU time. A thread in the running OS state means it is running on the CPU.

A thread is said to be in a blocked state if it was trying to enter (or re-enter) a synchronized method or block but the monitor is being used by another thread. A thread in the entry set that is waiting to acquire a monitor lock is in the blocked state. A thread in the wait set that is waiting to reacquire the monitor lock after it has been woken up is also in a blocked state.

A thread may place itself in a waiting state by calling one of the methods listed in Table 6-2. A thread may place itself in a timed-waiting state by calling one of the methods listed in Table 6-3. I will discuss the usage of the parkNanos() and parkUntil() methods later in this chapter.

Table 6-2. *Methods That Place a Thread in Waiting State*

Method	Description
wait()	This is the wait() method of the Object class, which a thread may call if it wants to wait for a specific condition to hold. Recall that a thread must own the monitor's lock of an object to call the wait() method on that object. Another thread must call the notify() or notifyAll() method on the same object in order for the waiting thread to transition to the runnable state.
join()	This is the join() method of the Thread class. A thread that calls this method wants to wait until the thread on which this method is called terminates.
park()	This is the park() method of the LockSupport class, which is in the java.util.concurrent.locks package. A thread that calls this method may wait until a permit is available by calling the unpark() method on a thread. I will cover the LockSupport class later in this chapter.

Table 6-3. *Methods That Place a Thread in a Timed-Waiting State*

Method	Description
sleep()	This method is in the Thread class.
wait (long millis) wait(long millis, int nanos)	These methods are in the Object class.
join(long millis) join(long millis, int nanos)	These methods are in the Thread class.
parkNanos (long nanos) parkNanos (Object blocker, long nanos)	These methods are in the LockSupport class, which is in the java.util.concurrent.locks package.
parkUntil (long deadline) parkUntil (Object blocker, long nanos)	These methods are in the LockSupport class, which is in the java.util.concurrent.locks package.

A thread that has completed its execution is said to be in the terminated state. A thread is terminated when it exits its run() method or its stop() method is called. A terminated thread cannot transition to any other state. You can use the isAlive() method of a thread after it has been started to know if it is alive or terminated.

You can use the getState() method of the Thread class to get the state of a thread at any time. This method returns one of the constants of the Thread.State enum type. Listing 6-14 and Listing 6-15 demonstrate the transition of a thread from one state to another. The output of Listing 6-15 shows some of the states the thread transitions to during its life cycle.

Listing 6-14. A ThreadState Class

```
// ThreadState.java
package com.jdojo.threads;

public class ThreadState extends Thread {
        private boolean keepRunning = true;
        private boolean wait = false;
        private Object syncObject = null;

        public ThreadState(Object syncObject) {
                this.syncObject = syncObject;
        }

        public void run() {
                while (keepRunning) {
                        synchronized (syncObject) {
                                if (wait) {
                                        try {
                                                syncObject.wait();
                                        }
                                        catch (InterruptedException e) {
                                                e.printStackTrace();
                                        }
                                }
                        }
                }
        }
```

```
        public void setKeepRunning(boolean keepRunning) {
                this.keepRunning = keepRunning;
        }

        public void setWait(boolean wait) {
                this.wait = wait;
        }
}
```

Listing 6-15. A ThreadStateTest Class to Demonstrate the States of a Thread

```
// ThreadStateTest.java
package com.jdojo.threads;

public class ThreadStateTest {
        public static void main(String[] args) {
                Object syncObject = new Object();
                ThreadState ts = new ThreadState(syncObject);
                System.out.println("Before start()-ts.isAlive():" + ts.isAlive());
                System.out.println("#1:" + ts.getState());

                // Start the thread
                ts.start();
                System.out.println("After start()-ts.isAlive():" + ts.isAlive());
                System.out.println("#2:" + ts.getState());
                ts.setWait(true);

                // Make the current thread sleep, so ts thread starts waiting
                sleepNow(100);

                synchronized (syncObject) {
                        System.out.println("#3:" + ts.getState());
                        ts.setWait(false);

                        // Wake up the waiting thread
                        syncObject.notifyAll();
                }

                // Make the current thread sleep, so ts thread wakes up
                sleepNow(2000);
                System.out.println("#4:" + ts.getState());
                ts.setKeepRunning(false);

                // Make the current thread sleep, so the ts thread will wake up
                sleepNow(2000);
                System.out.println("#5:" + ts.getState());
                System.out.println("At the end. ts.isAlive():" + ts.isAlive());
        }
```

```
        public static void sleepNow(long millis) {
                try {
                        Thread.currentThread().sleep(millis);
                }
                catch (InterruptedException e) {
                }
        }
}
```

```
Before start()-ts.isAlive():false
#1:NEW
After start()-ts.isAlive():true
#2:RUNNABLE
#3:WAITING
#4:RUNNABLE
#5:TERMINATED
At the end. ts.isAlive():false
```

Priority of a Thread

All threads have a priority. The priority is indicated by an integer between 1 and 10. A thread with the priority of 1 is said to have the lowest priority. A thread with the priority of 10 is said to have the highest priority. There are three constants defined in the Thread class to represent three different thread priorities as listed in Table 6-4.

Table 6-4. *Thread's Priority Constants Defined in the Thread Class*

Thread Priority Constants	Integer Value
MIN_PRIORITY	1
NORM_PRIORITY	5
MAX_PRIORITY	10

The priority of a thread is a hint to the scheduler that indicates the importance (or the urgency) with which it should schedule the thread. The higher priority of a thread indicates that the thread is of higher importance and the scheduler should give priority in giving the CPU time to that thread. Note that the priority of a thread is just a hint to the scheduler; it is up to the scheduler to respect that hint. It is not recommended to depend on the thread priority for the correctness of a program. For example, if there are ten maximum priority threads and one minimum priority thread, that does not mean that the scheduler will schedule the minimum priority thread after all ten maximum priority threads have been scheduled and finished. This scheduling scheme will result in a *thread starvation*, where a lower priority thread will have to wait indefinitely or for a long time to get CPU time.

The setPriority() method of the Thread class sets a new priority for the thread. The getPriority() method returns the current priority for a thread. When a thread is created, its priority is set to the priority of the thread that creates it.

Listing 6-16 demonstrates how to set and get the priority of a thread. It also demonstrates how a new thread gets the priority of the thread that creates it. In the example, threads t1 and t2 get the priority of the main thread at the time they are created.

Listing 6-16. Setting and Getting a Thread's Priority

```java
// ThreadPriority.java
package com.jdojo.threads;

public class ThreadPriority {
    public static void main(String[] args) {
        // Get the reference of the current thread
        Thread t = Thread.currentThread();
        System.out.println("main Thread Priority:" + t.getPriority());

        // Thread t1 gets the same priority as the main thread at this point
        Thread t1 = new Thread();
        System.out.println("Thread(t1) Priority:" + t1.getPriority());

        t.setPriority(Thread.MAX_PRIORITY);
        System.out.println("main Thread Priority:" + t.getPriority());

        // Thread t2 gets the same priority as main thread at this point, which is
        // Thread.MAX_PRIORITY (10)
        Thread t2 = new Thread();
        System.out.println("Thread(t2) Priority:" + t2.getPriority());

        // Change thread t2 priority to minimum
        t2.setPriority(Thread.MIN_PRIORITY);
        System.out.println("Thread(t2) Priority:" + t2.getPriority());
    }
}
```

```
main Thread Priority:5
Thread(t1) Priority:5
main Thread Priority:10
Thread(t2) Priority:10
Thread(t2) Priority:1
```

Is It a Demon or a Daemon?

A thread can be a daemon thread or a user thread. The word "daemon" is pronounced the same as "demon." However, the word daemon in a thread's context has nothing to do with a demon!

A daemon thread is a kind of a service provider thread, whereas a user thread (or non-daemon thread) is a thread that uses the services of daemon threads. A service provider should not exist if there is no service consumer. The JVM applies this logic. When it detects that all threads in an application are only daemon threads, it exits the application. Note that if there are only daemon threads in an application, the JVM does not wait for those daemon threads to finish before exiting the application.

You can make a thread a daemon thread by using the setDaemon() method by passing true as its argument. You must call the setDaemon() method of a thread before you start the thread. Otherwise, an java.lang. IllegalThreadStateException is thrown. You can use the isDaemon() method to check if a thread is a daemon thread.

▨ **Tip** The JVM starts a garbage collector thread to collect all unused object's memory as a daemon thread.

When a thread is created, its daemon property is the same as the thread that creates it. In other words, a new thread inherits the daemon property of its creator thread.

Listing 6-17 creates a thread and sets the thread as a daemon thread. The thread prints an integer and sleeps for some time in an infinite loop. At the end of the main() method, the program prints a message to the standard output stating that it is exiting the main() method. Since thread t is a daemon thread, the JVM will terminate the application when the main() method is finished executing. You can see this in the output. The application prints only one integer from the thread before it exits. You may get a different output when you run this program.

Listing 6-17. A Daemon Thread Example

```java
// DaemonThread.java
package com.jdojo.threads;

public class DaemonThread {
    public static void main(String[] args) {
        Thread t = new Thread(DaemonThread::print);
        t.setDaemon(true);
        t.start();
        System.out.println("Exiting main method");
    }

    public static void print() {
        int counter = 1 ;
        while(true) {
            try {
                System.out.println("Counter:" + counter++);
                Thread.sleep(2000); // sleep for 2 seconds
            }
            catch(InterruptedException e) {
                e.printStackTrace();
            }
        }
    }
}
```

```
Exiting main method
Counter:1
```

Listing 6-18 is the same program as Listing 6-17, except that it sets the thread as a non-daemon thread. Since this program has a non-daemon (or a user) thread, the JVM will keep running the application, even after the main() method finishes. You will have to stop this application forcibly because the thread runs in an infinite loop.

Listing 6-18. A Non-Daemon Thread Example

```java
// NonDaemonThread.java
package com.jdojo.threads;

public class NonDaemonThread {
    public static void main(String[] args) {
        Thread t = new Thread(NonDaemonThread::print);

        // t is already a non-daemon thread because the "main" thread that runs
        // the main() method is a non-daemon thread. You can verify it by using
        // t.isDaemon() method. It will return false.
        // Still we will use the following statement to make it clear that we
        // want t to be a non-daemon thread.
        t.setDaemon(false);
        t.start();
        System.out.println("Exiting main method");
    }

    public static void print() {
        int counter = 1;
        while(true) {
            try {
                System.out.println("Counter:" + counter++);
                Thread.sleep(2000); // sleep for 2 seconds
            }
            catch(InterruptedException e) {
                e.printStackTrace();
            }
        }
    }
}
```

```
Exiting main method
Counter:1
Counter:2
...
```

Am I Interrupted?

You can interrupt a thread that is alive by using the interrupt() method. This method invocation on a thread is just an indication to the thread that some other part of the program is trying to draw its attention. It is up to the thread how it responds to the interruption. Java implements the interruption mechanism using an interrupted status flag for every thread.

A thread could be in one of the two states when it is interrupted: running or blocked. If a thread is interrupted when it is running, its interrupted status is set by the JVM. The running thread can check its interrupted status by calling the Thread.interrupted() static method, which returns true if the current thread was interrupted. The call to the Thread.interrupted() method clears the interrupted status of a thread. That is, if you call this method again on the same thread and if the first call returned true, the subsequent calls will return false, unless the thread is interrupted after the first call but before the subsequent calls.

Listing 6-19 shows the code that interrupts the main thread and prints the interrupted status of the thread. Note that the second call to the Thread.interrupted() method returns false, as indicated in the output #3:false. This example also shows that a thread can interrupt itself. The main thread that is responsible for running the main() method is interrupting itself in this example.

Listing 6-19. A Simple Example of Interrupting a Thread

```java
// SimpleInterrupt.java
package com.jdojo.threads;

public class SimpleInterrupt {
        public static void main(String[] args) {
                System.out.println("#1:" + Thread.interrupted());

                // Now interrupt the main thread
                Thread.currentThread().interrupt();

                // Check if it has been interrupted
                System.out.println("#2:" + Thread.interrupted());

                // Check again if it has been interrupted
                System.out.println("#3:" + Thread.interrupted());
        }
}
```

```
#1:false
#2:true
#3:false
```

Let's have another example of the same kind. This time, one thread will interrupt another thread. Listing 6-20 starts a thread that increments a counter until the thread is interrupted. At the end, the thread prints the value of the counter. The main() method starts the thread; it sleeps for one second to let the counter thread do some work; it interrupts the thread. Since the thread checks whether it has been interrupted or not before continuing in the while-loop, it exits the loop once it is interrupted. You may a different output when you run this program.

Listing 6-20. A Thread Interrupting Another Thread

```java
// SimpleInterruptAnotherThread.java
package com.jdojo.threads;

public class SimpleInterruptAnotherThread {
        public static void main(String[] args) {
                Thread t = new Thread(SimpleInterruptAnotherThread::run);
                t.start();

                // Let the main thread sleep for 1 second
                try {
                        Thread.currentThread().sleep(1000);
                }
                catch (InterruptedException e) {
                        e.printStackTrace();
                }
```

```
                        // Now interrupt the thread
                        t.interrupt();
        }

        public static void run() {
                int counter = 0;

                while (!Thread.interrupted()) {
                        counter++;
                }
                System.out.println("Counter:" + counter);
        }
}
```

```
Counter:1630140
```

The Thread class has a non-static isInterrupted() method that can be used to test if a thread has been interrupted. When you call this method, unlike the interrupted() method, the interrupted status of the thread is not cleared. Listing 6-21 demonstrates the difference between the two methods: interrupted() and isInterrupted().

Listing 6-21. Difference Between the interrupted() and isInterrupted() Methods

```java
// SimpleIsInterrupted.java
package com.jdojo.threads;

public class SimpleIsInterrupted {
        public static void main(String[] args) {
                // Check if the main thread is interrupted
                System.out.println("#1:" + Thread.interrupted());

                // Now interrupt the main thread
                Thread mainThread = Thread.currentThread();
                mainThread.interrupt();

                // Check if it has been interrupted
                System.out.println("#2:" + mainThread.isInterrupted());

                // Check if it has been interrupted
                System.out.println("#3:" + mainThread.isInterrupted());

                // Now check if it has been interrupted using the static method
                // which will clear the interrupted status
                System.out.println("#4:" + Thread.interrupted());

                // Now, isInterrupted() should return false, because previous
                // statement Thread.interrupted() has cleared the flag
                System.out.println("#5:" + mainThread.isInterrupted());
        }
}
```

```
#1:false
#2:true
#3:true
#4:true
#5:false
```

You may interrupt a blocked thread. Recall that a thread may block itself by executing one of the sleep(), wait(), and join() methods. If a thread blocked on these three methods is interrupted, an InterruptedException is thrown and the interrupted status of the thread is cleared because the thread has already received an exception to signal the interruption.

Listing 6-22 starts a thread that sleeps for one second and prints a message until it is interrupted. The main thread sleeps for five seconds, so the sleeping thread gets a chance to sleep and print messages a few times. When the main thread wakes up, it interrupts the sleeping thread. You may get a different output when you run the program.

Listing 6-22. Interrupting a Blocked Thread

```java
// BlockedInterrupted.java
package com.jdojo.threads;

public class BlockedInterrupted {
        public static void main(String[] args) {
                Thread t = new Thread(BlockedInterrupted::run);
                t.start();

                // main thread sleeps for 5 seconds
                try {
                        Thread.sleep(5000);
                }
                catch (InterruptedException e) {
                        e.printStackTrace();
                }

                // Interrupt the sleeping thread
                t.interrupt();
        }

        public static void run() {
                int counter = 1;
                while (true) {
                        try {
                                Thread.sleep(1000);
                                System.out.println("Counter:" + counter++);
                        }
                        catch (InterruptedException e) {
                                System.out.println("I got interrupted!");
```

```
                                // Terminate the thread by returning
                                return;
                        }
                }

        }
}
```

```
Counter:1
Counter:2
Counter:3
I got interrupted!
```

If a thread is blocked on an I/O, interrupting a thread does not really do anything if you are using the old I/O API. However, if you are using the New I/O API, your thread will receive a ClosedByInterruptException, which is declared in the java.nio.channels package. I will discuss I/O in detail in subsequent chapters.

Threads Work in a Group

A thread is always a member of a thread group. By default, the thread group of a thread is the group of its creator thread. The JVM creates a thread group called main and a thread in this group called main, which is responsible for running the main() method of the class at startup. A thread group in a Java program is represented by an object of the java.lang.ThreadGroup class. The getThreadGroup() method of the Thread class returns the reference to the ThreadGroup of a thread. Listing 6-23 demonstrates that, by default, a new thread is a member of the thread group of its creator thread.

Listing 6-23. Determining the Default Thread Group of a Thread

```java
// DefaultThreadGroup.java
package com.jdojo.threads;

public class DefaultThreadGroup {
        public static void main(String[] args) {
                // Get the current thread, which is called "main"
                Thread t1 = Thread.currentThread();

                // Get the thread group of the main thread
                ThreadGroup tg1 = t1.getThreadGroup();

                System.out.println("Current thread's name: " + t1.getName());
                System.out.println("Current thread's group name: " + tg1.getName());

                // Creates a new thread. Its thread group is the same that of the main thread.
                Thread t2 = new Thread("my new thread");

                ThreadGroup tg2 = t2.getThreadGroup();
                System.out.println("New thread's name: " + t2.getName());
                System.out.println("New thread's group name: " + tg2.getName());
        }
}
```

```
Current thread's name: main
Current thread's group name: main
New thread's name: my new thread
New thread's group name: main
```

You can also create a thread group and place a new thread in that thread group. To place a new thread in your thread group, you must use one of the constructors of the Thread class that accepts a ThreadGroup object as an argument. The following snippet of code places a new thread in a particular thread group:

```
// Create a new ThreadGroup
ThreadGroup myGroup = new ThreadGroup("My Thread Group");

// Make the new thread a member of the myGroup thread group
Thread t = new Thread(myGroup, "myThreadName");
```

Thread groups are arranged in a tree-like structure. A thread group can contain another thread group. The getParent() method of the ThreadGroup class returns the parent thread group of a thread group. The parent of the top-level thread group is null.

The activeCount() method of the ThreadGroup class returns an estimate of the number of active threads in the group. The enumerate() method of the ThreadGroup class can be used to get the threads in a thread group.

A thread group in a Java program can be used to implement a group-based policy that applies to all threads in a thread group. For example, by calling the interrupt() method of a thread group, you can interrupt all threads in the thread group.

Volatile Variables

I have discussed the use of the synchronized keyword in previous sections. Two things happen when a thread executes a synchronized method/block.

- The thread must obtain the monitor lock of the object on which the method/block is synchronized.

- The thread's working copy of the shared variables is updated with the values of those variables in the main memory just after the thread gets the lock. The values of the shared variables in the main memory are updated with thread's working copy value just before the thread releases the lock. That is, at the start and at the end of a synchronized method/block, the values of the shared variables in thread's working memory and the main memory are synchronized.

What can you do to achieve only the second point without using a synchronized method/block? That is, how can you keep the values of variables in a thread's working memory in sync with their values in the main memory? The answer is the keyword volatile. You can declare a variable volatile like so:

```
volatile boolean flag = true;
```

For every read request for a volatile variable, a thread reads the value from the main memory. For every write request for a volatile variable, a thread writes the value to the main memory. In other words, a thread does not cache the value of a volatile variable in its working memory. Note that using a volatile variable is useful only in a multi-threaded environment for variables that are shared among threads. It is faster and cheaper than using a synchronized block.

You can declare only a class member variable (instance or static fields) as volatile. You cannot declare a local variable as volatile because a local variable is always private to the thread, which is never shared with other threads. You cannot declare a volatile variable final because the volatile keyword is used with a variable that changes.

You can use a volatile variable to stop a thread by using the variable's value as a flag. If the flag is set, the thread can keep running. If another thread clears the flag, the thread should stop. Since two threads share the flag, you need to declare it volatile, so that on every read the thread will get its updated value from the main memory.

Listing 6-24 demonstrates the use of a volatile variable. If the keepRunning variable is not declared volatile, the JVM is free to run the while-loop in the run() method forever, as the initial value of keepRunning is set to true and a thread can cache this value in its working memory. Since the keepRunning variable is declared volatile, the JVM will read its value from the main memory every time it is used. When another thread updates the keepRunning variable's value to false using the stopThread() method, the next iteration of the while-loop will read its updated value and stop the loop. Your program may work the same way as in Listing 6-23 even if you do not declare the keepRunning as volatile. However, according to the JVM specification, this behavior is not guaranteed. If the JVM specification is implemented correctly, using a volatile variable in this way ensures the correct behavior for your program.

Listing 6-24. Using a volatile Variable in a Multi-Threaded Program

```java
// VolatileVariable.java
package com.jdojo.threads;

public class VolatileVariable extends Thread {
    private volatile boolean keepRunning = true;

    public void run() {
        System.out.println("Thread started...");

        // keepRunning is volatile. So, for every read, the thread reads its
        // latest value from the main memory
        while (keepRunning) {
            try {
                System.out.println("Going to sleep ...");
                Thread.sleep(1000);
            }
            catch (InterruptedException e) {
                e.printStackTrace();
            }
        }
        System.out.println("Thread stopped...");
    }

    public void stopThread() {
        this.keepRunning = false;
    }

    public static void main(String[] args) {
        // Create the thread
        VolatileVariable vv = new VolatileVariable();

        // Start the thread
        vv.start();
```

```
                // Let the main thread sleep for 3 seconds
                try {
                        Thread.sleep(3000);
                }
                catch (InterruptedException e) {
                        e.printStackTrace();
                }

                // Stop the thread
                System.out.println("Going to set the stop flag to true...");
                vv.stopThread();
        }
}
```

```
Thread started...
Going to sleep...
Going to sleep...
Going to sleep...
Going to set the stop flag to true...
Thread stopped...
```

▓ **Tip** A volatile variable of long and double types is treated atomically for read and write purposes. Recall that a non-volatile variable of long and double types is treated non-atomically. That is, if two threads are writing two different values, say v1 and v2 to a non-volatile long or double variable, respectively, your program may see a value for that variable that is neither v1 nor v2. However, if that long or double variable is declared volatile, your program sees the value v1 or v2 at a given point in time. You cannot make array elements as volatile.

Stopping, Suspending, and Resuming a Thread

The stop(), suspend(), and resume() methods in the Thread class let you stop a thread, suspend a thread, and resume a suspended thread, respectively. These methods have been deprecated because their use is error-prone.

You can stop a thread by calling the stop() method. When the stop() method of a thread is called, the JVM throws a java.lang.ThreadDeath error. Because of throwing this error, all monitors locked by the thread being stopped are unlocked. Monitor locks are used to protect some important shared resources (typically Java objects). If any of the shared resources protected by the monitors were in inconsistent states when the thread was stopped, other threads may see that inconsistent state of those resources. This will result in an incorrect behavior of the program. This is the reason that the stop() method is deprecated; you are advised not to use it in your program.

How can you stop a thread without using its stop() method? You can stop a thread by setting a flag that the running thread will check regularly. If the flag is set, the thread should stop executing. This way of stopping a thread was illustrated in Listing 6-24 in the previous section.

You can suspend a thread by calling its suspend() method. To resume a suspended thread, you need to call its resume() method. However, the suspend() method has been deprecated because it is error-prone and it may cause a deadlock. Let's assume that the suspended thread holds the monitor lock of an object. The thread that will resume the suspended thread is trying to obtain the monitor lock of the same object. This will result in a deadlock. The suspended thread will remain suspended because there is no one who will resume it, and the thread that will resume it will remain blocked because the monitor lock it is trying to obtain is held by the suspended thread. This is the reason that the suspend() method has been deprecated. The resume() method is also deprecated because it is called in conjunction with the suspend() method. You can use a similar technique to simulate the suspend() and resume() methods of the Thread class in your program as you did to simulate the stop() method.

Listing 6-25 demonstrates how to simulate the stop(), suspend(), and resume() methods of the Thread class in your thread.

Listing 6-25. Stopping, Suspending, and Resuming a Thread

```java
// StopSuspendResume.java
package com.jdojo.threads;

public class StopSuspendResume extends Thread {
    private volatile boolean keepRunning = true;
    private boolean suspended = false;

    public synchronized void stopThread() {
        this.keepRunning = false;

        // Notify the thread in case it is suspended when this method
        // is called, so  it will wake up and stop.
        this.notify();
    }

    public synchronized void suspendThread() {
        this.suspended = true;
    }

    public synchronized void resumeThread() {
        this.suspended = false;
        this.notify();
    }

    public void run() {
        System.out.println("Thread started...");
        while (keepRunning) {
            try {
                System.out.println("Going to sleep...");
                Thread.sleep(1000);

                // Check for a suspended condition must be made inside a
                // synchronized block to call the wait() method
                synchronized (this) {
                    while (suspended) {
                        System.out.println("Suspended...");
                        this.wait();
                        System.out.println("Resumed...");
                    }
                }
            }
        }
```

```java
                catch (InterruptedException e) {
                        e.printStackTrace();
                }
        }
        System.out.println("Thread stopped...");
}

public static void main(String[] args) {
        StopSuspendResume t = new StopSuspendResume();

        // Start the thread
        t.start();

        // Sleep for 2 seconds
        try {
                Thread.sleep(2000);
        }
        catch (InterruptedException e) {
                e.printStackTrace();
        }

        // Suspend the thread
        t.suspendThread();

        // Sleep for 2 seconds
        try {
                Thread.sleep(2000);
        }
        catch (InterruptedException e) {
                e.printStackTrace();
        }

        // Resume the thread
        t.resumeThread();

        try {
                Thread.sleep(2000);
        }
        catch (InterruptedException e) {
                e.printStackTrace();
        }

        // Stop the thread
        t.stopThread();
    }
}
```

```
Thread started...
Going to sleep...
Going to sleep...
Going to sleep...
Suspended...
Resumed...
Going to sleep...
Going to sleep...
Going to sleep...
Thread stopped...
```

Note that you have two instance variables for the StopSuspendResume class. The suspended instance variable is not declared volatile. It is not necessary to declare it volatile because it is always accessed inside a synchronized method/block. The following code in the run() method is used to implement the suspend and resume features:

```
synchronized (this) {
        while (suspended) {
                System.out.println("Suspended...");
                this.wait();
                System.out.println("Resumed...");
        }
}
```

When the suspended instance variable is set to true, the thread calls the wait() method on itself to wait. Note the use of the synchronized block. It uses this as the object to synchronize. This is the reason that you can call this.wait() inside the synchronized block because you have obtained the lock on this object before entering the synchronized block. Once the this.wait() method is called, the thread releases the lock on this object and keeps waiting in the wait set until another thread calls the resumeThread() method to notify it. I also use the this.notify() method call inside the stopThread() method because if the thread is suspended when the stopThread() method is called, the thread will not stop; rather, it will remain suspended.

The thread in this example sleeps for only one second in its run() method. Suppose your thread sleeps for an extended period. In such a case, calling the stopThread() method will not stop the thread immediately because the thread will stop only when it wakes up and checks its keepRunning instance variable value in its next loop iteration. In such cases, you can use the interrupt() method inside the stopThread() method to interrupt sleeping/waiting threads, and when InterruptedException is thrown, you need to handle it appropriately.

If you use the technique used in Listing 6-25 to stop a thread, you may run into problems in some situations. The while-loop inside the run() method depends on the keepRunning instance variable, which is set in the stopThread() method. The example in this listing is simple. It is just meant to demonstrate the concept of how to stop, suspend, and resume a thread. Suppose inside the run() method, your code waits for other resources like calling a method someBlockingMethodCall() as shown:

```
while (keepRunning) {
        try {
                someBlockingMethodCall();
        }
        catch (InterruptedException e) {
                e.printStackTrace();
        }
}
```

If you call the stopThread() method while this thread is blocked on the method call someBlockingMethodCall(), this thread will not stop until it returns from the blocked method call or it is interrupted. To overcome this problem, you need to change the strategy for how to stop a thread. It is a good idea to rely on the interruption technique of a thread to stop it prematurely. The stopThread() method can be changed to

```java
public void stopThread() {
        // interrupt this thread
        this.interrupt();
}
```

In addition, the while-loop inside the run() method should be modified to check if the thread is interrupted. You need to modify the exception handling code to exit the loop if this thread is interrupted while it is blocked. The following snippet of code illustrates this logic:

```java
public void run() {
        while (Thread.currentThread().isInterrupted())) {
                try {
                        // Do the processing
                }
                catch (InterruptedException e) {
                        // Stop the thread by exiting the loop
                        break;
                }
        }
}
```

Handling an Uncaught Exception in a Thread

You can handle an uncaught exception thrown in your thread. It is handled using an object of a class that implements the java.lang.Thread.UncaughtExceptionHandler interface. The interface is defined as a nested static interface in the Thread class. It has the following one method defined, where t is the thread object reference that throws the exception and e is the uncaught exception thrown:

```java
void uncaughtException(Thread t, Throwable e);
```

Listing 6-26 has the code for a class whose object can be used as an uncaught exception handler for a thread.

Listing 6-26. An Uncaught Exception Handler for a Thread

```java
// CatchAllThreadExceptionHandler.java
package com.jdojo.threads;

public class CatchAllThreadExceptionHandler implements Thread.UncaughtExceptionHandler {
        public void uncaughtException(Thread t, Throwable e) {
                System.out.println("Caught Exception from Thread:" + t.getName());
        }
}
```

The class simply prints a message and the thread name stating that an uncaught exception from a thread has been handled. Typically, you may want to do some cleanup work or log the exception to a file or a database in the uncaughtException() method of the handler. The thread class contains two methods to set an uncaught exception handler for a thread: one is a static setDefaultUncaughtExceptionHandler() method and another is a non-static setUncaughtExceptionHandler() method. Use the static method to set a default handler for all threads in your application. Use the non-static method to set a handler for a particular thread. When a thread has an uncaught exception, the following steps are taken:

- If the thread sets an uncaught exception handler using the setUncaughtExceptionHandler() method, the uncaughtException() method of that handler is invoked.

- If a thread does not have an uncaught exception handler set, its thread group's uncaughtException() method is called. If the thread group has a parent thread group, it calls the uncaughtException() method of its parent. Otherwise, it checks if there is a default uncaught exception handler set. If it finds a default uncaught exception handler, it calls the uncaughtException() method on it. If it does not find a default uncaught exception handler, a message is printed on the standard error stream. It does not do anything if it does not find a default uncaught exception handler and a ThreadDeath exception is thrown.

Listing 6-27 demonstrates how to set a handler for uncaught exceptions in a thread. It creates an object of class CatchAllThreadExceptionHandler and sets it as a handler for the uncaught exceptions for the main thread. The main thread throws an unchecked exception in its last statement. The output shows that the handler handles the exception thrown in the main() method.

Listing 6-27. Setting an Uncaught Exception Handler for a Thread

```java
// UncaughtExceptionInThread.java
package com.jdojo.threads;

public class UncaughtExceptionInThread {
    public static void main(String[] args) {
        CatchAllThreadExceptionHandler handler = new CatchAllThreadExceptionHandler();

        // Set an uncaught exception handler for main thread
        Thread.currentThread().setUncaughtExceptionHandler(handler);

        // Throw an exception
        throw new RuntimeException();
    }
}
```

```
Caught Exception from Thread:main
```

New Thread Concurrency Packages

Although Java had support for multi-threading built into the language from the very beginning, it was not easy to develop a multi-threaded Java program that used an advanced level of concurrency constructs. For example, the synchronized keyword, used to lock an object's monitor, has existed since the beginning. However, a thread that tries to lock an object's monitor simply blocks if the lock is not available. In this case, a programmer had no choice but to back out. Wouldn't it be nice to have a construct that is based on a "try and lock" philosophy rather than a "lock or block" philosophy? In this strategy, if an object's monitor lock is not available, the call to lock the monitor returns immediately.

The package java.util.concurrent and its two subpackages, java.util.concurrent.atomic and java.util.concurrent.locks, include very useful concurrency constructs. You use the constructs available in these packages only when you are developing an advanced level multi-threaded program. I will not cover all new concurrency constructs in this section because describing everything available in these packages could take more than a hundred pages. I will briefly cover some of the most useful concurrency constructs available in these packages. We can broadly categorize these concurrency features into four categories:

- Atomic variables

- Locks

- Synchronizers

- Concurrent collections (Please refer to Chapter 12 for concurrent collections)

Atomic Variables

Typically, when you need to share an updateable variable among threads, synchronization is used. Synchronization among multiple threads used to be achieved using the synchronized keyword and it was based on an object's monitor. If a thread is not able to acquire an object's monitor, that thread is suspended and it has to be resumed later. This way of synchronization (suspending and resuming) uses a great deal of system resources. The problem is not in the locking and unlocking mechanism of the monitor lock; rather it is in suspending and resuming the threads. If there is no contention for acquiring a lock, using the keyword synchronized to synchronize threads does not hurt much.

An atomic variable uses a lock-free synchronization of a single variable. Note that if your program needs to synchronize on more than one shared variable, you still need to use the old synchronization methods. By lock-free synchronization, I mean that multiple threads can access a shared variable safely using no object monitor lock. JDK takes advantage of a hardware instruction called *"compare-and-swap"* (CAS) to implement the lock-free synchronization for one variable.

CAS is based on three operands: a memory location M, an expected old value O, and a new value N. If the memory location M contains a value O, CAS updates it atomically to N; otherwise, it does not do anything. CAS always returns the current value at the location M that existed before the CAS operation started. The pseudo code for CAS is as follows:

```
CAS(M, O, N) {
        currentValueAtM = get the value at Location M;

        if (currentValueAtM == O) {
                set value at M to N;
        }

        return currentValueAtM;
}
```

The CAS instruction is lock free. It is directly supported in most modern computers' hardware. However, CAS is not always guaranteed to succeed in a multi-threaded environment. CAS takes an optimistic approach by assuming that there are no other threads updating the value at location M; if the location M contains value O, update it to N; if the value at location M is not O, do not do anything. Therefore, if multiple threads attempt to update the value at location M to different values simultaneously, only one thread will succeed and others will fail.

The synchronization using locks takes a pessimistic approach by assuming that other threads may be working with location M and acquires a lock before it starts working at location M, so that other threads will not access location M while one is working with it. In case CAS fails, the caller thread may try the action again or give up; the caller thread using CAS never blocks. However, in case of synchronization using a lock, the caller thread may have to be suspended and resumed if it could not acquire the lock. Using synchronization, you also run the risk of a *deadlock*, a *livelock*, and other synchronization-related failures.

Atomic variable classes are named like AtomicXxx, and can be used to execute multiple instructions on a single variable atomically without using any lock. Here, Xxx is replaced with different words to indicate different classes that are used for different purposes; for example, the AtomicInteger class is used to represent an int variable, which is supposed to be manipulated atomically. Twelve classes in the Java class library support read-modify-write operations on a single variable atomically. They are in the java.util.concurrent.atomic package. They can be categorized in four categories, which will be discussed in the following sections.

Scalar Atomic Variable Classes

The AtomicInteger, AtomicLong, and AtomicBoolean classes support operations on primitive data types int, long, and boolean, respectively.

If you need to work with other primitive data types, use the AtomicInteger class. You can use it directly to work with byte and short data types. Use it to work with the float data type by using the Float.floatToIntBits() method to convert a float value to the int data type and the AtomicInteger.floatValue() method to convert an int value to the float data type back.

You can use the AtomicLong class to work with the double data type by using the Double.doubleToLongBits() method to convert a double value to the long data type and the AtomicLong.doubleValue() method to convert the long value to the double data type.

The AtomicReference class is used to work with a reference data type when a reference variable needs to be updated atomically.

Atomic Arrays Classes

There are three classes called AtomicIntegerArray, AtomicLongArray, and AtomicReferenceArray that represent an array of int, long, and reference types whose elements can be updated atomically.

Atomic Field Updater Classes

There are three classes called AtomicLongFieldUpdater, AtomicIntegerFieldUpdater, and AtomicReferenceFieldUpdater that can be used to update a volatile field of a class atomically using reflection. These classes have no constructors. To get a reference to an object of these classes, you need to use their factory method called newUpdater().

Atomic Compound Variable Classes

CAS works by asking "Is the value at location M still 0?" If the answer is yes, it updates the value at location M from 0 to N. In a typical scenario, one thread may read the value from location M as 0. By the time this thread tries to update the value from 0 to N, another thread has changed the value at location M from 0 to P, and back from P to 0. Therefore, the call CAS(M, 0, N) will succeed because the value at location M is still 0, even though it was changed (0 to P and back to 0) twice after the thread read the value 0 last time. In some cases, it is fine. The thread that wants to update the value at location M does not care if the old value 0 that it read last time was updated before its own update as long as the value at location M is 0 at the time it is updating the value to N. However, in some cases, it is not acceptable. If a thread reads the value 0 from a location M, this thread wants to make sure that after it read the value, no other thread has updated the value. In such cases, CAS needs to ask "Has the value at location M changed since I last read it as 0?" To achieve this functionality, you need to store a pair of values: the value you want to work with and its version number. Each update will also update the version number. The AtomicMarkableReference and AtomicStampedReference classes fall into this category of atomic compound variable class.

Let's look at a simple example that uses an atomic class. If you want to write a class to generate a counter using built-in Java synchronization, it will resemble the code in Listing 6-28.

Listing 6-28. A Counter Class That Uses Synchronization

```java
// SynchronizedCounter.java
package com.jdojo.threads;

public class SynchronizedCounter {
        private long value;

        public synchronized long next() {
                return ++value;
        }
}
```

You would rewrite the SynchronizedCounter class using the AtomicLong class as shown in Listing 6-29.

Listing 6-29. A Counter Class Using Atomic Variable

```java
// AtomicCounter.java
package com.jdojo.threads;

import java.util.concurrent.atomic.AtomicLong;

public class AtomicCounter {
        private AtomicLong value = new AtomicLong(0L);

        public long next() {
                return value.incrementAndGet();
        }
}
```

Note that the AtomicCounter class does not use any explicit synchronization. It takes advantage of CAS hardware instruction. The call to the incrementAndGet() method inside the next() method of the AtomicCounter class is performed atomically for you. You can also use an object of the AtomicLong class as a thread-safe counter object like so:

```java
AtomicLong aCounter = new AtomicLong(0L);
```

Then you can use the aCounter.incrementAndGet() method to generate a new counter. The incrementAndGet() method of the AtomicLong class increments its current value and returns the new value. You also have its counterpart method called getAndIncrement(), which increments its value and returns its previous value.

The AtomicXxx variable classes have a compareAndSet() method. It is a variant of compare and swap (CAS). The only difference is that the compareAndSet() method returns a boolean. It returns true if it succeeds; otherwise it returns false. The following is the pseudo code representation of the compareAndSet() method:

```java
compareAndSet(M, O, N) {
        // Call CAS (see CAS pseudo code) if CAS succeeded, return true;
        // otherwise, return false.
        return (CAS(M, O, N) == O)
}
```

Explicit Locks

Explicit locking mechanism can be used to coordinate access to shared resources in a multi-threaded environment without using the keyword synchronized. The Lock interface, which is declared in the java.util.concurrent.locks package, defines the explicit locking operations. The ReentrantLock class, in the same package, is the concrete implementation of the Lock interface. The Lock interface is declared as follows:

```
public interface Lock {
        void lock();
        Condition newCondition();
        void lockInterruptibly() throws InterruptedException;
        boolean tryLock();
        boolean tryLock(long time, TimeUnit unit) throws InterruptedException;
        void unlock();
}
```

The use of the lock() method to acquire a lock behaves the same as the use of the synchronized keyword. The use of the synchronized keyword requires that a thread should acquire and release an object's monitor lock in the same block of code. When you use the synchronized keyword to acquire an object's monitor lock, the lock is released by the JVM when the program leaves the block in which the lock was acquired. This feature makes working with intrinsic locks very simple and less error prone. However, in the case of the Lock interface, the restriction of acquiring and releasing of the lock in the same block of code does not apply. This makes it a little flexible to use; however, it is more error prone because the responsibility of acquiring as well as releasing the lock is on the programmer. It is not difficult to acquire the lock and forget to release it, resulting in hard-to-find bugs. You must make sure that you release the lock by calling the unlock() method of the Lock interface after you are done with the lock. You can use the lock() and unlock() methods in their simplest form, shown in Listing 6-30. Note the use of a try-finally block to release the lock in the updateResource() method. The use of a try-finally block is necessary in this case because no matter how you finish returning from this method after you call myLock.lock(), you would like to release the lock. This can be assured only if you place the call to the unlock() method inside the finally block.

Listing 6-30. Using an Explicit Lock in its Simplest Form

```
// SimpleExplicitLock.java
package com.jdojo.threads;

import java.util.concurrent.locks.Lock;
import java.util.concurrent.locks.ReentrantLock;

public class SimpleExplicitLock {
        // Instantiate the lock object
        private Lock myLock = new ReentrantLock();

        public void updateResource() {
                // Acquire the lock
                myLock.lock();

                try {
                        // Logic for updating/reading the shared resource goes here
                }
```

```
        finally {
                // Release the lock
                myLock.unlock();
        }
    }
}
```

You may wonder why you would use the code structure listed in Listing 6-30 when you could have used the synchronized keyword to achieve the same effect, like so:

```
public void updateResource() {
        // Acquire the lock and the lock will be released automatically by the
        // JVM when your code exits the block
        synchronized (this) {
                // Logic for updating/reading the shared resource goes here
        }
}
```

You are correct in thinking that using the synchronized keyword would have been better in this case. It is much simpler and less error prone to use the synchronized keyword in such situations. The power of using the new Lock interface becomes evident when you come across situations where using the synchronized keyword is not possible or very cumbersome. For example, if you want to acquire the lock in the updateResource() method and release it in some other methods, you cannot use the synchronized keyword. If you need to acquire two locks to work with a shared resource and if only one lock is available, you want to do something else rather than waiting for the other lock. If you use the synchronized keyword or the lock() method of the Lock interface to acquire a lock, the call blocks if the lock is not available immediately, which gives you no option to back off once you asked for the lock. Such blocked threads cannot be interrupted either. The two methods of the Lock interface, tryLock() and lockInterruptibly(), give you the ability to try to acquire a lock (rather than acquire a lock or block). The thread that has acquired the lock can be interrupted if it is blocked. The syntax to acquire and release a lock using the Lock interface should use a try-finally or a try-catch-finally block structure to avoid unintended bugs by placing the unlock() call in a finally block.

You will solve a classic synchronization problem known as the dining-philosophers problem using the explicit lock constructs. The problem goes like this: five philosophers spend all of their time either thinking or eating. They sit around a circular table with five chairs and five forks, as shown in Figure 6-7. There are only five forks and all five philosophers need to pick the two nearest (one from his left and one from his right) forks to eat.

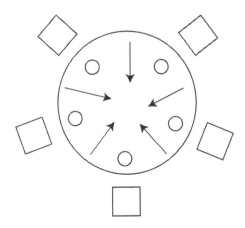

Figure 6-7. *Five philosophers at a dining table*

Once a philosopher finishes eating, he puts down both forks and starts thinking. A philosopher cannot pick up a fork if his neighbor is using it. What happens if each of the five philosophers picks up one fork from his right and waits for his left fork to be released by his neighbor? This would be a deadlock situation and no philosopher would be able to eat. This deadlock condition can be avoided easily by using the tryLock() method of the Lock interface. This method returns immediately and it never blocks. If the lock is available, it gets the lock and returns true. If the lock is not available, it returns false. The class in Listing 6-31 can be used to model the philosophers assuming that an object of the ReentrantLock class represents a fork.

Listing 6-31. A Philosopher Class to Represent a Philosopher

```java
// Philosopher.java
package com.jdojo.threads;

import java.util.concurrent.locks.Lock;

public class Philosopher {
        private Lock leftFork;
        private Lock rightFork;
        private String name; // Philosopher's name
        public Philosopher(Lock leftFork, Lock rightFork, String name) {
                this.leftFork  = leftFork;
                this.rightFork = rightFork;
                this.name = name;
        }

        public void think() {
                System.out.println(name + " is thinking...");
        }

        public void eat() {
                // Try to get the left fork
                if (leftFork.tryLock()) {
                        try {
                                // try to get the right fork
                                if (rightFork.tryLock()) {
                                        try {
                                                // Got both forks. Eat now
                                                System.out.println(name + " is eating...");
                                        }
                                        finally {
                                                // release the right fork
                                                rightFork.unlock();
                                        }
                                }
                        }
                        finally {
                                // release the left fork
                                leftFork.unlock();
                        }
                }
        }
}
```

To create a philosopher, you would use code like:

```
Lock fork1 = new ReentrantLock();
Lock fork2 = new ReentrantLock();
...
Lock fork5 = new ReentrantLock();

Philosopher p1 = new Philosopher(fork1, fork2, "John");
Philosopher p2 = new Philosopher(fork2, fork3, "Wallace");
...
Philosopher p5 = new Philosopher(fork5, fork1, "Charles");
```

It is left for the reader as an exercise to complete the code and run all five philosophers in five different threads to simulate the dining-philosophers problem. You can also think about how to use the synchronized keyword to solve the same problem. Read the code in the eat() method carefully. It tries to get the left and right forks one at a time. If you can get only one fork and not the other, you put down the one you got so others can have it. The code in the eat() method has only the logic to get the forks. In a real program, if you cannot get both forks, you would like to wait for some time and try again to pick up the forks. You will have to write that logic.

You can specify the fairness of a lock when you instantiate the ReentrantLock class. The fairness indicates the way of allocating the lock to a thread when multiple threads are waiting to get the lock. In a fair lock, threads acquire the lock in the order they request it. In a non-fair lock, jumping ahead by a thread is allowed. For example, in a non-fair lock, if some threads are waiting for a lock and another thread, which requests the same lock later, gets the lock before the waiting threads if the lock becomes available at the time this thread requested it. This may sound a little strange because it is not fair to the waiting threads to leave them waiting and granting the lock to the thread that requested it later. However, it has a performance gain. The overhead of suspending and resuming a thread is reduced using non-fair locking. The tryLock() method of the ReentrantLock class always uses a non-fair lock. You can create fair and non-fair locks as follows:

```
Lock nonFairLock1 = new ReentrantLock();       // A non-fair lock (Default is non-fair)
Lock nonFairLock2 = new ReentrantLock(false);  // A non-fair lock
Lock fairLock2 = new ReentrantLock(true);      // A fair lock
```

A ReentrantLock provides a mutually exclusive locking mechanism. That is, only one thread can own the ReentrantLock at a time. If you have a data structure guarded by a ReentrantLock, a writer thread as well as a reader thread must acquire the lock one at a time to modify or to read the data. This restriction of ReentrantLock, to be owned by only one thread at a time, may downgrade the performance if your data structure is read frequently and modified infrequently. In such situations, you may want multiple reader threads to have concurrent access to the data structure. However, if the data structure is being modified, only one writer thread should have the access to the data structure. The Read-Write lock allows you to implement this kind of locking mechanism using an instance of the ReadWriteLock interface. It has two methods: one to get the reader lock and another to get the writer lock, as shown:

```
public interface ReadWriteLock {
        Lock readLock();
        Lock writeLock();
}
```

A ReentrantReadWriteLock class is an implementation of the ReadWriteLock Interface. Only one thread can hold the write lock of ReentrantReadWriteLock, whereas multiple threads can hold its read lock. Listing 6-32 demonstrates the usage of ReentrantReadWriteLock. Note that in the getValue() method, you use read lock so multiple threads can read the data concurrently. The setValue() method uses a write lock so only one thread can modify the data at a given time.

Listing 6-32. Using a ReentrantReadWriteLock to Guard a Read-Mostly Data Structure

```java
// ReadMostlyData.java
package com.jdojo.threads;

import java.util.concurrent.locks.Lock;
import java.util.concurrent.locks.ReentrantReadWriteLock;

public class ReadMostlyData {
        private int value;
        private ReentrantReadWriteLock rwLock = new ReentrantReadWriteLock();
        private Lock rLock = rwLock.readLock();
        private Lock wLock = rwLock.writeLock();

        public ReadMostlyData(int value) {
                this.value = value;
        }

        public int getValue() {
                // Use the read lock, so multiple threads may read concurrently
                rLock.lock();
                try {
                        return this.value;
                }
                finally {
                        rLock.unlock();
                }
        }

        public void setValue(int value) {
                // Use the write lock, so only one thread can write at a time
                wLock.lock();
                try {
                        this.value = value;
                }
                finally {
                        wLock.unlock();
                }
        }
}
```

■ **Tip** The ReadWriteLock allows you have a read and a write version of the same lock. Multiple threads can own a read lock as long as another thread does not own the write lock. However, only one thread can own the write lock at a time.

Synchronizers

I have discussed how to coordinate access to a critical section by multiple threads using a mutually exclusive mechanism of intrinsic locks and explicit locks. Some classes known as synchronizers are used to coordinate the control flow of a set of threads in a situation that needs other than mutually exclusive access to a critical section. A synchronizer object is used with a set of threads. It maintains a state, and depending on its state, it lets a thread pass through or forces it to wait. This section will discuss four types of synchronizers:

- Semaphores
- Barriers
- Latches
- Exchangers

Other classes can also act as a synchronizer such as a blocking queue.

Semaphores

A semaphore is used to control the number of threads that can access a resource. A synchronized block also controls the access to a resource that is the critical section. So, how is a semaphore different from a synchronized block? A synchronized block allows only one thread to access a resource (a critical section), whereas a semaphore allows N threads (N can be any positive number) to access a resource.

If N is set to one, a semaphore can act as a synchronized block to allow a thread to have mutually exclusive access to a resource. A semaphore maintains a number of virtual permits. To access a resource, a thread acquires a permit and it releases the permit when it is done with the resource. If a permit is not available, the requesting thread is blocked until a permit becomes available. You can think of a semaphore's permit as a token.

Let's discuss a daily life example of using a semaphore. Suppose there is a restaurant with three dining tables. Only three people can eat in that restaurant at a time. When a person arrives at the restaurant, he must take a token for a table. When he is done eating, he will return the token. Each token represents a dining table. If a person arrives at the restaurant when all three tables are in use, he must wait until one is available. If a table is not available immediately, you have a choice to wait until one becomes available or to go to another restaurant. Let's simulate this example using a semaphore. You will have a semaphore with three permits. Each permit will represent a dining table. The Semaphore class in the java.util.concurrent package represents the semaphore synchronizer. You create a semaphore using one of its constructors, like so:

```
final int MAX_PERMITS = 3;
Semaphore s = new Semaphores(MAX_PERMITS);
```

Another constructor for the Semaphore class takes fairness as the second argument as in

```
final int MAX_PERMITS = 3;
Semaphore s = new Semaphores(MAX_PERMITS, true); // A fair semaphore
```

The fairness of a semaphore has the same meaning as that for locks. If you create a fair semaphore, in the situation of multiple threads asking for permits, the semaphore will guarantee first in, first out (FIFO). That is, the thread that asked for the permit first will get the permit first.

To acquire a permit, use the acquire() method. It returns immediately if a permit is available. It blocks if a permit is not available. The thread can be interrupted while it is waiting for the permit to become available. Other methods of the Semaphore class let you acquire one or multiple permits in one go.

To release a permit, use the release() method.

Listing 6-33 has the code for a Restaurant class. It takes the number of tables available in a restaurant and creates a semaphore, which has the number of permits that is equal to the number of tables. A customer uses its getTable() and returnTable() methods to get and return a table, respectively. Inside the getTable() method, you acquire a permit. If a customer calls the getTable() method and no table is available, he must wait until one becomes available. This class depends on a RestaurantCustomer class that is declared in Listing 6-34.

Listing 6-33. A Restaurant Class, Which Uses a Semaphore to Control Access to Tables

```java
// Restaurant.java
package com.jdojo.threads;

import java.util.concurrent.Semaphore;

public class Restaurant {
    private Semaphore tables;

    public Restaurant(int tablesCount) {
        // Create a semaphore using number of tables we have
        this.tables = new Semaphore(tablesCount);
    }

    public void getTable(int customerID) {
        try {
            System.out.println("Customer #" + customerID + " is trying to get a table.");

            // Acquire a permit for a table
            tables.acquire();

            System.out.println("Customer #" + customerID + " got a table.");
        }
        catch (InterruptedException e) {
            e.printStackTrace();
        }
    }

    public void returnTable(int customerID) {
        System.out.println("Customer #" + customerID + " returned a table.");
        tables.release();
    }

    public static void main(String[] args) {
        // Create a restaurant with two dining tables
        Restaurant restaurant = new Restaurant(2);

        // Create five customers
        for (int i = 1; i <= 5; i++) {
            RestaurantCustomer c = new RestaurantCustomer(restaurant, i);
            c.start();
        }
    }
}
```

```
Customer #1 is trying to get a table.
Customer #1 got a table.
Customer #2 is trying to get a table.
Customer #1 will eat for 17 seconds.
Customer #2 got a table.
Customer #2 will eat for 19 seconds.
Customer #3 is trying to get a table.
...
```

Listing 6-34 contains the code for a RestaurantCustomer class whose object represents a customer in a restaurant. The run() method of the customer thread gets a table from the restaurant, eats for a random amount of time, and returns the table to the restaurant. When you run the Restaurant class, you may get similar but not the same output. You may observe that you have created a restaurant with only two tables and five customers are trying to eat. At any given time, only two customers are eating, as shown by the output.

Listing 6-34. A RestaurantCustomer Class to Represent a Customer in a Restaurant

```java
// RestaurantCustomer.java
package com.jdojo.threads;

import java.util.Random;

class RestaurantCustomer extends Thread {
        private Restaurant r;
        private int customerID;
        private static final Random random = new Random();

        public RestaurantCustomer(Restaurant r, int customerID) {
                this.r = r;
                this.customerID = customerID;
        }

        public void run() {
                r.getTable(this.customerID); // Get a table
                try {
                        // Eat for some time. Use number between 1 and 30 seconds
                        int eatingTime = random.nextInt(30) + 1 ;
                        System.out.println("Customer #" + this.customerID +
                                            " will eat for " + eatingTime +
                                            " seconds.");
                        Thread.sleep(eatingTime * 1000);
                        System.out.println("Customer #" + this.customerID +
                                            " is done eating.");
                }
                catch(InterruptedException e) {
                        e.printStackTrace();
                }
                finally {
                        r.returnTable(this.customerID);
                }
        }
}
```

■ **Tip** A semaphore is not limited to the number of permits it was created with. Each `release()` method adds one permit to it. Therefore, if you call the `release()` method more than the times you call its `acquire()` method, you end up having more permits than the one you started with. A permit is not acquired on a per thread basis. One thread can acquire a permit from a semaphore and another can return it. This leaves the burden of the correct usage of acquiring and releasing a permit on programmers. A semaphore has other methods to acquire a permit, which will let you back off instead of forcing you to wait if a permit is not immediately available, such as `tryAcquire()` and `acquireUninterruptibly()` methods.

Barriers

A barrier is used to make a group of threads meet at a barrier point. A thread from a group arriving at the barrier waits until all threads in that group arrive. Once the last thread from the group arrives at the barrier, all threads in the group are released. You can use a barrier when you have a task that can be divided into subtasks; each subtask can be performed in a separate thread and each thread must meet at a common point to combine their results. Figure 6-8 through Figure 6-11 depict how a barrier synchronizer lets a group of three threads meet at the barrier point and lets them proceed.

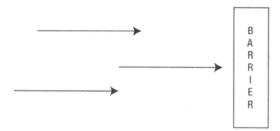

Figure 6-8. *Three threads arrive at a barrier*

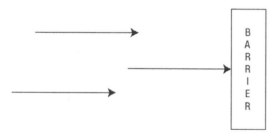

Figure 6-9. *One thread waits for two other threads to arrive at the barrier*

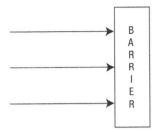

Figure 6-10. *All three threads arrive at the barrier. Now they are released at once*

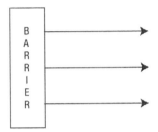

Figure 6-11. *All three threads pass the barrier successfully*

The CyclicBarrier class in the java.util.concurrent package provides the implementation of the barrier synchronizer. It is called a cyclic barrier because once all waiting threads at the barrier point are released, you can reuse the barrier by calling its reset() method. It also allows you to associate a barrier action to it, which is a Runnable task (an object of a class that implements the Runnable interface). The barrier action is executed just before all threads are released. You can think of the barrier action as a "party time" when all threads meet at the barrier, but before they are released.

Here are the steps you need to perform to use a barrier in a program:

- Create an object of the CyclicBarrier class with the number of threads in the group.

  ```
  CyclicBarrier barrier = new CyclicBarrier(5); // 5 threads
  ```

  If you want to execute a barrier action when all threads meet at the barrier, you can use another constructor of the CyclicBarrier class.

  ```
  // Assuming a BarrierAction class implements the Runnable //interface
  Runnable barrierAction = new BarrierAction();
  CyclicBarrier barrier = new CyclicBarrier(5, barrierAction);
  ```

- When a thread is ready to wait at the barrier, the thread executes the await() method of the CyclicBarrier class. The await() method comes in two flavors. One lets you wait for all other threads unconditionally and the other lets you specify a timeout.

The program in Listing 6-35 demonstrates how to use a cyclic barrier. You may get a different output when you run the program. However, the sequence of events will be the same: all three threads will work for some time, wait at the barrier for others to arrive, have a party time, and pass the barrier.

Listing 6-35. A Class That Demonstrates How to Use a CyclicBarrier in a Program

```java
// MeetAtBarrier.java
package com.jdojo.threads;

import java.util.Random;
import java.util.concurrent.CyclicBarrier;
import java.util.concurrent.BrokenBarrierException;

public class MeetAtBarrier extends Thread {
        private CyclicBarrier barrier;
        private int ID;
        private static Random random = new Random();

        public MeetAtBarrier(int ID, CyclicBarrier barrier) {
                this.ID = ID;
                this.barrier = barrier;
        }

        public void run() {
                try {
                        // Generate a random number between 1 and 30 to wait
                        int workTime = random.nextInt(30) + 1;

                        System.out.println("Thread #" + ID + " is going to work for " +
                                            workTime + " seconds");

                        // Yes. Sleeping is working for this thread!!!
                        Thread.sleep(workTime * 1000);

                        System.out.println("Thread #" + ID + " is waiting at the barrier...");

                        // Wait at barrier for other threads in group to arrive
                        this.barrier.await();

                        System.out.println("Thread #" + ID + " passed the barrier...");
                }
                catch (InterruptedException e) {
                        e.printStackTrace();
                }
                catch (BrokenBarrierException e) {
                        System.out.println("Barrier is broken...");
                }
        }

        public static void main(String[] args) {
                // Create a barrier for a group of three threads with a barrier action
                Runnable barrierAction
                        = () -> System.out.println("We are all together. It's party time...");
                CyclicBarrier barrier = new CyclicBarrier(3, barrierAction);
```

```
        for (int i = 1; i <= 3; i++) {
                MeetAtBarrier t = new MeetAtBarrier(i, barrier);
                t.start();
        }
    }
}
```

```
Thread #1 is going to work for 22 seconds
Thread #2 is going to work for 16 seconds
Thread #3 is going to work for 27 seconds
Thread #2 is waiting at the barrier...
Thread #1 is waiting at the barrier...
Thread #3 is waiting at the barrier...
We are all together. It's party time...
Thread #2 passed the barrier...
Thread #1 passed the barrier...
Thread #3 passed the barrier...
```

You might have noticed that inside the run() method of the MeetAtBarrier class, you are catching BrokenBarrierException. If a thread times out or it is interrupted while waiting at the barrier point, the barrier is considered *broken*. The thread that times out is released with a TimeoutException, whereas all waiting threads at the barrier are released with a BrokenBarrierException.

■ **Tip** The await() method of the CyclicBarrier class returns the arrival index of the thread calling it. The last thread to arrive at the barrier has an index of zero and the first has an index of the number of threads in the group minus one. You can use this index to do any special processing in your program. For example, the last thread to arrive at the barrier may log the time when a particular round of computation is finished by all participating threads.

Phasers

The Phaser class in the java.util.concurrent package provides an implementation for another synchronization barrier called *phaser*. A Phaser provides functionality similar to the CyclicBarrier and CountDownLatch synchronizers. However, it is more powerful and flexible. It provides the following features:

- Like a CyclicBarrier, a Phaser is also reusable.

- Unlike a CyclicBarrier, the number of parties to synchronize on a Phaser can change dynamically. In a CyclicBarrier, the number of parties is fixed at the time the barrier is created. However, in a Phaser, you can add or remove parties at any time.

- A Phaser has an associated phase number, which starts at zero. When all registered parties arrive at a Phaser, the Phaser advances to the next phase and the phase number is incremented by one. The maximum value of the phase number is Integer.MAX_VALUE. After its maximum value, the phase number restarts at zero.

- A Phaser has a termination state. All synchronization methods called on a Phaser in a termination state return immediately without waiting for an advance. The Phaser class provides different ways to terminate a phaser.

241

- A Phaser has three types of parties count: a registered parties count, an arrived parties count, and an unarrived parties count. The registered parties count is the number of parties that are registered for synchronization. The arrived parties count is the number of parties that have arrived at the current phase of the phaser. The unarrived parties count is the number of parties that have not yet arrived at the current phase of the phaser. When the last party arrives, the phaser advances to the next phase. Note that all three types of party counts are dynamic.

- Optionally, a Phaser lets you execute a phaser action when all registered parties arrive at the phaser. Recall that a CyclicBarrier lets you execute a barrier action, which is a Runnable task. Unlike a CyclicBarrier, you specify a phaser action by writing code in the onAdvance() method of your Phaser class. It means you need to use your own Phaser class by inheriting it from the Phaser class and override the onAdvance() method to provide a Phaser action. I will discuss an example of this kind shortly.

Figure 6-12 shows a phaser with three phases. It synchronizes on different number of parties in each phase. An arrow in the figure represents a party.

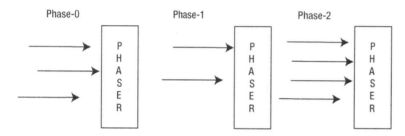

Figure 6-12. *A Phaser with three phases with a different number of parties in each phase*

There are several steps to work with a Phaser. You can create a Phaser with no initially registered party using its default constructor.

```
Phaser phaser = new Phaser(); // A phaser with no registered parties
```

Another constructor lets you register parties when the Phaser is created.

```
Phaser phaser = new Phaser(5); // A phaser with 5 registered parties
```

A Phaser may be arranged in a tree-like structure. Other constructors let you create a Phaser by specifying the parent of the newly created Phaser.

Once you have created a Phaser, the next step is to register parties that are interested in synchronizing on the phaser. You can register a party with a Phaser in the following ways:

- By specifying the number of parties to register in the constructor of the Phaser class when you create a Phaser object

- By using the register() method of the Phaser class to register one party at a time

- By using the bulkRegister(int parties) method of the Phaser class to register the specified number of parties in bulk

The registered parties of a Phaser may change at any time by registering new parties or deregistering the already registered parties. You can deregister a registered party using the arriveAndDeregister() method of the Phaser class. This method lets a party arrive at the Phaser and deregister without waiting for other parties to arrive. If a party is deregistered, the number of parties is reduced by one in the next phase of the Phaser.

Typically, a party in a Phaser means a thread. However, a Phaser does not associate the registration of a party with a specific thread. It simply maintains a count that is increased by one when a party is registered and decreased by one when a party is deregistered.

The most important part of a Phaser is the way multiple parties synchronize on it. A typical way to synchronize on a Phaser is to let the registered number of parties arrive and wait at the Phaser for other registered parties to arrive. Once the last registered party arrives at the Phaser, all parties advance to the next phase of the Phaser.

The arriveAndAwaitAdvance() method of the Phaser class lets a party arrive at the Phaser and waits for other parties to arrive before it can proceed.

The arriveAndDeregister() method of the Phaser class lets a party arrive at the Phaser and deregister without waiting for other parties to arrive. Upon deregistration, the number of parties required to advance to the future phase reduces by one. Typically, the arriveAndDeregister() method is used by a controller party whose job is to control the advance of other parties without participating in the advance itself. Typically, the controller party registers itself with the Phaser and waits for some conditions to occur; when the required condition occurs, it arrives and deregisters itself from the Phaser so parties can synchronize on the Phaser and advance.

Let's walk through an example of using a Phaser to synchronize a group of tasks so they can all start at the same time. An instance of the StartTogetherTask class, shown in Listing 6-36, represents a task in the example. This class inherits from the Thread class. Its constructor accepts a task name and a Phaser instance. In its run() method, it prints a message that it is initializing. It fakes its initialization by sleeping for a random period of 1 to 5 seconds. After that, it prints a message that it is initialized. At this stage, it waits on a Phaser advance by calling the arriveAndAwaitAdvance() method of the Phaser. This method will block until all registered parties arrive at the Phaser. When this method returns, it prints a message that the task has started.

Listing 6-36. A StartTogetherTask Class to Represent Tasks That Start Together by Synchronizing on a Phaser

```java
// StartTogetherTask.java
package com.jdojo.threads;

import java.util.Random;
import java.util.concurrent.Phaser;

public class StartTogetherTask extends Thread {
        private Phaser phaser;
        private String taskName;
        private static Random rand = new Random();

        public StartTogetherTask(String taskName, Phaser phaser) {
                this.taskName = taskName;
                this.phaser = phaser;
        }

        @Override
        public void run() {
                System.out.println(taskName + ":Initializing...");

                // Sleep for some time between 1 and 5 seconds
                int sleepTime = rand.nextInt(5) + 1;
                try {
                        Thread.sleep(sleepTime * 1000);
                }
                catch (InterruptedException e) {
                        e.printStackTrace();
                }
```

```
                    System.out.println(taskName + ":Initialized...");

                    // Wait for all parties to arrive to start the task
                    phaser.arriveAndAwaitAdvance();
                    System.out.println(taskName + ":Started...");
        }
}
```

Listing 6-37 has the code to test three tasks of StartTogetherTask type.

Listing 6-37. Testing Some Objects of the StartTogetherTask Class with a Phaser

```java
// StartTogetherTaskTest.java
package com.jdojo.threads;

import java.util.concurrent.Phaser;

public class StartTogetherTaskTest {
        public static void main(String[] args) {
                // Start with 1 registered party
                Phaser phaser = new Phaser(1);

                // Let's start three tasks
                final int TASK_COUNT = 3;
                for(int i = 1; i <= TASK_COUNT; i++) {
                        // Register a new party with the phaser for each task
                        phaser.register();

                        // Now create the task and start it
                        String taskName = "Task #" + i;
                        StartTogetherTask task = new StartTogetherTask(taskName, phaser);
                        task.start();
                }

                // Now, deregister the self, so all tasks can advance
                phaser.arriveAndDeregister();
        }
}
```

```
Task #1:Initializing...
Task #2:Initializing...
Task #3:Initializing...
Task #2:Initialized...
Task #1:Initialized...
Task #3:Initialized...
Task #3:Started...
Task #1:Started...
Task #2:Started...
```

First, the program creates a Phaser object by specifying 1 as the initially registered party.

```
// Start with 1 registered party
Phaser phaser = new Phaser(1);
```

You register a task with the Phaser one at a time. If a task (or a party) is registered and started before other tasks are registered, the first task will advance the phaser because there will be one registered party and it will arrive at the phaser by itself. This is the reason that you need to start with one registered party in the beginning. It acts like the controller party for other tasks.

You create three tasks in a loop. Inside the loop, you register a party (that represents a task) with the Phaser, create a task, and start it. Once you are done with setting up the tasks, you call the arriveAndDeregister() method of the Phaser. This takes care of one extra party that you had registered when created the Phaser. This method makes a party arrive at the Phaser and deregister without waiting for other registered parties to arrive. After this method call is over, it is up to the three tasks to arrive at the Phaser and advance. Once all three tasks arrive at the Phaser, they will all advance at the same time, thus making them start at the same time. You may get a different output. However, the last three messages in the output will always be about starting the three tasks.

If you do not want to use an additional party to act as a controller, you need to register all tasks in advance to make this program work correctly. You can rewrite the code in the main() method of the StartTogetherTaskTest class as follows:

```
public static void main(String[] args) {
        // Start with 0 registered party
        Phaser phaser = new Phaser();

        // Let's start three tasks
        final int TASK_COUNT = 3;

        // Initialize all tasksa in one go
        phaser.bulkRegister(TASK_COUNT);

        for(int i = 1; i <= TASK_COUNT; i++) {
                // Now create the task and start it
                String taskName = "Task #" + i;
                StartTogetherTask task = new StartTogetherTask(taskName, phaser);
                task.start();
        }
}
```

This time, you create a Phaser with no registered party. You register all the parties using the bulkRegister() method in one go. Note that you do not register a party inside the loop anymore. The new code has the same effect as the old one. It is just a different way to write the logic.

Like a CyclicBarrier, a Phaser lets you execute an action upon a phase advance using its onAdvance() method. You will need to create your own Phaser class by inheriting it from the Phaser class and override the onAdvance() method to write your custom Phaser action. On each phase advance, the onAdvance() method of the phaser is invoked. The onAdvance() method in the Phaser class is declared as follows. The first argument is the phase number and the second is the number of registered parties.

```
protected boolean onAdvance(int phase, int registeredParties)
```

Besides defining a phase advance action, the onAdvance() method of the Phaser class also controls the termination state of a Phaser. A Phaser is terminated if its onAdvance() method returns true. You can use the isTerminated() method of the Phaser class to check if a phaser is terminated or not. You can also terminate a phaser using its forceTermination() method.

Listing 6-38 demonstrates how to add a Phaser action. This is a trivial example. However, it demonstrates the concept of adding and executing a Phaser action. It uses an anonymous class to create a custom Phaser class. The anonymous class overrides the onAdvance() method to define a Phaser action. It simply prints a message in the onAdvance() method as the Phaser action. It returns false, which means the phaser will not be terminated from the onAdvance() method. Later, it registers the self as a party and triggers a phase advance using the arriveAndDeregister() method. On every phase advance, the Phaser action that is defined by the onAdvance() method is executed.

Listing 6-38. Adding a Phaser Action to a Phaser

```java
// PhaserActionTest.java
package com.jdojo.threads;

import java.util.concurrent.Phaser;

public class PhaserActionTest {
    public static void main(String[] args) {
        // Create a Phaser object using an anonymous class and override its
        // onAdvance() method to define a phaser action
        Phaser phaser = new Phaser() {
            protected boolean onAdvance(int phase, int parties) {
                System.out.println("Inside onAdvance(): phase = " +
                            phase + ", Registered Parties = " + parties);

                // Do not terminate the phaser by returning false
                return false;
            }
        };

        // Register the self (the "main" thread) as a party
        phaser.register();

        // Phaser is not terminated here
        System.out.println("#1: isTerminated():" + phaser.isTerminated());

        // Since we have only one party registered, this arrival will advance
        // the phaser and registered parties reduces to zero
        phaser.arriveAndDeregister();

        // Trigger another phase advance
        phaser.register();
        phaser.arriveAndDeregister();

        // Phaser is still not terminated
        System.out.println("#2: isTerminated():" + phaser.isTerminated());
```

```
                // Terminate the phaser
                phaser.forceTermination();

                // Phaser is terminated
                System.out.println("#3: isTerminated():" + phaser.isTerminated());
        }
}
```

```
#1: isTerminated():false
Inside onAdvance(): phase = 0, Registered Parties = 0
Inside onAdvance(): phase = 1, Registered Parties = 0
#2: isTerminated():false
#3: isTerminated():true
```

Let's consider using a Phaser to solve a little complex task. This time, the Phaser works in multiple phases by synchronizing multiple parties in each phase. Multiple tasks generate random integers in each phase and add them to a List. After the Phaser is terminated, you compute the sum of all the randomly generated integers.

Listing 6-39 contains the code for a task. Let's call this task AdderTask. In its run() method, it creates a random integer between 1 and 10, adds the integer to a List, and waits for a Phaser to advance. It keeps adding an integer to the list in each phase of the Phaser until the Phaser is terminated.

Listing 6-39. An AdderTask Class Whose Instances Can Be Used with a Phaser to Generate Some Integers

```java
// AdderTask.java
package com.jdojo.threads;

import java.util.List;
import java.util.Random;
import java.util.concurrent.Phaser;

public class AdderTask extends Thread {
        private Phaser phaser;
        private String taskName;
        private List<Integer> list;
        private static Random rand = new Random();

        public AdderTask(String taskName, Phaser phaser, List<Integer> list) {
                this.taskName = taskName;
                this.phaser = phaser;
                this.list = list;
        }

        @Override
        public void run() {
                do {
                        // Generate a random integer between 1 and 10
                        int num = rand.nextInt(10) + 1;

                        System.out.println(taskName + " added " + num);
```

```
                // Add the integer to the list
                list.add(num);

                // Wait for all parties to arrive at the phaser
                phaser.arriveAndAwaitAdvance();
            }
            while (!phaser.isTerminated());
        }
    }
}
```

Listing 6-40 creates a Phaser by inheriting an anonymous class from the Phaser class. In its onAdvance() method, it terminates the phaser after the second advance, which is controlled by the PHASE_COUNT constant, or if the registered parties reduces to zero. You use a synchronized List to gather the random integers generated by the adder tasks. You plan to use three adder tasks, so you register four parties (one more than the number of tasks) with the phaser. The additional party will be used to synchronize each phase. It waits for each phase advance until the Phaser is terminated. At the end, sum of the random integers generated by all adder tasks is computed and displayed on the standard output.

Listing 6-40. A Program to Use Multiple AdderTask Tasks with a Phaser

```java
// AdderTaskTest.java
package com.jdojo.threads;

import java.util.List;
import java.util.ArrayList;
import java.util.Collections;
import java.util.concurrent.Phaser;

public class AdderTaskTest {
    public static void main(String[] args) {
        final int PHASE_COUNT = 2;
        Phaser phaser
            = new Phaser() {
                public boolean onAdvance(int phase, int parties) {
                    // Print the phaser details
                    System.out.println("Phase:" + phase
                            + ", Parties:" + parties
                            + ", Arrived:" + this.getArrivedParties());
                    boolean terminatePhaser = false;

                    // Terminate the phaser when we reach the PHASE_COUNT
                    // or there is no registered party
                    if (phase >=PHASE_COUNT - 1 || parties == 0) {
                        terminatePhaser = true;
                    }

                    return terminatePhaser;
                }
            };
```

```
        // Use a synchronized List
        List<Integer> list = Collections.synchronizedList(new ArrayList<Integer>());

        // Let's start three tasks
        final int ADDER_COUNT = 3;

        // Register parties one more than the number of adder tasks.
        // The extra party will synchronize to compute the result of
        // all generated integers by all adder tasks
        phaser.bulkRegister(ADDER_COUNT + 1);

        for (int i = 1; i <= ADDER_COUNT; i++) {
                // Create the task and start it
                String taskName = "Task #" + i;
                AdderTask task = new AdderTask(taskName, phaser, list);
                task.start();
        }

        // Wait for the phaser to terminate, so we can compute the sum
        // of all generated integers by the adder tasks
        while (!phaser.isTerminated()) {
                phaser.arriveAndAwaitAdvance();
        }

        // Phaser is terminated now. Compute the sum
        int sum = 0;
        for (Integer num : list) {
                sum = sum + num;
        }

        System.out.println("Sum = " + sum);
    }
}
```

```
(You may get a different output.)
Task #1 added 1
Task #2 added 6
Task #3 added 8
Phase:0, Parties:4, Arrived:4
Task #3 added 9
Task #2 added 7
Task #1 added 8
Phase:1, Parties:4, Arrived:4
Sum = 39
```

Latches

A latch works similar to a barrier in the sense that it also makes a group of threads wait until it reaches its terminal state. Once a latch reaches its terminal state, it lets all threads pass through. Unlike a barrier, it is a one-time object. Once it has reached its terminal state, it cannot be reset and reused. A latch can be used in situations where a number of activities cannot proceed until a certain number of one-time activities have completed. For example, a service should not start until all services that it depends on have started.

The CountDownLatch class in the `java.util.concurrent` package provides the implementation of a latch. It is initialized to a count using its constructor. All threads that call the `await()` method of the latch object are blocked until latch's `countDown()` method is called as many times as its count is set. When the number of calls to the `countDown()` method is the same as its count, it reaches its terminal state and all blocked threads are released. Once a latch reaches its terminal state, its `await()` method returns immediately. You can think of the count that is set for the latch as the same as the number of events that a group of thread will wait to occur. Each occurrence of an event will call its `countDown()` method.

Listing 6-41 and Listing 6-42 contain classes that represent a helper service and a main service, respectively. The main service depends on helper services to start. After all helper services have started, only then can the main service start.

Listing 6-41. A Class to Represent a Helper Service

```java
// LatchHelperService.java
package com.jdojo.threads;

import java.util.concurrent.CountDownLatch;
import java.util.Random;

public class LatchHelperService extends Thread {
        private int ID;
        private CountDownLatch latch;
        private Random random = new Random();

        public LatchHelperService(int ID, CountDownLatch latch) {
                this.ID = ID;
                this.latch = latch;
        }

        public void run() {
                try {
                        int startupTime = random.nextInt(30) + 1;

                        System.out.println("Service #" + ID + " starting in "
                            + startupTime + " seconds...");
                        Thread.sleep(startupTime * 1000);
                        System.out.println("Service #" + ID + " has started...");
                }
                catch (InterruptedException e) {
                        e.printStackTrace();
                }
                finally {
                        // Count down on the latch to indicate that it has started
                        this.latch.countDown();
                }
        }
}
```

Listing 6-42. A Class to Represent the Main Service That Depends on Helper Services to Start

```java
// LatchMainService.java
package com.jdojo.threads;

import java.util.concurrent.CountDownLatch;

public class LatchMainService extends Thread {
        private CountDownLatch latch;

        public LatchMainService(CountDownLatch latch) {
                this.latch = latch;
        }

        public void run() {
                try {
                        System.out.println("Main service is waiting for helper services to start...");
                        latch.await();
                        System.out.println("Main service has started...");
                }
                catch (InterruptedException e) {
                        e.printStackTrace();
                }
        }
}
```

Listing 6-43 lists a program to test the concept of helper and main services with a latch. You create a latch that is initialized to two. The main service thread is started first and it calls latch's await() method to wait for the helper service to start. Once both helper threads call the countDown() method of the latch, the main service starts. The output explains the sequence of events clearly.

Listing 6-43. A Class to Test the Concept of a Latch with Helper and Main Services

```java
// LatchTest.java
package com.jdojo.threads;

import java.util.concurrent.CountDownLatch;

public class LatchTest {
        public static void main(String[] args) {
                // Create a countdown latch with 2 as its counter
                CountDownLatch latch = new CountDownLatch(2);

                // Create and start the main service
                LatchMainService ms = new LatchMainService(latch);
                ms.start();
```

```
                    // Create and start two helper services
                    for (int i = 1; i <= 2; i++) {
                            LatchHelperService lhs = new LatchHelperService(i, latch);
                            lhs.start();
                    }
            }
}
```

```
Main service is waiting for helper services to start...
Service #2 starting in 8 seconds...
Service #1 starting in 15 seconds...
Service #2 has started...
Service #1 has started...
Main service has started...
```

Exchangers

An exchanger is another form of a barrier. Like a barrier, an exchanger lets two threads wait for each other at a synchronization point. When both threads arrive, they exchange an object and continue their activities. This is useful in building a system where two independent parties need to exchange information from time to time. Figure 6-13 through Figure 6-15 depict how an exchanger works with two threads and lets them exchange an object.

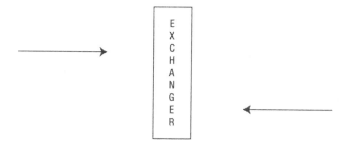

Figure 6-13. *Two threads perform their work independently*

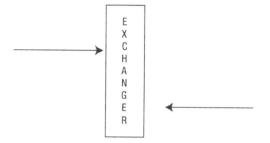

Figure 6-14. *One thread arrives at the exchange point and waits for another thread to arrive*

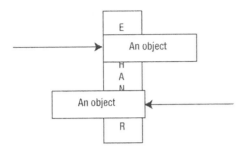

Figure 6-15. *Two threads meet at exchange point and exchange objects*

The Exchanger class provides an implementation for an exchanger synchronizer. It has one constructor, which takes no arguments. You can create an exchanger like so:

```
Exchanger exchanger = new Exchanger();
```

The exchanger created in the above statement will let two threads exchange any type of Java objects. However, if you know the type of the object the threads will exchange, you can specify that using generics while creating the exchanger like so:

```
Exchanger<ObjectType> exchanger = new Exchanger<ObjectType>();
```

The Exchanger class has only one method, exchange(). When a thread is ready to exchange an object with another thread, it calls the exchange() method of the exchanger and waits for another thread to exchange the object. A thread that is waiting to exchange an object may be interrupted. Another overloaded version of the exchange() method accepts a timeout period. If the timeout period is specified, the thread calling this method will wait for another thread to exchange an object until the timeout period is elapsed. The exchange() method takes the object to pass on to another thread as an argument and it returns the object passed by another thread. You call the exchange() method like so:

```
objectReceived = exchanger.exchange(objectedPassed);
```

Listing 6-44, Listing 6-45, and Listing 6-46 demonstrate the use of an exchanger in building a producer-consumer system that exchanges a buffer, which is an ArrayList of Integer objects. To declare an array list of integer objects, you have to declare it as

```
ArrayList<Integer> buffer = new ArrayList<Integer>();
```

In Listing 6-46, you have created an exchanger as

```
Exchanger<ArrayList<Integer>>exchanger = new Exchanger<ArrayList<Integer>>();
```

The type declaration Exchanger<ArrayList<Integer>>indicates that the exchanger will let two threads exchange objects of type ArrayList<Integer>. You can also note that the type declarations in the ExchangerProducer and ExchangerConsumer classes match the above declaration. The producer fills up the data and waits for some time to give user an impression that it is really filling up data. It waits for the consumer to exchange the filled buffer with an empty buffer from the consumer. The consumer does the opposite. It waits for the producer to exchange the buffer. When it gets a full buffer from the producer, it empties the buffer and again waits for the producer to exchange its empty buffer for a full one. Since the producer and consumer run in infinite loops, the program will not end. You will have to end the program manually. You will get a similar output to that shown for Listing 6-46.

Listing 6-44. A Producer Thread That Will Use an Exchanger to Exchange Data with a Consumer

```java
// ExchangerProducer.java
package com.jdojo.threads;

import java.util.concurrent.Exchanger;
import java.util.ArrayList;
import java.util.Random;

public class ExchangerProducer extends Thread {
    private Exchanger<ArrayList<Integer>>exchanger;
    private ArrayList<Integer> buffer = new ArrayList<Integer>();
    private int bufferLimit;
    private Random random = new Random();
    private int currentValue = 0; // to produce values

    public ExchangerProducer(Exchanger<ArrayList<Integer>>exchanger,
            int bufferLimit) {
        this.exchanger = exchanger;
        this.bufferLimit = bufferLimit;
    }

    public void run() {
        // keep producing integers
        while (true) {
            try {
                System.out.println("Producer is filling the buffer with data...");

                // Wait for some time by sleeping
                int sleepTime = random.nextInt(20) + 1;
                Thread.sleep(sleepTime * 1000);

                // Fill the buffer
                this.fillBuffer();
                System.out.println("Producer has produced:" + buffer);

                // Let's wait for the consumer to exchange data
                System.out.println("Producer is waiting to exchange the data...");
                buffer = exchanger.exchange(buffer);
            }
            catch (InterruptedException e) {
                e.printStackTrace();
            }
        }
    }

    public void fillBuffer() {
        for (int i = 1; i <= bufferLimit; i++) {
            buffer.add(++currentValue);
        }
    }
}
```

Listing 6-45. A Consumer Thread That Will Use an Exchanger to Exchange Data with a Producer

```java
// ExchangerConsumer.java
package com.jdojo.threads;

import java.util.concurrent.Exchanger;
import java.util.ArrayList;
import java.util.Random;

public class ExchangerConsumer extends Thread {
        private Exchanger<ArrayList<Integer>>exchanger;
        private ArrayList<Integer> buffer = new ArrayList<Integer>();
        private Random random = new Random();

        public ExchangerConsumer(Exchanger<ArrayList<Integer>>exchanger) {
                this.exchanger = exchanger;
        }

        public void run() {
                // keep consuming the integers
                while (true) {
                        try {
                                // Let's wait for the consumer to exchange data
                                System.out.println("Consumer is waiting to exchange the data...");

                                buffer = exchanger.exchange(buffer);
                                System.out.println("Consumer has received:" + buffer);
                                System.out.println("Consumer is emptying data from the buffer...");

                                // Wait for some time by sleeping
                                int sleepTime = random.nextInt(20) + 1;

                                // Sleep for some time
                                Thread.sleep(sleepTime * 1000);

                                // Empty the buffer
                                this.emptyBuffer();
                        }
                        catch (InterruptedException e) {
                                e.printStackTrace();
                        }
                }
        }

        public void emptyBuffer() {
                buffer.clear();
        }
}
```

Listing 6-46. A Class to Test a Producer/Consumer System with an Exchanger

```java
// ExchangerProducerConsumerTest.java
package com.jdojo.threads;

import java.util.concurrent.Exchanger;
import java.util.ArrayList;

public class ExchangerProducerConsumerTest {
        public static void main(String[] args) {
                Exchanger<ArrayList<Integer>>exchanger = new Exchanger<>();

                // The producer will produce 5 integers at a time
                ExchangerProducer producer = new ExchangerProducer(exchanger, 5);
                ExchangerConsumer consumer = new ExchangerConsumer(exchanger);

                producer.start();
                consumer.start();
        }
}
```

```
Producer is filling the buffer with data...
Consumer is waiting to exchange the data...
Producer has produced:[1, 2, 3, 4, 5]
Producer is waiting to exchange the data...
...
```

The Executor Framework

A task is a logical unit of work, and typically a thread is used to represent and execute a task. Many aspects of task execution should be considered before modeling it in a program. A few aspects of a task are as follows:

- How it is created.

- How it is submitted for execution.

- How it is executed. Is it executed synchronously or asynchronously?

- The time at which it is executed. Is it executed immediately upon submission or queued?

- Which thread executes it? Is it executed in the thread that submits it or in another thread?

- How do we get the result of a task when it is finished executing?

- How do we know the error that occurs during its execution?

- Does it depend on other tasks to finish its execution?

A task may be represented as a Runnable. If you want to manage tasks using threads, follow the steps described below. You can create a class to represent a task.

```
public class MyTask implements Runnable {
        public void run() {
                // Task processing logic goes here
        }
}
```

You create tasks as follows:

```
MyTask task1 = new MyTask();
MyTask task2 = new MyTask();
MyTask task3 = new MyTask();
```

To execute the tasks, you use threads as follows:

```
Thread t1 = new Thread(task1);
Thread t2 = new Thread(task2);
Thread t3 = new Thread(task3);
t1.start();
t2.start();
t3.start();
```

If you want to get the result of a task execution, you have to write additional code. You may notice that managing tasks as described above is difficult, if not impossible. There is another aspect of tasks execution that is very important: how many threads should be created to execute a group of tasks? One approach would be to create a thread per task. Creating a thread per task has the following disadvantages:

- Creating and destroying threads has overhead and it takes time, which in turn delays the start of the execution of the tasks.

- Each thread consumes resources. If the number of threads is more than the available CPUs, other threads will be sitting idle and will be consuming resources.

- Each platform has a limit of how many maximum threads it can support. If an application exceeds that limit, it may even crash!

Another approach is to create one thread and let it handle the execution of all tasks. This is another extreme case, which has the following disadvantages:

- Having one thread executing all tasks makes it a sequential executor.

- This policy is deadlock-prone if one task submits another task and it depends on the result of the task it has submitted.

- If you have long-running tasks, other tasks waiting for their execution seem to be unresponsive because of the long time it will take to start the pending tasks.

The executor framework attempts to solve all of these aspects of a task execution. The framework provides a way to separate task submission from task execution. You create a task and submit it to an executor. The executor takes care of the execution details of the task. It provides configurable policies to control many aspects of the task execution.

The Executor interface in the java.util.concurrent package is the foundation for the executor framework. It is an interface with only one method, as shown:

```
public interface Executor {
        void execute (Runnable command);
}
```

You can use the executor framework to execute the above-mentioned three tasks as follows:

```
// Get an executor instance.
// Method Executors.newCachedThreadPool() will be explainedshortly.
Executor executor = Executors.newCachedThreadPool();

// Submit three tasks to the executor
executor.execute(task1);
executor.execute(task2);
executor.execute(task3);
```

Note that when you used an executor, you did not create three threads to execute the three tasks. The executor will decide that for you. You just called the execute() method of the executor to submit a task. The executor will manage the threads that will execute the tasks and other details about the task execution.

The executor framework provides a class library to select the policies on the thread usage to execute the tasks. You can choose to run all tasks in one thread, in a fixed number of threads, or in a variable number of threads. In fact, you can choose a thread pool to execute your tasks, and the thread pool is configurable as to how many threads will be in the pool and how those threads will be maintained. In any case, all threads in the pool are reused as they become available. Using a thread pool to execute the submitted tasks has two important advantages:

- The overhead of creating and destroying new threads is reduced. The executor reuses the threads from the thread pool.

- If a thread is available in the thread pool at the time of a task submission, the task may start immediately. This eliminates the time delay between the thread creation and the task execution.

It is important to mention another interface called ExecutorService at this point. It provides some advanced features of an executor, which include managing the shutdown of the executor and checking the status of the submitted tasks. It inherits the Executor interface. Some of the important methods of this interface are shutdown(), shutdownNow(), submit(), and awaitTermination(). I will discuss them shortly.

It is important that you shut down the executor when it is no longer needed. The executor framework creates non-daemon threads to execute the tasks. Generally, when a thread is done executing a task, it is not destroyed. Rather it is kept in the thread pool for reuse in the future. (Whether a thread is destroyed or kept depends on the thread pool configuration). A Java application will not exit if some non-daemon threads are still alive. Therefore, if you forget to shut down the executor, your application may never exit.

How does an executor handle a task execution? To avoid a detailed and lengthy discussion, here is a simple explanation. You specify the type of thread pool that the executor should use to manage the tasks at the time you create the executor. All tasks that you submit to an executor are queued in a queue known as the *work queue*. As a thread becomes available, it removes a task from the work queue and executes it. When a thread is done executing a task, depending on your thread pool type, your executor either destroys the thread or puts it back into the pool so it can be reused to execute another task. You have a number of options to decide on what kind of thread pool to use for an executor:

- You can use one of the factory methods of the `Executors` class to get an executor, which has a preconfigured thread pool and lets you reconfigure it, if you desire so. You will use this approach to get an executor in your examples. You can also use this class to get a preconfigured executor that cannot be reconfigured. The commonly used methods of the `Executors` class to get an executor service are as follows:

    - `newCachedThreadPool()`: It returns an `ExecutorService` object. The thread pool reuses the previously created threads if they are available. Otherwise, it creates a new thread to execute a task. It destroys and removes idle threads from the pool. The thread pool has characteristics of expanding and shrinking depending on the workload.

    - `newFixedThreadPool(int nThreads)`: It returns an `ExecutorService` object. The thread pool maintains a fixed number of threads. At any time, the thread pool will have the maximum `nThread` number of threads. If a task arrives in the work queue and all threads are busy executing other tasks, the task has to wait for its execution until a thread becomes available. If a thread is terminated because of an unexpected failure during a task execution, it is replaced with a new thread.

    - `newSingleThreadExecutor()`: It returns an `ExecutorService` object. The thread pool maintains only one thread to execute all tasks. It guarantees that only one task will be executed at a time. If the lone thread dies unexpectedly, it is replaced with a new one.

- You can instantiate the `ThreadPoolExecutor` class and configure the thread pool.

- You can create your own executor from scratch.

Listing 6-47 and Listing 6-48 have the complete programs for an executor. An object of the `RunnableTask` class represents a task in your program. You will have a task that will sleep for some time and print a message on the standard output. The time to sleep will be determined randomly between 1 and 10 seconds. The task will repeat three times in its `run()` method. You have used an executor with its thread pool with a fixed number of threads. Your executor will have only three threads in its thread pool to execute only three tasks at a time. When the executor is done with one of the first three tasks, it starts the fourth one. Note the `exec.shutdown()` method call to shut down the executor after submitting all tasks. The `shutdownNow()` method call of executor attempts to stop the executing tasks by interrupting it and discards the pending tasks. It returns the list of all pending tasks that were discarded.

Listing 6-47. A Runnable Task

```
// RunnableTask.java
package com.jdojo.threads;

import java.util.Random;

public class RunnableTask implements Runnable {
        private int taskId;
        private int loopCounter;
        private Random random = new Random();

        public RunnableTask(int taskId, int loopCounter) {
                this.taskId = taskId;
                this.loopCounter = loopCounter;
        }
```

```
        public void run() {
            for(int i = 1; i <= loopCounter; i++) {
                try {
                    int sleepTime = random.nextInt(10) + 1;
                    System.out.println("Task #" + this.taskId +
                            " - Iteration #" + i +
                            " is going to sleep for " +
                            sleepTime + " seconds.");

                    Thread.sleep(sleepTime * 1000);
                }
                catch(Exception e) {
                    System.out.println("Task #" + this.taskId +
                                    " has been interrupted.");
                    break;
                }
            }
        }
    }
}
```

Listing 6-48. *A Class to Test an Executor to Run Some Runnable Tasks*

```java
// RunnableTaskTest.java
package com.jdojo.threads;

import java.util.concurrent.Executors;
import java.util.concurrent.ExecutorService;

public class RunnableTaskTest {
    public static void main(String[] args) {
        final int THREAD_COUNT = 3;
        final int LOOP_COUNT = 3;
        final int TASK_COUNT = 5;

        // Get an executor with three threads in its thread pool
        ExecutorService exec = Executors.newFixedThreadPool(THREAD_COUNT);

        // Create five tasks and submit them to the executor
        for(int i = 1; i <= TASK_COUNT; i++) {
            RunnableTask task = new RunnableTask(i, LOOP_COUNT);
            exec.submit(task);
        }

        // Let's shutdown the executor
        exec.shutdown();
    }
}
```

```
Task #1 - Iteration #1 is going to sleep for 9 seconds.
Task #2 - Iteration #1 is going to sleep for 2 seconds.
Task #3 - Iteration #1 is going to sleep for 7 seconds.
Task #2 - Iteration #2 is going to sleep for 5 seconds.
Task #2 - Iteration #3 is going to sleep for 7 seconds.
Task #3 - Iteration #2 is going to sleep for 2 seconds.
...
```

Result-Bearing Tasks

How do you get the result of a task when it is complete? The task that can return a result upon its execution has to be represented as an instance of the Callable<V> interface. The type parameter V is type of the result of the task. Note that the run() method of the Runnable interface cannot return a value and it cannot throw any checked exception. The Callable interface has a call() method. It can return a value of any type. It allows you to throw an exception. It is declared as follows:

```
public interface Callable<V> {
        V call() throws Exception;
}
```

Let's redo your RunnableTask class from Listing 6-47 as CallableTask, which is shown in Listing 6-49.

Listing 6-49. A Callable Task

```
// CallableTask.java
package com.jdojo.threads;

import java.util.Random;
import java.util.concurrent.Callable;

public class CallableTask implements Callable<Integer> {
        private int taskId;
        private int loopCounter;
        private Random random = new Random();

        public CallableTask(int taskId, int loopCounter) {
                this.taskId = taskId;
                this.loopCounter = loopCounter;
        }

        public Integer call() throws InterruptedException {
                int totalSleepTime = 0 ;
                for (int i = 1; i <= loopCounter; i++) {
                        try {
                                int sleepTime = random.nextInt(10) + 1;
                                System.out.println("Task #" + this.taskId +
                                        " - Iteration #" + i +
                                        " is going to sleep for " +
                                        sleepTime + " seconds.");
```

```
                            Thread.sleep(sleepTime * 1000);
                            totalSleepTime = totalSleepTime + sleepTime;
                    }
                    catch(InterruptedException e) {
                            System.out.println("Task #" + this.taskId +
                                              " has been interupted.");
                            throw e;
                    }
            }
            return totalSleepTime;
    }
}
```

The `call()` method of the task returns the sum of all its sleeping periods. Listing 6-50 illustrates the use of the Callable task.

Listing 6-50. A Class to Demonstrate How to Use a Callable Task with an Executor

```java
// CallableTaskTest.java
package com.jdojo.threads;

import java.util.concurrent.Executors;
import java.util.concurrent.ExecutorService;
import java.util.concurrent.Future;
import java.util.concurrent.ExecutionException;

public class CallableTaskTest {
        public static void main(String[] args) {
                // Get an executor with three threads in its thread pool
                ExecutorService exec = Executors.newFixedThreadPool(3);

                // Create the callable task with loop counter as 3
                CallableTask task = new CallableTask(1, 3);

                // Submit the callable task to executor
                Future<Integer> submittedTask = exec.submit(task);

                try {
                        Integer result = submittedTask.get();
                        System.out.println("Task's total sleep time: " + result + " seconds");
                }
                catch (ExecutionException e) {
                        System.out.println("Error in executing the task.");
                }
                catch (InterruptedException e) {
                        System.out.println("Task execution has been interrupted.");
                }

                // Let's shutdown the executor
                exec.shutdown();
        }
}
```

(You may get a different output.)
Task #1 - Iteration #1 is going to sleep for 8 seconds.
Task #1 - Iteration #2 is going to sleep for 9 seconds.
Task #1 - Iteration #3 is going to sleep for 5 seconds.
Task's total sleep time: 22 seconds

I will explain the logic in the two listings step by step:

- The CallableTask class defines the call() method, which contains the logic for task processing. It sums up all the sleep times for the task and returns it.

- The CallableTaskTest class uses an executor with three threads in its thread pool.

- The ExecutorService.submit() method returns a Future object. Future is an interface that lets you track the progress of the task that you submit. It is declared as follows:

```
public interface Future<V> {
    boolean cancel(boolean mayInterruptIfRunning);
    V get() throws InterruptedException, ExecutionException;
    V get(long timeout, TimeUnit unit) throws InterruptedException,
                                ExecutionException, TimeoutException;
    boolean isCancelled();
    boolean isDone();
}
```

The get() method returns the result of the task execution, which is the same as the returned value from the call() method of a Callable object. If the task has not yet finished executing, the get() method blocks. You can use another version of the get() method to specify a timeout period for waiting for the result of a task execution.

The cancel() method cancels a submitted task. Its call has no effect on a completed task. It accepts a boolean argument to indicate if the executor should interrupt the task if the task is still running. If you use cancel(true) to cancel a task, make sure the task responds to the interruption properly.

The isDone() method tells you if the task has finished executing. It returns true if the task is finished executing normally, it has been cancelled, or it had an exception during its execution.

In the CallableTaskTest class, you keep the returned Future object in the submittedTask variable. The Future<Integer> declaration indicates that your task returns an Integer object as its result.

```
Future<Integer> submittedTask = exec.submit(task);
```

- Another important method call is the get() method on submittedTask.

```
Integer result = submittedTask.get();
```

I have placed the call to the get() method in a try-catch block because it may throw an exception. If the task has not finished executing, the get() method will block. The program prints the result of the task execution, which is the total time that the task spent sleeping during its execution.

- Finally, you shut down the executor using its shutdown() method.

Scheduling a Task

The executor framework lets you schedule a task that will run in future. You can run a task to execute after a given delay or periodically. Scheduling a task is done using an object of the ScheduledExecutorService interface, which you can get using one of the static factory methods of the Executors class. You can also use the concrete implementation of this interface, which is the ScheduledThreadPoolExecutor class. To get an object of the ScheduledExecutorService interface, use the following snippet of code:

```
// Get scheduled executor service with 3 threads
ScheduledExecutorService sexec = Executors.newScheduledThreadPool(3);
```

To schedule a task (say task1) after a certain delay (say 10 seconds), use

```
sexec.schedule(task1, 10, TimeUnit.SECONDS);
```

To schedule a task (say task2) after a certain delay (say 10 seconds), and repeat after a certain period (say 25 seconds), use

```
sexec.scheduleAtFixedRate(task2, 10, 25, TimeUnit.SECONDS);
```

After a 10 second delay, task2 will execute for the first time. Subsequently, it will keep executing after 10 + 25 seconds, 10 + 2 * 25 seconds, 10 + 3 * 25 seconds, and so on.

You can also schedule a task with a set delay period between the end of an execution and the start of the next execution. To schedule task3, for the first time after 40 seconds, and every 60 seconds after every execution finishes, use

```
sexec.scheduleWithFixedDelay(task3, 40, 60, TimeUnit.SECONDS);
```

The ScheduledExecutorService interface does not provide a method to schedule a task using an absolute time. However, you can schedule a task to execute at an absolute time using the following technique. Suppose scheduledDateTime is the date and time at which you want to execute the task.

```
import java.time.LocalDateTime;
import static java.time.temporal.ChronoUnit.SECONDS;
import java.util.concurrent.TimeUnit;
...
LocalDateTime scheduledDateTime = get the scheduled date and time for the task...

// Compute the delay from the time you schedule the task
long delay = SECONDS.between(LocalDateTime.now(), scheduledDateTime);

// Schedule the task
sexec.schedule(task, delay, TimeUnit.MILLISECONDS);
```

▦ **Tip**   The submit() method of ExecutorService submits the task for immediate execution. You can submit a task for immediate execution using ScheduledExecutorService.schedule() method by specifying an initial delay of zero. A negative initial delay schedules a task for immediate execution.

Listing 6-51 contains the code for a Runnable task. It simply prints the date and time when it is run. Listing 6-52 demonstrates how to schedule a task. The second task has been scheduled to run repeatedly. To let it run for a few times, make the main thread sleep for 60 seconds before you shut down the executor. Shutting down an executor discards any pending tasks. A good way to stop a scheduled task that repeats is to cancel it after a certain delay using another scheduled task.

Listing 6-51. A Scheduled Task

```java
// ScheduledTask.java
package com.jdojo.threads;

import java.time.LocalDateTime;

public class ScheduledTask implements Runnable {
        private int taskId;

        public ScheduledTask(int taskId) {
                this.taskId = taskId;
        }

        public void run() {
                LocalDateTime currentDateTime = LocalDateTime.now();
                System.out.println("Task #" + this.taskId + " ran at " + currentDateTime);
        }
}
```

Listing 6-52. A Class to Test Scheduled Task Executions Using the Executor Framework

```java
// ScheduledTaskTest.java
package com.jdojo.threads;

import java.util.concurrent.Executors;
import java.util.concurrent.ScheduledExecutorService;
import java.util.concurrent.TimeUnit;

public class ScheduledTaskTest {
        public static void main(String[] args) {
                // Get an executor with 3 threads
                ScheduledExecutorService sexec = Executors.newScheduledThreadPool(3);

                // Task #1 and Task #2
                ScheduledTask task1 = new ScheduledTask(1);
                ScheduledTask task2 = new ScheduledTask(2);

                // Task #1 will run after 2 seconds
                sexec.schedule(task1, 2, TimeUnit.SECONDS);

                // Task #2 runs after 5 seconds delay and keep running every 10 seconds
                sexec.scheduleAtFixedRate(task2, 5, 10, TimeUnit.SECONDS);
```

```
                    // Let the current thread sleep for 60 seconds and shut down the executor that
                    // will cancel the task #2 because it is scheduled to run after every 10 seconds
                    try {
                            TimeUnit.SECONDS.sleep(60);
                    }
                    catch(InterruptedException e) {
                            e.printStackTrace();
                    }

                    // Shut down the executor
                    sexec.shutdown();
            }
    }
}
```

```
(You may get a different output.)
Task #1 ran at 2014-04-23T11:22:14.089
Task #2 ran at 2014-04-23T11:22:17.032
Task #2 ran at 2014-04-23T11:22:27.033
Task #2 ran at 2014-04-23T11:22:37.033
Task #2 ran at 2014-04-23T11:22:47.034
Task #2 ran at 2014-04-23T11:22:57.034
Task #2 ran at 2014-04-23T11:23:07.035
```

Handling Uncaught Exceptions in a Task Execution

What happens when an uncaught exception occurs during a task execution? The executor framework handles occurrences of any uncaught exception during task execution nicely for you. If you execute a Runnable task using the execute() method of the Executor object, any uncaught runtime exceptions will halt the task execution, and the exception stack trace will be printed on the console, as shown in the output of Listing 6-53.

Listing 6-53. Printing the Runtime Stack Trace from the execute() Method of the Executor

```
// BadRunnableTask.java
package com.jdojo.threads;

import java.util.concurrent.ExecutorService;
import java.util.concurrent.Executors;

public class BadRunnableTask {
        public static void main(String[] args) {
                Runnable badTask = () -> {
                        throw new RuntimeException("Throwing exception from task execution...");
                };

                ExecutorService exec = Executors.newSingleThreadExecutor();
                exec.execute(badTask);
                exec.shutdown();
        }
}
```

```
Exception in thread "pool-1-thread-1" java.lang.RuntimeException: Throwing exception from task
execution...
        at com.jdojo.threads.BadRunnableTask.lambda$main$0(BadRunnableTask.java:10)
        at com.jdojo.threads.BadRunnableTask$$Lambda$1/2536472.run(Unknown Source)
        at java.util.concurrent.ThreadPoolExecutor.runWorker(ThreadPoolExecutor.java:1142)
        at java.util.concurrent.ThreadPoolExecutor$Worker.run(ThreadPoolExecutor.java:617)
        at java.lang.Thread.run(Thread.java:745)
```

If you are submitting a task using the submit() method of the ExecutorService, the executor framework handles the exception and indicates that to you when you use the get() method to get the result of the task execution. The get() method on the Future object throws a ExecutionException, wrapping the actual exception as its cause. Listing 6-54 illustrates this kind of example. You can use the get() method of the Future object even if you submit a Runnable task. On successful execution of the task, the get() method will return a Void object. If an uncaught exception is thrown during the task execution, it throws an ExecutionException.

Listing 6-54. Future's get() Method Throws ExecutionException, Wrapping the Actual Exception Thrown in Task Execution as Its Cause

```java
// BadCallableTask.java
package com.jdojo.threads;

import java.util.concurrent.ExecutorService;
import java.util.concurrent.Executors;
import java.util.concurrent.Callable;
import java.util.concurrent.Future;
import java.util.concurrent.ExecutionException;

public class BadCallableTask {
        public static void main(String[] args) {
                Callable<Object> badTask = () -> {
                        throw new RuntimeException("Throwing exception from task execution...");
                };

                // CReate an executor service
                ExecutorService exec = Executors.newSingleThreadExecutor();

                // Submit a task
                Future submittedTask = exec.submit(badTask);

                try {
                        // The get method should throw ExecutionException
                        Object result = submittedTask.get();
                }
                catch(ExecutionException e) {
                        System.out.println("Execution exception has occurred: " +
                                                e.getMessage());
                        System.out.println("Execution exception cause is: " +
                                                e.getCause().getMessage());
                }
```

```
            catch(InterruptedException e) {
                    e.printStackTrace();
            }

            exec.shutdown();
        }
}
```

Execution exception has occurred: java.lang.RuntimeException: Throwing exception from task execution...
Execution exception cause is: Throwing exception from task execution...

Executor's Completion Service

In the previous sections, I discussed how to fetch the result of a task execution using a Future object. To fetch the result of a submitted task, you must keep the reference of the Future object returned from the executor, as demonstrated in Listing 6-50. However, if you have a number of tasks that you have submitted to an executor and you want to know their results as they become available, you need to use the completion service of the executor. It is represented by an instance of the CompletionService interface. It combines an executor and a blocking queue to hold the completed tasks references. The ExecutorCompletionService class is a concrete implementation of the CompletionService interface. Here are the steps to use it:

- Create an executor object.

  ```
  ExecutorService exec = Executors.newScheduledThreadPool(3);
  ```

- Create an object of ExecutorCompletionService class, passing the executor created in the previous step to its constructor.

  ```
  ExecutorCompletionService CompletionService = new
  ExecutorCompletionService(exec);
  ```

  The executor completion service uses a blocking queue internally to hold the completed task. Using another constructor, you can use your own blocking queue to hold the completed tasks.

- The take() method of the completion service returns the reference of a completed task. It blocks if no completed task is present. If you do not want to wait, in case there is no completed task, you can use the poll() method, which returns null if there is no completed task in the queue. Both methods remove the completed task from the queue if they find one.

Listing 6-55, Listing 6-56, and Listing 6-57 illustrate the use of the completion service. An instance of the TaskResult class represents the result of a task. It was necessary to have a custom object like a TaskResult to represent the result of a task because the completion service just tells you that a task is completed and you get its result. It does not tell you which task is completed. To identify the task that was completed, you need to identify the task in the result of the task. Your SleepingTask returns a TaskResult from its call() method by embedding the task id and the total sleeping time for the task.

Listing 6-55. A Class to Represent the Result of a Task

```
// TaskResult.java
package com.jdojo.threads;

public class TaskResult {
        private int taskId;
        private int result;
```

```
        public TaskResult(int taskId, int result) {
                this.taskId = taskId;
                this.result = result;
        }

        public int getTaskId() {
                return taskId;
        }

        public int getResult() {
                return result;
        }

        public String toString() {
                return "Task Name: Task #" + taskId + ", Task Result:" + result + " seconds";
        }
}
```

Listing 6-56. A Class Whose Object Represents a Callable Task. It Produces a TaskResult as Its Result.

```
// SleepingTask.java
package com.jdojo.threads;

import java.util.Random;
import java.util.concurrent.Callable;

public class SleepingTask implements Callable<TaskResult> {
        private int taskId;
        private int loopCounter;
        private Random random = new Random();

        public SleepingTask(int taskId, int loopCounter) {
                this.taskId = taskId;
                this.loopCounter = loopCounter;
        }

        public TaskResult call() throws InterruptedException {
                int totalSleepTime = 0 ;
                for (int i = 1; i <= loopCounter; i++) {
                        try {
                                int sleepTime = random.nextInt(10) + 1;
                                System.out.println("Task #" + this.taskId + " - Iteration #" + i
                                        + " is going to sleep for " + sleepTime + " seconds.");
                                Thread.sleep(sleepTime * 1000);
                                totalSleepTime = totalSleepTime + sleepTime;
                        }
                        catch(InterruptedException e) {
                                System.out.println("Task #" + this.taskId +
                                                        " has been interupted.");
```

```
                                        throw e;
                        }
                }

                return new TaskResult(taskId, totalSleepTime);
        }
}
```

Listing 6-57. A Class to Test the Completion Service

```java
// CompletionServiceTest.java
package com.jdojo.threads;

import java.util.concurrent.Future;
import java.util.concurrent.Executors;
import java.util.concurrent.ExecutorService;
import java.util.concurrent.ExecutionException;
import java.util.concurrent.ExecutorCompletionService;

public class CompletionServiceTest {
        public static void main(String[] args) {
                // Get an executor with three threads in its thread pool
                ExecutorService exec = Executors.newFixedThreadPool(3);

                // Completed task returns an object of the TaskResult class
                ExecutorCompletionService<TaskResult> completionService =
                        new ExecutorCompletionService<>(exec);

                // Submit five tasks and each task will sleep three times for a random period
                // between 1 and 10 seconds
                for(int i = 1; i <= 5; i++) {
                        SleepingTask task = new SleepingTask(i, 3);
                        completionService.submit(task);
                }

                // Print the result of each task as they are completed
                for(int i = 1; i <= 5; i++) {
                        try {
                                Future<TaskResult> completedTask =
                                                completionService.take();
                                TaskResult result= completedTask.get();
                                System.out.println("Completed a task - " + result);
                        }
                        catch (ExecutionException ex) {
                                System.out.println("Error in executing the task.");
                        }
                        catch (InterruptedException ex) {
                                System.out.println("Task execution has been interrupted.");
                        }
                }
```

```
                    // Let's shut down the executor
                    exec.shutdown();
            }
}
```

```
Task #1 - Iteration #1 is going to sleep for 4 seconds.
Task #2 - Iteration #1 is going to sleep for 6 seconds.
Task #3 - Iteration #1 is going to sleep for 9 seconds.
...
Completed a task - Task Name: Task #1, Task Result:20 seconds
...
```

The Fork/Join Framework

The fork/join framework is an implementation of the executor service whose focus is to solve those problems efficiently, which may use the divide-and-conquer algorithm by taking advantage of the multiple processors or multiple cores on a machine. The framework helps solve the problems that involve parallelism. Typically, the fork/join framework is suitable in a situation where

- A task can be divided in multiple subtasks that can be executed in parallel.

- When subtasks are finished, the partial results can be combined to get the final result.

The fork/join framework creates a pool of threads to execute the subtasks. When a thread is waiting on a subtask to finish, the framework uses that thread to execute other pending subtasks of other threads. The technique of an idle thread executing other thread's task is called *work-stealing*. The framework uses the work-stealing algorithm to enhance the performance.

The following four classes in the java.util.concurrent package are central to learning the fork/join framework:

- ForkJoinPool

- ForkJoinTask

- RecursiveAction

- RecursiveTask

An instance of the ForkJoinPool class represents a thread pool. An instance of the ForkJoinTask class represents a task. The ForkJoinTask class is an abstract class. It has two concrete subclasses: RecursiveAction and RecursiveTask. Java 8 added an abstract subclass of the ForkJoinTask class that is called CountedCompleter. The framework supports two types of tasks: a task that does not yield a result and a task that yields a result. An instance of the RecursiveAction class represents a task that does not yield a result. An instance of the RecursiveTask class represents a task that yields a result. A CountedCompleter task may or may not yield a result.

Both classes, RecursiveAction and RecursiveTask, provide an abstract compute() method. Your class whose object represents a fork/join task should inherit from one of these classes and provide an implementation for the compute() method. Typically, the logic inside the compute() method is written similar to the following:

```
if (Task is small) {
        Solve the task directly.
}
```

```
else {
        Divide the task into subtsaks.
        Launch the subtasks asynchronously (the fork stage).
        Wait for the subtasks to finish (the join stage).
        Combine the results of all subtasks.
}
```

The following two methods of the ForkJoinTask class provide two important features during a task execution:

- The fork() method launches a new subtask from a task for an asynchronous execution.

- The join() method lets a task wait for another task to complete.

Steps in Using the Fork/Join Framework

Using the fork/join framework involves the following five steps.

Step 1: Declaring a Class to Represent a Task

Create a class inheriting from the RecursiveAction or RecursiveTask class. An instance of this class represents a task that you want to execute. If the task yields a result, you need to inherit it from the RecursiveTask class. Otherwise, you will inherit it from the RecursiveAction class. The RecursiveTask is a generic class. It takes a type parameter, which is the type of the result of your task. A MyTask class that returns a Long result may be declared as follows:

```
public class MyTask extends RecursiveTask<Long> {
        // Code for your task goes here
}
```

Step 2: Implementing the compute() Method

The logic to execute your task goes inside the compute() method of your class. The return type of the compute() method is the same as the type of the result that your task returns. The declaration for the compute() method of the MyTask class look like the following:

```
public class MyTask extends RecursiveTask<Long> {
        public Long compute() {
                // Logic for the task goes here
        }
}
```

Step 3: Creating a Fork/Join Thread Pool

You can create a pool of worker threads to execute your task using the ForkJoinPool class. The default constructor of this class creates a thread of pool, which has the same parallelism as the number of processors available on the machine.

```
ForkJoinPool pool = new ForkJoinPool();
```

Other constructors let you specify the parallelism and other properties of the pool.

Step 4: Creating the Fork/Join Task

You need to create an instance of your task.

```
MyTask task = MyTask();
```

Step 5: Submitting the Task to the Fork/Join Pool for Execution

You need to call the invoke() method of the ForkJoinPool class, passing your task as an argument. The invoke() method will return the result of the task if your task returns a result. The following statement will execute your task:

```
long result = pool.invoke(task);
```

A Fork/Join Example

Let's consider a simple example of using the fork/join framework. Your task will generate a few random integers and compute their sum. Listing 6-58 has the complete code for your task.

Listing 6-58. A ForkJoinTask Class to Compute the Sum of a Few Random Integers

```java
// RandomIntSum.java
package com.jdojo.threads;

import java.util.ArrayList;
import java.util.List;
import java.util.Random;
import java.util.concurrent.RecursiveTask;

public class RandomIntSum extends RecursiveTask<Long> {
        private static Random randGenerator = new Random();
        private int count;

        public RandomIntSum(int count) {
                this.count = count;
        }

        @Override
        protected Long compute() {
                long result = 0;

                if (this.count <= 0) {
                        return 0L; // We do not have anything to do
                }

                if (this.count == 1) {
                        // Compute the number directly and return the result
                        return (long) this.getRandomInteger();
                }
```

```
                    // Multiple numbers. Divide them into many single tasks. Keep the references of
                    // all tasks to call thier join() method later
                    List<RecursiveTask<Long>>forks = new ArrayList<>();

                    for(int i = 0; i < this.count; i++) {
                            RandomIntSum subTask = new RandomIntSum(1);
                            subTask.fork(); // Launch the subtask

                            // Keep the subTask references to combine the results later
                            forks.add(subTask);
                    }

                    // Now wait for all subtasks to finish and combine the result
                    for(RecursiveTask<Long> subTask : forks) {
                            result = result + subTask.join();
                    }

                    return result;
            }

    public int getRandomInteger() {
                    // Generate the next randon integer between 1 and 100
                    int n = randGenerator.nextInt(100) + 1;

                    System.out.println("Generated a random integer: " + n);
                    return n;
            }
}
```

The class is named RandomIntSum. It extends RecursiveTask<Long> because it yields a result of the type Long. The result is the sum of all random integers. It declares a randGenerator instance variable that is used to generate a random number. The count instance variable stores the number of random numbers that you want to use. The value for the count instance variable is set in the constructor.

The getRandomInteger() method of the RandomIntSum class generates a random integer between 1 and 100, prints the integer value on the standard output, and returns the random integer.

The compute() method contains the main logic to perform the task. If the number of random numbers to use is one, it computes the result and returns it to the caller. If the number of random number is more than one, it launches as many subtasks as the number of random numbers. Note that if you use ten random numbers, it will launch ten subtasks because each random number can be computed independently. Finally, you need to combine the results from all subtasks. Therefore, you need to keep the references of the subtask for later use. You used a List to store the references of all subtasks. Note the use of the fork() method to launch a subtask. The following snippet of code performs this logic:

```
List<RecursiveTask<Long>>forks = new ArrayList<>();
for(int i = 0; i < this.count; i++) {
        RandomIntSum subTask = new RandomIntSum(1);
        subTask.fork(); // Launch the subtask

        // Keep the subTask references to combine the results at the end
        forks.add(subTask);
}
```

Once all subtasks are launched, you need to wait for all subtasks to finish and combine all random integers to get the sum. The following snippet of code performs this logic. Note the use of the join() method, which will make the current task wait for the subtask to finish.

```
for(RecursiveTask<Long> subTask : forks) {
        result = result + subTask.join();
}
```

Finally, the compute() method returns the result, which is the sum of all the random integers.
Listing 6-59 has the code to execute a task, which is an instance of the RandomIntSum class.

Listing 6-59. Using a Fork/Join Pool to Execute a Fork/Join Task

```
// ForkJoinTest.java
package com.jdojo.threads;

import java.util.concurrent.ForkJoinPool;

public class ForkJoinTest {
        public static void main(String[] args) {
                // Create a ForkJoinPool to run the task
                ForkJoinPool pool = new ForkJoinPool();

                // Create an instance of the task
                RandomIntSum task = new RandomIntSum(3);

                // Run the task
                long sum = pool.invoke(task);

                System.out.println("Sum is " + sum);
        }
}
```

```
(You may get a different output.)
Generated a random integer: 62
Generated a random integer: 46
Generated a random integer: 90
Sum is 198
```

This is a very simple example of using the fork/join framework. You are advised to explore the fork/join framework classes to know more about the framework. Inside the compute() method of your task, you can have complex logic to divide tasks into subtasks. Unlike in this example, you may not know in advance how many subtasks you need to launch. You may launch a subtask that may launch another subtask and so on.

Thread-Local Variables

A thread-local variable provides a way to maintain a separate value for a variable for each thread. The ThreadLocal class in the java.lang package provides the implementation of a thread-local variable. It has four methods: get(), set(), remove(), and initialValue(). The get() and set() methods are used to get and set the value for a thread-local variable, respectively. You can remove the value by using the remove() method. The initialValue() method is used to set the initial value of the variable, and it has a protected access. To use it, you need to subclass the ThreadLocal class and override this method.

Let's create a CallTracker class, shown in Listing 6-60, to keep track of the number of time times a thread calls its call() method.

Listing 6-60. A Class That Uses a ThreadLocal Object to Track Calls to Its Method

```java
// CallTracker.java
package com.jdojo.threads;

public class CallTracker {
        // threadLocal variable is used to store counters for all threads
        private static ThreadLocal<Integer> threadLocal = new ThreadLocal<Integer>();

        public static void call() {
                int counter = 0 ;
                Integer counterObject = threadLocal.get();

                if (counterObject == null) {
                        counter = 1;
                }
                else {
                        counter = counterObject.intValue();
                        counter++;
                }

                // Set the new counter
                threadLocal.set(counter);

                // Print how many times this thread has called this method
                String threadName = Thread.currentThread().getName();
                System.out.println("Call counter for " + threadName + " = " + counter);
        }
}
```

The get() method of the ThreadLocal class works on a thread basis. It returns the value set by the set() method by the same thread, which is executing the get() method. If a thread calls the get() method the very first time, it returns null. The program sets the call counter for the caller thread to 1 if it is its first call. Otherwise, it increments the call counter by 1. It sets the new counter back in the threadLocal object. At the end of the call, you print a message about how many times the current thread has called this method.

Listing 6-61 uses the CallTracker class in three threads. Each thread calls this method a random number of times between 1 and 5. You can observe in the output that the counter is maintained for each thread's call separately.

Listing 6-61. A Test Class for the CallTracker Class

```java
// CallTrackerTest.java
package com.jdojo.threads;

import java.util.Random;

public class CallTrackerTest {
    public static void main(String[] args) {
        // Let's start three threads to the CallTracker.call() method
        new Thread(CallTrackerTest::run).start();
        new Thread(CallTrackerTest::run).start();
        new Thread(CallTrackerTest::run).start();
    }

    public static void run() {
        Random random = new Random();

        // Generate a random value between 1 and 5
        int counter = random.nextInt(5) + 1;

        // Print the thread name and teh generated random number by the thread
        System.out.println(Thread.currentThread().getName() +
                           " generated counter: " + counter);

        for (int i = 0; i < counter; i++) {
            CallTracker.call();
        }
    }
}
```

```
(You may get a different output.)
Thread-0 generated counter: 4
Thread-1 generated counter: 2
Thread-2 generated counter: 3
Call counter for Thread-0 = 1
Call counter for Thread-2 = 1
Call counter for Thread-1 = 1
Call counter for Thread-2 = 2
Call counter for Thread-0 = 2
Call counter for Thread-2 = 3
Call counter for Thread-1 = 2
Call counter for Thread-0 = 3
Call counter for Thread-0 = 4
```

The initialValue() method sets the initial value of the thread-local variable for each thread. If you have set the initial value, the call to the get() method, before you call the set() method, will return that initial value. It is a protected method. You must override it in a subclass. You can set the initial value for the call counter to 1000 by using an anonymous class as shown:

```
// Create an anonymous subclass ThreadLocal class and override its initialValue() method to
// return 1000 as the initial value
private static ThreadLocal<Integer> threadLocal = new ThreadLocal<Integer>() {
                                    @Override
                                    public Integer initialValue() {
                                            return 1000;
                                    }
                    };
```

Subclassing the ThreadLocal class just to have an instance of ThreadLocal with an initial value was overkill. Finally, the class designers realized it (in Java 8) and provided a factory method called withInitial() in the ThreadLocal class that can specify an initial value. The method is declared as follows:

```
public static <S> ThreadLocal<S> withInitial(Supplier<? extends S> supplier)
```

The specified supplier provides the initial value for the ThreadLocal. The get() method of the supplier is used to get the initial value. You can rewrite above logic and replace the anonymous class, like so:

```
// Create a ThreadLocal with an initial value of 1000
ThreadLocal<Integer> threadLocal = ThreadLocal.withInitial(() -> 1000);
```

Having a Supplier as the supplier for the initial value, you can generate the initial value lazily and based on some logic. The following statement creates a ThreadLocal with initial value as the second part of the current time when the initial value is retrieved:

```
// Return the second of the current time as the initial value
ThreadLocal<Integer> threadLocal = ThreadLocal.withInitial(() -> LocalTime.now().getSecond());
```

You can use the remove() method to reset the value of the thread-local variable for a thread. After the call to the remove() method, the first call to the get() method works as if it was called the first time by returning the initial value.

The typical use of a thread-local variable is to store user id, transaction id, or transaction context for a thread. The thread sets those values in the beginning, and any code during the execution of that thread can use those values. Sometimes a thread may start child threads that may need to use the value set for a thread-local variable in the parent thread. You can achieve this by using an object of the InheritableThreadLocal class, which is inherited from the ThreadLocal class. The child thread inherits its initial value from the parent thread. However, the child thread can set its own value using the set() method.

Setting Stack Size of a Thread

Each thread in a JVM is allocated its own stack. A thread uses its stack to store all local variables during its execution. Local variables are used in constructors, methods, or blocks (static or non-static). The stack size of each thread will limit the number of threads that you can have in a program. Local variables are allocated memory on stack during their scope. Once they are out of scope, the memory used by them is reclaimed. It is essential to optimize the stack size of a thread in your program if it uses too many threads. If the stack size is too big, you can have a fewer number of threads in your program. The number of threads will be limited by the available memory to the JVM. If the stack size is too small to store all local variables used at a time, you may encounter a StackOverflowError. To set the stack size for each thread, you can use a non-standard JVM option called -Xssn, where n is the size of the thread stack. To set the stack size to 512 KB while running a Test class, you can use a command, like so:

```
java -Xss512k com.jdojo.threads.Test
```

Summary

A thread is a unit of execution in a program. An instance of the Thread class represents a thread in Java programs. The thread starts its execution in the run() method of the Thread class or its subclass. To execute your code in a thread, you need to subclass the Thread class and override its run() method; you can also use an instance of the Runnable interface as the target for a thread. Beginning from Java 8, you can use a method reference of any method that takes no parameters and returns void as the target for a thread. A thread is scheduled by using the start() method of the Thread class.

There are two types of threads: daemon and non-daemon. A non-daemon thread is also known as a user thread. The JVM exits when only threads running are all daemon threads.

Each thread in Java has a priority that is an integer between 1 and 10, 1 being the lowest priority and 10 being the highest priority. The priority of a thread is a hint, which can be ignored, to the operating system about its importance for getting the CPU time.

In a multi-threaded program, a section of code that may have undesirable effects on the outcome of the program if executed by multiple threads concurrently is called a *critical section*. You can mark a critical section in a Java program using the keyword synchronized. Methods can also be declared as synchronized. Only one synchronized instance method of an object can be executed at a time by any threads. Only one synchronized class method of a class can be executed at a time by any threads.

A thread in a Java program goes through a set of states that determines its life cycle. A thread can be in any one of these states: new, runnable, blocked, waiting, timed-waiting, terminated. States are represented by constants of the Thread.State enum. Use the getState() method of the Thread class to get the current state of the thread.

A thread can be interrupted, stopped, suspended, and resume. A stopped thread or a thread that has finished executing cannot be restarted.

Atomic variables, explicit locks, the synchronizer, the executor framework, and the fork/join framework are provided as class libraries to the Java developers to assist in developing concurrent application. Atomic variables provide variables that can be atomically updated without using explicit synchronization. Explicit locks have features that let you acquire locks and back off if the locks are not available. The executor framework helps schedule tasks. The fork/join framework is written on top of the executor framework to assist in working with tasks that can be divided in subtasks and finally their results can be combined.

Thread-local variables are implemented through the ThreadLocal class. They store values based on threads. They are suitable for values that are local to threads and that cannot be seen by other threads.

CHAPTER 7

■ ■ ■

Input/Output

In this chapter, you will learn

- What input/output is in Java
- How to work with a File object that represents an abstract pathname for a file or a directory in a file system
- The decorator pattern
- Byte-based and character-based input/output streams
- Reading data from a file and writing data to a file
- Reading and writing primitive type and reference type data to input/output streams
- Object serialization and deserialization
- How to develop custom input/output stream classes
- The Console and Scanner classes to interact with the console
- The StringTokenizer and StreamTokenizer classes to split text into tokens based on delimiters

What Is Input/Output?

Input/output (I/O) deals with reading data from a source and writing data to a destination. Data is read from the input source (or simply input) and written to the output destination (or simply output). For example, your keyboard works as a standard input, letting you read data entered using the keyboard into your program. You have been using the System.out.println() method to print text on the standard output from the very first Java program without your knowledge that you have been performing I/O.

Typically, you read data stored in a file or you write data to a file using I/O. However, your input and output are not limited to only files. You may read data from a String object and write it to another String object. In this case, the input is a String object; the output is also a String object. You may read data from a file and write it to a String object, which will use a file as an input and a String object as an output. Many combinations for input and output are possible. Input and output do not have to be used together all the time. You may use only input in your program, such as reading the contents of a file into a Java program. You may use only output in your program, such as writing the result of a computation to a file.

The java.io and java.nio (nio stands for New I/O) packages contain Java classes that deal with I/O. The java.io package has an overwhelming number of classes to perform I/O. It makes learning Java I/O a little complex. The situation where the number of classes increases to an unmanageable extent is called a *class explosion* and the java.io package is a good example of that. It is no wonder that there are some books in the market that deal only with Java

I/O. These books describe all Java I/O classes one by one. This chapter looks at Java I/O from a different perspective. First, you will look at the design pattern that was used to design the Java I/O classes. Once you understand the design pattern behind it, it is easy to understand how to use those classes to perform I/O in your program. After all, I/O is all about reading and writing data and it should not be that hard to understand! Before you start looking at the design pattern for the I/O classes, you will learn how to deal with a file in the next section.

Working with Files

How do you refer to a file in your computer? You refer to it by its pathname. A file's pathname is a sequence of characters by which you can identify it uniquely in a file system. A pathname consists of a file name and its unique location in the file system. For example, on a Windows platform, C:\users\dummy.txt is the pathname for a file named dummy.txt, which is located in the directory named users, which in turn is located in the root directory in the C: drive. On a UNIX platform, /users/dummy is the pathname for a file named dummy, which is located in the directory named users, which in turn is located in the root directory.

A pathname can be either absolute or relative. An absolute pathname points to the same location in a file system irrespective of the current working directory. For example, on a Windows platform, C:\users\dummy.txt is an absolute pathname.

A relative pathname is resolved with respect to the working directory. Suppose dummy.txt is your pathname. If your working directory is C:\, this pathname points to C:\dummy.txt. If your working directory is C:\users, it points to C:\users\dummy.txt. Note that if you specify a relative pathname for a file, it points to a different file depending on the current working directory. A pathname that starts with a root is an absolute pathname. The forward slash (/) is the root on the UNIX platform and a drive letter such as A: or C: defines the root for the Windows platform.

Tip The pathname syntax is platform-dependent. Programs using any platform-dependent syntax to represent pathnames may not work correctly on other platforms. In this chapter, most of the time I use the term "file" to mean a file or a directory.

Creating a File Object

An object of the File class is an abstract representation of a pathname of a file or a directory in a platform-independent manner. You can create a File object from

- A pathname
- A parent pathname and a child pathname
- A URI (uniform resource identifier)

Use one of the following constructors of the File class to create a file:

- File(String pathname)
- File(File parent, String child)
- File(String parent, String child)
- File(URI uri)

If you have a file pathname string of dummy.txt, you can create an abstract pathname (or a File object), like so:

```
File dummyFile = new File("dummy.txt");
```

Note that a file named dummy.txt does not have to exist to create a File object using this statement. The dummyFile object represents an abstract pathname, which may or may not point to a real file in a file-system.

The File class has several methods to work with files and directories. Using a File object, you can create a new file, delete an existing file, rename a file, change permissions on a file, and so on. You will see all these operations on a file in action in subsequent sections.

■ **Tip**   The File class contains two methods, isFile() and isDirectory(). Use these methods to know whether a File object represents a file or a directory.

Knowing the Current Working Directory

The concept of the current working directory is related to operating systems, not the Java programming language or Java I/O. When a process starts, it uses the current working directory to resolve the relative paths of files. When you run a Java program, the JVM runs as a process, and therefore it has a current working directory. The value for the current working directory for a JVM is set depending on how you run the java command.

You can get the current working directory for the JVM by reading the user.dir system property as follows:

```
String workingDir = System.getProperty("user.dir");
```

At this point, you may be tempted to use the System.setProperty() method to change the current working directory for the JVM in a running Java program. The following snippet of code will not generate any errors; it will not change the current working directory either:

```
System.setProperty("user.dir", "C:\\kishori");
```

After you try to set the current working directory in your Java program, the System.getProperty("user.dir") will return the new value. However, to resolve the relative file paths, the JVM will continue to use the current working directory that was set when the JVM was started, not the one changed using the System.setProperty() method.

■ **Tip**   Java designers found it too complex to allow changing the current working directory for the JVM in the middle of a running Java program. For example, if it were allowed, the same relative pathname would resolve to different absolute paths at different times in the same running JVM, giving rise to inconsistent behavior of the program.

You can also specify the current working directory for the JVM as the user.dir property value as a JVM option. To specify C:\test as the user.dir system property value on Windows, you run your program like so:

```
java -Duser.dir=C:\test your-java-class
```

Checking for a File's Existence

You can check if the abstract pathname of a File object exists using the exists() method of the File class, like so:

```
// Create a File object
File dummyFile = new File("dummy.txt");

// Check for the file's existence
boolean fileExists = dummyFile.exists();
if (fileExists) {
        System.out.println("The dummy.txt file exists.");
}
else {
        System.out.println("The dummy.txt file does not exist.");
}
```

I have used dummy.txt as the file name that is a relative path for this file. Where in the file system does the exists() method look for this file for its existence? There could be no file with this name or there could be multiple files with this name. When a relative file path is used, the JVM prepends the current working directory to the file path and uses the resulting absolute path for all file-related actual operations. Note that the absolute path is constructed in a platform-dependent way. For example, if the current working directory on Windows is C:\ksharan, the file name will be resolved to C:\ksharan\dummy.txt; if the current working directory on UNIX is /users/ksharan, the file name will be resolved to /users/ksharan/dummy.txt.

Which Path Do You Want to Go?

In addition to a relative path, a file has an absolute path and a canonical path. The absolute path identifies the file uniquely on a file system. A canonical path is the simplest path that uniquely identifies the file on a file system. The only difference between the two paths is that the canonical path is simplest in its form. For example, on Windows, if you have pathname dummy.txt whose absolute pathname is C:\users\dummy.txt, the pathname C:\users\sharan\..\dummy.txt also represents an absolute pathname for the same file. The two consecutive dots in the pathname represent one level up in the file hierarchy. Among the two absolute paths, the second one is not the simplest one. The canonical path for dummy.txt is the simplest absolute path C:\users\dummy.txt. You can use the getAbsolutePath() and getCanonicalPath() methods to get the absolute and canonical paths represented by a File object, respectively. Note that in a Java program you need to use double backslashes in a string literal to represent one backward slash; for example, the path C:\users\\sharan needs to be written as "C:\\users\\sharan" as a string.

Listing 7-1 illustrates how to get the absolute and canonical paths of a file. You may get a different output when you run the program; the output is shown running the program on Windows.

Listing 7-1. Getting the Absolute and Canonical Paths of a File

```
// FilePath.java
package com.jdojo.io;

import java.io.File;
import java.io.IOException;

public class FilePath {
        public static void main(String[] args) {
                String workingDir = System.getProperty("user.dir");
                System.out.println("Working Directory: " + workingDir);
```

```
                    System.out.println("---------------------");
                    printFilePath("dummy.txt");

                    System.out.println("---------------------");
                    printFilePath(".." + File.separator + "notes.txt");
        }

        public static void printFilePath(String pathname){
                    File f = new File(pathname);
                    System.out.println("File Name: " + f.getName());
                    System.out.println("File exists: " + f.exists());
                    System.out.println("Absolute Path: " + f.getAbsolutePath());

                    try {
                            System.out.println("Canonical Path: " + f.getCanonicalPath());
                    }
                    catch(IOException e){
                            e.printStackTrace();
                    }
        }
}
```

```
Working Directory: C:\book\javabook
---------------------
File Name: dummy.txt
File exists: false
Absolute Path: C:\book\javabook\dummy.txt
Canonical Path: C:\book\javabook\dummy.txt
---------------------
File Name: notes.txt
File exists: false
Absolute Path: C:\book\javabook\..\notes.txt
Canonical Path: C:\book\notes.txt
```

Different operating systems use a different character to separate two parts in a pathname. For example, Windows uses a backslash (\) as a name separator in a pathname, whereas UNIX uses a forward slash (/). The File class defines a constant named separatorChar, which is the system-dependent name separator character. You can use the File.separatorChar constant to get the name separator as a character. The File.separator constant gives you the name separator as a String. I used the name separator constant of the File class to build the following pathname:

```
printFilePath(".." + File.separator + "notes.txt");
```

Using the name separator in your program will make your Java code work on different platforms. The above statement on Windows will be the same as the following statement because Windows uses a backslash (\) as a name separator:

```
printFilePath("..\\notes.txt");
```

On UNIX, it will be the same as the following statement because UNIX uses a forward slash (/) as the file separator:

```
printFilePath("../notes.txt");
```

The benefit of using the File.separator constant in your code is that Java will use the appropriate file separator character in your file pathname depending on the operating system your program is executed.

If the pathname used to construct the File object is not absolute, the getAbsolutePath() method uses the working directory to get the absolute path.

You have to deal with two "devils" when you work with I/O in Java. If you do not specify the absolute pathname, your absolute path will be decided by the Java runtime and the operating system. If you specify the absolute pathname, your code may not run on different operating systems. One way to handle this situation is to use a configuration file, where you can specify a different file pathname for different operating systems, and you pass the configuration file path to your program at startup.

The canonical path of a file is system-dependent and the call to the getCanonicalPath() may throw an IOException. You must place this method call inside a try-catch block or throw an IOException from the method in which you invoke this method. Some of the I/O method calls throw an IOException in situations when the requested I/O operation fails.

Creating, Deleting, and Renaming Files

You can create a new file using the createNewFile() method of the File class:

```
// Create a File object to represent the abstract pathname
File dummyFile = new File("dummy.txt");

// Create the file
boolean fileCreated = dummyFile.createNewFile();
```

The createNewFile() method creates a new, empty file if the file with the specified name does not already exist. It returns true if the file is created successfully; otherwise, it returns false. The method throws an IOException if an I/O error occurs.

You can also create a temporary file in the default temporary file directory or a directory of your choice. To create a temporary file in the default temporary directory, use the createTempFile() static method of the File class, which accepts a prefix (at least three characters in length) and a suffix to generate the temporary file name.

```
File tempFile = File.createTempFile("kkk", ".txt");
```

You can use the mkdir() or mkdirs() method to create a new directory. The mkdir() method creates a directory only if the parent directories specified in the pathname already exists. For example, if you want to create a new directory called home in the users directory in the C: drive on Windows, you construct the File object representing this pathname like so:

```
File newDir = new File("C:\\users\\home");
```

Now the newDir.mkdir() method will create the home directory only if the C:\users directory already exists. However, the newDir.mkdirs() method will create the users directory if it does not exist in the C: drive, and hence, it will create the home directory under the C:\users directory.

Deleting a file is easy. You need to use the delete() method of the File class to delete a file/directory. A directory must be empty before you can delete it. The method returns true if the file/directory is deleted; otherwise, it returns false. You can also delay the deletion of a file until the JVM terminates by using the deleteOnExit() method. This is useful if you create temporary files in your program that you want to delete when your program exits.

```
// To delete the dummy.txt file immediately
File dummyFile = new File("dummy.txt");
dummyFile.delete();
```

286

```
// To delete the dummy.txt file when the JVM terminates
File dummyFile = new File("dummy.txt");
dummyFile.deleteOnExit();
```

■ **Tip** The call to the `deleteOnExit()` method is final. That is, once you call this method, there is no way for you to change your mind and tell the JVM not to delete this file when it terminates. You can use the `delete()` method to delete the file immediately even after you have requested the JVM to delete the same file on exit.

To rename a file, you can use the `renameTo()` method, which takes a `File` object to represent the new file:

```
// Rename old-dummy.txt to new_dummy.txt
File oldFile = new File("old_dummy.txt");
File newFile = new File("new_dummy.txt");

boolean fileRenamed = oldFile.renameTo(newFile);
if (fileRenamed) {
        System.out.println(oldFile + " renamed to " + newFile);
}
else {
        System.out.println("Renaming " + oldFile + " to " + newFile + " failed.");
}
```

The `renameTo()` method returns `true` if renaming of the file succeeds; otherwise, it returns `false`. You are advised to check the return value of this method to make sure the renaming succeeded because the behavior of this method is very system-dependent.

■ **Tip** The `File` object is immutable. Once created, it always represents the same pathname, which is passed to its constructor. When you rename a file, the old `File` object still represents the original pathname. An important thing to remember is that a `File` object represents a pathname, not an actual file in a file system.

Listing 7-2 illustrates the use of some of the methods described above to create, delete, and rename a file. You may get a different output; the output is shown when the program was run on Windows. When you run the program the second time, you may get a different output because it may not be able to rename the file if it already existed from the first run.

Listing 7-2. Creating, Deleting, and Renaming a File

```
// FileCreateDeleteRename.java
package com.jdojo.io;

import java.io.File;
import java.io.IOException;

public class FileCreateDeleteRename {
        public static void main(String[] args) {
                try {
```

```
File newFile = new File("my_new_file.txt");
System.out.println("Before creating the new file:");
printFileDetails(newFile);

// Create a new file
boolean fileCreated = newFile.createNewFile();
if (!fileCreated) {
        System.out.println(newFile + " could not be created.");
}

System.out.println("After creating the new file:");
printFileDetails(newFile);

// Delete the new file
newFile.delete();

System.out.println("After deleting the new file:");
printFileDetails(newFile);

// Let's recreate the file
newFile.createNewFile();

System.out.println("After recreating the new file:");
printFileDetails(newFile);

// Let's tell the JVM to delete this file on exit
newFile.deleteOnExit();

System.out.println("After using deleteOnExit() method:");
printFileDetails(newFile);

// Create a new file and rename it
File firstFile = new File("my_first_file.txt");
File secondFile = new File("my_second_file.txt");

fileCreated = firstFile.createNewFile();
if (fileCreated || firstFile.exists()) {
        System.out.println("Before renaming file:");
        printFileDetails(firstFile);
        printFileDetails(secondFile);

        boolean renamedFlag = firstFile.renameTo(secondFile);
        if (!renamedFlag) {
                System.out.println("Could not rename " + firstFile);
        }

        System.out.println("After renaming file:");
        printFileDetails(firstFile);
        printFileDetails(secondFile);
}
}
```

```
               catch(IOException e){
                       e.printStackTrace();
               }
        }

        public static void printFileDetails(File f) {
               System.out.println("Absolute Path: " + f.getAbsoluteFile());
               System.out.println("File exists: " + f.exists());
               System.out.println("-----------------------------");
        }
}
```

```
Before creating the new file:
Absolute Path: C:\javabook\my_new_file.txt
File exists: false
-----------------------------
After creating the new file:
Absolute Path: C:\javabook\my_new_file.txt
File exists: true
-----------------------------
After deleting the new file:
Absolute Path: C:\javabook\my_new_file.txt
File exists: false
-----------------------------
After recreating the new file:
Absolute Path: C:\javabook\my_new_file.txt
File exists: true
-----------------------------
After using deleteOnExit() method:
Absolute Path: C:\javabook\my_new_file.txt
File exists: true
-----------------------------
Before renaming file:
Absolute Path: C:\javabook\my_first_file.txt
File exists: true
-----------------------------
Absolute Path: C:\javabook\my_second_file.txt
File exists: false
-----------------------------
After renaming file:
Absolute Path: C:\javabook\my_first_file.txt
File exists: false
-----------------------------
Absolute Path: C:\javabook\my_second_file.txt
File exists: true
-----------------------------
```

Working with File Attributes

The File class contains methods that let you get/set attributes of files and directories in a limited ways. You can set a file as read-only, readable, writable, and executable using the setReadOnly(), setReadable(), setWritable(), and setExecutable() methods, respectively. You can use the lastModified() and setLastModified() methods to get and set the last modified date and time of a file. You can check if a file is hidden using the isHidden() method. Note that the File class does not contain a setHidden() method as the definition of a hidden file is platform-dependent.

■ **Tip**   I will discuss working with file attributes using the New Input/Output 2 (NIO.2) API in Chapter 10. NIO.2 has extensive support for file attributes.

Copying a File

The File class does not provide a method to copy a file. To copy a file, you must create a new file, read the content from the original file, and write it into the new file. I will discuss how to copy the contents of a file into another file later in this chapter, after I discuss the input and output streams. The NIO 2.0 API, which was added in Java 7, provides a direct way to copy a file contents and its attributes. Please refer to Chapter 10 for more details.

Knowing the Size of a File

You can get the size of a file in bytes using the length() method of the File class.

```
File myFile = new File("myfile.txt");
long fileLength = myFile.length();
```

If a File object represents a non-existent file, the length() method returns zero. If it is a directory name, the return value is not specified. Note that the return type of the length() method is long, not int.

Listing All Files and Directories

You can get a list of the available root directories in a file system by using the listRoots() static method of the File class. It returns an array of File objects.

```
// Get the list of all root directories
File[] roots = File.listRoots();
```

Root directories are different across platforms. On Windows, you have a root directory for each drive (e.g. C:\, A:\, D:\, etc.). On UNIX, you have a single root directory represented by a forward slash.

Listing 7-3 illustrates how to get the root directories on a machine. The output is shown when this program was run on Windows. You may get a different output when you run this program on your machine. The output will depend on the operating system and the drives that are attached to your machine.

Listing 7-3. Listing All Available Root Directories on a Machine

```java
// RootList.java
package com.jdojo.io;

import java.io.File;;

public class RootList {
        public static void main(String[] args) {
                File[] roots = File.listRoots();
                System.out.println("List of root directories:");
                for(File f : roots){
                        System.out.println(f.getPath());
                }
        }
}
```

```
List of root directories:
C:\
D:\
```

You can list all files and directories in a directory by using the `list()` or `listFiles()` methods of the File class. The only difference between them is that the `list()` method returns an array of String, whereas the `listFiles()` method returns an array of File. You can also use a file filter with these methods to exclude some files and directories from the returned results.

Listing 7-4 illustrates how to list the files and directories in a directory. Note that the `list()` and `listFiles()` methods do not list the files and directories recursively. You need to write the logic to list files recursively. You need to change the value of the `dirPath` variable in the `main()` method. You may get a different output. The output shown is the output when the program was run on Windows.

Listing 7-4. Listing All Files and Directories in a Directory

```java
// FileLists.java
package com.jdojo.io;

import java.io.File;

public class FileLists {
        public static void main(String[] args) {
                // Change the dirPath value to list files from your directory
                String dirPath = "C:\\";

                File dir = new File(dirPath);
                File[] list = dir.listFiles();

                for(File f : list){
                        if (f.isFile()) {
                                System.out.println(f.getPath() + " (File)");
                        }
                        else if(f.isDirectory()){
                                System.out.println(f.getPath() + " (Directory)");
                        }
```

```
            }
        }
}
```

```
C:\WINDOWS  (Directory)
C:\MSDOS.SYS  (File)
C:\CONFIG.SYS  (File)
...
```

Suppose you wanted to exclude all files from the list with an extension .SYS. You can do this by using a file filter that is represented by an instance of the functional interface FileFilter. It contains an accept() method that takes the File being listed as an argument and returns true if the File should be listed. Returning false does not list the file. The following snippet of code creates a file filter that will filter files with the extension .SYS. Note that the code uses lambda expressions that were introduced in Java 8.

```
// Create a file filter to exclude any .SYS file
FileFilter filter = file -> {
        if (file.isFile()) {
                String fileName = file.getName().toLowerCase();
                if (fileName.endsWith(".sys")) {
                        return false;
                }
        }
        return true;
};
```

Using lambda expressions makes it easy to build the file filters. The following snippet of code creates two file filters—one filters only files and another only directories:

```
// Filters only files
FileFilter fileOnlyFilter = File::isFile;

// Filters only directories
FileFilter dirOnlyFilter = File::isDirectory;
```

Listing 7-5 illustrates how to use a file filter. The program is the same as in Listing 7-4 except that it uses a filter to exclude all .SYS files from the list. You can compare the output of these two listings to see the effect of the filter.

Listing 7-5. Using FileFilter to Filter Files

```
// FilteredFileList.java
package com.jdojo.io;

import java.io.File;
import java.io.FileFilter;

public class FilteredFileList {
        public static void main(String[] args) {
                // Change the dirPath value to list files from your directory
                String dirPath = "C:\\";
                File dir = new File(dirPath);
```

```
        // Create a file filter to exclude any .SYS file
        FileFilter filter = file -> {
                if (file.isFile()) {
                        String fileName = file.getName().toLowerCase();
                        if (fileName.endsWith(".sys")) {
                                return false;
                        }
                }
                return true;
        };

        // Pass the filter object to listFiles() method
        // to exclude the .sys files
        File[] list = dir.listFiles(filter);

        for (File f : list) {
                if (f.isFile()) {
                        System.out.println(f.getPath() + " (File)");
                }
                else if (f.isDirectory()) {
                        System.out.println(f.getPath() + " (Directory)");
                }
        }
    }
}
```

```
C:\WINDOWS (Directory)
...
```

The Decorator Pattern

Suppose you need to design classes for a bar that sells alcoholic drinks. The available drinks are rum, vodka, and whiskey. It also sells two drink flavorings: honey and spices. You have to design classes for a Java application so that when a customer orders a drink, the application will let the user print a receipt with the drink name and its price.

What are the things that you need to maintain in the classes to compute the price of a drink and get its name? You need to maintain the name and price of all ingredients of the drink separately. When you need to print the receipt, you will concatenate the names of all ingredients and add up the prices for all ingredients. One way to design the classes for this application would be to have a Drink class with two instance variables: name and price. There would be a class for each kind of drink; the class would inherit from the Drink class. Some of the possible classes would be as follows:

- Drink
- Rum
- Vodka
- Whiskey
- RumWithHoney

293

- RumWithSpices

- VodkaWithHoney

- VodkaWithSpices

- WhiskeyWithHoney

- WhiskeyWithSpices

- WhiskeyWithHoneyAndSpices

Note that we have already listed eleven classes and the list is not complete yet. Consider ordering whiskey with two servings of honey. You can see that the number of classes involved is huge. If you add some more drinks and flavorings, the classes will increase tremendously. With this class design, you will have a problem maintaining the code. If the price of honey changes, you will need to revisit every class that has honey in it and change its price. This design will produce a class explosion. Fortunately, there is a design pattern to deal with such a problem. It is called the *decorator* pattern. Typically, classes are organized as shown in Figure 7-1 to use the decorator pattern.

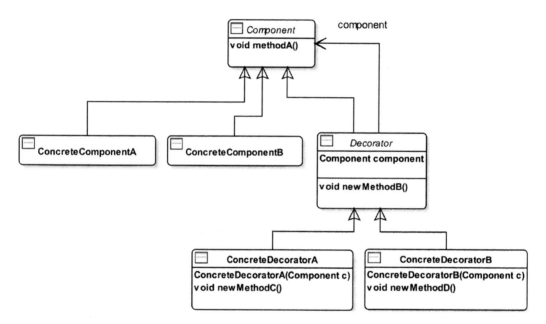

Figure 7-1. *A generic class diagram based on the decorator pattern*

The decorator pattern requires you to have a common abstract superclass from which you inherit your concrete component classes and an abstract decorator class. Name the common superclass Component. You can use an interface instead of an abstract class. Concrete components, shown as ConcreteComponentA and ConcreteComponentB in the class diagram, are inherited from the Component class. The Decorator class is the abstract decorator class, which is inherited from the Component class. Concrete decorators, shown as ConcreteDecoratorA and ConcreteDecoratorB in the class diagram, are inherited from the Decorator class. The Decorator class keeps a reference to its superclass Component. The reference of a concrete component is passed to a concrete decorator as an argument in its constructor as follows:

```
ConcreteComponentA ca = new ConcreteComponentA();
ConcreteDecoratorA cd = new ConcreteDecoratorA(ca);
```

When a method is called on a concrete decorator, it takes some actions and calls the method on the component it encloses. The decorator may decide to take its action before and/or after it calls the method on the component. This way, a decorator extends the functionality of a component. This pattern is called a decorator pattern because the decorator class adds functionality (or decorates) the component it encloses. It is also known as the *wrapper* pattern for the same reason: it encloses (wraps) the component that it decorates.

The decorator has the same interface as the concrete components because both of them are inherited from the common superclass, Component. Therefore, you can use a Decorator object wherever a Component object is expected. Sometimes decorators add additional functionalities by adding new methods that are not present in the component, as shown in the class diagram: newMethodB(), newMethodC() and newMethodD().

Let's apply this discussion about the generic class diagram of the decorator pattern to model classes for your drink application. The class diagram is shown in Figure 7-2.

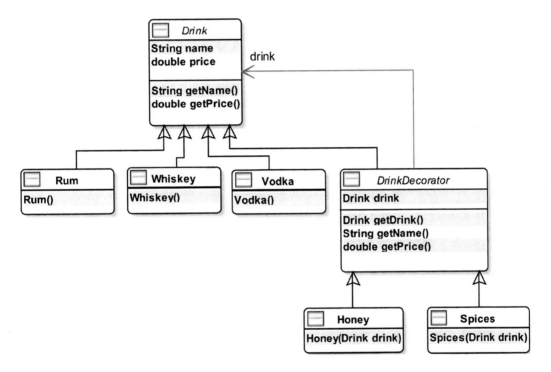

Figure 7-2. *The class diagram for the drink application based on the decorator pattern*

In the drink application, Rum, Vodka, and Whiskey are the concrete components (main drinks). Honey and Spices are the two decorators that are added to decorate (or to change the flavor) of the main drinks.

The Drink class, shown in Listing 7-6, serves as the abstract common ancestor class for the main drinks and decorators. The name and price instance variables in the Drink class hold the name and price of a drink; the class also contains the getters for these instance variables. These methods define the common interface for the main drinks as well as flavors.

Listing 7-6. An Abstract Drink Class to Model the Abstract Component in the Decorator Pattern

```java
// Drink.java
package com.jdojo.io;

public abstract class Drink {
        protected String name;
        protected double price;

        public String getName() {
                return name;
        }

        public double getPrice() {
                return price;
        }
}
```

Listing 7-7 contains the code for the Rum class that inherits from the Drink class. It sets the name and price in its constructor. Listing 7-8 and Listing 7-9 list the Vodka and Whiskey classes, respectively. The three classes are similar.

Listing 7-7. A Rum Class

```java
// Rum.java
package com.jdojo.io;

public class Rum extends Drink {
        public Rum() {
                this.name = "Rum";
                this.price = 0.9;
        }
}
```

Listing 7-8. A Vodka Class

```java
// Vodka.java
package com.jdojo.io;

public class Vodka extends Drink {
        public Vodka() {
                this.name = "Vodka";
                this.price = 1.2;
        }
}
```

Listing 7-9. A Whiskey Class

```java
// Whiskey.java
package com.jdojo.io;

public class Whiskey extends Drink {
        public Whiskey() {
```

```
                this.name = "Whisky";
                this.price = 1.5;
        }
}
```

The DrinkDecorator, shown in Listing 7-10, is the abstract decorator class that is inherited from the Drink class. The concrete decorators Honey and Spices inherit from the DrinkDecorator class. It has an instance variable named drink, which is of the type Drink. This instance variable represents the Drink object that a decorator will decorate. It overrides the getName() and getPrice() methods for decorators. In its getName() method, it gets the name of the drink it is decorating and appends its own name to it. This is what I mean by adding functionality to a component by a decorator. The getPrice() method works the same way. It gets the price of the drink it decorates and adds its own price to it.

Listing 7-10. An Abstract DrinkDecorator Class

```java
// DrinkDecorator.java
package com.jdojo.io;

public abstract class DrinkDecorator extends Drink {
        protected Drink drink;

        @Override
        public String getName() {
                // Append its name after the name of the drink it is decorating
                return drink.getName() + ", " + this.name;
        }

        @Override
        public double getPrice() {
                // Add its price to the price of the drink it is decorating/
                return drink.getPrice() + this.price;
        }

        public Drink getDrink() {
                return drink;
        }
}
```

Listing 7-11 lists a concrete decorator, the Honey class, which inherits from the DrinkDecorator class. It accepts a Drink object as an argument in its constructor. It requires that before you can create an object of the Honey class, you must have a Drink object. In its constructor, it sets its name, price, and the drink it will work with. It will use the getName() and getPrice() methods of its superclass DrinkDecorator class.

Listing 7-11. A Honey Class, a Concrete Decorator

```java
// Honey.java
package com.jdojo.io;

public class Honey extends DrinkDecorator{
        public Honey(Drink drink) {
                this.drink = drink;
                this.name = "Honey";
```

```
                            this.price = 0.25;
            }
}
```

Listing 7-12 lists another concrete decorator, the Spices class, which is implemented the same way as the Honey class.

Listing 7-12. A Spices Class, a Concrete Decorator

```
// Spices.java
package com.jdojo.io;

public class Spices extends DrinkDecorator {
        public Spices(Drink drink) {
                this.drink = drink;
                this.name = "Spices";
                this.price = 0.10;
        }
}
```

It is the time to see the drink application in action. Let's order whiskey with honey. How will you construct the objects to order whiskey with honey? It's simple. You always start with creating the concrete component. Concrete decorators are added to the concrete component. Whiskey is your concrete component and honey is your concrete decorator. You always work with the last component object you create in the series. Typically, the last component that you create is one of the concrete decorators unless you are dealing with only a concrete component.

```
// Create a Whiskey object
Whiskey w = new Whiskey();

// Add Honey to the Whiskey. Pass the object w in Honey's constructor
Honey h = new Honey(w);

// At this moment onwards, we will work with the last component we have
// created, which is h (a honey object). To get the name of the drink,
// call the getName() method on the honey object
String drinkName = h.getName();
```

Note that the Honey class uses the getName() method, which is implemented in the DrinkDecorator class. It will get the name of the drink, which is Whiskey in your case, and add its own name. The h.getName() method will return "Whiskey, Honey".

```
// Get the price
double drinkPrice = h.getPrice();
```

The h.getPrice() method will return 1.75. It will get the price of whiskey, which is 1.5 and add the price of honey, which is 0.25.

You do not need a two-step process to create a whiskey with honey drink. You can use the following one statement to create it:

```
Drink myDrink = new Honey(new Whiskey());
```

By using the above coding style, you get a feeling that Honey is really enclosing (or decorating) Whiskey. You ordered a drink: whiskey with honey. Therefore, it is better to store the reference of the final drink to a Drink variable (Drink myDrink) rather than a Honey variable (Honey h). However, if the Honey class implemented some additional methods than those inherited from the Drink class and you intended to use one of those additional methods, you need to use a variable of the Honey class to store the final reference.

```
// If our Honey class has additional methods, which are not defined in Drink
// class, store the reference in Honey type variable
Honey h = new Honey(new Whiskey());
```

How would you order a drink of whiskey with two servings of honey? It's simple. Create a Whiskey object, enclose it in a Honey object, and enclose the Honey object in another Honey object, like so:

```
// Create a drink of whiskey with double honey
Drink myDrink = new Honey(new Honey(new Whiskey()));
```

Similarly, you can create a drink of vodka with honey and spices, and get its name and price as follows:

```
// Create a drink of vodka with honey and spices
Drink myDrink = new Spices(new Honey(new Vodka()));
String drinkName = myDrink.getName();
double drinkPrice = myDrink.getPrice();
```

Sometimes reading the construction of objects based on the decorator pattern may be confusing because of several levels of object wrapping in the constructor call. You need to read the object's constructor starting from the innermost level. The innermost level is always a concrete component and all subsequent levels will be concrete decorators. In the previous example of vodka with honey and spices, the inner most level is the creation of vodka, new Vodka(), which is wrapped in honey, new Honey(new Vodka()), which in turn is wrapped in spices, new Spices(new Honey(new Vodka())). Figure 7-3 depicts how these three objects are arranged. Listing 7-13 demonstrates how to use your drink application.

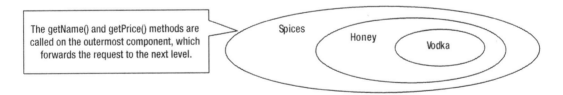

Figure 7-3. *The arrangement of components in the decorator pattern*

Listing 7-13. Testing the Drink Application

```
// DrinkTest.java
package com.jdojo.io;

public class DrinkTest {
    public static void main(String[] args) {
        // Have Whiskey only
        Drink d1 = new Whiskey();
        printReceipt(d1);
```

```
                // Have Whiskey with Honey
                Drink d2 = new Honey(new Whiskey());
                printReceipt(d2);

                // Have Vodka with Spices
                Drink d3 = new Spices(new Vodka());
                printReceipt(d3);

                // Have Rum with double Honey and Spices
                Drink d4 = new Spices(new Honey(new Honey(new Rum())));
                printReceipt(d4);
        }

        public static void printReceipt(Drink drink) {
                String name = drink.getName();
                double price = drink.getPrice();
                System.out.println(name + " - $" + price);
        }
}
```

```
Whisky - $1.5
Whisky, Honey - $1.75
Vodka, Spices - $1.3
Rum, Honey, Honey, Spices - $1.5
```

You need to consider the other aspects of the decorator pattern:

- The abstract Component class (the Drink class in the example) can be replaced by an interface. Note that you have included two instance variables in the Drink class. If you want to replace the Drink class with an interface, you must move these two instance variables down the class hierarchy.

- You may add any number of new methods in abstract decorators and concrete decorators to extend the behavior of its component.

- With the decorator pattern, you end up with lots of small classes, which may make your application hard to learn. However, once you understand the class hierarchy, it is easy to customize and use them.

- The goal of the decorator pattern is achieved by having a common superclass for the concrete components and concrete decorators. This makes it possible for a concrete decorator to be treated as a component, which in turn allows for wrapping a decorator inside another decorator. While constructing the class hierarchy, you can introduce more classes or remove some. For example, you could have introduced a class named MainDrink between the Drink class, and Rum, Vodka and Whiskey classes.

- The concrete decorator need not be inherited from an abstract decorator class. Sometimes you may want to inherit a concrete decorator directly from the abstract Component class. For example, the ObjectInputStream class is inherited from the InputStream class in the java.io package, not from the FilterInputStream class. Please refer to Figure 7-5 for details. The main requirement for a concrete decorator is that it should have the abstract component as its immediate or non-immediate superclass and it should accept an abstract component type argument in its constructor.

Input/Output Streams

The literal meaning of the word stream is *"an unbroken flow of something."* In Java I/O, a stream means an unbroken flow (or sequential flow) of data. The data in the stream could be bytes, characters, objects, etc.

A river is a stream of water where the water flows from a source to its destination in an unbroken sequence. Similarly, in Java I/O, the data flows from a source known as a *data source* to a destination known as a *data sink*. The data is read from a data source to a Java program. A Java program writes data to a data sink. The stream that connects a data source and a Java program is called an *input stream*. The stream that connects a Java program and a data sink is called an *output stream*. In a natural stream, such as a river, the source and the destination are connected through the continuous flow of water. However, in Java I/O, a Java program comes between an input stream and an output stream. Data flows from a data source through an input stream to a Java program. The data flows from the Java program through an output stream to a data sink. In other words, a Java program reads data from the input stream and writes data to the output stream. Figure 7-4 depicts the flow of data from an input stream to a Java program and from a Java program to an output stream.

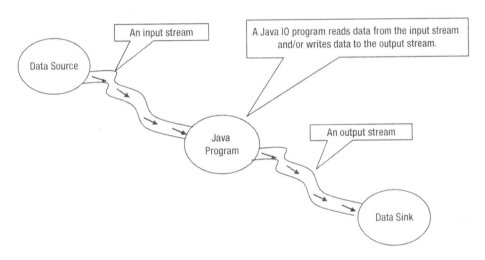

Figure 7-4. *Flow of data using an input/output stream in a Java program*

To read data from a data source into a Java program, you need to perform the following steps:

- Identify the data source. It may be a file, a string, an array, a network connection, etc.

- Construct an input stream using the data source that you have identified.

- Read the data from the input stream. Typically, you read the data in a loop until you have read all the data from the input stream. The methods of an input stream return a special value to indicate the end of the input stream.

- Close the input stream. Note that constructing an input stream itself opens it for reading. There is no explicit step to open an input stream. However, you must close the input stream when you are done reading data from it. From Java 7, you can use a `try-with-resources` block, which closes the input stream automatically.

To write data to a data sink from a Java program, you need to perform the following steps:

- Identify the data sink. That is, identify the destination where data will be written. It may be a file, a string, an array, a network connection, etc.

- Construct an output stream using the data sink that you have identified.

- Write the data to the output stream.

- Close the output stream. Note that constructing an output stream itself opens it for writing. There is no explicit step to open an output stream. However, you must close the output stream when you are done writing data to it. From Java 7, you can use a `try-with-resources` block, which closes the output stream automatically.

Input/output stream classes in Java are based on the decorator pattern. By now, you know that a class design based on the decorator pattern results in several small classes. So is the case with Java I/O. There are many classes involved in Java I/O. Learning each class at a time is no easy task. However, learning these classes can be made easy by comparing them with the class arrangements in the decorator pattern. I will compare the Java I/O classes with the decorator pattern later. In the next two sections, you will see input/output streams in action using simple programs, which will read data from a file and write data to a file.

Reading from File Using an Input Stream

In this section, I will show you how to read data from a file. The data will be displayed on the standard output. You have a file called `luci1.txt`, which contains the first stanza from the poem *Lucy* by William Wordsworth (1770-1850). One stanza from the poem is as follows:

```
STRANGE fits of passion have I known:
And I will dare to tell,
But in the lover's ear alone,
What once to me befell.
```

You can create a `luci1.txt` file with the text and save it in your current working directory. The following steps are needed to read from the file:

- Identify the data source, which is the file path in this case.

- Create an input stream using the file.

- Read the data from the file using the input stream.

- Close the input stream.

Identifying the Data Source

Your data source could be simply the file name as a string or a `File` object representing the pathname of the file. Let's assume that the `luci1.txt` file is in the current working directory.

```
// The data source
String srcFile = "luci1.txt";
```

Creating the Input Stream

To read from a file, you need to create an object of the FileInputStream class, which will represent the input stream.

```
// Create a file input stream
FileInputStream fin = new FileInputStream(srcFile);
```

When the data source for an input stream is a file, Java wants you to make sure that the file exists when you construct the file input stream. The constructor of the FileInputStream class throws a FileNotFoundException if the file does not exist. To handle this exception, you need to place your code in a try-catch block, like so:

```
try {
        // Create a file input stream
        FileInputStream fin = new FileInputStream(srcFile);
}
catch (FileNotFoundException e){
        // The error handling code goes here
}
```

Reading the Data

The FileInputStream class has an overloaded read() method to read data from the file. You can read one byte or multiple bytes at a time using the different versions of this method. Be careful when using the read() method. Its return type is int, though it returns a byte value. It returns -1 if the end of the file is reached, indicating that there are no more bytes to read. You need to convert the returned int value to a byte to get the byte read from the file. Typically, you read a byte at a time in a loop, like so:

```
int data;
byte byteData;

// Read the first byte
data = fin.read();
while (data != -1) {
        // Display the read data on the console. Note the cast
        // from int to byte - (byte)data
        byteData = (byte)data;

        // Cast the byte data to char to display the data
        System.out.print((char)byteData);

        // Try reading another byte
        data = fin.read();
}
```

You can rewrite the file-reading logic in a compact form, like so:

```
byte byteData;
while ((byteData = (byte)fin.read()) != -1){
        System.out.print((char)byteData);
}
```

We will use the compact form of reading the data from an input stream in subsequent examples. You need to place the code for reading data from an input stream in a try-catch block because it may throw an IOException.

Closing the Input Steam

Finally, you need to close the input stream using its close() method.

```
// Close the input stream
fin.close();
```

The close() method may throw an IOException, and because of that, you need to enclose this call inside a try-catch block.

```
try {
        // Close the input stream
        fin.close();
}
catch (IOException e) {
        e.printStackTrace();
}
```

Typically, you construct an input stream inside a try block and close it in a finally block to make sure it is always closed after you are done with it.

All input/output streams are auto closeable. You can use a try-with-resources to create their instances, so they will be closed automatically regardless of an exception being thrown or not, avoiding the need to call their close() method explicitly. The following snippet of code shows using a try-with-resources to create a file input stream:

```
String srcFile = "luci1.txt";
try (FileInputStream fin = new FileInputStream(srcFile)) {
        // Use fin to read data from the file here
}
catch (FileNotFoundException e) {
        // Handle the exception here
}
```

A Utility Class

You will frequently need to perform things such as closing an input/output stream and printing a message on the standard output when a file is not found, etc. Listing 7-14 contains the code for a FileUtil class that you will use in the example programs.

Listing 7-14. A Utility Class Containing Convenience Methods to Work with I/O Classes

```
// FileUtil.java
package com.jdojo.io;

import java.io.Closeable;
import java.io.IOException;

public class FileUtil {
        // Prints the location details of a file
```

```java
        public static void printFileNotFoundMsg(String fileName) {
                String workingDir = System.getProperty("user.dir");
                System.out.println("Could not find the file '" +
                                    fileName + "' in '" + workingDir + "' directory ");
        }

        // Closes a Closeable resource such as an input/output stream
        public static void close(Closeable resource) {
                if (resource != null ) {
                        try {
                                resource.close();
                        }
                        catch (IOException e) {
                                e.printStackTrace();
                        }
                }
        }
}
```

Completing the Example

Listing 7-15 illustrates the steps involved in reading the file luci1.txt. If you receive an error message indicating that the file does not exist, it will also print the directory where it is expecting the file. You may use an absolute path of the source file instead of a relative path by replacing the statement

```java
String srcFile = "luci1.txt";
```

with

```java
// Absolute path like c:\smith\luci1.txt on Windows or /users/smith/luci1.txt
// on UNIX. Note that you must use "c:\\smith\\luci1.txt"
// (two backslashes to escape a backslash) when you construct a string that
// contains a backslash
String srcFile = "absolute path of luci1.txt file";
```

By simply using luci1.txt as the data source file path, the program expects that the file is present in your current working directory when you run the program.

Listing 7-15. Reading a Byte at a Time from a File Input Stream

```java
// SimpleFileReading.java
package com.jdojo.io;

import java.io.FileInputStream;
import java.io.FileNotFoundException;
import java.io.IOException;

public class SimpleFileReading {
        public static void main(String[] args) {
                String dataSourceFile = "luci1.txt";
                try (FileInputStream fin = new FileInputStream(dataSourceFile)) {
```

```
                    byte byteData;
                    while ((byteData = (byte) fin.read()) != -1) {
                            System.out.print((char) byteData);
                    }
            }
            catch (FileNotFoundException e) {
                    FileUtil.printFileNotFoundMsg(dataSourceFile);
            }
            catch (IOException e) {
                    e.printStackTrace();
            }
        }
}
```

STRANGE fits of passion have I known:
And I will dare to tell,
But in the lover's ear alone,
What once to me befell.

Writing Data to a File Using an Output Stream

In this section, I will show you how to write a stanza from the poem *Lucy* by William Wordsworth to a file named luci2.txt. The stanza is as follows:

When she I loved look'd every day
Fresh as a rose in June,
I to her cottage bent my way,
Beneath an evening moon.

The following steps are needed to write to the file:

- Identify the data sink, which is the file to which the data will be written.

- Create an output stream using the file.

- Write the data to the file using the output stream.

- Flush the output stream.

- Close the output stream.

Identifying the Data Sink

Your data sink could be simply the file path as a string or a File object representing the pathname of the file. Let's assume that the luci2.txt file is in the current working directory.

```
// The data sink
String destFile = "luci2.txt";
```

Creating the Output Stream

To write to a file, you need to create an object of the FileOutputStream class, which will represent the output stream.

```
// Create a file output stream
FileOutputStream fos = new FileOutputStream(destFile);
```

When the data sink for an output stream is a file, Java tries to create the file if the file does not exist. Java may throw a FileNotFoundException if the file name that you have used is a directory name, or if it could not open the file for any reason. You must be ready to handle this exception by placing your code in a try-catch block, as shown:

```
try {
        FileOutputStream fos = new FileOutputStream(srcFile);
}
catch (FileNotFoundException e){
        // Error handling code goes here
}
```

If your file contains data at the time of creating a FileOutputStream, the data will be erased. If you want to keep the existing data and append the new data to the file, you need to use another constructor of the FileOutputStream class, which accepts a boolean flag for appending the new data to the file.

```
// To append data to the file, pass true in the second argument
FileOutputStream fos = new FileOutputStream(destFile, true);
```

Writing the Data

Write data to the file using the output stream. The FileOutputStream class has an overloaded write() method to write data to a file. You can write one byte or multiple bytes at a time using the different versions of this method. You need to place the code for writing data to the output stream in a try-catch block because it may throw an IOException if data cannot be written to the file.

Typically, you write binary data using a FileOutputStream. If you want to write a string such as "Hello" to the output stream, you need to convert the string to bytes. The String class has a getBytes() method that returns an array of bytes that represents the string. You write a string to the FileOutputStream as follows:

```
String text = "Hello";
byte[] textBytes = text.getBytes();
fos.write(textBytes);
```

You want to write four lines of text to luci2.txt. You need to insert a new line after every line for the first three lines of text. A new line is different on different platforms. You can get a new line for the platform on which your program is running by reading the line.separator system variable as follows:

```
// Get the newline for the platform
String lineSeparator = System.getProperty("line.separator");
```

Note that a line separator may not necessarily be one character. To write a line separator to a file output stream, you need to convert it to a byte array and write that byte array to the file as follows:

```
fos.write(lineSeparator.getBytes());
```

Flushing the Output Stream

You need to flush the output stream using the flush() method.

```
// Flus the output stream
fos.flush();
```

Flushing an output stream indicates that if any written bytes were buffered, they may be written to the data sink. For example, if the data sink is a file, you write bytes to a FileOutputStream, which is an abstraction of a file. The output stream passes the bytes to the operating system, which is responsible for writing them to the file. For a file output stream, if you call the flush() method, the output stream passes the bytes to the operating system for writing. It is up to the operating system when it writes the bytes to the file, If an implementation of an output stream buffers the written bytes, it flushes the bytes automatically when its buffer is full or when you close the output stream by calling its close() method.

Closing the Output Steam

Closing an output stream is similar to closing an input stream. You need to close the output stream using its close() method.

```
// Close the output stream
fos.close();
```

The close() method may throw an IOException. Use a try-with-resources to create an output stream if you want tit to be closed automatically.

Completing the Example

Listing 7-16 illustrates the steps involved in writing to a file named luci2.txt. If the file does not exist in your current directory, the program will create it. If it exists, it will be overwritten. The file path displayed in the output may be different when you run the program.

Listing 7-16. Writing Bytes to a File Output Stream

```java
// SimpleFileWriting.java
package com.jdojo.io;

import java.io.File;
import java.io.FileNotFoundException;
import java.io.FileOutputStream;
import java.io.IOException;

public class SimpleFileWriting {
        public static void main(String[] args) {
                String destFile = "luci2.txt";

                // Get the line separator for the current platform
                String lineSeparator = System.getProperty("line.separator");

                String line1 = "When she I loved look'd every day";
                String line2 = "Fresh as a rose in June," ;
```

```
            String line3 = "I to her cottage bent my way,";
            String line4 = "Beneath an evening moon.";

            try (FileOutputStream fos = new FileOutputStream(destFile)){
                    // Write all four lines to the output stream as bytes
                    fos.write(line1.getBytes());
                    fos.write(lineSeparator.getBytes());

                    fos.write(line2.getBytes());
                    fos.write(lineSeparator.getBytes());

                    fos.write(line3.getBytes());
                    fos.write(lineSeparator.getBytes());

                    fos.write(line4.getBytes());

                    // Flush the written bytes to the file
                    fos.flush();

                    // Display the output file path
                    System.out.println("Text has been written to " +
                                    (new File(destFile)).getAbsolutePath());
            }
            catch (FileNotFoundException e1) {
                    FileUtil.printFileNotFoundMsg(destFile);
            }
            catch (IOException e2) {
                    e2.printStackTrace();
            }
    }
}
```

```
Text has been written to C:\book\javabook\luci2.txt
```

Input Stream Meets the Decorator Pattern

Figure 7-5 depicts the class diagram that includes some commonly used input stream classes. You can refer to the API documentation of the java.io package for the complete list of the input stream classes. The comments in the class diagram compare input stream classes with the classes in the decorator pattern. Notice that the class diagram for the input streams is similar to the class diagram for your drink application, which was also based on the decorator pattern. Table 7-1 compares the classes in the decorator pattern, the drink application, and the input streams.

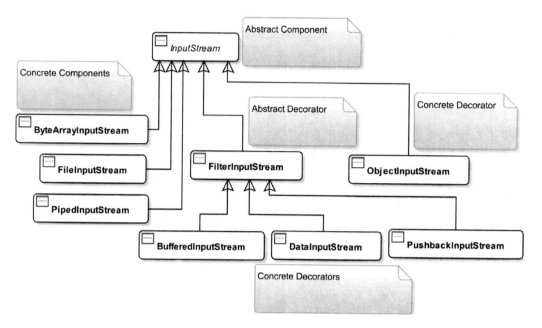

Figure 7-5. *Commonly used classes for input streams compared with the decorator pattern*

Table 7-1. *Comparing the Class Design in the Decorator Pattern, the Drink Application, and Input Streams*

Decorator Pattern	Drink Application	Input Stream
Component	Drink	InputStream
ConcreteComponentA ConcreteComponentB	Rum Vodka Whisky	FileInputStream ByteArrayInputStream PipedInputStream
Decorator	DrinkDecorator	FilterInputStream
ConcreteDecoratorA ConcreteDecoratorB	Honey Spices	BufferedInputStream PushbackInputStream DataInputStream ObjectInputStream

The abstract base component is the InputStream class, which is similar to the Drink class. You have concrete component classes of FileInputStream, ByteArrayInputStream, and PipedInputStream, which are similar to the Rum, Vodka, and Whiskey classes. You have a FilterInputStream class, which is similar to the DrinkDecorator class. Notice the decorator class in the input stream family does not use the word "Decorator" in its class name; it is named as FilterInputStream instead. It is also not declared abstract as you had declared the DrinkDecorator class. Not declaring it abstract seems to be an inconsistency in the class design. You have concrete decorator classes of BufferedInputStream, DataInputStream, and PushbackInputStream, which are similar to the Honey and Spices classes in the drink application. One noticeable difference is that the ObjectInputStream class is a concrete decorator and it is inherited from the abstract component InputStream, not from the abstract decorator FilterInputStream. Note that the requirement for a concrete decorator is that it should have the abstract component class in its immediate or non-immediate superclass and it should have a constructor that accepts an abstract component as its argument. The ObjectInputStream class fulfills these requirements.

Once you understand that the class design for input streams in Java I/O is based on the decorator pattern, it should be easy to construct an input stream using these classes. The superclass InputStream contains the basic methods to read data from an input stream, which are supported by all concrete component classes as well as all concrete decorator classes. The basic operation on an input stream is to read data from it. Some important methods defined in the InputStream class are listed in Table 7-2. Note that you have already used two of these methods, read() and close(), in the SimpleFileReading class to read data from a file.

Table 7-2. *Some Important Methods of the InputStream Class*

Method	Description
read()	Reads one byte from the input stream and returns the read byte as an int. It returns –1 when the end of the input stream is reached.
read(byte[] buffer)	Reads maximum up to the length of the specified buffer. It returns the number of bytes read in the buffer. It returns –1 if the end of the input stream is reached.
read(byte[] buffer, int offset, int length)	Reads maximum up to the specified length bytes. The data is written in the buffer starting from the offset index. It returns the number of bytes read or –1 if the end of the input stream is reached.

Note: The read() method blocks until the input data is available for reading, the end of the input stream is reached, or an exception is thrown.

close()	Closes the input stream
available()	Returns the estimated number of bytes that can be read from this input stream without blocking.

Let's briefly discuss the four input stream concrete decorators: BufferedInputStream, PushbackInputStream, DataInputStream, and ObjectInputStream. I will discuss BufferedInputStream and PushbackInputStream in this section. I will discuss DataInputStream in the "Reading and Writing Primitive Data Types" section. I will discuss ObjectInputStream in the "Object" section.

BufferedInputStream

A BufferedInputStream adds functionality to an input stream by buffering the data. It maintains an internal buffer to store bytes read from the underlying input stream. When bytes are read from an input stream, the BufferedInputStream reads more bytes than requested and buffers them in its internally maintained buffer. When a byte read is requested, it checks if the requested byte already exists in its buffer. If the requested byte exists in its buffer, it returns the byte from its buffer. Otherwise, it reads some more bytes in its buffer and returns only the requested bytes. It also adds support for the mark and reset operations on an input stream to let you reread bytes from an input stream. The main benefit of using BufferedInputStream is faster speed because of buffering.

Listing 7-17 demonstrates how to use a BufferedInputStream to read contents of a file. The code in this listing reads the text in the luci1.txt file. The only difference between SimpleFileReading in Listing 7-15 and BufferedFileReading in Listing 7-17 is that the latter uses a decorator BufferedInputStream for a FileInputStream and the former simply uses a FileInputStream. In SimpleFileReading, you construct the input stream as follows:

```
String srcFile = "luci1.txt";
FileInputStream fis = new FileInputStream(srcFile);
```

In BufferedFileReading, you construct the input stream as follows:

```
String srcFile = "luci1.txt";
BufferedInputStream bis = new BufferedInputStream(new FileInputStream(srcFile));
```

You may not find any noticeable speed gain using BufferedFileReading over SimpleFileReading in this example because the file size is small. You are reading one byte at a time in both examples to keep the code simpler to read. You should be using another version of the read() method of the input stream so you can read more bytes at a time.

Listing 7-17. Reading from a File Using a BufferedInputStream for Faster Speed

```java
// BufferedFileReading.java
package com.jdojo.io;

import java.io.BufferedInputStream;
import java.io.FileInputStream;
import java.io.FileNotFoundException;
import java.io.IOException;

public class BufferedFileReading {
        public static void main(String[] args) {
                String srcFile = "luci1.txt";

                try (BufferedInputStream bis =
                        new BufferedInputStream(new FileInputStream(srcFile))) {
                        // Read one byte at a time and display it
                        byte byteData;
                        while ((byteData = (byte) bis.read()) != -1) {
                                System.out.print((char) byteData);
                        }
                }
                catch (FileNotFoundException e1) {
                        FileUtil.printFileNotFoundMsg(srcFile);
                }
                catch (IOException e2) {
                        e2.printStackTrace();
                }
        }
}
```

```
STRANGE fits of passion have I known:
And I will dare to tell,
But in the lover's ear alone,
What once to me befell.
```

PushbackInputStream

A PushbackInputStream adds functionality to an input stream that lets you unread bytes (or push back the read bytes) using its unread() method. There are three versions of the unread() method. One lets you push back one byte and other two let you push back multiple bytes. If you call the read() method on the input stream after you have called its unread() method, you will first read those bytes that you have pushed back. Once all unread bytes are read again, you start reading fresh bytes from the input stream. For example, suppose your input stream contains a string of bytes, HELLO. If you read two bytes, you would have read HE. If you call unread((byte)'E') to push back the last byte you have read, the subsequent read will return E and the next reads will read LLO.

Listing 7-18 illustrates how to use the PushbackInputStream to unread bytes to the input stream and reread them. This example reads the first stanza of the poem *Lucy* by William Wordsworth from the luci1.txt in the current working directory. It reads each byte from the file twice as shown in the output. For example, STRANGE is read as SSTTRRAANNGGEE. You may notice a blank line between two lines because each new line is read twice.

Listing 7-18. Using the PushbackInputStream Class

```java
// PushbackFileReading.java
package com.jdojo.io;

import java.io.PushbackInputStream;
import java.io.FileInputStream;
import java.io.FileNotFoundException;
import java.io.IOException;

public class PushbackFileReading {
        public static void main(String[] args) {
                String srcFile = "luci1.txt";

                try (PushbackInputStream pis = new PushbackInputStream(
                        new FileInputStream(srcFile))) {

                        // Read one byte at a time and display it
                        byte byteData;
                        while ((byteData = (byte) pis.read()) != -1) {
                                System.out.print((char) byteData);

                                // Unread the last byte that we have just read
                                pis.unread(byteData);

                                // Reread the byte we unread (or pushed back)
                                byteData = (byte) pis.read();
                                System.out.print((char) byteData);
                        }
                }
                catch (FileNotFoundException e1) {
                        FileUtil.printFileNotFoundMsg(srcFile);
                }
                catch (IOException e2) {
                        e2.printStackTrace();
                }
        }
}
```

```
SSTTRRAANNGGEE  ffiittss  ooff  ppaassssiioonn  hhaavvee  II  kknnoowwnn::
AAnndd  II  wwiillll  ddaarree  ttoo  tteellll,,
BBuutt  iinn  tthhee  lloovveerr''ss  eeaarr  aalloonnee,,
WWhhaatt  oonnccee  ttoo  mmee  bbeeffeellll..
```

Output Stream Meets the Decorator Pattern

Figure 7-6 depicts the class diagram that includes some commonly used output stream classes. You can refer to the API documentation of the java.io package for the complete list of the output stream classes. The comments in the class diagram compare the output stream classes with the classes required to implement the decorator pattern. Notice that the class diagram for the output stream is similar to that of the input stream and the drink application.

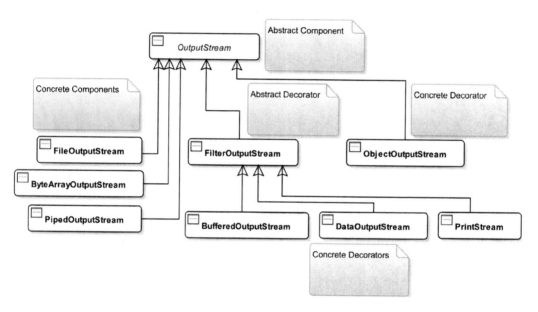

Figure 7-6. *Some commonly used classes for output streams compared with the decorator pattern*

Most of the times, if you know the name of the input stream class, you can get the corresponding output stream class by replacing the word "Input" in the class name with the word "Output." For example, for the FileInputStream class, you have a corresponding FileOutputStream class; for the BufferedInputStream class, you have a corresponding BufferedOutputStream class, and so on. You may not find a corresponding output stream class for every input stream class; for example, PushbackInputStream class has no corresponding output stream class. You may find some new classes that are not in the input stream class hierarchy because they do not make sense while reading data; for example, you have a new concrete decorator class PrintStream in the output stream class hierarchy. Table 7-3 compares the classes in the decorator pattern, your drink application, and the output streams.

Table 7-3. *Comparing Classes in the Decorator Pattern, the Drink Application, and the Output Streams*

Decorator Pattern	Drink Application	Output Stream
Component	Drink	OutputStream
ConcreteComponentA ConcreteComponentB	Rum Vodka Whisky	FileOutputStream ByteArrayOutputStream PipedOutputStream
Decorator	DrinkDecorator	FilterOutputStream
ConcreteDecoratorA ConcreteDecoratorB	Honey Spices	BufferedOutputStream DataOutputStream ObjectOutputStream

There are three important methods defined in the abstract superclass OutputStream: write(), flush(), and close(). The write() method is used to write bytes to an output stream. It has three versions that let you write one byte or multiple bytes at a time. You used it to write data to a file in the SimpleFileWriting class in Listing 7-16. The flush() method is used to flush any buffered bytes to the data sink. The close() method closes the output stream.

The technique to use concrete decorators with the concrete component classes for the output stream is the same as for the input stream classes. For example, to use the BufferedOutputStream decorator for better speed to write to a file, use the following statement:

```
BufferedOutputStream bos = new BufferedOutputStream(
                    new FileOutputStream("your output file path")
            );
```

To write data to a ByteArrayOutputStream, use

```
ByteArrayOutputStream baos = new ByteArrayOutputStream();
baos.write(buffer); // buffer is a byte array
```

ByteArrayOutputStream provides some important methods: reset(), size(), toString(), and writeTo(). The reset() method discards all bytes written to it; the size() method returns the number of bytes written to the stream; the toString() method returns the string representation of the bytes in the stream; the writeTo() method writes the bytes in the stream to another output stream. For example, if you have written some bytes to a ByteArrayOutputStream called baos and want to write its content to a file represented by FileOutputStream named fos, you would use the following statement:

```
// All bytes written to baos is written to fos
baos.writeTo(fos);
```

I will not discuss any more examples of writing to an output stream in this section. You can use SimpleFileWriting class in Listing 7-16 as an example to use any other output stream. You can use any output stream's concrete decorators by using them as an enclosing object for a concrete component or another concrete decorator. I will discuss DataOutputStream, ObjectOutputStream, and PrintStream classes with examples in subsequent sections.

PrintStream

The PrintStream class is a concrete decorator for the output stream as shown in Figure 7-6. It adds the following functionality to an output stream:

- It contains methods that let you print any data type values, primitive or object, in a suitable format for printing.

- Its methods to write data to the output stream do not throw an IOException. If a method call throws an IOException, it sets an internal flag, rather than throwing the exception to the caller. The flag can be checked using its checkError() method, which returns true if an IOException occurs during the method execution.

- It has an auto-flush capability. You can specify in its constructor that it should flush the contents written to it automatically. If you set the auto-flush flag to true, it will flush its contents when a byte array is written, one of its overloaded println() methods is used to write data, a newline character is written, or a byte ('\n') is written.

Some of the important methods in PrintStream class are as follows:

- print(Xxx arg)
- println(Xxx arg)
- printf()

Here Xxx is any primitive data type (int, char, float, etc.), String, or Object.

The print(Xxx arg) method writes the specified arg value to the output stream in a printable format. For example, you can use print(10) to write an integer to an output stream. Xxx also includes two reference types: String and Object. If your argument is an object, the toString() method on that object is called, and the returned string is written to the output stream. If the object type argument is null, a string "null" is written to the output stream. Note that all input and output streams are byte based. When I mention that the print stream writes a "null" string to the output stream, it means that the print stream converts the string "null" into bytes and writes those bytes to the output stream. The character-to-byte conversion is done based on the platform's default character encoding. You can also provide the character encoding to use for such conversions in some of the constructors of the PrintStream class.

The println(XXX arg) method works like the print(XXX arg) method with one difference. It appends a line separator string to the specified arg. That is, it writes an arg value and a line separator to the output stream. The method println() with no argument is used to write a line separator to the output stream. The line separator is platform dependent and it is determined by the system property line.separator.

The printf() method is used to write a formatted string to the output stream. For example, if you want to write a string in the form "Today is: <<today's date>>" to a output stream, you can use its printf() method as follows:

```
// Assuming that date format is mm/dd/yyyy and ps is the PrintStream object reference
ps.printf("Today is: %1$tm/%1$td/%1$tY", new java.time.LocalDate.now());
```

Listing 7-19 illustrates how to use a PrintStream to write to a file. It writes another stanza from the poem *Lucy* by William Wordsworth to a file named luci3.txt. The contents of the file after you run this program would be as follows:

```
Upon the moon I fix'd my eye,
All over the wide lea;
With quickening pace my horse drew nigh
Those paths so dear to me.
```

Listing 7-19 is very similar in structure to Listing 7-16. It creates a PrintStream object using the data sink file name. You can also create a PrintStream object using any other OutputStream object. You may notice that you do not have to handle the IOException in the catch block because unlike another output stream, a PrintStream object does not throw this exception. In addition, you use the println() and print() methods to write the four lines of text without worrying about converting them to bytes. If you want to use auto-flush in this program, you need to create the PrintStream object using another constructor as in

```
boolean autoFlush = true;
PrintStream ps = new PrintStream(new FileOutputStream(destFile), autoFlush);
```

Listing 7-19. Using the PrintStream Class to Write to a File

```java
// FileWritingWithPrintStream.java
package com.jdojo.io;

import java.io.File;
import java.io.FileNotFoundException;
import java.io.PrintStream;

public class FileWritingWithPrintStream {
        public static void main(String[] args) {
                String destFile = "luci3.txt";

                try (PrintStream ps = new PrintStream(destFile)) {
                        // Write data to the file. println() appends a new line
                        // and print() does not apend a new line
                        ps.println("Upon the moon I fix'd my eye,");
                        ps.println("All over the wide lea;");
                        ps.println("With quickening pace my horse drew nigh");
                        ps.print("Those paths so dear to me.");

                        // flush the print stream
                        ps.flush();

                        System.out.println("Text has been written to " +
                                        (new File(destFile).getAbsolutePath()));
                }
                catch (FileNotFoundException e1) {
                        FileUtil.printFileNotFoundMsg(destFile);
                }
        }
}
```

```
Text has been written to C:\book\javabook\luci3.txt
```

Using Pipes

A pipe connects an input stream and an output stream. A piped I/O is based on the producer-consumer pattern, where the producer produces data and the consumer consumes the data, without caring about each other. It works similar to a physical pipe, where you inject something at one end and gather it at the other end. In a piped I/O, you create two streams representing two ends of the pipe. A PipedOutputStream object represents one end and a PipedInputStream object the other end. You connect the two ends using the connect() method on the either object. You can also connect them by passing one object to the constructor when you create another object. You can imagine the logical arrangement of a piped input stream and a piped output stream as depicted in Figure 7-7.

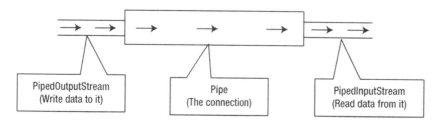

Figure 7-7. *The logical arrangement of piped input and output streams*

The following snippet of code shows two ways of creating and connecting the two ends of a pipe:

```
// Method #1: Create piped input and output streams and connect them
PipedInputStream pis = new PipedInputStream();
PipedOutputStream pos = new PipedOutputStream();
pis.connect(pos); /* Connect the two ends */

// Method #1: Create piped input and output streams and connect them
PipedInputStream pis = new PipedInputStream();
PipedOutputStream pos = new PipedOutputStream(pis);
```

You can produce and consume data after you connect the two ends of the pipe. You produce data by using one of the write() methods of the PipedOutputStream object. Whatever you write to the piped output stream automatically becomes available to the piped input stream object for reading. You use the read() method of PipedInputStream to read data from the pipe. The piped input stream is blocked if data is not available when it attempts to read from the pipe.

Have you wondered where the data is stored when you write it to a piped output stream? Similar to a physical pipe, a piped stream has a buffer with a fixed capacity to store data between the time it is written to and read from the pipe. You can set the pipe capacity when you create it. If a pipe's buffer is full, an attempt to write on the pipe will block.

```
// Create piped input and output streams with the buffer capacity of 2048 bytes
PipedOutputStream pos = new PipedOutputStream();
PipedInputStream pis = new PipedInputStream(pos, 2048);
```

■ **Tip** Typically, a pipe is used to transfer data from one thread to another. One thread will produce data and another thread will consume the data. Note that the synchronization between two threads is taken care of by the blocking read and write.

Listing 7-20 demonstrates how to use a piped I/O. The main() method creates and connects a piped input and a piped output stream. The piped output stream is passed to the produceData() method, producing numbers from 1 to 50. The thread sleeps for a half second after producing a number. The consumeData() method reads data from the piped input stream. I used a quick and dirty way of handling the exceptions to keep the code smaller and readable. Data is produced and read in two separate threads.

Listing 7-20. Using Piped Input and Output Streams

```
// PipedStreamTest.java
package com.jdojo.io;

import java.io.PipedInputStream;
import java.io.PipedOutputStream;

public class PipedStreamTest {
        public static void main(String[] args) throws Exception {
                // Create and connect piped input and output streams
                PipedInputStream pis = new PipedInputStream();
                PipedOutputStream pos = new PipedOutputStream();
                pos.connect(pis);

                // Creates and starts two threads, one to produce data (write data)
                // and one to consume data (read data)
                Runnable producer = () -> produceData(pos);
                Runnable consumer = () -> consumeData(pis);
                new Thread(producer).start();
                new Thread(consumer).start();
        }

        public static void produceData(PipedOutputStream pos) {
                try {
                        for (int i = 1; i <= 50; i++) {
                                pos.write((byte) i);
                                pos.flush();
                                System.out.println("Writing: " + i);
                                Thread.sleep(500);
                        }
                        pos.close();
                }
                catch (Exception e) {
                        e.printStackTrace();
                }
        }
```

```
        public static void consumeData(PipedInputStream pis) {
            try {
                    int num = -1;
                    while ((num = pis.read()) != -1) {
                            System.out.println("Reading: " + num);
                    }
                    pis.close();
            }
            catch (Exception e) {
                    e.printStackTrace();
            }

        }
}
```

```
Writing: 1
Reading: 1
...
Writing: 50
Reading: 50
```

Reading and Writing Primitive Data Types

An object of the DataInputStream class is used to read Java primitive data type values in a machine-independent way from an input stream. An object of the DataOutputStream class is used to write Java primitive data type values in a machine-independent way to an output stream.

The DataInputStream class contains readXxx() methods to read a value of data type Xxx, where Xxx is a Java primitive data type such as int, char, etc. For example, to read an int value, it contains a readInt() method; to read a char value, it has a readChar() method, etc. It also supports reading strings using the readUTF() method.

The DataOutputStream class contains a writeXxx(Xxx value) method corresponding to each the readXxx() method of the DataInputStream class, where Xxx is a Java primitive data type. It supports writing a string to an output stream using the writeUTF(String text) method. Note that these classes are concrete decorators, which provide you a convenient way to read and write Java primitive data type values and strings using input and output streams, respectively. You must have an underlying concrete component linked to a data source or a data sink to use these classes. For example, to write Java primitive data type values to a file named primitives.dat, you construct an object of DataOutputStream as follows:

```
DataOutputStream dos = new DataOutputStream(new FileOutputStream("primitives.dat"));
```

Listing 7-21 writes an int value, a double value, a boolean value, and a string to a file named primitives.dat. The file path in the output may be different when you run this program. Listing 7-22 reads those values back. Note that you must read the values using DataInputStream in the same order they were written using DataOutputStream. You need to run the WritingPrimitives class before you run the ReadingPrimitives class.

Listing 7-21. Writing Java Primitive Values and Strings to a File

```java
// WritingPrimitives.java
package com.jdojo.io;

import java.io.DataOutputStream;
import java.io.File;
import java.io.FileNotFoundException;
import java.io.FileOutputStream;
import java.io.IOException;

public class WritingPrimitives {
        public static void main(String[] args) {
                String destFile = "primitives.dat";

                try (DataOutputStream dos = new DataOutputStream(
                                        new FileOutputStream(destFile))) {

                        // Write some primitive values and a string
                        dos.writeInt(765);
                        dos.writeDouble(6789.50);
                        dos.writeBoolean(true);
                        dos.writeUTF("Java Input/Output is cool!");

                        // Flush the written data to the file
                        dos.flush();

                        System.out.println("Data has been written to " +
                                        (new File(destFile)).getAbsolutePath() );
                }
                catch (FileNotFoundException e) {
                        FileUtil.printFileNotFoundMsg(destFile);
                }
                catch (IOException e) {
                        e.printStackTrace();
                }
        }
}
```

```
Data has been written to C:\book\javabook\primitives.dat
```

Listing 7-22. Reading Primitive Values and Strings from a File

```java
// ReadingPrimitives.java
package com.jdojo.io;

import java.io.IOException;
import java.io.FileInputStream;
import java.io.FileNotFoundException;
import java.io.DataInputStream;
```

```java
public class ReadingPrimitives {
        public static void main(String[] args) {
                String srcFile = "primitives.dat";

                try (DataInputStream dis = new DataInputStream(
                        new FileInputStream(srcFile))) {
                        // Read the data in the same order they were written
                        int intValue = dis.readInt();
                        double doubleValue = dis.readDouble();
                        boolean booleanValue = dis.readBoolean();
                        String msg = dis.readUTF();

                        System.out.println(intValue);
                        System.out.println(doubleValue);
                        System.out.println(booleanValue);
                        System.out.println(msg);
                }
                catch (FileNotFoundException e) {
                        FileUtil.printFileNotFoundMsg(srcFile);
                }
                catch (IOException e) {
                        e.printStackTrace();
                }
        }
}
```

```
765
6789.5
true
Java Input/Output is cool!
```

Object Serialization

You create an object using the new operator. For example, if you have a Person class that accepts a person's name, gender, and height as arguments in its constructor, you can create a Person object as follows:

```java
Person john = new Person("John", "Male", 6.7);
```

What would you do if you wanted to save the object john to a file and later restore it in memory without using the new operator again? You have not learned how to do it yet. This is the subject of the discussion in this section.

The process of converting an object in memory to a sequence of bytes and storing the sequence of bytes in a storage medium such as a file is called *object serialization*. You can store the sequence of bytes to permanent storage such as a file or a database. You can also transmit the sequence of bytes over a network. The process of reading the sequence of bytes produced by a serialization process and restoring the object back in memory is called *object deserialization*. The serialization of an object is also known as *deflating* or *marshalling* the object. The deserialization of an object is also known as *inflating* or *unmarshalling* the object. You can think of serialization as writing an object from memory to a storage medium and deserialization as reading an object into memory from a storage medium.

An object of the ObjectOutputStream class is used to serialize an object. An object of the ObjectInputStream class is used to deserialize an object. You can also use objects of these classes to serialize values of the primitive data types such as int, double, boolean, etc.

The ObjectOutputStream and ObjectInputStream classes are the concrete decorator classes for output and input streams, respectively. However, they are not inherited from their abstract decorator classes. They are inherited from their respective abstract component classes. ObjectOutputStream is inherited from OutputStream and ObjectInputStream is inherited from InputStream. This seems to be an inconsistency. However, this still fits into the decorator pattern.

Your class must implement the Serializable or Externalizable interface to be serialized or deserialized. The Serializable interface is a marker interface. If you want the objects of a Person class to be serialized, you need to declare the Person class as follows:

```
public class Person implements Serializable {
        // Code for the Person class goes here
}
```

Java takes care of the details of reading/writing a Serializable object from/to a stream. You just need to pass the object to write/read to/from a stream to one of the methods of the stream classes.

Implementing the Externalizable interface gives you more control in reading and writing objects from/to a stream. It inherits the Serializable interface. It is declared as follows:

```
public interface Externalizable extends Serializable {
        void readExternal(ObjectInput in) throws IOException, ClassNotFoundException;
        void writeExternal(ObjectOutput out) throws IOException;
}
```

Java calls the readExternal() method when you read an object from a stream. It calls the writeExternal() method when you write an object to a stream. You have to write the logic to read and write an object's fields inside the readExternal() and writeExternal() methods, respectively. Your class implementing the Externalizable interface looks like the following:

```
public class Person implements Externalizable {
        public void readExternal(ObjectInput in) throws IOException, ClassNotFoundException {
                // Write the logic to read the Person object fields from the stream
        }

        public void writeExternal(ObjectOutput out) throws IOException {
                // Write the logic to write Person object fields to the stream
        }
}
```

Serializing Objects

To serialize an object, you need to perform the following steps:

- Have the references of the objects to be serialized.
- Create an object output stream for the storage medium to which the objects will be written.
- Write objects to the output stream.
- Close the object output stream.

Create an object of the ObjectOutputStream class by using it as a decorator for another output stream that represents the storage medium to save the object. For example, to save an object to a person.ser file, create an object output stream as follows:

```
// Create an object output stream to write objects to a file
ObjectOutputStream oos = new ObjectOutputStream(new FileOutputStream("person.ser"));
```

To save an object to a ByteArrayOutputStream, you construct an object output stream as follows:

```
// Creates a byte array output stream to write data to
ByteArrayOutputStream baos = new ByteArrayOutputStream();
```

```
// Creates an object output stream to write objects to the byte array output stream
ObjectOutputStream oos = new ObjectOutputStream(baos);
```

Use the writeObject() method of the ObjectOutputStream class to serialize the object by passing the object reference as an argument, like so:

```
// Serializes the john object
oos.writeObject(john);
```

Finally, use the close() method to close the object output stream when you are done writing all objects to it:

```
// Close the object output stream
oos.close();
```

Listing 7-23 defines a Person class that implements the Serializable interface. The Person class contains three fields: name, gender, and height. It overrides the toString() method and returns the Person description using the three fields. I have not added getters and setters for the fields in the Person class to keep the class short and simple. Listing 7-24 demonstrates how to write Person objects to a person.ser file. The output displays the objects written to the file and the absolute path of the file, which may be different on your machine.

Listing 7-23. A Person Class That Implements the Serializable Interface

```
// Person.java
package com.jdojo.io;

import java.io.Serializable;

public class Person implements Serializable {
        private String name   = "Unknown";
        private String gender = "Unknown" ;
        private double height = Double.NaN;

        public Person(String name, String gender, double height) {
                this.name = name;
                this.gender = gender;
                this.height = height;
        }
```

```java
        @Override
        public String toString() {
                return "Name: " + this.name + ", Gender: " + this.gender +
                        ", Height: " + this.height;
        }
}
```

Listing 7-24. Serializing an Object

```java
// PersonSerializationTest.java
package com.jdojo.io;

import java.io.File;
import java.io.FileOutputStream;
import java.io.IOException;
import java.io.ObjectOutputStream;

public class PersonSerializationTest {
        public static void main(String[] args) {
                // Create three Person objects
                Person john = new Person("John", "Male", 6.7);
                Person wally = new Person("Wally", "Male", 5.7);
                Person katrina = new Person("Katrina", "Female", 5.4);

                // The output file
                File fileObject = new File("person.ser");

                try (ObjectOutputStream oos =
                        new ObjectOutputStream(new FileOutputStream(fileObject))) {

                        // Write (or serialize) the objects to the object output stream
                        oos.writeObject(john);
                        oos.writeObject(wally);
                        oos.writeObject(katrina);

                        // Display the serialized objects on the standard output
                        System.out.println(john);
                        System.out.println(wally);
                        System.out.println(katrina);

                        // Print the output path
                        System.out.println("Objects were written to " +
                                                fileObject.getAbsolutePath());
                }
                catch (IOException e) {
                        e.printStackTrace();
                }
        }
}
```

Name: John, Gender: Male, Height: 6.7
Name: Wally, Gender: Male, Height: 5.7
Name: Katrina, Gender: Female, Height: 5.4
Objects were written to C:\book\javabook\person.ser

Deserializing Objects

It is time to read the objects back from the person.ser file. Reading a serialized object is just the opposite of serializing it. To deserialize an object, you need to perform the following steps:

- Create an object input stream for the storage medium from which objects will be read.

- Read the objects.

- Close the object input stream.

Create an object of the ObjectInputStream class by using it as a decorator for another input stream that represents the storage medium where serialized objects are stored. For example, to read an object from a person.ser file, create an object input stream as follows:

```
// Create an object input stream to read objects from a file
ObjectInputStream ois = new ObjectInputStream(new FileInputStream("person.ser"));
```

To read objects from a ByteArrayInputStream, create an object output stream as follows:

```
// Create an obejct input stream to read obejcts from a byte array input stream
ObjectInputStream ois = new ObjectInputStream(Byte-Array-Input-Stream-Reference);
```

Use the readObject() method of the ObjectInputStream class to deserialize the object, like so:

```
// Read an object from the stream
Object obj = oos.readObject();
```

Make sure to call the readObject() method to read objects in the same order you called the writeObject() method to write objects. For example, if you wrote three pieces of information in the order object-1, a float, and object-2, you must read them in the same order: object-1, a float, and object-2.

Finally, close the object input stream as follows:

```
// Close the object input stream
ois.close();
```

Listing 7-25 demonstrates how to read objects from the person.ser file. Make sure that the person.ser file exists in your current directory. Otherwise, the program will print an error message with the expected location of this file.

Listing 7-25. Reading Objects from a File

```
// PersonDeserializationTest.java
package com.jdojo.io;

import java.io.File;
import java.io.FileInputStream;
```

```
import java.io.FileNotFoundException;
import java.io.IOException;
import java.io.ObjectInputStream;

public class PersonDeserializationTest {
        public static void main(String[] args) {
                // The input file
                File fileObject = new File("person.ser");

                try (ObjectInputStream ois =
                        new ObjectInputStream(new FileInputStream(fileObject))) {

                        // Read (or deserialize) the three objects
                        Person john = (Person)ois.readObject();
                        Person wally = (Person)ois.readObject();
                        Person katrina = (Person)ois.readObject();

                        // Let's display the objects that are read
                        System.out.println(john);
                        System.out.println(wally);
                        System.out.println(katrina);

                        // Print the input path
                        System.out.println("Objects were read from " +
                                        fileObject.getAbsolutePath());
                }
                catch(FileNotFoundException e) {
                        FileUtil.printFileNotFoundMsg(fileObject.getPath());
                }
                catch(ClassNotFoundException | IOException e) {
                        e.printStackTrace();
                }
        }
}
```

```
Name: John, Gender: Male, Height: 6.7
Name: Wally, Gender: Male, Height: 5.7
Name: Katrina, Gender: Female, Height: 5.4
Objects were read from C:\book\javabook\person.ser
```

Externalizable Object Serialization

In the previous sections, I showed you how to serialize and deserialize Serializable objects. In this section, I will show you how to serialize and deserialize Externalizable objects. I have modified the Person class to implement the Externalizable interface. The new class is called PersonExt and is shown in Listing 7-26.

Listing 7-26. A PersonExt Class That Implements the Externalizable Interface

```java
// PersonExt.java
package com.jdojo.io;

import java.io.Externalizable;
import java.io.IOException;
import java.io.ObjectInput;
import java.io.ObjectOutput;

public class PersonExt implements Externalizable {
        private String name   = "Unknown";
        private String gender = "Unknown" ;
        private double height = Double.NaN;

        // We must define a no-arg constructor for this class. It is
        // used to construct the object during deserialization process
        // before the readExternal() method of this class is called
        public PersonExt() {
        }

        public PersonExt(String name, String gender, double height) {
                this.name   = name;
                this.gender = gender;
                this.height = height;
        }

        // Override the toString() method to return the person description
        public String toString() {
                return "Name: " + this.name + ", Gender: " + this.gender +
                        ", Height: " + this.height ;
        }

        public void readExternal(ObjectInput in) throws IOException, ClassNotFoundException {
                // Read name and gender in the same order they were written
                this.name   = in.readUTF();
                this.gender = in.readUTF();
        }

        public void writeExternal(ObjectOutput out) throws IOException {
                // we write only the name and gender to the stream
                out.writeUTF(this.name);
                out.writeUTF(this.gender);
        }
}
```

Java will pass the reference of the object output stream and object input stream to the writeExternal() and readExternal() methods of the PersonExt class, respectively.

In the writeExternal() method, you write the name and gender fields to the object output stream. Note that the height field is not written to the object output stream. It means that you will not get the value of the height field back when you read the object from the stream in the readExternal() method. The writeUTF() method is used to write strings (name and gender) to the object output stream.

In the readExternal() method, you read the name and gender fields from the stream and set them in the name and gender instance variables.

Listing 7-27 and Listing 7-28 contain the serialization and deserialization logic for PersonExt objects. The output of Listing 7-28 demonstrates that the value of the height field is the default value (Double.NaN) after you deserialize a PersonExt object.

Here are the steps to take to serialize and deserialize an object using Externalizable interface:

- When you call the writeObject() method to write an Externalizable object, Java writes the identity of the object to the output stream, and calls the writeExternal() method of its class. You write the data related to the object to the output stream in the writeExternal() method. You have full control over what object-related data you write to the stream in this method. If you want to store some sensitive data, you may want to encrypt it before you write it to the stream and decrypt the data when you read it from the stream.

- When you call the readObject() method to read an Externalizable object, Java reads the identity of the object from the stream. Note that for an Externalizable object, Java writes only the object's identity to the output stream, not any details about its class definition. It uses the object class's no-args constructor to create the object. This is the reason that you must provide a no-args constructor for an Externalizable object. It calls the object's readExternal() method, so you can populate object's fields values.

Listing 7-27. Serializing PersonExt Objects That Implement the Externalizable Interface

```java
// PersonExtSerializationTest.java
package com.jdojo.io;

import java.io.File;
import java.io.FileOutputStream;
import java.io.IOException;
import java.io.ObjectOutputStream;

public class PersonExtSerializationTest {
    public static void main(String[] args) {
        // Create three Person objects
        PersonExt john = new PersonExt("John", "Male", 6.7);
        PersonExt wally = new PersonExt("Wally", "Male", 5.7);
        PersonExt katrina = new PersonExt("Katrina", "Female", 5.4);

        // The output file
        File fileObject = new File("personext.ser");

        try (ObjectOutputStream oos = new ObjectOutputStream (
                new FileOutputStream(fileObject))) {

            // Write (or serialize) the objects to the object output stream
            oos.writeObject(john);
            oos.writeObject(wally);
            oos.writeObject(katrina);

            // Display the serialized objects on the standard output
            System.out.println(john);
            System.out.println(wally);
            System.out.println(katrina);
```

```
                        // Print the output path
                        System.out.println("Objects were written to " +
                                            fileObject.getAbsolutePath());
                }
                catch(IOException e1) {
                        e1.printStackTrace();
                }
        }
}
```

```
Name: John, Gender: Male, Height: 6.7
Name: Wally, Gender: Male, Height: 5.7
Name: Katrina, Gender: Female, Height: 5.4
Objects were written to C:\book\javabook\personext.ser
```

Listing 7-28. Deserializing PersonExt Objects That Implement the Externalizable Interface

```
// PersonExtDeserializationTest.java
package com.jdojo.io;

import java.io.File;
import java.io.FileInputStream;
import java.io.FileNotFoundException;
import java.io.IOException;
import java.io.ObjectInputStream;

public class PersonExtDeserializationTest {
        public static void main(String[] args) {
                // The input file
                File fileObject = new File("personext.ser");

                try (ObjectInputStream ois
                        = new ObjectInputStream(new FileInputStream(fileObject))) {

                        // Read (or deserialize) the three objects
                        PersonExt john = (PersonExt) ois.readObject();
                        PersonExt wally = (PersonExt) ois.readObject();
                        PersonExt katrina = (PersonExt) ois.readObject();

                        // Let's display the objects that are read
                        System.out.println(john);
                        System.out.println(wally);
                        System.out.println(katrina);

                        // Print the input path
                        System.out.println("Objects were read from " +
                                            fileObject.getAbsolutePath());
                }
                catch (FileNotFoundException e) {
```

```
                    FileUtil.printFileNotFoundMsg(fileObject.getPath());
            }
            catch (ClassNotFoundException | IOException e) {
                    e.printStackTrace();
            }
        }
    }
}
```

```
Name: John, Gender: Male, Height: NaN
Name: Wally, Gender: Male, Height: NaN
Name: Katrina, Gender: Female, Height: NaN
Objects were read from C:\book\javabook\personext.ser
```

For a Serializable object, the JVM serializes only instance variables that are not declared as transient. I will discuss serializing transient variables in the next section. For an Externalizable object, you have full control over what pieces of data are serialized.

Serialization of transient Fields

The keyword transient is used to declare a class's field. As the literal meaning of the word "transient" implies, a transient field of a Serializable object is not serialized. The following code for an Employee class declares the ssn and salary fields as transient:

```
public class Employee implements Serializable {
        private String name;
        private String gender;
        private transient String ssn;
        private transient double salary;
}
```

The transient fields of a Serializable object are not serialized when you use the writeObject() method of the ObjectOutputStream class.

Note that if your object is Externalizable, not Serializable, declaring a field transient has no effect because you control what fields are serialized in the writeExternal() method. If you want transient fields of your class to be serialized, you need to declare the class Externalizable and write the transient fields to the output stream in the writeExternal() method of your class. I will not cover any examples of serializing transient fields because the logic will be the same as shown in Listing 7-26, except that you will declare some instance variables as transient and write them to the output stream in the writeExternal() method.

Advanced Object Serialization

The following sections discuss advanced serialization techniques. They are designed for experienced developers. If you are a beginner or an intermediate level developer, you may skip the following sections; you should, however, revisit them after you gain more experience with Java I/O.

Writing an Object More Than Once to a Stream

The JVM keeps track of object references it writes to the object output stream using the writeObject() method. Suppose you have a PersonMutable object named john and you use an ObjectOutputStream object oos to write it to a file as follows:

```
PersonMutable john = new PersonMutable("John", "Male", 6.7);
oos.writeObject(john);
```

At this time, Java makes a note that the object john has been written to the stream. You may want to change some attributes of the john and write it to the stream again as follows:

```
john.setName("John Jacobs");
john.setHeight(5.9);
oos.writeObject(john);
```

At this time, Java does not write the john object to the stream. Rather, the JVM back references it to the john object that you wrote the first time. That is, all changes made to the name and height fields are not written to the stream separately. Both writes for the john object share the same object in the written stream. When you read the objects back, both objects will have the same name, gender, and height.

An object is not written more than once to a stream to keep the size of the serialized objects smaller. Listing 7-29 shows this process. The MultipleSerialization class as shown in Listing 7-30, in its serialize() method, writes an object, changes object's attributes, and serializes the same object again. It reads the objects in its deserialize() method. The output shows that Java did not write the changes made to the object when it wrote the object the second time.

Listing 7-29. A MutablePerson Class Whose Name and Height Can Be Changed

```java
// MutablePerson.java
package com.jdojo.io;

import java.io.Serializable;

public class MutablePerson implements Serializable {
        private String name   = "Unknown";
        private String gender = "Unknown" ;
        private double height = Double.NaN;

        public MutablePerson(String name, String gender, double height) {
                this.name   = name;
                this.gender = gender;
                this.height = height;
        }

        public void setName(String name) {
                this.name = name;
        }

        public String getName() {
                return name;
        }
```

```java
        public void setHeight(double height) {
                this.height = height;
        }

        public double getHeight() {
                return height;
        }

        public String toString() {
                return "Name: " + this.name + ", Gender: " + this.gender +
                        ", Height: " + this.height ;
        }
}
```

Listing 7-30. Writing an Object Multiple Times to the Same Output Stream

```java
// MultipleSerialization.java
package com.jdojo.io;

import java.io.File;
import java.io.FileInputStream;
import java.io.FileOutputStream;
import java.io.IOException;
import java.io.ObjectInputStream;
import java.io.ObjectOutputStream;

public class MultipleSerialization {
        public static void main(String[] args) {
                String fileName = "mutableperson.ser";

                // Write the same object twice to the stream
                serialize(fileName);

                System.out.println("-------------------------------------");

                // Read the two objects back
                deserialize(fileName);
        }

        public static void serialize(String fileName) {
                // Create a MutablePerson objects
                MutablePerson john = new MutablePerson("John", "Male", 6.7);

                File fileObject = new File(fileName);
                try (ObjectOutputStream oos =
                        new ObjectOutputStream(new FileOutputStream(fileObject))) {

                        // Let's display the objects we have serialized on the console
                        System.out.println("Objects are written to " +
                                        fileObject.getAbsolutePath());
```

```
                        // Write the john object first time to the stream
                        oos.writeObject(john);
                        System.out.println(john); // Display what we wrote

                        // Change john object's name and height
                        john.setName("John Jacobs");
                        john.setHeight(6.9);

                        // Write john object again with changed name and height
                        oos.writeObject(john);
                        System.out.println(john); // display what we wrote again

                }
                catch(IOException e1) {
                        e1.printStackTrace();
                }
        }

        public static void deserialize(String fileName) {
                // personmutable.ser file must exist in the current directory
                File fileObject = new File(fileName);

                try (ObjectInputStream ois =
                        new ObjectInputStream(new FileInputStream(fileObject))) {

                        // Read the two objects that were written in the serialize() method
                        MutablePerson john1 = (MutablePerson)ois.readObject();
                        MutablePerson john2 = (MutablePerson)ois.readObject();

                        // Display the objects
                        System.out.println("Objects are read from " +
                                                fileObject.getAbsolutePath());
                        System.out.println(john1);
                        System.out.println(john2);
                }
                catch(IOException | ClassNotFoundException e) {
                        e.printStackTrace();
                }
        }
}
```

```
Objects are written to C:\book\javabook\mutableperson.ser
Name: John, Gender: Male, Height: 6.7
Name: John Jacobs, Gender: Male, Height: 6.9
--------------------------------------
Objects are read from C:\book\javabook\mutableperson.ser
Name: John, Gender: Male, Height: 6.7
Name: John, Gender: Male, Height: 6.7
```

If you do not want Java to share an object reference, use the writeUnshared() method instead of the writeObject() method of the ObjectOutputStream class to serialize an object. An object written using the writeUnshared() method is not shared or back referenced by any subsequent call to the writeObject() method or the writeUnshared() method on the same object. You should read the object that was written using the writeUnshared() using the readUnshared() method of the ObjectInputStream class. If you replace the call to writeObject() with writeUnshared() and the call to readObject() with readUnshared() in MutipleSerialization class, you get the changed state of the object back when you read the object again.

You can control the serialization of a Serializable object in another way by defining a field named serialPersistentFields, which is an array of ObjectStreamField objects. This field must be declared private, static, and final. It declares that all the fields mentioned in this array are serializable. Note that this is just the opposite of using the transient keyword with a field. When you use a transient keyword, you state that this field is not serializable, whereas by declaring a serialPersistentFields array, you state that these fields are serializable. The declaration of serialPersistentFields takes over the declaration of transient fields in a class. For example, if you declare a field transient and include that field in the serialPersistentFields field, that field will be serialized. The following snippet of code shows how to declare a serialPersistentFields field in a Person class:

```
class Person implements Serializable {
        private String name;
        private String gender;
        private double height;

        // Declare that only name and height fields are serializable
        private static final ObjectStreamField[] serialPersistentFields
                = {new ObjectStreamField("name", String.class),
                   new ObjectStreamField("height", double.class)};
}
```

Class Evolution and Object Serialization

Your class may evolve (or change) over time. For example, you may remove an existing field or a method from a class. You may add new fields or methods to a class. During an object serialization, Java uses a number that is unique for the class of the object you serialize. This unique number is called the *serial version unique ID* (SUID). Java computes this number by computing the hash code of the class definition. If you change the class definition such as by adding new fields, the SUID for the class will change. When you serialize an object, Java also saves the class information to the stream. When you deserialize the object, Java computes the SUID for the class of the object being deserialized by reading the class definition from the stream. It compares the SUID computed from the stream with the SUID of the class loaded into the JVM. If you change the definition of the class after you serialize an object of that class, the two numbers will not match and you will get a java.io.InvalidClassException during the deserialization process. If you never serialize the objects of your class or you never change your class definition after you serialize the objects and before you deserialize them, you do not need to worry about the SUID of your class. What should you do to make your objects deserialize properly, even if you change your class definition, after serializing objects of your class? You should declare a private, static, and final instance variable in your class that must be of the long type and named serialVersionUID.

```
public class MyClass {
        // Declare the SUID field. L in "801890L" denotes a long value
        private static final long serialVersionUID = 801890L;

        // More code goes here
}
```

The MyClass uses 801890 as the value for serialVersionUID. This number was chosen arbitrarily. It does not matter what number you choose for this field. The JDK ships with a serialver tool that you can use to generate the value for the serialVersionUID field of your class. You can use this tool at the command prompt as follows:

```
serialver -classpath <your-class-path> <your-class-name>
```

When you run this tool with your class name, it prints the declaration of the serialVersionUID field for your class with the generated SUID for it. You just need to copy and paste that declaration into your class declaration.

■ **Tip** Suppose you have a class that does not contain a serialVersionUID field and you have serialized its object. If you change your class and try to deserialize the object, the Java runtime will print an error message with the expected serialVersionUID. You need to add the serialVersionUID field in your class with the same value and try deserializing the objects.

Stopping Serialization

How do you stop the serialization of objects of your class? Not implementing the Serializable interface in your class seems to be an obvious answer. However, it is not a valid answer in all situations. For example, if you inherit your class from an existing class that implements the Serializable interface, your class implements the Serializable interface implicitly. This makes your class automatically serializable. To stop objects of your class from being serialized all the time, you can add writeObject() and readObject() methods in your class. These methods should simply throw an exception. Note that in Listing 7-31 you are implementing the Serializable interface and still it is not serializable because you are throwing an exception in the readObject() and writeObject() methods.

Listing 7-31. Stopping a Class from Serializing

```java
// NotSerializable.java
package com.jdojo.io;

import java.io.IOException;
import java.io.ObjectInputStream;
import java.io.ObjectOutputStream;
import java.io.Serializable;

public class NotSerializable implements Serializable {
        private void readObject(ObjectInputStream ois)
                        throws IOException, ClassNotFoundException {
                // Throw an exception
                throw new IOException("Not meant for serialization!!!");
        }

        private void writeObject(ObjectOutputStream os) throws IOException {
                // Throw an exception
                throw new IOException("Not meant for serialization!!!");
        }

        // Other code for the class goes here
}
```

Readers and Writers

Input and output streams are byte-based streams. In this section, I will discuss readers and writers, which are character-based streams. A reader is used when you want to read character-based data from a data source. A writer is used when you want to write character-based data to a data sink.

Figure 7-8 and Figure 7-9 show some classes, and the relationship between them, for the Reader and Writer stream families. Recall that the input and output stream class names end with the words "InputStream" and "OutputStream," respectively. The Reader and Writer class names end with the words "Reader" and "Writer," respectively.

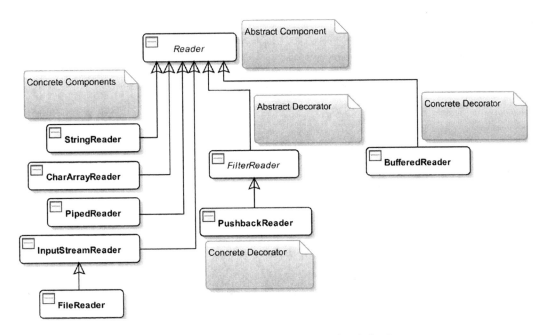

Figure 7-8. *Commonly used classes for Reader streams compared with the decorator pattern*

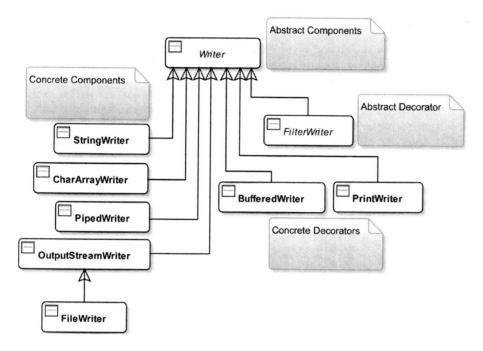

Figure 7-9. *Commonly used classes for Writer streams compared with the decorator pattern*

Table 7-4 and Table 7-5 compare classes in byte-based and character-bases input/output streams.

Table 7-4. *Comparing Classes in Byte-based and Character-based Input Streams*

Byte-based Input Stream Class	Character-based Input Stream Class
InputStream	Reader
ByteArrayInputStream	CharArrayReader
StringBufferInputStream	StringReader
PipedInputStream	PipedReader
FileInputStream	FileReader
No corresponding class	InputStreamReader
FilterInputStream	FilterReader
BufferedInputStream	BufferedReader
PushbackInputStream	PushbackReader
DataInputStream	No corresponding class
ObjectInputStream	No corresponding class

Table 7-5. *Comparing Classes from Byte-based Output Streams and Character-based Output Streams*

Byte-based Output Stream Class	Character-based Output Stream Class
OutputStream	Writer
ByteArrayOutputStream	CharArrayWriter
No corresponding class	StringWriter
PipedOutputStream	PipedWriter
FileOutputStream	FileWriter
No corresponding class	OutputStreamWriter
FilterOutputStream	FilterWriter
BufferedOutputStream	BufferedWriter
DataOutputStream	No corresponding class
ObjectOutputStream	No corresponding class
PrintStream	PrintWriter

Some of the classes in the byte-based input/output streams do not have the corresponding character-based classes and vice versa. For example, reading and writing primitive data and objects are always byte-based; therefore, you do not have any classes in the reader/writer class family corresponding to the data/object input/output streams.

I have discussed how to use the byte-based input/output classes in detail in the previous sections. You will find the classes in the reader/writer and the input/output categories similar. They are also based on the decorator pattern.

In the reader class hierarchy, BufferedReader, which is a concrete decorator, is directly inherited from the Reader class instead of the abstract decorator FilterReader class. In the writer class hierarchy, all concrete decorators have been inherited from the Writer class instead of the FilterWriter. No concrete decorator inherits the FilterWriter class.

The two classes, InputStreamReader and OutputStreamWriter, in the reader/writer class family provide the bridge between the byte-based and character-based streams. If you have an instance of InputStream and you want to get a Reader from it, you can get that by using the InputStreamReader class. That is, you need to use the InputStreamReader class if you have a stream that supplies bytes and you want to read characters by getting those bytes decoded into characters for you. For example, if you have an InputStream object called iso, and you want to get a Reader object instance, you can do so as follows:

```
// Create a Reader object from an InputStream object using the
// platform default encoding
Reader reader = new InputStreamReader(iso);
```

If you know the encoding used in the byte-based stream, you can specify it while creating a Reader object as follows:

```
// Create a Reader object from an InputStream using the "US-ASCII" encoding
Reader reader = new InputStreamReader(iso, "US-ASCII");
```

Similarly, you can create a Writer object to spit out characters from a bytes-based output stream as follows, assuming that oso is an OutputStream object:

```
// Create a Writer object from OutputStream using the platform default encoding
Writer writer = new OutputStreamWriter(oso);
```

```
// Create a Writer object from OutputStream using the "US-ASCII" encoding
Writer writer = new OutputStreamWriter(oso, "US-ASCII");
```

You do not have to write only a character at a time or a character array when using a writer. It has methods that let you write a String and a CharSequence object.

Let's write another stanza from the poem *Lucy* by William Wordsworth to a file and read it back into the program. This time, you will use a BufferedWriter to write the text and a BufferedReader to read the text back. Here are the four lines of text for the stanza:

```
And now we reach'd the orchard-plot;
And, as we climb'd the hill,
The sinking moon to Lucy's cot
Came near and nearer still.
```

The text is saved in a luci4.txt file in the current directory. Listing 7-32 illustrates how to use a Writer object to write the text to this file. You may get a different output when you run the program because it prints the path of the output file that depends on the current working directory.

Listing 7-32. Using a Writer Object to Write Text to a File

```java
// FileWritingWithWriter.java
package com.jdojo.io;

import java.io.BufferedWriter;
import java.io.File;
import java.io.FileNotFoundException;
import java.io.FileWriter;
import java.io.IOException;

public class FileWritingWithWriter {
    public static void main(String[] args) {
        // The output file
        String destFile = "luci4.txt";

        try (BufferedWriter bw = new BufferedWriter(new FileWriter(destFile))) {
            // Write the text to the writer
            bw.append("And now we reach'd the orchard-plot;");
            bw.newLine();
            bw.append("And, as we climb'd the hill,");
            bw.newLine();
            bw.append("The sinking moon to Lucy's cot");
            bw.newLine();
            bw.append("Came near and nearer still.");

            // Flush the written text
            bw.flush();

            System.out.println("Text was written to " +
                            (new File(destFile)).getAbsolutePath());
        }
        catch (FileNotFoundException e1) {
            FileUtil.printFileNotFoundMsg(destFile);
```

```
            }
            catch (IOException e2) {
                    e2.printStackTrace();
            }
        }
    }
}
```

Text was written to C:\book\javabook\luci4.txt

If you compare the code in this listing to any other listings, which write data to a stream, you will not find any basic differences. The differences lie only in using classes to construct the output stream. In this case, you used the BufferedWriter and FileWriter classes to construct a Writer object. You used the append() method of the Writer class to write the strings to the file. You can use the write() method or the append() method to write a string using a Writer object. However, the append() method supports writing any CharSequence object to the stream whereas the write() method supports writing only characters or a string. The BufferedWriter class provides a newLine() method to write a platform specific new line to the output stream.

How would you read the text written to the file luci4.txt using a Reader object? It's simple. Create a BufferedReader object by wrapping a FileReader object and read one line of text at a time using its readLine() method. The readLine() method considers a linefeed ('\n'), a carriage return ('\r'), and a carriage return immediately followed by a linefeed as a line terminator. It returns the text of the line excluding the line terminator. It returns null when the end of the stream is reached. The following is the snippet of code to read the text from the luci4.txt file. You can write the full program as an exercise.

```
String srcFile = "luci4.txt";
BufferedReader br = new BufferedReader(new FileReader(srcFile));
String text = null;

while ((text = br.readLine()) != null) {
    System.out.println(text);
}

br.close();
```

Converting a byte-based stream to a character-based stream is straightforward. If you have an InputStream object, you can get a Reader object by wrapping it inside an InputStreamReader object, like so:

```
InputStream is = create your InputStream object here;
Reader reader = new InputStreamReader(is);
```

If you want to construct a BufferedReader object from an InputStream object, you can do that as follows:

```
InputStream is = create your InputStream object here;
BufferedReader br = new BufferedReader(new InputStreamReader(is));
```

You can construct a Writer object from an OutputStream object as follows:

```
OutputStream os = create your OutputStream object here;
Writer writer = new OutputStreamWriter(os);
```

Custom Input/Output Streams

Can you have your own I/O classes? The answer is yes. How difficult is it to have your own I/O classes? It is not that difficult if you understand the decorator pattern. Having your own I/O class is just a matter of adding a concrete decorator class in the I/O class hierarchy. In this section, you will add a new reader class that is called LowerCaseReader. It will read characters from a character-based stream and convert all characters to lowercase.

The LowerCaseReader class is a concrete decorator class in the Reader class family. It should inherit from the FilterReader class. It needs to provide a constructor that will accept a Reader object.

```java
public class LowerCaseReader extends FilterReader {
        public LowerCaseReader(Reader in) {
                // Code for the constructor goes here
        }
        // More code goes here
}
```

There are two versions of the read() method in the FilterReader class to read characters from a character-based stream. You need to override just one version of the read() method as follows. All other versions of the read() method delegate the reading job to this one.

```java
public class LowerCaseReader extends FilterReader {
        public LowerCaseReader(Reader in) {
                // Code for the constructor goes here
        }

        @Override
        public int read(char[] cbuf, int off, int len) throws IOException {
                // Code goes here
        }
}
```

That is all it takes to have your own reader class. You can provide additional methods in your class, if needed. For example, you may want to have a readLine() method that will read a line in lowercase. Alternatively, you can also use the readLine() method of the BufferedReader class by wrapping an object of LowerCaseReader in a BufferedReader object. Using the new class is the same as using any other reader class. You can wrap a concrete reader component such as a FileReader or a concrete decorator such as a BufferedReader inside a LowerCaseReader object. Alternatively, you can wrap a LowerCaseReader object inside any other concrete reader decorator such as a BufferedReader.

■ **Tip**   The Reader class has four versions of the read() method. The read(), read(CharBuffer target), and read(char[] cbuf) methods call the read(char[] cbuf, int off, int len) methods. Therefore, you need to override only the read(char[] cbuf, int off, int len) methods to implement your LowerCaseReader class.

Listing 7-33 has the complete code for the new LowerCaseReader class.

Listing 7-33. A Custom Java I/O Reader Class Named LowerCaseReader

```java
// LowerCaseReader.java
package com.jdojo.io;

import java.io.Reader;
import java.io.FilterReader;
import java.io.IOException;

public class LowerCaseReader extends FilterReader{
        public LowerCaseReader(Reader in) {
                super(in);
        }

        @Override
        public int read(char[] cbuf, int off, int len) throws IOException {
                int count = super.read(cbuf, off, len);
                if (count != -1) {
                        // Convert all read characters to lowercase
                        int limit = off + count;
                        for (int i = off; i < limit; i++) {
                                cbuf[i] = Character.toLowerCase(cbuf[i]);
                        }
                }
                return count;
        }
}
```

Listing 7-34 shows how to use your new class. It reads from the file luci4.txt. It reads the file twice: the first time by using a LowerCaseReader object and the second time by wrapping a LowerCaseReader object inside a BufferedReader object. Note that while reading the licu4.txt file the second time, you are taking advantage of the readLine() method of the BufferedReader class. The test class throws an exception in the declaration of its main() method to keep the code readable. The luci4.txt file should exist in your current working directory. Otherwise, you will get an error when you run the test program.

Listing 7-34. Testing the Custom Reader Class, LowerCaseReader

```java
// LowerCaseReaderTest.java
package com.jdojo.io;

import java.io.FileReader;
import java.io.BufferedReader;

public class LowerCaseReaderTest {
        public static void main(String[] args) throws Exception {
                String fileName = "luci4.txt";
                LowerCaseReader lcr = new LowerCaseReader(new FileReader(fileName));

                System.out.println("Reading luci4.txt using LowerCaseReader:");
                int c = -1;
                while ((c = lcr.read()) != -1) {
                        System.out.print((char) c);
```

```
                    }
                    lcr.close();

                    System.out.println("\n\nReading luci4.txt using " +
                                       "LowerCaseReader and BufferedReader:");

                    BufferedReader br = new BufferedReader(
                            new LowerCaseReader(new FileReader(fileName)));

                    String str = null;
                    while ((str = br.readLine()) != null) {
                            System.out.println(str);
                    }
                    br.close();
          }
}
```

```
Reading luci4.txt using LowerCaseReader:
and now we reach'd the orchard-plot;
and, as we climb'd the hill,
the sinking moon to lucy's cot
came near and nearer still.

Reading luci4.txt using LowerCaseReader and BufferedReader:
and now we reach'd the orchard-plot;
and, as we climb'd the hill,
the sinking moon to lucy's cot
came near and nearer still.
```

Random Access Files

A FileInputStream lets you read data from a file whereas a FileOutputStream lets you write data to a file. A random access file is a combination of both. Using a random access file, you can read from a file as well as write to the file. Reading and writing using the file input and output streams are a sequential process. Using a random access file, you can read or write at any position within the file (hence the name random access).

An object of the RandomAccessFile class facilitates the random file access. It lets you read/write bytes and all primitive types values to a file. It also lets you work with strings using its readUTF() and writeUTF() methods. The RandomAccessFile class is not in the class hierarchy of the InputStream and OutputStream classes.

A random access file can be created in four different access modes. In its constructor, you must specify the access mode. The access mode value is a string. They are listed as follows:

- "r": The file is opened in a read-only mode. You will receive an IOException if you attempt to write to the file.

- "rw": The file is opened in a read-write mode. The file is created if it does not exist.

- "rws": Same as the "rw" mode, except that any modifications to the file's content and its metadata are written to the storage device immediately.

- "rwd": Same as the "rw" mode, except that any modifications to the file's content are written to the storage device immediately.

You create an instance of the RandomAccessFile class by specifying the file name and the access mode as shown:

```
RandomAccessFile raf = new RandomAccessFile("randomtest.txt", "rw");
```

A random access file has a file pointer that is advanced when you read data from it or write data to it. The file pointer is a kind of cursor where your next read or write will start. Its value indicates the distance of the cursor from the beginning of the file in byes. You can get the value of file pointer by using its getFilePointer() method. When you create an object of the RandomAccessFile class, the file pointer is set to zero, which indicates the beginning of the file. You can set the file pointer at a specific location in the file using the seek() method.

The length() method of a RandomAccessFile returns the current length of the file. You can extend or truncate a file by using its setLength() method. If you extend a file using this method, the contents of the extended portion of the file are not defined.

Reading from and writing to a random access file is performed the same way you have been reading/writing from/to any input and output streams. Listing 7-35 demonstrates the use of a random access file. When you run this program, it writes two things to a file: the file read counter, which keeps track of how many times a file has been read using this program, and a text message of "Hello World!". The program increments the counter value in the file every time it reads the file. The counter value keeps incrementing when you run this program repeatedly. You may get a different output every time you run this program.

Listing 7-35. Reading and Writing Files Using a RandomAccessFile Object

```java
// RandomAccessFileReadWrite.java
package com.jdojo.io;

import java.io.File;
import java.io.IOException;
import java.io.RandomAccessFile;

public class RandomAccessFileReadWrite {
        public static void main(String[] args) throws IOException {
                String fileName = "randomaccessfile.txt";
                File fileObject = new File(fileName);

                if (!fileObject.exists()) {
                        initialWrite(fileName);
                }

                // Read the file twice
                readFile(fileName);
                readFile(fileName);
        }

        public static void readFile(String fileName) throws IOException{
                // Open the file in read-write mode
                RandomAccessFile raf = new RandomAccessFile(fileName, "rw");

                int counter = raf.readInt();
                String msg = raf.readUTF();

                System.out.println("File Read Counter: " + counter);
                System.out.println("File Text: " + msg);
                System.out.println("--------------------------");
```

```
                    // Increment the file read counter by 1
                    incrementReadCounter(raf);

                    raf.close();
            }

        public static void incrementReadCounter(RandomAccessFile raf) throws IOException {
                    // Read the current file pointer position so that we can restore it at the end
                    long currentPosition = raf.getFilePointer();

                    // Set the file pointer in the beginning
                    raf.seek(0);

                    // Read the counter and increment it by 1
                    int counter = raf.readInt();
                    counter++;

                    // Set the file pointer to zero again to overwrite the value of the counter
                    raf.seek(0);
                    raf.writeInt(counter);

                    // Restore the file pointer
                    raf.seek(currentPosition);
            }

        public static void initialWrite(String fileName) throws IOException{
                    // Open the file in read-write mode
                    RandomAccessFile raf = new RandomAccessFile(fileName, "rw");

                    // Write the file read counter as zero
                    raf.writeInt(0);

                    // Write a message
                    raf.writeUTF("Hello world!");
                    raf.close();
            }
}
```

```
File Read Counter: 0
File Text: Hello world!
----------------------------
File Read Counter: 1
File Text: Hello world!
----------------------------
```

Copying the Contents of a File

After you learn about input and output streams, it is simple to write code that copies the contents of a file to another file. You need to use the byte-based input and output streams (InputStream and OutputStream objects) so that your file copy program will work on all kinds of files. The main logic in copying a file is to keep reading from the input stream until the end of file and keep writing to the output stream as data is read from the input stream. The following snippet of code shows this file-copy logic:

```
// Copy the contents of a file
int count = -1;
byte[] buffer = new byte[1024];
while ((count = in.read(buffer)) != -1) {
        out.write(buffer, 0, count);
}
```

■ **Tip**   The file-copy logic copies only the file's contents. You will have to write logic to copy file's attributes. The NIO 2.0 API, covered in Chapter 10, provides a copy() method in the java.nio.file.Files class to copy the contents and attributes of a file to another file. Please use the Files.copy() method to copy a file.

Standard Input/Output/Error Streams

A standard input device is a device defined and controlled by the operating system from where your Java program may receive the input. Similarly, the standard output and error are other operating system-defined (and controlled) devices where your program can send an output. Typically, a keyboard is a standard input device, and a console acts as a standard output and a standard error device. Figure 7-10 depicts the interaction between the standard input, output, and error devices, and a Java program.

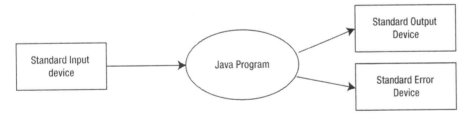

Figure 7-10. *Interaction between a Java program and standard input, output, and error devices*

What happens when you use the following statement to print a message?

```
System.out.println("This message goes to the standard output device!");
```

Typically, your message is printed on the console. In this case, the console is the standard output device and the Java program lets you send some data to the standard output device using a high level println() method call. You saw a similar kind of println() method call in the previous section when you used the PrintStream class that is a concrete decorator class in the OutputStream class family. Java makes interacting with a standard output device on a computer easier. It creates an object of the PrintStream class and gives you access to it through a public static variable out in the System class. Look at the code for the System class; it declares three public static variables (one for each device: standard input, output, and error) as follows:

```
public class System {
        public static PrintStream out; // the standard output
        public static InputStream in;  // the standard input
        public static PrintStream err; // the standard error

        // More code for the System class goes here
}
```

The JVM initializes the three variables to appropriate values. You can use the System.out and System.err object references wherever you can use an OutputStream object. You can use the System.in object wherever you can use an InputStream object.

Java lets you use these three objects in the System class in one more way. If you do not want the three objects to represent the standard input, output, and error devices, you can supply your own devices; Java will redirect the data flow to/from these objects to your devices.

Suppose, whenever you call the System.out.println() method to print a message on the console, you want to send all messages to a file instead. You can do so very easily. After all, System.out is just a PrintStream object and you know how to create a PrintStream object using a FileOutputStream object (refer to Listing 7-19) to write to a file. The System class provides three static setter methods, setOut(), setIn(), and setErr(), to replace these three standard devices with your own devices. To redirect all standard output to a file, you need to call the setOut() method by passing a PrintStream object that represents your file. If you want to redirect the output to a file named stdout.txt in your current directory, you do so by executing the following piece of code:

```
// Redirect all standard ouputs to the stdout.txt file
PrintStream ps = new PrintStream(new FileOutputStream("stdout.txt"));
System.setOut(ps);
```

Listing 7-36 demonstrates how to redirect the standard output to a file. You may get a different output on the console. You will see the following two messages in the stdout.txt file in your current working directory, after you run this program:

```
Hello world!
Java I/O is cool!
```

You may get a different output when you run the program as it prints the path to the stdout.txt file using your current working directory.

Listing 7-36. Redirecting Standard Outputs to a File

```
// CustomStdOut.java
package com.jdojo.io;

import java.io.PrintStream;
import java.io.FileOutputStream;
import java.io.File;

public class CustomStdOut {
        public static void main(String[] args) throws Exception{
                // Create a PrintStream for file stdout.txt
                File outFile = new File("stdout.txt");
                PrintStream ps = new PrintStream(new FileOutputStream(outFile));

                //Print a message on console
                System.out.println("Messages will be redirected to " +
                                outFile.getAbsolutePath());
```

```
        // Set the standard out to the file
        System.setOut(ps);

        // The following messages will be sent to the stdout.txt file
        System.out.println("Hello world!");
        System.out.println("Java I/O is cool!");
    }
}
```

Messages will be redirected to C:\book\javabook\stdout.txt

Generally, you use System.out.println() calls to log debugging messages. Suppose you have been using this statement all over your application and it is time to deploy your application to production. If you do not take out the debugging code from your program, it will keep printing messages on the user's console. You do not have time to go through all your code to remove the debugging code. Can you think of an easy solution? There is a simple solution to swallow all your debugging messages. You can redirect your debugging messages to a file as you did in Listing 7-36. Another solution is to create your own concrete component class in the OutputStream class family. Let's call the new class DummyStandardOutput, as shown in Listing 7-37.

Listing 7-37. *A Dummy Output Stream Class That Will Swallow All Written Data*

```
// DummyStandardOutput.java
package com.jdojo.io;

import java.io.OutputStream;
import java.io.IOException;

public class DummyStandardOutput extends OutputStream {
        public void write(int b) throws IOException {
                // Do not do anything. Swallow whatever is written
        }
}
```

You need to inherit the DummyStandardOutput class from the OutputStream class. The only code you have to write is to override the write(int b) method and do not do anything in this method. Then, create a PrintStream object by wrapping an object of the new class and set it as the standard output using the System.setOut() method shown in Listing 7-38. If you do not want to go for a new class, you can use an anonymous class to achieve the same result, as follows:

```
System.setOut(new PrintStream(new OutputStream() {
                        public void write(int b) {
                                // Do nothing
                }}));
```

Listing 7-38. *Swallowing All Data Sent to the Standard Output*

```
// SwallowOutput.java
package com.jdojo.io;

import java.io.PrintStream;

public class SwallowOutput {
```

```java
        public static void main(String[] args) {
                PrintStream ps = new PrintStream(new DummyStandardOutput());

                // Set the dummy standard output
                System.setOut(ps);

                // The following messages are not going anywhere
                System.out.println("Hello world!");
                System.out.println("Is someone listening?");
                System.out.println("No. We are all taking a nap!!!");
        }
}
```

(No output will be printed.)

You can use the System.in object to read data from a standard input device (usually a keyboard). You can also set the System.in object to read from any other InputStream object of your choice, such as a file. You can use the read() method of the InputStream class to read bytes from this stream. System.in.read() reads a byte at a time from the keyboard. Note that the read() method of the InputStream class blocks until data is available for reading. When a user enters data and presses the Enter key, the entered data becomes available, and the read() method returns one byte of data at a time. The last byte read will represent a new-line character. When you read a new-line character from the input device, you should stop further reading or the read() call will block until the user enters more data and presses the Enter key again. Listing 7-39 illustrates how to read data entered using the keyboard.

Listing 7-39. Reading from the Standard Input Device

```java
// EchoStdin.java
package com.jdojo.io;

import java.io.IOException;

public class EchoStdin {
        public static void main(String[] args) throws IOException{
                // Prompt the user to type a message
                System.out.print("Please type a message and press enter: ");

                // Display whatever user types in
                int c = '\n';
                while ((c = System.in.read()) != '\n') {
                        System.out.print((char) c);
                }
        }
}
```

Since System.in is an instance of InputStream, you can use any concrete decorator to read data from the keyboard; for example, you can create a BufferedReader object and read data from the keyboard one line at a time as string. Listing 7-40 illustrates how to use System.in object with a BufferedReader. Note that this is the kind of situation when you will need to use the InputStreamReader class to get a character-based stream (BufferedReader) from a byte-based stream (System.in). The program keeps prompting the user to enter some text until the user enters Q or q to quit the program.

Listing 7-40. Using System.in with a BufferedReader

```java
// EchoBufferedStdin.java
package com.jdojo.io;

import java.io.BufferedReader;
import java.io.InputStreamReader;
import java.io.IOException;

public class EchoBufferedStdin {
    public static void main(String[] args) throws IOException {
        // Get a BufferedReader from System.in object. Note the use of
        // InputStreamReader, the bridge class between the byte-based and
        // the character-based stream
        BufferedReader br = new BufferedReader(new InputStreamReader(System.in));

        String text = "q";
        while (true) {
            // Prompt user to type some text
            System.out.print("Please type a message (Q/q to quit) " +
                                "and press enter: ") ;

            // Read the text
            text = br.readLine();
            if (text.equalsIgnoreCase("q")) {
                System.out.println("You have decided to exit the program");
                break;
            }
            else {
                System.out.println("You typed: " + text);
            }
        }
    }
}
```

If you want your standard input to come from a file, you will have to create an input stream object to represent that file and set that object using the System.setIn() method as in

```java
FileInputStream fis = new FileInputStream("stdin.txt");
System.setIn(fis); // Now System.in.read() will read from stdin.txt file
```

The standard error device (generally the console) is used to display any error message. Its use in your program is the same as a standard output device. Instead of System.out for a standard output device, Java provides another PrintStream object called System.err. You use it as follows:

```java
System.err.println("This is an error message.");
```

Console and Scanner Classes

Although Java gives you three objects to represent the standard input, output, and error devices, it is not easy to use them for reading numbers from the standard input. The purpose of the Console class is to make the interaction between a Java program and the console easier. I will discuss the Console class in this section. I will also discuss the Scanner class used for parsing the text read from the console.

The Console class is a utility class in the java.io package that gives access to the system console, if any, associated with the JVM. The console is not guaranteed to be accessible in a Java program on all machines. For example, if your Java program is run as a service, no console will be associated to the JVM and you will not have access to it either. You get the instance of the Console class by using the static console() method of the System class as follows:

```
Console console = System.console();
if (console != null) {
        console.printf("Console is available.")
}
```

The Console class has a printf() method that is used to display formatted string on the console. You also have a printf() method in the PrintStream class to write the formatted data. Please refer to Chapter 13 in *Beginning Java Fundamentals* (ISBN: 978-1-4302-6652-5) for more details on using the printf() method and how to use the Formatter class to format text, numbers, and dates.

Listing 7-41 illustrates how to use the Console class. If the console is not available, it prints a message and the program exits. If you run this program using an IDE such as NetBeans, the console may not be available. Try to run this program using a command prompt. The program prompts the user to enter a user name and a password. If the user enters password *letmein*, the program prints a message. Otherwise, it prints that the password is not valid. The program uses the readLine() method to read a line of text from the console and the readPassword() method to read the password. Note that when the user enters a password, it is not visible; the program receives it in a character array.

Listing 7-41. Using the Console Class to Enter User Name and Password

```java
// ConsoleLogin.java
package com.jdojo.io;

import java.io.Console;

public class ConsoleLogin {
        public static void main(String[] args) {
                Console console = System.console();
                if (console != null) {
                        console.printf("Console is available.%n");
                }
                else {
                        System.out.println("Console is not available.%n");
                        return; // A console is not available
                }

                String userName = console.readLine("User Name: ");
                char[] passChars = console.readPassword("Password: ");
                String passString = new String(passChars);
                if (passString.equals("letmein")) {
                        console.printf("Hello %s", userName);
```

```
            }
            else {
                    console.printf("Invalid password");
            }
        }
    }
}
```

If you want to read numbers from the standard input, you have to read it as a string and parse it to a number. The Scanner class in java.util package reads and parses a text, based on a pattern, into primitive types and strings. The text source can be an InputStream, a file, a String object, or a Readable object. You can use a Scanner object to read primitive type values from the standard input System.in. It has many methods named liked hasNextXxx() and nextXxx(), where Xxx is a data type, such as int, double, etc. The hasNextXxx() method checks if the next token from the source can be interpreted as a value of the Xxx type. The nextXxx() method returns a value of a particular data type.

Listing 7-42 illustrates how to use the Scanner class by building a trivial calculator to perform addition, subtraction, multiplication, and division.

Listing 7-42. Using the Scanner Class to Read Inputs from the Standard Input

```java
// Calculator.java
package com.jdojo.io;

import java.util.Scanner;

public class Calculator {
    public static void main(String[] args) {
        // Read three tokens from the console: operand-1 operation operand-2
        String msg = "You can evaluate an arithmetic expressing.\n" +
                     "Expression must be in the form: a op b\n" +
                     "a and b are two numbers and op is +, -, * or /." +
                     "\nPlease enter an expression and press Enter: ";
        System.out.print(msg);

        // Build a scanner for the standard input
        Scanner scanner = new Scanner(System.in);
        double n1 = Double.NaN;
        double n2 = Double.NaN;
        String operation = null;

        try {
            n1 = scanner.nextDouble();
            operation = scanner.next();
            n2 = scanner.nextDouble();

            double result = calculate(n1, n2, operation);
            System.out.printf("%s %s %s = %.2f%n", n1,
                                    operation, n2, result);
        }
        catch (Exception e) {
            System.out.println("An invalid expression.");
        }
    }
```

```java
    public static double calculate(double op1, double op2, String operation) {
        switch(operation) {
            case "+":
                return op1 + op2;
            case "-":
                return op1 - op2;
            case "*":
                return op1 * op2;
            case "/":
                return op1 / op2;
        }

        return Double.NaN;
    }
}
```

```
You can evaluate an arithmetic expressing.
Expression must be in the form: a op b
a and b are two numbers and op is +, -, * or /.
Please enter an expression and press Enter: 10 + 19
10.0 + 19.0 = 29.00
```

StringTokenizer and StreamTokenizer

Java has some utility classes that let you break a string into parts called tokens. A token in this context is a part of the string. You define the sequence of characters that are considered tokens by defining delimiter characters. Suppose you have a string "This is a test, which is simple". If you define a space as a delimiter, this string has the following seven tokens:

1. This

2. is

3. a

4. test,

5. which

6. is

7. simple

If you define a comma as a delimiter, the same string has the following two tokens:

1. This is a test

2. which is simple

The StringTokenizer class is in the java.util package. The StreamTokenizer class is in the java.io package. A StringTokenizer lets you break a string into tokens whereas a StreamTokenizer gives you access to the tokens in a character-based stream.

A StringTokenizer object lets you break a string into tokens based on your definition of delimiters. It returns one token at a time. You also have the ability to change the delimiter anytime. You can create a StringTokenizer by specifying the string and accepting the default delimiters, which are a space, a tab, a new line, a carriage return, and a line-feed character (" \t\n\r\f") as follows:

```
// Create a string tokenizer
StringTokenizer st = new StringTokenizer("here is my string");
```

You can specify your own delimiters when you create a StringTokenizer as follows:

```
// Have a space, a comma and a semi-colon as delimiters
String delimiters = " ,;";
StringTokenizer st = new StringTokenizer("my text...", delimiters);
```

You can use the hasMoreTokens() method to check if you have more tokens and the nextToken() method to get the next token from the string.

You can also use the split() method of the String class to split a string into tokens based on delimiters. The split() method accepts a regular expression as a delimiter. Listing 7-43 illustrates how to use the StringTokenizer and the split() method of the String class.

Listing 7-43. Breaking a String into Tokens Using a StringTokenizer and the String.split() Method

```
// StringTokens.java
package com.jdojo.io;

import java.util.StringTokenizer;

public class StringTokens {
        public static void main(String[] args) {
                String str = "This is a test, which is simple";
                String delimiters = " ,"; // a space and a comma
                StringTokenizer st = new StringTokenizer(str, delimiters);

                System.out.println("Tokens using a StringTokenizer:");
                String token = null;
                while(st.hasMoreTokens()) {
                        token = st.nextToken();
                        System.out.println(token);
                }

                // Split the same string using String.split() method
                System.out.println("\nTokens using the String.split() method:");
                String regex = "[ ,]+" ; /* a space or a comma */
                String[] s = str.split(regex);
                for(int i = 0 ; i < s.length; i++) {
                        System.out.println(s[i]);
                }
        }
}
```

Tokens using a StringTokenizer:
This
is
a
test
which
is
simple

Tokens using the String.split() method:
This
is
a
test
which
is
simple

The StringTokenizer and the split() method of the String class return each token as a string. Sometimes you may want to distinguish between tokens based on their types; your string may contain comments. You can have these sophisticated features while breaking a character-based stream into tokens using the StreamTokenizer class. Listing 7-44 illustrates how to use a StreamTokenizer class.

Listing 7-44. Reading Tokens from a Character-based Stream

```java
// StreamTokenTest.java
package com.jdojo.io;

import java.io.StreamTokenizer;
import static java.io.StreamTokenizer.*;
import java.io.StringReader;
import java.io.IOException;

public class StreamTokenTest {
        public static void main(String[] args) throws Exception{
                String str = "This is a test, 200.89 which is simple 50";
                StringReader sr = new StringReader(str);
                StreamTokenizer st = new StreamTokenizer(sr);

                try {
                        while (st.nextToken() != TT_EOF) {
                                switch (st.ttype) {
                                        case TT_WORD: /* a word has been read */
                                                System.out.println("String value: " +
                                                                st.sval);
                                                break;
                                        case TT_NUMBER: /* a number has been read */
                                                System.out.println("Number value: " +
                                                                st.nval);
                                                break;
                                }
                        }
```

```
            }
            catch(IOException e) {
                    e.printStackTrace();
            }
        }
    }
}
```

```
String value: This
String value: is
String value: a
String value: test
Number value: 200.89
String value: which
String value: is
String value: simple
Number value: 50.0
```

The program uses a StringReader object as the data source. You can use a FileReader object or any other Reader object as the data source. The syntax to get the tokens is not easy to use. The nextToken() method of StreamTokenizer is called repeatedly. It populates three fields of the StreamTokenizer object: ttype, sval, and nval. The ttype field indicates the token type that was read. The following are the four possible values for the ttype field:

- TT_EOF: End of the stream has been reached.

- TT_EOL: End of line has been reached.

- TT_WORD: A word (a string) has been read as a token from the stream.

- TT_NUMBER: A number has been read as a token from the stream.

If the ttype has TT_WORD, the string value is stored in its field sval. If it returns TT_NUBMER, its number value is stored in nval field.

StreamTokenizer is a powerful class to break a stream into tokens. It creates tokens based on a predefined syntax. You can reset the entire syntax by using its resetSyntax() method. You can specify your own set of characters that can make up a word by using its wordChars() method. You can specify your custom whitespace characters using its whitespaceChars() method.

Summary

Reading data from a data source and writing data to a data sink is called input/output. A stream represents a data source or data sink for serial reading or writing. The Java I/O API contains several classes to support input and output streams. Java I/O classes are in the java.io and java.nio packages. The input/output stream classes in Java are based on the decorator pattern.

You refer to a file in your computer by its pathname. A file's pathname is a sequence of characters by which you can identify it uniquely in a file system. A pathname consists of a file name and its unique location in the file system. An object of the File class is an abstract representation of a pathname of a file or a directory in a platform-independent manner. The pathname represented by a File object may or may not exist in the file system. The File class provides several methods to work with files and directories.

Java I/O supports two types of streams: byte-based streams and character-based streams. Byte-based streams are inherited from the InputStream or OutputStream classes. Character-based stream classes are inherited from the Reader or Writer classes.

The process of converting an object in memory to a sequence of bytes and storing the sequence of bytes in a storage medium such as a file is called *object serialization*. The process of reading the sequence of bytes produced by a serialization process and restoring the object back in memory is called *object deserialization*. Java supports serialization and deserialization of object through the ObjectInputStream and ObjectOutputStream classes. An object must implement the Serializable interface to be serialized.

The Java I/O API provides the Console and Scanner classes to interact with the console.

You can use the StringTokenizer and StreamTokenizer classes to split text into tokens based on delimiters. The String class contains a convenience method split() to split a string into tokens based on a regular expression.

■ ■ ■

CHAPTER 8

Working with Archive Files

In this chapter, you will learn

- What archive files are

- What data compression is and how to compress and decompress data

- How to compute checksum for data using different algorithms

- How to create files in ZIP, GZIP, and JAR file formats and read data from them

- How to use the `jar` command-line tool to work with JAR files

What Is an Archive File?

An archive file consists of one or more files. It also contains metadata that may include the directory structure of the files, comments, error detection and recovery information, etc. An archive file may also be encrypted. Typically, but not necessarily, an archive file is stored in a compressed format. An archive file is created using file archiver software. For example, the WinZip, 7-zip, etc. utilities are used to create a file archive in a ZIP format on Microsoft Windows; the `tar` utility is used to create archive files on UNIX-based operating systems. An archive file makes it easier to store and transmit multiple files as one file. This chapter discusses in detail how to work with archive files using the Java I/O API and the `jar` command line utility that is included in the JDK.

Data Compression

Data compression is a process of applying an encoding algorithm to the given data to represent it in a smaller size. Suppose you have a string, 777778888. One way to encode it is 5748, which can be interpreted as "five sevens and four eights." By this encoding, you have reduced the length of the string from nine to five characters. The algorithm you have applied to compress 777778888 as 5748 is called *Run Length Encoding* (RLE). The RLE encodes the data by replacing the repeated sequence of data by the counter number and one copy of data. The RLE is easy to implement. It is suitable only in situations where you have more repeated data.

The reverse of data compression is called data decompression. Here, you apply an algorithm to the compressed data to get back the original data.

There are two types of data compression: lossless and lossy. In lossless data compression, you get your original data back when you decompress the compressed data. For example, if you decompress 5748, you can get your original data (777778888) back without losing any information. You can get the information back in this example because RLE is a lossless data compression algorithm. Other lossless data compression algorithms are LZ77, LZ78, LZW, Huffman coding, Dynamic Markov Compression (DMC), etc.

In lossy data compression, you lose some of the data during the compression process and you will not be able to recover the original data fully when you decompress the compressed data. Lossy data compression is acceptable in some situations, such as viewing pictures, audios, and videos, where the audience will not see a noticeable difference when they use the decompressed data. Compared to the lossless data compression, lossy data compression achieves a higher compression ratio at the cost of the lower data quality. Examples of lossy data compression algorithms are Discrete Cosine Transform (DCT), A-Law Compander, Mu-Law Compander, Vector Quantization, etc.

DEFLATE is a lossless data compression algorithm, which is used for compressing data in ZIP and GZIP file formats. GZIP is an abbreviation for GNU ZIP. GNU is a recursive acronym for GNU's Not Unix. The ZIP file format is used for data compression and file archival. A file archival is the process of combining multiple files into one file for convenience of storage. Typically, you compress multiple files and put them together in an archive file.

You may have worked with files with an extension of .zip. A ZIP file uses the ZIP file format. It combines multiple files into one .zip file by, optionally, compressing them.

If you are a UNIX user, you must have worked with a .tar or .tar.gz file. Typically, on UNIX, you use a two-step process to create a compressed archive file. First, you combine multiple files into a .tar archive file using the tar file format (tar stands for **Tape Ar**chive), you compress that archive file using the GZIP file format to get a .tar.gz or .tgz file. A .tar.gz or .tgz file is also called a tarball. A tarball is more compressed as compared to a zip file. A zip file compresses multiple files separately and archives them. A tarball archives the multiple files first and then compresses them. Because a tarball compresses the combined files together, it takes advantage of data repetition among all files during compression, resulting in a better compression than a zip file.

ZLIB is a general-purpose lossless data compression library. It is free and not covered by any patents. Java provides support for data compression using the ZLIB library. Deflater and Inflater are two classes in the java.util.zip package that support general-purpose data compression/decompression functionality in Java using the ZLIB library. Java provides classes to support ZIP and GZIP file formats. It also supports another file format called the jar file format, which is a variation of the ZIP file format. I will discuss examples of the file formats supported by Java in the next few sections.

Checksum

A checksum is a number that is computed by applying an algorithm on a stream of bytes. Typically, it is used when data is transmitted across the network to check for errors during data transmission. The sender computes a checksum for a packet of data and sends that checksum with the packet to the receiver. The receiver computes the checksum for the packet of data it receives and compares it with the checksum it received from the sender. If the two match, the receiver may assume that there were no errors during the data transmission. The sender and the receiver must agree to compute the checksum for the data by applying the same algorithm. Otherwise, the checksum will not match. Using a checksum is not a data security measure to authenticate the data. It is used as an error-detection method. A hacker can alter some bits of the data and you may still get the same checksum as for the original data.

Let's discuss an algorithm to compute a checksum. The algorithm is called Adler-32 after its inventor Mark Adler. Its name has the number 32 in it because it computes a checksum by computing two 16-bit checksums and concatenating them into a 32-bit integer. Let's call the two 16-bit checksums A and B, and the final checksum C. A is the sum of all bytes plus one in the data. B is the sum of individual values of A from each step. In the beginning, A is set to 1 and B is set to 0. A and B are computed based on modulus 65521. That is, if the value of A or B exceeds 65521, their values become their current values modulo 65521. The final checksum is computed as follows:

C = B * 65536 + A

The final checksum is computed by concatenating the 16-bit B and A values. You need to multiply the value of B by 65536 and add the value of A to it to get the decimal value of that 32-bit final checksum number.

Let's apply the Adler-32 checksum algorithm to compute a checksum for a string HELLO, as shown in Table 8-1.

Table 8-1. *Computing the Adler-32 checksum for the String HELLO*

Character	ASCII Value (Base 10)	A	B
H	72	1 + 72 = 73	0 + 73 = 73
E	69	73 + 69 = 142	73 + 142 = 215
L	76	142 + 76 = 218	215 + 218 = 433
L	76	218 + 76 = 294	433 + 294 = 727
O	79	294 + 79 = 373	727 + 373 = 1100

```
C = B * 65536 + A
  = 1100 * 65536 + 373
  = 72089973
```

Java provides an Adler32 class in the java.util.zip package to compute the Adler-32 checksum for bytes of data. You need to call the update() method of this class to pass bytes to it. Once you have passed all bytes to it, call its getValue() method to get the checksum. CRC32 (**C**yclic **R**edundancy **C**heck 32-bit) is another algorithm to compute a 32-bit checksum. There is also another class named CRC32 in the same package, which lets you compute a checksum using the CRC32 algorithm. Listing 8-1 illustrates how to use the Adler32 and CRC32 classes to compute checksums.

Listing 8-1. Computing Adler32 and CRC32 Checksums

```java
// ChecksumTest.java
package com.jdojo.archives;

import java.util.zip.Adler32;
import java.util.zip.CRC32;

public class ChecksumTest {
        public static void main(String[] args) throws Exception {
                String str = "HELLO";
                byte[] data = str.getBytes("UTF-8");
                System.out.println("Adler32 and CRC32 checksums for " + str);

                // Compute Adler32 checksum
                Adler32 ad = new Adler32();
                ad.update(data);
                long adler32Checksum = ad.getValue();
                System.out.println("Adler32: " + adler32Checksum);

                // Compute CRC32 checksum
                CRC32 crc = new CRC32();
                crc.update(data);
                long crc32Checksum = crc.getValue();
                System.out.println("CRC32: " + crc32Checksum);
        }
}
```

```
Adler32 and CRC32 checksums for HELLO
Adler32: 72089973
CRC32: 3242484790
```

Adler32 is faster than CRC32. However, CRC32 gives a more robust checksum. Checksum is frequently used to check for data corruption. CheckedInputStream and CheckedOutputStream are two concrete decorator classes in the InputStream/OutputStream class family. They are in the java.util.zip package. They work with a Checksum object. Note that Checksum is an interface, and the Adler32 and CRC32 classes implement the interface. CheckedInputStream computes a checksum as you read data from a stream and CheckedOutputStream computes the checksum as you write data to a stream. The ZipEntry class lets you compute the CRC32 checksum for an entry in a ZIP file using its getCrc() method.

Compressing Byte Arrays

You can use the Deflater and Inflater classes in the java.util.zip package to compress and decompress data in a byte array, respectively. These classes are the basic building blocks for compression and decompression in Java. You may not use them directly very often. You have other high-level, easy-to-use classes in Java to deal with data compression. Those classes are DeflaterInputStream, DeflaterOutputStream, GZIPInputStream, ZipFile, GZIPOutputStream, ZipInputStream, and ZipOutputStream. I will discuss these classes in detail in subsequent sections.

Using the Deflater and Inflater classes is not straightforward. You need to use the following steps to compress data in a byte array.

1. Create a Deflater object.

2. Set the input data to be compressed using the setInput() method.

3. Call the finish() method indicating that you have supplied all input data.

4. Call the deflate() method to compress the input data.

5. Call the end() method to end the compression process.

You can create an object of the Deflater class using one of its constructors.

```
// Uses the no-args constructor
Deflater compressor = new Deflater();
```

Other constructors of the Deflater class let you specify the level of compression. You can specify the compression level using one of the constants in the Deflater class. Those constant are BEST_COMPRESSION, BEST_SPEED, DEFAULT_COMPRESSION, and NO_COMPRESSION. There is a trade-off in choosing between the best compression and the best speed. The best speed means lower compression ratio and the best compression means slower compression speed.

```
// Uses the best compression
Deflater compressor = new Deflater(Deflater.BEST_COMPRESSION);
```

By default, the compressed data using the Deflater object will be in the ZLIB format. If you want the compressed data to be in GZIP or PKZIP format, you need to specify that by using the boolean flag as true in the constructor.

```
// Uses the best speed compression and GZIP format
Deflater compressor = new Deflater(Deflater.BEST_SPEED, true);
```

You can supply the input data to the Deflater object in a byte array.

```
byte[] input = get a data filled byte array;
compressor.setInput(input);
```

You call the finish() method to indicate that you have supplied all the input data.

```
compressor.finish();
```

You call the deflate() method to compress the input data. It accepts a byte array as its argument. It fills the byte array with the compressed data and returns the number of bytes in the byte array it has filled. After every call to the deflate() method, you need to call the finished() method to check if the compression process is over. Typically, you would place this check in a loop as follows:

```
// Try to read the compressed data 1024 bytes at a time
byte[] readBuffer = new byte[1024];
int readCount = 0;

while(!compressor.finished())
        readCount = compressor.deflate(readBuffer);

        /* At this point, the readBuffer array has the compressed data
           from index 0 to readCount - 1.
        */
}
```

You call the end() method to release any resources the Deflater object has held.

```
// Indicates that the compression process is over
compressor.end();
```

Follow the following steps to decompress data in a byte array. The steps are just the reverse of what you did to compress a byte array.

1. Create an Inflater object.

2. Set the input data to be decompressed using the setInput() method.

3. Call the inflate() method to decompress the input data.

4. Call the end() method to end the decompression process.

You can create an object of the Inflater class using one of its constructors.

```
// Uses the no-args constructor
Inflater decompressor = new Inflater();
```

If the compressed data is in GZIP or PKZIP format, you use another constructor and pass true as its argument.

```
// Creates a decompressor to decompress data that is
// in GZIP or PKZIP format
Inflater decompressor = new Inflater(true);
```

You set the input for the decompressor, which is the compressed data in a byte array.

```
byte[] input = get the compressed data in the byte array;
decompressor.setInput(input);
```

You call the `inflate()` method to decompress the input data. It accepts a byte array as its argument. It fills the byte array with the decompressed data and returns the number of bytes in the byte array. After every call to this method, you need to call the `finished()` method to check if the compression process is over. Typically, you use a loop, as follows:

```
// Try to read the decompressed data 1024 bytes at a time
byte[] readBuffer = new byte[1024];
int readCount = 0;

while(!decompressor.finished()){
        readCount = decompressor.inflate(readBuffer);

        /* At this point, the readBuffer array has the decompressed
           data from index 0 to readCount - 1.
        */
}
```

You need to call the end() method to release any resources held by the `Inflater` object.

```
// Indicates that the decompression process is over
decompressor.end();
```

Listing 8-2 illustrates how to use the `Deflater` and `Inflater` classes. The `compress()` and `decompress()` methods accept the inputs and return the compressed and decompressed data, respectively. In this example, I have tried to compress a small string of Hello world!. It is 12 bytes in length. It became 20 bytes after I compressed it. The goal of compression is to reduce, not to increase, the size of data. However, you cannot achieve reducing the data size just because you have attempted to compress it. The output of the program in Listing 8-2 is one such example. When you compress the data, the compressed format has to add some information to it to do some housekeeping. If the data you are attempting to compress is very small in size, as was the case in my example, or if it is already compressed, the compressed size of the data may increase because of additional information added by the compression process.

Listing 8-2. Compressing and Decompressing a byte Array Using Deflater and the Inflater classes

```
// DeflateInflateTest.java
package com.jdojo.archives;

import java.io.ByteArrayOutputStream;
import java.io.IOException;
import java.util.zip.DataFormatException;
import java.util.zip.Deflater;
import java.util.zip.Inflater;

public class DeflateInflateTest {
        public static void main(String[] args) throws Exception {
                String input = "Hello world!";
                byte[] uncompressedData = input.getBytes("UTF-8");
```

```java
        // Compress the data
        byte[] compressedData = compress(uncompressedData,
                Deflater.BEST_COMPRESSION, false);

        // Decompress the data
        byte[] decompressedData = decompress(compressedData, false);

        String output = new String(decompressedData, "UTF-8");

        // Display the statatistics
        System.out.println("Input String: " + input);
        System.out.println("Uncompressed data length: " + uncompressedData.length);
        System.out.println("Compressed data length: " + compressedData.length);
        System.out.println("Decompressed data length: " + decompressedData.length);
        System.out.println("Output String: " + output);
    }

    public static byte[] compress(byte[] input, int compressionLevel,
                boolean GZIPFormat) throws IOException {

        // Create a Deflater object to compress data
        Deflater compressor = new Deflater(compressionLevel, GZIPFormat);

        // Set the input for the compressor
        compressor.setInput(input);

        // Call the finish() method to indicate that we have
        // no more input for the compressor object
        compressor.finish();

        // Compress the data
        ByteArrayOutputStream bao = new ByteArrayOutputStream();
        byte[] readBuffer = new byte[1024];
        int readCount = 0 ;

        while(!compressor.finished()){
                readCount = compressor.deflate(readBuffer);
                if (readCount > 0) {
                        // Write compressed data to the output stream
                        bao.write(readBuffer, 0, readCount);
                }
        }

        // End the compressor
        compressor.end();

        // Return the written bytes from output stream
        return bao.toByteArray();
    }
```

```
        public static byte[] decompress(byte[] input, boolean GZIPFormat)
                        throws IOException, DataFormatException {
            // Create an Inflater object to compress the data
            Inflater decompressor = new Inflater(GZIPFormat);

            // Set the input for the decompressor
            decompressor.setInput(input);

            // Decompress data
            ByteArrayOutputStream bao = new ByteArrayOutputStream();
            byte[] readBuffer = new byte[1024];
            int readCount = 0 ;

            while(!decompressor.finished()){
                    readCount = decompressor.inflate(readBuffer);
                    if (readCount > 0) {
                            // Write the data to the output stream
                            bao.write(readBuffer, 0, readCount);
                    }
            }

            // End the decompressor
            decompressor.end();

            // Return the written bytes from the output stream
            return bao.toByteArray();
        }
}
```

```
Input String: Hello world!
Uncompressed data length: 12
Compressed data length: 20
Decompressed data length: 12
Output String: Hello world!
```

You can use DeflaterInputStream and DeflaterOutputStream to compress data in the input and output streams. There are also InflaterInputStream and InflaterOutputStream classes for decompressing data in the input and output streams. The four classes are concrete decorators in the InputStream and OutputStream class families. Please refer to Chapter 7 for more details on the decorator pattern and the concrete decorator classes.

Working with ZIP File Format

Java has direct support for the ZIP file format. Typically, you would be using the following four classes from the java.util.zip package to work with the ZIP file format:

- ZipEntry

- ZipInputStream

- ZipOutputStream

- ZipFile

A ZipEntry object represents an entry in an archive file in a ZIP file format. If you have archived 10 files in a file called test.zip, each file in the archive is represented by a ZipEntry object in your program. A zip entry may be compressed or uncompressed. When you read all files from a ZIP file, you read each of them as a ZipEntry object. When you want to add a file to a ZIP file, you add a ZipEntry object to the ZIP file. The ZipEntry class has methods to set and get information about an entry in a ZIP file.

ZipInputStream is a concrete decorator class in the InputStream class family; you use it to read data from a ZIP file for each entry. ZipOutputStream is a concrete decorator class in the OutputStream class family; you use this class to write data to a ZIP file for each entry. ZipFile is a utility class to read the entries from a ZIP file. You have the option to use either the ZipInputStream class or the ZipFile class when you want to read entries from a ZIP file.

Here are the steps to create a ZIP file.

1. Create a ZipOutputStream object.

2. Create a ZipEntry object to represent an entry in the ZIP file.

3. Add the ZipEntry to the ZipOutputStream.

4. Write the contents of the entry to the ZipOutputStream.

5. Close the ZipEntry.

6. Repeat the previous four steps for each zip entry you want to add to the archive.

7. Close the ZipOutputStream.

You can create an object of ZipOutputStream using the name of the ZIP file. You need to create a FileOutputStream object and wrap it inside a ZipOutputStream object as follows:

```
// Create a zip output stream
ZipOutputStream zos = new ZipOutputStream(
                            new FileOutputStream("ziptest.zip"));
```

You may use any other output stream concrete decorator to wrap your FileOutputStream object. For example, you may want to use BufferedOutputStream for a better speed as follows:

```
ZipOutputStream zos = new ZipOutputStream(new BufferedOutputStream(
                            new FileOutputStream("ziptest.zip")));
```

Optionally, you can set the compression level for the ZIP file entries. By default, the compression level is set to DEFAULT_COMPRESSION. For example, the following statement sets the compression level to BEST_COMPRESSION:

```
// Set the compression level for zip entries
zos.setLevel(Deflater.BEST_COMPRESSION);
```

You create a ZipEntry object using the file path for each entry and add the entry to the ZipOutputStream object using its putNextEntry() method, like so:

```
ZipEntry ze = new ZipEntry("test1.txt")
zos.putNextEntry(ze);
```

Optionally, you can set the storage method for the zip entry to indicate if the zip entry is stored compressed or uncompressed. By default, a zip entry is stored in a compressed form.

```
// To store the zip entry in a compressed form
ze.setMethod(ZipEntry.DEFLATED);

// To store the zip entry in an uncompressed form
ze.setMethod(ZipEntry.STORED);
```

Write the content of the entry you have added in the previous step to the ZipOutputStream object. Since a ZipEntry object represents a file, you will need to read the file by creating a FileInputStream object.

```
// Create an input stream to read data for the entry file
BufferedInputStream bis = new BufferedInputStream(
                                   new FileInputStream("test1.txt"));
byte[] buffer = new byte[1024];
int count = -1;

// Write the data for the entry
while((count = bis.read(buffer)) != -1) {
        zos.write(buffer, 0, count);
}

bis.close();
```

Now, close the entry using the closeEntry() method of the ZipOutputStream.

```
// Close the zip entry
zos.closeEntry();
```

Repeat the previous steps for each entry that you want to add to the zip file.
Finally, you need to close the ZipOutputStream.

```
// Close the zip entry
zos.close()
```

Listing 8-3 demonstrates how to create a ZIP file. It adds two files called test1.txt and notes\test2.txt to the testzip.zip file. The program expects these files in the current working directory. If the files do not exist, the program prints an error message with the path of the expected files. When the program finishes successfully, a testzip.zip file is created in the current directory that you can open using a ZIP file utility such as WinZip on Windows. The program prints the path of the newly created ZIP file. You may get a different output when you run the program.

Listing 8-3. Creating a ZIP File

```
// ZipUtility.java
package com.jdojo.archives;

import java.util.zip.ZipOutputStream;
import java.util.zip.ZipEntry;
import java.io.FileOutputStream;
import java.io.FileNotFoundException;
import java.io.IOException;
import java.io.BufferedInputStream;
import java.io.FileInputStream;
import java.io.BufferedOutputStream;
```

```java
import java.io.File;
import java.util.zip.Deflater;

public class ZipUtility {
    public static void main(String[] args) {
        // we want to create a ziptest.zip file in the current
        // directory. We want to add two files to this zip file.
        // Both file paths are relative to the current directory.
        String zipFileName = "ziptest.zip";
        String[] entries = new String[2];
        entries[0] = "test1.txt";
        entries[1] = "notes" + File.separator + "test2.txt";
        zip(zipFileName, entries);
    }

    public static void zip(String zipFileName, String[] zipEntries) {
        // Get the current directory for later use
        String currentDirectory = System.getProperty("user.dir");

        try (ZipOutputStream zos =
                new ZipOutputStream(
                    new BufferedOutputStream(
                        new FileOutputStream(zipFileName)))) {

            // Set the compression level to best compression
            zos.setLevel(Deflater.BEST_COMPRESSION);

            // Add each entry to the ZIP file
            for (int i = 0; i < zipEntries.length; i++) {
                // Make sure the entry file exists
                File entryFile = new File(zipEntries[i]);
                if (!entryFile.exists()) {
                    System.out.println("The entry file "
                            + entryFile.getAbsolutePath()
                            + " does not exist");
                    System.out.println(
                            "Aborted processing.");
                    return;
                }

                // Create a ZipEntry object
                ZipEntry ze = new ZipEntry(zipEntries[i]);

                // Add zip entry object to the ZIP file
                zos.putNextEntry(ze);

                // Add the contents of the entry to the ZIP file
                addEntryContent(zos, zipEntries[i]);

                // We are done with the current entry
                zos.closeEntry();
            }
```

```
                    System.out.println("Output has been written to " +
                        currentDirectory + File.separator + zipFileName);
            }
            catch (IOException e) {
                    e.printStackTrace();
            }
        }

        public static void addEntryContent(ZipOutputStream zos,
                                    String entryFileName)
                throws IOException, FileNotFoundException {

            // Create an input stream to read data from the entry file
            BufferedInputStream bis = new BufferedInputStream(
                                new FileInputStream(entryFileName));

            byte[] buffer = new byte[1024];
            int count = -1;
            while ((count = bis.read(buffer)) != -1) {
                    zos.write(buffer, 0, count);
            }
            bis.close();
        }
}
```

```
Output has been written to C:\book\javabook\ziptest.zip
```

Reading contents from a ZIP file is just the opposite of writing contents to it. Here are the steps to read the contents (or extract entries) of a ZIP file.

1. Create a ZipInputStream object.

2. Get a ZipEntry from the input stream calling the getNextEntry() method of the ZipInputStream object.

3. Read the data for the ZipEntry from the ZipInputStream object.

4. Repeat the previous two steps to read another zip entry from the archive.

5. Close the ZipInputStream.

You can create a ZipInputStream object using the ZIP file name as follows:

```
ZipInputStream zis = new ZipInputStream(
                        new BufferedInputStream(
                                new FileInputStream(zipFileName)));
```

The following snippet of code gets the next entry from the input stream:

```
ZipEntry entry = zis.getNextEntry();
```

Now, you can read the data from the ZipInputStream object for the current zip entry. You can save the data for the zip entry in a file or any other storage medium. You can check if the zip entry is a directory by using its isDirectory() method of the ZipEntry class.

Listing 8-4 illustrates how to read contents of a ZIP file. The example does not check for some of the errors. It does not check if a file already exists before overwriting it. It also assumes that all entries are files. The program expects a ziptest.zip file in your current working directory. It extracts all files from the ZIP file and outputs the path of the directory containing the extracted files. You may get a different output.

Listing 8-4. Reading Contents of a ZIP File

```java
// UnzipUtility.java
package com.jdojo.archives;

import java.util.zip.ZipEntry;
import java.io.FileOutputStream;
import java.io.FileNotFoundException;
import java.io.IOException;
import java.io.BufferedInputStream;
import java.io.FileInputStream;
import java.io.BufferedOutputStream;
import java.io.File;
import java.util.zip.ZipInputStream;

public class UnzipUtility {
    public static void main(String[] args) {
        String zipFileName = "ziptest.zip";
        String unzipdirectory = "extracted";
        unzip(zipFileName, unzipdirectory);
    }

    public static void unzip(String zipFileName, String unzipdir) {
        try (ZipInputStream      zis = new ZipInputStream(
                new BufferedInputStream(
                    new FileInputStream(zipFileName)))) {

            // Read each entry from the ZIP file
            ZipEntry entry = null;
            while((entry = zis.getNextEntry()) != null) {
                // Extract teh entry's contents
                extractEntryContent(zis, entry, unzipdir);
            }

            System.out.println(
                "ZIP file's contents have been extracted to " +
                (new File(unzipdir)).getAbsolutePath());
        }
        catch (IOException e) {
            e.printStackTrace();
        }
    }
```

```java
    public static void extractEntryContent(ZipInputStream zis,
                                           ZipEntry entry,
                                           String unzipdir)
                            throws IOException, FileNotFoundException {

        String entryFileName = entry.getName();
        String entryPath = unzipdir + File.separator + entryFileName;

        // Create the entry file by creating necessary directories
        createFile(entryPath);

        // Create an output stream to extract the content of the
        // zip entry and write to the new file
        BufferedOutputStream bos = new BufferedOutputStream(
                new FileOutputStream(entryPath));

        byte[] buffer = new byte[1024];
        int count = -1;
        while((count = zis.read(buffer)) != -1) {
                bos.write(buffer, 0, count);
        }

        bos.close();
    }

    public static void createFile(String filePath) throws IOException {
        File file = new File(filePath);
        File parent = file.getParentFile();

        // Create all parent directories if they do not exist
        if (!parent.exists()) {
                parent.mkdirs();
        }
        file.createNewFile();
    }
}
```

```
ZIP file's contents have been extracted to C:\books\javabook\extracted
```

It is easier to use the ZipFile class to read the contents of a ZIP file or list its entries. For example, ZipFile allows random access to ZIP entries, whereas ZipInputStream allows sequential access. The entries() method of a ZipFile object returns an enumeration of all zip entries in the file. Its getInputStream() method returns the input stream to read the content of a ZipEntry object. The following snippet of code shows how to use the ZipFile class. You can rewrite the code in Listing 8-4 using the ZipFile class instead of the ZipOutputStream class as an exercise. The ZipFile class comes in handy when you just want to list the entries in a ZIP file.

```java
import java.io.InputStream;
import java.util.Enumeration;
import java.util.zip.ZipEntry;
import java.util.zip.ZipFile;
...
```

```
// Create a ZipFile object using the ZIP file name
ZipFile zf = new ZipFile("ziptest.zip");

// Get the enumeration for all zip entries and loop through them
Enumeration<? extends ZipEntry> e = zf.entries();
ZipEntry entry = null;

while (e.hasMoreElements()) {
        entry = e.nextElement();

        // Get the input stream for the current zip entry
        InputStream is = zf.getInputStream(entry);

        /* Read data for the entry using the is object */

        // Print the name of the entry
        System.out.println(entry.getName());
}
```

Java 8 added a new stream() method to the ZipFile class that returns a Stream of ZipEntry objects. I will cover the Stream class in Chapter 13. Let's rewrite the above code using the Stream class and a lambda expression. The revised code uses the latest addition to the Java languages: the Stream class and the lambda expression.

```
import java.io.IOException;
import java.io.InputStream;
import java.util.stream.Stream;
import java.util.zip.ZipEntry;
import java.util.zip.ZipFile;
...

// Create a ZipFile object using the ZIP file name
ZipFile zf = new ZipFile("ziptest.zip");

// Get the Stream of all zip entries and apply some actions on each of them
Stream<? extends ZipEntry> entryStream = zf.stream();
entryStream.forEach(entry -> {
        try {
                // Get the input stream for the current zip entry
                InputStream is = zf.getInputStream(entry);

                /* Read data for the entry using the is object */
        }
        catch(IOException e) {
                e.printStackTrace();
        }

        // Print the name of the entry
        System.out.println(entry.getName());
});
```

Working with GZIP File Format

The GZIPInputStream and GZIPOutputStream classes are used to work with the GZIP file format. They are concrete decorator classes in the InputStream and OutputStream class families. Their usage is similar to any other concrete decorator classes for I/O. You need to wrap your OutputStream object inside an object of GZIPOutputStream to apply GZIP compression to your data. You need to wrap your InputStream object inside a GZIPInputStream object to apply GZIP decompression. The following snippet of code illustrates how to use these classes to compress and decompress data:

```
// Create a GZIPOutputStream object to compress data in GZIP format
// and write it to gziptest.gz file.
GZIPOutputStream gos = new GZIPOutputStream(new FileOutputStream("gziptest.gz"));

// Write uncompressed data to GZIP output stream and it will be compressed and written to //
gziptest.gz file
gos.write(byteBuffer);
```

If you want buffered writing for better speed, you should wrap the GZIPOutputStream inside a BufferedOutputStream and write the data to the BufferedOutputStream.

```
BufferedOutputStream bos = new BufferedOutputStream(new GZIPOutputStream(
                               new FileOutputStream("gziptest.gz")));
```

How would you compress an object while serializing it? It is simple. Just wrap the GZIPOutputStream inside an ObjectOutputStream object. When you write an object to your ObjectOutputStream, its serialized form will be compressed using a GZIP format.

```
ObjectOutputStream oos = new ObjectOutputStream(new GZIPOutputStream(
                              new FileOutputStream("gziptest.ser")));
```

Apply the reverse logic to read the compressed data in GZIP format for decompressing. The following snippet of code shows how to construct an InputStream object to decompress data, which is in GZIP format:

```
// Decompress data in GZIP format from gziptest.gz file and read it
GZIPInputStream gis = new GZIPInputStream(new FileInputStream("gziptest.gz"));

/* Read uncompressed data from GZIP input stream, e.g., gis.read(byteBuffer);*/

// Construct a BufferedInputStream to read data, which is in GZIP format
BufferedInputStream bis = new BufferedInputStream (new GZIPInputStream(
                               new FileInputStream(gziptest.gz")));

// Construct an ObjectInputStream to read compressed object
ObjectInputStream ois = new ObjectInputStream (new GZIPInputStream(
                               new FileInputStream("gziptest.ser")));
```

Working with JAR File Format

JAR (**Java Ar**chive) is a file format based on the ZIP file format. It is used to bundle resources, class files, sound files, images, etc. for a Java application or applet. It also provides data compression. Originally, it was developed to bundle resources for an applet to reduce download time over an HTTP connection.

You can think of a JAR file as a special kind of a ZIP file. A JAR file provides many features that are not available in a ZIP file. You can digitally sign the contents of a JAR file to provide security. It provides a platform-independent file format. You can use the JAR API to manipulate a JAR file in a Java program.

A JAR file can have an optional META-INF directory to contain files and directories containing information about application configuration. Table 8-2 lists the entries in a META-INF directory.

Table 8-2. *Contents of META-INF Directory of a JAR File*

Name	Type	Purpose
MANIFEST.MF	File	It contains extension and package related data.
INDEX.LIST	File	It contains location information of packages. Class loaders use it to speed up the class searching and loading process.
X.SF	File	X is the base file name. It stores the signature for the jar file.
X.DSA	File	X is the base file name. It stores the digital signature of the corresponding signature file.
/services	Directory	This directory contains all service provider configuration files.

The JDK ships a jar tool to create and manipulate JAR files. You can also create and manipulate a JAR file using the Java API using classes in the java.util.jar package. Most of the classes in this package are similar to the classes in the java.util.zip package. In fact, most of the classes in this package are inherited from the classes that deal with the ZIP file format. For example, the JarEntry class inherits from the ZipEntry class; the JarInputStream class inherits from the ZipInputStream class; the JarOutputStream class inherits from the ZipOutputStream class, etc. The JAR API has some new classes to deal with a manifest file. The Manifest class represents a manifest file. I will discuss how to use the JAR API later in this chapter. I will discuss the jar tool in this section.

To create a JAR file using the jar tool, many command-line options are available. There are four basic operations that you perform using the jar tool.

- Create a JAR file.
- Update a JAR file.
- Extract entries from a JAR file.
- List the contents of a JAR file.

Table 8-3 lists the command-line options for the jar tool.

Table 8-3. *Command-line Options for the jar Tool*

Option	Description
-c	Create a new JAR file.
-u	Update an existing JAR file.
-x	Extract a named file or all files from a JAR file.
-t	List the table of contents of a JAR file.
-f	Specify the JAR file name.
-m	Include the manifest information from the specified file.

(*continued*)

Table 8-3 (*continued*)

Option	Description
-M	Do not create a manifest file.
-i	Generate index information for the specified JAR file. It creates an INDEX.LIST file in JAR file under the META-INF directory.
-0	Do not compress the entries in the JAR file. Only store them. The option value is zero, which means zero compression.
-e	Add the specified class name as the value for the Main-Class entry in the main section of the manifest file.
-v	Generate verbose output on the standard output
-C	Change to the specified directory and include the following files in a JAR file. Note that the option is in uppercase (C). The lowercase (c) is used to indicate the create JAR file option.

Creating a JAR File

Use the following command to create a test.jar JAR file with two class files called A.class and B.class:

```
jar cf test.jar A.class B.class
```

If you get an error such as "jar is not recognized as a command" when you run this command, you need to use the full path of the jar command or add the directory containing the jar command in the PATH environment variable on your machine. On Windows, if you install the JDK in the C:\java8 directory, the jar command is stored in the C:\java8\bin directory.

In the above command, the option c indicates that you are creating a new JAR file and the option f indicates that you are specifying a JAR file name, which is test.jar. At the end of the command, you can specify one or more file names or directory names to include in the JAR file.

To view the contents of the test.jar file, you can execute the following command:

```
jar tf test.jar
```

The option t in this command indicates that you are interested in the table of contents of a JAR file. The option f indicates that you are specifying the JAR file name, which is test.jar in this case. The above command will generate the following output:

```
META-INF/
META-INF/MANIFEST.MF
A.class
B.class
```

Note that the jar command had automatically created two extra things for you: one directory called META-INF and a file named MANIFEST.MF in the META-INF directory.

The following command will create a test.jar file by including everything in the current working directory. Note the use of an asterisk as the wild-card character to denote everything in the current working directory.

```
jar cf test.jar *
```

The following command will create a JAR file with all class files in the book/archives directory and all images from the book/images directory. Here, book is a subdirectory in the current working directory.

```
jar cf test.jar book/archives/*.class book/images
```

You can specify a manifest file using the command-line option while creating a JAR file. The manifest file you specify will be a text file that contains all manifest entries for your JAR file. Note that your manifest file must have a blank line at the end of the file. Otherwise, the last entry in the manifest file will not be processed. I will discuss the contents of a manifest file in detail shortly.

The following command will use a manifest.txt file while creating test.jar file including all files and sub-directories in the current directory. Note the use of the option m.

```
jar cfm test.jar manifest.txt *
```

The order of the options used in the above command matters. I have specified the option as cfm. That is, f occurs before m and therefore, you must specify the JAR file name, test.jar, before the manifest file name manifest.txt. You can rewrite the above command as follows:

```
jar cmf manifest.txt test.jar *
```

Updating a JAR File

Use the option u to update an existing JAR file entries or its manifest file. The following command will add a C.class file to an existing test.jar file:

```
jar uf test.jar C.class
```

Suppose you have a test.jar file and you want to change the Main-Class entry in its manifest file to HelloWorld class. You can do that by using the following command:

```
jar ufe test.jar HelloWorld
```

In this command, the option u indicates that you are updating a JAR file; the option f indicates that you are specifying the JAR file name, which is test.jar, and the option e indicates that you are specifying the Main-Class entry's value as HelloWorld for the MANIFEST.MF file in test.jar file.

Indexing a JAR File

You can generate an index file for your JAR file. It is used to speed up class loading. You must use the option i with the jar command in a separate command, after you have created a JAR file.

```
jar i test.jar
```

This command will add a META-INF/INDEX.LIST file to the test.jar file. You can verify it by listing the table of contents of the test.jar file by using the following command:

```
jar tf test.jar
```

The generated INDEX.LIST file contains location information for all packages in all JAR files listed in the Class-Path attribute of the test.jar file. You can include an attribute called Class-Path in the manifest file of a JAR file. It is a space-separated list of JAR files. The attribute value is used to search and load classes when you run the JAR file.

Extracting an Entry from a JAR File

You can extract all or some entries from a JAR file using the option x with the jar command. To extract all entries from a test.jar file, you use

```
jar xf test.jar
```

The option x indicates that you want to extract the entries from the JAR file. The option f indicates that you are specifying the file name, which is test.jar. The above command will extract all entries from test.jar file in the current working directory. It will create the same directory structure as it exists in the test.jar file. For example, if book/HelloWorld.class is an entry in the test.jar file, the above command will create a book directory in the current working directory and extract the HelloWorld.class file into the book directory. Any existing file during the extraction of an entry is overwritten. The JAR file, test.jar in this example, is unchanged by the above command.

To extract individual entries from a JAR file, you need to list them at the end of the command. The entries should be separated by a space. The following command will extract A.class and book/HelloWorld.class entries from a test.jar file:

```
jar xf test.jar A.class book/HelloWorld.class
```

To extract all class files from a book directory, you can use the following command:

```
jar xf test.jar book/*.class
```

Listing the Contents of a JAR File

Use the option t with the jar command to list the table of contents of a JAR file on the standard output.

```
jar tf test.jar
```

The Manifest File

A JAR file differs from a ZIP file in that it may optionally contain a manifest file named MANIFEST.MF in the META-INF directory. The manifest file contains information about the JAR file and its entries. It can contain information about the CLASSPATH setting for the JAR file. Its main entry class is a class with the main() method to start a stand-alone application, version information about packages, etc.

A manifest file is divided into sections separated by a blank line. Each section contains name-value pairs. A new line separates each name-value pair. A colon separates a name and its corresponding value. A manifest file must end with a new line. The following is a sample of the content of a manifest file:

```
Manifest-Version: 1.0
Created-By: 1.8.0_20-ea-b05 (Oracle Corporation)
Main-Class: com.jdojo.intro.Welcome
Profile: compact1
```

The above manifest file has one section with four attributes:

- `Manifest-Version`
- `Created-By`
- `Main-Class`
- `Profile`

There are two kinds of sections in a manifest file: the main section and the individual section. A blank line must separate any two sections. Entries in the main section apply to the entire JAR file. Entries in the individual section apply to a particular entry. An attribute in an individual section overrides the same attribute in the main section. An individual entry starts with a "Name" attribute, whose value is the name of the entry in the JAR file and it is followed by other attributes for that entry. For example, suppose you have a manifest file with the following contents:

```
Manifest-Version: 1.0
Created-By: 1.6.0 (Sun Microsystems Inc.)
Main-Class: com.jdojo.chapter2.Welcome
Sealed: true

Name: book/data/
Sealed: false

Name: images/logo.bmp
Content-Type: image/bmp
```

The manifest file contains three sections: one main section and two individual sections. Note that there is a blank line between the two sections. The first individual section indicates that the package book/data is not sealed. This individual section attribute of "Sealed: false" will override the main section's attribute of "Sealed: true". Another individual section is for an entry called images/logo.bmp. It states that the content type of the entry is an image of bmp type.

The jar command can create a default manifest file and add it to the JAR file. The default manifest file contains only two attributes: Manifest-Version and Created-By. You can use the option M to tell the jar tool to omit the default manifest file. The following command will create a test.jar file without adding a default manifest file:

```
jar cMf test.jar book/*.class
```

The jar command gives you an option to customize the contents of the manifest file. You can use the option m to specify your file that has the contents for the manifest file. The jar command will read the name-value pairs from the specified manifest file and add them to the MANIFEST.MF file. Suppose you have a file named manifest.txt with one attribute entry in it. Make sure to add a new line at the end of the file. The file's contents are as follows:

```
Main-Class: com.jdojo.intro.Welcome
```

To add the Main-Class attribute value from manifest.txt file in a new test.jar file by including all class files in the current working directory, you execute the following command:

```
jar cfm test.jar manifest.txt *.class
```

Note that when you specify the option m, you must also specify the manifest file name. The order in which you specify the new JAR file name and the manifest file name must match the order of options m and f. For example, you can change the above command by specifying the f and m options in a different order as follows:

```
jar cmf manifest.txt test.jar *.class
```

This command will add a manifest file with the following contents to the test.jar file:

```
Manifest-Version: 1.0
Created-By: 1.8.0_20-ea (Oracle Corporation)
Main-Class: com.jdojo.intro.Welcome
```

If you do not specify the Manifest-Version and Created-By attribute in your manifest file, the tool adds them. It defaults the Manifest-Version to 1.0. The Created-By is defaulted to the JDK version you use.

You have been running a Java program by using the java command and specifying the class name that has the main() method as follows:

```
java com.jdojo.intro.Welcome
```

You can also run a jar file using the -jar option with the java command as follows:

```
java -jar test.jar
```

When you run the above command, the JVM will look for the value of the Main-Class attribute in the MANIFEST.MF file in the test.jar file and attempt to run that class. If you have not included a Main-Class attribute in the test.jar file, the above command will generate an error.

You can also add the Main-Class attribute value in the manifest file without creating your own manifest file. Use the option e with the jar tool when you create/update a jar file. The following command will add com.jdojo.intro.Welcome as the value of the Main-Class in the MANIFEST.MF file in the test.jar file:

```
jar cfe test.jar com.jdojo.intro.Welcome *.class
```

The following command will add com.jdojo.intro.Welcome as the value of the Main-Class in the MANIFEST.MF file in an existing test.jar file by using the option u for update:

```
jar ufe test.jar com.jdojo.intro.Welcome
```

You can set the CLASSPATH for a JAR file in its manifest file. The attribute name is called Class-Path, which you must specify in a custom manifest file. It is a space-separated list of jar files, zip files, and directories. The Class-Path attribute in a manifest file looks like

```
Class-Path: chapter8.jar file:/c:/book/ http://www.jdojo.com/jutil.jar
```

The above entry has three items for the CLASSPATH: a JAR file chapter8.jar, a directory using the file protocol file:/c:/book/, and another JAR file using a HTTP protocol http://www.jdojo.com/jutil.jar. Note that a directory name must end with a forward slash. Suppose this Class-Path setting is included in the manifest file for the test.jar file. When you run the test.jar file using the following java command, this CLASSPATH will be used to search and load classes.

```
java -jar test.jar
```

When you run a JAR file with the -jar option using the java command, any CLASSPATH setting outside the manifest file of the JAR file (test.jar file in the above case) is ignored. Another use of the Class-Path attribute is to generate an index of all packages using the option i of the jar tool. The following command will generate an index for all packages in all JAR files listed in the Class-Path attribute of the manifest file in the test.jar file:

```
jar i test.jar
```

Sealing a Package in a JAR File

You can seal a package in a JAR file. Sealing a package in a JAR file means that all classes declared in that package must be archived in the same JAR file. Typically, you seal a package to easily maintain versions of the package. If you change anything in the package, you just recreate a JAR file. To seal a package in a JAR file, you need to include two attributes: Name and Sealed. The value for the Name attribute is the name of the package and the Sealed attribute has value as true. The following entries in a manifest file will seal a package named com.jdojo.archives. Note that the package name must end with a forward slash (/).

```
Name: com/jdojo/archives/
Sealed: true
```

By default, all packages in a JAR file are not sealed. If you want to seal the JAR file itself, you can include a Sealed attributed, as shown:

```
Sealed: true
```

Sealing the JAR file will seal all packages in that JAR file. However, you can override it by not sealing a package individually. The following entries in a manifest file will seal all packages in the JAR file, except the book/chapter8/ package:

```
Sealed: true

Name: book/chapter8/
Sealed: false
```

Using the JAR API

Using JAR API is very similar to using the ZIP API, except that the JAR API includes classes for working with a manifest file. An object of the Manifest class represents a manifest file. You create a Manifest object in your code as follows:

```
Manifest manifest = new Manifest();
```

There are two things you can do with a manifest file: read entries from it and write entries to it. There are separate ways to deal with entries in the main and individual sections. To add an entry into a main section, get an instance of the Attributes class using the getMainAttributes() method of the Manifest class and keep adding a name-value pair to it using its put() method. The following snippet of code adds some attributes to the main section of a manifest object. The known attribute names are defined as constants in the Attributes.Name class. For example, the constant Attributes.Name.MANIFEST_VERSION represents the Manifest-Version attribute name.

```
// Create a Manifest object
Manifest manifest = new Manifest();
```

```
/* Add main attributes
   1. Manifest Version
   2. Main-Class
   3. Sealed
*/
Attributes mainAttribs = manifest.getMainAttributes();
mainAttribs.put(Attributes.Name.MANIFEST_VERSION, "1.0");
mainAttribs.put(Attributes.Name.MAIN_CLASS, "com.jdojo.intro.Welcome");
mainAttribs.put(Attributes.Name.SEALED, "true");
```

Adding an individual entry to the manifest file is a little more complex than adding the main entry. Suppose you want to add the following individual entry to a manifest file:

```
Name: "com/jdojo/archives/"
Sealed: false
```

You need to perform the following steps.

1. Get the Map object that stores the individual entries for a manifest.

2. Create an Attributes object.

3. Add the name-value pair to the Attributes object. You can add as many name-value pairs as you want.

4. Add the Attributes object to the attribute Map using the name of the individual section as the key.

The following snippet of code shows you how to add an individual entry to a Manifest object:

```
// Get the Attribute map for the Manifest
Map<String,Attributes> attribsMap = manifest.getEntries();

// Create an Attributes object
Attributes attribs = new Attributes();

// Create an Attributes.Name object for the "Sealed" attribute
Attributes.Name name = new Attributes.Name("Sealed");

// Add the "name: value" pair (Sealed: false) to the attributes objects
attribs.put(name, "false");

// Add the Sealed: false attitute to the attributes map
attribsMap.put("com/jdojo/archives/", attribs);
```

If you want to add a manifest file to a JAR file, you can specify it in one of the constructors of the JarOutputStream class. For example, the following snippet of code creates a jar output stream to create a test.jar file with a Manifest object:

```
// Create a Manifest object
Manifest manifest = new Manifest();
```

```
// Create a JarOutputStream with a Manifest object
JarOutputStream jos = new JarOutputStream(new BufferedOutputStream(
                        new FileOutputStream("test.jar")), manifest);
```

Listing 8-5 contains the code to create a JAR file that includes a manifest file. The code is similar to creating a ZIP file. The main() method contains the file names used to create the JAR file. All files are expected to be in the current working directory.

- It creates a JAR file named jartest.jar.

- It adds an images/logo.bmp and com/jdojo/archives/Test.class files to the jartest.jar file.

If the input files do not exist in your current working directory, you will get an error message when you run the program. If you want to add other files to the JAR file, please change the code in the main() method accordingly.

Listing 8-5. Creating a JAR File Using the JAR API

```
// JARUtility.java
package com.jdojo.archives;

import java.util.jar.Manifest;
import java.util.jar.Attributes;
import java.util.Map;
import java.util.jar.JarOutputStream;
import java.io.FileOutputStream;
import java.io.IOException;
import java.io.BufferedInputStream;
import java.io.FileInputStream;
import java.io.FileNotFoundException;
import java.io.File;
import java.util.zip.Deflater;
import java.io.BufferedOutputStream;
import java.util.jar.JarEntry;

public class JARUtility {
        public static void main(String[] args) throws Exception {
                // Create a Manifest object
                Manifest manifest = getManifest();

                // Store jar entries in a String array
                String jarFileName = "jartest.jar";
                String[] entries = new String[2];
                entries[0] = "images/logo.bmp";
                entries[1] = "com/jdojo/archives/Test.class";

                createJAR(jarFileName, entries, manifest);
        }

        public static void createJAR(String jarFileName,
                                    String[] jarEntries,
                                    Manifest manifest) {
```

```java
            // Get the current directory for later use
            String currentDirectory = System.getProperty("user.dir");

            // Create the JAR file
            try (JarOutputStream jos = new JarOutputStream(
                              new BufferedOutputStream(
                                      new FileOutputStream(jarFileName)
                              ), manifest)) {

                // Set the compression level to best compression
                jos.setLevel(Deflater.BEST_COMPRESSION);

                // Add each entry to JAR file
                for (int i = 0; i < jarEntries.length; i++) {
                    // Make sure the entry file exists
                    File entryFile = new File(jarEntries[i]);
                    if (!entryFile.exists()) {
                        System.out.println("The entry file " +
                                entryFile.getAbsolutePath() +
                                " does not exist");
                        System.out.println("Aborted processing.");
                        return;
                    }

                    // Create a JarEntry object
                    JarEntry je = new JarEntry(jarEntries[i]);

                    // Add jar entry object to JAR file
                    jos.putNextEntry(je);

                    // Add the entry's contents to the JAR file
                    addEntryContent(jos, jarEntries[i]);

                    // Inform the JAR output stream that we are done
                    // working with the current entry
                    jos.closeEntry();
                }

                System.out.println("Output has been written to " +
                        currentDirectory + File.separator + jarFileName);
            }
            catch (IOException e) {
                e.printStackTrace();
            }
    }

    public static void addEntryContent(JarOutputStream jos, String entryFileName)
                            throws IOException, FileNotFoundException {

        // Create an input stream to read data from the entry file
        BufferedInputStream bis =
                new BufferedInputStream(new FileInputStream(entryFileName));
```

```
                byte[] buffer = new byte[1024];
                int count = -1;
                while ((count = bis.read(buffer)) != -1) {
                        jos.write(buffer, 0, count);
                }

                bis.close();
        }

        public static Manifest getManifest() {
                Manifest manifest = new Manifest();

                /* Add main attributes
                 1. Manifest Version
                 2. Main-Class
                 3. Sealed
                */
                Attributes mainAttribs = manifest.getMainAttributes();
                mainAttribs.put(Attributes.Name.MANIFEST_VERSION, "1.0");
                mainAttribs.put(Attributes.Name.MAIN_CLASS, "com.jdojo.archives.Test");
                mainAttribs.put(Attributes.Name.SEALED, "true");

                /* Add two individual sections */
                /* Do not seal the com/jdojo/archives/ package. Note that you
                    have sealed the whole JAR file and to exclude this package
                    you we must add a Sealed: false attribute for this package
                    separately.
                */
                Map<String, Attributes> attribsMap = manifest.getEntries();

                // Create an attribute "Sealed : false" and
                // add it for individual entry "Name: com/jdojo/archives/"
                Attributes a1 = getAttribute("Sealed", "false");
                attribsMap.put("com/jdojo/archives/", a1);

                // Create an attribute "Content-Type: image/bmp" and
                // add it for images/logo.bmp
                Attributes a2 = getAttribute("Content-Type", "image/bmp");
                attribsMap.put("images/logo.bmp", a2);

                return manifest;
        }

        public static Attributes getAttribute(String name, String value) {
                Attributes a = new Attributes();
                Attributes.Name attribName = new Attributes.Name(name);
                a.put(attribName, value);
                return a;
        }
}
```

You can read the entries from a JAR file using similar code to that you used to read entries from a ZIP file. To read the entries from a manifest file of a JAR file, you need to get the object of the Manifest class using the getManifest() class of the JarInputStream as follows:

```
// Create a JAR input stream object
JarInputStream jis = new JarInputStream(new FileInputStream("jartest.jar"));

// Get the manifest file from the JAR file. Will return null if
// there is no manifest file in the JAR file.
Manifest manifest = jis.getManifest();

if (manifest != null) {
        // Get the attributes from main section
        Attributes mainAttributes = manifest.getMainAttributes();
        String mainClass = mainAttributes.getValue("Main-Class");

        // Get the attributes from individual section
        Map<String, Attributes> entries = manifest.getEntries();
}
```

This section does not include code examples on reading entries from a JAR file. Please refer to the code in the UnzipUtility class, which has the code to read entries from a ZIP file. The code to read from a JAR file would be similar, except you would be using JAR-related classes from the java.util.jar package instead of the ZIP-related classes from the java.util.zip package.

Accessing Resources from a JAR File

How would you get access to the resources stored in a JAR file? For example, how would you get access to a file named images/logo.bmp in a JAR file, so that you can display the bmp file as an image in your java application?

You can construct a URL object by using the reference of a resource in a JAR file. The JAR file URL syntax is of the form

```
jar:<url>!/{entry}
```

The following URL refers to an images/logo.bmp JAR entry in a test.jar file on www.jdojo.com using the HTTP protocol:

```
jar:http://www.jdojo.com/test.jar!/images/logo.bmp
```

The following URL refers to an images/logo.bmp JAR entry in a test.jar file on the local file system in the c:\ jarfiles\ directory using the file protocol:

```
jar:file:/c:/jarfiles/test.jar!/images/logo.bmp
```

If you want to read the images/logo.bmp file from a JAR file in the classpath, you can get an input stream object using a class object as follows:

```
// Assuming that the Test class is in the CLASSPATH
Class cls = Test.class;
InputStream in = cls.getResourceAsStream("/images/logo.bmp")
```

You can also get a URL object (URL class is in `java.net` package) for an entry in your JAR file, which is in your classpath as follows:

```
URL url = cls.getResource("/images/logo.bmp");
```

Summary

An archive file consists of one or more files. Optionally, the files in an archive file may be compressed. It also contains metadata that may include the directory structure of the files, comments, error detection and recovery information, etc. An archive file may be encrypted as well.

A checksum is a number that is computed by applying an algorithm on a stream of bytes. Typically, it is used when data is transmitted across the network to check for errors during data transmission. The sender and receiver use the same algorithm to compute the checksum for the transmitted data. A mismatch signals an error in data transmission. Java contains `Adler32` and `CRC32` classes to compute checksum for data using the Adler32 and CRC32 algorithms, respectively. Java provides `Deflater` and `Inflater` classes to work with data compression and decompression.

The JDK supports creating and manipulating archive files in ZIP, GZIP, and JAR formats through APIs and tools. The APIs are in the `java.util.zip` and `java.util.jar` packages. In addition to the JAR API to work with JAR files, the JDK provides a `jar` command-line tool that can be used create, read, and update JAR files.

CHAPTER 9

■ ■ ■

New Input/Output

In this chapter, you will learn

- What the New Input/Ouput is

- How to create different types of buffers

- How to read data from buffers and write data to buffers

- How to manipulate position, limit, and mark properties of a buffer

- How to create different types of views of a buffer

- How to encode/decode data in a buffer using different charsets

- What channels are and how to use channels to read/write files' contents

- How to use memory-mapped files for faster I/O

- How to use file locks

- How to know the byte order of a machine and how to deal with byte order when using buffers

What Is NIO?

The stream-based I/O uses streams to transfer data between a data source/sink and a Java program. The Java program reads from or writes to a stream a byte at a time. This approach to performing I/O operations is slow. The New Input/Ouput (NIO) solves the slow speed problem in the older stream-based I/O.

In NIO, you deal with channels and buffers for I/O operations. A channel is like a stream. It represents a connection between a data source/sink and a Java program for data transfer. There is one difference between a channel and a stream. A stream can be used for one-way data transfer. That is, an input stream can only transfer data from a data source to a Java program; an output stream can only transfer data from a Java program to a data sink. However, a channel provides a two-way data transfer facility. You can use a channel to read data as well as to write data. You can obtain a read-only channel, a write-only channel, or a read-write channel depending on your needs.

In stream-based I/O, the basic unit of data transfer is a byte. In channel-based NIO, the basic unit of data transfer is a buffer. A buffer is a bounded data container. That is, a buffer has a fixed capacity that determines the upper limit of the data it may contain. In stream-based I/O, you write data directly to the stream. In channel-based I/O, you write data into a buffer; you pass that buffer to the channel, which writes the data to the data sink. Similarly, when you want to read data from a data source, you pass a buffer to a channel. The channel reads data from the data source into a buffer. You read data from the buffer. Figure 9-1 depicts the interaction between a channel, a buffer, a data source, a data sink, and a Java program. It is evident that the most important parts in this interaction are reading from a buffer and writing into a buffer. I will discuss buffers and channels in detail in subsequent sections.

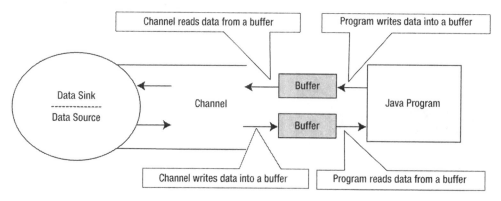

Figure 9-1. *Interaction between a channel, buffers, a Java program, a data source, and a data sink*

Buffers

A buffer is a fixed-length data container. There is a separate buffer type to hold data for each type of primitive value, except for boolean type values. A buffer is an object in your program. You have a separate class to represent each type of buffer. All buffer classes are inherited from an abstract Buffer class. Buffer classes that hold primitive values are as follows:

- ByteBuffer

- ShortBuffer

- CharBuffer

- IntBuffer

- LongBuffer

- FloatBuffer

- DoubleBuffer

An object of an XxxBuffer class is used to hold data of the Xxx primitive data type. For example, a ByteBuffer is used to hold byte values; a ShortBuffer is used to hold short values; a CharBuffer is used to hold characters, and so on.

The following are the four important properties of a buffer, which you must understand to use buffers effectively:

- Capacity

- Position

- Limit

- Mark

The capacity of a buffer is the maximum number of elements that it can hold. The capacity of a buffer is fixed when the buffer is created. You can think of the capacity of a buffer as the length of an array. Once you create an array, its length is fixed. Similarly, once you create a buffer, its capacity is fixed. However, a buffer is not necessarily backed by an array. You can check if a buffer is backed by an array by calling its hasArray() method that returns true if the buffer is backed by an array. You can get access to the backing array of a buffer by using the array() method of the buffer object. Once you get access to the backing array of a buffer, any changes made to that array will be reflected in the buffer. A buffer has a capacity() method that returns its capacity.

You can create a buffer of a particular kind in many ways. You can create a buffer by using the `allocate()` factory method of a particular buffer class as follows:

```
// Create a byte buffer with the capacity as 8
ByteBuffer bb = ByteBuffer.allocate(8);

// Assigns 8 to the capacity variable
int capacity = bb.capacity();

// Create a character buffer with the capacity as 1024
CharBuffer cb = CharBuffer.allocate(1024);
```

A byte buffer gets special treatment in NIO. It has an extra method called `allocateDirect()` that creates a byte buffer. This method creates a byte buffer for which the memory is allocated from the operating system memory, not from the JVM heap. This avoids copying the contents to intermediate buffers during I/O operations. A direct buffer has an additional creation cost. However, it is faster during an I/O operation. You should use a direct byte buffer when a buffer is long-lived. You can use the `isDirect()` method of the `ByteBuffer` class to check if a buffer is direct or non-direct.

```
// Create a direct byte buffer of 512 bytes capacity
ByteBuffer bbd = ByteBuffer.allocateDirect(512);
```

Another way to create a buffer is to wrap an array using the buffer's static `wrap()` method, like so:

```
// Have an array of bytes
byte[] byteArray = new byte[512];

// Create a byte buffer by wrapping the byteArray
ByteBuffer bb = ByteBuffer.wrap(byteArray);
```

You can use the same technique to create a buffer to store other primitive values. I will discuss other ways of creating a buffer later in this section.

When you create a buffer, all elements of the buffer are initialized to a value of zero. Each element of a buffer has an index. The first element has an index of 0 and the last element has an index of `capacity - 1`.

Position and limit are two properties of a buffer. When a buffer is created, its position is set to 0 and its limit is equal to its capacity. Figure 9-2 shows the state of a buffer with a capacity of 8 just after its creation. All its elements have a value of 0. Its position is set to zero. Its limit is set to 8, which is equal to its capacity. In the figure, P and L denote the position and the limit of the buffer, respectively. Note that the figure shows the index at 8, which is out of range for the buffer, to show the value of the limit.

Buffer Elements >>	0	0	0	0	0	0	0	0	
Element's Index >>	0	1	2	3	4	5	6	7	8
	P								L

Figure 9-2. *A buffer of capacity 8 after its creation*

You can get/set the position of a buffer using its overloaded `position()` method. The `position()` method returns the current value of the position of a buffer. The `position(int newPosition)` method sets the position of the buffer to the specified `newPosition` value and returns the reference of the buffer.

You can get/set the limit of a buffer using its overloaded `limit()` method. The `limit()` method returns the current value of the limit of a buffer. The `limit(int newLimit)` method sets the limit of a buffer to the specified `newLimit` value and returns the reference of the buffer.

You can bookmark a position of a buffer by using the mark() method. When you call the mark() method, the buffer stores the current value of its position as its mark value. You can set the position of a buffer to its previously bookmarked value by using the reset() method. The buffer's mark is not defined when it is created. You must call the reset() method on a buffer only when its mark is defined. Otherwise, the reset() method throws an InvalidMarkException.

The following invariant must hold during the lifetime of a buffer:

```
0 <= mark <= position <= limit <= capacity
```

Since the capacity of a buffer never changes and mark has limited use through the mark() and reset() methods, I will limit the discussion only to the position and limit properties of a buffer. There are some indirect consequences of changing the position and limit values. Since the mark cannot be greater than the position, the mark is discarded if the position is set less than the current mark value. If you set the limit less than the position, the position is automatically set equal to the limit value.

So far, you have read a great deal on buffers. It's time to see a buffer in action. Listing 9-1 contains the code to create a new buffer and display its four properties.

Listing 9-1. Mark, Position, Limit, and Capacity of a New Buffer

```java
// BufferInfo.java
package com.jdojo.nio;

import java.nio.ByteBuffer;
import java.nio.InvalidMarkException;

public class BufferInfo {
        public static void main(String[] args) {
                // Create a byte buffer of capacity 8
                ByteBuffer bb = ByteBuffer.allocate(8);

                System.out.println("Capacity: " + bb.capacity());
                System.out.println("Limit: " + bb.limit());
                System.out.println("Position: " + bb.position());

                // The mark is not set for a new buffer. Calling the
                // reset() method throws a runtime exception if the mark is not set.
                // If the mark is set, the position is set to the mark value.
                try {
                        bb.reset();
                        System.out.println("Mark: " + bb.position());
                }
                catch (InvalidMarkException e) {
                        System.out.println("Mark is not set");
                }
        }
}
```

```
Capacity: 8
Limit: 8
Position: 0
Mark is not set
```

Reading from and Writing to a Buffer

There are two ways to read data from a buffer:

- Using absolute position

- Using relative position

In an absolute position read, you specify the index in the buffer from which you want to read the data. The position of the buffer is unchanged after an absolute position read.

In a relative position read, you specify how many data elements you want to read. The current position of the buffer determines which data elements will be read. In a relative position read, the read starts at the current position of the buffer and it is incremented by one after reading each data element.

The get() method is used to read data from a buffer. The get() method is overloaded. It has four versions. Just replace the data type byte with another data type for other primitive type buffers in the following methods:

- get(int index): It returns the data at the given index. For example, get(2) will return the data at index 2 from the buffer. It is an absolute way of reading data from a buffer because you provide the absolute position of the element from which you want to read the data. This method does not change the current position of the buffer.

- get(): It returns the data from the current position in the buffer and increases the position by 1. For example, if position is set at index 2, calling the get() method will return the value at index 2 from the buffer and set the position to 3. It is a relative way of reading data from a buffer because you read the data relative to the current position.

- get(byte[] destination, int offset, int length): It is used to read data from a buffer in bulk. It reads length number of bytes from the current position of the buffer and puts them in the specified destination array starting at the specified offset. If it cannot read the length number of bytes from the buffer, it throws a BufferUnderflowException. If there is no exception, it increases the current position by length. It is a relative read from a buffer.

- get(byte[] destination): It fills the specified destination array by reading data from the current position of the buffer and incrementing the current position by one each time it reads a data element. If there is not enough data to fill the array, it will throw a BufferUnderflowException. It is a relative way of reading data from a buffer. This method call is the same as calling get(byte[] destination, 0, destination.length).

Writing data to a buffer is the opposite of reading data from it. The put() method is used to write data to a buffer. The put() method has five versions: one for absolute position write and four for relative position write. The absolute version of the put() method does not affect the position of the buffer. The relative versions of the put() method write the data and advance the position of the buffer by one for each written element. Different buffer classes have different versions of the put() method; however, there are five versions that are common among all types of buffers. The following are the five versions of the put() method for ByteBuffer. Just replace the data type byte with another data type for other primitive type buffers in the following methods.

- put(int index, byte b): It writes the specified b data at the specified index. The call to this method does not change the current position of the buffer.

- put(byte b): It is a relative put() method that writes the specified byte at the current position of the buffer and increments the position by 1.

- put(byte[] source, int offset, int length): It reads the length number of bytes from the source array starting at offset and writes them to the buffer starting at the current position. It throws a BufferOverflowException if there is not enough room in the buffer to write all bytes. The position of the buffer is incremented by length.

- put(byte[] source): It is the same as calling put(byte[] source, 0, source.length).

- ByteBuffer put(ByteBuffer src): It reads the remaining bytes from the specified byte buffer src and writes them to the buffer. If the remaining space in the target buffer is less than the remaining bytes in the source buffer, a runtime BufferOverflowException is thrown.

Let's have some pictorial views of the state of a buffer and its properties after each read and write. Figure 9-3 through 9-6 depict how the position of a buffer with a capacity of 8 is advanced after each write in the buffer. After the eighth write in the buffer, the position and the limit become equal. If you attempt to write a ninth time, you would get a BufferOverflowException. Note that I have used a relative write using the put(byte b) method.

Buffer Elements >>	0	0	0	0	0	0	0	0	
Element's Index >>	0	1	2	3	4	5	6	7	8
	P								L

Figure 9-3. Buffer state with capacity 8 after creation. Buffer state - (position=0, limit=8)

Buffer Elements >>	50	0	0	0	0	0	0	0	
Element's Index >>	0	1	2	3	4	5	6	7	8
		P							L

Figure 9-4. Buffer state after calling put((byte)50). Buffer state - (position= 1, limit=8)

Buffer Elements >>	50	51	0	0	0	0	0	0	
Element's Index >>	0	1	2	3	4	5	6	7	8
			P						L

Figure 9-5. Buffer state after calling put((byte)51). Buffer state – (position= 2, limit=8)

Buffer Elements >>	50	51	52	53	54	55	56	57	
Element's Index >>	0	1	2	3	4	5	6	7	8
									L
									P

Figure 9-6. Buffer state after calling put((byte)52), put((byte)53), put((byte)54), put((byte)55), put((byte)56), and put((byte)57). Buffer state - (position= 8, limit=8)

Let's read the data that you have just written into the buffer whose state is shown in Figure 9-6. Note that the position of the buffer is 8 and its limit is also 8. If you call the get() method (a relative read) to read data from this buffer, you would get a BufferUnderflowException. You have just filled the buffer with data. However, when you attempt to read the data, you get an exception because the get() method returns data from the current position of the buffer, which is out of range in this case. The get() method will return data only if the position of the buffer is in the range of 0 and 7. Let's not lose hope, and try to read the data using an absolute position with the get(int index) method. If you call get(0), get(1) ... get(7), you will be surprised to know that you can read all the data you had written. Listing 9-2 demonstrates this.

Listing 9-2. Writing to and Reading from a Buffer

```java
// BufferReadWrite.java
package com.jdojo.nio;

import java.nio.ByteBuffer;

public class BufferReadWrite {
        public static void main(String[] args) {
                // Create a byte buffer with a capacity of 8
                ByteBuffer bb = ByteBuffer.allocate(8);

                // Print the buffer info
                System.out.println("After creation:");
                printBufferInfo(bb);

                // Populate buffer elements from 50 to 57
                for (int i = 50; i < 58; i++) {
                        bb.put((byte) i);
                }

                // Print the buffer info
                System.out.println("After populating data:");
                printBufferInfo(bb);
        }

        public static void printBufferInfo(ByteBuffer bb) {
                int limit = bb.limit();
                System.out.println("Position = " + bb.position() +
                                    ", Limit = " + limit);

                // Use absolute reading without affecting the position
                System.out.print("Data: ");
                for (int i = 0; i < limit; i++) {
                        System.out.print(bb.get(i) + " ");
                }
                System.out.println();
        }
}
```

```
After creation:
Position = 0, Limit = 8
Data: 0 0 0 0 0 0 0 0
After populating data:
Position = 8, Limit = 8
Data: 50 51 52 53 54 55 56 57
```

Now you understand that there is a big difference in using relative and absolute methods for reading from and writing to a buffer. Both methods have a working range. The data must be read and written in the working range. The working range for relative and absolute methods is different.

The working range for a relative read/write is the indices between position and limit – 1 of the buffer, where position is less than limit -1. That is, you can read/write data using the relative get() and put() methods if the position of the buffer is less than its limit.

The working range for the absolute read/write is the index between zero and limit -1. So, how do you read all the data from a buffer using a relative position read, after you have finished writing data into the buffer? One way to accomplish this is to set the limit of the buffer equal to its position and set its position to 0. The following snippet of code shows this technique:

```
// Create a byte buffer of capacity 8 and populate its elements
ByteBuffer bb = ByteBuffer.allocate(8);
for(int i = 50; i < 58; i++) {
        bb.put((byte)i);
}

// Set the limit the same as the position and set the position to 0
bb.limit(bb.position());
bb.position(0);

// Now bb is set to read all data using relative get() method
int limit = bb.limit();
for(int i = 0; i < limit; i++) {
        byte b = bb.get(); // Uses a relative read
        System.out.println(b);
}
```

The Buffer class has a method to accomplish just what you have coded in the above snippet of code. You can set the limit of the buffer to its position and set the position to 0 by using its flip() method. Figure 9-7 shows the state of a buffer, which has capacity of 8, after it has been created and after its two elements at index 0 and 1 have been written. Figure 9-8 shows the state of the buffer after its flip() method is called. The flip() method discards the mark of a buffer if it is defined.

Buffer Elements >>	50	51	0	0	0	0	0	0	
Element's Index >>	0	1	2	3	4	5	6	7	8
			P						L

Figure 9-7. *Buffer's state just after you have written two elements at indexes 0 and 1*

Buffer Elements >>	50	51	0	0	0	0	0	0	
Element's Index >>	0	1	2	3	4	5	6	7	8
	P	L							

Figure 9-8. *Buffer's state after writing two elements at indexes 0 and 1 and calling the flip() method*

In the previous snippet of code, you used a for-loop to read the data from the buffer. The index of the for-loop runs from zero to limit –1. However, there is an easier way to read/write data from/to a buffer using relative read/write method. The hasRemaining() method of a buffer returns true if you can use relative get() or put() method on the buffer to read/write at least one element. You can also get the maximum number of elements you can read/write using relative get() or put() methods by using its remaining() method. Listing 9-3 demonstrates the use of these methods.

Listing 9-3. Using the flip() and hasRemaining() Methods of a Buffer Between Relative Reads and Writes

```java
// BufferReadWriteRelativeOnly.java
package com.jdojo.nio;

import java.nio.ByteBuffer;

public class BufferReadWriteRelativeOnly {
        public static void main(String[] args) {
                // Create a byte buffer of capacity 8
                ByteBuffer bb = ByteBuffer.allocate(8);

                // Print the buffer info
                System.out.println("After creation:");
                printBufferInfo(bb);

                // Must call flip() to reset the position to zero because
                // the printBufferInfo() method uses relative get() method,
                // which increments the position
                bb.flip();

                // Populate buffer elements from 50 to 57
                int i = 50;
                while (bb.hasRemaining()) {
                        bb.put((byte)i++);
                }

                // Call flip() again to reset the position to zero,
                // because the above put() call incremented the position
                bb.flip();

                // Print the buffer info
                System.out.println("After populating data:");
                printBufferInfo(bb);
        }

        public static void printBufferInfo(ByteBuffer bb) {
                int limit = bb.limit();
                System.out.println("Position = " + bb.position() +
                                ", Limit = " + limit);
```

```
                // We use absolute method of reading the data, so that we do
                // not affect the position of the buffer
                System.out.print("Data: ");
                while (bb.hasRemaining()) {
                        System.out.print(bb.get() + " ");
                }
                System.out.println();
        }
}
```

```
After creation:
Position = 0, Limit = 8
Data: 0 0 0 0 0 0 0 0
After populating data:
Position = 0, Limit = 8
Data: 50 51 52 53 54 55 56 57
```

Apart from the flip() method, there are three more methods of a buffer that change its mark, position, and/or limit. They are clear(), reset(), and rewind().

The clear() method of a buffer sets the position to zero, limit to its capacity, and discards its mark. That is, it sets the buffer's properties as if the buffer has just been created. Note that it does not change any data in the buffer. Figure 9-9 and 9-10 show the mark, position, and limit of a buffer before and after calling the clear() method. Typically, you call the clear() method on a buffer before you start filling it with fresh data.

Buffer Elements >>	50	51	52	53	54	0	0	0	
Element's Index >>	0	1	2	3	4	5	6	7	8
		M	P			L			

Figure 9-9. Buffer's state before calling its clear() method

Buffer Elements >>	50	51	52	53	54	0	0	0	
Element's Index >>	0	1	2	3	4	5	6	7	8
	P								L

Figure 9-10. Buffer's state after calling its clear() method. The clear() method discarded the mark

The reset() method sets the position of a buffer equal to its mark. If mark is not defined, it throws an InvalidMarkException. It does not affect the limit and data of the buffer. Typically, it is called to revisit (for rereading or rewriting) the buffer's elements starting from the previously marked position and up to the current position. The mark of the buffer remains unchanged by the reset() method. Figure 9-11 and 9-12 show the states of a buffer before and after its reset() method is called.

Buffer Elements >>	50	51	52	53	54	0	0	0	
Element's Index >>	0	1	2	3	4	5	6	7	8
		M	P			L			

Figure 9-11. Buffer's state before calling its reset() method

Buffer Elements >>	50	51	52	53	54	0	0	0	
Element's Index >>	0	1	2	3	4	5	6	7	8
		M P				L			

Figure 9-12. Buffer's state after calling its reset() method

The rewind() method sets the position of the buffer to zero and discards its mark. It does not affect the limit. Typically, you call this method between multiple read/write operations to use the same number of data elements in the buffer multiple times. Figure 9-13 and 9-14 show the state of a buffer before and after calling its rewind() method.

Buffer Elements >>	50	51	52	53	54	0	0	0	
Element's Index >>	0	1	2	3	4	5	6	7	8
			P			L			

Figure 9-13. Buffer's state before calling its rewind() method

Buffer Elements >>	50	51	52	53	54	0	0	0	
Element's Index >>	0	1	2	3	4	5	6	7	8
	P					L			

Figure 9-14. Buffer's state after calling its rewind() method

Read-Only Buffers

A buffer can be read-only or read-write. You can only read the contents of a read-only buffer. Any attempt to change the contents of a read-only buffer results in a ReadOnlyBufferException. Note that the properties of a read-only buffer such as its position, limit, and mark can be changed during the read operations, but not its data.

You may want to get a read-only buffer from a read-write buffer, so you can pass it as an argument to a method to make sure the method does not modify its contents. You can get a read-only buffer by calling the asReadOnlyBuffer() method of the specific buffer class. You can check if a buffer is read-only by calling the isReadOnly() method as follows:

```
// Create a buffer that is read-write by default
ByteBuffer bb = ByteBuffer.allocate(1024);
boolean readOnly = bb.isReadOnly(); // Assigns false to readOnly
```

```
// Get a read-only buffer
ByteBuffer bbReadOnly = bb.asReadOnlyBuffer();
readOnly = bbReadOnly.isReadOnly(); // Assigns true to readOnly
```

The read-only buffer returned by the asReadOnlyBuffer() method is a different view of the same buffer. That is, the new read-only buffer shares data with its original buffer. Any modifications to the contents of the original buffer are reflected in the read-only buffer. A read-only buffer has the same value of position, mark, limit, and capacity as its original buffer at the time of creation and it maintains them independently afterwards.

Different Views of a Buffer

You can obtain different views of a buffer. A view of a buffer shares data with the original buffer and maintains its own position, mark, and limit. I discussed getting a read-only view of a buffer in the previous section that does not let its contents be modified. You can also duplicate a buffer, in which case they share contents, but maintain mark, position, and limit independently. Use the duplicate() method of a buffer to get a copy of the buffer as follows:

```
// Create a buffer
ByteBuffer bb = ByteBuffer.allocate(1024);

// Create a duplicate view of the buffer
ByteBuffer bbDuplicate = bb.duplicate();
```

You can also create a sliced view of a buffer. That is, you can create a view of a buffer that reflects only a portion of the contents of the original buffer. You use the slice() method of a buffer to create its sliced view as follows:

```
// Create a buffer
ByteBuffer bb = ByteBuffer.allocate(8);

// Set the position and the limit before getting a slice
bb.position(3);
bb.limit(6);

// bbSlice buffer will share data of bb from index 3 to 5.
// bbSlice will have position set to 0 and its limit set to 3.
ByteBuffer bbSlice = bb.slice();
```

You can also get a view of a byte buffer for different primitive data types. For example, you can get a character view, a float view, etc. of a byte buffer. The ByteBuffer class contains methods such as asCharBuffer(), asLongBuffer(), asFloatBuffer(), etc. to obtain a view for primitive data types.

```
// Create a byte buffer
ByteBuffer bb = ByteBuffer.allocate(8);

// Create a char view of the byte buffer
CharBuffer cb = bb.asCharBuffer();

// Create a float view of the byte buffer
FloatBuffer fb = bb.asFloatBuffer();
```

Character Set

A character is not always stored in one byte. The number of bytes used to store a character depends on the coded character set and the character-encoding scheme. A coded-character set is a mapping between a set of abstract characters and a set of integers. A character-encoding scheme is a mapping between a coded-character set and a set of octet sequence. Please refer to Appendix A in *Beginning Java Fundamentals* (ISBN: 978-1-4302-6652-5) for more details on character set and character encoding.

An instance of the java.nio.charset.Charset class represents a character set and a character-encoding scheme in a Java program. Examples of some character set names are US-ASCII, ISO-8859-1, UTF-8, UTF-16BE, UTF-16LE, and UTF-16.

The process of converting a character into a sequence of bytes based on an encoding scheme is called *character encoding*. The process of converting a sequence of bytes into a character based on an encoding scheme is called *decoding*.

In NIO, you have the ability to convert a Unicode character to a sequence of bytes and vice versa using an encoding scheme. The java.nio.charset package provides classes to encode/decode a CharBuffer to a ByteBuffer and vice versa. An object of the Charset class represents the encoding scheme. The CharsetEncoder class performs the encoding. The CharsetDecoder class performs the decoding. You can get an object of the Charset class using its forName() method by passing the name of the character set as its argument.

The String and InputStreamReader classes support character encoding and decoding. When you use str.getBytes("UTF-8"), you are encoding the Unicode-characters stored in the string object str to a sequence of bytes using the UTF-8 encoding-scheme. When you use the constructor of the String class String(byte[] bytes, Charset charset) to create a String object, you are decoding the sequence of bytes in the bytes array from the specified character set to the Unicode-character set. You are also decoding a sequence of bytes from an input stream into Unicode-characters when you create an object of the InputStreamReader class using a character set.

For simple encoding and decoding tasks, you can use the encode() and decode() methods of the Charset class. Let's encode a sequence of characters in the string Hello stored in a character buffer and decode it using the UTF-8 encoding-scheme. The snippet of code to achieve this is as follows:

```
// Get a Charset object for UTF-8 encoding
Charset cs = Charset.forName("UTF-8");

// Character buffer to be encoded
CharBuffer cb = CharBuffer.wrap("Hello");

// Encode character buffer into a byte buffer
ByteBuffer encodedData = cs.encode(cb);

// Decode the byte buffer back to a character buffer
CharBuffer decodedData = cs.decode(encodedData);
```

The encode() and decode() methods of the Charset class are easy to use. However, they cannot be used in all situations. They require you to know the inputs in advance. Sometimes you do not know the data to be encoded/decoded in advance.

CharsetEncoder and CharsetDecoder classes provide much more power during the encoding and decoding process. They accept a chunk of input to be encoded or decoded. The encode() and decode() methods of the Charset class return the encoded and decoded buffers to you. However, CharsetEncoder and CharsetDecoder will let you use your buffers for input and output data. The power comes with a little complexity! If you want more powerful encoding/decoding, you will need to use the following five classes instead of just the Charset class:

- Charset

- CharsetEncoder

- CharsetDecoder

- CoderResult

- CodingErrorAction

You will still need to use the Charset class to represent a character set. A CharsetEncoder object lets you encode characters into a sequence of bytes using its encode() method. A sequence of bytes is decoded using the decode() method of a CharsetDecoder object. The newEncoder() method of a Charset object returns an instance of the CharsetEncoder class whereas its newDecoder() method returns an instance of the CharsetDecoder class.

```
// Get encoder and decoder objects from a Charset object
Charset cs = Charset.forName("UTF-8");
CharsetEncoder encoder = cs.newEncoder();
CharsetDecoder decoder = cs.newDecoder();
```

Two buffers, an input buffer and an output buffer, are needed for encoding and decoding. A character buffer supplies the input characters to the encoding process and receives the decoded characters from the decoding process. The encoding process writes the encoded result into a byte buffer and the decoding process reads its input from a byte buffer. The following snippet of code illustrates the few steps in using an encoder and a decoder:

```
// Encode characters in inputChars buffer.
// outputBytes buffer will receive encoded bytes.
CharBuffer inputChars = get input characters to be encoded;
ByteBuffer outputBytes = get the output buffer for the encoded data;

boolean eoi = true; // Indicates the end of the input
CoderResult result = encoder.encode(inputChars, outputBytes, eoi);

// Decode bytes in inputBytes buffer.
// outputChars buffer will receive the decoded characters.
ByteBuffer inputBytes = get the input bytes to be decoded;
CharBuffer outputChars = get the output buffer for the decoded characters;

boolean eoi = true; // Indicates the end of the input
CoderResult result = encoder.decode(inputBytes, outputChars, eoi);
```

Consider a situation of encoding 16 characters stored in a character buffer using a 4-byte buffer. The encoding process cannot encode all characters in one call to the encode() method. There must be a way to read all encoded output repeatedly. You can apply the same argument for the decoding process. You can pass an input to the encoding/decoding process and receive an output from them in chunks. The encoder's encode() method and decoder's decode() method return an object of the CoderResult class, which contains the status of the encoding/decoding process. There are two important results that this object can indicate: an Underflow or an Overflow.

- Underflow: It indicates that the process needs more input. You can test for this condition by using the isUnderflow() method of the CoderResult object. You can also test this condition by comparing the return value of the encode() or decode() method with CoderResult.UNDERFLOW object as follows:

  ```
  CoderResult result = encoder.encode(input, output, eoi);
  if (result == CoderResult.UNDERFLOW) {
    // Supply some more input
  }
  ```

- Overflow: It indicates that the process has produced more output than the capacity of the output buffer. You need to empty the output buffer and call the encode()/decode() method again to get more output. You can test for this condition by using the isOverflow() method of the CoderResult object. You can also test for this condition by comparing the return value of the encode() or decode() method with CoderResult.OVERFLOW object as follows:

```
CoderResult result = encoder.encode(input, output, eoi);
if (result == CoderResult.OVERFLOW) {
   // Empty output buffer to make some room for more output
}
```

Tip Apart from reporting buffer underflow and overflow, a CoderResult object is also capable of reporting a malformed-input error and an unmappable-character error. You can also customize the default action of the encoding/decoding engine for these error conditions by using their onMalformedInput() and onUnmappableCharacter() methods.

The last argument to the encode()/decode() method is a boolean value indicating the end of the input. You should pass true for the end of the input argument when you pass the last chunk of data for encoding or decoding.

After passing the last chunk of data, you need to call the flush() method to flush the internal buffer of the engine. It returns an object of CoderResult that can indicate underflow or overflow. If there is an overflow, you need to empty the output buffer and call the flush() method again. You need to keep calling the flush() method until its return value indicates an underflow. The flush() method call should be placed in a loop, so you get all of the encoded/decoded data.

Listings 9-4 and 9-5 demonstrate how to use a character set encoder/decoder. The DataSourceSink class serves as a data source and a data sink. I have created this class only for illustration purposes; you would not need a class like this in a real-world application. It supplies a stanza from the poem *Lucy* by William Wordsworth in a character buffer. The getCharData() method fills the character buffer. It returns -1 when there are no more characters to supply. You use this method during the encoding process. The storeByteData() method is used to accumulate the encoded bytes during encoding process. The getByteData() method is used during the decoding process to supply the encoded bytes in chunks that you accumulate during the encoding process. The encode() and decode() methods of the CharEncoderDecoder class have the encoding and decoding logic. This example displays the decoded characters on the standard output.

Listing 9-4. A Data Source and Sink that Supplies Character Data, Stores and Supplies Byte Data

```java
// DataSourceSink.java
package com.jdojo.nio;

import java.nio.ByteBuffer;
import java.nio.CharBuffer;

public class DataSourceSink {
        private CharBuffer cBuffer = null;
        private ByteBuffer bBuffer = null;

        public DataSourceSink() {
                String text = getText();
                cBuffer = CharBuffer.wrap(text);
        }
```

```java
    public int getByteData(ByteBuffer buffer) {
        if (!bBuffer.hasRemaining()) {
            return -1;
        }

        int count = 0;
        while (bBuffer.hasRemaining() && buffer.hasRemaining()) {
            buffer.put(bBuffer.get());
            count++;
        }
        return count;
    }

    public int getCharData(CharBuffer buffer) {
        if (!cBuffer.hasRemaining()) {
            return -1;
        }

        int count = 0;
        while (cBuffer.hasRemaining() && buffer.hasRemaining()) {
            buffer.put(cBuffer.get());
            count++;
        }

        return count;
    }

    public void storeByteData(ByteBuffer byteData) {
        if (this.bBuffer == null) {
            int total = byteData.remaining();
            this.bBuffer = ByteBuffer.allocate(total);
            while (byteData.hasRemaining()) {
                this.bBuffer.put(byteData.get());
            }
            this.bBuffer.flip();
        }
        else {
            this.bBuffer = this.appendContent(byteData);
        }
    }

    private ByteBuffer appendContent(ByteBuffer content) {
        // Create a new buffer to accommodate new data
        int count = bBuffer.limit() + content.remaining();
        ByteBuffer newBuffer = ByteBuffer.allocate(count);

        // Set the position of bBuffer that has some data
        bBuffer.clear();
        newBuffer.put(bBuffer);
        newBuffer.put(content);
```

```
                bBuffer.clear();
                newBuffer.clear();
                return newBuffer;
        }

        public String getText() {
                String newLine = System.getProperty("line.separator");
                StringBuilder sb = new StringBuilder();
                sb.append("My horse moved on; hoof after hoof");
                sb.append(newLine);
                sb.append("He raised, and never stopped:");
                sb.append(newLine);
                sb.append("When down behind the cottage roof,");
                sb.append(newLine);
                sb.append("At once, the bright moon dropped.");

                return sb.toString();
        }
}
```

Listing 9-5. Charset Encoder and Decoder Using a DataSourceSink as a Data Supplier/Consumer for Encoding/Decoding

```
// CharEncoderDecoder.java
package com.jdojo.nio;

import java.nio.ByteBuffer;
import java.nio.CharBuffer;
import java.nio.charset.Charset;
import java.nio.charset.CharsetDecoder;
import java.nio.charset.CharsetEncoder;
import java.nio.charset.CoderResult;

public class CharEncoderDecoder {
        public static void main(String[] args) throws Exception {
                DataSourceSink dss = new DataSourceSink();

                // Display the text we are going to encode
                System.out.println("Original Text:");
                System.out.println(dss.getText());
                System.out.println("--------------------");

                // Encode the text using UTF-8 encoding. We will store
                // encoded bytes in the dss object during the encoding process
                encode(dss, "UTF-8");

                // Decode bytes stored in the dss object using UTF-8 encoding
                System.out.println("Decoded Text:");
                decode(dss, "UTF-8");
        }
```

```java
public static void encode(DataSourceSink ds, String charset) {
        CharsetEncoder encoder = Charset.forName(charset).newEncoder();

        CharBuffer input = CharBuffer.allocate(8);
        ByteBuffer output = ByteBuffer.allocate(8);

        // Initialize variables for loop
        boolean endOfInput = false;
        CoderResult result = CoderResult.UNDERFLOW;

        while (!endOfInput) {
                if (result == CoderResult.UNDERFLOW) {
                        input.clear();
                        endOfInput = (ds.getCharData(input) == -1);
                        input.flip();
                }

                // Encode the input characters
                result = encoder.encode(input, output, endOfInput);

                // Drain output when
                // 1. It is an overflow. Or,
                // 2. It is an underflow and it is the end of the input

                if (result == CoderResult.OVERFLOW ||
                        (endOfInput && result == CoderResult.UNDERFLOW)) {
                        output.flip();
                        ds.storeByteData(output);
                        output.clear();
                }
        }

        // Flush the internal state of the encoder
        while (true) {
                output.clear();
                result = encoder.flush(output);
                output.flip();
                if (output.hasRemaining()) {
                        ds.storeByteData(output);
                        output.clear();
                }

                // Underflow means flush() method has flushed everything
                if (result == CoderResult.UNDERFLOW) {
                        break;
                }
        }
}
```

```java
public static void decode(DataSourceSink dss, String charset) {
        CharsetDecoder decoder = Charset.forName(charset).newDecoder();
        ByteBuffer input = ByteBuffer.allocate(8);
        CharBuffer output = CharBuffer.allocate(8);

        boolean endOfInput = false;
        CoderResult result = CoderResult.UNDERFLOW;

        while (!endOfInput) {
                if (result == CoderResult.UNDERFLOW) {
                        input.clear();
                        endOfInput = (dss.getByteData(input) == -1);
                        input.flip();
                }

                // Decode the input bytes
                result = decoder.decode(input, output, endOfInput);

                // Drain output when
                // 1. It is an overflow. Or,
                // 2. It is an underflow and it is the end of the input
                if (result == CoderResult.OVERFLOW ||
                        (endOfInput && result == CoderResult.UNDERFLOW)) {

                        output.flip();
                        while (output.hasRemaining()) {
                                System.out.print(output.get());
                        }
                        output.clear();

                }
        }

        // Flush the internal state of the decoder
        while (true) {
                output.clear();
                result = decoder.flush(output);
                output.flip();
                while (output.hasRemaining()) {
                        System.out.print(output.get());
                }

                if (result == CoderResult.UNDERFLOW) {
                        break;
                }
        }
    }
}
```

```
Original Text:
My horse moved on; hoof after hoof
He raised, and never stopped:
When down behind the cottage roof,
At once, the bright moon dropped.
--------------------
Decoded Text:
My horse moved on; hoof after hoof
He raised, and never stopped:
When down behind the cottage roof,
At once, the bright moon dropped.
```

You can get the list of all available character sets supported by the JVM using the static method availableCharsets() of the Charset class, which returns a Map. The key of the Map is a character set name and the value is the Charset object that represents the character set.

■ **Tip** You can create your own character encoder/decoder by using the CharsetProvider class in java.nio.charset.spi package. You need to explore the java.nio.charset and java.nio.charset.spi packages for details on how to create and install your own character set. This book does not cover how to create and install a custom character set.

Listing 9-6 demonstrates how to list all character sets supported by a JVM. A partial output is shown. When you run the program, you may get a different output.

Listing 9-6. List of Available Character Sets Supported by Your JVM

```java
// AvailableCharsets.java
package com.jdojo.nio;

import java.util.Map;
import java.nio.charset.Charset;
import java.util.Set;

public class AvailableCharsets {
        public static void main(String[] args) {
                Map<String, Charset> map = Charset.availableCharsets();
                Set<String> keys = map.keySet();
                System.out.println("Available Character Set Count: " + keys.size());

                for(String charsetName : keys) {
                        System.out.println(charsetName);
                }
        }
}
```

```
Available Character Set Count: 160
Big5
ISO-8859-1
US-ASCII
UTF-16
UTF-16BE
UTF-16LE
UTF-32
UTF-32BE
UTF-32LE
UTF-8
windows-1250
x-iso-8859-11
...
```

Channels

A channel is an open connection between a data source/data sink and a Java program to perform some I/O operations. The Channel interface is in the java.nio.channels package. It is used as a base to implement channels in Java. It declares only two methods: close() and isOpen(). When a channel is created, it is open and its isOpen() method returns true. Once you are finished using a channel, you should call its close() method to close it. At that point, isOpen() returns false. Figure 9-15 depicts the class diagram for the Channel interface.

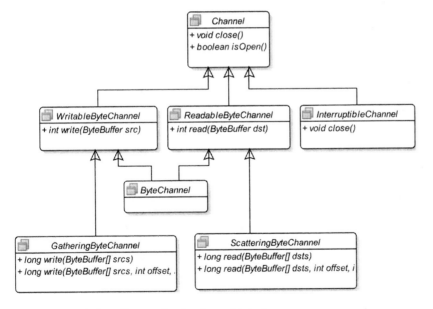

Figure 9-15. *A class diagram for the channel interface*

Your Java program interacts with a channel for an I/O operation using byte buffers. That is, even if you have many different kinds of buffers, you will need to convert them to a byte buffer before you can pass them to a channel for reading/writing data.

A ReadableByteChannel is used to read data from a data source into a byte buffer using its read() method. A WritableByteChannel is used to write data from a byte buffer to a data sink using its write() method. A ByteChannel is capable of both reading and writing byte data using its read() and write() methods, respectively.

A ScatteringByteChannel reads data from a data source into multiple byte buffers. It is useful to read data from a known file format or a similar data source, where data is supplied in some fixed-length headers followed by a variable length body. For example, suppose a file has a 256-byte fixed-length header and a variable length body. An object of the ScatteringByteChannel class is used to read data from this kind of file using two byte buffers. The first byte buffer will be of capacity 256. The second buffer will be of a size of your choice. When you pass these two buffers to this channel, the fixed-length header of 256 bytes will be read in the first buffer. The second buffer will have the file data and you may have to use the second buffer multiple times to read the rest of bytes from the file. The advantage of using this channel is separating the fixed-length header data from other data.

A GatheringByteChannel performs just the opposite of what a ScatteringByteChannel performs. It writes data from multiple byte buffers to a data sink. It is used to write data in a format that is grouped in some fixed-length headers, followed by a variable length body.

An InterruptibleChannel channel can be closed asynchronously. If a thread is blocked on an I/O operation on this channel, another thread can call its close() method to close it. The blocked thread will receive an AsynchronousCloseException. If a thread is blocked on an I/O operation on this channel, another thread can call the interrupt() method on the blocked thread. This channel is closed, and the blocked thread receives a ClosedByInterruptException exception.

Typically, you do not deal with these channel interfaces directly in your Java program. You will be dealing with concrete channel classes that implement one or more of these interfaces. Unlike streams, you do not create a channel directly. You get it indirectly by calling a method. To obtain a channel for a data source and a data sink, you will need to create an object of InputStream and OutputStream using old ways of working with I/O using classes in the java.io package. The Channels class in the java.nio.channels package is a utility class that has many static methods to convert streams into channels and vice versa. The Channels class also provides methods to convert readers/writers to channels and vice versa. For example, if you have an input stream object named myInputStream, you can obtain a ReadableByteChannel as follows:

```
// Get a ReadableByteChannel from an InputStream
ReadableByteChannel rbc = Channels.newChannel(myInputStream);
```

If you have a ReadableByteChannel named rbc, you can obtain the underlying InputStream object as follows:

```
// Get the InputStream of the ReadableByteChannel
InputStream myInputStream = Channels.newInputStream(rbc);
```

For NIO, the FileInputStream and FileOutputStream classes have been modified to work with channels. They have a new method called getChannel() to return a FileChannel object. A FileChannel is used to read and write data to a file. The FileChannel object obtained from a FileInputStream is opened in a read-only mode. A FileChannel object obtained from a FileOutputStream object is opened in a write-only mode. If you obtain a FileChannel from a RandomAccessFile, it is opened in a read-only, write-only, or read-write mode, depending on the way you create that RandomAccessFile object. The following snippet of code obtains FileChannel objects for different kinds of file streams:

```
FileInputStream fis = new FileInputStream("luci1.txt");
FileChannel fcReadOnly = fis.getChannel(); // A read-only channel

FileOutputStream fos = new FileOutputStream("luci1.txt");
FileChannel fcWriteOnly = fos.getChannel(); // A write-only channel
```

```
// Open file in a read-only mode
RandomAccessFile raf1 = new RandomAccessFile("luci1.txt", "r");
FileChannel rafReadOnly = raf1.getChannel(); // A read-only channel

// Open file in a read-write mode
RandomAccessFile raf2 = new RandomAccessFile("luci1.txt", "rw");
FileChannel rafReadWrite = raf2.getChannel(); // A read-write channel
```

■ **Tip** Starting from Java 7, you can obtain a FileChannel using the FileChannel.open() static method. This avoids the need to create an input/output stream to create a FileChannel. The new open() method uses a Path object, which is part of NIO 2. Please refer to Chapter 9 on NIO 2 for more details on using a Path object.

Reading/Writing Files

I have covered the basic concepts of buffers and channels. A FileChannel object maintains a position variable as a buffer does. The read() and write() methods for FileChannel come in two varieties: relative position read/write and absolute position read/write. The meanings of relative and absolute position read/write are the same as in the context of a buffer read/write. When you open a FileChannel, its position is set to 0, which is the beginning of the file. When you read from a FileChannel using a relative read() method, its position is incremented by the number of bytes read. An absolute position read from a FileChannel does not affect its position. You can get the current value of the position of a FileChannel object using its position() method. You can set its position to a new position using its position(int newPosition) method. You need to follow a few easy steps to read data from a file and to write data to a file using NIO.

The steps to read data from a file using buffer and channel are as follows:

- Create an object of FileInputStream.

- Get a FileChannel object using the getChannel() method of FileInputStream.

- Create a ByteBuffer object to read data from the file.

- Call the read() method of the FileChannel object by passing the ByteBuffer object. Make sure that before you pass the byte buffer, the buffer's position and limit are set appropriately. A simple rule of thumb is to always call the clear() method on the byte buffer before passing it to a channel to read data into it. The read() method of a channel returns the number of bytes read into the buffer.

- Call the flip() method of the buffer, so you can read data into your Java program from the buffer. The previous step will change the position of the buffer because the channel reads data into it. You may need to use a CharsetDecoder object to decode the byte buffer into a character buffer if the bytes you have read represent characters.

- Read data from the buffer into your Java program.

- Repeat the process of reading data from the FileChannel into the buffer by calling its read() method until the read() method returns 0 or –1.

- Close the channel using its close() method.

■ **Tip** Like input/output streams, channels are also `AutoCloseable`. If you use a `try-with-resources` statement to obtain a channel, the channel will be closed automatically, thus avoiding a need for you to call the `close()` method of the channel explicitly.

Listing 9-7 puts all of the above steps together. It reads text from a file named `luci1.txt`. The file should be in your current working directory. If the file does not exist, the program prints a message with the full path of where the file is expected to exist. If you do not have this file, create it and enter the following text in the file, before you run the program:

```
STRANGE fits of passion have I known:
And I will dare to tell,
But in the lover's ear alone,
What once to me befell.
```

You need to pay close attention to the call to the `clear()` and `flip()` methods on a buffer. When you call the `read()` or `write()` method of a channel, it performs a relative position read/write on the buffer. Therefore, you must call the `flip()` method of the buffer to read data from it after the channel writes data into the buffer.

Listing 9-7. Reading from a File Using a Buffer and a Channel

```java
// FileChannelRead.java
package com.jdojo.nio;

import java.io.File;
import java.io.FileInputStream;
import java.io.IOException;
import java.nio.ByteBuffer;
import java.nio.channels.FileChannel;

public class FileChannelRead {
    public static void main(String[] args) {
        // The input file to read from
        File inputFile = new File("luci1.txt");

        // Make sure the input file exists
        if (!inputFile.exists()) {
            System.out.println("The input file " +
                inputFile.getAbsolutePath() + " does not exist.");
            System.out.println("Aborted the file reading process.");
            return;
        }

        // Obtain channel for luci1.txt file to read from it
        try (FileChannel fileChannel
                    = new FileInputStream(inputFile).getChannel()) {

            // Create a buffer
            ByteBuffer buffer = ByteBuffer.allocate(1024);
```

```
                  // Read all data from the channel
                  while (fileChannel.read(buffer) > 0) {
                          // Flip the buffer before we can read data from it
                          buffer.flip();

                          // Display the read data as characters on the console
                          // Note that we are assuming that a byte represents a
                          // character, which is not true all the time. In a
                          // real world application, you should use
                          // CharsetDecoder to decode the bytes into character
                          // before you display/use them.
                          while (buffer.hasRemaining()) {
                                  byte b = buffer.get();

                                  // Assuming a byte represents a character
                                  System.out.print((char) b);
                          }

                          // Clear the buffer before next read into it
                          buffer.clear();
                  }
          }
          catch (IOException e) {
                  e.printStackTrace();
          }
     }
}
```

STRANGE fits of passion have I known:
And I will dare to tell,
But in the lover's ear alone,
What once to me befell.

The steps to write data to a file using a buffer and a channel are as follows:

- Create an object of FileOutputStream.

- Get a FileChannel object using the getChannel() method of FileOutputStream.

- Create a ByteBuffer object to write data to the file.

- Fill the ByteBuffer with data.

- Call the flip() method of the buffer to get it ready to be read by the channel.

- Call the write() method of the FileChannel object by passing the ByteBuffer object filled with data .

- Close the channel by calling its close() method.

Listing 9-8 puts all the above steps together to write the following text to luci5.txt file:

In one of those sweet dreams I slept,
Kind Nature's gentlest boon!
And all the while my eyes I kept
On the descending moon.

The code creates a string from the text inserting a platform-dependent new line character between two lines. It converts the text into a byte array, creates a byte buffer by wrapping the byte array, and writes the buffer to the file channel. Note that you do not need to use the flip() method on the buffer because, before passing it to the channel for writing, your buffer object was just created with the text, and its position and limit were set appropriately by the wrap() method. The program prints the path of the file in which the text was written that may be different on your machine.

Listing 9-8. Writing to a File Using a Buffer and a Channel

```java
// FileChannelWrite.java
package com.jdojo.nio;

import java.io.File;
import java.nio.channels.FileChannel;
import java.io.IOException;
import java.nio.ByteBuffer;
import java.io.FileOutputStream;

public class FileChannelWrite {
        public static void main(String[] args) {
                // The output file to write to
                File outputFile = new File("luci5.txt");

                try (FileChannel fileChannel =
                        new FileOutputStream(outputFile).getChannel()) {

                        // Get the text as string
                        String text = getText();

                        // Convert text into byte array
                        byte[] byteData = text.toString().getBytes("UTF-8");

                        // Create a ByteBuffer using the byte array
                        ByteBuffer buffer = ByteBuffer.wrap(byteData);

                        // Write bytes to the file
                        fileChannel.write(buffer);

                        System.out.println("Data has been written to " +
                                        outputFile.getAbsolutePath());
                }
                catch (IOException e1) {
                        e1.printStackTrace();
                }
        }

        public static String getText() {
                String lineSeparator = System.getProperty("line.separator");
                StringBuilder sb = new StringBuilder();
                sb.append("In one of those sweet dreams I slept,");
                sb.append(lineSeparator);
                sb.append("Kind Nature's gentlest boon!");
                sb.append(lineSeparator);
```

```
                sb.append("And all the while my eyes I kept");
                sb.append(lineSeparator);
                sb.append("On the descending moon.");

                return sb.toString();
        }
}
```

```
Data has been written to C:\book\javabook\luci5.txt
```

A file has two kinds of data associated with it. One is its contents and the other is metadata such as creation time, last-modified time, etc. When you write data to a file channel, the data may not be actually written to the storage device (for example, the hard disk) immediately. To write the data to the storage device immediately, after a call to the write() method on a file channel, you can call its force(boolean metaData) method. It guarantees that the file's contents and metadata are written to its storage device. If you call force(false), only the file's metadata is written to the storage device. If you call force(true), both the file's content and its metadata are written to the storage device. In fact, this is guaranteed only if the storage device is local. Otherwise, the JVM tries its best to write the data to the storage device.

■ **Tip**   A file channel works only with byte buffers. In the examples in this section, I have assumed that a character is represented in a byte, which is true only when you are using an encoding such as US-ASCII or UTF-8 for English alphabets. Please refer to the "Character Set" section on how to encode a character buffer into a byte buffer and how to decode a byte buffer into a character buffer.

Memory-Mapped File I/O

There is another way to perform I/O on a file, which is by mapping a region of the file into physical memory and treating it as a memory array. This is the fastest way available to perform file I/O in Java. Using a special kind of byte buffer called MappedByteBuffer lets you perform memory-mapped file I/O.

For memory-mapped file I/O, start by obtaining a FileChannel object for the file, and use the map() method of the FileChannel to get a MappedByteBuffer. Read or write directly to the mapped byte buffer instead of using the read() or write() method of the FileChannel object. When you read from the mapped byte buffer, you read from the file's region you have mapped. When you write to the mapped byte buffer, you write to the mapped region of the file. If you want to write the written data to the mapped byte buffer immediately to the storage device, you need to use the force() method of the mapped byte buffer. There is no boolean argument to force() related to metadata.

Once you obtain the mapped byte buffer from a FileChannel, closing the channel has no effect on your buffer. You can keep reading/writing the mapped byte buffer, even after the FileChannel is closed.

You can map a region of a file in a read-only, read-write, or private mode. In a read-only mode, you can only read from the mapped byte buffer. In a read-write mode, you can read from as well as write to the mapped byte buffer. The private mode needs a little explanation. This mode is also called a *copy-on-write* mode. When multiple programs map the same region of a file, a separate copy of that region is not created for each program. Rather, all programs share the same region of the file. However, when a program modifies the mapped region, a separate copy of that region is created only for that program, which is its private copy. Any modification made to the private copy is not visible to other programs.

The following snippet of code maps the whole file luci5.txt in a read-only mode. It reads the file and displays the contents on the standard output.

```
FileInputStream fis = new FileInputStream("luci5.txt");
FileChannel fc = fis.getChannel();

long startRegion = 0;
long endRegion = fc.size();
MappedByteBuffer mbb = fc.map(FileChannel.MapMode.READ_ONLY,
                             startRegion, endRegion);
while(mbb.hasRemaining()) {
   System.out.print((char)mbb.get());
}

fc.close();
```

File Locking

NIO supports file locking to synchronize access to a file. You have the ability to lock a region of a file or the entire file. The file locking mechanism is handled by the operating system and therefore its exact effect is platform-dependent. On some operating systems, a file lock is advisory, whereas on some, it is mandatory. Since it is handled by the operating system, its effect is visible to other programs as well as to Java programs running in other JVMs.

■ **Tip** An advisory lock lets other users use the file on which you have acquired the lock, but prevents them from acquiring a lock on the same file. A mandatory lock forces the user to acquire a lock on the file before the file can be used.

There are two kinds of file locking: *exclusive* and *shared*. Only one program can hold an exclusive lock on a region of a file. Multiple programs can hold shared locks on the same region of a file. You cannot mix an exclusive lock and a shared lock on the same region of a file. If a program has a shared lock on a region, another program must wait to get an exclusive lock on that region and vice versa. Some operating systems do not support a shared file lock, and in that case, the request for a shared file lock is converted to a request for an exclusive file lock.

An object of the FileLock class, which is in the java.nio.channels package, represents a file lock. You acquire a lock on a file by using the lock() or tryLock() method of the FileChannel object. The lock() method blocks if the lock on the requested region of the file is not available. The tryLock() method does not block; it returns immediately. It returns an object of the FileLock class if the lock was acquired; otherwise, it returns null.

Both lock() and tryLock() methods have two versions: one without an argument and another with three arguments. The version without an argument locks the entire file. The version with three arguments accepts the starting position of the region to lock, the number of bytes to lock, and a boolean flag to indicate if the lock is shared. The isShared() method of the FileLock object returns true if the lock is shared; otherwise, it returns false.

The following snippet of code shows different ways of obtaining locks on a file. The exception handling code is omitted for readability.

```
// Create a random access file and obtain a channel for it
RandomAccessFile raf = new RandomAccessFile("test.txt", "rw");
FileChannel fileChannel = raf.getChannel();

// Get an exclusive lock on the file
FileLock lock = fileChannel.lock();
```

```
// Get an exclusive lock on first 10 bytes
FileLock lock = fileChannel.lock(0, 10, false);

// Try to get an exclusive lock on the entire file
FileLock lock = fileChannel.tryLock();
if (lock == null) {
        // Could not get the lock
}
else {
        // Got the lock
}

// Try to lock 100 bytes starting from the 11th byte in a shared mode
FileLock lock = fileChannel.tryLock(11, 100, true);
if (lock == null) {
        // Could not get the lock
}
else {
        // Got the lock
}
```

The file region that you lock may not be contained in the range of the file size. Suppose you have a file with a size of 100 bytes. When you request a lock on this file, you can specify that you want to lock a region of this file starting at byte 11 and covering 5000 bytes. Note that this file contains only 100 bytes; you are locking 5000 bytes. In such a case, if the file size grows beyond 100 bytes, your lock covers the additional region of the file. Suppose you locked 0 to 100 bytes of a 100-byte file. If this file grows to 150 bytes, your lock does not cover the last 50 bytes that was added after you acquired the lock. The lock() and tryLock() methods of the FileChannel object, where you do not specify any argument, lock a region from 0 to Long.MAX_VALUE of the file. The two method calls fc.lock() and fc.lock(0, Long.MAX_VALUE, false) have the same effect.

When you are done with the file lock, you need to release it by using the release() method. A file lock is released in three ways: by calling its release() method, by closing the file channel it is obtained from, and by shutting down the JVM. It is good practice to use a try-catch-finally block to acquire and release a file lock as follows:

```
RandomAccessFile raf = new RandomAccessFile("test.txt", "rw");
FileChannel fileChannel = raf.getChannel();
FileLock lock = null;
try {
        lock = fileChannel.lock(0, 10, true);

        /* Work with the file here */
}
catch(IOException e) {
        // Handle the exception
}
finally {
        if (lock != null) {
                try {
                        lock.release();
                }
```

```
        catch(IOException e) {
                // Handle the exception
        }
    }
}
```

Copying Contents of a File

You can use buffers and channels to copy a file much faster. Copying the contents of a file to another file is just one method call when you use a FileChannel. Get the FileChannel object for the source file and the destination file, and call the transferTo() method on the source FileChannel object or call the transferFrom() method on the sink FileChannel object. The following snippet of code shows how to copy file luci5.txt to luci5_copy.txt:

```
// Obtain the source and sink channels
FileChannel sourceChannel = new FileInputStream(sourceFile).getChannel();
FileChannel sinkChannel = new FileOutputStream(sinkFile).getChannel();

// Copy source file contents to the sink file
sourceChannel.transferTo(0, sourceChannel.size(), sinkChannel);

// Instead of using the transferTo() method on the source channel,
// you can also use the transferFrom() method on the sink channel
sinkChannel.transferFrom(sourceChannel, 0, sourceChannel.size());
```

Listing 9-9 contains the complete code. The program prints the path of the source and destination files when the file copy succeeds.

Listing 9-9. Copying a File's Contents Using a FileChannel

```
// FastestFileCopy.java
package com.jdojo.nio;

import java.io.IOException;
import java.io.File;
import java.io.FileInputStream;
import java.io.FileOutputStream;
import java.nio.channels.FileChannel;

public class FastestFileCopy {
    public static void main(String[] args) {
        File sourceFile = new File("luci5.txt");
        File sinkFile = new File("luci5_copy.txt");
        try {
            copy(sourceFile, sinkFile, false);
            System.out.println(sourceFile.getAbsoluteFile() +
                            " has been copied to " +
                            sinkFile.getAbsolutePath());
        }
        catch (IOException e) {
            System.out.println(e.getMessage());
        }
    }
```

```java
    public static void copy(File sourceFile,
            File sinkFile, boolean overwrite) throws IOException {

        String msg = "";

        // Perform some error checks
        if (!sourceFile.exists()) {
            msg = "Source file " + sourceFile.getAbsolutePath() +
                    " does not exist.";
            throw new IOException(msg);
        }

        if (sinkFile.exists() && !overwrite) {
            msg = "Destination file " +
                    sinkFile.getAbsolutePath() +
                    " already exists.";
            throw new IOException(msg);
        }

        // Obtain source and sink file channels in a
        // try-with-resources block, so they are closed automatically.
        try (FileChannel srcChannel =
                    new FileInputStream(sourceFile).getChannel();
             FileChannel sinkChannel =
                    new FileOutputStream(sinkFile).getChannel()) {

            // Copy source file contents to the sink file
            srcChannel.transferTo(0, srcChannel.size(), sinkChannel);
        }
    }
}
```

Knowing the Byte Order of a Machine

If you ever wanted to know the byte order (also called endian-ness) of your machine, you need to use the nativeOrder() method of the ByteOrder class, shown in Listing 9-10. The byte order of a machine/buffer is discussed in detail in the next section. The program prints the byte order of the machine on which it is run. You may get a different output.

Listing 9-10. Knowing the Endia-ness (Byte Order) of Your Machine

```java
// MachineByteOrder.java
package com.jdojo.nio;

import java.nio.ByteOrder;

public class MachineByteOrder {
    public static void main(String args[]) {
        ByteOrder b = ByteOrder.nativeOrder();
```

```
                if (b.equals(ByteOrder.BIG_ENDIAN)) {
                        System.out.println("Big endian");
                }
                else {
                        System.out.println("Little endian");
                }
        }
}
```

```
Little endian
```

Byte Buffer and Its Byte Order

A byte order is the order in which bytes of a multi-byte value are stored. Suppose you have a short value 300 stored in a variable as follows:

```
short s = 300;
```

A short value is stored in two bytes. The value 300 can be represented in 16-bits as 0000000100101100, where the rightmost bit is the least significant bit and the leftmost bit is the most significant bit. You can split the 16-bit into two bytes as 00000001 and 00101100. At the byte level, you can think of 00000001 as the most significant byte and 00101100 as the least significant byte. If you consider two bytes separately for a short value, you may store them as either 00000001 followed by 00101100 or 00101100 followed by 00000001. As long as you know the order of the bytes in which they are stored, you would be able to compute the correct value 300 using either form of the 16-bits: 0000000100101100 or 0010110000000001.

A byte order is called *big endian* if the bytes of a multi-bytes value are stored from the most significant byte to the least significant byte. If the bytes of a multi-byte value are stored from the least significant byte to the most significant byte, it is known as little endian. To remember the two definitions easily, you can replace the word "big" with "most significant," "little" with "least significant," and "endian" with "first". That is, remember "big endian" as "most significant first" and "little endian" as "least significant first."

If you store a short value of 300 as 0000000100101100, you are using the big endian byte order. In the little endian byte order, you would store 300 as 0010110000000001, which seems backwards for representing a 16-bit value.

When you deal with byte data in a byte buffer, you may be considering each byte as an independent byte. A byte in a byte buffer may be part of a bigger value. When a byte value in a byte buffer is independent, the byte order is not a consideration. When a byte in a byte buffer is part of a bigger value (e.g. two bytes of a short value 300), the byte order becomes very important in reading. If you read two bytes from a byte buffer to compute a short value, you must know how those two bytes are stored. Suppose you read two bytes as 0000000100101100. If it is in a big endian byte order, it represents a value 300. If it is in a little endian byte order, it represents a value of 11265.

Java uses a big-endian byte order to store data. By default, a byte buffer uses a big endian byte order. An instance of the java.nio.ByteOrder class represents a byte order. You will not need to instantiate this class because you always use the value that represents a byte order; you don't create a new byte order. In fact, this class has no public constructor. You can use two constants, BIG_ENDIAN and LITTLE_ENDIAN, which are defined in the ByteOrder class to represent these byte orders.

■ **Tip** A byte order is meaningful only in a multi-byte value stored in a byte buffer. You may also need to deal with byte orders when you are dealing with two different systems that use different byte orders.

Listing 9-11 demonstrates how to get and set byte order for a byte buffer. You use the order() method of the ByteBuffer class to get or set the byte order. The program stores a short value of 300 in two bytes of a byte buffer. It displays the values stored in the first and the second bytes using both big endian and little endian byte orders. The output shows the values of bytes in decimal as 1 and 44, whose binary equivalents are 00000001 and 00101100, respectively.

Listing 9-11. Setting the Byte Order of a Byte Buffer

```java
// ByteBufferOrder.java
package com.jdojo.nio;

import java.nio.ByteBuffer;
import java.nio.ByteOrder;

public class ByteBufferOrder {
    public static void main(String[] args) {
        ByteBuffer bb = ByteBuffer.allocate(2);
        System.out.println("Default Byte Order: " + bb.order());
        bb.putShort((short) 300);
        bb.flip();
        showByteOrder(bb);

        // Repopulate the buffer in little endian byte order
        bb.clear();
        bb.order(ByteOrder.LITTLE_ENDIAN);
        bb.putShort((short)300);
        bb.flip();
        showByteOrder(bb);
    }

    public static void showByteOrder(ByteBuffer bb) {
        System.out.println("Byte Order: " + bb.order());
        while (bb.hasRemaining()) {
            System.out.print(bb.get() + "  ");
        }
        System.out.println();
    }
}
```

```
Default Byte Order: BIG_ENDIAN
Byte Order: BIG_ENDIAN
1  44
Byte Order: LITTLE_ENDIAN
44  1
```

Summary

New Input/Ouput (NIO) provides faster I/O compared to the stream-based input/output. NIO uses buffers and channels for I/O operations. A channel represents a connection between a data source/sink and a Java program for data transfer. A buffer contains data to be written to a file or data that is read from a file. Buffers for holding different types of primitive values are supported as instances of separate classes. You can use only a ByteBuffer for file I/O operations. NIO also supports memory-mapped file I/O that is the fastest way to read/write files.

A buffer maintains several properties that are affected by reading its data or writing data to it. The position property of a buffer is the index in the buffer that is the starting position to be read or written in the next read/write operation. The limit property of a buffer is the index in the buffer that is the starting index indicating the invalid read/write position. The buffer's position may change as you read from the buffer or write to the buffer.

Buffer related classes contain methods to manipulate those properties directly as well. A buffer supports absolute as well as relative read/write. In absolute read/write, the buffer's position is unaffected. In a relative read/write, the position property of the buffer is automatically advanced.

Byte buffers support different views. You can use a view of a buffer to access the data buffer's data as different primitive type values or to see only part of the buffer's data.

A FileChannel along with buffers are used to read/write files. You can obtain a FileChannel from an InputStream, an OutputStream, or using the factory method of the FileChannel class. You can also lock a file in exclusive or shared mode using the lock() method of the FileChannel class.

The byte order is the order in which bytes of a multi-byte value are stored. A byte order is called *big endian* if the bytes of a multi-bytes value are stored from the most significant byte to the least significant byte. If the bytes of a multi-byte value are stored from the least significant byte to the most significant byte, it is known as little endian. You need to deal with the byte order of a byte buffer if the buffer represents multi-byte data. The java.nio.ByteOrder class represents the byte order. It contains two constants, BIG_ENDIAN and LITTLE_ENDIAN, to represent big-endian and little-endian byte orders, respectively.

CHAPTER 10

■ ■ ■

New Input/Output 2

In this chapter, you will learn

- What New Input/Output 2 is

- How to work with a file system and file store

- How to represent a platform-dependent abstract pathname using a `Path`

- How to perform different file operations on a `Path` object

- How to traverse a file tree

- How to manage file attributes

- How to watch a directory for changes

- How to perform asynchronous file I/O operations

What Is New Input/Output 2?

Java 7 introduced New Input/Output 2 (NIO.2) API, which provides a new I/O API. It provides many features that were lacking in the original File I/O API. The features provided in NIO.2 are essential for working with a file system efficiently. It adds three packages to the Java class library: `java.nio.file`, `java.nio.file.attribute`, and `java.nio.file.spi`. The following are some of the new features of NIO.2:

- It lets you deal with all file systems in a uniform way. The file system support provided by NIO.2 is extensible. You can use the default implementation for a file system or you can choose to implement your own file system.

- It supports basic file operations (copy, move, and delete) on all file systems. It supports an atomic file move operation. It has improved exception handling support.

- It has support for symbolic links. Whenever applicable, operations on a symbolic link are redirected to the target file.

- One of the most important additions to NIO.2 is the support for accessing the attributes of file systems and files.

- It lets you create a watch service to watch for any events on a directory such as adding a new file or a subdirectory, deleting a file, etc. When such an event occurs on the directory, your program receives a notification through the watch service.

- It added an API that lets you walk through a file tree. You can perform a file operation on a node as you walk through the file tree.

- It supports asynchronous I/O on network sockets and files.

- It supports multicasting using a DatagramChannel.

Working with a File System

An object of the FileSystem class represents a file system in a Java program. A FileSystem object is used to perform two tasks:

- It acts as an interface between a Java program and a file system.

- It acts as a factory for creating many types of file system-related objects and services.

A FileSystem object is platform-dependent. You do not create an object of the FileSystem class directly. To obtain the default FileSystem object for a platform, you need to use the getDefault() static method of the FileSystems class as follows:

```
// Create the platform-specific default file system object
FileSystem fs = FileSystems.getDefault();
```

Typically, a file system consists of one or more file stores. A file store provides storage for files. The getFileStores() method of the FileSystem class returns an Iterator for the FileStore objects.

A file system may be represented differently on different platforms. One platform may represent a file system in a single hierarchy of files with one top-level root directory, whereas another may represent it in multiple hierarchies of files with multiple top-level directories. The getRootDirectories() method of the FileSystem class returns an iterator of Path objects, which represent paths to all top-level directories. I will discuss the Path class in detail in the next section.

You can use the isReadOnly() method of the FileSystem object to test if it only allows read-only access to the file stores. You will work with the FileSystem class in subsequent sections to create the file system-related objects and services.

Listing 10-1 demonstrates how to use a FileSystem object. It uses the default file system for the platform. The output shows the file system information when the program was run on Windows; you may get a different output when you run the program.

Listing 10-1. Retrieving Information About a File System

```
// FileSystemTest.java
package com.jdojo.nio2;

import java.nio.file.FileStore;
import java.nio.file.FileSystem;
import java.nio.file.FileSystems;
import java.nio.file.Path;
import java.io.IOException;

public class FileSystemTest {
        public static void main(String[] args) {
                // Create the platform-specific default file system object
                FileSystem fs = FileSystems.getDefault();
```

```
                System.out.println("Read-only file system: " + fs.isReadOnly());
                System.out.println("File name separator: " + fs.getSeparator());

                System.out.println("\nAvailable file-stores are");

                for(FileStore store : fs.getFileStores()) {
                        printDetails(store);
                }

                System.out.println("\nAvailable root directories are");

                for(Path root : fs.getRootDirectories()) {
                        System.out.println(root);
                }
        }

        public static void printDetails(FileStore store) {
                try {
                        String desc = store.toString();
                        String type = store.type();
                        long totalSpace = store.getTotalSpace();
                        long unallocatedSpace = store.getUnallocatedSpace();
                        long availableSpace = store.getUsableSpace();
                        System.out.println(desc + ", Total: " + totalSpace +
                                                ", Unallocated: " + unallocatedSpace +
                                                ", Available: " + availableSpace);
                }
                catch (IOException e) {
                        e.printStackTrace();
                }
        }
}
```

```
Read-only file system: false
File name separator: \

Available file-stores are
Local Disk (C:), Total: 1000097181696, Unallocated: 924354596864, Available: 924354596864
DataE (F:), Total: 1759213608960, Unallocated: 365291376640, Available: 365291376640
DataE (H:), Total: 1759213608960, Unallocated: 365291376640, Available: 365291376640

Available root directories are
C:\
D:\
E:\
F:\
H:\
```

Working with Paths

Typically, a file system stores objects (files, directories, symbolic links, etc.) in a hierarchical fashion. A file system uses one or more root nodes that serve as the root of the hierarchy. An object in a file system has a path, which is typically represented as a string, such as C:\home\test.txt on Windows, and /home/test.txt on UNIX-like operating systems. A path string may contain multiple components separated by a special character called *separator* or *delimiter*. For example, the path C:\home\test.txt consists of three components: C:\ as the root, home as a directory, and test.txt as a file name. A backslash is a path separator on Windows. UNIX-like operating systems use a forward slash (/) as the path separator. Note that path representation is platform-dependent.

A path can be absolute or relative. If a path starts with a root node, it is an absolute path. A relative path does not start with a root node. No additional information is needed to locate an object referred in a file system by an absolute path. Additional information is needed to locate an object referred in a file system by a relative path. For example, on Windows, the path C:\home\test.txt is an absolute path because it starts with the root node C:\, whereas the path luci1.txt is a relative path. To locate the luci1.txt file, you need more information, such as the path of the directory in which it exists.

A Path object is a programmatic representation of a path of an object in a file system such as a file, a directory, and a symbolic link. A file system path is platform-dependent, so is a Path object.

Path is an interface in the java.nio.file package. When you work with a Path object, it is most likely that you will also need to work with its two companion classes: Paths and Files. A path does not have to exist in a file system to create a Path object to represent it in a Java program.

■ **Tip**   As a developer, you will be using Path objects most of the time when working with NIO.2 API. The Path API meets most of the file I/O-related needs of a developer. It has been designed to work with the old java.io.File API. You can get a Path object from a File object using the method toPath()of the File class. You can get a File object from a Path object using the toFile() method of a Path object.

You can perform two kinds of operations on a Path object:

- Path-related operations

- File I/O operations

The methods in the Path interface let you perform path-related operations on a Path object that may include the following:

- Accessing the components of a path such as the file name, root name, etc.

- Comparing and testing paths. For example, checking if a path ends with .txt, comparing if two paths are identical, checking if a path is absolute or relative, etc.

- Combining and resolving paths.

The Path interface does not include any methods to perform file I/O operations. You need to use the Files class to perform the file I/O operations on a Path object. The Files class consists of all static methods. I will cover using the Files class shortly.

Creating a Path Object

A FileSystem object acts as a factory to create a Path object. You can use the getPath() method of the FileSystem class to create a Path object. The following snippet of code creates a Path object for file path C:\poems\luci1.txt on Windows:

```
Path p1 = FileSystems.getDefault().getPath("C:\\poems\\luci1.txt");
```

You can pass components of a path separately to the getPath() method when constructing a Path object. Java will take care of using an appropriate platform-dependent file name separators. The following statement creates a Path object to represent the C:\poems\luci1.txt path on Windows:

```
Path p2 = FileSystems.getDefault().getPath("C:", "poems", "luci1.txt");
```

The Path API includes a utility class called Paths whose sole job is to create a Path object from the components of a path string or a URI. The Paths.get() static method creates a Path object. Internally, it delegates the call to the default FileSystem object. The following snippet of code creates Path objects to represent the same path, C:\poems\luci1.txt:

```
Path p3 = Paths.get("C:\\poems\\luci1.txt");
Path p4 = Paths.get("C:", "poems", "luci1.txt");
```

■ **Tip**   You can create a Path object from an empty path such as Paths.get(""). A Path object with an empty path refers to the default directory of the file system. A default directory is the same as the current working directory.

Accessing Components of a Path

A path in a file system consists of one or more components. The methods of the Path interface let you access those components.

The getNameCount() method returns the number of components in a Path object excluding the root. For example, the path C:\poems\luci1.txt consists of three components: a root of C:, and two components named poems and luci1.txt. In this case, the getNameCount() method will return 2. The getName(int index) method returns the component name at the specified index. The component that is closest to the root has an index of 0. The component that is farthest from the root has an index of count - 1. In the path C:\poems\luci1.txt, the poems component has an index of 0 and the luci1.txt component has an index of 1.

The getParent() method returns the parent of a path. If a path does not have a parent, it returns null. The parent of a path is the path itself without the farthest component from the root. For example, the parent of the path C:\poems\luci.txt is C:\poems. The relative path test.txt has no parent.

The getRoot() method returns the root of the path. If a path does not have a root, it returns null. For example, the path C:\poems\luci1.txt on Windows has C:\ as its root.

The getFileName() method returns the file name denoted by the path. If a path has no file name, it returns null. The file name is the farthest component from the root. For example, in the path C:\poems\luci1.txt, luci1.txt is the file name.

You can check if a path represents an absolute path by using the isAbsolute() method. Note that a path does not have to exist in the file system to get information about its components. The Path API uses the information provided in the path string to give you all these pieces of information.

Listing 10-2 demonstrates how to access components of a Path object. One of the paths used in this example is a Windows-based path. If you are not running the program on Windows, please change the path in the main() method to represent a valid path on your platform. You may get a different output when you run the program.

Listing 10-2. Demonstrating How to Access Components of a Path

```java
// PathComponentsTest.java
package com.jdojo.nio2;

import java.nio.file.Path;
import java.nio.file.Paths;

public class PathComponentsTest {
	public static void main(String[] args) {
		Path p1 = Paths.get("C:\\poems\\luci1.txt");
		printDetails(p1);

		System.out.println("----------------------");

		Path p2 = Paths.get("luci1.txt");
		printDetails(p2);
	}

	public static void printDetails(Path p) {
		System.out.println("Details for path: " + p);

		int count = p.getNameCount();
		System.out.println("Name count: " + count);

		for(int i = 0; i < count; i++) {
			Path name = p.getName(i);
			System.out.println("Name at index " + i + " is " + name);
		}

		Path parent = p.getParent();
		Path root = p.getRoot();
		Path fileName = p.getFileName();
		System.out.println("Parent: " + parent + ", Root: " + root +
		                   ", File Name: " + fileName);
		System.out.println("Absolute Path: " + p.isAbsolute());
	}
}
```

```
Details for path: C:\poems\luci1.txt
Name count: 2
Name at index 0 is poems
Name at index 1 is luci1.txt
Parent: C:\poems, Root: C:\, File Name: luci1.txt
Absolute Path: true
----------------------
```

```
Details for path: luci1.txt
Name count: 1
Name at index 0 is luci1.txt
Parent: null, Root: null, File Name: luci1.txt
Absolute Path: false
```

Comparing Paths

You can compare two Path objects for equality based on their textual representation. The equals() method tests for the equality of two Path objects by comparing their string forms. Whether the equality test is case-sensitive depends on the file system. For example, the path comparison for equality is case-insensitive on Windows. The following snippet of code shows how to compare Windows paths:

```
Path p1 = Paths.get("C:\\poems\\luci1.txt");
Path p2 = Paths.get("C:\\POEMS\\LUCI1.TXT");
Path p3 = Paths.get("C:\\poems\\..\\poems\\luci1.txt");
boolean b1 = p1.equals(p2); // Returns true on Windows
boolean b2 = p1.equals(p3); // Returns false on Windows
```

In this snippet of code, p1.equals(p3) returns false, even though p1 and p3 refer to the same file; this is so because the equals() method compares two paths textually without resolving the actual file references.

■ **Tip** The Path.equals() method does not test a Path for existence in the file system.

The Path interface implements the java.lang.Comparable interface. You can use its compareTo() method to compare it with another Path object textually. The compareTo() method returns an int value, which is 0, less than 0, or greater than 0, when the two paths are equal, the path is less than the specified path, or the path is greater than the specified path, respectively. It is useful in sorting multiple paths in the textual order. The file system is not accessed when paths are compared using the compareTo() method. The ordering used by this method to compare two paths is platform-dependent. The following snippet of code shows examples of using the compareTo() method on Windows:

```
Path p1 = Paths.get("C:\\poems\\luci1.txt");
Path p2 = Paths.get("C:\\POEMS\\Luci1.txt");
Path p3 = Paths.get("C:\\poems\\..\\poems\\luci1.txt");
int v1 = p1.compareTo(p2); // Assigns 0 to v1
int v2 = p1.compareTo(p3); // Assigns 30 to v2
```

You can use the endsWith() and startsWith() methods to test if a path ends with and starts with a given path, respectively. It is important to note that endsWith() and startsWith() do not test if a path ends and starts with a text, respectively. They test if a path ends and starts with components of another path, respectively. The following snippet of code shows some examples of using these methods with paths on Windows:

```
Path p1 = Paths.get("C:\\poems\\luci1.txt");
Path p2 = Paths.get("luci1.txt");
Path p3 = Paths.get("poems\\luci1.txt");
Path p4 = Paths.get(".txt");
```

```
// Using endsWith()
boolean b1 = p1.endsWith(p2); // Assigns true to b1
boolean b2 = p1.endsWith(p3); // Assigns true to b2
boolean b3 = p1.endsWith(p4); // Assigns false to b3

// Using startsWith()
Path p5 = Paths.get("C:\\");
Path p6 = Paths.get("C:\\poems");
Path p7 = Paths.get("C:\\poem");

boolean b4 = p1.startsWith(p5); // Assigns true to b4
boolean b5 = p1.startsWith(p6); // Assigns true to b5
boolean b6 = p1.startsWith(p7); // Assigns false to b6
```

The endsWith() method compares the components, not the text, of a path with the specified path. For example, the path C:\poems\luci1.txt ends with luci1.txt, poems\luci1.txt, and C:\poems\luci1.txt. The same logic is used by the startsWith() method, though in the reverse order.

You can use the isSameFile(Path p1, Path p2) method of the Files class to check if two paths refer to the same file. If p1.equals(p2) returns true, this method returns true without verifying the existence of the paths in the file system. Otherwise, it checks with the file system, if both paths locate the same file. The file system implementation may require this method to access or open both files. The isSameFile() throws an IOException when an I/O error occurs.

Listing 10-3 demonstrates how the isSameFile() method works. Let's assume that the file denoted by the path C:\poems\luci1.txt exists. Since paths p1 and p2 are not equal using the equals() method, the isSameFile() method looks for these two paths in the file system for existence. It returns true, because p1 and p2 will resolve to the same file in the file system. Assume that the file denoted by path C:\abc.txt does not exist. The isSameFile(p3, p4) method call returns true because both paths are textually equal. The output depends on the existence and non-existence of these files. The program may print the stack trace of an error if it does not find files at the same location. Please change the file paths in the program to play with these methods. If you are running the program on the platform other than Windows, you must change the file path to conform to the path syntax used on your platform.

Listing 10-3. Checking If Two Paths Will Locate the Same File

```
// SameFileTest.java
package com.jdojo.nio2;

import java.io.IOException;
import java.nio.file.Files;
import java.nio.file.Path;
import java.nio.file.Paths;

public class SameFileTest {
    public static void main(String[] args) {
        // Assume that C:\poems\luci1.txt file exists
        Path p1 = Paths.get("C:\\poems\\luci1.txt");
        Path p2 = Paths.get("C:\\poems\\..\\poems\\luci1.txt");

        // Assume that C:\abc.txt file does not exist
        Path p3 = Paths.get("C:\\abc.txt");
        Path p4 = Paths.get("C:\\abc.txt");
```

```
            try {
                    boolean isSame = Files.isSameFile(p1, p2);
                    System.out.println("p1 and p2 are the same: " + isSame);

                    isSame = Files.isSameFile(p3, p4);
                    System.out.println("p3 and p4 are the same: " + isSame);
            }
            catch (IOException e) {
                    e.printStackTrace();
            }
        }
    }
}
```

```
p1 and p2 are the same: true
p3 and p4 are the same: true
```

Normalizing, Resolving, and Relativizing Paths

In a file system, it is common to use a dot and two dots to represent the current directory and the parent directory, respectively. Sometimes it is also acceptable to specify more than one consecutive delimiter between a file name and a directory name. The normalize() method of the Path interface returns a Path after removing these extra characters. This method does not access the file system. Sometimes a normalized path may not locate the same file as the original path if the original path contained a symbolic link. The following snippet of code shows some examples of normalizing paths on Windows. Please change the paths to conform to your platform if you run this code on a platform other than Windows.

```
Path p1 = Paths.get("C:\\poems\\..\\\\\poems\\luci1.txt");
Path p1n = p1.normalize();
System.out.println(p1 + " normalized to " + p1n);

Path p2 = Paths.get("C:\\poems\\luci1.txt");
Path p2n = p2.normalize();
System.out.println(p2 + " normalized to " + p2n);

Path p3 = Paths.get("a\\..\\.\\test.txt");
Path p3n = p3.normalize();
System.out.println(p3 + " normalized to " + p3n);
```

```
C:\poems\..\poems\luci1.txt normalized to C:\poems\luci1.txt
C:\poems\luci1.txt normalized to C:\poems\luci1.txt
a\..\.\test.txt normalized to test.txt
```

You can combine two paths using the resolve(Path p) method of the Path interface. If the specified path is an absolute path, it returns the specified path. It returns the path if the specified path is an empty path. In other cases, it simply combines the two paths and returns the result, so the returned path ends with the specified path. The path on which this method is invoked is assumed to be a directory. The following snippet of code has some examples of resolving paths on Windows. Please change the paths to conform to your platform if you run this code on a platform other than Windows.

```
Path p1 = Paths.get("C:\\poems");
Path p2 = Paths.get("luci1.txt");
System.out.println(p1.resolve(p2));

Path p3 = Paths.get("C:\\test.txt");
System.out.println(p1.resolve(p3));

Path p4 = Paths.get("");
System.out.println(p1.resolve(p4));

Path p5 = Paths.get("poems\\Luci");
Path p6 = Paths.get("luci4.txt");
System.out.println(p5.resolve(p6));
```

```
C:\poems\luci1.txt
C:\test.txt
C:\poems
poems\Luci\luci4.txt
```

Relativizing is the process of getting a relative path for a given path against another path. The relativize(Path p) method of the Path interface does this job. The relative path that is returned from this method, when resolved against the same path against which the path was relativized, returns the same given path. A relative path cannot be obtained if one of the paths has a root element. Whether a relative path can be obtained is platform-dependent if both paths have root elements. The following snippet of code has some examples of getting relative paths. When there is no common sub-path between the two paths, it is assumed that both paths locate sibling objects. For example, when getting a relative path for Doug against Bobby, it is assumed that Doug and Bobby are siblings. The output is shown when the program was run on Windows. On other platforms, you may get a slightly different output.

```
Path p1 = Paths.get("poems");
Path p2 = Paths.get("poems", "recent", "Luci");
System.out.println(p1.relativize(p2));
System.out.println(p2.relativize(p1));

Path p3 = Paths.get("Doug");
Path p4 = Paths.get("Bobby");
System.out.println(p3.relativize(p4));
System.out.println(p4.relativize(p3));
```

```
recent\Luci
..\..
..\Bobby
..\Doug
```

Symbolic Links

A *symbolic link* is a special type of file that contains a reference to another file or directory. A symbolic link is also known as *symlink* or *soft link*. The file referenced by a symbolic link is known as the target file for the symbolic link. Some operating systems that support symbolic links are UNIX-like operating systems (Linux, Mac OS X, etc.), Windows Vista, Windows 7, etc.

Operations on a symbolic link are transparent to the application. When an operation is performed on a symbolic link, the operating system performs the operation on the target of the link. For example, performing a read/write operation on a symbolic link performs a read/write on its target. However, the delete, move, and rename operations are performed directly on the link, rather than on its target. Sometimes it is possible to have a circular reference in a symbolic link, where the target of a symbolic link points back to the original link.

The NIO.2 API fully supports symbolic links. It has safeguards in place to detect a circular reference in a symbolic link. You can work with symbolic links using the java.nio.file.Files class. You can use its isSymbolicLink(Path p) method to check if the file denoted by the specified path is a symbolic link. The createSymbolicLink() method of the Files class is used to create a symbolic link. Note that the createSymbolicLink() is an optional operation, which may not be supported on all platforms.

```
Path existingFilePath = Paths.get("C:\\poems\\luci1.txt");
Path symLinkPath = Paths.get("C:\\luci1_link.txt");
try {
        Files.createSymbolicLink(symLinkPath, existingFilePath);
}
catch (IOException e) {
        e.printStackTrace();
}
```

The NIO.2 API follows the symbolic link by default. In some cases, you can specify whether you want to follow a symbolic link or not. The option not to follow a symbolic link is indicated by using the enum constant LinkOption. NOFOLLOW_LINKS. The LinkOption enum is declared in the java.nio.file package. Methods supporting this option let you pass an argument of the LinkOption type.

■ **Tip** The NIO.2 API also supports regular links (also known as hard links). You can use the createLink(Path newLink, Path existingPath) method of the Files class to create a hard link.

Different Forms of a Path

You can get different type of representations for a path. Suppose you create a Path object as follows:

```
// Create a Path object to represent a relative path
Path p1 = Paths.get("test.txt");
```

Here, p1 is a relative path. You can get the absolute path that is represented by p1 using its toAbsolutePath() method as follows:

```
// Get the absolute path represented by p1
Path p1AbsPath = p1.toAbsolutePath();
```

Now the p1AbsPath is the absolute path for p1. For example, on Windows, p1AbsPath may look like C:\testapp\ test.txt. If a path is not an absolute path, the toAbsolutePath() method uses a platform-dependent default directory to resolve the path to give you the absolute path. If the path is an absolute path, the toAbsolutePath() method returns the same path.

You can use the toRealPath() method to get the real path of an existing file. It returns a canonical path to an existing file. If the path represents a symbolic link, it returns the real path of the target file. You can pass a link option to this method indicating whether you do not want to follow the symbolic link to its target. If the file represented by the path does not exist, the toRealPath() throws an IOException. The following snippet of code demonstrates how to get the real path from a Path object:

```java
import java.io.IOException;
import java.nio.file.LinkOption;
import java.nio.file.Path;
import java.nio.file.Paths;
...
try {
        Path p2 = Paths.get("test2.txt");

        // Follow link for p2, if it is a symbolic link
        Path p2RealPath = p2.toRealPath();

        System.out.println("p2RealPath:" + p2RealPath);
}
catch (IOException e) {
        e.printStackTrace();
}

try {
        Path p3 = Paths.get("test3.txt");

        // Do not follow link for p3, if it is a symbolic link
        Path p3RealPath = p3.toRealPath(LinkOption.NOFOLLOW_LINKS);

        System.out.println("p3RealPath:" + p3RealPath);
}
catch (IOException e) {
        e.printStackTrace();
}
```

You can use the toUri() method of a Path object to get its URI representation. A URI representation of a path is highly platform-dependent. Typically, a URI form of a path can be used in a browser to open the file indicated by the path. The following snippet of code shows how to get the URI form of a path. The output was generated on Windows. You may get a different output.

```java
Path p2 = Paths.get("test2.txt");
java.net.URI p2UriPath = p2.toUri();
System.out.println("Absolute Path: " + p2.toAbsolutePath());
System.out.println("URI Path: " + p2UriPath);
```

```
Absolute Path: C:\java_code\testapp\test2.txt
URI Path: file:///C:/java_code/testapp/test2.txt
```

Performing File Operations on a Path

The java.nio.file.Files class consists of all static methods that let you perform most of the file operations on a Path object.

Creating New Files

The Files class provides several methods to create regular files, directories, symbolic links, and temporary files/directories. These methods throw an IOException when an I/O error occurs during the file creation; for example, they throw an IOException if you attempt to create a file that already exists. Most of the methods accept a varargs parameter of the FileAttribute type, which lets you specify the file attributes. I will discuss file attributes shortly.

You can use the createFile() method to create a new regular file. The new file, if created, is empty. The file creation fails in case the file already exists, or the parent directory does not exist. Listing 10-4 shows how to create a new file. It attempts to create a text.txt file in your default directory. The program prints the details of the file creation status.

Listing 10-4. Creating a New File

```java
// CreateFileTest.java
package com.jdojo.nio2;

import java.io.IOException;
import java.nio.file.FileAlreadyExistsException;
import java.nio.file.Files;
import java.nio.file.NoSuchFileException;
import java.nio.file.Path;
import java.nio.file.Paths;

public class CreateFileTest {
    public static void main(String[] args) {
        Path p1 = Paths.get("test.txt");
        try {
            Files.createFile(p1);
            System.out.format("File created: %s%n", p1.toRealPath());
        }
        catch (FileAlreadyExistsException e) {
            System.out.format("File %s already exists.%n",
                              p1.normalize());
        }
        catch (NoSuchFileException e) {
            System.out.format("Directory %s does not exists.%n",
                              p1.normalize().getParent());
        }
        catch (IOException e) {
            e.printStackTrace();
        }
    }
}
```

The createDirectory() and createDirectories() methods are used to create a new directory. If the parent directory of the new directory does not exist, the createDirectory() method fails. The createDirectories() method creates a non-existent parent directory. You can use the createTempDirectory() and createTempFile() methods to create a temporary directory and a temporary file respectively.

The following snippet of code shows how to create temporary files and directories. The output was generated when the program was run on Windows 7. The name generation for a temporary directory/file is implementation dependent. Attempts are made to use the supplied prefix and suffix for the temporary file/directory. You will need to change the paths to conform to your platform and you may get a different output.

```java
try {
        String dirPrefix = "KDir";
        Path tDir = Files.createTempDirectory(dirPrefix);
        System.out.println("Temp directory: " + tDir);
        String fPrefix = "KF_";
        String fSuffix = ".txt";
        Path tFile1 = Files.createTempFile(fPrefix, fSuffix);
        System.out.println("Temp file1: " + tFile1);

        Path p1 = Paths.get("C:\\temp");
        Path tFile2 = Files.createTempFile(p1, fPrefix, fSuffix);
        System.out.println("Temp file2: " + tFile2);
}
catch (IOException e) {
        e.printStackTrace();
}
```

```
Temp directory: C:\Users\ksharan\AppData\Local\Temp\KDir6632178761947534022
Temp file1: C:\Users\ksharan\AppData\Local\Temp\KF_6811753793376220963.txt
Temp file2: C:\temp\KF_4190593797467345768.txt
```

A temporary file/directory is not automatically deleted. You may want to use the deleteOnExit() method of the java.io.File class to delete the file when the JVM exits.

```java
Path tempFile = Files.createTempFile("myTempFile", ".txt");

// Delete the file when the JVM exits
tempFile.toFile().deleteOnExit();
```

Deleting Files

The Files class has two methods called delete(Path p) and deleteIfExists(Path p) to delete a file, a directory, and a symbolic link.

The delete() method throws an exception if the deletion fails. For example, it throws a NoSuchFileException if the file being deleted does not exist and throws a DirectoryNotEmptyException if the directory being deleted is not empty.

The deleteIfExists() method does not throw a NoSuchFileException if the file being deleted does not exist. It returns true if it deletes the file. Otherwise, it returns false. It throws a DirectoryNotEmptyException if the directory being deleted is not empty.

The following snippet of code shows how to delete a file and handle exceptions:

```
// Create a Path object on Windows
Path p = Paths.get("C:\\poems\\luci1.txt");

try {
        // Delete the file
        Files.delete(p);
        System.out.println(p + " deleted successfully.");
}
catch (NoSuchFileException e) {
        System.out.println(p + " does not exist.");
}
catch (DirectoryNotEmptyException e) {
        System.out.println("Directory " + p + " is not empty.");
}
catch (IOException e) {
        e.printStackTrace();
}
```

Checking for Existence of a File

The Files class provides two methods called exists(Path p, LinkOption... options) and notExists(Path p, LinkOption... options) to check for the existence and non-existence of a file, respectively. Note that these two methods are not the opposite of each other. If it is not possible to determine whether a file exists, both methods return false. If you need to take an action when a file exists, use the exists() method in your logic. If you need to take an action when a file does not exist, use the notExists() method.

Copying and Moving Files

The Files class provides a copy(Path source, Path target, CopyOption... options) method to copy contents and attributes of the specified source path to the specified target path. If the specified source file is a symbolic link, the target of the symbolic link is copied, not the symbolic link. If the specified source file is a directory, an empty directory at the target location is created without copying the contents of the directory. This method is overloaded. You can use the other two versions of this method to copy all bytes from an input stream to a file and all bytes in a file to an output stream. If the specified source and target files are the same, the copy() method does not do anything.

You can specify one or more of the following copy options with the copy() method:

- StandardCopyOption.REPLACE_EXISTING

- StandardCopyOption.COPY_ATTRIBUTES

- LinkOption.NOFOLLOW_LINKS

If the target file already exists, the copy() method throws a FileAlreadyExistsException. You can specify the REPLACE_EXISTING option to replace the existing target file. If the target file is a non-empty directory, specifying the REPLACE_EXISTING option throws a DirectoryNotEmptyException. If the target file is a symbolic link and if it exists, the symbolic link is replaced by specifying the REPLACE_EXISTING option, not the target of the symbolic link.

The COPY_ATTRIBUTES option copies the attributes of the source file to the target file. The file attributes that are copied are highly platform- and file system-dependent. At least, the last-modified-time attribute of the source file is copied to the target file, if supported by both file stores.

If the NOFOLLOW_LINKS option is used, the copy() method copies the symbolic link, not the target of the symbolic link.

Listing 10-5 demonstrates the use of the copy() method to copy a file. It handles the possible exceptions if the copy operation fails. You will need to change the paths for the source and target files before running the program.

Listing 10-5. Copying a File, a Directory, and a Symbolic Link Using the Files.copy() Method

```java
// CopyTest.java
package com.jdojo.nio2;

import java.nio.file.Path;
import java.nio.file.Paths;
import java.nio.file.Files;
import java.io.IOException;
import java.nio.file.FileAlreadyExistsException;
import java.nio.file.DirectoryNotEmptyException;
import static java.nio.file.StandardCopyOption.REPLACE_EXISTING;
import static java.nio.file.StandardCopyOption.COPY_ATTRIBUTES;

public class CopyTest {
    public static void main(String[] args) {
        // Change the paths for teh source and target files
        // before you run the program
        Path source = Paths.get("C:\\poems\\luci1.txt");
        Path target = Paths.get("C:\\poems\\luci1_backup.txt");

        try {
            Path p = Files.copy(source, target,
                            REPLACE_EXISTING, COPY_ATTRIBUTES);
            System.out.println(source + " has been copied to " + p);
        }
        catch (FileAlreadyExistsException e) {
            System.out.println(target+ " already exists.");
        }
        catch (DirectoryNotEmptyException e) {
            System.out.println(target + " is not empty.");
        }
        catch (IOException e) {
            e.printStackTrace();
        }
    }
}
```

The move(Path source, Path target, CopyOption... options) method of the Files class lets you move or rename a file. The move operation fails if the specified target file already exists. You can specify the REPLACE_EXISTING option to replace the existing target file. If the file to move is a symbolic link, it moves the symbolic link, not the target of the symbolic link. The move() method can only be used to move an empty directory. A DirectoryNotEmptyException is thrown if the directory is not empty.

Apart from the REPLACE_EXISTING CopyOption, you can use the ATOMIC_MOVE as another CopyOption. If the ATOMIC_MOVE option is used, it throws an AtomicMoveNotSupportedException if the file could not be moved atomically. If ATOMIC_MOVE option is specified, all other options are ignored. The following snippet of code shows how to move a file by handling possible exceptions:

```java
import java.io.IOException;
import java.nio.file.AtomicMoveNotSupportedException;
import java.nio.file.DirectoryNotEmptyException;
import java.nio.file.FileAlreadyExistsException;
import java.nio.file.Files;
import java.nio.file.NoSuchFileException;
import java.nio.file.Path;
import java.nio.file.Paths;
import static java.nio.file.StandardCopyOption.ATOMIC_MOVE;
...
// Create source and target paths using the syntax supoprted by your platform
Path source = Paths.get("C:\\poems\\luci1.txt");
Path target = Paths.get("C:\\poems\\dir2\\luci1.txt");

try {
        // Try moving the source to target atomically
        Path p = Files.move(source, target, ATOMIC_MOVE);
        System.out.println(source + " has been moved to " + p);
}
catch (NoSuchFileException e) {
        System.out.println("Source/target does not exist.");
}
catch (FileAlreadyExistsException e) {
        System.out.println(target + " already exists. Move failed.");
}
catch (DirectoryNotEmptyException e) {
        System.out.println(target + " is not empty. Move failed.");
}
catch (AtomicMoveNotSupportedException e){
        System.out.println("Atomic move is not supported. MOve failed.");
}
catch (IOException e) {
        e.printStackTrace();
}
```

Commonly Used File Attributes

The Files class has many methods that let you access the commonly used attributes of a file. For example, you can use the Files.isHidden(Path p) method to test if a file is hidden. The following methods in the Files class let you access various types of commonly used attributes of a file. Please refer to the "Managing File Attributes" section for managing advanced file attributes.

- long size(Path)

- boolean isHidden(Path path)

- boolean isRegularFile(Path path, LinkOption... options)

- boolean isDirectory(Path path, LinkOption... options)

- boolean isSymbolicLink(Path path)

- FileTime getLastModifiedTime(Path path, LinkOption... options)

Probing the Content Type of a File

You can use the Files.probeContentType(Path path) method to probe the content type of a file. The method returns the content type in the string form of the value of a Multipurpose Internet Mail Extension (MIME) content type. If the content type of a file cannot be determined, it returns null.

Listing 10-6 shows how to probe the content type of a file. You may get a different output when you run this program. The program uses the file path C:\poems\luci1.txt. Please change this path to the path of the file whose content type you want to know.

Listing 10-6. Probing the Content Type of a File

```
// ProbeFileContent.java
package com.jdojo.nio2;

import java.nio.file.Files;
import java.nio.file.Path;
import java.nio.file.Paths;
import java.io.IOException;

public class ProbeFileContent {
        public static void main(String[] args) {
                Path p = Paths.get("C:\\poems\\luci1.txt");

                try {
                        String contentType = Files.probeContentType(p);
                        System.out.format("Content type of %s is %s%n", p, contentType);
                }
                catch (IOException e) {
                        e.printStackTrace();
                }
        }
}
```

```
Content type of C:\poems\luci1.txt is text/plain
```

Reading the Contents of a File

The NIO.2 API supports reading the contents of a file in the following three ways:

- As bytes or lines of text
- Using InputStream and BufferedReader using the java.io API
- Using channel API using a SeekableByteChannel object

The Files class contains the following methods to read the contents of a file as bytes and lines of text:

- static byte[] readAllBytes(Path path)
- static List<String> readAllLines(Path path)
- static List<String> readAllLines(Path path, Charset cs)

All three methods may throw an IOException. The readAllBytes()method reads all bytes from a file. The readAllLines() method reads the entire contents of a file lines of text. The readAllLines() method uses a carriage return, a line feed, and a carriage returned followed by a line feed as a line terminator. The lines that are returned do not contain the line terminator. The version of this method that takes only the Path of the source file as an argument assumes the contents of the file in the UTF-8 charset.

▨ **Tip** The readAllBytes() and readAllLines() method in the Files class are intended to read the contents of a small file. Both methods take care of opening/closing the file before/after reading.

The Files class provides methods to obtain InputStream and BufferedReader objects from a Path object. The newInputStream(Path path, OpenOption... options) method returns an InputStream object for the specified path. The newBufferedReader(Path path) and newBufferedReader(Path path, Charset cs) method returns a BufferedReader; the former assumes that the file's contents are in the UTF-8 charset whereas the latter lets you specify the charset. Please refer to Chapter 7 for more details on how to use InputStream and BufferedReader to read the contents of a file.

The Files class provides methods to obtain a SeekableByteChannel object from a Path object using its newByteChannel(Path path, OpenOption... options) method. A SeekableByteChannel object provides random access to a file using the channel API. It can be used to read from and write to a file. You can cast a SeekableByteChannel to a FileChannel to use advance features of the channel API such as locking a region of the file and mapping a region of the file directly into memory. It maintains a current position where you can start reading or writing. Please refer to Chapter 9 for more details on how to use channels to read data from a file. I will discuss an example of using a SeekableByteChannel to read/write the contents of a file later in this chapter.

Many of the methods of the Files class that deal with reading from and writing to files accept an optional argument of OpenOption type. This option lets you configure the file being opened. Table 10-1 lists the values with their descriptions for the OpenOption type. OpenOption is an interface in the java.nio.file package. The StandardOpenOption enum in the java.nio.file package implements the OpenOption interface. Therefore, each enum constant in the StandardOpenOption represents a value of the OpenOption type.

Table 10-1. *List of OpenOption Type Values That are Enum Constants in the StandardOpenOption Enum*

StandardOpenOption Constant	Description
APPEND	Appends the written data to the existing file, if the file is opened for writing.
CREATE	Creates a new file, if it does not exist.
CREATE_NEW	Creates a new file, if it does not exist. If the file already exists, it fails the operation.
DELETE_ON_CLOSE	Deletes the file when the stream is closed. It is useful when used with a temporary file.
DSYNC	Keeps the contents of the file synchronized with the underlying storage.
READ	Opens a file with a read access.
SPARSE	If it is used with the CREATE_NEW option, it is a hint to the file system that the new file should be a sparse file. If a sparse file is not supported by a file system, this option is ignored.
SYNC	Keeps the content and the metadata of the file synchronized with the underlying storage.
TRUNCATE_EXISTING	Truncates the length of an existing file to zero if the file is opened for a write access.
WRITE	Opens a file for a write access.

The following snippet of code obtains a SeekableByteChannel object for luci2.txt file in the default directory. It opens the file for a READ and WRITE access. It uses the CREATE option, so the file is created if it does not exist.

```
import java.nio.file.Path;
import java.nio.file.Paths;
import java.nio.file.Files;
import java.nio.channels.SeekableByteChannel;
import static java.nio.file.StandardOpenOption.READ;
import static java.nio.file.StandardOpenOption.WRITE;
import static java.nio.file.StandardOpenOption.CREATE;
...
Path src = Paths.get("luci2.txt");
SeekableByteChannel sbc = Files.newByteChannel(src, READ, WRITE, CREATE);
```

Listing 10-7 demonstrates how to read and display the contents of a file luci1.txt in your default directory. The program displays an error message if the file does not exist.

Listing 10-7. *Using the Files.readAllLines( ) Method to Read Contents of a File*

```
// ReadAllLines.java
package com.jdojo.nio2;

import java.nio.file.Files;
import java.nio.file.Path;
import java.nio.file.Paths;
import java.util.List;
```

```
import java.nio.charset.Charset;
import java.io.IOException;
import java.nio.file.NoSuchFileException;

public class ReadAllLines {
        public static void main(String[] args) {
                Charset cs = Charset.forName("US-ASCII");
                Path source = Paths.get("luci1.txt");

                try {
                        // Read all lines in one go
                        List<String> lines = Files.readAllLines(source, cs);

                        // Print each line
                        for (String line : lines) {
                                System.out.println(line);
                        }
                }
                catch (NoSuchFileException e) {
                        System.out.println(source.toAbsolutePath() + " does not exist.");
                }
                catch (IOException e) {
                        e.printStackTrace();
                }
        }
}
```

Writing to a File

The NIO.2 API supports writing to a file in the following three ways:

- Writing an array of bytes or a collection of lines of texts to a file in one shot.

- Writing to a file using an OutputStream and a BufferedWriter using the java.io API.

- Writing to a file using the channel API using a SeekableByteChannel object.

You can use the following write() methods of the Files class to write contents to a file in one shot:

- static Path write(Path path, byte[] bytes, OpenOption... options)

- static Path write(Path path, Iterable<? extends CharSequence> lines, OpenOption... options)

- static Path write(Path path, Iterable<? extends CharSequence> lines, Charset cs, OpenOption... options)

These methods are designed to write smaller contents to a file. You are advised to use other methods (discussed below) to write bigger contents to a file.

The write() method opens the file, writes the passed in contents to the file, and closes it. If no open options are present, it opens the file with CREATE, TRUNCATE_EXISTING, and WRITE options. If you are writing lines of text to a file, it writes a platform-dependent line separator after every line of text. If charset is not specified when lines of text are written, UTF-8 charset is assumed.

Listing 10-8 demonstrates how to write lines of texts to a file using the write() method. The program writes a few lines of text in a file named twinkle.txt in the default directory. It prints the path of the file. You may get a different output when you run this program.

Listing 10-8. Writing Some Lines of Text to a File in One Shot Using the NIO.2 API

```java
// WriteLinesTest.java
package com.jdojo.nio2;

import java.io.IOException;
import java.nio.charset.Charset;
import java.nio.file.Files;
import java.nio.file.Path;
import java.nio.file.Paths;
import java.util.ArrayList;
import java.util.List;
import static java.nio.file.StandardOpenOption.WRITE;
import static java.nio.file.StandardOpenOption.CREATE;

public class WriteLinesTest {
        public static void main(String[] args) {
                // Prepare the lines of text to write in a List
                List<String> texts = new ArrayList<>();
                texts.add("Twinkle, twinkle, little star,");
                texts.add("How I wonder what you are.");
                texts.add("Up above the world so high,");
                texts.add("Like a diamond in the sky.");

                Path dest = Paths.get("twinkle.txt");
                Charset cs = Charset.forName("US-ASCII");
                try {
                        Path p = Files.write(dest, texts, cs, WRITE, CREATE);
                        System.out.println("Text was written to " +
                                        p.toAbsolutePath());
                }
                catch (IOException e) {
                        e.printStackTrace();
                }
        }
}
```

```
Text was written to C:\book\javabook\twinkle.txt
```

The Files class contains newOutputStream(Path path, OpenOption... options) that returns an OutputStream for the specified path. The class contains a newBufferedWriter(Path path, Charset cs, OpenOption... options) method that returns a BufferedWriter for the specified path. You can use the java.io API to write contents to a file using the OutputStream and BufferedWriter. Please refer to Chapter 7 for more details on how to use the java.io API.

You can use the newByteChannel(Path path, OpenOption... options) method to get a SeekableByteChannel for the specified path. You can use the write(ByteBuffer src) method of the SeekableByteChannel to write data to a file. Please refer to Chapter 9 for more details on how to use the channel API to write to a file. I will discuss an example of using SeekableByteChannel in the next section.

Random Access to a File

A SeekableByteChannel object provides random access to a file using the channel API. You can use it to read data from and write data to a file. It is an interface declared in the java.nio.channels package. The FileChannel class in the java.nio.channels package implements this interface. You can get a SeekableByteChannel object for a Path using the newByteChannel() method of the Files class as follows:

```
Path src = Paths.get("twinkle2.txt");
SeekableByteChannel seekableChannel =
        Files.newByteChannel(src, READ, WRITE, CREATE, TRUNCATE_EXISTING);
```

A SeekableByteChannel is connected to an entity such as a file. It maintains a current position. When you write to the channel, the data is written at the current position. If you read from it, the data is read from the current position. You can get the current position using its position() method. To set its current position, you need to use its position(long newPosition) method.

You can get the size of the entity of a SeekableByteChannel in bytes using its size() method. As the data is truncated or written to the channel, the size is updated.

The truncate(long size) method of the SeekableByteChannel lets you truncate the size of the entity to the specified size. If the specified size is less than the current size of the entity, it truncates the data to the specified size. If the specified size is greater than or equal to the current size of the entity, this method does not modify the entity.

Use the read(ByteBuffer source) and write(ByteBuffer destination) methods to read data from the channel and write data to the channel, respectively. Make sure to set the current position correctly, before you perform the read and write operations on the channel.

Listing 10-9 shows how to read from and write to a file using a SeekableByteChannel. It creates a file named twinkle2.txt in the default directory and writes a few lines of text to it. It resets the position to zero after writing the data and reads the texts to print them on the standard output. At every step, it prints the size and the current position.

Listing 10-9. A Sample Program That Uses a SeekableByteChannel to Read Data from and Write Data to a File

```
// SeekableByteChannelTest.java
package com.jdojo.nio2;

import java.nio.ByteBuffer;
import java.nio.charset.Charset;
import java.io.IOException;
import java.nio.CharBuffer;
import java.nio.channels.SeekableByteChannel;
import java.nio.file.Path;
import java.nio.file.Paths;
import java.nio.file.Files;
import static java.nio.file.StandardOpenOption.READ;
import static java.nio.file.StandardOpenOption.WRITE;
import static java.nio.file.StandardOpenOption.CREATE;
import static java.nio.file.StandardOpenOption.TRUNCATE_EXISTING;

public class SeekableByteChannelTest {
        public static void main(String[] args) {
                Path src = Paths.get("twinkle2.txt");
```

```java
            // Get the file encoding for the system
            String encoding = System.getProperty("file.encoding");
            Charset cs = Charset.forName(encoding);

            try (SeekableByteChannel seekableChannel =
                    Files.newByteChannel(src,
                    READ, WRITE, CREATE, TRUNCATE_EXISTING)) {

                // Print the details
                printDetails(seekableChannel, "Before writing data");

                // First, write some data to the file
                writeData(seekableChannel, cs);

                // Print the details
                printDetails(seekableChannel, "After writing data");

                // Reset the position of the seekable channel to 0,
                // so we can read the data from the beginning
                seekableChannel.position(0);

                // Print the details
                printDetails(seekableChannel,
                             "After resetting position to 0");

                // Read the data from the file
                readData(seekableChannel, cs);

                // Print the details
                printDetails(seekableChannel, "After reading data");
            }
            catch (IOException e) {
                e.printStackTrace();
            }
    }

    public static void writeData(SeekableByteChannel seekableChannel,
                            Charset cs) throws IOException {
        // Get the platform-dependent line separator
        String separator = System.getProperty("line.separator");

        // Prepare the text to write to the file
        StringBuilder sb = new StringBuilder();
        sb.append("When the blazing sun is gone,");
        sb.append(separator);
        sb.append("When he nothing shines upon,");
        sb.append(separator);
        sb.append("Then you show your little light,");
        sb.append(separator);
        sb.append("Twinkle, twinkle, all the night");
        sb.append(separator);
```

```
                   // Wrap the text into a char buffer
                   CharBuffer charBuffer = CharBuffer.wrap(sb);

                   // Encode the char buffer data into a byte buffer
                   ByteBuffer byteBuffer = cs.encode(charBuffer);

                   // Write the data to the file
                   seekableChannel.write(byteBuffer);
        }

        public static void readData(SeekableByteChannel seekableChannel,
                                    Charset cs) throws IOException {
               ByteBuffer byteBuffer = ByteBuffer.allocate(128);
               String encoding = System.getProperty("file.encoding");

               while (seekableChannel.read(byteBuffer) > 0) {
                      byteBuffer.rewind();
                      CharBuffer charBuffer = cs.decode(byteBuffer);
                      System.out.print(charBuffer);
                      byteBuffer.flip();
               }
        }

        public static void printDetails(SeekableByteChannel seekableChannel, String msg) {
               try {
                      System.out.println(msg + ": Size = " +
                             seekableChannel.size() +
                             ", Position = " + seekableChannel.position());
               }
               catch (IOException e) {
                      e.printStackTrace();
               }
        }
    }
}
```

```
Before writing data: Size = 0, Position = 0
After writing data: Size = 128, Position = 128
After resetting position to 0: Size = 128, Position = 0
When the blazing sun is gone,
When he nothing shines upon,
Then you show your little light,
Twinkle, twinkle, all the night
After reading data: Size = 128, Position = 128
```

Traversing a File Tree

NIO.2 provides a FileVisitor API to recursively process all files and directories in a file tree. The FileVisitor API is useful when you want to perform some actions on all or some files or directories in a file tree. For example, you cannot delete a directory until it is empty. Before you delete a directory, you must delete all files and directories underneath it, which can be achieved easily using the FileVisitor API.

447

You need to use the following steps to traverse a file tree:

- Create a file visitor class by implementing the java.nio.file.FileVisitor interface.

- To start visiting the file tree, use the walkFileTree() method of the Files class by specifying the start directory and a file visitor object of the class created in the previous step. One of the methods of the FileVisitor interface is called when a file/directory is visited or a file/directory visit fails.

■ **Tip** The NIO.2 API provides the SimpleFileVisitor class, which is a basic implementation of the FileVisitor interface. The methods in the SimpleFileVisitor class do not do anything when a file/directory is visited. When a failure occurs, it rethrows the original exception. You can inherit your file visitor class from the SimpleFileVisitor class and override only the methods that fit your needs.

Table 10-2 lists the methods of the FileVisitor interface with their descriptions. All methods throw an IOException and they all return an enum constant of FileVisitResult type. Table 10-3 lists the constants defined by the FileVisitResult enum type with their descriptions.

Table 10-2. *Methods of the FileVisitor Interface*

Method	Description
FileVisitResult preVisitDirectory(T dir, BasicFileAttributes attrs) throws IOException	This method is called once before visiting entries in a directory.
FileVisitResult postVisitDirectory(T dir, IOException exc) throws IOException	This method is called after entries in a directory (and all of their descendants) have been visited. It is invoked even if there are errors during the visit of entries in a directory.
	If there was any exception thrown during the iteration of a directory, the exception object is passed to this method as the second argument. If the second argument to this method is null, there was no exception during the directory iteration.
FileVisitResult visitFile(T file, BasicFileAttributes attrs) throws IOException	This method is called when a file in a directory is visited.
FileVisitResult visitFileFailed(T file, IOException exc) throws IOException	This method is called when a file or directory could not be visited for any reason.

Table 10-3. *Enum Constants of FileVisitResult and Their Descriptions*

Enum Constant	Description
CONTINUE	Continues processing
SKIP_SIBLINGS	Continues processing without visiting the siblings of the file or directory. If it is returned from the preVisitDirectory() method, the entries in the current directory is also skipped and the postVisitDirectory() method is not called on that directory.
SKIP_SUBTREE	Continues processing without visiting entries in the directory. It is meaningful only when returned from the preVisitDirectory() method. Otherwise, its effect is the same as CONTINUE.
TERMINATE	Terminates the file visiting process.

You do not need to write logic in all four methods of your file visitor class. For example, if you want to copy a directory, you would like the code in the preVisitDirectory() method to create a new directory and the visitFile() method to copy the file. If you want to delete a directory, you need to delete the entries first. In this case, you will implement the visitFile() method to delete the files and the postVisitDirectory() method to delete the directory afterwards.

Let's implement a file visitor that will print the names of all files and subdirectories of a directory. It will also print the size of the files in bytes.

Listing 10-10 contains the complete program. It prints the details of files and subdirectories of the default directory. You may get a different output when you run this program.

Listing 10-10. A Program to the Print the Names of Subdirectories and Files of a Directory

```java
// WalkFileTreeTest.java
package com.jdojo.nio2;

import java.io.IOException;
import java.nio.file.FileVisitor;
import java.nio.file.Path;
import java.nio.file.Paths;
import java.nio.file.SimpleFileVisitor;
import java.nio.file.attribute.BasicFileAttributes;
import java.nio.file.FileVisitResult;
import java.nio.file.Files;
import static java.nio.file.FileVisitResult.CONTINUE;

public class WalkFileTreeTest {
    public static void main(String[] args) {
        // Get the Path obejct for the default directory
        Path startDir = Paths.get("");

        // Get a file visitor object
        FileVisitor<Path> visitor = getFileVisitor();

        try {
            // Traverse the contents of the startDir
            Files.walkFileTree(startDir, visitor);
        }
        catch (IOException e) {
            e.printStackTrace();
        }
    }

    public static FileVisitor<Path> getFileVisitor() {
        // Declare a local class DirVisitor that
        // inherits fron the SimpleFileVisitor<Path> class
        class DirVisitor<Path> extends SimpleFileVisitor<Path> {
            @Override
            public FileVisitResult preVisitDirectory(Path dir,
                                        BasicFileAttributes attrs) {
```

```
                              System.out.format("%s [Directory]%n", dir);
                              return CONTINUE;
                   }

                   @Override
                   public FileVisitResult visitFile(Path file,
                                         BasicFileAttributes attrs) {

                       System.out.format("%s [File, Size: %s bytes]%n",
                                           file, attrs.size());
                       return CONTINUE;
                   }
              }

              // Create an obejct of the DirVisitor
              FileVisitor<Path> visitor = new DirVisitor<>();

              return visitor;
         }
}
```

```
build [Directory]
build\built-jar.properties [File, Size: 84 bytes]
build\classes [Directory]
twinkle.txt [File, Size: 117 bytes]
twinkle2.txt [File, Size: 128 bytes]
```

The getFileVisitor() method creates a FileVisitor object by using the SimpleFileVisitor class to inherit a file visitor class. In the preVisitDirectory() method, it prints the name of the directory and returns FileVisitResult.CONTINUE to indicate that it wants to continue processing the entries in the directory. In the visitFile() method, it prints the name and size of the file and continues the processing. The FileVisitor API traverses a file tree in depth-first order. However, it does not guarantee the order of the visits of the subdirectories of a directory. To traverse a file tree, you need to call the walkFileTree() method of the Files class. The walkFileTree() method will automatically call the method of the visitor object as it walks through the file tree.

The FileVisitor API is very useful whenever you want to take some actions on all entries or some selective entries in a file tree. Operations such as copying a directory tree, deleting a non-empty directory, finding a file, etc. can be implemented easily using the FileVisitor API. Listing 10-11 demonstrates how to use the FileVisitor API to delete a directory tree. You need to specify the path to the directory to be deleted before you run the program. Note that you will not be able to get the contents of the deleted directory back. Therefore, be careful in experimenting with this program and do not delete any useful directory accidently.

Listing 10-11. Using the FileVisitor API to Delete a Directory Tree

```java
// DeleteDirectoryTest.java
package com.jdojo.nio2;

import java.io.IOException;
import java.nio.file.FileVisitResult;
import static java.nio.file.FileVisitResult.CONTINUE;
import static java.nio.file.FileVisitResult.TERMINATE;
import java.nio.file.FileVisitor;
```

```java
import java.nio.file.Files;
import java.nio.file.Path;
import java.nio.file.Paths;
import java.nio.file.SimpleFileVisitor;
import java.nio.file.attribute.BasicFileAttributes;

public class DeleteDirectoryTest {
        public static void main(String[] args) {
                /* WARNING!!!
                   Replace YOUR_DIR_PATH_TO_DELETE in the following statement with
                   the path of the directory whose contents you want to delete.
                   You will not be able to get the contents of the directory back
                   after you run this program.
                */
                Path dirToDelete = Paths.get("YOUR_DIR_PATH_TO_DELETE");
                FileVisitor<Path> visitor = getFileVisitor();

                try {
                        Files.walkFileTree(dirToDelete, visitor);
                }
                catch (IOException e) {
                        System.out.println(e.getMessage());
                }
        }

        public static FileVisitor<Path> getFileVisitor() {
                // A inner local class that is used as a file visitor to
                // delete a directory
                class DeleteDirVisitor extends SimpleFileVisitor<Path> {
                        @Override
                        public FileVisitResult postVisitDirectory(Path dir,
                                        IOException e) throws IOException {

                                FileVisitResult result = CONTINUE;

                                // Now, delete the directory at the end
                                if (e != null) {
                                        System.out.format("Error deleting %s. %s%n",
                                                        dir, e.getMessage());
                                        result = TERMINATE;
                                }
                                else {
                                        Files.delete(dir);
                                        System.out.format("Deleted directory %s%n",
                                                        dir);
                                }
                                return result;
                        }
```

451

```
                        @Override
                        public FileVisitResult visitFile(Path file,
                                   BasicFileAttributes attrs) throws IOException {

                                   // Delete the file that we are visiting
                                   Files.delete(file);

                                   System.out.format("Deleted file %s%n", file);
                                   return CONTINUE;
                        }
                }

                // Create an obejct of the DirVisitor
                FileVisitor<Path> visitor = new DeleteDirVisitor();

                return visitor;
        }
}
```

By default, the Files.walkFileTree() method does not follow symbolic links. If you want the FileVisitor API to follow the symbolic links, you need to use another version of the walkFileTree() method that lets you specify the FileVisitOption.FOLLOW_LINKS as an option. It also lets you specify the maximum depth, which is the maximum number of levels of a directory to visit. Specifying the depth as 0 visits only the starting file. You can specify Integer.MAX_VALUE as the depth to visit all levels. The following snippet of code shows how to use the walkFileTree() method to follow a symbolic link:

```
import java.util.Set;
import java.util.EnumSet;
import java.nio.file.Path;
import java.nio.file.Files;
import java.io.IOException;
import java.nio.file.FileVisitor;
import java.nio.file.FileVisitOption;
import static java.nio.file.FileVisitOption.FOLLOW_LINKS;
...
Path startDir = get the path to the starting directory;
FileVisitor<Path> visitor = get a file visitor;

// Prepare the set of options
Set<FileVisitOption> options = EnumSet.of(FOLLOW_LINKS);

// Visit all levels
int depth = Integer.MAX_VALUE;

// Walk the file tree with all levels and following the symbolic links
Files.walkFileTree(startDir, options, depth, visitor);
```

Matching Paths

The NIO.2 API lets you perform pattern matching on the string form of Path objects using the *glob* and *regex* patterns. An instance of the PathMatcher interface is used to perform the match. The PathMatcher interface is a functional interface. It contains a method matches(Path path) method that returns true if the specified path matches the pattern.

It is a three-step process to match a pattern to a path:

- Prepare a glob or regex pattern string.

- Get a PathMatcher object using the getPathMatcher() method of a FileSystem object.

- Call the matches() method with a Path object to check if the specified path matches the pattern.

The pattern string consists of two parts, syntax and pattern, separated by a colon:

syntax:pattern

The value for syntax is either glob or regex. The pattern part follows the syntax that depends on the value of the syntax part. I will list the syntax rules for the glob pattern briefly. For the regex pattern syntax rules, please refer to Chapter 14 in the book *Beginning Java Fundamentals* (ISBN: 978-1-4302-6652-5).

The glob pattern uses the following syntax rules:

- An asterisk (*) matches zero or more characters without crossing directory boundaries.

- Two consecutive asterisks (**) match zero or more characters crossing directory boundaries.

- A question mark (?) matches exactly one character.

- A backslash (\) is used to escape the special meaning of the following character. For example, \\ matches a single backslash, and * matches an asterisk.

- Characters placed inside brackets ([]) are called a bracket expression, which matches a single character. For example, [aeiou] matches a, e, i, o, or u. A dash between two characters specifies a range. For example, [a-z] matches all alphabets between a and z. The exclamation mark (!) after the left bracket is treated as negation. For example, [!tyu] matches all characters except t, y, and u.

- You can use a group of subpatterns by specifying comma-separated subpatterns inside braces ({}). For example, {txt, java, doc} matches txt, java, and doc.

- The matching of the root component of a path is implementation-dependent.

Listing 10-12 demonstrates how to use a PathMatcher object to match a path against a glob pattern. The program uses a glob pattern to match a path on Windows. Please change the path syntax to conform to your platform before you run the program.

Listing 10-12. Matching a Path Against a Glob/Regex Pattern

```
// PathMatching.java
package com.jdojo.nio2;

import java.nio.file.FileSystems;
import java.nio.file.Path;
import java.nio.file.PathMatcher;
import java.nio.file.Paths;
```

```java
public class PathMatching {
        public static void main(String[] args) {
                String globPattern = "glob:**txt";
                PathMatcher matcher =
                        FileSystems.getDefault().getPathMatcher(globPattern);
                Path path = Paths.get("C:\\poems\\luci1.txt");
                boolean matched = matcher.matches(path);
                System.out.format("%s matches %s: %b%n",
                                globPattern, path, matched);
        }
}
```

```
glob:**txt matches C:\poems\luci1.txt: true
```

Managing File Attributes

Through the File class, the java.io API provides support for accessing very basic file attributes such as the last modified time of a file. NIO.2 has extensive support for managing (reading and writing) the file attributes across platforms. The java.nio.attribute package contains the attribute-related classes. It bundles the file attributes in the following six types of views.

1. BasicFileAttributeView: This attribute view allows you to manage the basic file attributes such as creation time, last access time, last modified time, size, file type (regular file, directory, symbolic link, or other), and file key (a unique number for a file). It lets you modify the creation time, the last accessed time, and the last modified time of a file. This view is supported on all platforms.

2. DosFileAttributeView: It extends the BasicFileAttributeView. As the name suggests, it allows you to access the file attributes that are specific to DOS. It provides the support to check if a file is a hidden file, a system file, an archive file, and a read-only file. It is available only on the systems that support DOS such as Microsoft Windows.

3. PosixFileAttributeView: POSIX stands for Portable Operating System Interface for UNIX. It extends the BasicFileAttributeView and adds support for attributes that are available on the systems that support POSIX standards such as UNIX. Apart from basic file attributes, it lets you manage owner, group, and [related access] permissions.

4. FileOwnerAttributeView: This attribute view lets you manage the owner of a file.

5. AclFileAttributeView: ACL stands for Access Control List. It is a list of permissions attached to a file. It lets you manage the ACL for a file.

6. UserDefinedFileAttributeView: This view lets you manage a set of user-defined attributes for a file in the form of name-value pairs. Sometimes the user-defined attributes of a file are also known as *extended attributes*. The name of an attribute is a String. The value of an attribute could be of any data type.

Some attribute views are available across platforms and some only on specific platforms. An implementation may provide additional file attribute views.

Checking for a File Attribute View Support

Not all file attribute views are supported on all platforms, except the basic view. You can use the supportsFileAttributeView() method of the FileStore class to check whether a specific file attribute view is supported by a file store. The method accepts the class reference of the type of the file attribute view you want to check for support. If the specified file attribute view is supported, it returns true; otherwise, it returns false. The following snippet of code shows how to check for file attribute support:

```
Path path = get a path reference to a file store;

// Get the file store reference for the path
FileStore fs = Files.getFileStore(path);

// Check if POSIX file attribute is supported by the file store
boolean supported =    fs.supportsFileAttributeView(PosixFileAttributeView.class);
if (supported) {
        System.out.println("POSIX file attribute view is supported.");
}
else {
        System.out.println("POSIX file attribute view is not supported.");
}
```

Listing 10-13 demonstrates how to check if a file store supports a file attribute view. It checks for the file attribute support for the C: drive on Windows. Please change the file store path in the main() method to check for the supported file attribute views for the file store. You may get a different output when you run the program.

Listing 10-13. Checking for Supported File Attribute Views by a File Store

```
// SupportedFileAttribViews.java
package com.jdojo.nio2;

import java.io.IOException;
import java.nio.file.FileStore;
import java.nio.file.Files;
import java.nio.file.Path;
import java.nio.file.Paths;
import java.nio.file.attribute.AclFileAttributeView;
import java.nio.file.attribute.BasicFileAttributeView;
import java.nio.file.attribute.DosFileAttributeView;
import java.nio.file.attribute.FileAttributeView;
import java.nio.file.attribute.FileOwnerAttributeView;
import java.nio.file.attribute.PosixFileAttributeView;
import java.nio.file.attribute.UserDefinedFileAttributeView;

public class SupportedFileAttribViews {
        public static void main(String[] args) {
                // Use C: as the file store path on Windwos
                Path path = Paths.get("C:");
```

```
            try {
                    FileStore fs = Files.getFileStore(path);
                    printDetails(fs, AclFileAttributeView.class);
                    printDetails(fs, BasicFileAttributeView.class);
                    printDetails(fs, DosFileAttributeView.class);
                    printDetails(fs, FileOwnerAttributeView.class);
                    printDetails(fs, PosixFileAttributeView.class);
                    printDetails(fs, UserDefinedFileAttributeView.class);
            }
            catch (IOException ex) {
                    ex.printStackTrace();
            }
        }

        public static void printDetails(FileStore fs,
                        Class<? extends FileAttributeView> attribClass) {
            // Check if the file attribute view is supported
            boolean supported = fs.supportsFileAttributeView(attribClass);

            System.out.format("%s is supported: %s%n",
                            attribClass.getSimpleName(), supported);
        }
}
```

```
AclFileAttributeView is supported: true
BasicFileAttributeView is supported: true
DosFileAttributeView is supported: true
FileOwnerAttributeView is supported: true
PosixFileAttributeView is supported: false
UserDefinedFileAttributeView is supported: true
```

Reading and Updating File Attributes

The NIO.2 API provides many ways to work with file attributes. Sometimes it may be confusing to decide the method that you want to use to manage the attributes of a file.

You may need to work with only one attribute or many attributes of a file at a time. If you need to read or update the value of only one attribute of a file, you need to look at the available methods in the Files class that let you read/update that specific attribute. For example, if you want to check if a file is a directory, use the Files.isDirectory() method. If you want to read the owner of a file, use the Files.getOwner() method. If you want to update the owner of a file, use the Files.setOwner() method. The Files class has the following two static methods that let you read and update a file attribute using the attribute name as a string:

- Object getAttribute(Path path, String attribute, LinkOption... options)

- Path setAttribute(Path path, String attribute, Object value, LinkOption... options)

If you need to read or update multiple attributes of a file, you need to work with a specific file attribute view. The type of attributes determines the file attribute view that you need to use. For most of the file attribute views, you have to work with two interfaces named as XxxAttributes and XxxAttributeView. For example, for the basic file attributes, you have the BasicFileAttributes and BasicFileAtrributeView interfaces. The XxxAttributes lets you read the attributes. The XxxAttributeView lets you read as well as update the attributes. If you only want to read the attributes, use XxxAttributes. If you want to read and update attributes, use XxxAttributeView as well as XxxAttributes.

The following two methods of the Files class let you read the file attributes in a bulk, which is much more efficient than reading one attribute at a time.

- `<A extends BasicFileAttributes> A readAttributes(Path path, Class<A> type, LinkOption... options)`

- `Map<String,Object> readAttributes(Path path, String attributes, LinkOption... options)`

The last argument of both methods lets you specify how a symbolic link is handled. By default, if a file is a symbolic link, the attributes of the target of the symbolic link are read. If you specify NOFOLLOW_LINKS as the option, the attributes of the symbolic link are read, not the attributes of its target.

The first readAttributes() method returns all file attributes of a specified type in an XxxAttributes object. For example, you would write the following snippet of code to read the basic file attributes:

```
// Create the Path object representing the path of the file
Path path = Paths.get("C:\\poems\\luci1.txt");

// Read the basic file attributes
BasicFileAttributes bfa =
        Files.readAttributes(path, BasicFileAttributes.class);

// Get the last modified time
FileTime lastModifiedTime = bfa.lastModifiedTime();

// Get the size of the file
long size = bfa.size();
```

The second readAttributes() method returns all or some of the attributes of a specific type. The list of attributes to read is supplied in a string form. The string form of an attribute list uses the following syntax:

```
view-name:comma-separated-attributes
```

The view-name is the name of the attribute view that you want to read, such as basic, posix, acl, etc. If view-name is omitted, it defaults to basic. If view-name is present, it is followed by a colon. You can read all attributes of a specific view type by specifying an asterisk as the attributes list. For example, you can specify "basic:*" or "*" to read all basic file attributes. To read the size and the last modified time of the basic view, you would use "basic:size,lastModifiedTime" or "size,lastModifiedTime". To read the owner attribute of a file using an ACL view, you would use a string "acl:owner". To read all posix attributes of a file, you would use "posix:*". The following snippet of code prints the size and the last modified time of the file C:\poems\luci1.txt. Note that the file path uses Windows syntax.

```
// Get a Path object
Path path = Paths.get("C:\\poems\\luci1.txt");

// Prepare the attribute list
String attribList = "basic:size,lastModifiedTime";
```

```
// Raad the attributes
Map<String, Object> attribs = Files.readAttributes(path, attribList);

// Display the attributes on the standard output
System.out.format("Size:%s, Last Modified Time:%s %n",
                  attribs.get("size"), attribs.get("lastModifiedTime"));
```

Listing 10-14 reads the basic file attributes of the file C:\poems\luci1.txt and prints some of them on the standard output. You will need to change the file path in the main() method to work with another file on your platform. You may get a different output when you run this program. If the specified file does not exist, a NoSuchFileException is thrown and the program prints the stack trace of the exception.

Listing 10-14. Reading the Basic File Attributes of a File

```
// BasicFileAttributesTest.java
package com.jdojo.nio2;

import java.io.IOException;
import java.nio.file.Files;
import java.nio.file.Path;
import java.nio.file.Paths;
import java.nio.file.attribute.BasicFileAttributes;

public class BasicFileAttributesTest {
        public static void main(String[] args) {
                // Change the file path of an existing file
                Path path = Paths.get("C:\\poems\\luci1.txt");

                try {
                        // Read basic file attributes
                        BasicFileAttributes bfa =
                            Files.readAttributes(path, BasicFileAttributes.class);

                        // Print some of the basic file attributes
                        System.out.format("Size:%s bytes %n", bfa.size());
                        System.out.format("Creation Time:%s %n",
                                        bfa.creationTime());
                        System.out.format("Last Access Time:%s %n",
                                        bfa.lastAccessTime());
                }
                catch (IOException e) {
                        e.printStackTrace();
                }
        }
}
```

```
Size:119 bytes
Creation Time:2014-05-05T20:52:16.589994Z
Last Access Time:2014-05-05T20:52:16.589994Z
```

You can also read file attributes using a specific view object. You can use the getFileAttributeView() method of the Files class to get a specific attribute view. It returns null if the file attribute view is not available. The method declaration is as follows:

- <V extends FileAttributeView> V getFileAttributeView(Path path, Class<V> type, LinkOption... options)

Once you get a view object of a specific view type, you can read all attributes of that view type using the view object's readAttributes() method. Note that not all views provide readAttributes() method. For example, the FileOwnerAttributeView provides only the getOwner() method to read the owner attribute of a file. If an attribute view is updateable, the view object provides appropriate setter methods to update the attributes. The following snippet of code reads all basic attributes for C:\poems\luci1.txt file using a basic view object:

```
// Get a Path object
Path path = Paths.get("C:\\poems\\luci1.txt");

// Get the basic view
BasicFileAttributeView bfv =
        Files.getFileAttributeView(path, BasicFileAttributeView.class);

// Read all basic attributes through the view
BasicFileAttributes bfa = bfv.readAttributes();
```

The basic view lets you update the last modified time, the last accessed time, and the creation time of a file. The setTimes() method lets you update all three types of times. If you pass a null value for a time, it means you do not want to update that time. The time you need to pass to the setTimes() method is of FileTime type.

Listing 10-15 demonstrates how to use the basic file attribute view to read and update basic file attributes. Please change the file path in the main() method to the path of an existing file whose attributes you want to read. The program uses a file path of C:\poems\luci1.txt on Windows that may not exist on your machine.

Listing 10-15. Using Basic File Attribute View to Read and Update Basic File Attributes

```
// BasicFileAttributeViewTest.java
package com.jdojo.nio2;

import java.io.IOException;
import java.nio.file.Files;
import java.nio.file.Path;
import java.nio.file.Paths;
import java.nio.file.attribute.BasicFileAttributeView;
import java.nio.file.attribute.BasicFileAttributes;
import java.nio.file.attribute.FileTime;
import java.time.Instant;

public class BasicFileAttributeViewTest {
    public static void main(String[] args) {
        // Change the path to point to your file
        Path path = Paths.get("C:\\poems\\luci1.txt");

        try {
            // Get the basic view
            BasicFileAttributeView bfv =
                    Files.getFileAttributeView(path,
                            BasicFileAttributeView.class);
```

```
                    // Read all basic attributes through the view
                    BasicFileAttributes bfa = bfv.readAttributes();

                    // Print some basic attributes
                    System.out.format("Size:%s bytes %n", bfa.size());
                    System.out.format("Creation Time:%s %n",
                               bfa.creationTime());
                    System.out.format("Last Access Time:%s %n",
                                     bfa.lastAccessTime());

                    // Update the create time to the current time
                    FileTime newLastModifiedTime = null;
                    FileTime newLastAccessTime = null;
                    FileTime newCreateTime = FileTime.from(Instant.now());

                    // A null for time means youdo not want to update that time
                    bfv.setTimes(newLastModifiedTime,
                               newLastAccessTime,
                               newCreateTime);
            }
            catch (IOException e) {
                    e.printStackTrace();
            }
        }
    }
}
```

Managing the Owner of a File

There are three ways to manage the owner of a file:

- Using Files.getOwner()and Files.setOwner() methods.

- Using Files.getAttribute() and Files.setAttribute() methods using "owner" as the
  attribute name.

- Using the FileOwnerAttributeView.

You need to work with UserPrincipal and GroupPrincipal interfaces to manage the owner of a file. The owner of a file could be a user or a group. A UserPrincipal represents a user whereas a GroupPrincipal represents a group. When you read the owner of a file, you get an instance of UserPrincipal. Use the getName() method on the UserPrincipal object to get the name of the user. When you want to set the owner of a file, you need to get an object of the UserPrincipal from a user name in a string form. To get a UserPrincipal from the file system, you need to use an instance of the UserPrincipalLookupService class, which you can get using the getUserPrincipalLookupService() method of the FileSystem class. The following snippet of code gets a UserPrincipal object for a user whose user id is ksharan:

```
FileSystem fs = FileSystems.getDefault();
UserPrincipalLookupService upls = fs.getUserPrincipalLookupService();

// Throws a UserPrincipalNotFoundException exception if the user ksharan does not exist
UserPrincipal user = upls.lookupPrincipalByName("ksharan");
System.out.format("User principal name is %s%n", user.getName());
```

You can use method chaining in the above snippet of code to avoid intermediate variables.

```
UserPrincipal user = FileSystems.getDefault()
                           .getUserPrincipalLookupService()
                           .lookupPrincipalByName("ksharan");
System.out.format("User principal name is %s%n", user.getName());
```

The user principal lookup service is an optional operation for a file system. You need to handle the UnsupportedOperationException that is thrown when the file system does not support it.

To get a GroupPrincipal instance, use the lookupPrincipalByGroupName() method of the user principal lookup service. Once you get a UserPrincipal or GroupPrincipal instance that represents the owner of the file, you can use any of the three methods described in the beginning of this section to update the owner of a file.

Listing 10-16 demonstrates how to read and update the owner of a file using the FileOwnerAttributeView. Please change the file path in the main() method to an existing file on your machine before you run the program. The program uses brice as the new user for the file. Please change the new user id to a user that exists on your machine. If the user does not exist on your machine, you may get a UserPrincipalNotFoundException exception. You may get a different output when you run the program.

Listing 10-16. Changing the Owner of a File Using the FileOwnerAttributeView

```
// FileOwnerManagement.java
package com.jdojo.nio2;

import java.io.IOException;
import java.nio.file.FileSystem;
import java.nio.file.FileSystems;
import java.nio.file.Files;
import java.nio.file.Path;
import java.nio.file.Paths;
import java.nio.file.attribute.FileOwnerAttributeView;
import java.nio.file.attribute.UserPrincipal;
import java.nio.file.attribute.UserPrincipalLookupService;

public class FileOwnerManagement {
        public static void main(String[] args) throws IOException {
                try {
                        // Change the file path to an existing file on your machine
                        Path path = Paths.get("C:\\poems\\luci1.txt");

                        FileOwnerAttributeView foav =
                         Files.getFileAttributeView(
                                path,FileOwnerAttributeView.class);

                        UserPrincipal owner = foav.getOwner();
                        System.out.format("Original owner of %s is %s%n",
                                        path, owner.getName());

                        FileSystem fs = FileSystems.getDefault();
                        UserPrincipalLookupService upls =
                                fs.getUserPrincipalLookupService();
```

```
                        // Change the file owner to brice
                        UserPrincipal newOwner =
                                upls.lookupPrincipalByName("brice");
                        foav.setOwner(newOwner);

                        UserPrincipal changedOwner = foav.getOwner();
                        System.out.format("New owner of %s is %s%n",
                                        path, changedOwner.getName());
                }
                catch (UnsupportedOperationException | IOException e) {
                        e.printStackTrace();
                }
        }
}
```

```
Original owner of C:\poems\luci1.txt is CORPORATE\ksharan
New owner of C:\poems\luci1.txt is CORPORATE\brice
```

The following snippet of code uses the Files.setOwner() method to update the owner of a file identified with the path C:\poems\luci1.txt on Windows:

```
UserPrincipal owner = get the owner;
Path path = Paths.get("C:\\poems\\luci1.txt");
Files.setOwner(path, owner);
```

Managing ACL File Permissions

In this section, I will cover managing the file permissions using AclFileAttributeView. Note that ACL type file attributes are supported on Microsoft Windows. An ACL consists of an ordered list of access control entries. Each entry consists of a UserPrincipal, the type of access, and the level of the access to an object. In NIO.2, an instance of the AclEntry class represents an entry in an ACL. You can get and set a List of AclEntry for a file using the getAcl() and setAcl() methods of the AclFileAttributeView. The following snippet of code gets the List of ACL entries for a file called C:\poems\luci1.txt:

```
Path path = Paths.get("C:\\poems\\luci1.txt");
AclFileAttributeView view =
        Files.getFileAttributeView(path, AclFileAttributeView.class);
List<AclEntry> aclEntries = view.getAcl();
```

The AclEntry class has methods to read various properties of an ACL entry. Its principal() method returns the UserPrincipal to identify the user or the group. Its permissions() method returns a Set of AclEntryPermission objects to identify the permissions. Its type() method returns an enum constant of the type AclEntryType such as ALARM, ALLOW, AUDIT, and DENY that indicates the type of the access. Its flags() method returns a Set of AclEntryFlag enum constants, which contains the inheritance flags of the ACL entry.

Listing 10-17 demonstrates how to read ACL entries for file C:\poems\luci1.txt. If the file does not exist, a NoSuchFileException is thrown. The program handles the exception and prints the stack trace of the exception. If you run the program on a UNIX-like platform, it will print an error message that the ACL view is not supported. A partial output is shown when the program was run on Windows. You may get a different output.

Listing 10-17. Reading ACL Entries and Related Permissions

```java
// AclReadEntryTest.java
package com.jdojo.nio2;

import java.io.IOException;
import java.nio.file.Files;
import java.nio.file.Path;
import java.nio.file.Paths;
import java.util.List;
import java.util.Set;
import java.nio.file.attribute.AclEntry;
import java.nio.file.attribute.AclEntryPermission;
import java.nio.file.attribute.AclFileAttributeView;

public class AclReadEntryTest {
        public static void main(String[] args) {
                // Change the path to an existing file on Windows
                Path path = Paths.get("C:\\poems\\luci1.txt");

                AclFileAttributeView aclView =
                        Files.getFileAttributeView(path, AclFileAttributeView.class);
                if (aclView == null) {
                        System.out.format("ACL view is not supported.%n");
                        return;
                }

                try {
                        List<AclEntry> aclEntries = aclView.getAcl();
                        for(AclEntry entry: aclEntries) {
                                System.out.format("Principal: %s%n", entry.principal());
                                System.out.format("Type: %s%n", entry.type());
                                System.out.format("Permissions are:%n");

                                Set<AclEntryPermission> permissions = entry.permissions();
                                for(AclEntryPermission p : permissions) {
                                        System.out.format("%s %n", p);
                                }

                                System.out.format("-----------------------%n");
                        }
                }
                catch (IOException e) {
                        e.printStackTrace();
                }
        }
}
```

```
Principal: CORPORATE\ksharan (User)
Type: ALLOW
Permissions are:
WRITE_OWNER
DELETE_CHILD
EXECUTE
READ_DATA
...
------------------------
Principal: NT AUTHORITY\SYSTEM (Well-known group)
Type: ALLOW
Permissions are:
WRITE_OWNER
...
```

Updating ACL entries for a file is more involved than reading them. You need to create an AclEntry object using the AclEntry.Builder class. The newBuilder() method of the AclEntry class returns an empty AclEntry.Builder object, which acts as a staging area for a new AclEntry object. You need to call various setter methods such as setPrincipal(), setType(), setPermissions(), etc. on the builder object. When you are finished with setting all properties, call the build() method on the builder object to create an AclEntry object. The following snippet of code demonstrates these steps, assuming that bRiceUser is a UserPrincipal and permissions is a Set of AclEntryPermission:

```
// Let's build an ACL entry
AclEntry.Builder builder = AclEntry.newBuilder();
builder.setPrincipal(bRiceUser);
builder.setType(AclEntryType.ALLOW);
builder.setPermissions(permissions);
AclEntry newEntry = builder.build();
```

Once you prepare a new AclEntry, you need to add it to the existing ACL entries for the file. The following snippet of code adds the new ACL entry to the existing ones and sets them back using an ACL attribute view:

```
// Get the ACL entry for the path
List<AclEntry> aclEntries = aclView.getAcl();

// Add the ACL entry to the existing list
aclEntries.add(newEntry);

// Update the ACL entries for the file
aclView.setAcl(aclEntries);
```

Listing 10-18 demonstrates how to add a new ACL entry for a user named brice. It adds DATA_READ and DATA_WRITE permissions for the user brice on the C:\poems\luci1.txt file. Make sure that the file C:\poems\luci1.txt and a user with the user id brice exist on the machine. Please change the file and user id that exist on the machine to set the ACL entries for another file and user id.

Listing 10-18. Updating ACL Entries for a File

```java
// AclUpdateEntryTest.java
package com.jdojo.nio2;

import java.io.IOException;
import java.nio.file.FileSystems;
import java.nio.file.Files;
import java.nio.file.Path;
import java.nio.file.Paths;
import java.util.List;
import java.util.Set;
import java.nio.file.attribute.AclEntry;
import java.nio.file.attribute.AclEntryPermission;
import java.nio.file.attribute.AclEntryType;
import java.nio.file.attribute.AclFileAttributeView;
import java.nio.file.attribute.UserPrincipal;
import java.util.EnumSet;
import static java.nio.file.attribute.AclEntryPermission.READ_DATA;
import static java.nio.file.attribute.AclEntryPermission.WRITE_DATA;

public class AclUpdateEntryTest {
        public static void main(String[] args) {
                Path path = Paths.get("C:\\poems\\luci1.txt");

                AclFileAttributeView aclView =
                        Files.getFileAttributeView(path, AclFileAttributeView.class);
                if (aclView == null) {
                        System.out.format("ACL view is not supported.%n");
                        return;
                }

                try {
                        // Get UserPrincipal for brice
                        UserPrincipal bRiceUser =
                                FileSystems.getDefault()
                                            .getUserPrincipalLookupService()
                                            .lookupPrincipalByName("brice");

                        // Prepare permissions set
                        Set<AclEntryPermission> permissions = EnumSet.of(READ_DATA, WRITE_DATA);

                        // Let us build an ACL entry
                        AclEntry.Builder builder = AclEntry.newBuilder();
                        builder.setPrincipal(bRiceUser);
                        builder.setType(AclEntryType.ALLOW);
                        builder.setPermissions(permissions);
                        AclEntry newEntry = builder.build();

                        // Get the ACL entry for the path
                        List<AclEntry> aclEntries = aclView.getAcl();
```

```
                        // Add the ACL entry for brice to the existing list
                        aclEntries.add(newEntry);

                        // Update the ACL entries
                        aclView.setAcl(aclEntries);

                        System.out.println("ACL entry added for brice successfully");
                }
            catch (IOException e) {
                        e.printStackTrace();
                }
        }
    }
}
```

Managing POSIX File Permissions

In this section, I will cover managing file permissions using PosixFileAttributeView. Note that UNIX supports POSIX standard file attributes. POSIX file permissions consist of nine components: three for the owner, three for the group, and three for others. The three types of permissions are read, write, and execute. A typical POSIX file permission in a string form looks like "rw-rw----", which has read and write permissions for the owner and the group. The PosixFilePermission enum type defines nine constants, one for each permission component. The nine constants are named as XXX_YYY, where XXX is OWNER, GROUP, and OTHERS, and YYY is READ, WRITE, and EXECUTE.

PosixFilePermissions is a utility class that has methods to convert the POSIX permissions of a file from one form to another. Its toString() method converts a Set of PosixFilePermission enum constants into a string of the rwxrwxrwx form. Its fromString() method converts the POSIX file permissions in a string of the rwxrwxrwx form to a Set of PosixFilePermission enum constants. Its asFileAttribute() method converts a Set of PosixFilePermission enum constants into a FileAttribute object, which you can use in the Files.createFile() method as an argument when creating a new file.

Reading POSIX file permissions is easy. You need to use the readAttributes() method of the PosixFileAttributeView class to get an instance of PosixFileAttributes. The permissions() method of PosixFileAttributes returns all POSIX file permissions as a Set of PosixFilePermission enum constants. The following snippet of code reads and prints POSIX file permissions in the rwxrwxrwx form for a file named luci in the default directory:

```
// Get a Path object for lici file
Path path = Paths.get("luci");

// Get the POSIX attribute view for the file
PosixFileAttributeView posixView =
        Files.getFileAttributeView(path, PosixFileAttributeView.class);

// Here, make sure posixView is not null

// Read all POSIX attributes
PosixFileAttributes attribs; attribs = posixView.readAttributes();

// Read the file permissions
Set<PosixFilePermission> permissions = attribs.permissions();

// Convert the file permissions into the rwxrwxrwx string form
String rwxFormPermissions = PosixFilePermissions.toString(permissions);
```

```
// Print the permissions
System.out.println(rwxFormPermissions);
```

Updating POSIX file permissions is also easy. You need to get all permissions in a Set of PosixFilePermission enum constants. To update the POSIX file permissions, call the setPermissions() method of PosixFileAttributeView, passing the Set of the PosixFilePermission enum constants as an argument. The following snippet of code shows how to set the POSIX file permissions:

```
// Get the permission in a string form
String rwxFormPermissions = "rw-r-----";

// Convert the permission in the string form to a Set of PosixFilePermission
Set<PosixFilePermission> permissions = PosixFilePermissions.fromString(rwxFormPermissions);

// Update the permissions
posixView.setPermissions(permissions);
```

Alternatively, you can also create a Set of PosixFilePermission enum constants directly and set it as the file permissions, like so:

```
Set<PosixFilePermission> permissions = EnumSet.of(OWNER_READ, OWNER_WRITE, GROUP_READ);
posixView.setPermissions(permissions);
```

Listing 10-19 demonstrates how to read and update POSIX file permissions for a file named luci on UNIX-like platforms. If the file does not exist, the program outputs the stack trace of a NoSuchFileException. If you run the program on a non-UNIX-like platform, it will print a message that POSIX attribute view is not supported. You may get a different output when you run this program.

Listing 10-19. Reading and Writing POSIX File Permissions

```
// PosixPermissionsTest.java
package com.jdojo.nio2;

import java.io.IOException;
import java.nio.file.Files;
import java.nio.file.Path;
import java.nio.file.Paths;
import java.util.EnumSet;
import java.util.Set;
import java.nio.file.attribute.PosixFileAttributeView;
import java.nio.file.attribute.PosixFileAttributes;
import java.nio.file.attribute.PosixFilePermission;
import java.nio.file.attribute.PosixFilePermissions;
import static java.nio.file.attribute.PosixFilePermission.OWNER_READ;
import static java.nio.file.attribute.PosixFilePermission.OWNER_WRITE;
import static java.nio.file.attribute.PosixFilePermission.GROUP_READ;

public class PosixPermissionsTest {
        public static void main(String[] args) {
                Path path = Paths.get("luci");
                PosixFileAttributeView posixView =
                        Files.getFileAttributeView(path, PosixFileAttributeView.class);
```

```
            if (posixView == null) {
                    System.out.format("POSIX attribute view is not supported%n.");
                    return;
            }

            readPermissions(posixView);
            updatePermissions(posixView);
    }

    public static void readPermissions(PosixFileAttributeView posixView) {
            try {
                    PosixFileAttributes attribs; attribs = posixView.readAttributes();
                    Set<PosixFilePermission> permissions = attribs.permissions();

                    // Convert the set of posix file permissions into rwxrwxrwx form
                    String rwxFormPermissions = PosixFilePermissions.toString(permissions);
                    System.out.println(rwxFormPermissions);
            }
            catch (IOException ex) {
                    ex.printStackTrace();
            }
    }

    public static void updatePermissions(PosixFileAttributeView posixView) {
            try {
                    Set<PosixFilePermission> permissions =
                            EnumSet.of(OWNER_READ, OWNER_WRITE, GROUP_READ);
                    posixView.setPermissions(permissions);
                    System.out.println("Permissions set successfully.");
            }
            catch (IOException ex) {
                    ex.printStackTrace();
            }
    }
}
```

```
rw-r--r--
Permissions set successfully.
```

Watching a Directory for Modifications

NIO.2 supports a watch service to notify a Java program when an object in a file system is modified. Currently, you can watch only directories for modifications. The watch service uses the native file event notification facility of the file system. If a file system does not provide a file event notification facility, it may use other mechanisms such as polling.

The following classes and interfaces in the java.nio.file package are involved in the implementation of a watch service:

- The Watchable interface

- The WatchService interface

- The WatchKey interface

- The `WatchEvent<T>` interface

- The `WatchEvent.Kind<T>` interface

- The `StandardWatchEventKinds` class

A `Watchable` object represents a file-system object that can be watched for changes. A `Watchable` object can be registered with a watch service. A `Path` object is a `Watchable` object. Therefore, you can register a `Path` object with a watch service.

A `WatchService` represents a watch service that watches registered objects for changes. When an object is registered with a `WatchService`, the `WatchService` returns a `WatchKey` that serves as a token for the registration. In other words, a `WatchKey` identifies the registration of an object with a `WatchService`.

A `WatchEvent` represents an event (or a repeated event) on an object registered with a watch service. Its `kind()` method returns the kind of event that occurs on the registered object. Its `context()` method returns a `Path` object that represents the entry on which the event occurs. The `Path` object represents a relative path between the registered directory with the watch service and the entry on which the event occurs. An event may be repeated before it is notified. The `count()` method returns the number of times the event occurs for a specific notification. If it returns a value greater than 1, it is a repeated event.

A `WatchEvent.Kind<T>` represents the kind of event that occurs on a registered object. The `StandardWatchEventKinds` class defines constants to represent the kind of an event.

The `StandardWatchEventKinds` class defines the following four constants to identify the kind of an event. Each constant is of the type `WatchEvent.Kind` type. It contains the following constants:

- `ENTRY_CREATE`

- `ENTRY_DELETE`

- `ENTRY_MODIFY`

- `OVERFLOW`

The names of the first three constants are self-explanatory. They represent events when an entry is created, deleted, and modified in a registered directory.

The last event kind is `OVERFLOW`, which represents a special kind of event to indicate that event may have been lost or discarded.

The following steps are needed to watch a directory for changes:

- Create a watch service.

- Register a directory with the watch service.

- Retrieve a watch key from the watch service queue.

- Process the events that occur on the registered directory.

- Reset the watch key after processing the events.

- Close the watch service.

Create a Watch Service

Create a watch service for the file system in which you want to watch a directory for changes as follows:

```
WatchService ws = FileSystems.getDefault().newWatchService();
```

Register the Directory with the Watch Service

You need to create a Path object for the directory you want to watch and invoke its register() method to register it with the watch service. At the time of registration, you need to specify the kinds of events for which you want to register your directory. The register() method will return a WatchKey object as a registration token.

```
// Get a Path object for C:\kishori directory to watch
Path dirToWatch = Paths.get("C:\\kishori");

// Register the dirToWatch for create, modify and delete events
WatchKey token = dirToWatch.register(ws, ENTRY_CREATE, ENTRY_MODIFY, ENTRY_DELETE);
```

You can cancel the registration of a directory with the watch service using the cancel() method of the WatchKey. When a directory is registered, its WatchKey is said to be in the *ready* state. You can register multiple directories with a watch service. Note that the directory must exist at the time of registration.

Retrieve a WatchKey from the Watch Service Queue

When an event occurs on a registered directory, the WatchKey for that registered directory is said to be in the *signaled* state and the WatchKey is queued to the watch service. Another event may occur on a registered directory when its WatchKey is in the *signaled* state. If an event occurs on a directory while its WatchKey is in the *signaled* state, the event is queued to the WatchKey, but the WatchKey itself is not re-queued to the watch service. A WatchKey in the *signaled* state remains in this state until its reset() method is called to change its state to the *ready* state.

You can use the take() or poll() method of the WatchService object to retrieve and remove a signaled and queued WatchKey. The take() method waits until a WatchKey is available. The poll() method lets you specify a timeout for the wait. Typically, an infinite loop is used to retrieve a signaled WatchKey.

```
while(true) {
        // Retrieve and remove the next available WatchKey from the watch service
        WatchKey key = ws.take();
}
```

Process the Events

Once you retrieve and remove a WatchKey from the watch service queue, you can retrieve and remove all pending events for that WatchKey. A WatchKey may have more than one pending events. The pollEvents() method of the WatchKey retrieves and removes all its pending events. It returns a List of WatchEvent. Each element of the List represents an event on the WatchKey. Typically, you will need to use the kind(), context(), and count() methods of the WatchEvent object to know the details of the event. The following snippet of code shows the typical logic for processing an event:

```
while(true) {
        // Retrieve and remove the next available WatchKey
        WatchKey key = ws.take();

        // Process all events of the WatchKey
        for(WatchEvent<?> event : key.pollEvents()) {
                // Process each event here
        }
}
```

Reset the WatchKey after Processing Events

You must reset the WatchKey object by calling its reset() method, so it may receive event notifications and be queued to the watch service again. The reset() method puts the WatchKey into the *ready* state. The reset() method returns true if the WatchKey is still valid. Otherwise, it returns false. A WatchKey may become invalid if it is cancelled or its watch service is closed.

```
// Reset the WatchKey
boolean isKeyValid = key.reset();
if (!isKeyValid) {
        System.out.println("No longer watching " + dirToWatch);
}
```

Close the Watch Service

When you are done with the watch service, close it by calling its close() method. You will need to handle the java.io.IOException when you call its close() method.

```
// Close the watch service
ws.close();
```

■ **Tip** The WatchService is AutoCloseable. If you create an object of the WatchService in a try-with-resources block, it will be automatically closed when the program exits the block.

Listing 10-20 has a complete program that watches a C:\kishori directory for changes. You can replace the directory path in the Watcher class with the directory path that you want to watch for changes. You will need to make changes to the watched directory, such as creating a new file and changing an existing file, after you run the Watcher class. The output will show the details of the events that occur on an entry in the watched directory. You may get a different output.

Listing 10-20. Implementing a Watch Service to Monitor Changes in a Directory

```
// Watcher.java
package com.jdojo.nio2;

import java.nio.file.WatchEvent.Kind;
import java.io.IOException;
import java.nio.file.FileSystems;
import java.nio.file.Path;
import java.nio.file.Paths;
import java.nio.file.WatchService;
import java.nio.file.WatchEvent;
import java.nio.file.WatchKey;
import static java.nio.file.StandardWatchEventKinds.ENTRY_CREATE;
import static java.nio.file.StandardWatchEventKinds.ENTRY_MODIFY;
import static java.nio.file.StandardWatchEventKinds.ENTRY_DELETE;
import static java.nio.file.StandardWatchEventKinds.OVERFLOW;
```

471

```java
public class Watcher {
    public static void main(String[] args) {
        try (WatchService ws = FileSystems.getDefault().newWatchService()) {
            // Get a Path object for C:\kishori directory to watch
            Path dirToWatch = Paths.get("C:\\kishori");

            // Register the path with the watch service for create,
            // modifiy and delete events
            dirToWatch.register(ws, ENTRY_CREATE, ENTRY_MODIFY, ENTRY_DELETE);

            System.out.println("Watching " + dirToWatch + " for events.");

            // Keep watching for events on the dirToWatch
            while(true) {
                // Retrieve and remove the next available WatchKey
                WatchKey key = ws.take();

                for(WatchEvent<?> event : key.pollEvents()) {
                    Kind<?> eventKind = event.kind();
                    if (eventKind == OVERFLOW) {
                        System.out.println("Event overflow occurred");
                        continue;
                    }

                    // Get the context of the event, which is the directory
                    // entry on which the event occurred.
                    WatchEvent<Path> currEvent = (WatchEvent<Path>)event;
                    Path dirEntry = currEvent.context();

                    // Print the event details
                    System.out.println(eventKind +
                                        " occurred on " + dirEntry);
                }

                // Reset the key
                boolean isKeyValid = key.reset();

                if (!isKeyValid) {
                    System.out.println("No longer watching " + dirToWatch);
                    break;
                }
            }
        }
        catch (IOException | InterruptedException e) {
            e.printStackTrace();
        }
    }
}
```

```
Watching C:\kishori for events.
ENTRY_DELETE occurred on temp
ENTRY_CREATE occurred on hello.txt
ENTRY_MODIFY occurred on hello.txt
```

Asynchronous File I/O

NIO.2 supports asynchronous file I/O. In a synchronous file I/O, the thread that requests the I/O operation waits until the I/O operation is complete. In an asynchronous file I/O, the Java application requests the system for an I/O operation and the operation is performed by the system asynchronously. When the system is performing the file I/O operation, the application continues doing other work. When the system finishes the file I/O, it notifies the application about the completion of its request.

The asynchronous file I/O model is scalable as compared to the synchronous file I/O model. The requests for an asynchronous file I/O and the completion notification to the application are performed by a pool of threads that are specially created for this purpose. The asynchronous file I/O API has options to let you use the default thread pool or a custom thread pool. It offers enhanced scalability by using a predefined dedicated pool of threads to handle all asynchronous file I/O operations, instead of creating a new thread for each I/O operation.

An instance of the java.nio.channels.AsynchronousFileChannel class represents an asynchronous file channel that is used to read, write, and perform other operations on a file asynchronously. Multiple I/O operations can be performed simultaneously on an asynchronous file channel. An asynchronous file channel does not maintain a current position where a read or a write operation starts. You need to provide the position for each read and write operation with each request.

The static open() method of the AsynchronousFileChannel class is used to get an instance of the AsynchronousFileChannel class. The method is overloaded. One version uses the default thread pool to handle the I/O operations and the completion notification. Another version lets you specify an ExecutorService to which the asynchronous tasks will be submitted for handling the I/O operations and the completion notifications. The following snippet of code gets an AsynchronousFileChannel on a file for writing. It creates the file if the file does not exist.

```
// Get a Path object
Path path = Paths.get("C:\\poems\\rainbow.txt");

// Get an asynchronous file channel for WRITE.
// Create the file, if it does not exist
AsynchronousFileChannel afc = AsynchronousFileChannel.open(path, WRITE, CREATE);
```

The AsynchronousFileChannel provides two ways to handle the result of an asynchronous file I/O operation.

- Using a java.util.concurrent.Future object.

- Using a java.nio.channels.CompletionHandler object.

Each method of the AsynchronousFileChannel class that supports asynchronous file I/O operation has two versions. One version returns a Future object, which you can use to handle the result of the requested asynchronous operation. The get() method of the Future object returns the number of bytes written to the file channel. The following snippet of code uses the version of the write() method that returns a Future object:

```
// Get the data to write in a ByteBuffer
ByteBuffer dataBuffer = get a byte buffer filled with data;

// Perform the asynchronous write operation
long startPosition = 0;
Future<Integer> result = afc.write(dataBuffer, startPosition);
```

Once you get a Future object, you can use a polling method or a blocked waiting method to handle the result of the asynchronous file I/O. The following snippet of code shows the polling method, where it keeps calling the isDone() method of the Future object to check if the I/O operation is finished:

```
while (!result.isDone()) {
        // Async file I/O is not done yet. Keep working on something else
}

// We are done with the async file I/O. Get the result
int writtenNumberOfBytes = result.get();
```

▨ **Tip** Note that the call to the Future.get() method blocks until the result is available. The call to the Future.isDone() method is non-blocking.

Another version of the methods of the AsynchronousFileChannel class that supports asynchronous file I/O lets you pass a CompletionHandler object whose methods are called when the requested asynchronous I/O operation completes or fails. The CompletionHandler interface has two methods: completed() and failed(). The completed() method is called when the requested I/O operation completes successfully. When the requested I/O operation fails, the failed() method is called. The API lets you pass an object of any type to the completed() and failed() methods. Such an object is called an *attachment*. You may want to pass an attachment such as the ByteBuffer or the reference to the channel, etc. to these methods so you can perform additional actions such as reading the data from the ByteBuffer inside these methods. Pass null as an attachment if you do not have anything useful to pass to these methods as an attachment. Suppose you intend to use an object of the following Attachment class as an attachment to you completion handler:

```
// Used as an attachment
public class Attachment {
        public Path path;
        public ByteBuffer buffer;
        public AsynchronousFileChannel asyncChannel;
}
```

Now you can declare your completion handler class as follows:

```
// A class to handle completion of an asynchronous I/O operation
public class MyHandler implements CompletionHandler<Integer, Attachment> {
        @Override
        public void completed(Integer result, Attachment attach) {
                // Handle completion of the I/O operation
        }

        @Override
        public void failed(Throwable e, Attachment attach) {
                // Handle failure of the I/O operation
        }
}
```

You can use an object of the MyHandler class to handle the completion of an asynchronous file I/O operation. The following snippet of code uses a MyHandler instance as a completion handler for an asynchronous write operation. The completed() or failed() method of the MyHandler instance will be called depending on the result of the I/O operation.

```
// Get a completion handler
MyHandler handler = new MyHandler();

// Get the data to write in a ByteBuffer
ByteBuffer dataBuffer = get a data buffer;

// Prepare the attachment
Attachment attach = new Attachment();
attach.asyncChannel = afc;
attach.buffer = dataBuffer;
attach.path = path;

// Perform the asynchronous write operation
afc.write(dataBuffer, 0, attach, handler);
```

> **Tip** The ByteBuffer that is used to read or write in an asynchronous file operation should not be used by the application between the time it is used in an asynchronous file I/O request and the time the request is completed. Otherwise, it will have an unpredictable result. You can close an AsynchronousFileChannel using its close() method. All pending operations are completed with a java.nio.channels.AsynchronousCloseException when its close() method is called.

Listing 10-21 demonstrates how to use a CompletionHandler object to handle the results of an asynchronous write to a file. After submitting the request for the asynchronous write on a file, the main thread sleeps for 5 seconds to give the asynchronous operation time to finish. In a real-world application, after submitting an asynchronous file I/O request, you would continue performing other tasks. The program writes some text to a rainbow.txt file in the default directory. You may get a different output.

Listing 10-21. Using a CompletionHandler Object to Handle the Result of an Asynchronous File Write

```
// AsyncFileWrite.java
package com.jdojo.nio2;

import java.nio.ByteBuffer;
import java.io.IOException;
import java.nio.file.Path;
import java.nio.file.Paths;
import java.nio.channels.CompletionHandler;
import java.nio.channels.AsynchronousFileChannel;
import java.nio.charset.Charset;
import static java.nio.file.StandardOpenOption.WRITE;
import static java.nio.file.StandardOpenOption.CREATE;
```

```java
public class AsyncFileWrite {
        // Used as an attachment to the CompletionHandler
        private static class Attachment {
                public Path path;
                public ByteBuffer buffer;
                public AsynchronousFileChannel asyncChannel;
        }

        // An inner class to handle completion of the asynchronous write operation
        private static class WriteHandler
                            implements CompletionHandler<Integer, Attachment> {
            @Override
            public void completed(Integer result, Attachment attach) {
                    System.out.format("%s bytes written to %s%n",
                                        result, attach.path.toAbsolutePath());

                    try {
                            // Close the channel
                            attach.asyncChannel.close();
                    }
                    catch (IOException e) {
                            e.printStackTrace();
                    }
            }

            @Override
            public void failed(Throwable e, Attachment attach) {
                    System.out.format("Write operation on %s file failed." +
                                        " The error is:  %s%n",
                                        attach.path, e.getMessage());
                    try {
                            // Close the channel
                            attach.asyncChannel.close();
                    }
                    catch (IOException e1) {
                            e1.printStackTrace();
                    }
            }
        }

        public static void main(String[] args) {
                Path path = Paths.get("rainbow.txt");

                try {
                        // Get an async channel
                        AsynchronousFileChannel afc =
                                AsynchronousFileChannel.open(path, WRITE, CREATE);

                        // Get a completion handler
                        WriteHandler handler = new WriteHandler();
```

```
                // Get the data to write in a ByteBuffer
                ByteBuffer dataBuffer = getDataBuffer();

                // Prepare the attachment
                Attachment attach = new Attachment();
                attach.asyncChannel = afc;
                attach.buffer = dataBuffer;
                attach.path = path;

                // Perform the asynchronous write operation
                afc.write(dataBuffer, 0, attach, handler);

                try {
                        // Let the thread sleep for five seconds,
                        // to allow the asynchronous write is complete
                        System.out.println("Sleeping for 5 seconds...");
                        Thread.sleep(5000);
                }
                catch (InterruptedException e) {
                        e.printStackTrace();
                }

                System.out.println("Done...");
        }
        catch (IOException e) {
                e.printStackTrace();
        }
}

public static ByteBuffer getDataBuffer() {
        String lineSeparator = System.getProperty("line.separator");

        StringBuilder sb = new StringBuilder();
        sb.append("My heart leaps up when I behold");
        sb.append(lineSeparator);
        sb.append("A Rainbow in the sky");
        sb.append(lineSeparator);
        sb.append(lineSeparator);
        sb.append("So was it when my life began;");
        sb.append(lineSeparator);
        sb.append("So is it now I am a man;");
        sb.append(lineSeparator);
        sb.append("So be it when I shall grow old,");
        sb.append(lineSeparator);
        sb.append("Or let me die!");
        sb.append(lineSeparator);
        sb.append(lineSeparator);
        sb.append("The Child is father of the man;");
        sb.append(lineSeparator);
        sb.append("And I could wish my days to be");
```

```
                String str = sb.toString();
                Charset cs = Charset.forName("UTF-8");
                ByteBuffer bb = ByteBuffer.wrap(str.getBytes(cs));

                return bb;
        }
}
```

```
Sleeping for 5 seconds...
228 bytes written to C:\book\javabook\rainbow.txt
Done...
```

Listing 10-22 demonstrates how to use a Future object to handle the results of an asynchronous write to a file. It uses a try-with-resources clause to open an AsynchronousFileChannel. It uses a polling method (Future.isDone() method calls) to check if the I/O operation has completed. The program writes some text to a file named rainbow.txt in the default directory. You may get a different output.

Listing 10-22. Using a Future Object to Handle the Result of an Asynchronous File Write

```java
// AsyncFileWriteFuture.java
package com.jdojo.nio2;

import java.util.concurrent.ExecutionException;
import java.util.concurrent.Future;
import java.nio.ByteBuffer;
import java.io.IOException;
import java.nio.file.Path;
import java.nio.file.Paths;
import java.nio.channels.AsynchronousFileChannel;
import static java.nio.file.StandardOpenOption.WRITE;
import static java.nio.file.StandardOpenOption.CREATE;

public class AsyncFileWriteFuture {
        public static void main(String[] args) {
                Path path = Paths.get("rainbow.txt");

                try (AsynchronousFileChannel afc =
                        AsynchronousFileChannel.open(path, WRITE, CREATE)) {

                        // Get the data to write in a ByteBuffer
                        ByteBuffer dataBuffer = AsyncFileWrite.getDataBuffer();

                        // Perform the asynchronous write operation
                        Future<Integer> result = afc.write(dataBuffer, 0);

                        // Keep polling to see if I/O has finished
                        while (!result.isDone()) {
                                try {
                                        // Let the thread sleep for 2 seconds
                                        // before the next polling
                                        System.out.println("Sleeping for 2 seconds...");
                                        Thread.sleep(2000);
                                }
```

```
                                catch (InterruptedException e) {
                                        e.printStackTrace();
                                }
                        }

                        // I/O is complete
                        try {
                                int writtenBytes = result.get();
                                System.out.format("%s bytes written to %s%n",
                                        writtenBytes, path.toAbsolutePath());
                        }
                        catch (InterruptedException | ExecutionException e) {
                                e.printStackTrace();
                        }
                }
        }
        catch (IOException e) {
                e.printStackTrace();
        }
    }
}
```

```
Sleeping for 2 seconds...
228 bytes written to C:\book\javabook\rainbow.txt
```

Listing 10-23 demonstrates how to use a CompletionHandler object to handle the results of an asynchronous read from a file. The program reads and prints the contents a rainbow.txt file in the default directory. To read the contents of a different file, change the path of the file in the main() method. You may get a different output.

Listing 10-23. Using a CompletionHandler to Handle the Result of an Asynchronous File Read

```java
// AsyncFileRead.java
package com.jdojo.nio2;

import java.nio.ByteBuffer;
import java.io.IOException;
import java.nio.file.Path;
import java.nio.file.Paths;
import java.nio.channels.CompletionHandler;
import java.nio.channels.AsynchronousFileChannel;
import java.nio.charset.Charset;
import static java.nio.file.StandardOpenOption.READ;

public class AsyncFileRead {
        // Used as an attachment to the CompletionHandler
        private static class Attachment {
                public Path path;
                public ByteBuffer buffer;
                public AsynchronousFileChannel asyncChannel;
        }
```

```
        // An inner class to handle completion of the asynchronous read operation
        private static class ReadHandler
                        implements CompletionHandler<Integer, Attachment> {
            @Override
            public void completed(Integer result, Attachment attach) {
                    System.out.format("%s bytes read from %s%n",
                                        result, attach.path);

                    System.out.format("Read data is:%n");

                    byte[] byteData = attach.buffer.array();
                    Charset cs = Charset.forName("UTF-8");
                    String data = new String(byteData, cs);
                    System.out.println(data);

                    try {
                            // Close the channel
                            attach.asyncChannel.close();
                    }
                    catch (IOException e) {
                            e.printStackTrace();
                    }
            }


            @Override
            public void failed(Throwable e, Attachment attach) {
                    System.out.format("Read operation on %s file failed." +
                                        "The error is: %s%n",
                                        attach.path, e.getMessage());

                    try {
                            // Close the channel
                            attach.asyncChannel.close();
                    }
                    catch (IOException e1) {
                            e1.printStackTrace();
                    }
            }
        }
    }

    public static void main(String[] args) {
            Path path = Paths.get("rainbow.txt");
            try {
                    // Get an async channel
                    AsynchronousFileChannel afc =
                            AsynchronousFileChannel.open(path, READ);

                    // Get a completion handler
                    ReadHandler handler = new ReadHandler();
```

```
                    // Get the data size in bytes to read
                    int fileSize = (int)afc.size();
                    ByteBuffer dataBuffer = ByteBuffer.allocate(fileSize);

                    // Prepare the attachment
                    Attachment attach = new Attachment();
                    attach.asyncChannel = afc;
                    attach.buffer = dataBuffer;
                    attach.path = path;

                    // Perform the asynchronous read operation
                    afc.read(dataBuffer, 0, attach, handler);

                    try {
                            // Let the thread sleep for five seconds,
                            // to allow the asynchronous read to complete
                            System.out.println("Sleeping for 5 seconds...");
                            Thread.sleep(5000);
                    }
                    catch (InterruptedException e) {
                            e.printStackTrace();
                    }

                    System.out.println("Done...");
            }
        catch (IOException e) {
                e.printStackTrace();
        }
    }
}
}
```

```
Sleeping for 5 seconds...
228 bytes read from rainbow.txt
Read data is:
My heart leaps up when I behold
A Rainbow in the sky

So was it when my life began;
So is it now I am a man;
So be it when I shall grow old,
Or let me die!

The Child is father of the man;
And I could wish my days to be
Done...
```

Listing 10-24 demonstrates how to use a Future object to handle the results of an asynchronous read from a file. It uses the wait method (a Future.get() method call) to wait for the asynchronous file I/O to complete. The program reads the contents of a rainbow.txt file in the default directory. Change the path of this file if you want to read the contents of a different file. You may get a different output.

Listing 10-24. Using a Future Object to Handle the Result of an Asynchronous File Read

```java
// AsyncFileReadFuture.java
package com.jdojo.nio2;

import java.util.concurrent.ExecutionException;
import java.util.concurrent.Future;
import java.nio.ByteBuffer;
import java.io.IOException;
import java.nio.file.Path;
import java.nio.file.Paths;
import java.nio.channels.AsynchronousFileChannel;
import java.nio.charset.Charset;
import static java.nio.file.StandardOpenOption.READ;

public class AsyncFileReadFuture {
    public static void main(String[] args) {
        Path path = Paths.get("rainbow.txt");

        try (AsynchronousFileChannel afc =
                AsynchronousFileChannel.open(path, READ)) {

            // Get a data buffer of the file size to read
            int fileSize = (int)afc.size();
            ByteBuffer dataBuffer = ByteBuffer.allocate(fileSize);

            // Perform the asynchronous read operation
            Future<Integer> result = afc.read(dataBuffer, 0);

            System.out.println("Waiting for reading to be finished...");
            try {
                // Let us wait until reading is finished
                int readBytes = result.get();

                System.out.format("%s bytes read from %s%n", readBytes, path);
                System.out.format("Read data is:%n");

                // Read the data from the buffer
                byte[] byteData = dataBuffer.array();
                Charset cs = Charset.forName("UTF-8");
                String data = new String(byteData, cs);

                System.out.println(data);
            }
            catch (InterruptedException | ExecutionException e) {
                e.printStackTrace();
            }
        }
        catch (IOException ex) {
            ex.printStackTrace();
        }
    }
}
```

Waiting for reading to be finished...
228 bytes read from rainbow.txt
Read data is:
My heart leaps up when I behold
A Rainbow in the sky

So was it when my life began;
So is it now I am a man;
So be it when I shall grow old,
Or let me die!

The Child is father of the man;
And I could wish my days to be

Summary

The New Input/Output 2 (NIO.2) is a new I/O API that provides improved, comprehensive support for working with platform-dependent file systems. An instance of the FileSystem class represents a platform-dependent file system.

An instance of the Path class represents an abstract pathname in the file system. It contains several methods to manipulate a path. A Path is used with a utility class called Files to work with the contents and attributes of the file that it represents. The Files class consists of all static convenience methods to work with files, such as for deleting, copying, and moving files.

NIO.2 has extensive support for reading and modifying file attributes. Attribute support is provided through different attribute views. Some views are supported on all platforms and some are platform specific. Some views are optional.

NIO.2 provides a watch service to watch for changes in a directory's contents. The Java program registers a directory with the watch service to get notified for specific events that occur in the directory, such as the creation of a new file/directory, change in the contents of a file, deletion of a file, etc. The watch service notifies the Java program when the event of interest occurs on the registered directories.

NIO.2 provides comprehensive support for asynchronous file I/O. An instance of the java.nio.channels. AsynchronousFileChannel class represents an asynchronous file channel that is used to read, write, and perform other operations on a file asynchronously. Multiple I/O operations can be performed simultaneously on an asynchronous file channel.

CHAPTER 11

■ ■ ■

Garbage Collection

In this chapter, you will learn

- What garbage collection is

- How garbage collection is implemented in Java

- How to pass a hint to the JVM to run the garbage collector

- How to implement the finalizers

- Different states of an object based on its reachability and finalization status

- The difference between strong and weak references

- How to use weak references to implement memory-sensitive cache

What Is Garbage Collection?

In a programming language, memory management is central to the development of a fast, efficient, and bug-free application. Memory management involves two activities:

- Memory allocation

- Memory reclamation

When a program needs memory, memory is allocated from a memory pool. When the program is finished with the memory, the memory is returned to the memory pool, so it can be reused by some other part of the program in the future. The process of returning memory to the pool is known as *memory reclamation* or *memory recycling*. The memory allocation and reclamation can be accomplished explicitly or implicitly.

In explicit memory allocation, the programmer decides how much memory is needed. The programmer requests that amount of memory from the program runtime environment known as the *memory allocator* or simply the *allocator*. The allocator allocates the requested memory and marks that memory as in-use, so it will not allocate the same memory block again. Here, we assumed that our request for new memory block to allocator is always fulfilled. This can happen only if we have an infinite amount of memory. However, that is not the case with any computer. Some computers may have megabytes of memory and some may have gigabytes. However, there is always a limit to the memory available on a computer. If we run a program that always allocates memory blocks from the memory pool and never returns the memory back to the pool, we will soon run out of memory and the program will stop.

In explicit memory reclamation, the programmer decides when to return the memory to the memory pool. The allocator is free to allocate the returned memory when it receives a new request for memory allocation. Explicit memory reclamation often leads to subtle bugs in programs. It also complicates the inter-modules interface design. Suppose there are two modules, m1 and m2, in an application. Module m1 allocates a block of memory and the reference to that memory is r1. Module m1 makes a call to module m2, passing the reference r1. Module m2 stores the reference r1 for future use. Which module should be responsible for the reclamation of the memory referenced by r1? There could be different scenarios depending on the program flow between the two modules. Suppose module m1 reclaims the memory immediately after a call to module m2. In such a case, you may come across two problems:

- At some point in the program execution, module m2 tries to access the memory using the reference r1. Because module m1 has already reclaimed the memory referenced by r1, the same memory might have been reallocated by the allocator and may have entirely different data stored at that memory location. In such a case, r1 is called a *dangling reference* because it is referencing a memory location that has already been reclaimed. If you try to read data using a dangling reference, the result would be unpredictable. You cannot have a dangling reference in Java.

- Module m1 may try to use reference r1 after it has reclaimed the memory referenced by r1. This will also lead to the problem of using a dangling reference.

If module m2 reclaims the memory referenced by r1, you may end up with the same dangling reference problem if any of the modules, m1 or m2, try to use reference r1. What happens if none of the modules reclaims the memory and never uses the reference r1 again? The memory will never be returned to the memory pool and will never be reused. This situation is known as a *memory leak* because the allocator has no knowledge of the memory block, which is not returned to it, even though it is never used again by the program. If memory leaks happen regularly, the program will eventually run out of memory and will cease to function. If your program runs for a short time with small memory leaks, you may not even notice this bug for years or the entire life of your program!

In a programming language that allows explicit memory management, programmers spend a substantial amount of effort in the memory management aspect of the program. In another kind of memory-related problem, a programmer may allocate a big amount of memory statically, so that he can use it throughout the life cycle of the program. The static memory allocation may not always succeed, since static memory has an upper limit. The hardest part of the memory management decision is to decide when to reclaim the memory to avoid dangling references and memory leaks.

In implicit memory allocation, a programmer indicates to the runtime system that he wants to allocate the memory to store a particular type of data. The runtime system computes the memory needed to store the requested type of data and allocates it to the running program. In implicit/automatic memory reclamation, a programmer does not need to worry about memory reclamation. The runtime system will automatically reclaim all memory blocks, which will never be used by the program again. The process of automatic reclamation of unused memory is known as *garbage collection*. The program that performs garbage collection is known as a *garbage collector* or simply a *collector*. The garbage collector may be implemented as part of the language runtime system or as an add-on library.

Memory Allocation in Java

In Java, programmers deal with objects. The memory required for an object is always allocated on the heap. The memory is allocated implicitly using the new operator. Suppose you have a class called Employee. You create an object of the Employee class.

```
Employee emp = new Employee();
```

Depending on the definition of the Employee class, the Java runtime computes how much memory is needed, allocates the needed memory on heap, and stores the reference to that memory block in the emp reference variable. Note that when you want to create an Employee object, you do not specify how much memory you need. The new Employee() part of the above statement indicates to Java that you want to create an object of the Employee class. Java queries the definition of the Employee class to compute the memory required to represent an Employee object.

Every Java object in memory has two areas: a *header area* and a *data area*. The header area stores bookkeeping information to be used by the Java runtime, for example, the pointer to the object class, information about the garbage collection status of the object, locking information about the object, length of an array if the object is an array, etc.

The data area is used to store the values for all instance variables of the object. The header area layout is fixed for a particular JVM implementation whereas the data area layout is dependent on the object type. The Java Hotspot virtual machine uses two machine-words (in 32-bit architecture one word is 4 bytes) for the object header. If the object is an array, it uses three machine-words for its header. One extra word in the header is used to store the array length. However, most JVMs use three-machine words for an object header. Figure 11-1 depicts the object layout for the Java Hotspot VM and the IBM VM.

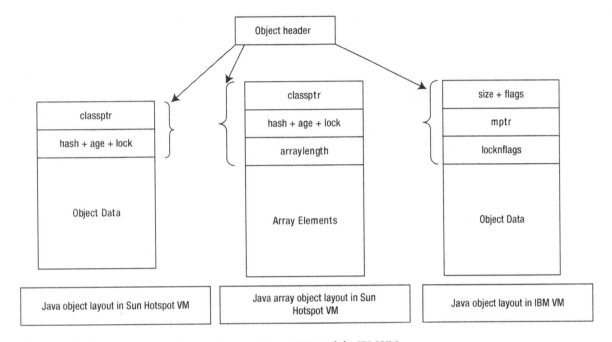

Figure 11-1. *The layout of an object in the Java Hotspot VM and the IBM VM*

The Java Hotspot VM uses a variable length object header to save memory on the heap. Since most Java objects are small, one machine-word savings per object for non-array objects is a significant heap space savings. The Java Hotspot VM's object header contains the following information:

- classptr: This is the first machine-word in the object layout. It contains a pointer to the class information of the object. The class information includes the object's method table, the object's size, and a pointer to a Class structure, which contains information about the class of the object, etc.

- hash + age + lock: This is the second machine-word in the object header. It contains the object's hash code, age information, and lock fields. Age information is used in the process of reclaiming the object's memory by the generational garbage collector. The generation garbage collector is a special type of garbage collector that uses the object's age in its algorithm to reclaim an object's memory.

- arraylength: This is the third machine-word in the object header. It is included only if the object is an array. It contains the length of the array. In this case, the object's data area contains the array elements.

The IBM VM uses three machine-words for the object header. All header fields hold the following information:

- `size + flags`: This field is the first machine-word of the object header. This field contains the size of the object and flags to indicate different states of the object. Because the size of the object is limited and all objects start at 8 bytes boundary, some of the bits are used to store flags indicating different states of the object.

- `mptr`: This field is the second machine-word in the object header. It can hold one of the two pieces of information depending on if the object is an array or not.

  - It holds a pointer to the method block, if the object is not an array. The method block has reference to class block, which can provide more information about the Java class to which the object belongs.

  - If the object is an array, this field holds the length of the array.

- `locknflags`: This field is the third machine-word in the object header. It is used to hold information about the object locking and some flags. A 1-bit flag is used to indicate whether the object is an array. If this bit is set, `mptr` contains the length of the array. Another 1-bit flag is used to indicate whether the object was hashed and moved. Note that objects are moved during some kind of garbage collection. Since the hash code of an object is its address in the memory and is supposed to be the same, the garbage collector that moves objects around during garbage collection uses this flag to preserve the hash code, if it was computed and used before the garbage collection.

■ **Tip** In Java, all objects are created on heap. Java uses the `new` operator to allocate memory for an object on heap. An array's length is not a part of its class definition. It is defined at runtime. It is stored in the object header. You will not find the `length` instance variable in the array's class definition when you perform introspection on an array's class.

Java does not provide any direct means to compute the size of an object. You should not write a Java program that depends on the size of the objects anyway. The size of primitive types, for example, `int`, `long`, `double`, etc. is fixed for all JVM implementations. The layout and size of an object depends on the JVM implementation. Therefore, any code that depends on the size of objects may work on one platform and not on others.

Garbage Collection in Java

The garbage collector is part of the Java platform. It runs in the background in a low priority thread. It automatically reclaims objects. However, before it reclaims objects, it makes sure that the running program in its current state will never use them again. This way, it ensures that the program will not have any dangling references. An object that cannot be used in the future by the running program is known as a *dead object* or *garbage*. An object that can be used in the future by the running program is known as a *live object*.

There are many algorithms to determine whether an object is live or dead. One of the simplest, but not very efficient, algorithms is based on reference counting, which stores the count of references that refer to an object. When an object's reference is assigned to a reference variable, the reference count is incremented by 1. When a reference variable no longer refers to an object, the reference count is decremented by 1. When the reference count for an object is zero, it becomes garbage. This algorithm has a lot of overhead of updating the reference count of objects. Another type of algorithm, which is called a *tracing algorithm*, is based on the concept of a root set. A root set includes

- Reference variables in the Java stack for each thread

- Static reference variables defined in loaded classes

- Reference variables registered using the Java Native Interface (JNI)

A garbage collector, which is based on the tracing algorithm, starts traversing references starting from the root set. Objects that can be reached (or accessed) from the reference variables in the root set are known as *reachable objects*. A reachable object is considered live. A reachable object from the root set may refer to other objects. These objects are also considered reachable. Therefore, all objects that can be reached directly or indirectly from the root set reference variables are considered live. Other objects are considered dead and are thus eligible for garbage collection.

An object may manage resources other than memory on heap. These resources may include network connections, file handles, memory managed explicitly by native code, etc. For example, an object may open a file when it is created. File handles that can be opened simultaneously may have an upper limit depending on your operating system. When the object is garbage collected, you may want to close those file handles. The garbage collector gives the dying object a chance to perform the cleanup work. It does this by executing a predefined block of code before the memory for the dying object is reclaimed. The process of performing the cleanup work, before the object is reclaimed by the garbage collector, is known as *finalization*. The block of code that is invoked by the garbage collector to perform finalization is known as the *finalizer*. In Java, you can define an instance method `finalize()` in a class, which serves as a finalizer for the objects of that class. The Java garbage collector invokes the `finalize()` method of an object before it reclaims the memory occupied by the object.

Invoking the Garbage Collector

Programmers have little control over the timing when the garbage collector is run. The JVM performs the garbage collection whenever it runs low in memory. The JVM tries its best to free up memory of all unused objects before it throws a `java.lang.OutOfMemoryError` error. The `gc()` method of the `java.lang.Runtime` class may be used to pass a hint to the JVM that it may run the garbage collector. The call to the `gc()` method is just a hint to the JVM. The JVM is free to ignore the call. The Java Language API Documentation describes the behavior of a call to the `gc()` as follows:

> *"Runs the garbage collector. Calling this method suggests that the Java virtual machine expend effort toward recycling unused objects in order to make the memory they currently occupy available for quick reuse. When control returns from the method call, the virtual machine has made its best effort to recycle all discarded objects..."*

Suggesting that the garbage collection should run can be invoked as shown:

```
// Get the Runtime instance
Runtime rt = Runtime.getRuntime();

// Invoke the garbage collector
rt.gc();
```

You can combine the above two statements into one statement, if you do not intend to use the `Runtime` instance, like so:

```
// Get runtime instance and invoke the garbage collector
Runtime.getRuntime().gc();
```

The System class contains a convenience method called gc(), which is equivalent to executing the Runtime.getRuntime().gc() statement. You can also use the following statement to run the garbage collector:

```
// Invoke the garbage collector
System.gc();
```

The program in Listing 11-1 demonstrates the use of the System.gc() method. The program creates 2,000 objects of the Object class in the createObjects() method. The references of the new objects are not stored. You cannot refer to these objects again, and hence, they are garbage. When you invoke the System.gc() method, you suggest to the JVM that it should try to reclaim the memory used by these objects. The memory freed by the garbage collector is displayed in the output section. Note that you will more than likely get a different output when you run this program.

Listing 11-1. Invoking Garbage Collection

```java
// InvokeGC.java
package com.jdojo.gc;

public class InvokeGC {
        public static void main(String[] args) {
                long m1, m2, m3;

                // Get a runtime instance
                Runtime rt = Runtime.getRuntime();

                for(int i = 0; i < 3; i++){
                        // Get free memory
                        m1 =  rt.freeMemory();

                        // Create some objects
                        createObjects(2000);

                        // Get free memory
                        m2 =  rt.freeMemory();

                        // Invoke garbage collection
                        System.gc();

                        // Get free memory
                        m3 =  rt.freeMemory();

                        System.out.println("m1=" + m1 + ", m2=" + m2 + ", m3=" +
                                        m3 + "\nMemory freed by gc()=" + (m3 - m2));

                        System.out.println("-------------------------");
                }
        }
}
```

```
        public static void createObjects(int count) {
                for(int i = 0; i < count; i++) {
                        // Do not store the references of new objects, so they are
                        // immediately eligible for garbage collection.
                        new Object();
                }
        }
}
```

```
m1=130944496, m2=130920640, m3=131670824
Memory freed by gc()=750184
------------------------
m1=131652360, m2=131636904, m3=131671208
Memory freed by gc()=34304
------------------------
m1=131652696, m2=131638504, m3=131671208
Memory freed by gc()=32704
------------------------
```

In general, it is not advisable to invoke the garbage collector programmatically. Invoking the garbage collector has some overhead. It may slow down performance if it is invoked arbitrarily. The Java runtime takes care of reclaiming unused object's memory automatically. You may get an OutOfMemoryError in your program. This error may be caused by many reasons. The Java runtime makes all efforts to free up memory, invoking the garbage collector before throwing the OutOfMemoryError error. Therefore, simply invoking the garbage collector programmatically will not make this error go away. To resolve this error, you can look at the following:

- Review your program to make sure that you are not holding onto some object references that you will never use again. Set these references to null after you are done with them. Setting all references to an object to null makes the object eligible for the garbage collection. If you are storing large objects in static variables, those objects will remain in memory until the class itself is unloaded. Generally, the objects stored in static variables will take up memory forever. Review your program and try to avoid storing large objects in static variables.

- Review your code and make sure that you are not caching large amounts of data in objects. You can use weak references to cache large amount of data in objects. Weak references have an advantage over regular references (regular references are also known as strong references) that the objects referenced by weak references are garbage collected before the Java runtime throws an OutOfMemoryError. I will discuss weak references later in this chapter.

- If none of the above solutions work for you, you may try to adjust the heap size.

Object Finalization

Finalization is an action that is automatically performed on an object before the memory used by the object is reclaimed by the garbage collector. The block of code that contains the action to be performed is known as a *finalizer*. The Object class has a finalize() method, which is declared as

```
protected void finalize() throws Throwable
```

Because all Java classes inherit from the Object class, the finalize() method can be invoked on all Java objects. Any class can override and implement its own version of the finalize() method. The finalize() method serves as a finalizer for Java objects. That is, the garbage collector automatically invokes the finalize() method on an object before reclaiming the object's memory. Understanding the correct use of the finalize() method is key to writing a good Java program, which manages resources other than the heap memory.

Let's first start with a simple example that demonstrates the fact that the finalize() method is called before an object is garbage collected. Listing 11-2 defines a method finalize() in the Finalizer class.

Listing 11-2. Using the finalize() Method

```java
// Finalizer.java
package com.jdojo.gc;

public class Finalizer {
        // id is used to identify the object
        private int id;

        // Constructor which takes the id as argument
        public Finalizer(int id){
                this.id = id;
        }

        // This is the finalizer for the object. The JVM will call
        // this method, before the object is garbage collected
        public void finalize(){
                // Just print a message indicating which object is being garbage
                // collected. Print message when id is a multiple of 100
                // just to avoid a bigger output.
                if (id % 100 == 0) {
                        System.out.println ("finalize() called for " + id ) ;
                }
        }

        public static void main(String[] args) {
                // Create 500000 objects of the Finalizer class
                for(int i = 1; i <= 500000; i++){
                        // Do not store reference to the new object
                        new Finalizer(i);
                }

                // Invoke the garbage collector
                System.gc();
        }
}
```

```
finalize() called for 5300
finalize() called for 6900
finalize() called for 7100
more output (not shown here)...
```

The finalize() method prints a message if the object being garbage collected has an id, which is a multiple of 100. The main() method creates 500,000 objects of the Finalizer class and calls System.gc() to invoke the garbage collector.

When the garbage collector determines that an object is unreachable, it marks that object for finalization and places that object in a queue. If you want the Java runtime to finalize all objects that are pending finalization, you can do so by calling the runFinalization() method of the Runtime class as shown:

```
Runtime rt = Runtime.getRuntime();
rt.runFinalization();
```

The System class has a runFinalization() convenience method, which is equivalent to calling the runFinalization() method of the Runtime class. It can be called as shown:

```
System.runFinalization();
```

Invoking the runFinalization() method is only a hint to the Java runtime to invoke the finalize() method of all objects pending finalization. Technically, you may call the finalize() method on an object in your code as many times as you want. However, it is meant for the garbage collector to call an object's finalize() method at most one time during the lifetime of the object. The garbage collector's one-time call to the finalize() method of an object is not affected by the fact that the finalize() method of the object was called programmatically before.

Programmers should not override the finalize() method in a class trivially. A finalize() method with no code, or which calls the finalize() method of the Object class, is an example of a trivially overridden finalize() method. The method in the Object class does nothing. If your class is a direct subclass of the Object class and you do not have any meaningful code in the finalize() method of your class, it is better not to include the finalize() method in your class at all. Memory reclamation is faster and sooner for the objects, which do not have an implementation of the finalize() method compared to those that have an implementation of the finalize() method.

Finally or Finalize?

The time when an object is finalized is not guaranteed. Finalizing all unreachable objects is also not guaranteed. In short, there is no guarantee when the finalize() method of an unreachable object will be called or if it will be called at all. So, what good is the finalize() method? The main purpose of a garbage collector in Java is to relieve programmers from the burden of freeing the memory of unused objects to avoid the problem of memory leaks and dangling references. Its secondary job is to run the finalization on the objects with no guarantee about the timing. As a programmer, you should not depend much on the finalization process of garbage collection. You should code the finalize() method with care. If you need to clean up resources for sure when you are done with them, you should use a try-finally clause, such as

```
try {
        /* Get your resources and work with them */
}
finally { /* Release your resources */
}
```

You can acquire resources and use them in a try block and release them in the associated finally block. A finally block is guaranteed to be executed after a try block is executed. This way, you can be sure that scarce resources in your program are always freed once you are done with them. However, it may not always be feasible, because of performance issues, to release resources immediately after you are done with them. For example, you may not want to open a network connection every time you need it. You may open a network connection once, use it, and close it when you no longer need it. Sometimes you may not know the exact point in a program from where you will not need that network connection. In such cases, you can code the finalize() method as a backup to free the resources if they have not been freed yet. You can call the finalize() method programmatically when you know for sure that the resources can be freed. The following FinalizeAsBackup class shows the skeleton of the code that uses such a technique:

```
/* Template of a class that uses finalize() method as a backup to free resources */
public class FinalizeAsBackup {
        /* Other codes go here */
        SomeResource sr;
        public void aMethod() {
                sr = Obtain the resources here...;

                /* Do some processing . . . */

                /* Note the conditional freeing of resources */
                if (some condition is true) {
                        /* Free resources here calling finalize() */
                        this.finalize();
                }
        }

        public void finalize() {
                /* Free the resources if they have not been freed yet */
                if (resources not yet freed ) {
                        free resources now;
                }
        }
}
```

The aMethod() method of the class gets the resource and stores its reference in the sr instance variable. Programmers call the finalize() method when they are sure they should free the resources. Otherwise, the garbage collector will call the finalize() method and resources will be freed. Note that the FinalizeAsBackup class is a template. It contains pseudocode to explain the technique. This class will not compile.

■ **Tip** The moral of the story about using the finalize() method is to use it with care and use it only as a last resort to free resources. You can use a try-finally block to free resources. The order in which objects are finalized is not defined. For example, if object obj1 becomes eligible for garbage collection before object obj2, it is not guaranteed that obj1 will be finalized before obj2. When an uncaught exception is thrown, the main program is halted. However, an uncaught exception in a finalizer halts the finalization of only that object, not the entire application.

Object Resurrection

Someone is about to die. God asks him for his last wish. He says, "Give me my life back." God grants his last wish and he gets back his life. When he was about to die the second time God kept quiet and let him die without asking him for his last wish. Otherwise, he would ask for his life repeatedly and he would never die. The same logic applies to an object's finalization in Java. The call to the finalize() method of an object is like the garbage collector asking the object for its last wish. Generally, the object responds, "I want to clean up all my mess." That is, an object responds to its finalize() method call by performing some cleanup work. It may respond to its finalize() method call by resurrecting itself by placing its reference in a reachable reference variable. Once it is reachable through an already reachable reference variable, it is back to life. The garbage collector marks an object using the object's header bits as finalized, after it calls the object's finalize() method. If an already finalized object becomes unreachable the next time during garbage collection, the garbage collector does not call the object's finalize() method again.

The resurrection of an object is possible because the garbage collector does not reclaim an object's memory just after calling its finalize() method. After calling the finalize() method, it just marks the object as finalized. In the next phase of the garbage collection, it determines again if the object is reachable. If the object is unreachable and finalized, only then will it reclaim the object's memory. If an object is reachable and finalized, it does not reclaim object's memory; this is a typical case of resurrection.

Resurrecting an object in its finalize() method is not a good programming practice. One simple reason is that if you have coded the finalize() method, you expect it to be executed every time an object dies. If you resurrect the object in its finalize() method, the garbage collector will not call its finalize() method again when it becomes unreachable a second time. After resurrection, you might have obtained some resources that you expect to be released in the finalize() method. This will leave subtle bugs in your program. It is also hard for other programmers to understand your program flow if your program resurrects objects in their finalize() methods. Listing 11-3 demonstrates how an object can resurrect using its finalize() method.

Listing 11-3. Object Resurrection

```java
// Resurrect.java
package com.jdojo.gc;

public class Resurrect {
        // Declare a static variable of the Resurrect type
        private static Resurrect res = null;

        // Declare an instance variable that stores the name of the object
        private String name = "";

        public Resurrect(String name) {
                this.name = name;
        }

        public static void main(String[] args) {
                // We will create objects of the Resurrect class and will not store
                // their references, so they are eligible for garbage collection immediately.
                for(int count = 1; count <= 1000; count++) {
                        new Resurrect("Object #" + count);

                        // For every 100 objects created invoke garbage collection
                        if (count % 100 == 0) {
                                System.gc();
                                System.runFinalization();
                        }
                }
        }

        public void sayHello() {
                System.out.println("Hello from " + name);
        }
```

```
        public static void resurrectIt(Resurrect r) {
                // Set the reference r to static variable res, which makes it reachable
                // as long as res is reachable.
                res = r ;

                // Call a method to show that we really got the object back
                res.sayHello();
        }

        public void finalize() {
                System.out.println("Inside finalize(): " + name);

                // Resurrect this object
                Resurrect.resurrectIt(this);
        }
}
```

```
(Partial output is shown below)
...
Inside finalize(): Object #14
Hello from Object #14
...
Inside finalize(): Object #997
Hello from Object #997
```

The Resurrect class creates 1,000 objects in the main() method. It does not store references of those new objects, so they become garbage as soon as they are created. After creating 100 new objects, it invokes the garbage collector using the System.gc() method. It also calls the System.runFinalization() method, so the finalizers are run for the garbage objects. When the garbage collector calls the finalize() method for an object, that object passes its reference to the resurrectIt() method. This method stores the dying object's reference in the static variable res, which is reachable. The method resurrectIt() also calls the sayHello() method on the resurrected object to show which object was resurrected. Note that once another object resurrects itself you are overwriting the static res variable with the recently resurrected object reference. The previously resurrected object becomes garbage again. The garbage collector will reclaim the memory for the previously resurrected object without calling its finalize() method again. You may get different output when you run the program.

State of an Object

The state of a Java object is defined based on two criteria:

- Finalization status
- Reachability

Based on the finalization status, an object can be in one of the following three states:

- Unfinalized
- Finalizable
- Finalized

When an object is instantiated, it is in the unfinalized state. For example,

```
Employee john = new Employee();
```

The object referred to by the john reference variable is in an unfinalized state after the above statement is executed. The finalizer of an unfinalized object had never been invoked automatically by the JVM. An object becomes finalizable when the garbage collector determines that the finalize() method can be invoked on the object. A finalized object has its finalize() method invoked automatically by the garbage collector.

Based on reachability, an object can be in one of three states:

- Reachable

- Finalizer-reachable

- Unreachable

An object is reachable if it can be accessed through any chain of references from the root set. A finalizer-reachable object can be reached through the finalizer of any finalizable object. A finalizer-reachable object may become reachable if the finalizer from which it is reachable stores its reference in an object that is reachable. This is the situation when an object resurrects. An object may resurrect itself in its finalize() method or through another object's finalize() method. An unreachable object cannot be reached by any means.

There are nine combinations of object states based on their finalization status and reachability status. One of the nine combinations, finalizable and unreachable, is not possible. The finalize() method of a finalizable object may be called in future. The finalize() method can still refer to the object using this keyword. Therefore, a finalizable object cannot also be unreachable. An object can exist in one of the following eight states:

- Unfinalized - Reachable

- Unfinalized - Finalizer-reachable

- Unfinalized - Unreachable

- Finalizable - Reachable

- Finalizable - Finalizer-reachable

- Finalized - Reachable

- Finalized - Finalizer-reachable

- Finalized - Unreachable

Weak References

Java 2 introduced the concept of weak references in Java garbage collection by including a new package called java.lang.ref. The concept of weak references in the context of garbage collection is not new to Java. It existed before in other programming languages, but Java included it in Java 2. So far, the object references I have discussed are strong references. That is, as long as the object reference is in scope, the object it refers to cannot be garbage collected. For example, consider the following object creation and reference assignment statement:

```
Employee john = new Employee("John Jacobs");
```

Here, john is a reference to the object created by the expression new Employee("John Jacobs"). The memory state that exists after executing the above statement is depicted in Figure 11-2.

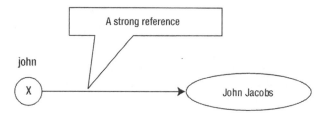

Figure 11-2. *An example of a strong reference*

If at least one strong reference to an object exists, the garbage collector will not reclaim that object. In the previous section, I discussed the object state based on its reachability. By stating that there is a strong reference to an object, I mean that the object is reachable. With the introduction of weak references, now there are three more states of an object based on its reachability:

- Softly reachable
- Weakly reachable
- Phantom reachable

Therefore, when I called an object *reachable* in the last section, I will call it *strongly reachable* now onwards. This change in terminology is because of the introduction of three new kinds of object reachability. Before I discuss the three new kinds of object reachability, you need to know about the classes included in java.lang.ref package. There are four classes of interest, as shown in Figure 11-3. I will not discuss the Reference class from the diagram.

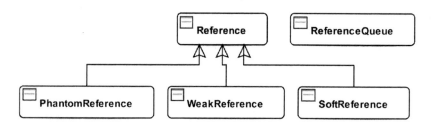

Figure 11-3. *A class diagram for some classes in the java.lang.ref package*

The Reference class is the superclass for the SoftReference, WeakReference, and PhantomReference classes. The Reference class is an abstract class. Therefore, you cannot create an object of this class. The SoftReference, WeakReference, and PhantomReference classes are used to create weak references. Note that by the phrase "weak reference," I mean a reference that is not a strong reference. By the phrase WeakReference, I mean the class java.lang.ref.WeakReference. I will describe a weak reference later in this section. The ReferenceQueue class is used to place the references of SoftReference, WeakReference, and PhantomReference objects in a queue. Let's look at different ways to create these three types of objects. The constructors for these three classes are shown in Table 11-1.

Table 11-1. *Constructors for the SoftReference, WeakReference, and PhantomReference classes*

Class	Constructors
SoftReference	SoftReference(Object referent) SoftReference(Object referent, ReferenceQueue q)
WeakReference	WeakReference(Object referent) WeakReference(Object referent, ReferenceQueue q)
PhantomReference	PhantomReference(Object referent, ReferenceQueue q)

You can create objects of SoftReference and WeakReference classes using an object of any class, or using an object of any class and an object of the ReferenceQueue class. You must create an object of the PhantomReference class using an object of any class and an object of the ReferenceQueue class. You can create an object of the SoftReference class as shown:

```
Employee john = new Employee ("John Jacobs");
SoftReference sr = new SoftReference(john);
```

The memory state after executing the above two statements is depicted in Figure 11-4.

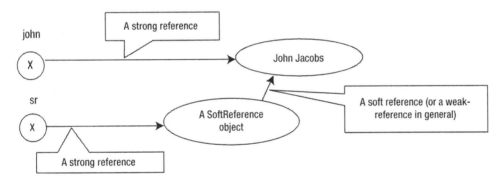

Figure 11-4. *An example of a soft reference*

In Figure 11-4, there are two strong references and one weak reference. All three weak reference classes have two instance variables: referent and queue. I will not discuss any other instance variables of these classes here. They are used to hold the reference of the object and reference queue passed in to the constructors of these classes. A reference to any object stored in the referent instance variable of any of these three classes is known as a weak reference in general—and a soft reference, weak reference, or phantom reference in particular, depending on the class being used. Therefore, the link from a soft reference object to the employee object shown in the figure is a weak reference. To be specific, I will call it a soft reference because I used an object of the SoftReference class. Any reference that does not involve the referent instance variable of any of these three classes is a strong reference in Java. Therefore, john and sr are strong references.

How are weak references different from strong references? The difference lies in how the garbage collector treats them. Weak references do not prevent the objects from being collected by the garbage collector. That is, if there is a weak reference to an object, the garbage collector can still reclaim the object. However, if there is at least one strong reference to an object, the garbage collector will not reclaim the object. Before you start looking at details of how to use these three reference classes in Java programs, let's discuss the reachability of an object when these classes are involved in a program.

- *Strongly reachable*: An object is strongly reachable if it can be reached from the root set through at least one chain of references, which does not involve any weak reference.

- *Softly reachable*: An object is softly reachable if it is not strongly reachable and it can be reached from the root set through at least one chain of references, which involves at least one soft reference, but no weak and phantom references.

- *Weakly reachable*: An object is weakly reachable if it is not strongly and softly reachable and it can be reached from the root set through at least one chain of references, which involves at least a weak reference and no phantom references.

- *Phantom reachable*: An object is phantom reachable if it is not strongly, softly, and weakly reachable and it can be reached from the root set through at least one chain of references, which involves at least a phantom reference. A phantom reachable object is finalized, but not reclaimed.

Among the three kinds of weak references, a soft reference is considered stronger than a weak reference and a phantom reference. A weak reference is considered stronger than a phantom reference. Therefore, the rule to identify the reachability of an object is that if an object is not strongly reachable, it is as reachable as the weakest reference in the reference chain leading to that object. That is, if a chain of references to an object involves a phantom reference, the object must be phantom reachable. If a chain of references to an object does not involve a phantom reference, but it involves a weak reference, the object must be weakly reachable. If a chain of references to an object does not involve a phantom reference and a weak reference, but it involves a soft reference, the object must be softly reachable.

How do you determine the reachability of an object when there is more than one chain of references to the object? In such cases, you determine the object's reachability using all possible chains of references and use the strongest one. That is, if an object is softly reachable through one chain of references and phantom reachable through another, the object is considered softly reachable. Figure 11-5 depicts the examples of how an object's reachability is determined. The elliptical shape at the end of every reference chain represents an object. The reachability of the object has been indicated inside the elliptical shape. The rectangles denote references.

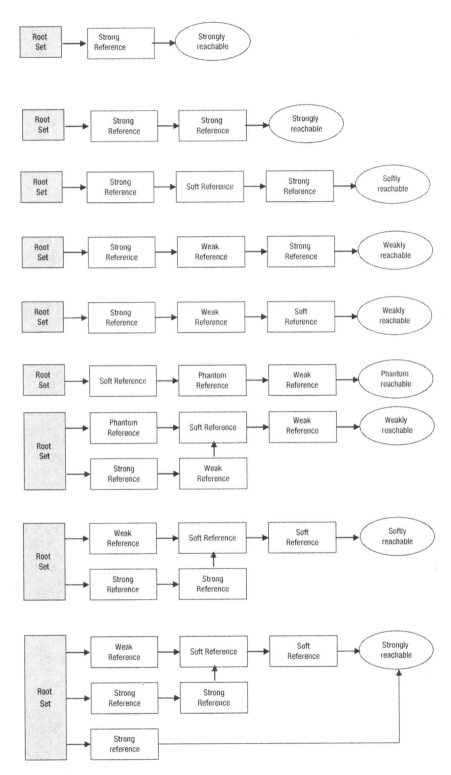

Figure 11-5. *Different kinds of an object's reachability*

Accessing and Clearing a Referent's Reference

You will use objects of a trivial class to demonstrate the use of reference classes. This class, called BigObject, is shown in Listing 11-4. It has a big array of long as an instance variable, so it uses a big chunk of memory. The id instance variable is used to track the objects of this class. The finalize() method prints a message on the console using the object's id.

Listing 11-4. A BigObject Class, Which Uses Big Memory

```java
// BigObject.java
package com.jdojo.gc;

public class BigObject {
        // Declare a 32KB array. This choice is arbitrary. We just wanted to use a large
        // amount of memory  when an object of this class is created.
        private long [] anArray = new long[4096];

        // Have an id to track the object
        private long id;

        public BigObject(long id) {
                this.id = id;
        }

        // Define finalize() to track the object's finalization
        public void finalize(){
                System.out.println("finalize() called for id:" + id);
        }

        public String toString() {
                return "BigObject: id = " + id;
        }
}
```

The object that you pass to the constructors of the WeakReference, SoftReference, and PhantomReference classes is called a *referent*. In other words, the object referred to by the object of these three reference classes is called a referent. To get the reference of the referent of a reference object, you need to call the get() method.

```java
// Create a big object with id as 101
BigObject bigObj = new BigObject(101);

/* At this point, the big object with id 101 is strongly reachable */

// Create a soft reference object using bigObj as referent
SoftReference<BigObject> sr = new SoftReference<BigObject>(bigObj);

/* At this point, the big object with id 101 is still strongly reachable,
because bigObj is a strong reference referring to it. It also has a soft reference
referring to it.
*/

// Set bigObj to null to make the object softly reachable
bigObj = null;
```

```
/* At this point, the big object with id 101 is softly reachable,
because  it can be reached only through a soft reference sr.
*/

// Get the reference of referent of soft reference object
BigObject referent = sr.get();

/* At this point, the big object with id 101 again becomes strongly reachable
because referent is a strong reference. It also has a soft reference referring to it.
*/
```

Figure 11-6 depicts the memory states with all the references after you execute each statement in this snippet of code.

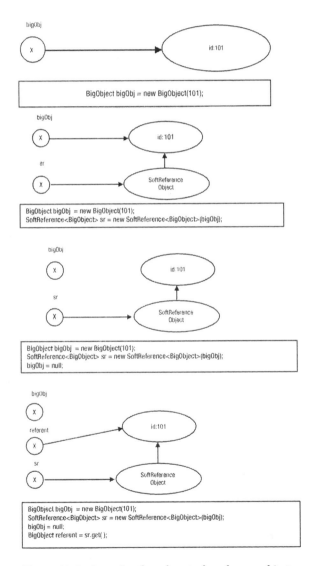

Figure 11-6. *Accessing the referent of a reference object*

The clear() method clears the link between the reference (weak, soft, or phantom) object and its referent. The following piece of code illustrates its use:

```
// Create a soft reference object. Use a BigObject with id 976 as its referent.
SoftReference<BigObject> sr1 = new SoftReference<BigObject> (new BigObject(976));

/* At this point, the BigObject with id 976 is softly reachable, because it is reachable only
through a soft reference sr.
*/

// Clear the referent
sr1.clear();

/* At this point, the big object with id 976 is unreachable (to be exact, it is finalizer-
reachable), because we cleared the only one reference soft reference) we had to the object.
*/
```

The memory state with all references, after each statement in the above snippet of code is executed, is depicted in Figure 11-7. After the referent's reference is cleared using the clear() method, the get() method returns null. Note that the get() method of a PhantomReference object always returns null.

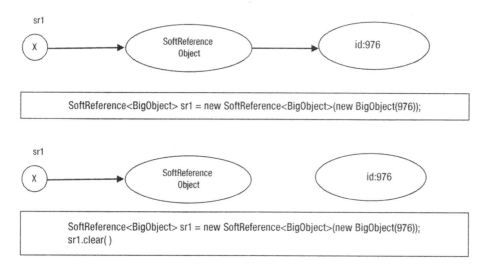

Figure 11-7. *Clearing referent*

Using the SoftReference Class

A softly reachable object is used to maintain memory-sensitive caches. That is, if you want to maintain a cache of objects as long as the program is not running low in memory, you can use softly reachable objects. When the program runs low in memory, the garbage collector clears the soft references to an object, making the object eligible for reclamation. At that point, your program will lose some or all objects from the cache. Java does not guarantee that soft references will not be cleared if the program is not running low in memory. However, it guarantees that all soft references will be cleared before the JVM throws an OutOfMemoryError. There is also no guarantee of the order in which soft references will be cleared. However, JVM implementations are encouraged to clear the least-recently created/used soft reference first.

It is very important to note that to take advantage of the garbage collector behavior with respect to soft references, you must not keep a strong reference to the object. As long as you keep strong references to the object, the garbage collector will not clear the soft references to it, even if the program is running low in memory. The garbage collector clears the soft reference only if an object is softly reachable. Listing 11-5 shows the wrong use of soft references to cache data.

Listing 11-5. An Incorrect Use of a Soft Reference

```
// WrongSoftRef.java
package com.jdojo.gc;

import java.lang.ref.SoftReference;
import java.util.ArrayList;

public class WrongSoftRef {
        public static void main(String[] args) {
                // Create a big object with an id 101 for caching
                BigObject bigObj = new BigObject(101);

                // Wrap soft reference inside a soft reference
                SoftReference<BigObject> sr = new SoftReference<BigObject>(bigObj);

                // Let us try to create many big objects storing their
                // references in an array list, just to use up big memory.
                ArrayList<BigObject> bigList = new ArrayList<BigObject>();
                long counter = 102;
                while (true) {
                        bigList.add(new BigObject(counter++) );
                }
        }
}
```

```
Exception in thread "main" java.lang.OutOfMemoryError: Java heap space
        at com.jdojo.gc.BigObject.<init>(BigObject.java:7)
        at com.jdojo.gc.WrongSoftRef.main(WrongSoftRef.java:20)
```

The intention of the programmer was to cache a big object with an id of 101 using a soft reference. If the program runs low in memory, the cached big object with id 101 may be reclaimed. The while-loop inside the program is trying to create many big objects to make the program run low in memory. The programmer is expecting that when the program is executed, it should reclaim memory used by the big object with id 101, before throwing an OutOfMemoryError.

The output shows that the program did not reclaim the memory used by the big object with id 101. Why did the garbage collector not behave the way it was expected to behave? There was a mistake in the code for the WrongSoftRef class. In fact, the big object with id 101 is strongly reachable because the bigObj reference to it is a strong reference. You must set the bigObj reference variable to null to make it softly reachable. Listing 11-6 shows the correct use of soft references. It is clear from the output that finalize() method for the big object with id 101 was called and it was reclaimed before JVM threw an OutOfMemoryError. You still got an OutOfMemoryError because you are creating many new objects inside a while-loop and all of them are strongly reachable from the array list. This proves the point that soft references are cleared and the referents are reclaimed by the garbage collector before JVM throws an OutOfMemoryError.

Listing 11-6. A Correct Use of a Soft Reference

```java
// CorrectSoftRef.java
package com.jdojo.gc;

import java.lang.ref.SoftReference;
import java.util.ArrayList;

public class CorrectSoftRef {
        public static void main(String[] args) {
                // Create a big object with an id 101 for caching
                BigObject bigObj = new BigObject(101);

                // Wrap soft reference inside a soft reference
                SoftReference<BigObject> sr = new SoftReference<BigObject>(bigObj);

                // Set bigObj to null, so the big object will be
                // softly reachable and can be reclaimed, if necessary.
                bigObj = null;

                // Let us try to create many big objects storing their
                // references in an array list, just to use up big memory.
                ArrayList<BigObject> bigList = new ArrayList<BigObject>();
                long counter = 102;
                while (true) {
                        bigList.add(new BigObject(counter++));
                }
        }
}
```

```
finalize() called for id:101
Exception in thread "main" java.lang.OutOfMemoryError: Java heap space
        at com.jdojo.gc.BigObject.<init>(BigObject.java:7)
        at com.jdojo.gc.CorrectSoftRef.main(CorrectSoftRef.java:24)
```

Listing 11-7 illustrates how to use soft references to implement memory-sensitive caches.

Listing 11-7. Creating a Cache Using Soft References

```java
// BigObjectCache.java
package com.jdojo.gc;

import java.lang.ref.SoftReference;

public class BigObjectCache {
        private static SoftReference<BigObject>[] cache = new SoftReference[10];

        public static BigObject getObjectById(int id) {
                // Check for valid cache id
                if (id < 0 || id >=cache.length) {
                        throw new IllegalArgumentException("Invalid id");
                }
```

```
                BigObject obj = null;

                // Check if we have a cache for this id
                if (cache[id] == null) {
                        // We have not cached the object yet. Cache and return it.
                        obj = createCacheForId(id);
                        return obj;
                }

                // Get the BigObject reference using a soft reference
                obj = cache[id].get();

                // Make sure the object has not yet been reclaimed
                if (obj == null) {
                        // Garbage collector has reclaimed the object.
                        // Cache it again and return the newly cached object.
                        obj = createCacheForId(id);
                }

                return obj;
        }


        // Creates cache for a given id
        private static BigObject createCacheForId(int id) {
                BigObject obj = null;
                if (id >=0 && id < cache.length) {
                        obj =  new BigObject(id);
                        cache[id] = new SoftReference<BigObject>(obj);
                }

                return obj;
        }
}
```

It can cache up to 10 objects of the BigObject class with ids from 0 to 9. To get the cached object for a given id, you need to call the getObjectById() method. If that id has not yet been cached or it was reclaimed by the garbage collector, the method caches the object. This example is very restrictive and its purpose is only to demonstrate the use of the SoftReference class to maintain a memory-sensitive cache. You can cache only objects with ids from 0 to 9. It can be modified to meet specific requirements. For example, you can use an ArrayList to cache the objects instead of using an array. You can use the BigObjectCache class as shown:

```
// Get the object from cache
BigObject cachedObject = BigObjectCache.getObjectById(5);

/* Do some processing...*/

// You must set the cachedObject to null after you are done with it, so the cached object
// becomes softly reachable and may be reclaimed by the garbage collector.
cachedObject = null;
```

If an object with an id of 5 is not already in the cache, it will be cached and the new object reference will be assigned to cachedObject. If an object with an id of 5 is already in the cache, the reference of that object from the cache will be returned and assigned to cachedObject.

Using the ReferenceQueue Class

An object of the ReferenceQueue class is used in conjunction with objects of the SoftReference, WeakReference, and PhantomReference classes when the object needs to be notified upon its reachability change. An object of any of these reference classes can be registered with a reference queue, as shown:

```
ReferenceQueue q = new ReferenceQueue();

SoftReference sr = new SoftReference(new BigObject(19), q);
WeakReference wr = new WeakReference(new BigObject(20), q);
PhantomReference pr = new PhantomReference(new BigObject(21), q);
```

It is optional to register the SoftReference and WeakReference objects with a reference queue. However, you must register a PhantomReference object with a reference queue. When a SoftReference or WeakReference is cleared by the garbage collector, the reference of the SoftReference or the WeakReference object is appended to the reference queue. Note the references of the SoftReference and WeakReference are placed in the queue, not the reference of their referent. For example, if the garbage collector clears the soft reference to a BigObject with id 19 in the above snippet of code, sr will be placed in the reference queue. In case of a PhantomReference, when its referent becomes phantom reachable, the garbage collector places the PhantomReference object in the reference queue. Unlike soft and weak references, the garbage collector does not clear the phantom references as it places them in their reference queue. The program must clear the phantom references by calling the clear() method.

There are two ways to determine if a reference object has been placed in its reference queue. You can call the poll() or remove() method on a ReferenceQueue object, or you can call the isEnqueued() method on the soft, weak, and phantom references. The poll() method removes a reference from the queue and returns it. If there is no reference available in the queue, it returns null. The remove() method works the same as the poll() method, except that if there is no reference available in the queue, it blocks until it becomes available. The isEnqueued() method for soft, weak, and phantom references returns true if they are placed in queue. Otherwise, it returns false. Listing 11-8 demonstrates how to use the ReferenceQueue class.

Listing 11-8. Using the ReferenceQueue Class

```
// ReferenceQueueDemo.java
package com.jdojo.gc;

import java.lang.ref.ReferenceQueue;
import java.lang.ref.WeakReference;

public class ReferenceQueueDemo {
        public static void main(String[] args) {
                // Create a reference queue
                ReferenceQueue<BigObject> q = new ReferenceQueue<BigObject>();

                // Wrap a BigObject inside a soft reference.
                // Also register the soft reference with the reference queue
                BigObject bigObj = new BigObject(131);
                WeakReference<BigObject> wr = new WeakReference<BigObject>(bigObj, q);
```

```
                // Clear the strong reference to the big object
                bigObj = null;

                // Check if weak reference has been queued
                System.out.println("Before calling gc():");
                printMessage(wr, q);

                // Invoke garbage collector. If it runs, it will clear the weak reference
                System.out.println("Invoking garbage collector...");
                System.gc();
                System.out.println("Garbage collector finished...");

                // Check if weak reference has been queued
                System.out.println("After calling gc():");
                printMessage(wr, q);
        }

        public static void printMessage(WeakReference<BigObject> wr,
                                        ReferenceQueue<BigObject> q) {
                System.out.println("wr.get()= " + wr.get());
                System.out.println("wr.isEnqueued()= " + wr.isEnqueued());
                WeakReference<BigObject> temp = (WeakReference<BigObject>)q.poll();
                if (temp == wr) {
                        System.out.println("q.poll() returned wr");
                }
                else {
                        System.out.println("q.poll()= " + temp);
                }
        }
}
```

```
Before calling gc():
wr.get()= BigObject: id = 131
wr.isEnqueued()= false
q.poll()= null
Invoking garbage collector...
Garbage collector finished...
After calling gc():
wr.get()= null
wr.isEnqueued()= false
q.poll()= null
finalize() called for id:131
```

Using the WeakReference Class

The only difference between a softly reachable and a weakly reachable object is that the garbage collector clears and reclaims weakly reachable objects whenever it runs, whereas it uses some algorithm to decide whether it needs to clear and reclaim a softly reachable object or not. In other words, the garbage collector may or may not reclaim a softly reachable object, whereas it always reclaims a weakly reachable object.

You may not see any important use of a weak reference because its referent is reclaimed when the garbage collector is run. Generally, weak references are not used to maintain caches. They are used to associate extra data with an object. Suppose you have a person's details and his address. If you lose his details, you will not be interested in his address. However, as long as the person's details are accessible, you want to keep his address information. This kind of information can be stored using weak references and a Hashtable. A Hashtable stores objects in key-value pairs. While adding a key-value pair to a Hashtable, you need to wrap the key object in a WeakReference object. The key and value are not garbage collected when the key is accessible or in use. When the key object is no longer in use, it will be garbage collected because it was wrapped inside a WeakReference. At that point, you can remove that entry from the Hashtable, so the value object will also be eligible for the garbage collection. The following is a sample snippet of code using Hashtable and WeakReference objects:

```
// Create a Hashtable object
Hashtable ht = new Hashtable();

// Create a reference queue, so  we can check when a key was garbage collected
Referencequeue q = new ReferenceQueue();

// Create key and value objects
key = your key object creation logic goes here
value = your value object creation logic goes here

// Create a weak reference object using the key object as the referent
WeakReference wKey = new WeakReference(key, q);

// Place the key-value pair in the Hashtable. Note that we place key wrapped
// in the weak reference. That is, we will use wKey as key
ht.put(wKey, value);

/* Use key and value objects in your program... */

// When done with the key object, set it to null, so it will not be strongly reachable.
key = null;

/* At this point, if garbage collector is run, weak reference to key object will be cleared and the
WeakReference, wr, will be placed in reference queue, q. */

// Your logic to remove the entry for garbage collected key object will be as follows
if (wr.isEnqueued()) {
        // This will make value object eligible for reclamation
        ht.remove(wr);
}
```

Note that using a WeakReference object to associate extra information with an object using a Hashtable involves some complex code and logic. The java.util.WeakHashMap class provides this functionality without writing any complex logic. You add the key-value pairs to a WeakHashMap without wrapping the key object inside a WeakReference. The WeakHashMap class takes care of creating a reference queue and wrapping the key object in a WeakReference. There is one important point to remember while using a WeakHashMap. The key object is reclaimed when it is not strongly reachable. However, the value object is not reclaimed immediately. The value object is reclaimed after the entry is removed from the map. The WeakHashMap removes the entry after the weak reference to the key has been cleared and one of its methods put(), remove(), or clear() is called. Listing 11-9 demonstrates the use of a WeakHashMap. The example uses objects of the BigObject class as keys as well as values. The messages in the output show when the key and value objects are reclaimed by the garbage collector. You may get different output when you run this program.

Listing 11-9. Using a WeakHashMap

```java
// WeakHashMapdemo.java
package com.jdojo.gc;

import java.util.WeakHashMap;

public class WeakHashMapDemo {
        public static void main(String[] args) {
                // Create a WeakHashMap
                WeakHashMap<BigObject, BigObject> wmap =
                                new WeakHashMap<BigObject, BigObject>();

                // Add two key-value pairs to WeakHashMap
                BigObject key1 = new BigObject(10);
                BigObject value1 = new BigObject(110);
                BigObject key2 = new BigObject(20);
                BigObject value2 = new BigObject(210);

                wmap.put(key1, value1);
                wmap.put(key2, value2);

                // Printa  message
                printMessage ("After adding two entries:", wmap);

                /* Invoke gc(). This gc() invocation will not reclaim any of
                   the key objects, because we are still having their strong references.
                */
                System.out.println("Invoking gc() first time...");
                System.gc();

                // Print a message
                printMessage ("After first gc() call:", wmap);

                // Now remove strong references to keys and values
                key1 = null;
                key2 = null;
                value1 = null;
                value2 = null;

                /* Invoke gc(). This gc() invocation will reclaim two key objects
                   with ids 10 and 20. However, the corresponding two value objects
                   will still /be strongly referenced by WeakHashMap internally and hence
                   will not be reclaimed at this point.
                */
                System.out.println("Invoking gc() second time...");
                System.gc();
```

```
                // Print a message
                printMessage("After second gc() call:", wmap);

                /* Both keys have been reclaimed by now. Just to make value
                   objects reclaimable, we will call clear() method on WeakHashMap.
                   Usually, you will not call this method here in your program.
                */
                wmap.clear();

                // Invoke gc() so that value object will be reclaimed
                System.out.println("Invoking gc() third time...");
                System.gc();

                // Print message
                printMessage("After calling clear() method:", wmap);
        }

        public static void printMessage(String msgHeader, WeakHashMap wmap){
                System.out.println(msgHeader) ;

                // Print the size and content of map */
                System.out.println("Size=" + wmap.size());
                System.out.println("Content=" + wmap);
                System.out.println();
        }
}
```

```
After adding two entries:
Size=2
Content={BigObject: id = 10=BigObject: id = 110, BigObject: id = 20=BigObject: id = 210}

Invoking gc() first time...
After first gc() call:
Size=2
Content={BigObject: id = 10=BigObject: id = 110, BigObject: id = 20=BigObject: id = 210}

Invoking gc() second time...
After second gc() call:
finalize() called for id:20
finalize() called for id:10
Size=0
Content={}

Invoking gc() third time...
After calling clear() method:
finalize() called for id:210
finalize() called for id:110
Size=0
Content={}
```

Using the PhantomReference Class

Phantom references work a little differently than soft and weak references. A PhantomReference object must be created with a ReferenceQueue. When the garbage collector determines that there are only phantom references to an object, it finalizes the object and adds the phantom references to their reference queues. Unlike soft and weak references, it does not clear the phantom references to the object automatically. Programs must clear the phantom reference to the object by calling the clear() method. A garbage collector will not reclaim the object until the program clears the phantom references to that object. Therefore, a phantom reference acts as a strong reference as long as reclaiming of objects is concerned. Why would you use a phantom reference instead of using a strong reference? A phantom reference is used to do post-finalization and pre-mortem processing. At the end of post-finalization processing, you must call the clear() method on the PhantomReference object, so its referent will be reclaimed by the garbage collector. Unlike the get() method of the soft and weak references, the phantom reference's get() method always returns null. An object is phantom reachable when it has been finalized. If a phantom reference returns the referent's reference from its get() method, it would resurrect the referent. This is why phantom reference's get() method always returns null.

Listing 11-10 demonstrates the use of a phantom reference to do some post-finalization processing for an object. Note that the post-finalization processing cannot involve the object itself because you cannot get to the object using the get() method of the phantom reference. You may get a different output when you run this program.

Listing 11-10. Using PhantomReference Objects

```
// PhantomRef.java
package com.jdojo.gc;

import java.lang.ref.PhantomReference;
import java.lang.ref.ReferenceQueue;

public class PhantomRef {
        public static void main(String[] args){
                BigObject bigObject = new BigObject(1857);
                ReferenceQueue<BigObject> q  = new ReferenceQueue<BigObject> ();
                PhantomReference<BigObject> pr = new PhantomReference<BigObject>(bigObject, q);

                /* You can use BigObject reference here */

                // Set BigObject to null, so garbage collector will find only the
                // phantom reference to it and finalize it.
                bigObject = null;

                // Invoke garbage collector
                printMessage(pr, "Invoking gc() first time:") ;
                System.gc();
                printMessage(pr, "After invoking gc() first time:");

                // Invoke garbage collector again
                printMessage(pr, "Invoking gc() second time:") ;
                System.gc();
                printMessage(pr, "After invoking gc() second time:");
        }
```

```java
    public static void printMessage(PhantomReference<BigObject> pr, String msg){
        System.out.println(msg);
        System.out.println("pr.isEnqueued = " + pr.isEnqueued());
        System.out.println("pr.get() = " + pr.get());

        // We will check if pr is queued. If it has been queued,
        // we will clear its referent's reference
        if (pr.isEnqueued() ) {
            pr.clear();
            System.out.println("Cleared the referent's reference");
        }
        System.out.println("-----------------------");
    }
}
```

```
Invoking gc() first time:
pr.isEnqueued = false
pr.get() = null
-----------------------
After invoking gc() first time:
pr.isEnqueued = false
pr.get() = null
-----------------------
finalize() called for id:1857
Invoking gc() second time:
pr.isEnqueued = false
pr.get() = null
-----------------------
After invoking gc() second time:
pr.isEnqueued = true
pr.get() = null
Cleared the referent's reference
-----------------------
```

You can also use phantom references to coordinate the post-finalization processing of more than one object. For example, suppose you have three objects called obj1, obj2, and obj3. All of them share a network connection. When all three objects become unreachable, you would like to close the shared network connection. You can achieve this by wrapping the three objects in a phantom reference object and using a reference queue. Your program can wait on a separate thread for all three phantom reference objects to be queued. When the last phantom reference is queued, you can close the shared network connection. Post-finalization coordination using a phantom reference is demonstrated in Listing 11-11. Note that the startThread() method of the PhantomRefDemo class uses a thread object and an anonymous class. The remove() method blocks until there is a phantom reference in the queue. You may get a different output when you run this program.

Listing 11-11. Post-finalization Coordination Using Phantom References

```java
// PhantomRefDemo.java
package com.jdojo.gc;

import java.lang.ref.PhantomReference;
import java.lang.ref.Reference;
import java.lang.ref.ReferenceQueue;
```

```
public class PhantomRefDemo {
    public static void main(String[] args) {
        final ReferenceQueue<BigObject> q = new ReferenceQueue<BigObject>();
        BigObject bigObject1 = new BigObject (101);
        BigObject bigObject2 = new BigObject (102);
        BigObject bigObject3 = new BigObject (103);
        PhantomReference<BigObject> pr1 =
                        new PhantomReference<BigObject>(bigObject1, q);
        PhantomReference<BigObject> pr2 =
                        new PhantomReference<BigObject>(bigObject2, q);
        PhantomReference<BigObject> pr3 =
                        new PhantomReference<BigObject>(bigObject3, q);

        /* This method will start a thread that will wait for the arrival of new
           phantom references in reference queue q
        */
        startThread(q);

        /* You can use bigObject1, bigObject2 and bigObject3 here */

        // Set the bigObject1, bigObject2 and bigObject3 to null,
        // so the objects they are referring to may become phantom reachable.
        bigObject1 = null;
        bigObject2 = null;
        bigObject3 = null;

        /* Let us invoke garbage collection in a loop. One garbage collection will
           just finalize the three big objects with ids 101, 102 and 103. They may
           not be placed in a reference queue. In another garbage collection run,
           they will become phantom reachable and they will be placed in a queue
           and the waiting thread will remove them from the queue and will clear
           their referent's reference. Note that we exit the application when all
           three objects are cleared inside run() method of thread. Therefore, the
           following infinite loop is ok for demonstration purpose. If System.gc()
           does not invoke the garbage collector on your machine, you should replace
           the following loop with a loop which would create many big objects keeping
           their references, so the garbage collector would run.
        */
        while (true) {
                System.gc();
        }
    }

    public static void startThread(final ReferenceQueue<BigObject> q ) {
        /* Create a thread and wait for the reference object's arrival in the queue */
        Thread t = new Thread(new Runnable() {
                public void run() {
                        Reference r = null;
                        try {
                                // Wait for first phantom reference to be queued
                                r =  q.remove();
```

```
                                        // Clear the referent's reference
                                        r.clear();

                                        // Wait for second phantom reference to be queued
                                        r = q.remove();

                                        // Clear the referent's reference
                                        r.clear();

                                        // Wait for third phantom reference to be queued
                                        r = q.remove();

                                        // Clear the referent's reference
                                        r.clear();

                                        System.out.println("All three objects have been " +
                                                            "queued and cleared.");

                                        /* Typically, you will release the network connection or
                                           any resources shared by three objects here.
                                        */

                                        // Exit the application
                                        System.exit(1);
                                    }
                                    catch (InterruptedException e) {
                                        System.out.println(e.getMessage());
                                    }
                                }
                        } );

                        // Start the thread, which will wait for three phantom
                        // references to be queued
                        t.start();
        }
}
```

```
finalize() called for id:103
finalize() called for id:102
finalize() called for id:101
All three objects have been queued and cleared.
```

Summary

The process of reclaiming the memory of dead objects is known as garbage collection. Garbage collection in Java is automatic. The Java runtime runs garbage collection in a low priority background thread. The JVM does its best to free up memory of dead objects before throwing an OutOfMemoryError. You can pass a hint, although not needed in an application, to the JVM by calling Runtime.getRuntime().gc(). You can also use the convenience method System.gc() to pass the hint to the JVM. The JVM is free to ignore the hint.

The memory occupied by an unreachable object is reclaimed in two phases. The first phase, called finalization, is an action automatically performed on an unreachable object before the memory used by the object is reclaimed by the garbage collector. The block of code that contains the action to be performed is known as a finalizer. A finalizer is implemented using the `finalize()` method of the object. In the `finalize()` method, the unreachable object may resurrect itself by storing its reference in a reachable object. In the second phase, if the object is still unreachable, the memory occupied by the object is reclaimed.

At times, you may want to use memory-sensitive objects, which are fine to be kept in memory if enough memory is available. However, if the application runs low in memory, it would be fine to reclaim those objects. Typically, objects cached for a better performance fall into this category of objects. Java provides `SoftReference`, `WeakReference`, and `PhantomReference` classes in the `java.lang.ref` package to work with such memory-sensitive objects.

■ ■ ■

CHAPTER 12

Collections

In this chapter, you will learn

- What collections are in Java

- What the Collections Framework is and its architecture

- Different ways for traversing a collection

- Different types of collections such as List, Set, Queue, Map, etc.

- Applying algorithms to collections

- Obtaining different views of a collection

- Creating empty and singleton collections

- How hash-based collections work internally

What Is a Collection?

A collection is an object that contains a group of objects. A collection is also known as a container. Each object in a collection is called an *element* of the collection.

The concept of collections in Java is no different from the concept of collections in our daily life. You see different kinds of collections every day. Every collection contains a group of objects. What distinguishes one type of collection from that of another type? One type of collection is distinguished from another type based on the way they manage their elements. Let's take a few examples of collections from our daily life.

Let's start with a money jar. A money jar is an example of a collection. It contains a group of coins. Do you put a coin in the money jar in a specific order? Do you retrieve the coins from the jar in a specific order? Can you put many coins of the same kind in the jar? Can you remove all coins from the jar in one go or must you take them out one at a time? Can you call your keyboard a collection? Isn't it a collection of keys? Does a keyboard have duplicate keys? No, you can't have duplicate keys in a keyboard. However, you can have duplicate coins in your money jar.

Consider a queue of customers at a counter in a post office. Is the queue of customers not a collection of customers? Definitely, it is. Does this queue follow any specific rule? Yes, it does follow a rule, which is first come, first served. You can rephrase the rule of first come, first served as First In, First Out (FIFO).

Consider a stack of books at your desk. Is it not also a collection of books? Yes, it is. Assuming that you deal with one book at a time, does it follow the rule that the book that was placed on the stack last will be removed first? All right, this rule seems to be the opposite of the rule about the collection of customers in a queue at the counter in the post office. This time, the stack of books is following the rule of Last In, First Out (LIFO).

I just mentioned quite a few examples of collections that follow different rules to manage their elements. What would you do if you had to model these collections of objects into a Java program? First, you would categorize all possible kinds of collections that you would deal with in your programs. Then, you would write some reusable generic interfaces and classes that you could use in a situation where you need to deal with collection of objects. The good news is that you do not need to write generic code to manage collections. The designers of the Java language realized the need for it and incorporated a framework in Java libraries, which is called the *Collections Framework*.

The Collections Framework consists of interfaces, implementation classes, and some utility classes that let you handle most types of collections that you would encounter in a Java application. If you encounter a collection type for which Java does not provide an implementation, you can always roll out your own implementation, which will work seamlessly with the Collections Framework. The Collections Framework is simple, powerful, and an exciting topic to learn. This chapter will explore the different types of collections available in the Collections Framework. Figure 12-1 shows five types of collections: a bag, a list, a queue, a stack, and a map.

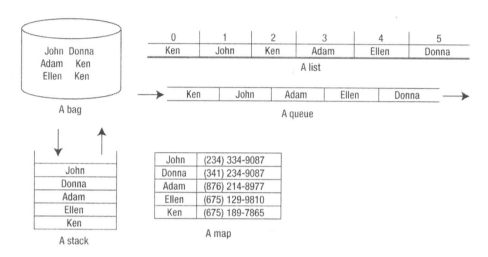

Figure 12-1. *A pictorial view of different types of collections*

One collection (the map) in the figure stands out: a collection of name-phone pairs. It maps a name to a phone number. At this point, these pictures are not associated with any specific types of collection classes in Java. They are just to help you visualize that Java collections are the same as collections in your daily life. Arrows in some collections indicate the entry and exit of an element to and from the collection. You may observe that some collections enforce that an element must be added in a certain way to the collection and it must exit (be removed) the collection in a certain way. For example, in a queue, elements enter from one end and exit from the other end; in a stack, elements enter and exit from the same end.

Need for a Collection Framework

The support for arrays of primitive and reference types is built into the Java language right from the beginning. Using an array is also one of the most efficient ways to store and retrieve a group of object references and primitive values. Why did we need the Collections Framework if we already had arrays in Java?

Using an array in Java has the following advantages:

- It can be used to store and retrieve values using indexes, and it is fast.

- It knows its type. It provides compile-time type checking such as you cannot store a double value in an int array, though if the array is of type Object, there is no compile-time type safety as anything can be stored in the array.

- You can have arrays of objects as well as primitives.

- You have the helper class `java.util.Arrays` to help you work with arrays. For example, it provides methods for searching through an array, sorting the array elements, etc.

Using an array in Java has the following disadvantages:

- Arrays are fixed in size. You must specify the size at the time of creation. Once created, the array size cannot be changed. That is, arrays cannot expand or shrink if you need them to.

- If you store an element in an array at specific position and later you want to remove it, there is no way to know that the element at that position was removed.

- Compile-time type checking, though an advantage, also becomes a disadvantage. It cannot store different kinds of values. For example, a reference array of a `Car` class will store only `Car` type objects. A primitive array of `double` will only store values of `double` type.

- You need to write a lot of code if you want to implement a specific type of collection using an array. For example, suppose you want to have a collection that should not allow duplicate values. Of course, you can develop a new class that uses an array to implement your collection. However, it is a time-consuming task.

The Collections Framework provides all the features provided by arrays, and then some. It provides many other features that are not provided by arrays. The Collections Framework team has already gone through the pain of designing, developing, and testing the interfaces and classes that are needed to use different kinds of collections. All you need to do is to learn those classes and interfaces, and use them in your Java programs.

You need to keep the following points in mind when you learn about collections:

- Collections are designed to work only with objects. To work with collections of primitive types, either you wrap and unwrap your primitive values in wrapper objects or you can take advantage of the built-in autoboxing features in Java that will wrap and unwrap the primitive values as needed.

- All collection classes in Java are declared generic. That is, you can specify the type of elements that your collection deals with as the type parameter.

Architecture of the Collection Framework

The Collections Framework consists of three main components:

- Interfaces

- Implementation Classes

- Algorithm Classes

An interface represents a specific type of collection in the framework. There is one interface defined for every type of collection in the framework; for example, the `List` interface represents a list, the `Set` interface represents a set, the `Map` interface represents a map, etc. Using an interface to define a collection (rather than a class) has the following advantages:

- Your code, which is written using interfaces, is not tied to any specific implementation.

- Classes that implement collections defined by interfaces may be changed without forcing you to change your code that was written using interfaces.

- You can have your own implementation for a collection interface to suit specific needs.

The Collections Framework provides implementations of collection interfaces, which are called implementation classes. You need to create objects of these classes that will represent a collection. It is advised to write code using interfaces, rather than using their implementation classes. The following snippet of code shows how to use the implementation class ArrayList to create a list and store the reference in a variable of the type List that is the interface representing a list:

```
// Create an instance of the ArrayList class storing the reference
// in a variable of the List interface
List<String> names = new ArrayList<>();

// Work with the names variable here onwards
```

Sometimes you need to perform different actions on a collection, such as searching through a collection, converting a collection of one type to another type, copying elements from one collection to another, sorting elements of a collection in a specific order, etc. The algorithm classes let you apply these kinds of algorithms to your collections.

Typically, you do not need to develop interfaces or classes in any of the three categories. The Collections Framework provides you with all the interfaces and classes you need. You can choose from a variety of collection interfaces and their implementations. Figure 12-2 shows the interfaces that define collections. I will discuss each type of collection in the subsequent sections.

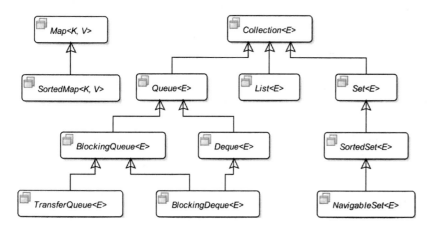

Figure 12-2. *A class diagram including most interfaces in the Collections Framework*

The Collection Interface

The Collection interface is the root of the collection interface hierarchy. It defines a generic collection. The Collections Framework does not provide an implementation for the Collection interface. This is the most generic type of collection. You can use it as an argument type in methods, where you do not care about the collection type of the argument, provided it isn't a map. It declares methods that are inherited by other types of collection interfaces. Non-map collection interfaces inherit from the Collection interface and add methods of their own to provide functionalities that are specific to their types.

Methods of the Collection interface may be classified into the following categories:

- Methods for basic operations
- Methods for bulk (or group) operations
- Methods for aggregate operations

- Methods for array operations

- Methods for comparison operations

Methods in the `Collection` interface are further classified as *optional* and *required*. An implementation class is not required to provide an implementation for the optional methods. If an implementation class chooses not to provide an implementation for optional methods, those methods must throw an `UnsupportedOperationException`.

Methods for Basic Operations

Methods for basic operations let you perform basic operations on a collection such as getting its size (number of elements), adding a new element to it, removing an element from it, checking if an object is an element of this collection, checking if the collection is empty, etc. Some of the methods in this category are as follows:

- `int size()`: Returns the number of elements in the collection.

- `boolean isEmpty()`: Returns true if the collection is empty. Otherwise, it returns false. This acts the same as checking `size()` for 0.

- `boolean contains(Object o)`: Returns true if the collection contains the specified object. Otherwise, it returns false.

- `boolean add(E o)`: Adds an element to the collection. It returns true if the collection changed. Otherwise, it returns false. If the implementation does not allow duplicate elements in a collection, this method will return false when you call it with an element that is already in the collection. If a collection is size constrained and there is no space, the method throws a `java.lang.IllegalStateException`.

- `boolean remove(Object o)`: Removes the specified object from the collection. Returns `true` if the collection changed because of this call. Otherwise, it returns `false`.

- `Iterator<E> iterator()`: Returns an iterator that can be used to traverse elements in the collection.

Methods for Bulk (or Group) Operations

Methods for bulk operations let you perform operations on a collection that involves a group of objects such as removing all elements from it, checking if a collection contains all elements from another collection, adding all elements of a collection to another collection, etc. Some of the methods in this category are as follows:

- `boolean addAll(Collection<? extends E> c)`: Adds all elements of the specified collection to this collection. Returns true if the collection changes because of this call. Otherwise, it returns false.

- `void clear()`: Removes all elements of the collection.

- `boolean containsAll(Collection<?> c)`: Returns true if all the elements in the specified collection are also elements of the collection. Otherwise, it returns false.

- `boolean removeAll(Collection<?> c)`: Removes all elements from the collection that are elements of the specified collection. Returns true if the collection changed as a result of this call. Otherwise, it returns false.

- `boolean retainAll(Collection<?> c)`: Retains only those elements that are also elements of the specified collection. That is, it will remove all elements from the collection that are not elements of the specified collection. Returns true if the collection changes as a result of this call. Otherwise, it returns false.

Methods for Aggregate Operations

Java 8 added support for aggregate operations on collections through streams. A stream is a sequence of elements that supports sequential and parallel aggregate operations such as computing the sum of all elements of a collection whose elements are integers. Streams are a vast topic and I will discuss them in Chapter 13. A stream is an instance of the Stream interface. The Stream interface is in the java.util.stream package. You can create a Stream object from a collection using the following methods of the Collection interface:

- default Stream<E> stream(): Returns a sequential Stream with the collection as the source of elements for the Stream.

- default Stream<E> parallelStream(): Returns a possibly parallel Stream with the collection as the source of elements for the Stream.

Methods for Array Operations

Methods for array operations let you convert a collection into an array. The following are the methods in this category:

- Object[] toArray(): Returns the elements of the collections in an array.

- <T> T[] toArray(T[] a): Returns an array of the specified type T that contains all elements of the collection. If the passed-in array length is equal to or greater than the size of the collection, all elements are copied to the passed-in array and the same array is returned. Any extra elements in the array are set to null. If the passed-in array's length is less that the size of the collection, it creates a new array of type T whose length is equal to the size of the collection, copies all elements of the collection to the new array, and returns the new array.

Methods for Comparison Operations

Methods for comparison operations let you compare two collections for equality. The following are the methods in this category:

- boolean equals(Object o): Returns true if two collections are equal. Otherwise, returns false. The specific collection type specifies the criteria for equality of two collections.

- int hashCode(): Returns the hash code for the collection. Suppose c1 and c2 are references of two collections. If c1.equals(c2) returns true, c1.hashCode() == c2.hashCode() must also return true.

A Quick Example

Before I discuss different types of collections, I will present a quick example of using a list that is a collection of objects. A list is an ordered list of objects. An instance of the List<E> interface represents a list. The ArrayList<E> class is an implementation of the List<E> interface. The program in Listing 12-1 creates a list to store names and manipulates the list using different methods of the Collection interface.

The program uses the add() method to add some names to the list. It uses the remove() method to remove a name from the list. The clear() method is used to remove all names from the list. At every stage, the program prints the size of the list and the elements in the list.

■ **Tip** The toString() method of the list (and all types of collections) returns a comma-separated list of elements enclosed in brackets. If a collection is empty, an empty pair of brackets ([ ]) is returned. The string is very useful for debugging purposes, provided each element has a reasonable toString() implementation.

Listing 12-1. Using a List to Store Names

```java
// NamesList.java
package com.jdojo.collections;

import java.util.ArrayList;
import java.util.List;

public class NamesList {
        public static void main(String[] args) {
                // Create a list of strings
                List<String> names = new ArrayList<>();

                // Print the list details
                System.out.printf("After creation: Size = %d, Elements = %s%n",
                                   names.size(), names);

                // Add some names to the list
                names.add("Ken");
                names.add("Lee");
                names.add("Joe");

                // Print the list details
                System.out.printf("After adding 3 elements: Size = %d, Elements = %s%n",
                        names.size(), names);

                // Remove Lee from the list
                names.remove("Lee");

                // Print the list details
                System.out.printf("After removing 1 element: Size = %d, Elements = %s%n",
                        names.size(), names);

                // Clear all elements
                names.clear();

                // Print the list details
                System.out.printf("After clearing all elements: Size = %d, Elements = %s%n",
                        names.size(), names);

        }
}
```

```
After creation: Size = 0, Elements = []
After adding 3 elements: Size = 3, Elements = [Ken, Lee, Joe]
After removing 1 element: Size = 2, Elements = [Ken, Joe]
After clearing all elements: Size = 0, Elements = []
```

Traversing Collections

Most often, you need to access all elements of a collection one at a time. Different types of collections store their elements differently using different types of data structures. Some collections impose ordering on their elements and some do not. The Collections Framework provides the following ways to traverse a collection:

- Using an Iterator

- Using a for-each loop

- Using the forEach() method

■ **Tip** Some collections, such as lists, assign each element an index and they let you access their elements using indexes. You can traverse those collections using a regular for-loop statement as well. You can also traverse collections by converting them into streams and performing an aggregate operation on those streams. I will discuss streams in Chapter 13.

Using an Iterator

A collection provides an iterator to iterate over all its elements. Sometimes an iterator is also known as a *generator* or a *cursor*. An iterator lets you perform the following three operations on a collection:

- Check if there are elements that have not been yet accessed using this iterator.

- Access the next element in the collection.

- Remove the last accessed element of the collection.

■ **Tip** The meaning of the term "next element" of a collection depends on the collection type. The iterator itself does not impose any ordering in which it returns the elements from a collection. However, if the collection imposes ordering on its elements, the iterator will maintain the same ordering. In general, the "next element" means any element in the collection that has not been returned by this iterator yet.

An iterator in Java is an instance of the Iterator<E> interface. You can get an iterator for a collection using the iterator() method the Collection interface. The following snippet of code creates a list of strings and gets an iterator for the list:

```
// Create a list of strings
List<String> names = new ArrayList<>();
```

```
// Get an iteratir for the list
Iterator<String> nameIterator = names.iterator();
```

The Iterator<E> interface contains the following methods:

- boolean hasNext()
- E next()
- default void remove()
- default void forEachRemaining(Consumer<? super E> action)

The hasNext() method returns true if there are more elements in the collection to iterate. Otherwise, it returns false. Typically, you call this method before asking the iterator for the next element from the collection.

The next() method returns the next element from the collection. You should always call the hasNext() method before calling the next() method. If you call the next() method and the iterator has no more elements to return, it throws a NoSuchElementException.

Typically, the hasNext() and next() methods are used together in a loop. The following snippet of code prints all elements of a list using an iterator:

```
List<String> names = // get a list;

// Get an iterator for the list
Iterator<String> nameIterator = names.iterator();

// Iterate over all elements in the list
while(nameIterator.hasNext()) {
        // Get the next element from the list
        String name = nameIterator.next();

        // Print the name
        System.out.println(name);
}
```

The remove() method removes the element of the collection that was returned last time by calling the next() method of the iterator. The remove() method can be called only once per call to the next() method. If the remove() method is called more than once per next() method call or before the first call to the next() method, it throws an IllegalStateException. The support for the remove() method is optional. Calling the remove() method of an iterator may throw an UnsupportedOperationException if the iterator does not support the remove operation.

The following snippet of code iterates over all elements of a list using an iterator and removes the element using the remove() method of the iterator if the element is only two characters long:

```
List<String> names = get a list;

// Get an iterator for the list
Iterator<String> nameIterator = names.iterator();

// Iterate over all elements in the list
while(nameIterator.hasNext()) {
        String name = nameIterator.next();
```

```
            // Remove the name if it is two characters
            if (name.length() == 2) {
                    nameIterator.remove();
            }
    }
}
```

The forEachRemaining() method is new to Java 8 and takes an action on each element of the collection that has not been accessed by the iterator yet. The action is specified as a Consumer. You can use the following snippet of code to print all elements of a list:

```
List<String> names = get a list;

// Get an iterator for the list
Iterator<String> nameIterator = names.iterator();

// Print the names in the list
nameIterator.forEachRemaining(System.out::println);
```

The code uses method reference System.out::println as a Consumer for the forEachRemaining() method. Notice that using the forEachRemaining() method helps shorten the code by eliminating the need for a loop using the hasNext() and next() methods. Please refer to Chapter 5 for more on using the Consumer interface and method references.

Listing 12-2 contains a complete program that uses an iterator and the forEachRemaining() of the iterator to print all elements of a list on the standard output. The program has combined the steps to obtain the iterator and call its forEachRemaining() method call into one statement.

Listing 12-2. Using an Iterator to Iterate Over Elements of a List

```
// NameIterator.java
package com.jdojo.collections;

import java.util.ArrayList;
import java.util.List;

public class NameIterator {
        public static void main(String[] args) {
                // Create a list of strings
                List<String> names = new ArrayList<>();

                // Add some names to the list
                names.add("Ken");
                names.add("Lee");
                names.add("Joe");

                // Print all elements of the names list
                names.iterator()
                    .forEachRemaining(System.out::println);
        }
}
```

Ken
Lee
Joe

The Collections Framework supports fast-fail concurrent iterators. You can obtain multiple iterators for a collection and all of them can be used to iterate over the same collection concurrently. If the collection is modified by any means, except using the remove() method of the same iterator after the iterator is obtained, the attempt to access the next element using the iterator will throw a ConcurrentModificationException. It means that you can have multiple iterators for a collection; however, all iterators must be accessing (reading) elements of the collection. If any of the iterators modify the collection using its remove() method, the iterator that modifies the collection will be fine and all other iterators will fail. If the collection is modified outside of all iterators, all iterators will fail.

■ **Tip** An Iterator is a one-time object. You cannot reset an iterator. It cannot be reused to iterate over the element of the collection. If you need to iterate over the elements of the same collection again, you need to obtain a new Iterator calling the iterator() method of the collection.

Using a for-each Loop

You can use the for-each loop to iterate over elements of a collection that hides the logic to set up an iterator for a collection. The general syntax for the for-each loop is as follows:

```
Collection<T> yourCollection = // get a collection here;

for(T element : yourCollection) {
        /* The body of the for-each loop is executed once for each element in yourCollection.
           Each time the body code is executed, the element variable holds the reference of the
           current element in the collection
        */
}
```

■ **Tip** You can use the for-each loop to iterate over any collection whose implementation class implements the Iterable interface. The Collection interface inherits from the Iterable interface, and therefore, you can use the for-each loop with all types of collections that implement the Collection interface. For example, the Map collection type does not inherit from the Collection interface, and therefore, you cannot use the for-each loop to iterate over entries in a Map.

The for-each loop is simple and compact. Behind the scenes, it gets the iterator for your collection and calls the hasNext() and next() methods for you. You can iterate over all elements of a list of string as follows:

```
List<String> names = // get a list;

// Print all elements of the names list using a for-each loop
for(String name : names) {
        System.out.println(name);
}
```

Listing 12-3 contains the complete program that shows how to use the for-each loop to iterate over elements of a list of strings. The program is simple and self-explanatory.

Listing 12-3. Using a for-each Loop to Iterate Over Elements of a List

```java
// ForEachLoop.java
package com.jdojo.collections;

import java.util.ArrayList;
import java.util.List;

public class ForEachLoop {
    public static void main(String[] args) {
        // Create a list of strings
        List<String> names = new ArrayList<>();

        // Add some names to the list
        names.add("Ken");
        names.add("Lee");
        names.add("Joe");

        // Print all elements of the names list
        for(String name : names) {
            System.out.println(name);
        }
    }
}
```

```
Ken
Lee
Joe
```

The for-each loop is not a replacement for using an iterator. The compactness of the for-each loop wins over using an iterator in most use cases. The for-each loop has several limitations, however.

You cannot use the for-each loop everywhere you can use an iterator. For example, you cannot use the for-each loop to remove elements from the collection. The following snippet of code will throw a ConcurrentModificationException exception:

```java
List<String> names = get a list;
for(String name : names) {
    // Throws a ConcurrentModificationException
    names.remove(name);
}
```

Another limitation of the for-each loop is that you must traverse from the first element to the last element of the collection. It provides no way to start from middle of the collection. The for-each loop provides no way to visit the previously visited elements, which is allowed by the iterator of some collection types such as lists.

Using the forEach() Method

The Iterable interface contains a new forEach(Consumer<? super T> action) method that you can use in all collection types that inherit from the Collection interface. The method iterates over all elements and applies the action. It works similar to the forEachRemaining(Consumer<? super E> action) method of the Iterator interface with a difference that the Iterable.forEach() method iterates over all elements whereas the Iterator.forEachRemaining() method iterates over the elements in the collections that have not yet been retrieved by the Iterator.

The forEach() method is available in all collection types that inherit from the Collection interface. Listing 12-4 shows how to use the forEach() method to print all elements of a list of strings. Notice that using the forEach() method is the most compact way of iterating over elements of a collection.

■ **Tip**   The Iterator is the fundamental (and a little cumbersome) way of iterating over elements of a collection. It has existed since the beginning. All other ways, such as the for-each loop, the forEach() method, and the forEachRemaining() method, are syntactic sugar for the Iterator. Internally, they all use an Iterator.

Listing 12-4. Using the forEach() Method of the Iterable Interface to Iterate Over Elements of a List

```java
// ForEachMethod.java
package com.jdojo.collections;

import java.util.ArrayList;
import java.util.List;

public class ForEachMethod {
        public static void main(String[] args) {
                // Create a list of strings
                List<String> names = new ArrayList<>();

                // Add some names to the list
                names.add("Ken");
                names.add("Lee");
                names.add("Joe");

                // Print all elements of the names list
                names.forEach(System.out::println);
        }
}
```

```
Ken
Lee
Joe
```

Using Different Types of Collections

In this section, I will discuss different types of collections and their variants, such as sets, lists, queues, maps, etc.

Working with Sets

A set is mathematical concept that represents a collection of unique objects. In mathematics, the ordering of elements in a set is irrelevant. The Collections Framework offers three types of sets:

- Mathematical set

- Sorted set

- Navigable set

The following sections cover all types of sets in detail.

Mathematical Set

The Set interface models a *set* in mathematics. In mathematics, a set is a collection of unique elements. That is, a set cannot contain duplicate elements. Java allows at most one null element in a Set because one null element is still distinguishable from all other non-null elements and thus, it is unique. Further, the ordering of the elements in a mathematical set is not important. Java follows the same rule; it does not guarantee the ordering of the elements in a Set. You can add elements to a Set in one order, and when you retrieve them, they may be supplied back in a different order. The only guarantee is that when looping through all elements of a Set, you get each element in the Set once.

The Collections Framework provides the HashSet class as an implementation for the Set interface. Listing 12-5 demonstrates how to create a Set and add elements to it. Note that you can attempt to add duplicate elements to a Set and they are ignored silently. Two elements in a Set are considered equal if comparing them using the equals() method returns true.

Listing 12-5. Using the Set Interface with HashSet as Its Implementation Class

```
// SetTest.java
package com.jdojo.collections;

import java.util.HashSet;
import java.util.Set;

public class SetTest {
        public static void main(String[] args) {
                // Create a set
                Set<String> s1 = new HashSet<>();

                // Add a few elements
                s1.add("John");
                s1.add("Donna");
                s1.add("Ken");
                s1.add("Ken"); // Duplicate!!! No effect

                // Create another set by copying s1
                Set<String> s2 = new HashSet<>(s1);
```

```
                // Add a few more elements
                s2.add("Ellen");
                s2.add("Sara");
                s2.add(null); // one null is fine
                s2.add(null); // Duplicate!!! No effect

                // Print the sets
                System.out.println("s1: " + s1);
                System.out.println("s1.size(): " + s1.size());

                System.out.println("s2: " + s2);
                System.out.println("s2.size(): " + s2.size());
        }
}
```

```
s1: [Donna, Ken, John]
s1.size(): 3
s2: [null, Ellen, Donna, Ken, John, Sara]
s2.size(): 6
```

The Collections Framework offers the LinkedHashSet class as another implementation class for the Set interface. The class adds one feature over the HashSet implementation. The HashSet implementation does not guarantee the ordering of elements during iteration. The LinkedHashSet implementation guarantees that the iterator of a Set will return the elements in the same order the elements were inserted (insertion order).

I will discuss maintaining ordering of elements in a Set in the next section when I discuss SortedSet. The LinkedHashSet class provides insertion ordering without incurring any overhead.

Listing 12-6 compares the use of HashSet and LinkedHashSet classes. The output shows that HashSet does not maintain any ordering on the elements whereas the LinkedHashSet maintains the insertion order.

Listing 12-6. Comparing the HashSet and LinkedHashSet Implementations of the Set Interface

```java
// LinkedHashSetTest.java
package com.jdojo.collections;

import java.util.Set;
import java.util.LinkedHashSet;
import java.util.HashSet;

public class LinkedHashSetTest {
        public static void main(String[] args) {
                Set<String> s1 = new LinkedHashSet<>();
                s1.add("John");
                s1.add("Adam");
                s1.add("Eve");
                s1.add("Donna");
                System.out.println("LinkedHashSet: " + s1);

                // Add the same elements to this set
                Set<String> s2 = new HashSet<>();
                s2.add("John");
                s2.add("Adam");
```

```
                s2.add("Eve");
                s2.add("Donna");
                System.out.println("HashSet: " + s2);

                System.out.println("s1.equals(s2): " + s1.equals(s2));
        }
}
```

```
LinkedHashSet: [John, Adam, Eve, Donna]
HashSet: [Adam, Donna, Eve, John]
s1.equals(s2): true
```

■ **Tip**   A Set has a very useful application. You can use it when you are supplied with an unknown number of objects and you have to keep only unique objects. You can create a Set and add all objects to it. It will keep only unique objects and ignore the duplicate ones. At the end, you will have only unique objects in your Set.

You can perform *union, intersection,* and *difference* (or *minus*) operations on mathematical sets. You can perform the same operations on sets in Java. For discussing these operations, I assume that you have two sets called s1 and s2. The union of two sets (written as s1 ∪ s2 in mathematics) contains elements from both sets with no duplicates. The intersection of two sets (written as s1 ∩ s2 in mathematics) contains elements that are common to both sets. The difference of two sets, s1 and s2 (written as s1 - s2), is a set that contains all elements of s1 that are not in s2. Here is how you perform these Set operations:

```
// Union of s1 and s2 will be stored in s1
s1.add(s2);

// Intersection of s1 and s2 will be stored in s1
s1.retainAll(s2);

// Difference of s1 and s2 will be stored in s1
s1.removeAll(s2);
```

Note that during the set operations such as union, intersection, and difference, the set on which you perform the operation is modified. For example, s1 is modified if you perform s1.addAll(s2) to compute the union of s1 and s2. If you want to compute the union of two sets and keep the original set unchanged, you must make a copy of the original set before you perform the union operation, like so:

```
// Compute the union of two sets by keeping the original set unchanged
Set s1Unions2 = new HashSet(s1); // Make a copy of s1

// Now, s1Unions2 is the union of s1 and s2 and both s1 and s2 are unchanged
s1Unions2.addAll(s2);
```

In mathematics, you can test if a set s1 is a subset of another set s2. Set s1 is a subset of set s2 if set s2 contains all elements that are also present in set s1. You can use the s2.containsAll(s1) method to test if s1 is a subset of s2. This method will return true if s1 is a subset of s2. Otherwise, it will return false.

Listing 12-7 demonstrates how to use the Set interface to perform mathematical set operations.

Listing 12-7. Performing Mathematical Set Operations Using the Set Interface

```java
// SetOperations.java
package com.jdojo.collections;

import java.util.HashSet;
import java.util.Set;

public class SetOperations {
        public static void main(String[] args) {
                // Create a set
                Set<String> s1 = new HashSet<>();
                s1.add("John");
                s1.add("Donna");
                s1.add("Ken");

                // Create another set
                Set<String> s2 = new HashSet<>();
                s2.add("Ellen");
                s2.add("Sara");
                s2.add("Donna");

                //Print  the elements of both sets
                System.out.println("s1: " + s1);
                System.out.println("s2: " + s2);

                // Perform set operations
                performUnion(s1, s2);
                performIntersection(s1, s2);
                performDifference(s1, s2);
                testForSubset(s1, s2);
        }

        public static void performUnion(Set<String> s1, Set<String> s2) {
                Set<String> s1Unions2 = new HashSet<>(s1);
                s1Unions2.addAll(s2);
                System.out.println("s1 union s2: " + s1Unions2);
        }

        public static void performIntersection(Set<String> s1, Set<String> s2) {
                Set<String> s1Intersections2 = new HashSet<>(s1);
                s1Intersections2.retainAll(s2);
                System.out.println("s1 intersection s2: " + s1Intersections2);
        }

        public static void performDifference(Set<String> s1, Set<String> s2) {
                Set<String> s1Differences2 = new HashSet<>(s1);
                s1Differences2.removeAll(s2);
```

```
                Set<String> s2Differences1 = new HashSet<>(s2);
                s2Differences1.removeAll(s1);

                System.out.println("s1 difference s2: " + s1Differences2);
                System.out.println("s2 difference s1: " + s2Differences1);
        }

        public static void testForSubset(Set<String> s1, Set<String> s2) {
                System.out.println("s2 is subset s1: " + s1.containsAll(s2));
                System.out.println("s1 is subset s2: " + s2.containsAll(s1));
        }
}
```

```
s1: [Donna, Ken, John]
s2: [Ellen, Donna, Sara]
s1 union s2: [Ellen, Donna, Ken, John, Sara]
s1 intersection s2: [Donna]
s1 difference s2: [Ken, John]
s2 difference s1: [Ellen, Sara]
s2 is subset s1: false
s1 is subset s2: false
```

In this example, I kept the two original sets, s1 and s2, unmodified inside methods that performed some operations on these two sets. However, they could have been modified inside any of these methods. It is not wise to pass a collection to a method like the way I did in this example if you do not want the method to modify your collection. The Collections Framework offers a way to get an unmodifiable view of a collection using the java.util.Collections class. I will discuss this class and all other features that it offers later in this chapter. The method Collections.unmodifiableSet(s1) will return the unmodifiable version of the s1 set. Any operation that attempts to modify an unmodifiable collection results in an UnsupportedOperationException.

Sorted Set

A sorted set is a set that imposes ordering on its elements. An instance of the SortedSet interface represents a sorted set.

The elements in a SortedSet can be sorted in a natural order or using a Comparator. A SortedSet must know how to sort its elements as they are added. The sorted set relies on two things to sort its elements:

- If its elements implement the Comparable interface, it will use the compareTo() method of elements to sort them. This is called sorting in natural order.

- You can supply a Comparator object to use a custom sorting. The implementation class for SortedSet is recommended to provide a constructor that will accept a Comparator object to use a custom sorting. If a Comparator is specified, the Comparator is used for sorting irrespective of the elements implementing the Comparable interface.

What would happen if the class of the elements of a SortedSet does not implement the Comparable interface and you don't supply a Comparator object? The answer is that, in such cases, you cannot add any elements to a SortedSet. Attempting to add an element results in a ClassCastException.

The TreeSet class is one of the predefined implementation classes for the SortedSet interface in the Collections Framework.

The String class implements the Comparable interface. If you are storing only strings in a SortedSet, its elements will be sorted using the natural order using the compareTo() method of the String class. Listing 12-8 demonstrates the use of SortedSet, which uses the natural order to sort its elements.

Listing 12-8. Using a SortedSet That Uses Natural Ordering to Sort Its Elements

```java
// SortedSetTest.java
package com.jdojo.collections;

import java.util.SortedSet;
import java.util.TreeSet;

public class SortedSetTest {
    public static void main(String[] args) {
        // Create a sorted set of some names
        SortedSet<String> sortedNames = new TreeSet<>();
        sortedNames.add("John");
        sortedNames.add("Adam");
        sortedNames.add("Eve");
        sortedNames.add("Donna");

        // Print the sorted set of names
        System.out.println(sortedNames);
    }
}
```

```
[Adam, Donna, Eve, John]
```

Let's discuss a real world example in which you want store a list of person objects in a SortedSet. Listing 12-9 contains the code for a Person class. It does not implement the Comparable interface. You will use the objects of the Person class in a SortedSet to demonstrate custom sorting.

Listing 12-9. A Person Class

```java
// Person.java
package com.jdojo.collections;

public class Person {
    private int id;
    private String name;

    public Person(int id, String name) {
        this.id = id;
        this.name = name;
    }

    public int getId() {
        return id;
    }
```

```java
        public void setId(int id) {
                this.id = id;
        }

        public String getName() {
                return name;
        }

        public void setName(String name) {
                this.name = name;
        }

        @Override
        public boolean equals(Object o) {
                if (!(o instanceof Person)) {
                        return false;
                }

                // id must be the same for two Persons to be equal
                Person p = (Person) o;
                if (this.id == p.getId()) {
                        return true;
                }

                return false;
        }

        @Override
        public int hashCode() {
                // A trivial implementaiton
                return this.id;
        }

        @Override
        public String toString() {
                return "(" + id + ", " + name + ")";
        }
}
```

You cannot add an object of the Person class in a SortedSet unless you also supply a Comparator object. The following code will throw a ClassCastException:

```java
Set<Person> persons = new TreeSet<>();
persons.add(new Person(1, "John"));
persons.add(new Person(2, "Donna"));
```

The following snippet of code creates a SortedSet of persons using a Comparator that sorts the persons using their names:

```java
SortedSet<Person> personsSortedByName = new TreeSet<>(Comparator.comparing(Person::getName));
```

The code uses a method reference to create a lambda expression for creating the Comparator object. Please refer to Chapter 5 for more details on the lambda expressions and method references.

If you add two Person objects to the personsSortedByName sorted set with the same name, the second one will be ignored because the supplied Comparator compares names of two Person objects for equality.

```
personsSortedByName.add(new Person(1, "John"));
personsSortedByName.add(new Person(2, "Donna"));
personsSortedByName.add(new Person(3, "Donna")); // A duplicate Person. Will be ignored
```

Listing 12-10 demonstrates how to use a Comparator object to apply custom sorting in a SortedSet. It uses two custom sortings for Person objects, one by id and one by name. The output shows that one SortedSet is sorted by id and another by name.

Listing 12-10. Using Custom Sorting in a SortedSet

```java
// SortedSetComparatorTest.java
package com.jdojo.collections;

import java.util.Comparator;
import java.util.SortedSet;
import java.util.TreeSet;

public class SortedSetComparatorTest {
    public static void main(String[] args) {
        // Create a sorted set sorted by id
        SortedSet<Person> personsById =
            new TreeSet<>(Comparator.comparing(Person::getId));

        // Add soem persons to the set
        personsById.add(new Person(1, "John"));
        personsById.add(new Person(2, "Adam"));
        personsById.add(new Person(3, "Eve"));
        personsById.add(new Person(4, "Donna"));
        personsById.add(new Person(4, "Donna")); // A duplicate Person

        // Print the set
        System.out.println("Persons by Id:");
        personsById.forEach(System.out::println);

        // Create a sorted set sorted by name
        SortedSet<Person> personsByName =
            new TreeSet<>(Comparator.comparing(Person::getName));
        personsByName.add(new Person(1, "John"));
        personsByName.add(new Person(2, "Adam"));
        personsByName.add(new Person(3, "Eve"));
        personsByName.add(new Person(4, "Donna"));
        personsByName.add(new Person(4, "Kip")); // Not a duplicate person

        System.out.println("Persons by Name: ");
        personsByName.forEach(System.out::println);
    }
}
```

```
Persons by Id:
(1, John)
(2, Adam)
(3, Eve)
(4, Donna)
Persons by Name:
(2, Adam)
(4, Donna)
(3, Eve)
(1, John)
(4, Kip)
```

Suppose you have a group of strings and you want to remove duplicates and sort them in ascending order of their length. How difficult will it be to achieve this using your current knowledge of collections? The following snippet of code shows how to do this:

```java
// Sort the names based on their length
SortedSet<String> names = new TreeSet<>(Comparator.comparing(String::length));
names.add("Ken");
names.add("Lo");
names.add("Ellen");
names.add("Don"); // A duplicate that is ignored

// Print the sorted names
names.forEach(System.out::println);
```

```
Lo
Ken
Ellen
```

The SortedSet interface inherits all methods of the Set interface; it also adds some more methods to give you access to its subsets. For example, if you want to get a subset of the SortedSet, you can use its subSet(E fromElement, E toElement) method to get the elements between fromElement (inclusive) and toElement (exclusive). Listing 12-11 demonstrates how to use some of the methods of the SortedSet interface to get a subset of its elements.

Listing 12-11. Accessing Subsets of a SortedSet

```java
// SortedSetSubset.java
package com.jdojo.collections;

import java.util.SortedSet;
import java.util.TreeSet;

public class SortedSetSubset {
        public static void main(String[] args) {
                // Create a sorted set of names
                SortedSet<String> names = new TreeSet<>();
                names.add("John");
                names.add("Adam");
                names.add("Eve");
                names.add("Donna");
```

```
                    // Print the sorted set
                    System.out.println("Sorted Set: " + names);

                    // Print the first and last elements in the sorted set
                    System.out.println("First: " + names.first());
                    System.out.println("Last: " + names.last());

                    SortedSet ssBeforeDonna = names.headSet("Donna");
                    System.out.println("Head Set Before Donna: " + ssBeforeDonna);

                    SortedSet ssBetwenDonnaAndJohn = names.subSet("Donna", "John");
                    System.out.println("Subset between Donna and John (exclusive): " +
                                        ssBetwenDonnaAndJohn);

                    // Note the trick "John" + "\0" to include "John" in the subset
                    SortedSet ssBetwenDonnaAndJohn2 = names.subSet("Donna", "John" + "\0");
                    System.out.println("Subset between Donna and John (Inclusive): " +
                                        ssBetwenDonnaAndJohn2);

                    SortedSet ssDonnaAndAfter = names.tailSet("Donna");
                    System.out.println("Subset from Donna onwards: " + ssDonnaAndAfter);
        }
}
```

```
Sorted Set: [Adam, Donna, Eve, John]
First: Adam
Last: John
Head Set Before Donna: [Adam]
Subset between Donna and John (exclusive): [Donna, Eve]
Subset between Donna and John (Inclusive): [Donna, Eve, John]
Subset from Donna onwards: [Donna, Eve, John]
```

How is a null element stored in a SortedSet? If a SortedSet uses natural order (uses the Comparable interface's compareTo() method), adding a null element will throw a NullPointerException. If you use a Comparator object to apply the ordering, it is up to you to allow a null element in the SortedSet. If you allow a null element in the SortedSet, you can decide whether the null element will be placed in the beginning or at the end of the Set. The following snippet of code creates a SortedSet using a Comparator that places the null element first:

```
// Sort the names based on their length, placing null first
SortedSet<String> names =
        new TreeSet<>(Comparator.nullsFirst(Comparator.comparing(String::length)));
names.add("Ken");
names.add("Lo");
names.add("Ellen");
names.add(null); // Adds a null

// Print the names
names.forEach(System.out::println);
```

```
null
Lo
Ken
Ellen
```

Navigable Set

A navigable set is a specialized type sorted set that lets you work with its subsets in a variety of ways. An instance of the NavigableSet represents a navigable set. The NavigableSet interface inherits from the SortedSet interface and defines some additional methods to extend the functionality provided by the SortedSet. It extends SortedSet in four ways:

- It lets you navigate the set in reverse order. The reverse order is the opposite order in which your SortedSet would be sorted normally. Its descendingSet() method returns a NavigableSet object, which is another view of the same NavigableSet in the reverse order. If you modify the original NavigableSet or the one returned from the descendingSet() method, the modifications will be reflected in both sets.

- It adds another version of the three methods headSet(), tailSet(), and subSet() in SortedSet, which accept a boolean flag to include the element at the beginning or the end of the subset boundary.

It provides four methods, lower(), floor(), higher(), and ceiling(), that are used to search for an element based on search criteria. The lower() method returns the greatest element in the NavigableSet that is less than the specified element. The floor() method is similar to the lower() method that returns the greatest element in the NavigableSet that is less than or equal to the specified element. The higher() method returns the least element in the NavigableSet that is greater than the specified element. The ceiling() method is similar to the higher() method that returns the least element in the NavigableSet that is greater than or equal to a specified element.

It provides two methods, pollFirst() and pollLast(), that retrieve and remove the first and the last element of the NavigableSet, respectively. If the NavigableSet is empty, they return null.

The TreeSet class is one of the implementation classes for the NavigableSet interface. Since a NavigableSet is also a SortedSet and a SortedSet is also a Set, you can use an object of TreeSet as a set, a sorted set, and a navigable set. If you do not need ordering of the elements in a set, you are better off using the HashSet implementation class rather than the TreeSet implementation class.

Listing 12-12 demonstrates how to use navigable sets. It uses integers as the elements of the NavigableSet because numbers seem to be more intuitive when you perform methods like higher() and lower(). The output shows how a NavigableSet performs all its operations on its elements.

Listing 12-12. Using a NavigableSet to Get a Subset of a Set

```java
// NavigableSetTest.java
package com.jdojo.collections;

import java.util.TreeSet;
import java.util.NavigableSet;

public class NavigableSetTest {
    public static void main(String[] args) {
        // Create a navigable set and add some integers
        NavigableSet<Integer> ns = new TreeSet<>();
        ns.add(1);
        ns.add(2);
```

```
        ns.add(3);
        ns.add(4);
        ns.add(5);

        // Get a reverse view of the navigable set
        NavigableSet reverseNs = ns.descendingSet();

        // Print the normal and reverse views
        System.out.println("Normal View of the Set: " + ns);
        System.out.println("Reverse view of the set: " + reverseNs);

        // Get and print a subset of the navigable set
        System.out.println("\nGetting subset of the set");

        NavigableSet threeOrMore = ns.tailSet(3, true);
        System.out.println("3 or more: " + threeOrMore);

        // Search the navigable set
        System.out.println();
        System.out.println("Searching through the set");

        System.out.println("lower(3): " + ns.lower(3));
        System.out.println("floor(3): " + ns.floor(3));
        System.out.println("higher(3): " + ns.higher(3));
        System.out.println("ceiling(3): " + ns.ceiling(3));

        // Poll the navigable set
        System.out.println();
        System.out.println("Polling elements from the set");

        // Poll elements one by one and look at the set
        System.out.println("pollFirst(): " + ns.pollFirst());
        System.out.println("Navigable Set: " + ns);

        System.out.println("pollLast(): " + ns.pollLast());
        System.out.println("Navigable Set: " + ns);

        System.out.println("pollFirst(): " + ns.pollFirst());
        System.out.println("Navigable Set: " + ns);

        System.out.println("pollFirst(): " + ns.pollFirst());
        System.out.println("Navigable Set: " + ns);

        System.out.println("pollFirst(): " + ns.pollFirst());
        System.out.println("Navigable Set: " + ns);

        // Since the set is empty, polling will return null
        System.out.println("pollFirst(): " + ns.pollFirst());
        System.out.println("pollLast(): " + ns.pollLast());
    }
}
```

```
Normal View of the Set: [1, 2, 3, 4, 5]
Reverse view of the set: [5, 4, 3, 2, 1]

Getting subset of the set
3 or more: [3, 4, 5]

Searching through the set
lower(3): 2
floor(3): 3
higher(3): 4
ceiling(3): 3

Polling elements from the set
pollFirst(): 1
Navigable Set: [2, 3, 4, 5]
pollLast(): 5
Navigable Set: [2, 3, 4]
pollFirst(): 2
Navigable Set: [3, 4]
pollFirst(): 3
Navigable Set: [4]
pollFirst(): 4
Navigable Set: []
pollFirst(): null
pollLast(): null
```

Working with Lists

A *list* is an ordered collection of objects. Sometimes a list is also known as a *sequence*. An instance of the List interface represents a list in the Collections Framework. A list can have duplicate elements. You can also store multiple null values in a list.

The List interface inherits the Collection interface. It adds methods to support access to elements of the List using indexes. It also allows you to add an element to the end of the List or at any position identified by an integer called the *index*. The index of an element in a List is zero-based. That is, the first element of the List has an index of 0, the second element has an index of 1, and so on. Figure 12-3 shows a List with four elements and their indexes.

Index >>	0	1	2	3
Element >>	John	Richard	Donna	Ken

Figure 12-3. *A pictorial view of a List with four elements*

A List provides the following additional features over a generic collection:

- It provides access to its elements using indexes. You can use its add(int index, E element), addAll(int index, Collection<? extends E> c), get(int index), remove(int index) and set(int index, E element) methods to add, get, remove, and replace its elements using indexes.

- You can search for the position of an element in the List using indexOf(Object o) or lastIndexOf(Object o) methods. The indexOf() method searches for the specified object in the List from the beginning and it returns the index of the first occurrence of the object. The lastIndexOf() method does the same starting from the end of the list. Both methods return –1 if the List does not contain the specified object.

- It provides a method called subList(int fromIndex, int toIndex) that gives you a sublist of the original list starting at index fromIndex (inclusive) to index toIndex (exclusive).

- It provides a specialized iterator for its elements, which is an instance of the ListIterator interface. This iterator lets you iterate over its elements in both directions (forward and backward) at the same time. You can get the ListIterator for a List using its listIterator() method. Note that the Iterator returned from the iterator() method of the Collection interface returns a forward-only iterator.

The following are two of many implementation classes for the List interface:

- ArrayList
- LinkedList

An ArrayList is backed up by an array. A LinkedList is backed up by a linked list. An ArrayList performs better if you access (get and set) the elements of the list frequently. Accessing elements in an ArrayList is faster because the index of an element becomes the index in the backing array, and accessing an element from an array is always fast. Adding or removing elements from a list backed by an ArrayList performs slower, unless done from the end, because an ArrayList has to perform an array copy internally to keep the elements in sequence. The LinkedList performs better as compared to ArrayList for adding and removing elements from the middle of the list. However, it is slower for accessing elements of the list, unless at the head of the list.

You can create and add some elements to a list as follows:

```
// Create a list of strings
List<String> nameList = new ArrayList<>();
nameList.add("John");    // Adds John at the index 0
nameList.add("Richard"); // Adds Richard at the index 1
```

The add(E element) method of the List interface appends the element to the end of the List. The remove(Object o) method of List removes the first occurrence of the element from the beginning of the list.

You can also add elements to a List using positional indexes. Note that the index that you use to access any element must be between 0 and size, where size is the size of the List. You can use add(int index, E element) method to insert the specified element at the specified index. For example, nameList.add(1, "Sara") will insert "Sara" at index 1, which is the second element in the List. When you use an index to add an element to a List, the element at the specified index and elements to the right of the specified index are shifted to the right and their indexes are incremented by 1. Suppose you have a List as shown in Figure 12-3 and you execute the following code:

```
// Add an element at index 1
nameList.add(1, "Sara");
```

Now the List will look as shown in Figure 12-4.

Index >>	0	1	2	3	4
Element >>	John	Sara	Richard	Donna	Ken

Figure 12-4. *The resulting List after a new element is added at index 1 in the List in Figure 12-3*

■ **Tip**   Note that a List does not allow inserting an element at any arbitrary index by using the add(int index, E element) method. If the List is empty, you can use only 0 as the index to add the first element to the list. If you have five elements in a List, you must use indexes between 0 and 5 to add a new element to the List. The index from 0 to 4 will insert an element between existing elements. The index of 5 will append the element to the end of the List. This implies that a List must grow sequentially. You cannot have a sparse List such as a List with first element and tenth element, leaving second to ninth elements non-populated. This is the reason that a List is also known as a *sequence*.

Listing 12-13 demonstrates how to use a List. It shows how to add, remove, and iterate over its elements using indexes.

Listing 12-13. Using a List with the ArrayList as Its Implementation

```java
// ListTest.java
package com.jdojo.collections;

import java.util.List;
import java.util.ArrayList;

public class ListTest {
        public static void main(String[] args) {
                // Create a List and add few elements
                List<String> list = new ArrayList<>();
                list.add("John");
                list.add("Richard");
                list.add("Donna");
                list.add("Ken");

                System.out.println("List: " + list);

                int count = list.size();
                System.out.println("Size of List: " + count);

                // Print each element with its index
                for(int i = 0; i < count; i++) {
                        String element = list.get(i);
                        System.out.println("Index=" + i + ", Element=" + element);
                }

                List<String> subList = list.subList(1, 3);
                System.out.println("Sub List 1 to 3(excluded): " + subList);
```

```
                   // Remove "Donna" from the list
                   list.remove("Donna"); // Same as list.remove(2);
                   System.out.println("List (after removing Donna): " + list);
        }
}
```

```
List: [John, Richard, Donna, Ken]
Size of List: 4
Index=0, Element=John
Index=1, Element=Richard
Index=2, Element=Donna
Index=3, Element=Ken
Sub List 1 to 3(excluded): [Richard, Donna]
List (after removing Donna): [John, Richard, Ken]
```

A List lets you iterate over its elements using a specialized iterator represented by an instance of the ListIterator interface. The ListIterator interface inherits the Iterator interface; it adds a few more methods to give you access to elements in the list from the current position in the backward direction. You can get a list iterator for all elements of the list or a sublist, like so:

```
List<String> list = new ArrayList<>();

// Populate the list here...

// Get a full list iterator
ListIterator<String> fullIterator = list.listIterator();

// Get a list iterator, which will start at index 5 in the forward direction.
// You can iterate to an index that's less than 5 if you choose to.
ListIterator<String> partialIterator = list.listIterator(5);
```

The hasPrevious() method of the ListIterator returns true if there is an element before the current position in the list iterator. To get the previous element, you need to use its previous() method. You can observe that the hasPrevious() and previous() methods do the same work but in the opposite direction of the hasNext() and next() methods. You can also get to the index of the next and previous element from the current position using its nextIndex() and previousIndex() methods. It also has methods to insert, replace, and remove an element at the current location.

Listing 12-14 demonstrates how to use a ListIterator. It iterates over elements of a List, first in the forward direction and then in the backward direction. You do not need to recreate the ListIterator again to iterate in the backward direction.

Listing 12-14. Iterating Over the Elements in a List in Forward and Backward Directions

```
// ListIteratorTest.java
package com.jdojo.collections;

import java.util.ArrayList;
import java.util.List;
import java.util.ListIterator;
```

```java
public class ListIteratorTest {
        public static void main(String[] args) {
                List<String> list = new ArrayList<>();
                list.add("John");
                list.add("Richard");
                list.add("Donna");
                list.add("Ken");

                System.out.println("List: " + list);

                // Get the list iterator
                ListIterator<String> iterator = list.listIterator();

                System.out.println();
                System.out.println("List Iterator in forward direction:");
                while (iterator.hasNext()) {
                        int index = iterator.nextIndex();
                        String element = iterator.next();
                        System.out.println("Index=" + index + ", Element=" + element);
                }

                System.out.println();
                System.out.println("List Iterator in backward direction:");

                // Reuse the iterator to iterate from the end to the beginning
                while (iterator.hasPrevious()) {
                        int index = iterator.previousIndex();
                        String element = iterator.previous();
                        System.out.println("Index=" + index + ", Element=" + element);
                }
        }
}
```

```
List: [John, Richard, Donna, Ken]

List Iterator in forward direction:
Index=0, Element=John
Index=1, Element=Richard
Index=2, Element=Donna
Index=3, Element=Ken

List Iterator in backward direction:
Index=3, Element=Ken
Index=2, Element=Donna
Index=1, Element=Richard
Index=0, Element=John
```

■ **Tip** A ListIterator lets you look ahead or look back in a List. If you use its next() method followed by the previous() method, the iterator goes back to the same position. The call to the next() method moves it one index forward and the call to the previous() method moves it one index backward.

Working with Queues

A queue is a collection based on the notion of a real-world queue. A queue is a collection of objects on which some kind of processing is applied one element at a time. A queue has two ends known as head and tail. In the simple queue, objects are added to the tail and removed from the head; the object added first will be removed first. However, queues can be categorized based on the way it allows insertion and removal of its elements. In this section, I will discuss the following types of queues:

- A *simple queue* allows insertion at the tail and removal from the head.

- A *priority queue* associates a priority with every element of the queue and allows the element with the highest priority to be removed next from the queue.

- A *delay queue* associates a delay with every element of the queue and allows for the removal of the element only when its delay has elapsed.

- A *doubly ended queue* allows for insertion and removal of its elements from the head as well as the tail.

- A *blocking queue* blocks the thread that adds elements to it when it is full and it blocks the thread removing elements from it when it is empty.

- A *transfer queue* is a special type of blocking queue where a handoff of an object occurs between two threads (a producer and a consumer).

- A *blocking doubly ended queue* is a combination of a doubly ended queue and a blocking queue.

Simple Queues

Simple queues are represented by an instance of the Queue interface. Typically, you hold a group of objects in a queue for some kind of processing that is applied to one element at a time. For example, the line of customers at a counter in a post office is an example of a queue. You can classify a queue based on many criteria.

How many elements can a queue hold? Sometimes you have an unlimited (at least theoretically) number of elements in a queue, and sometimes it has a predefined number of elements. When the length of a queue is unlimited, it is called an *unbounded queue*. When the length of the queue is predefined, it is called a *bounded queue*. The bound of a queue defines its behavior when an element is added to a full bounded queue. Attempting to add an element to a full queue may throw an exception; it may fail silently; it may wait indefinitely (or for a predefined time period) for the queue to have room to accommodate the new element, etc. The exact behavior depends on the type of the queue.

Which element of the queue comes out next? A queue always has an entry point and an exit point for its elements. The exit point is called the *head* of the queue and the entry point is called the *tail*. The head and the tail may be the same. If the head and the tail of a queue are the same, it is called a Last In, First Out (LIFO) queue. A LIFO queue is also known as a *stack*. The head and the tail of a queue may be different. If a queue follows a rule that the element entering the queue first will leave the queue first (first come, first served rule), it is called a First In, First Out (FIFO) queue. Have you ever had a chance to stand in a queue for a long time and as soon as your turn comes, another person, who showed up after you, is served before you, based on a priority? Java also has this kind of queue and it is called a *priority queue*. In a priority queue, you define the priority using a Comparator object or implement the Comparable interface in an element's class, and the next element in the queue to come out will be decided based on the priority of the elements in the queue.

▨ **Tip** Typically, a null element does not make sense in a Queue. After all, the purpose of having a queue is to apply some processing logic on its elements or use the elements to perform some logic. In either case, a null value does not make sense. It is up to the implementation of the Queue interface to allow or disallow null values. The use of null elements in a queue is not recommended. If you use null elements in a queue, you will not be able to distinguish between the null value returned from its method to indicate a special situation and the null value of the element.

A queue lets you perform three basic operations:

- Add an element to its tail
- Remove an element from its head
- Peek the element at its head

The Queue interface defines two methods for each of the three operations. One method throws an exception if the operation is not possible; the other method returns a value (false or null) to indicate the failure. The method you use to perform the specific operation depends on your requirements. The Queue interface adds six methods to provide the functionality of a FIFO queue. They are listed in Table 12-1.

Table 12-1. *Additional Methods Declared by the Queue Interface*

Category	Method	Description
Adding an element to the queue	boolean add(E e)	Adds an element to the queue if it is possible. Otherwise, it throws an exception.
	boolean offer(E e)	Adds an element to the queue without throwing an exception if the element cannot not be added. It returns false on failure and true on success. It is the preferred way to add an element in a bounded queue.
Removing an element from the queue	E remove()	Retrieves and removes the head of the queue. It throws an exception if the queue is empty.
	E poll()	Performs the same job as the remove() method. However, it returns null if the queue is empty instead of throwing an exception.
Peeking at the head of the queue	E element()	Retrieves the head of the queue without removing it from the queue. It throws an exception if the queue is empty.
	E peek()	Performs the same job as the element() method. However, it returns null if the queue is empty instead of throwing an exception.

The LinkedList and PriorityQueue are two implementation classes for the Queue interface. Note that the LinkedList class is also the implementation class for the List interface. The LinkedList class is a multi-purpose collection implementation class. I will mention its name a few more times in this chapter.

Listing 12-15 demonstrates how to use a LinkedList as a FIFO queue. In fact, it is the Queue interface that represents a FIFO queue. An instance of the LinkedList class can be used as a FIFO queue or a LIFO queue.

Listing 12-15. Using a FIFO Queue Using LinkedList as the Implementation Class

```java
// QueueTest.java
package com.jdojo.collections;

import java.util.Queue;
import java.util.LinkedList;
import java.util.NoSuchElementException;

public class QueueTest {
    public static void main(String[] args) {
        Queue<String> queue = new LinkedList<>();
        queue.add("John");

        // offer() will work the same as add()
        queue.offer("Richard");
        queue.offer("Donna");
        queue.offer("Ken");

        System.out.println("Queue: " + queue);

        // Let's remove elements until the queuee is empty
        while (queue.peek() != null) {
            System.out.println("Head Element: " + queue.peek());
            queue.remove();
            System.out.println("Removed one element from Queue");
            System.out.println("Queue: " + queue);
        }

        // Now Queue is empty. Try  calling the peek(),
        // element(), poll() and remove() methods
        System.out.println("queue.isEmpty(): " + queue.isEmpty());

        System.out.println("queue.peek(): " + queue.peek());
        System.out.println("queue.poll(): " + queue.poll());

        try {
            String str = queue.element();
            System.out.println("queue.element(): " + str);
        }
        catch (NoSuchElementException e) {
            System.out.println("queue.element(): Queue is empty.");
        }
```

```
                    try {
                            String str = queue.remove();
                            System.out.println("queue.remove(): " + str);
                    }
                    catch (NoSuchElementException e) {
                            System.out.println("queue.remove(): Queue is empty.");
                    }
            }
    }
}
```

```
Queue: [John, Richard, Donna, Ken]
Head Element: John
Removed one element from Queue
Queue: [Richard, Donna, Ken]
Head Element: Richard
Removed one element from Queue
Queue: [Donna, Ken]
Head Element: Donna
Removed one element from Queue
Queue: [Ken]
Head Element: Ken
Removed one element from Queue
Queue: []
queue.isEmpty(): true
queue.peek(): null
queue.poll(): null
queue.element(): Queue is empty.
queue.remove(): Queue is empty.
```

How do you create a LIFO queue? An instance of the Stack class represents a LIFO queue. The Stack class was not designed properly. It inherits the java.util.Vector class. You can roll out your own representation of a LIFO queue using the LinkedList class easily. I will discuss the Deque collection interface in the next section and you will see how to use it as a LIFO queue. You will also develop your own LIFO queue.

Priority Queues

A priory queue is a queue in which each element has an associated priority. The element with the highest priority is removed next from the queue. Java provides PriorityQueue as an implementation class for an unbounded priority queue. You can use natural order of the elements of the queue as its priority. In this case, the elements of the queue must implement the Comparable interface. You can also supply a Comparator object, which will determine the priority order of the elements. When you add a new element to a priority queue, it is positioned in the queue based on its priority. How the priority is decided in the queue is up to you to implement.

Let's develop a priority queue based on natural ordering of its elements. Let's extend your Person class to implement the Comparable interface. You will call your new class ComparablePerson. The priority of a ComparablePerson will be decided on two criteria, id and name. If the id is higher, its priority is lower. If persons have the same id, the name will be used to decide the priority based on the alphabetical order of the names. Listing 12-16 has the code for the ComparablePerson class.

Listing 12-16. A ComparablePerson Class

```java
// ComparablePerson.java
package com.jdojo.collections;

public class ComparablePerson extends Person implements Comparable {
        public ComparablePerson(int id, String name) {
                super(id, name);
        }

        @Override
        public int compareTo(Object o) {
                ComparablePerson cp = (ComparablePerson) o;
                int cpId = cp.getId();
                String cpName = cp.getName();

                if (this.getId() < cpId) {
                        return -1;
                }

                if (this.getId() > cpId) {
                        return 1;
                }

                if (this.getId() == cpId) {
                        return this.getName().compareTo(cpName);
                }

                // Should not reach here
                return 0;
        }
}
```

Listing 12-17 demonstrates how to use a priority queue.

Listing 12-17. Using a Priority Queue

```java
// PriorityQueueTest.java
package com.jdojo.collections;

import java.util.Queue;
import java.util.PriorityQueue;

public class PriorityQueueTest {
        public static void main(String[] args) {
                Queue<ComparablePerson> pq = new PriorityQueue<>();
                pq.add(new ComparablePerson(1, "John"));
                pq.add(new ComparablePerson(4, "Ken"));
                pq.add(new ComparablePerson(2, "Richard"));
                pq.add(new ComparablePerson(3, "Donna"));
                pq.add(new ComparablePerson(4, "Adam"));

                System.out.println("Priority queue: " + pq);
```

553

```
                   while (pq.peek() != null) {
                           System.out.println("Head Element: " + pq.peek());
                           pq.remove();
                           System.out.println("Removed one element from Queue");
                           System.out.println("Priority queue: " + pq);
                   }
           }
}
```

```
Priority queue: [(1, John), (3, Donna), (2, Richard), (4, Ken), (4, Adam)]
Head Element: (1, John)
Removed one element from Queue
Priority queue: [(2, Richard), (3, Donna), (4, Adam), (4, Ken)]
Head Element: (2, Richard)
Removed one element from Queue
Priority queue: [(3, Donna), (4, Ken), (4, Adam)]
Head Element: (3, Donna)
Removed one element from Queue
Priority queue: [(4, Adam), (4, Ken)]
Head Element: (4, Adam)
Removed one element from Queue
Priority queue: [(4, Ken)]
Head Element: (4, Ken)
Removed one element from Queue
Priority queue: []
```

There is one important thing that you will notice in the output. When you print the queue, its elements are not ordered the way you would expect. You would expect that the element returned by the next call to the peek() method should be at head of the queue. Note that a queue is never used to iterate over its elements. Rather, it is used to remove one element from it, process that element, and then remove another element. The PriorityQueue class does not guarantee any ordering of the elements when you use an iterator. Its toString() method uses its iterator to give you the string representation of its elements. This is the reason that when we print the priority queue, its elements are not ordered according to their priority. However, when we use the peek() or remove() method, the correct element is peeked at or removed, which is based on the element's priority. In your case, id and name are used to order the elements. Therefore, the element with the least id and name (alphabetical order) has the highest priority.

Using a Comparator object in a priority queue is easy. You must specify your Comparator object when you create an object of the PriorityQueue class. Listing 12-18 demonstrates how to use a Comparator object to have a priority queue for the list of ComparablePerson. It uses the alphabetical ordering of the name of a ComparablePerson as the criterion to determine its priority. The person whose name comes first in the alphabetical order has higher priority.

Listing 12-18. Using a Comparator Object in a Priority Queue

```
// PriorityQueueComparatorTest.java
package com.jdojo.collections;

import java.util.Queue;
import java.util.PriorityQueue;
import java.util.Comparator;

public class PriorityQueueComparatorTest {
        public static void main(String[] args) {
```

```
            int initialCapacity = 5;
            Comparator<ComparablePerson> nameComparator =
                    Comparator.comparing(ComparablePerson::getName);

            Queue<ComparablePerson> pq =
                    new PriorityQueue<>(initialCapacity, nameComparator);
            pq.add(new ComparablePerson(1, "John"));
            pq.add(new ComparablePerson(4, "Ken"));
            pq.add(new ComparablePerson(2, "Richard"));
            pq.add(new ComparablePerson(3, "Donna"));
            pq.add(new ComparablePerson(4, "Adam"));

            System.out.println("Priority queue: " + pq);

            while (pq.peek() != null) {
                    System.out.println("Head Element: " + pq.peek());
                    pq.remove();
                    System.out.println("Removed one element from Queue");
                    System.out.println("Priority queue: " + pq);
            }
    }
}
```

```
Priority queue: [(4, Adam), (3, Donna), (2, Richard), (4, Ken), (1, John)]
Head Element: (4, Adam)
Removed one element from Queue
Priority queue: [(3, Donna), (1, John), (2, Richard), (4, Ken)]
Head Element: (3, Donna)
Removed one element from Queue
Priority queue: [(1, John), (4, Ken), (2, Richard)]
Head Element: (1, John)
Removed one element from Queue
Priority queue: [(4, Ken), (2, Richard)]
Head Element: (4, Ken)
Removed one element from Queue
Priority queue: [(2, Richard)]
Head Element: (2, Richard)
Removed one element from Queue
Priority queue: []
```

Double Ended Queues

A doubly ended queue or deque is an extended version of a queue to allow insertion and removal of elements from both ends (the head and the tail). An instance of Deque represents a doubly ended queue. The name Deque does not mean opposite of Queue. Rather, it means "**D**ouble **e**nded **que**ue". It is pronounced "deck," not "de queue."

The Deque interface extends the Queue interface. It declares additional methods to facilitate all the operations for a queue at the head as well as at the tail. It can be used as a FIFO queue or a LIFO queue. You already know what a Queue is and how to use it. A Deque is just another version of a queue that can be used to represent different kinds of queues, not just a FIFO queue. All you have to do in this section is learn about the new methods that the Deque interface offers.

Table 12-2 lists the new methods that are declared in the Deque interface to facilitate insertion, removal, and peeking at either end (head or tail) of a Deque. In the method names, first means head and last means tail.

Table 12-2. *New Methods in Deque Interface for Insertion, Removal, and Peek Operations at Both Ends*

Category	Method	Description
Adding an element to the Deque	void addFirst(E) void addLast(E)	The addXxx() methods add an element at the head or tail, and they throw an exception if an element cannot be added, such as in a full bounded Deque.
	boolean offerFirst(E) boolean offerLast(E)	The offerXxx() methods work the same way as the addXxx() methods. However, they do not throw an exception on failure. Rather, they return false if the specified element cannot be added to a Deque.
Removing an element from the Deque	E removeFirst() E removeLast()	The removeXxx() methods retrieve and remove the element from the head or tail of the Deque. They throw an exception if the Deque is empty.
	E pollFirst() E pollLast()	The pollXxx() methods perform the same job as the removeXxx() methods. However, they return null if the Deque is empty.
Peeking at an element at end of the Deque	E getFirst() E getLast()	The getXxx() methods retrieve without removing the element at the head or the tail of the Deque. They throw an exception if the Deque is empty.
	E peekFirst() E peekLast()	The peekXxx() methods perform the same job as the getXxx()methods. However, they return null if the Deque is empty instead of throwing an exception.

Since Deque inherits from Queue, a Deque can also act like a FIFO queue. Table 12-3 compares the methods in the Queue interface and their equivalent methods in the Deque interface.

Table 12-3. *Method Comparison of the Queue and Deque Interfaces*

Method in Queue	Equivalent Method in Deque
add(e)	addLast(e)
offer(e)	offerLast(e)
remove()	removeFirst()
poll()	pollFirst()
element()	getFirst()
peek()	peekFirst()

Since, in a FIFO queue, you always add an element at the tail (or Last), the add() method in the Queue interface does the same thing as what the addLast() method does in the Deque interface.

You can also use a Deque as a stack (a LIFO queue) using familiar methods such as push(), pop(), and peek(). The push() method pushes (or adds) an element to the top of the stack that is the same as using the method addFirst(). The pop() method pops (or removes) the element from the top of the stack that is the same as calling the removeFirst() method. The peek() method retrieves, but does not remove, the element at the top of the stack; if the stack is empty, it returns null. Calling the peek() method is the same as calling the peekFirst() method. A stack needs four methods to perform its operations: isEmpty(), push(), pop() and peek(). Table 12-4 lists the stack specific methods in the Deque interface and their alternate versions.

Table 12-4. *Deque Methods Named Specifically to be Used with Stacks*

Stack Specific Methods in Deque	Equivalent Alternate Methods in Deque
isEmpty()	Inherited from the Collection interface
push(E e)	addFirst(E e)
pop()	removeFirst()
peek()	peekFirst()

Looking at the methods that you have seen so far in the Deque interface, you can say that it is a huge interface. A programmer can easily get confused if he does not learn this interface by breaking its methods down into separate categories. The Deque interface has methods that fall into the following four categories:

- Methods that let you insert, remove, and peek elements at the head and tail of the Deque, as listed in Table 12-2. All these methods are enough to use a Deque as any queue you want. However, it offers some more methods with different names to accomplish the same thing.

- Methods that let you use a Deque as a FIFO queue (or simply as Queue). They are listed in Table 12-3.

- Methods that let you use familiar method names that are used with stacks. Note that these methods are not performing anything new other than insertion, removal, and peeking. They just have different names. They are listed in Table 12-4.

- Some utility methods that help you work with a Deque in specific situations. For example, its descendingIterator() method returns an Iterator object that lets you iterate over its elements in a reverse order (from tail to head). It also adds two methods called removeFirstOccurrence(Object o) and removeLastOccurrence(Object o) that let you remove the first occurrence (starting from the head and going towards the tail) and last occurrence (starting from the tail and going towards the head) of an object in the Deque, respectively. Now you can relax—there are no more new methods in the Deque to learn.

The ArrayDeque and LinkedList classes are two implementation classes for the Deque interface. The ArrayDeque class is backed by an array whereas the LinkedList class is backed by a linked list. You should use the ArrayDeque as a Deque implementation if you are using a Deque as a LIFO queue (or a stack). The LinkedList implementation performs better if you use a Deque as a FIFO queue (or simply as a Queue).

Listing 12-19 demonstrates how to use a Deque as a FIFO queue. If you compare this program with the program in Listing 12-15, in this program you have just used Deque-specific methods to perform the same thing as what you accomplished with the methods of the Queue interface. Suppose a method accepts an argument of type Queue. If you pass a Deque to that method, your Deque will be used as a FIFO queue inside that method.

Listing 12-19. Using a Deque as a FIFO Queue

```java
// DequeAsQueue.java
package com.jdojo.collections;

import java.util.Deque;
import java.util.LinkedList;
import java.util.NoSuchElementException;

public class DequeAsQueue {
    public static void main(String[] args) {
        // Create a Deque and add elements at its tail using
        // addLast() or offerLast() method
        Deque<String> deque = new LinkedList<>();
        deque.addLast("John");
        deque.offerLast("Richard");
        deque.offerLast("Donna");
        deque.offerLast("Ken");

        System.out.println("Deque: " + deque);

        // Let's remove elements from the Deque until it is empty
        while (deque.peekFirst() != null) {
            System.out.println("Head Element: " + deque.peekFirst());
            deque.removeFirst();
            System.out.println("Removed one element from Deque");
            System.out.println("Deque: " + deque);
        }

        // Now, the Deque is empty. Try to call its peekFirst(),
        // getFirst(), pollFirst() and removeFirst() methods
        System.out.println("deque.isEmpty(): " + deque.isEmpty());

        System.out.println("deque.peekFirst(): " + deque.peekFirst());
        System.out.println("deque.pollFirst(): " + deque.pollFirst());

        try {
            String str = deque.getFirst();
            System.out.println("deque.getFirst(): " + str);
        }
        catch (NoSuchElementException e) {
            System.out.println("deque.getFirst(): Deque is empty.");
        }

        try {
            String str = deque.removeFirst();
            System.out.println("deque.removeFirst(): " + str);
        }
        catch (NoSuchElementException e) {
            System.out.println("deque.removeFirst(): Deque is empty.");
        }
    }
}
```

```
Deque: [John, Richard, Donna, Ken]
Head Element: John
Removed one element from Deque
Deque: [Richard, Donna, Ken]
Head Element: Richard
Removed one element from Deque
Deque: [Donna, Ken]
Head Element: Donna
Removed one element from Deque
Deque: [Ken]
Head Element: Ken
Removed one element from Deque
Deque: []
deque.isEmpty(): true
deque.peekFirst(): null
deque.pollFirst(): null
deque.getFirst(): Deque is empty.
deque.removeFirst(): Deque is empty.
```

Listing 12-20 demonstrates how to use a Deque as a stack (or LIFO queue).

Listing 12-20. Using a Deque as a Stack

```java
// DequeAsStack.java
package com.jdojo.collections;

import java.util.ArrayDeque;
import java.util.Deque;

public class DequeAsStack {
        public static void main(String[] args) {
                // Create a Deque and use it as stack
                Deque<String> deque = new ArrayDeque<>();
                deque.push("John");
                deque.push("Richard");
                deque.push("Donna");
                deque.push("Ken");

                System.out.println("Stack: " + deque);

                // Let's remove all elements from the Deque
                while (deque.peek() != null) {
                        System.out.println("Element at top: " + deque.peek());
                        System.out.println("Popped: " + deque.pop());
                        System.out.println("Stack: " + deque);
                }

                System.out.println("Stack is empty: " + deque.isEmpty());
        }
}
```

```
Stack: [Ken, Donna, Richard, John]
Element at top: Ken
Popped: Ken
Stack: [Donna, Richard, John]
Element at top: Donna
Popped: Donna
Stack: [Richard, John]
Element at top: Richard
Popped: Richard
Stack: [John]
Element at top: John
Popped: John
Stack: []
Stack is empty: true
```

Note that even if the Deque provides all the methods that you need to use it as a stack, it does not give a programmer a collection type that can be truly used as a stack. If you need a stack in a method as its argument, you will need to declare it as a Deque type as shown:

```
public class MyClass {
        public void myMethod(Deque stack){
                /* This method is free to use (or misuse) stack argument
                   as a FIFO even though it needs only a LIFO queue
                */
        }
}
```

The myMethod() is passed a Deque when it needs a stack. If you trust myMethod(), it's fine. Otherwise, it can access elements of the Deque in any way the Deque interface allows. It is not limited to use only as a stack. The only way you can stop the user of your Deque to use it only as a stack is to roll out your own interface and an implementation class. The Stack class works as a stack. However, you are advised not to use the Stack class to work with a stack as it has the same problem that you are trying to solve.

You can create an interface named LIFOQueue with four methods: isEmpty(), push(), pop(), and peek(). You can create an implementation class named ArrayLIFOQueue, which implements the LIFOQueue interface. Your ArrayLIFOQueue class will wrap an ArrayDeque object. All of its methods will be delegated to ArrayDeque. And that is all. Note that by creating a new LIFOQueue interface and its implementation, you are diverting from the Collections Framework. Your new interface and classes will be outside the Collections Framework. However, if you do need to implement your own version of a data structure that can be used strictly as a stack, you can do so.

There is another way to create a stack from a Deque. You can convert a Deque to a LIFO Queue using the asLifoQueue() static method of the Collections class. The method signature is as follows:

- `public static <T> Queue<T> asLifoQueue(Deque<T> deque)`

The following snippet of code creates a stack from a Deque:

```
Deque<String> deque = create a Deque ;
// Get a LIFO queue from Deque
Queue<String> stack = Collections.asLifoQueue(deque);

// Now, you can pass around stack reference, which can be used only as a LIFO queue
```

Blocking Queues

You have seen the behavior of a Queue in two extreme cases:

- When you want to add an element to it when it is full

- When you want to remove an element from it when it is empty

A queue specifies two types of methods to deal with insertion, removal, and peeking in these two extreme cases: one type of method throws an exception whereas the other type of method returns a special value.

A blocking queue extends the behavior of a queue in dealing with these extreme cases. It adds two more sets of methods: one set of methods blocks indefinitely and another set of methods lets you specify a time period to block.

An instance of the BlockingQueue interface represents a blocking queue. The BlockingQueue interface inherits from the Queue interface. Here are two additional features that the BlockingQueue interface offers:

- It adds two methods called put() and offer() to let you add an element to the blocking queue at its tail. The put() method blocks indefinitely if the blocking queue is full until space becomes available in the queue. The offer() method lets you specify the time period to wait for space to become available in the blocking queue. It returns true if the specified element was added successfully; it returns false if the specified time period elapsed before the space became available for the new element.

- It adds two methods called take() and poll() to let you retrieve and remove the head from the blocking queue. The take() method blocks indefinitely if the blocking queue is empty. The poll() method lets you specify a time period to wait if the blocking queue is empty; it returns null if the specified time elapses before an element became available.

If you use methods from the Queue interface with a BlockingQueue, they would behave as if you are using a Queue. A BlockingQueue is designed to be thread-safe. Usually it is used in a producer/consumer-like situation where some threads (called producers) add elements to it and some threads (called consumers) remove elements from it.

A blocking queue does not allow a null element. A blocking queue can be bounded or unbounded. It adds another method called remainingCapacity() that returns the number of elements that can be added to the blocking queue without blocking. You need to be careful in basing your decision on the return value of this method. There may be other threads attempting to add elements to the blocking queue at the same time you call this method. In such cases, when you attempt to add new elements based on the return value of this method, your elements may not be added, even though you know that there is some space available. The real test whether an element can be added to a blocking queue or not is to attempt to add one and check the return value of the put() or offer() method.

There is one more thing that is related to a blocking queue: *fairness*. Fairness is used to handle situations where multiple threads are blocked to perform insertion or removal. If a blocking queue is fair, it will allow the longest waiting thread to perform the operation when a condition arises that allows the operation to proceed. If the blocking queue is not fair, the order in which the blocked threads are allowed to perform the operation is not specified. Specific implementations determine fairness availability.

The BlockingQueue interface and all its implementation classes are in the java.util.concurrent package. The following are the implementation classes for the BlockingQueue interface:

- ArrayBlockingQueue: It is a bounded implementation class for BlockingQueue. It is backed by an array. It also lets you specify the fairness of the blocking queue in its constructor. By default, it is not fair.

- LinkedBlockingQueue: It is another implementation class for BlockingQueue. It can be used as a bounded or unbounded blocking queue. It does not allow specifying a fairness rule for the blocking queue.

- PriorityBlockingQueue: It is an unbounded implementation class for BlockingQueue. It works the same way as PriortyQueue for ordering the elements in the blocking queue. It adds the blocking feature to PriorityQueue.

- SynchronousQueue: It is a special type of implementation of BlockingQueue. It does not have any capacity. The put operation waits for the take operation to take the element being put. It facilitates a kind of handshake between two threads. One thread tries to put an element to the blocking queue that must wait until there is a thread that tries to take the element. It facilitates an exchange of an object between two threads. You can also specify the fairness rule for the queue. For all practical purposes, this blocking queue is always empty. It seems to have an element only when there are two threads: one trying to add an element and one trying to remove an element. Its isEmpty() method always returns true.

- DelayQueue: It is another unbounded implementation class for BlockingQueue. It allows an element to be taken out only if a specified delay has passed for that element. If there are multiple elements in the blocking queue whose specified delay has passed, the element whose delay passed earliest will be placed at the head of the blocking queue.

Let's start with an example of a producer/consumer application. Listing 12-21 has the code for a producer. It accepts a blocking queue and a producer name in its constructor. It generates a string and adds it to the blocking queue after waiting for a random number of seconds between 1 and 5. If the blocking queue is full, it will wait until the space is available in the queue.

Listing 12-21. The Producer Class for a Blocking Queue

```java
// BQProducer.java
package com.jdojo.collections;

import java.util.concurrent.BlockingQueue;
import java.util.Random;

public class BQProducer extends Thread {
        private final BlockingQueue<String> queue;
        private final String name;
        private int nextNumber = 1;
        private final Random random = new Random();

        public BQProducer(BlockingQueue<String> queue, String name) {
                this.queue = queue;
                this.name = name;
        }

        @Override
        public void run() {
                while (true) {
                        try {
                                String str = name + "-" + nextNumber;
                                System.out.println(name + " is trying to add: " +
                                        str + ". Remaining capacity: " +
                                        queue.remainingCapacity());
                                this.queue.put(str);
                                nextNumber++;
                                System.out.println(name + " added: " + str);

                                // Sleep between 1 and 5 seconds
                                int sleepTime = (random.nextInt(5) + 1) * 1000;
                                Thread.sleep(sleepTime);
                        }
```

```
                    catch (InterruptedException e) {
                            e.printStackTrace();
                            break;
                    }
            }
        }
}
```

Listing 12-22 has code for a consumer. It does the opposite of what a producer does. It removes elements from the blocking queue. If the blocking queue is empty, it waits indefinitely for an element to become available. Both the producer and consumer run in an infinite loop.

Listing 12-22. The Consumer Class for a Blocking Queue

```
// BQConsumer.java
package com.jdojo.collections;

import java.util.concurrent.BlockingQueue;
import java.util.Random;

public class BQConsumer extends Thread {
        private final BlockingQueue<String> queue;
        private final String name;
        private final Random random = new Random();

        public BQConsumer(BlockingQueue<String> queue, String name) {
                this.queue = queue;
                this.name = name;
        }

        @Override
        public void run() {
                while (true) {
                        try {
                                System.out.println(name +
                                        " is trying to take an element. " +
                                        "Remaining capacity: " +
                                        queue.remainingCapacity());

                                String str = this.queue.take();
                                System.out.println(name + " took: " + str);

                                // Sleep between 1 and 5 seconds
                                int sleepTime = (random.nextInt(5) + 1) * 1000;
                                Thread.sleep(sleepTime);
                        }
                        catch (InterruptedException e) {
                                e.printStackTrace();
                                break;
                        }
                }
        }
}
```

Listing 12-23 creates a bounded and fair blocking queue. It creates one producer and two consumers. Each producer/consumer is created in a separate thread. A partial output has been shown. You will have to stop the application manually. You may experiment with adding more producers or consumers and adjusting their sleep times. Note that the messages printed in the output may not appear in the order that makes sense; this is typical in a multi-threaded program. A thread performs an action and it is preempted before it can print a message stating that it did perform the action. Meanwhile, you will see messages from another thread.

Listing 12-23. A Class to Run the Producer/Consumer Program

```java
// BQProducerConsumerTest.java
package com.jdojo.collections;

import java.util.concurrent.BlockingQueue;
import java.util.concurrent.ArrayBlockingQueue;

public class BQProducerConsumerTest {
        public static void main(String[] args) {
                int capacity = 5;
                boolean fair = true;
                BlockingQueue<String> queue = new ArrayBlockingQueue<>(capacity, fair);

                // Create one producer and two consumer and let them produce
                // and consume indefinitely
                new BQProducer(queue, "Producer1").start();
                new BQConsumer(queue, "Consumer1").start();
                new BQConsumer(queue, "Consumer2").start();
        }
}
```

```
Consumer1 is trying to take an element. Remaining capacity: 5
Consumer2 is trying to take an element. Remaining capacity: 5
Producer1 is trying to add: Producer1-1. Remaining capacity: 5
Producer1 added: Producer1-1
Consumer1 took: Producer1-1
Producer1 is trying to add: Producer1-2. Remaining capacity: 5
Producer1 added: Producer1-2
Consumer2 took: Producer1-2
Consumer1 is trying to take an element. Remaining capacity: 5
Consumer2 is trying to take an element. Remaining capacity: 5
...
```

I will not discuss an example of `PriorityBlockingQueue`. You can use the `PriorityBlockingQueue` implementation class to create the blocking queue in Listing 12-23 and the same example will work. Note that a `PriorityBlockingQueue` is an unbounded queue. You may also want to use a different type of element (other than a string), which will emulate the priority of elements in a better way. Please refer to Listing 12-17 for an example of a simple non-blocking priority queue.

Delay Queues

Let's see an example of a DelayQueue. A DelayQueue is one of the implementation classes for the BlockingQueue interface. It lets you implement a queue whose elements must stay in a queue for a certain amount of time (known as a *delay*). How does the DelayQueue know about the amount of time an element has to be kept in the queue? It makes use of an interface called Delayed to know the time an element must stay in the queue. The interface is in the java.util.concurrent package. Its declaration is as follows:

```
public interface Delayed extends Comparable<Delayed> {
        long getDelay(TimeUnit timeUnit);
}
```

It extends the Comparable interface whose compareTo() method accepts a Delayed object. The DelayQueue calls the getDelay() method of each element to know how long that element must be kept in the queue before it can be taken out. The DelayQueue will pass a TimeUnit to this method. Your job is to convert the delay time of an element to the TimeUnit being passed and return the value. For example, if you want to keep an element in the queue for 10 seconds, your getDelay(TimeUnit timeUnit) method will be implemented as follows:

```
public class DelayClass implement Delayed {
        public long getDelay(TimeUnit timeUnit){
                long delay = timeUnit.convert(10, TimeUnit.SECONDS);
                return delay;
        }
}
```

The element stays in the DelayQueue as long as the delay returned from the getDelay() method is a positive number. When the getDelay() method returns a zero or a negative number, it is time for the element to get out of the queue. However, there must be someone to take the element out of the queue when it is ready to get out. Typically, you would call the take() method to take an element out of the queue. There may be many elements that are ready (whose delay time has expired) to come out of the queue. Which one of the expired elements will be placed as the head of the queue? The queue determines this by calling the compareTo() method of the elements. This method determines the priority of an expired element to be removed from the queue with respect to the other expired elements. Typically, you would decide that the element that has expired latest would be the first one to be removed. However, it is up to you to decide which expired element will be ready to be removed next. You may decide just the opposite, such as the element that has expired earliest should be removed first.

Listing 12-24 has code for a DelayedJob class. It implements the Delayed interface. Its constructor takes a job name and a scheduled time for the job as arguments. The scheduled time could be in the past, the present, or in the future. It is specified as a number, which represents the milliseconds passed between the specified time and midnight, January 1, 1970 UTC. Its getDelay() method returns the delay time for this job. Its compareTo() method uses the getDelay() method, so that the earliest expired element will be removed first. Its toString() method simply prints its job name and scheduled time.

Listing 12-24. A DelayedJob Class That Implements the Delayed Interface

```
// DelayedJob.java
package com.jdojo.collections;

import java.time.Instant;
import java.util.concurrent.Delayed;
import java.util.concurrent.TimeUnit;
import static java.util.concurrent.TimeUnit.MILLISECONDS;
import static java.time.temporal.ChronoUnit.MILLIS;
```

```java
public class DelayedJob implements Delayed {
        private final Instant scheduledTime;
        String jobName;

        public DelayedJob(String jobName, Instant scheduledTime) {
                this.scheduledTime = scheduledTime;
                this.jobName = jobName;
        }

        @Override
        public long getDelay(TimeUnit unit) {
                // Positive delay means it should stay in queue. Zero or negative delay
                // means that it ready to be removed from the queue.
                long delay = MILLIS.between(Instant.now(), scheduledTime);

                // Convert the delay in millis into the specified unit
                long returnValue = unit.convert(delay, MILLISECONDS);
                return returnValue;
        }

        @Override
        public int compareTo(Delayed job) {
                long currentJobDelay = this.getDelay(MILLISECONDS);
                long jobDelay = job.getDelay(MILLISECONDS);

                int diff = 0;
                if (currentJobDelay > jobDelay) {
                        diff = 1;
                }
                else if (currentJobDelay < jobDelay) {
                        diff = -1;
                }
                return diff;
        }

        @Override
        public String toString() {
                String str = "(" + this.jobName + ", " + "Scheduled Time: " +
                                this.scheduledTime + ")";
                return str;
        }
}
```

The program in Listing 12-25 shows how to use the DelayedJob objects as elements in a DelayQueue. It adds three jobs ("Print Data", "Populate Data", and "Balance Data") to the queue that are scheduled to run 9m, 3m, and 6000 seconds after the current time on your computer, respectively. Note the sequence of adding these jobs in the queue. I have not added the job to be run first as the first element. It is the job of the DelayQueue to arrange the elements in its queue based on their delay time returned from their getDelay() method. When you run this program, there will be a delay of about 3 seconds because no elements will be expired and the take() method on the queue will be blocked. When elements start expiring, you will see them getting removed one by one by the take() method in the while-loop. You may get a different output when you run the program.

Listing 12-25. Using a DelayQueue with Instances of DelayedJob as Its Element

```java
// DelayQueueTest.java
package com.jdojo.collections;

import java.time.Instant;
import java.util.concurrent.BlockingQueue;
import java.util.concurrent.DelayQueue;

public class DelayQueueTest {
        public static void main(String[] args) throws InterruptedException {
                BlockingQueue<DelayedJob> queue = new DelayQueue<>();
                Instant now = Instant.now();

                // Create three delayed job and add them to the queue
                // Jobs should run in a sequence as
                // 1. Populate Data (After 3 seeconds)
                // 2. Balance Data (After 6 seconds)
                // 3. Print Data (After 9 seconds)
                queue.put(new DelayedJob("Print Data", now.plusSeconds(9)));
                queue.put(new DelayedJob("Populate Data", now.plusSeconds(3)));
                queue.put(new DelayedJob("Balance Data", now.plusSeconds(6)));

                while (queue.size() > 0) {
                        System.out.println("Waiting to take a job from the queue...");
                        DelayedJob job = queue.take();
                        System.out.println("Took Job: " + job);
                }

                System.out.println("Finished running all jobs.");
        }
}
```

```
Waiting to take a job from the queue...
Took Job: (Populate Data, Scheduled Time: 2014-05-09T02:35:44.721Z)
Waiting to take a job from the queue...
Took Job: (Balance Data, Scheduled Time: 2014-05-09T02:35:47.721Z)
Waiting to take a job from the queue...
Took Job: (Print Data, Scheduled Time: 2014-05-09T02:35:50.721Z)
Finished running all jobs.
```

Transfer Queues

The transfer queue extends the functionality of a blocking queue. An instance of the TransferQueue represents a transfer queue. In a TransferQueue, a producer will wait to hand off an element to a consumer. This is a useful feature in a message passing application, where a producer makes sure that its message has been consumed by a consumer. A producer hands off an element to a consumer using the transfer(E element) method of the TransferQueue. When a producer invokes this method, it waits until a consumer takes its element. If the TransferQueue has some elements, all its elements must be consumed before the element added by the transfer() method is consumed. The tryTransfer() method provides a non-blocking and a timeout version of the method, which lets a producer transfer an element immediately if a consumer is already waiting or wait for a specified amount of time.

The TransferQueue has two more methods to get more information about the waiting consumers. The getWaitingConsumerCount() method returns the number of waiting consumers. The hasWaitingConsumer() method returns true if there is a waiting consumer; otherwise, it returns false.

The LinkedTransferQueue is an implementation class for the TransferQueue interface. It provides an unbounded TransferQueue. It is based on FIFO. That is, the element that enters the TransferQueue first is removed from the queue first.

Listing 12-26 contains code for a TQProducer class whose instance represents a producer for a TransferQueue. The producer sleeps for a random number of seconds between 1 and 5. It generates an integer. If the integer is even, it puts it in the queue. If the integer is odd, it tries to hand it off to a consumer using the transfer() method. Note that if the TransferQueue has some elements, the consumer will consume those elements first, before it consumes the element that a producer is trying to hand off using the transfer() method.

Listing 12-26. A TQProducer Class That Represents a Producer for a TransferQueue

```java
// TQProducer.java
package com.jdojo.collections;

import java.util.Random;
import java.util.concurrent.TransferQueue;
import java.util.concurrent.atomic.AtomicInteger;

public class TQProducer extends Thread {
    private final String name;
    private final TransferQueue<Integer> tQueue;
    private final AtomicInteger sequence;
    private Random rand = new Random();

    public TQProducer(String name, TransferQueue<Integer> tQueue, AtomicInteger sequence) {
        this.name = name;
        this.tQueue = tQueue;
        this.sequence = sequence;
    }

    @Override
    public void run() {
        while (true) {
            try {
                // Sleep for 1 tp 5 random number of seconds
                int sleepTime = rand.nextInt(5) + 1;
                Thread.sleep(sleepTime * 1000);

                // Generate a sequence number
                int nextNum = this.sequence.incrementAndGet();

                // An even number is enqueued. An odd number is handed off
                // to a consumer
                if (nextNum % 2 == 0) {
                    System.out.format("%s: Enqueuing: %d%n", name, nextNum);
                    tQueue.put(nextNum); // Enqueue
                }
```

```
                else {
                        System.out.format("%s: Handing off: %d%n",
                                            name, nextNum);
                        System.out.format("%s: has a waiting consumer: %b%n",
                                            name, tQueue.hasWaitingConsumer());
                        tQueue.transfer(nextNum); // A hand off
                }
            }
            catch (InterruptedException e) {
                    e.printStackTrace();
            }
        }
    }
}
```

Listing 12-27 contains the code for a consumer that consumes elements from a TransferQueue. It sleeps for 1 to 5 seconds randomly and consumes an element from the TransferQueue.

Listing 12-27. A TQConsumer Class That Represents a Consumer for a TransferQueue

```java
// TQConsumer.java
package com.jdojo.collections;

import java.util.Random;
import java.util.concurrent.TransferQueue;

public class TQConsumer extends Thread {
        private final String name;
        private final TransferQueue<Integer> tQueue;
        private final Random rand = new Random();

        public TQConsumer(String name, TransferQueue<Integer> tQueue) {
                this.name = name;
                this.tQueue = tQueue;
        }

        @Override
        public void run() {
                while (true) {
                        try {
                                // Sleep for 1 tp 5 random number of seconds
                                int sleepTime = rand.nextInt(5) + 1;
                                Thread.sleep(sleepTime * 1000);

                                int item = tQueue.take();
                                System.out.format("%s removed: %d%n", name, item);
                        }
                        catch (InterruptedException e) {
                                e.printStackTrace();
                        }
                }
        }
}
```

Listing 12-28 contains the code to test a TransferQueue. You may get a different output when you run the program.

Listing 12-28. A Class to Test a TransferQueue

```java
// TQProducerConsumerTest.java
package com.jdojo.collections;

import java.util.concurrent.LinkedTransferQueue;
import java.util.concurrent.TransferQueue;
import java.util.concurrent.atomic.AtomicInteger;

public class TQProducerConsumerTest {
        public static void main(String[] args) {
                final TransferQueue<Integer> tQueue = new LinkedTransferQueue<>();
                final AtomicInteger sequence = new AtomicInteger();

                // Initialize transfer queue with five items
                for(int i = 0; i < 5; i++) {
                        try {
                                tQueue.put(sequence.incrementAndGet());
                        }
                        catch (InterruptedException e) {
                                e.printStackTrace();
                        }
                }

                System.out.println("Initial queue: " + tQueue);

                // Create and start a producer and a consumer
                new TQProducer("Producer-1", tQueue, sequence).start();
                new TQConsumer("Consumer-1", tQueue).start();
        }
}
```

```
Initial queue: [1, 2, 3, 4, 5]
Producer-1: Enqueuing: 6
Consumer-1 removed: 1
Consumer-1 removed: 2
Producer-1: Handing off: 7
Producer-1: has a waiting consumer: false
Consumer-1 removed: 3
Consumer-1 removed: 4
Consumer-1 removed: 5
Consumer-1 removed: 6
Consumer-1 removed: 7
Producer-1: Enqueuing: 8
Consumer-1 removed: 8
...
```

The program creates a `TransferQueue` and adds five elements to it. It creates and starts a producer and a consumer. Its output needs a little explanation. You added five elements initially to make sure the consumer will have some elements to consume from the `TransferQueue` when the producer tries to transfer an element. The producer got the first go. It puts the integer 6 into the queue. The consumer removed the integer 1 from the queue. At this time, the producer tried to hand off the integer 7 to the consumer, leaving five elements (2, 3, 4, 5, and 6) still queued in the `TransferQueue`. The consumer must remove all these elements from the `TransferQueue`, before it will accept the transfer request for the integer 7 from the producer. This is evident from the output. The consumer removes the elements 2, 3, 4, 5, and 6, and then the element 7. Both the producer and the consumer run in infinite loops. You need to stop the program manually.

Blocking Doubly Ended Queues

A blocking, doubly ended queue provides the functionality of a doubly ended queue and a blocking queue. An instance of the `BlockingDeque` interface represents a blocking, doubly ended queue. It inherits from the `Deque` and `BlockingQueue` interfaces. It adds eight more methods to add and remove elements from the head and the tail. These methods block indefinitely or for a specified amount of time, as in the case of a `BlockingQueue`. The new methods are `putXxx()`, `offerXxx()`, `takeXxx()`, and `pollXxx()`, where `Xxx` is `First` or `Last`. The method with the suffix `First` is used to put or take an element from the head of the `Deque`, whereas the method with the suffix `Last` is used to put or take an element from its tail. Please refer to the "Double Ended Queues" and "Blocking Queue" sections described earlier in this chapter for more details on using these methods.

The `LinkedBlockingDeque` class is an implementation class for the `BlockingDeque` interface. It supports bounded as well as unbounded blocking deque.

Working with Maps

A map represents a type of collection that is different from the collections that you have seen so far. It contains `key-value` mappings. It is easy to visualize a map as a table with two columns. The first column of the table contains keys; the second column contains the values associated with the keys. Table 12-5 shows person names as keys and their phone numbers as values. You can think of this table representing a map that contains mapping between names and phone numbers. Sometimes a map is also known as a *dictionary*. In a dictionary, you have a word and you look up its meanings. Similarly, in a map, you have a key and you look up its value.

Table 12-5. A Table with Two Columns, Key and Value. Each Row Contains a Key-Value Pair.

Key	Value
John	(342)113-9878
Richard	(245)890-9045
Donna	(205)678-9823
Ken	(205)678-9823

If you still have problem visualizing a map, you can think of it as a collection in which each element represents a key-value pair as <key, value>. A <key, value> pair is also known as an *entry* in the map. The key and the value must be reference types. You cannot use primitive types (`int`, `double`, etc.) for either keys or values in a map.

A map is represented by an instance of the `Map<K,V>` interface. The `Map` interface is not inherited from the `Collection` interface. A `Map` does not allow any duplicate keys. Each key is mapped to exactly one value. In other words, each key in a `Map` has exactly one value. Values do not have to be unique. That is, two keys may map to the same value.

A Map allows for at most one null value as its key and multiple null values as its values. However, an implementation class may restrict null as a value in a Map.

The methods in the Map interface may be classified in the following four categories depending on the operations they perform:

- Methods for basic operations

- Methods for bulk operations

- Methods for view operations

- Methods for comparison operations

The methods in the basic operations category let you perform basic operations on a Map, for example, putting an entry into a Map, getting the value for a specified key, getting the number of entries, removing an entry, checking if the Map is empty, etc. Examples of methods in this category are as follows:

- `int size()`

- `boolean isEmpty()`

- `boolean containsKey (Object key)`

- `boolean containsValue (Object value)`

- `V get(Object key)`

- `V getOrDefault(Object key, V defaultValue)`

- `V put(K key, V value)`

- `V putIfAbsent(K key, V value)`

- `V remove (Object key)`

- `boolean remove(Object key, Object value)`

- `boolean replace(K key, V oldValue, V newValue)`

The methods in the bulk operations category let you perform bulk operations on a Map such as copying entries to a Map from another Map and removing all entries from the Map. Examples of methods in this category are as follows:

- `void clear()`

- `void putAll (Map<? extends K, ? extends V> t)`

- `void replaceAll(BiFunction<? super K,? super V,? extends V> function)`

The view operations category contains three methods. Each returns a different view of a Map. You can view all keys in a Map as a Set, all values as a Collection, and all <key, value> pairs as a Set. Note that all keys and all <key, value> pairs are always unique in a Map and that is the reason why you get their Set views. Since a Map may contain duplicate values, you get a Collection view of its values. Examples of methods in this category are as follows:

- `Set<K> keySet()`

- `Collection<V> values()`

- `Set<Map. Entry<K, V>>entrySet()`

The comparison operations methods deal with comparing two Maps for equality. Examples of methods in this category are as follows:

- boolean equals (Object o)
- int hashCode()

The HashMap, LinkedHashMap, and WeakHashMap are three of the available implementation classes for the Map interface.

The HashMap allows one null value as a key and multiple null values as the values. The following snippet of code demonstrates how to create and use a Map. A HashMap does not guarantee any specific iteration order of entries in the Map.

```
// Create a map using HashMap as the implementation class
Map<String, String> map = new HashMap<>();

// Put an entry to the map - "John" as the key and "(342)113-9878" as the value
map.put("John", "(342)113-9878");
```

The LinkedHashMap is another implementation class for the Map interface. It stores entries in the Map using a doubly linked list. It defines the iteration ordering as the insertion order of the entries. If you want to iterate over entries in a Map in its insertion order, you need to use LinkedHashMap instead of HashMap as the implementation class.

Listing 12-29 demonstrates how to use a Map. Note that the methods remove() and get() return the value of a key. If the key does not exist in the Map, they return a null. You must use the containsKey() method to check if a key exists in a Map or use the getOrDefault() method that lets you specify the default value in case the key does not exist in the map. The toString() method returns a well-formatted string for all entries in the Map. It places all entries inside braces ({}). Each entry is formatted in key=value format. A comma separates two entries. The toString() method of the Map returns a string like {key1=value1, key2=value2, key3=value3 ...}.

Listing 12-29. Using a Map

```
// MapTest.java
package com.jdojo.collections;

import java.util.HashMap;
import java.util.Map;

public class MapTest {
        public static void main(String[] args) {
                // Create a map and add some key-value pairs
                Map<String,String> map = new HashMap<>();
                map.put("John", "(342)113-9878");
                map.put("Richard", "(245)890-9045");
                map.put("Donna", "(205)678-9823");
                map.put("Ken", "(205)678-9823");

                // Print the details
                printDetails(map);

                // Remove all entries from the map
                map.clear();

                System.out.printf("%nRemoved all entries from the map.%n%n");
```

```
                        // Print the details
                        printDetails(map);
                }

        public static void printDetails(Map<String,String> map) {
                        // Get the value for the "Donna" key
                        String donnaPhone = map.get("Donna");

                        // Print details
                        System.out.println("Map: " + map);
                        System.out.println("Map Size: " + map.size());
                        System.out.println("Map is empty: " + map.isEmpty());
                        System.out.println("Map contains Donna key: " + map.containsKey("Donna"));
                        System.out.println("Donna Phone: " + donnaPhone);
                        System.out.println("Donna key is removed: " + map.remove("Donna"));
                }
}
```

```
Map: {Donna=(205)678-9823, Ken=(205)678-9823, John=(342)113-9878, Richard=(245)890-9045}
Map Size: 4
Map is empty: false
Map contains Donna key: true
Donna Phone: (205)678-9823
Donna key is removed: (205)678-9823

Removed all entries from the map.

Map: {}
Map Size: 0
Map is empty: true
Map contains Donna key: false
Donna Phone: null
Donna key is removed: null
```

The WeakHashMap class is another implementation for the Map interface. As the name of the class implies, it contains *weak keys*. When there is no reference to the key except in the map, keys are candidates for garbage collection. If a key is garbage collected, its associated entry is removed from the Map. You use a WeakHashMap as implementation class for a Map when you want to maintain a cache of key-value pairs and you do not mind if your key-value pairs are removed from the Map by the garbage collector. The WeakHashMap implementation allows a null key and multiple null values. Please refer to Chapter 11 for a complete example of using the WeakHashMap class.

Sometimes you want to iterate over keys, values, or entries of a Map. The keySet(), values() and entrySet() methods of a map returns a Set of keys, a Collection of values, and a Set of entries, respectively. Iterating over elements of a Set or a Collection is the same as described in the "Traversing Collections" section.

The following snippet of code shows how to print all keys of a map:

```
Map<String,String> map = new HashMap<>();
map.put("John", "(342)113-9878");
map.put("Richard", "(245)890-9045");
map.put("Donna", "(205)678-9823");
map.put("Ken", "(205)678-9823");
```

```
// Get the set of keys
Set<String> keys = map.keySet();

// Print all keys using the forEach() method.
// You can use a for-each loop, an iterator, etc. to do the same.
keys.forEach(System.out::println);
```

```
Donna
Ken
John
Richard
```

Each key-value pair in a map is called an entry. An entry is represented by an instance of the Map.Entry<K,V> interface. Map.Entry is an inner static interface of the Map interface. It has three commonly used methods called getKey(), getValue(), and setValue(), which return the key of the entry, the value of the entry, and sets a new value in the entry, respectively. A typical iteration over an entry set of a Map is written as follows:

```
Map<String, String> map = new HashMap<>();
map.put("John", "(342)113-9878");
map.put("Richard", "(245)890-9045");
map.put("Donna", "(205)678-9823");
map.put("Ken", "(205)678-9823");

// Get the entry Set
Set<Map.Entry<String,String>>entries = map.entrySet();

// Print all key-value pairs using the forEach() method of the Collection interace.
// You can use a for-each loop, an iterator, etc. to do the same.
entries.forEach((Map.Entry<String,String> entry) -> {
        String key = entry.getKey();
        String value = entry.getValue();
        System.out.println("key=" + key + ", value=" + value);
});
```

```
key=Donna, value=(205)678-9823
key=Ken, value=(205)678-9823
key=John, value=(342)113-9878
key=Richard, value=(245)890-9045
```

Java 8 added a forEach(BiConsumer<? super K,? super V> action) method to the Map interface that lets you iterate over all entries in the map in a cleaner way. The method takes a BiConsumer instance whose first argument is the key and second argument is the value for the current entry in the map. You can rewrite the above snippet of code as follows:

```
Map<String, String> map = new HashMap<>();
map.put("John", "(342)113-9878");
map.put("Richard", "(245)890-9045");
map.put("Donna", "(205)678-9823");
map.put("Ken", "(205)678-9823");
```

```
// Use the forEach() method of the Map interface
map.forEach((String key, String value) -> {
        System.out.println("key=" + key + ", value=" + value);
});
```

```
key=Donna, value=(205)678-9823
key=Ken, value=(205)678-9823
key=John, value=(342)113-9878
key=Richard, value=(245)890-9045
```

Listing 12-30 demonstrates how to get three different views of a Map and iterate over the elements in those views.

Listing 12-30. Using Keys, Values, and Entries Views of a Map

```java
// MapViews.java
package com.jdojo.collections;

import java.util.HashMap;
import java.util.Map;
import java.util.Set;
import java.util.Collection;

public class MapViews {
        public static void main(String[] args) {
                Map<String, String> map = new HashMap<>();
                map.put("John", "(342)113-9878");
                map.put("Richard", "(245)890-9045");
                map.put("Donna", "(205)678-9823");
                map.put("Ken", "(205)678-9823");

                System.out.println("Map: " + map.toString());

                // Print keys, values, and entries in the map
                listKeys(map);
                listValues(map);
                listEntries(map);
        }

        public static void listKeys(Map<String,String> map) {
                System.out.println("Key Set:");
                Set<String> keys = map.keySet();
                keys.forEach(System.out::println);
                System.out.println();
        }

        public static void listValues(Map<String,String> map) {
                System.out.println("Values Collection:");
                Collection<String> values = map.values();
                values.forEach(System.out::println);
                System.out.println();
        }
```

```
        public static void listEntries(Map<String,String> map) {
                System.out.println("Entry Set:");

                // Get the entry Set
                Set<Map.Entry<String, String>>entries = map.entrySet();
                entries.forEach((Map.Entry<String, String> entry) -> {
                        String key = entry.getKey();
                        String value = entry.getValue();
                        System.out.println("key=" + key + ", value=" + value);
                });
        }
}
```

```
Map: {Donna=(205)678-9823, Ken=(205)678-9823, John=(342)113-9878, Richard=(245)890-9045}
Key Set:
Donna
Ken
John
Richard

Values Collection:
(205)678-9823
(205)678-9823
(342)113-9878
(245)890-9045

Entry Set:
key=Donna, value=(205)678-9823
key=Ken, value=(205)678-9823
key=John, value=(342)113-9878
key=Richard, value=(245)890-9045
```

Sorted Maps

A sorted map stores entries in a map in an ordered way. It sorts the map entries on keys based on either natural sort order or a custom sort order. The natural sort order is defined by the Comparable interface of the keys. If the keys do not implement the Comparable interface, you must use a Comparator object to sort the entries. If the keys implement the Comparable interface and you use a Comparator object, the Comparator object will be used to sort the keys.

An instance of the SortedMap interface represented a sorted map. The SortedMap interface inherits from the Map interface. A SortedMap is to a Map what a SortedSet is to a Set.

The SortedMap interface contains methods that let you take advantage of the sorted keys in the map. It has methods that let you get the first and the last key or a submap based on a criteria, etc. Those methods are as follows:

- Comparator<? super K> comparator(): It returns the Comparator object used for custom sorting of the keys in the SortedMap. If you have not used a Comparator object, it returns null and natural ordering will be used based on the implementation of the Comparable interface for the keys.

- K firstKey(): It returns the key of the first entry in the SortedMap. If the SortedMap is empty, it throws a NoSuchElementException.

- SortedMap<K, V> headMap(K toKey): It returns a view of the SortedMap whose entries will have keys less than the specified toKey. If you add a new entry to the view, its key must be less than the specified toKey. Otherwise, it will throw an exception. The view is backed by the original SortedMap.

- K lastKey(): It returns the key of the last entry in the SortedMap. If the SortedMap is empty, it throws a NoSuchElementException.

- SortedMap<K, V> subMap(K fromKey, K toKey): It returns a view of the SortedMap whose entries will have keys ranging from the specified fromKey (inclusive) and toKey (exclusive). The original SortedMap backs the partial view of the SortedMap. Any changes made to either map will be reflected in both. You can put new entries in the sub map whose keys must fall in the range fromKey (inclusive) and toKey (Exclusive).

- SortedMap<K, V> tailMap(K fromKey): It returns a view of the SortedMap whose entries will have keys equal to or greater than the specified fromKey. If you add a new entry to the view, its key must be equal to or greater than the specified fromKey. Otherwise, it will throw an exception. The original SortedMap backs the tail view.

The TreeMap class is the implementation class for the SortedMap interface. For basic operations, you work with a SortedMap the same way as you work with a Map. Listing 12-31 demonstrates how to use a SortedMap.

Listing 12-31. Using a SortedMap

```
// SortedMapTest.java
package com.jdojo.collections;

import java.util.SortedMap;
import java.util.TreeMap;

public class SortedMapTest {
    public static void main(String[] args) {
        SortedMap<String,String> sMap = new TreeMap<>();
        sMap.put("John", "(342)113-9878");
        sMap.put("Richard", "(245)890-9045");
        sMap.put("Donna","(205)678-9823");
        sMap.put("Ken", "(205)678-9823");

        System.out.println("Sorted Map: " + sMap);

        // Get a sub map from Donna (inclusive) to Ken(exclusive)
        SortedMap<String,String> subMap = sMap.subMap("Donna", "Ken");
        System.out.println("Sorted Submap from Donna to Ken(exclusive): " + subMap);

        // Get the first and last keys
        String firstKey = sMap.firstKey();
        String lastKey = sMap.lastKey();
        System.out.println("First Key: " + firstKey);
        System.out.println("Last key: " + lastKey);
    }
}
```

```
Sorted Map: {Donna=(205)678-9823, John=(342)113-9878, Ken=(205)678-9823, Richard=(245)890-9045}
Sorted Submap from Donna to Ken(exclusive): {Donna=(205)678-9823, John=(342)113-9878}
First Key: Donna
Last key: Richard
```

If you want to use a `Comparator` object to sort the entries based keys in a `SortedMap`, you need use the constructor of the `TreeMap` class that takes a `Comparator` as an argument. The following snippet of code shows how to sort entries in a sorted map based on the length of their keys followed by the alphabetical order of the keys ignoring the case:

```java
// Sort entries on key's length and then on keys ignoring case
Comparator<String> keyComparator =
        Comparator.comparing(String::length)
                  .thenComparing(String::compareToIgnoreCase);
SortedMap<String, String> sMap = new TreeMap<>(keyComparator);
sMap.put("John", "(342)113-9878");
sMap.put("Richard", "(245)890-9045");
sMap.put("Donna", "(205)678-9823");
sMap.put("Ken", "(205)678-9823");
sMap.put("Zee", "(205)679-9823");

System.out.println("Sorted Map: " + sMap);
```

```
Sorted Map: {Ken=(205)678-9823, Zee=(205)679-9823, John=(342)113-9878, Donna=(205)678-9823,
Richard=(245)890-9045}
```

Please refer to the "Sorted Set" section for more details on using a `Comparator` object for sorting keys. A `Comparator` object in a `SortedMap` works the same way for keys as it works for the elements in a `SortedSet`.

Navigable Maps

A navigable map is represented by an instance of the `NavigableMap` interface. It extends the `SortedMap` interface by adding some useful features like getting the closest match for a key, getting a view of the map in reverse order, etc. It also adds some methods that are similar to methods added by `SortedMap`, but they return an entry (a `Map.Entry` object) rather than just the key.

The `TreeMap` class is the implementation class for the `NavigableMap` interface.

Please replace Xxx with `Entry` or `Key` in methods names of the `NavigableMap` interface mentioned in this paragraph. The `lowerXxx(K key)` method returns the greatest entry or key that is lower than the specified key. The `floorXxx(K key)` method returns the greatest entry or key that is equal to or lower than the specified key. The `higherXxx(K key)` method returns the least entry or key that is higher than the specified key. The `ceilingXxx(K key)` method returns the least entry of key that is equal to or higher than the specified key.

The `NavigableMap` contains two methods called `firstEntry()` and `lastEntry()` that return the first and the last entries as `Map.Entry` objects; they return `null` if the map is empty. It contains methods to retrieve and remove the first and the last entries from the map using `pollFirstEntry()` and `pollLastEntry()` methods. It adds other versions of the `headMap()`, `tailMap()`, and `subMap()` methods declared in `SortedMap`, which accept a boolean flag to indicate if you want to include the extreme values in the submap returned from these methods. Finally, it adds `descendingKeySet()` and `descendingMap()` methods that give you a view of keys and the map itself in the reverse order. Listing 12-32 shows how to use a `NavigableMap`.

Listing 12-32. Using a NavigableMap

```java
// NavigableMapTest.java
package com.jdojo.collections;

import java.util.TreeMap;
import java.util.NavigableMap;
import java.util.Map.Entry;

public class NavigableMapTest {
        public static void main(String[] args) {
                // Create a sorted map sorted on string keys alphabetically
                NavigableMap<String,String> nMap = new TreeMap<>();
                nMap.put("John", "(342)113-9878");
                nMap.put("Richard", "(245)890-9045");
                nMap.put("Donna", "(205)678-9823");
                nMap.put("Ken", "(205)678-9823");

                System.out.println("Navigable Map:" + nMap);

                // Get the closest lower and higher matches for Ken
                Entry<String,String> lowerKen = nMap.lowerEntry("Ken");
                Entry<String,String> floorKen = nMap.floorEntry("Ken");
                Entry<String,String> higherKen = nMap.higherEntry("Ken");
                Entry<String,String> ceilingKen = nMap.ceilingEntry("Ken");

                System.out.println("Lower Ken: " + lowerKen);
                System.out.println("Floor Ken: " + floorKen);
                System.out.println("Higher Ken: " + higherKen);
                System.out.println("Ceiling Ken: " + ceilingKen);

                // Get the reverse order view of the map
                NavigableMap<String,String> reverseMap = nMap.descendingMap();
                System.out.println("Navigable Map(Reverse Order):" + reverseMap);
        }
}
```

```
Navigable Map:{Donna=(205)678-9823, John=(342)113-9878, Ken=(205)678-9823, Richard=(245)890-9045}
Lower Ken: John=(342)113-9878
Floor Ken: Ken=(205)678-9823
Higher Ken: Richard=(245)890-9045
Ceiling Ken: Ken=(205)678-9823
Navigable Map(Reverse Order):{Richard=(245)890-9045, Ken=(205)678-9823, John=(342)113-9878,
Donna=(205)678-9823}
```

Concurrent Maps

Sometimes you need to perform multiple operations on a map atomically when the map is used by multiple threads concurrently. For example, you may want to put a new key-value pair in a map only if the key does not already exist in the map. Your code may look as follows:

```
Map<String,String> map = ...;
String key = ...;
String value = ...;

// Need to lock the entire map
synchronized(map) {
        if (map.containsKey(key)) {
                // Key is already in the map
        }
        else {
                map.put(key, value); // Add the new key-value
        }
}
```

In this code, you had to lock the entire map just to put a new key-value pair if the key was absent in the map. Locking the map was necessary because you needed to perform two things atomically: testing for a key existence and putting the key-value if the test fails. When these two operations are being performed on the map by a thread, no other thread can lock the map for any other operations. A ConcurrentMap enables you to perform concurrent operations, like the one I discussed, without resorting to locking the map.

You can choose the level of concurrency when you create a concurrent map using its implementation class. The level of concurrency is specified as the estimated number of threads that would perform the write operations on the map. The map will try to adjust those many threads concurrently. A ConcurrentMap does not lock the entire map. Even if it locks the entire map, other threads will still be able to perform read and write operations on it because it uses fine-grained synchronization mechanism based on a *compare-and-set* primitive.

The ConcurrentHashMap class is an implementation class for the ConcurrentMap interface. Both of them are in the java.util.concurrent package.

Listing 12-33 demonstrates the use of a ConcurrentMap. The example simply shows how to create and use some of the methods of a ConcurrentMap. Typically, you should use a ConcurrentMap in a multi-threaded environment. The program does not use multiple threads to access the map. It only demonstrates use of some of the methods of the ConcurrentMap interface.

Listing 12-33. Using a ConcurrentMap

```
// ConcurrentMapTest.java
package com.jdojo.collections;

import java.util.concurrent.ConcurrentHashMap;
import java.util.concurrent.ConcurrentMap;

public class ConcurrentMapTest {
        public static void main(String[] args) {
                ConcurrentMap<String,String> cMap = new ConcurrentHashMap<>();
                cMap.put("one", "one");

                System.out.println("Concurrent Map: " + cMap);
```

```
                System.out.println(cMap.putIfAbsent("one", "nine"));
                System.out.println(cMap.putIfAbsent("two", "two"));
                System.out.println(cMap.remove("one", "two"));
                System.out.println(cMap.replace("one", "two"));

                System.out.println("Concurrent Map: " + cMap);
        }
}
```

```
Concurrent Map: {one=one}
one
null
false
one
Concurrent Map: {one=two, two=two}
```

Concurrent and Navigable Maps

A concurrent navigable map is the concurrent and navigable version of the map. An instance of the ConcurrentNavigableMap interface represents a concurrent and navigable map. The interface inherits from the ConcurrentMap and NavigableMap interfaces.

The ConcurrentSkipListMap is the implementation class for the ConcurrentNavigableMap interface.

I have discussed both the concurrent map and navigable map. Please refer to the examples of both kinds for using the ConcurrentNavigableMap.

Applying Algorithms to Collections

The Collections Framework lets you apply many types of algorithms on all or a few elements of a collection. It lets you search through a collection for a value; sort and shuffle elements of a collection; get a read-only view of a collection; etc. The good news is that all of these features are provided in one class named Collections. Notice that we have a similarly named interfaced called Collection, which is the ancestor of most of the collection interfaces defined in the Collections Framework. The Collections class consists of all static methods. If you want to apply any algorithm to a collection, you need to look at the list of methods in this class before you writing your own code.

Sorting a List

You can use one of the following two static methods in the Collections class to sort the elements of a List:

- `<T extends Comparable<? super T>> void sort(List<T> list)`: It sorts the elements in a List in the *natural order* defined by the Comparable interface that is implemented by the elements in the List. Each element in the List must implement the Comparable interface and they must be comparable to each other.

- `<T> void sort(List<T> list, Comparator<? super T> c)`: It lets you pass a Comparator object to define a custom ordering of the elements.

■ **Tip** Java 8 added a default method called sort(Comparator<? super E> c) in the List<E> interface that allows you to sort a List without using the Collections class.

The following snippet of code demonstrates how to sort a List:

```
import java.util.ArrayList;
import java.util.Collections;
import java.util.List;
...
List<String> list = new ArrayList<>();
list.add("John");
list.add("Richard");
list.add("Donna");
list.add("Ken");

System.out.println("List: " + list);

// Uses Comparable implementation in String to sort the list in natural order
Collections.sort(list);
System.out.println("Sorted List: " + list);
```

```
List: [John, Richard, Donna, Ken]
Sorted List: [Donna, John, Ken, Richard]
```

The following snippet of code sorts the same list in ascending order of the length of their elements using the sort() method in the List interface:

```
import java.util.ArrayList;
import java.util.Comparator;
import java.util.List;
...
List<String> list = new ArrayList<>();
list.add("John");
list.add("Richard");
list.add("Donna");
list.add("Ken");

System.out.println("List: " + list);

// Uses List.sort() method with a Comparator
list.sort(Comparator.comparing(String::length));

System.out.println("Sorted List: " + list);
```

```
List: [John, Richard, Donna, Ken]
Sorted List: [Ken, John, Donna, Richard]
```

The sort() method uses a modified *mergesort* algorithm. It is a stable sort. That is, equal elements will stay at their current positions after the sort operation. Internally, all elements are copied to an array, sorted in the array, and copied back to the List. Sorting is guaranteed to give n*log(n) performance, where n is the number of elements in the List.

Searching a List

You can use one of the following two static binarySearch() method in the Collections class to search for a key in a List.

- `<T> int binarySearch(List<? extends Comparable<? super T>>list, T key)`
- `<T> int binarySearch(List<? extends T> list, T key, Comparator<? super T> c)`

A List must be sorted in ascending order using the natural order or the Comparator object before you use the binarySearch() method on the List. If the List is not sorted, the result of the binarySearch() method is not defined. If the key is found in the List, the method returns the index of the key in the List. Otherwise, it returns (-(insertion index) -1), where the insertion index is the index in the List where this key would have been placed, if it were present. This return value makes sure that you will get a negative value only if the key is not found in the List. If you get a negative number as the retuned value from this method, you can use the absolute value of the return index as the basis of the insertion point into the list-((return value) + 1). This method uses the binary search algorithm to perform the search. If the List supports random access, the search runs in log(n) time. If the List does not support random access, the search runs in n×log(n) time. The following snippet of code shows how to use this method:

```
List<String> list = new ArrayList<>();
list.add("John");
list.add("Richard");
list.add("Donna");
list.add("Ken");

// Must sort before performing the binary search
Collections.sort(list);
System.out.println("List: " + list);

// Find Donna
int index = Collections.binarySearch(list, "Donna");
System.out.println("Donna in List is at " + index);

// Find Ellen
index = Collections.binarySearch(list, "Ellen");
System.out.println("Ellen in List is at " + index);
```

```
List: [Donna, John, Ken, Richard]
Donna in List is at 0
Ellen in List is at -2
```

Since "Ellen" is not in the List, the binary search returned -2. It means that if you insert "Ellen" in the List, it will be inserted at index 1, which is computed using the expression (-(-2+1)). Note that "Donna" has an index of 0 and "John" has an index of 1. If "Ellen" is added to the list, its index will be the same as the current index for "John" and "John" will be moved to the right at index 2.

Shuffling, Reversing, Swapping, and Rotating a List

In this section, I will discuss applying different kinds of algorithms to a List such as shuffling , reversing, swapping, and rotating its elements.

Shuffling gives you a random permutation of the elements in a List. The concept of shuffling elements of a List is the same as shuffling a deck of cards. You shuffle the elements of a List by using the Collections.shuffle() static method. You can supply a java.util.Random object or the shuffle() method can use a default randomizer. The two versions of the shuffle() methods are as follows:

- void shuffle(List<?> list)

- void shuffle(List<?> list, Random rnd)

Reversing is the algorithm that puts the elements of a List in the reverse order. You can use the following reverse() static method of the Collections class to accomplish this:

- void reverse(List<?> list)

Swapping lets you swap the position of two elements in a List. You can perform swapping using the swap() static method of the Collections class, which is defined as follows:

- void swap(List<?> list, int i, int j)

Here i and j are indexes of two elements to be swapped and they must be between 0 and size - 1, where size is the size of the List. Otherwise, it throws an IndexOutOfBoundsException.

Rotating involves moving all elements of a List forward or backward by a distance. Suppose you have a List as [a, b, c, d]. You need to visualize that the List is a circular list and its first element is next to its last element. If you rotate this List by a distance of 1, the resulting List becomes [d, a, b, c]. If you rotate the [a, b, c, d] list by a distance of 2, the List becomes [c, d, a, b]. You can also rotate a List backwards by using a negative distance. If you rotate the [a, b, c, d] list by a distance of -2, the List becomes [c, d, a, b]. You can also rotate only part of a List using a sublist view. Suppose list is a reference variable of type List and it has [a, b, c, d] elements. Consider executing the following statement:

```
Collections.rotate(list.subList(1, 4), 1);
```

The statement will change the list to [a, d, b, c]. Note that list.subList(1, 4) returns a view of [b, c, d] elements and the above statement rotates only the three elements that are in the sublist.

The following snippet of code shows how to reorder elements of a List using these methods. You may get a different output when you run the following code because shuffle() uses a random algorithm to shuffle the elements of the List.

```
List<String> list = new ArrayList<>();
list.add("John");
list.add("Richard");
list.add("Donna");
list.add("Ken");

System.out.println("List: " + list);

// Shuffle
Collections.shuffle(list);
System.out.println("After Shuffling: " + list);
```

```
// Reverse the list
Collections.reverse(list);
System.out.println("After Reversing: " + list);

// Swap elements at indexes 1 and 3
Collections.swap(list, 1, 3);
System.out.println("After Swapping (1 and 3): " + list);

// Rotate elements by 2
Collections.rotate(list, 2);
System.out.println("After Rotating by 2: " + list);
```

```
List: [John, Richard, Donna, Ken]
After Shuffling: [Ken, Donna, Richard, John]
After Reversing: [John, Richard, Donna, Ken]
After Swapping (1 and 3): [John, Ken, Donna, Richard]
After Rotating by 2: [Donna, Richard, John, Ken]
```

Creating Different Views of a Collection

You can get a LIFO Queue view of a Deque using the asLifoQueue() static method of the Collections class:

- <T> Queue<T> asLifoQueue(Deque<T> deque)

Some Map implementations have corresponding Set implementations too. For example, for HashMap, you have a HashSet; for TreeMap, you have a TreeSet. If you want to use a Map's implementation as a Set implementation, you can use the newSetFromMap() static method of the Collections class:

- <E> Set<E> newSetFromMap(Map<E, Boolean> map)

Note that the idea is to use the implementation of the Map as a Set, not to share elements between a Map and a Set. This is the reason that the Map must be empty when you use it in this method and you are not supposed to use the Map directly at all. There is a WeakHashMap implementation class for the Map. However, there is no corresponding WeakHashSet implementation class for the Set. Here is how you can get a weak hash set implementation:

```
Map map = new WeakHashMap(); // Do not populate and use the map
Set wSet = Collections.newSetFromMap(map); // You can use wSet
```

Use the weak hash set wSet as a Set and it acts as the WeakHashMap implementation. Since you are not supposed to use the Map object, it is better to use the following statement to create the set using the WeakHashMap implementation class:

```
// Do not keep the reference of the Map
Set wSet = Collections.newSetFromMap(new WeakHashMap());
```

When the JVM needs memory, the garbage collector can remove elements from wSet as it does from any WeakHashMap. By using one line of code, you get a Set that has features of a WeakHashMap.

Read-Only Views of Collections

You can get a read-only view (also called unmodifiable view) of a collection. This is useful when you want to pass around your collection to other methods and you do not want the called method to modify your collection. In such cases, you need to pass a read-only view of your collection to those methods.

The Collections class offers the following methods to get read-only views of different types of collections:

- `<T> Collection<T> unmodifiableCollection(Collection<? extends T> c)`

- `<T> List<T> unmodifiableList(List<? extends T> list)`

- `<K,V> Map<K,V> unmodifiableMap(Map<? extends K,? extends V> m)`

- `<K,V> NavigableMap<K,V> unmodifiableNavigableMap(NavigableMap<K,? extends V> m)`

- `<T> Set<T> unmodifiableSet(Set<? extends T> s)`

- `<T> NavigableSet<T> unmodifiableNavigableSet(NavigableSet<T> s)`

- `static <T> SortedSet<T> unmodifiableSortedSet(SortedSet<T> s)`

- `<K,V> SortedMap<K,V> unmodifiableSortedMap(SortedMap<K,? extends V> m)`

Using any of these methods is straightforward. You pass a collection of a specific type and you get a read-only collection of the same type.

Synchronized View of a Collection

Most collections that are members of the Collections Framework discussed in this chapter are not thread-safe and you should not use them in a multithreaded environment. Note that the collections whose names have the word "concurrent" in them are designed to be thread-safe. You can get a synchronized view of a collection using one of the following static methods of the Collections class. You have one method for each collection type to return the same type of synchronized version of the collection. The methods are

- `<T> Collection<T> synchronizedCollection(Collection<T> c)`

- `<T> List<T> synchronizedList(List<T> list)`

- `<K,V> Map<K,V> synchronizedMap(Map<K,V> m)`

- `<K,V> NavigableMap<K,V> synchronizedNavigableMap(NavigableMap<K,V> m)`

- `<T> NavigableSet<T> synchronizedNavigableSet(NavigableSet<T> s)`

- `<T> Set<T> synchronizedSet(Set<T> s)`

- `<T> SortedSet<T> synchronizedSortedSet(SortedSet<T> s)`

- `<K,V> SortedMap<K,V> synchronizedSortedMap (SortedMap<K,V> m)`

You need to pay attention when working with a synchronized view of a collection. All reads and writes through the synchronized view will be thread-safe, except when you are iterating over elements of the collection using an iterator. You must synchronize the entire collection during the time you get the iterator and use it. The following snippet of code illustrates this concept:

```
// Suppose you have a Set
Set s = ...; // unsynchronized set
```

```
// Get a synchronized view of the Set, s
Set ss = Collections.synchronizedSet(s);

// We need to iterate over elements of ss.
// Must get a lock on ss first (not on s)
synchronized(ss) {
        Iterator iterator = ss.iterator();
        // use iterator while holding the lock
        while (iterator.hasNext()) {
                Object obj = iterator.next();

                // Do something with obj here
        }
}
```

You need to follow the same logic while iterating over the key, value, or entry views of a synchronized Map. That is, you must get a lock on the synchronized view of the Map while iterating over any of its views.

Checked Collections

Generics provide compile-time type-safety for collections. If a compiler determines that collections may have elements violating its type declaration, it issues an unchecked compile-time warning. If you ignore the warning, your code may bypass the generics rules at runtime. Let's consider the following snippet of code:

```
Set<String> s = new HashSet<>();
s.add("Hello");
a.add(new Integer(123)); // A compile-time error
```

You have declared the Set as a Set of String objects. You tried to add an Integer object to the Set. The compiler made sure that you do not succeed in doing this.

Let's bypass the compiler check this time by using the following snippet of code:

```
Set<String> s = new HashSet< >();
s.add("Hello");

Set anythingGoesSet = s;
anythingGoesSet.add(new Integer(123)); // No runtime exception
```

This time, the compiler will issue an unchecked warning for the anythingGoesSet.add(new Integer(123)) statement because it has no way to know that you are adding an incorrect type of object to the Set. The result of the above snippet of code is that you declared a Set of String objects and you were able to add an Integer object to it. You will get a runtime exception when you try to read the Integer object as a String object, and it will be too late to find out which line of code did it!

The Collections class helps you create a checked collection in which you will get a ClassCastException when a piece of code attempts to add an element that violates the rule. This makes debugging the code easier. When you create a checked collection, you mention the class type of the element it must hold. Adding any other type of element will throw a ClassCastException. You can use the following static methods of the Collections class to get a checked collection of a specific type:

- `<E> Collection<E> checkedCollection(Collection<E> c, Class<E> type)`

- `<E> List<E> checkedList(List<E> list, Class<E> type)`

- `<K,V> Map<K,V> checkedMap(Map<K,V> m, Class<K> keyType, Class<V> valueType)`

- `<K,V> NavigableMap<K,V> checkedNavigableMap(NavigableMap<K,V> m, Class<K> keyType, Class<V> valueType)`

- `<E> NavigableSet<E> checkedNavigableSet(NavigableSet<E> s, Class<E> type)`

- `<E> Queue<E> checkedQueue(Queue<E> queue, Class<E> type)`

- `<E> Set<E> checkedSet(Set<E> s, Class<E> type)`

- `<K,V> SortedMap<K,V> checkedSortedMap(SortedMap<K,V> m, Class<K> keyType, Class<V> valueType)`

- `<E> SortedSet<E> checkedSortedSet(SortedSet<E> s, Class<E> type)`

Here is the solution of the previous example that will throw a ClassCastException when an attempt is made to add an Integer to the Set of String:

```
// Work with a checked Set of String type
Set<String> checkedSet = Collections.checkedSet(new HashSet<String>(), String.class);

Set anythingGoesSet = checkedSet;
anythingGoesSet.add(new Integer(123)); // Throws ClassCastException
```

■ **Tip**   Using a checked collection does not stop you from bypassing the compiler. Rather, it helps you identify the offending code easily and exactly at runtime.

Creating Empty Collections

Sometimes you need to call a method that accepts a collection. However, you do not have any elements for the collection to pass. In such cases, you do not need to go through the hassle of creating a collection object. The Collections class provides an immutable empty collection object of each type as a return value of its static methods. It also provides methods that return an empty Iterator. The following is a list of such static methods in the Collections class:

- `<T> List<T> emptyList()`

- `<K,V> Map<K,V> emptyMap()`

- `<T> Set<T> emptySet()`

- `<T> Iterator<T> emptyIterator()`

- `<T> ListIterator<T> emptyListIterator()`

Using these methods is straightforward. Suppose there is a method called m1(Map<String,String> map). If you want to pass an empty map to this method, your call would be m1(Collections.emptyMap()).

Creating Singleton Collections

Sometimes you want to create a collection that needs to have one and only one element in it. This kind of situation arises when a method accepts a collection as its argument and you have only one object to pass to that method. Instead of going through the hassle of creating a new collection and adding a lone element to it, you can use one of the three static methods of the Collections class, which will create an *immutable* collection with the one specified element. Those methods are as follows:

- `<T> Set<T> singleton(T o)`
- `<T> List<T> singletonList(T o)`
- `<K,V> Map<K,V> singletonMap(K key, V value)`

Depending on the collection type that you need, you need to pass one or two objects. For a Set and a List, you need to pass one object, whereas for a Map you need to pass two objects (one for the key and one for the corresponding value). The following snippet of code creates a singleton set:

```
Set<String> singletonSet = Collections.singleton("Lonely");

// Throws a runtime exception as a singleton set is immutable
singletonSet.add("Hello");
```

Understanding Hash-based Collections

You have used many implementation classes for collections that have the word "hash" in their names, such as HashSet, LinkedHashSet, HashMap, etc. They are known as hash-based collections. They facilitate fast and efficient storage and retrieval of objects. This section discusses the internal workings of hash-based collections in brief.

Let's start with a daily life example. Assume that you have been given many pieces of paper. Each piece of paper has a number written on it. Your task is to organize (or store) those pieces of paper so that you can tell us as quickly as possible whether a specific number exists in the collection of pieces of paper that you were given. You may be given more pieces of paper with a number on them in the future.

One way to organize all your numbers is to place them all in one bucket, as shown in Figure 12-5.

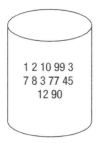

1 2 10 99 3
7 8 3 77 45
12 90

Figure 12-5. *Placing all numbers in one bucket*

When you are asked to verify the existence of number 89, you will have to look at all of the numbers in your bucket, one at a time, and finally you will say that number 89 does not exist in the collection. In the worst-case scenario, you will have to search the entire bucket to tell if a specific number exists in the bucket. In the best-case scenario, you may find the number on the very first attempt. The average time that it takes you to verify the existence of a number is proportional to the size of the collection. You may realize that organizing your number in one bucket is not very efficient for retrieval. As the numbers increase, you will take more time to search through them for a specific number.

Let's try to find a more efficient way to organize the numbers. Let's use more buckets, say 4, to store them. Any number that is given to you will be stored in one of the four buckets. If you place a number in one of the four buckets arbitrarily, it poses the same problem in searching. In the worst-case scenario, you will have to search all four buckets for a number because you do not know which bucket contains a specific number. To avoid this inefficiency, let's use an algorithm to place a specific number into a bucket.

To keep the algorithm simple, you will compute the modulus of the number by the number of buckets (four in your case) and place the number in the bucket that corresponds to the modulus value. If you compute a modulus of a number using 4, the value will be 0, 1, 2, or 3. You will name your four buckets as bucket-0, bucket-1, bucket-2, and bucket-3. Which bucket will hold the number 17? The result of 17 modulus 4 is 1. Therefore, the number 17 will go to the bucket-1. Where will number 31 go? The result of 31 modulus 4 is 3. Therefore, the number 31 will go to the bucket-3. Figure 12-6 shows an arrangement in which you have used four buckets to store some numbers based on this algorithm.

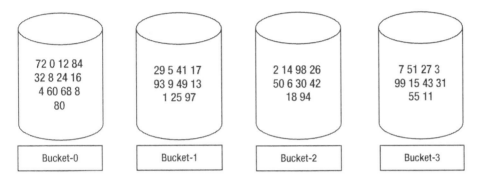

Figure 12-6. *Using four buckets to hold numbers*

Let's walk through the steps to store a number in one of your four buckets. Suppose you are handed the number 94. Which one of the four buckets will store the number 94? First, you evaluate the result of 94 modulus 4, which is 2. Therefore, the number 94 will be stored in the bucket-2. You will follow this logic to decide the bucket for every number that you need to store.

Now, let's walk through the steps of verifying if a number exists in one of the buckets. Suppose you are asked to verify if the number 67 exists in the collection. First, you compute the result of 67 modulus 4, which is 3. According to the logic of storing a number, if the number 67 exists in the collection, it must exist in bucket-3. Once you know the bucket number, you look at each number in the bucket (bucket-3 in this case) for that number. In this case (see Figure 12-6), there are ten numbers in bucket-3 and none of them is 67. After looking at ten numbers in bucket-3, you respond that the number 67 does not exist in the collection. Note that you looked at numbers in only one of the buckets to tell whether the number 67 existed in the collection or not. You did not have to look at numbers in all four buckets. By using an algorithm to store and retrieve a number from the collection, you have shortened the time it takes to search for a number in the collection.

The story is not over yet. Let's consider using four buckets to store numbers where all numbers are a multiple of 4 such as 4, 8, 12, 16, 20, 24, etc. The value of N modulus 4 for all N, which are multiple of 4 is 0. This means that all such numbers will be stored in only one bucket, which is the bucket-0. Is this scenario better than storing all numbers in only one bucket? The answer is no. Using multiple buckets helps in the search process only if the numbers that are stored are uniformly distributed among all buckets. The best-case scenario is when all buckets have only one number in them. In that case, you will be able to tell if a number exists in the collection by just looking at one number in one of the buckets. The search performance may degrade as the size of the collection increases even if numbers are distributed uniformly among the buckets. For example, suppose you have 100 numbers and they are uniformly distributed among four buckets. In the worst-case scenario, you need to search through 25 numbers in a bucket. Suppose the numbers increase to 10,000 and they are still uniformly distributed among the four buckets. Now, in the worst-case scenario, you need to search through 2,500 numbers. To keep your search process fast, you can increase the number of buckets as the numbers in one bucket increases to a point where the time taken to search for a number becomes a performance concern.

The hash-based collections in Java work similar to the collection of numbers that I discussed. Note that a Java collection stores only objects. They do not allow storing of primitive type values. Two methods in the Object class are central to the working of hash-based collections. Those methods are equals() and hashCode().

Hash-based collections maintain a number of buckets to store objects. When you add an object to a hash-based collection, Java gets the hash code value of the object by calling object's hashCode() method. Then, it applies an algorithm to the hash code value to compute the bucket in which the object should be placed. When you want to check if an object exists in a hash-based collection, Java applies the same logic to compute the bucket in which the object might have been placed. It calls the hashCode() method of the object and applies some algorithm to compute the bucket in which it might have been placed. Then, it uses the equals() method of the object to compare the object with existing objects in the bucket to check if the object exists in that bucket.

The internal workings of the hash-based collections in Java sound easy. However, it is full of complications for programmers if the hashCode() and equals() methods are not implemented correctly in the class whose objects are stored in hash-based collections. Let's consider the code for a BadKey class, shown in Listing 12-34.

Listing 12-34. A BadKey Class That Is Not a Good Candidate for Keys in Hash-based Collections

```java
// BadKey.java
package com.jdojo.collections;

public class BadKey {
        private int id;

        public BadKey(int id) {
                this.id = id;
        }

        public int getId() {
                return this.id;
        }

        public void setId(int id) {
                this.id = id;
        }

        @Override
        public int hashCode() {
                // Return the value of id as its hash code value
                return id;
        }

        @Override
        public boolean equals(Object obj) {
                if (obj == this) {
                        return true;
                }
```

```
        if (obj instanceof BadKey) {
                BadKey bk = (BadKey) obj;
                if (bk.getId() == this.id) {
                        return true;
                }
        }

        return false;
    }

    @Override
    public String toString() {
            return String.valueOf(this.id);
    }
}
```

The BadKey class stores an integer value. It is a mutable class. You can modify its state by calling the setId() method and supplying a new value for its id. It overrides the equals() and hashCode() methods of the Object class. The implementation of the hashCode() method is simple. It returns the value of the id instance variable as the hash code value. The equals() method checks if the id instance variable's value for two BadKey objects are the same or not. If two BadKey objects have the same id, they are considered equal.

Consider the program in Listing 12-35 that uses BadKey objects in a Set. Can you spot a problem by looking at the program and the output? Don't worry if you do not see the problem. I will explain it.

Listing 12-35. Using BadKey Objects in a Set

```
// BadKeyTest.java
package com.jdojo.collections;

import java.util.HashSet;
import java.util.Set;

public class BadKeyTest {
        public static void main(String[] args) {
                Set<BadKey> s = new HashSet<>();
                BadKey bk1 = new BadKey(100);
                BadKey bk2 = new BadKey(200);

                // Add two objects bk1 and bk2 to the set
                s.add(bk1);
                s.add(bk2);

                System.out.println("Set contains:" + s);
                System.out.println("Set contains bk1: " + s.contains(bk1));

                // Set the id for bk1 to 300
                bk1.setId(300);
                System.out.println("Set contains:" + s);
                System.out.println("Set contains bk1: " + s.contains(bk1));
        }
}
```

```
Set contains:[100, 200]
Set contains bk1: true
Set contains:[300, 200]
Set contains bk1: false
```

The program adds two BadKey objects called bk1 and bk2 to the Set. The first line in the output confirms that the set contains the two objects. Then, the value for the id of bk1 object is changed from 100 to 300, which is confirmed by the third line in the output. Since you have not removed the object bk1 from the set, the fourth line of the output is unexpected. The fourth line of the output states that the object bk1 does not exist in the set, whereas the third line of the output states that bk1 object is in the set.

What's wrong? Is the object bk1 in the set or not? The answer is that the object bk1 is in the set until you remove it. If you use a for-each loop or an iterator to access all objects in the set, you will be able to get to it. However, the collection (the set in this case) will not be able to find the object bk1. The reason why the set is not able to find the bk1 object is that the hash code value of the object bk1 changed after it was added to the set. Recall that HashSet is a hash-based collection in Java. It uses the hash code of the object to locate the bucket in which the object will be placed. When s.contains(bk1) is executed the second time, the hash code value of bk1 will be 300, which is the returned value from its hashCode() method. When the object bk1 was placed in the set, its hash code was 200. Since the hash code of the object bk1 has changed, the set will mistakenly identify a different bucket to locate it. Since the set is looking for the object bk1 in a different bucket than the one in which it was placed, it does not find it. Where is the problem? The problem lies in the hashCode() method of the BadKey class. The BadKey class is a mutable class and the mutable state of this class (the id instance variable) has been used to compute its hash code, which is causing the problem in locating the object in the set.

One way to fix this problem of apparently losing the BadKey objects in the set is to return a constant value from its hashCode() method, say 99. The following is a valid implementation (not a good one, though) of the hashCode() method of the BadKey class:

```java
// BadKey.java
package com.jdojo.collections;

public class BadKey {

        // Other code goes here...

        public int hashCode() {
                // Return the same value 99 all the time
                return 99;
        }
}
```

The above code will fix the problem of losing the object bk1 in the example shown in Listing 12-36 because hash code value for an object of the BadKey class never changes. However, it introduces another issue that is related to the performance of the hash-based collection. If you store objects of the BadKey class in a hash-based collection, say a set, all objects will hash to the same bucket because all objects of the BadKey class will have the same hash code value, which is 99. You fixed one problem and introduced another!

The main issue with the BadKey class is its mutability. It has only one instance variable id that is mutable. You should consider the following guidelines when you work with mutable objects with hash-based collection:

- You should avoid using objects of a mutable class as elements in a Set and as keys in a Map, if possible. Consider using objects of immutable classes such String, Integer, or your own immutable class as keys for a Map and elements for a Set.

- Implement the equals() and hashCode() methods of your mutable class very carefully. You must return the same value from the hashCode() method of the object of the mutable class. Otherwise, you will lose track of the objects of your mutable class in hash-based collections. If a mutable class has some part of its state that is immutable, use those immutable parts of the class to compute its hash code value so that the hash code value does not change for an object of the mutable class. As a last resort, which is not recommended, consider returning a constant integer from the hashCode() method of your mutable class.

Make sure that the contracts for the equals() and hashCode() methods are fulfilled.

Summary

A collection is a group of objects. Java provides a Collections Framework containing several interfaces and classes for working with a wide range of collection types such as lists, queues, sets, and maps. The Collections Framework provides an interface to represent a specific type of collection. Each interface in the framework has at least one implementation class. Collection-related interfaces and classes are in the java.util package. Collection classes to be used in multi-threaded programs where synchronization is needed are in the java.util.concurrent package.

The Collections Framework contains a Collection interface that is the root for most of the collections. The Collection interface contains most of the methods used with all types of collection (except for the Map-based collections). The interface provides methods for adding elements, removing elements, knowing the size of the collection, etc. Specific subinterfaces of the Collection interface provide additional methods to work with the specific type of collections.

The Collections Framework provides a uniform way for traversing elements of all types of collections using iterators. An instance of the Iterator interface represents an iterator. All collections support traversing their elements using the for-each loop and a forEach() method.

In mathematics, a set is a collection of unordered unique elements. An instance of the Set interface represents a set in the Collections Framework. HashSet is the implementation class for the mathematical set.

An instance of the SortedSet represents an ordered unique set. TreeSet is the implementation class for the SortedSet interface. Elements in a sorted set can be sorted in natural order or in a custom order using a Comparator.

A queue is a collection of objects that are used for processing objects one at a time. Objects enter the queue from one end and exit the queue from another end. The Queue interface in the Collections Framework represents a queue. The Collections Framework provides several implementation classes for the Queue interface to support different types of queues, such as a simple queue, blocking queue, priority queue, delay queue, etc.

A list is an ordered collection of objects. An instance of the List interface represents a list in the Collections Framework. ArrayList and LinkedList are two implementation classes for the List interface that are backed up by an array and a linked list, respectively. Each element in the list has an index that starts from 0. The List interface provides methods that let you access its elements sequentially or randomly using indexes of the elements. The Collections Framework supports only a dense list; that is, there cannot be a gap between two elements in the list.

A map is another type of collection that stores key-value pairs. Keys in a map must be unique. An instance of the Map interface represents a map in the Collections Framework. HashMap is the simple implementation class for the Map interface. The Collections Framework also supports sorted, navigable, and concurrent maps. A sorted map stores all key-value pairs sorted based on keys. An instance of the SortedMap interface represents a sorted map. TreeMap is the implementation class for the SortedMap interface. An instance of the NavigableMap and ConcurrentMap represent a navigable map and concurrent map, respectively.

The Collections Framework contains a utility class called Collections that contains only static methods. Methods in this class let you apply different types of algorithms to a collection—for example, shuffling elements in a collection, rotating its elements, sorting elements of a list, etc. The class also provides methods to obtain different views of collections, such as read-only view, synchronized view, unmodifiable view, etc.

A hash-based collection uses buckets to store its elements. The number of buckets is determined based on the number of elements in the collection and the required performance. When an element is added to the collection, the element's hash code is used to determine the bucket in which the element will be stored. A reverse process is used when an element is searched in the collection. Hash-based collections provide faster element storage and retrieval.

CHAPTER 13

■ ■ ■

Streams

In this chapter, you will learn

- What streams are

- Differences between collections and streams

- How to create streams from different types of data sources

- How to represent an optional value using the Optional class

- Applying different types of operations on streams

- Collecting data from streams using collectors

- Grouping and partitioning a stream's data

- Finding and matching data in streams

- How to work with parallel streams

What Is a Stream?

An *aggregate operation* computes a single value from a collection of values. The result of an aggregate operation may be simply a primitive value, an object, or a void. Note that an object may represent a single entity such as a person or a collection of values such as a list, a set, a map, etc.

A *stream* is a sequence of data elements supporting sequential and parallel aggregate operations. Computing the sum of all elements in a stream of integers, mapping all names in list to their lengths, etc. are examples of aggregate operations on streams.

Looking at the definition of streams, it seems that they are like collections. So, how do streams differ from collections? Both are abstractions for a collection of data elements. Collections focus on storage of data elements for efficient access whereas streams focus on aggregate computations on data elements from a data source that is typically, but not necessarily, collections.

In this section, I will discuss the following features of streams, comparing them with collections when necessary:

- Streams have no storage.

- Streams can represent a sequence of infinite elements.

- The design of streams is based on internal iteration.

- Streams are designed to be processed in parallel with no additional work from the developers.

- Streams are designed to support functional programming.

- Streams support lazy operations.

- Streams can be ordered or unordered.

- Streams cannot be reused.

The following sections will present brief snippets of code using streams. The code is meant to give you a feel for the Streams API and to compare the Streams API with the Collections API. You do not need to understand the code fully at this point. I will explain it later in detail.

Streams Have No Storage

A collection is an in-memory data structure that stores all its elements. All elements must exist in memory before they are added to the collection. A stream has no storage; it does not store elements. A stream pulls elements from a data source on-demand and passes them to a pipeline of operations for processing.

Infinite Streams

A collection cannot represent a group of infinite elements whereas a stream can. A collection stores all its elements in memory, and therefore, it is not possible to have an infinite number of elements in a collection. Having a collection of an infinite number of elements will require an infinite amount of memory and the storage process will continue forever. A stream pulls its elements from a data source that can be a collection, a function that generates data, an I/O channel, etc. Because a function can generate an infinite number of elements and a stream can pull data from it on demand, it is possible to have a stream representing a sequence of infinite data elements.

Internal Iteration vs. External Iteration

Collections are based on external iteration. You obtain an iterator for a collection and process elements of the collections in serial using the iterator. Suppose you have a list of integers from 1 to 5. You would compute the sum of squares of all odd integers in the list as follows:

```
List<Integer> numbers = Arrays.asList(1, 2, 3, 4, 5);
int sum = 0;
for (int n : numbers) {
        if (n % 2 == 1) {
                int square = n * n;
                sum = sum + square;
        }
}
```

The code uses a for-each loop that performs an external iteration on the list of integers. Simply put, the client code (the for-loop in this case) pulls the elements out of collection and applies the logic to get the result.

Consider the following code that uses a stream to compute the sum of all odd integers in the same list:

```
int sum = numbers.stream()
                .filter(n -> n % 2 == 1)
                .map(n -> n * n)
                .reduce(0, Integer::sum);
```

Did you notice the power and the simplicity of streams? You have replaced five statements with just one statement. However, the code brevity is not the point that I want to make. The point is that you did not iterate over the elements in the list when you used the stream. The stream did that for you internally. This is what I meant by internal iteration supported by streams. You specify to a stream what you want by passing an algorithm using lambda expressions to the stream and the stream applies your algorithm to its data element by iterating over its elements *internally* and gives you the result.

Using external iteration, typically, produces sequential code; that is, the code can be executed only by one thread. For example, when you wrote the logic to compute the sum using a for-each loop, the loop must be executed only by one thread. All modern computers come with a multicore processor. Wouldn't it be nice to take advantage of the multicore processor to execute the logic in parallel? The Java library provides a Fork/Join framework to divide a task into subtasks recursively and execute the subtasks in parallel, taking advantage of a multicore processor. However, the Fork/Join framework is not so simple to use, especially for beginners.

Streams come to your rescue! They are designed to process their elements in parallel without you even noticing it! This does not mean that streams automatically decide for you when to process their elements in serial or parallel. You just need to tell a stream that you want to use parallel processing and the stream will take care of the rest. Streams take care of the details of using the Fork/Join framework internally. You can compute the sum of squares of odd integers in the list in parallel, like so:

```
int sum = numbers.parallelStream()
                 .filter(n -> n % 2 == 1)
                 .map(n -> n * n)
                 .reduce(0, Integer::sum);
```

All you had to do was replace the method called stream() with parallelStream()! The Streams API will use multiple threads to filter the odd integers, compute their squares, and add them to compute partial sums. Finally, it will join the partial sums to give you the result. In this example, you have only five elements in the list. Using multiple threads to process them is overkill. You will not use parallel processing for such a trivial computation. I have presented this example to drive home the point that parallelizing your computation using streams is free; you get it by just using a different method name! The second point is that parallelizing the computation was made possible because of the internal iteration provided by the stream.

Streams are designed to use internal iteration. They provide an iterator() method that returns an Iterator to be used for external iteration of its elements. You will "never" need to iterate elements of a stream yourself using its iterator. If you ever need it, here is how to use it:

```
// Get a list of integers from 1 to 5
List<Integer> numbers = Arrays.asList(1, 2, 3, 4, 5);
...
// Get an iterator from the stream
Iterator<Integer> iterator = numbers.stream().iterator();
while(iterator.hasNext()) {
        int n = iterator.next();
        ...
}
```

Imperative vs. Functional

Collections support imperative programming whereas streams support declarative programming. This is an offshoot of collections supporting external iteration whereas streams support internal iteration. When you use collections, you need to know "what" you want and "how" to get it; this is the feature of imperative programming. When you use streams, you specify only "what" you want in terms of stream operations; the "how" part is taken care by the Streams API. The Streams API supports the functional programming. Operations on a stream produce a result without modifying the data source. Like in the functional programming, when you use streams, you specify "what" operations you want to perform on its elements using the built-in methods provided by the Streams API, typically by passing a lambda expressions to those methods, customizing the behavior of those operations.

Stream Operations

A stream supports two types of operations:

- Intermediate operations

- Terminal operations

Intermediate operations are also known as *lazy* operations. Terminal operations are also known as *eager* operations. Operations are known as lazy and eager based on the way they pull the data elements from the data source. A lazy operation on a stream does not process the elements of the stream until another eager operation is called on the stream.

Streams connect though a chain of operations forming a stream pipeline. A stream is inherently lazy until you call a terminal operation on it. An intermediate operation on a stream produces another stream. When you call a terminal operation on a stream, the elements are pulled from the data source and pass through the stream pipeline. Each intermediate operation takes elements from an input stream and transforms the elements to produce an output stream. The terminal operation takes inputs from a stream and produces the result.

Figure 3-1 shows a stream pipeline with a data source, three streams, and three operations. The *filter* and *map* operations are intermediate operations and the *reduce* operation is a terminal operation.

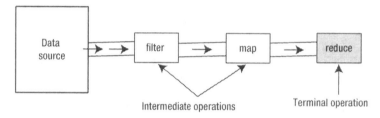

Figure 13-1. *A stream pipeline*

In the figure, the first stream (on the left) pulls data from the data source and becomes the input source for the filter operation. The filter operation produces another stream containing data for which the filter condition is true. The stream produced by the filter operation becomes the input for the map operation. The map operation produces another stream that contains the mapped data. The stream produced by the map operation becomes the input for the reduce operation. The reduce operation is a terminal operation. It computes and returns the result, and then the processing of stream is over.

■ **Tip** I have used the phrase "a stream pulls/consumes elements from its data source" in the preceding discussion. This does not mean that the stream removes the elements from the data source; it only reads them. Streams are designed to support functional programming in which data elements are read and operations on the read data elements produce new data elements. However, the data elements are not modified (or at least should not be modified).

Stream processing does not start until a terminal operation is called. If you just call intermediate operations on a stream, nothing exciting happens, except that they create another stream objects in memory, without reading data from the data source. This implies that you must use a terminal operation on a stream for it to process the data to produce a result. This is also the reason that the terminal operation is called a result-bearing operation and intermediate operations are also called non result-bearing operations.

You have seen the following code that uses a pipeline of stream operations to compute the sum of odd integers from 1 to 5:

```
List<Integer> numbers = Arrays.asList(1, 2, 3, 4, 5);
int sum = numbers.stream()
                .filter(n -> n % 2 == 1)
                .map(n -> n * n)
                .reduce(0, Integer::sum);
```

Figure 3-2 through Figure 3-5 show the states of the stream pipeline as operations are added. Notice that no data flows through the stream until the reduce operation is called. The last figure shows the integers in the input stream for an operation and the mapped (or transformed) integers produced by the operation. The reduce terminal operation produces the result 35.

```
1, 2,
3, 4,
5
```

numbers.stream( )

Figure 13-2. *The stream pipeline after the stream object is created*

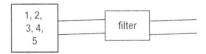

numbers.stream( ).filter(n -> n % 2 == 1)

Figure 13-3. *The stream pipeline after the filter operation is called*

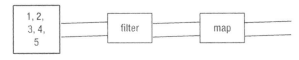

numbers.stream( ).filter(n -> n % 2 == 1). map(n -> n * n)

Figure 13-4. *The stream pipeline after the map operation is called*

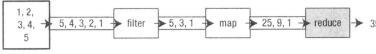

numbers.stream( ).filter(n -> n % 2 == 1).map(n -> n * n).reduce(0, Integer::sum)

Figure 13-5. *The stream pipeline after the reduce operation is called*

Ordered Streams

A stream can be ordered or unordered. An ordered stream preserves the order of its elements. The Streams API lets you convert an ordered stream into an unordered stream. A stream can be ordered because it represents an ordered data source such as a list or a sorted set. You can also convert an unordered stream into an ordered stream by applying an intermediate operation such as sorting.

A data source is said to have an encounter order if the order in which the elements are traversed by an iterator is predictable and meaningful. For example, arrays and lists always have an encounter order that is from the element at index 0 to the element at the last index. All ordered data sources have an encounter order for their elements. Streams based on data sources having an encounter order also have an encounter order for their elements. Sometimes a stream operation may impose an encounter order on an otherwise unordered stream. For example, a HashSet does not have an encounter order for its elements. However, applying a sort operation on a stream based on a HashSet imposes an encounter order so that elements are yielded in sorted order.

Streams Are Not Reusable

Unlike collections, streams are not reusable. They are one-shot objects. A stream cannot be reused after calling a terminal operation on it. If you need to perform a computation on the same elements from the same data source again, you must recreate the stream pipeline. A stream implementation may throw an IllegalStateException if it detects that the stream is being reused.

Architecture of the Streams API

Figure 13-6 shows a class diagram for the stream-related interfaces. Stream-related interfaces and classes are in the java.util.stream package.

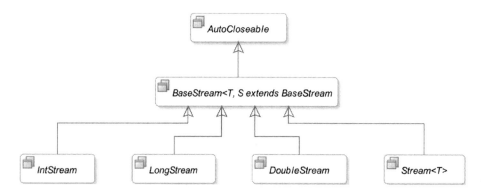

Figure 13-6. *A class diagram for stream-related interfaces in the Streams API*

All stream interfaces inherit from the BaseStream interface, which inherits from the AutoCloseable interface from the java.lang package. In practice, most streams use collections as their data source, and collections do not need to be closed. When a stream is based on a closeable data source such as a file I/O channel, you may create the instance of the stream using a try-with-resources statement to get it closed automatically. Methods common to all types of streams are declared in the BaseStream interface.

- Iterator<T> iterator(): It returns an iterator for the stream. You will almost never need to use this method in your code. This is a terminal operation. After calling this method, you cannot call any other methods on the stream.

- S sequential(): It returns a sequential stream. If the stream is already sequential, it returns itself. Use this method to convert a parallel stream into a sequential stream. This is an intermediate operation.

- S parallel(): It returns a parallel stream. If the stream is already parallel, it returns itself. Use this method to convert a parallel stream into a sequential stream. This is an intermediate operation.

- boolean isParallel(): It returns true if the stream is parallel, false otherwise. The result is unpredictable when this method is called after invoking a terminal stream operation method.

- S unordered(): It returns an unordered version of the stream. If the stream is already unordered, it returns itself. This is an intermediate operation.

The Stream<T> interface represents a stream of the element type T; for example, a Stream<Person> represents a stream of Person objects. The interface contains methods representing intermediate and terminal operations such as filter(), map(), reduce(), collect(), max(), min(), etc. When you work with streams, you will use these methods most of the time. I will discuss each method in detail shortly.

Note that the Stream<T> interface takes a type parameter T, which means that you can use it only to work with the elements of the reference type. If you have to work with a stream of primitive type such as int, long, etc., using Stream<T> will involve an additional cost of boxing and unboxing the elements when primitive values are needed. For example, adding all elements of a String<Integer> will require unboxing all Integer elements to int. The designers of the Streams API realized this and they have provided three specialized stream interfaces called IntStream, LongStream, and DoubleStream to work with primitives; these interfaces contain methods to deal with primitive values. Note that you do not have stream interfaces representing other primitive types such as float, short, etc. because the three stream types can be used to represent other primitive type streams.

A Quick Example

Let's have a quick example of using streams. The code reads a list of integers and computes the sum of the squares of all odd integers in the list.

The stream() method in the Collection interface returns a sequential stream where the Collection acts as the data source. The following snippet of code creates a List<Integer> and obtains a Stream<Integer> from the list:

```
// Get a list of integers from 1 to 5
List<Integer> numbersList = Arrays.asList(1, 2, 3, 4, 5);

// Get the stream from the list
Stream<Integer> numbersStream = numbersList.stream();
```

The filter() method of the Stream<T> interface takes a Predicate<T> as argument and returns a Stream<T> with elements of the original stream for which the specified Predicate returns true. The following statement obtains a stream of only odd integers:

```
// Get a stream of odd integers
Stream<Integer> oddNumbersStream= numbersStream.filter(n -> n % 2 == 1);
```

Notice the use of the lambda expression as the argument for the filter() method. The lambda expression returns true if the element in the stream is not divisible by 2.

The map() method of the Stream<T> interface takes a Function as argument. Each element in the stream is passed to the Function and a new stream is generated containing the returned values from the Function. The following statement takes all odd integers and maps them to their squares:

```
// Get a stream of the squares of odd integers
Stream<Integer> squaredNumbersStream = oddNumbersStream.map(n -> n * n);
```

Finally, you need to add the squares of all odd integers to get the result. The reduce(T identity, BinaryOperator<T> accumulator) method of the Stream interface performs a reduction operation on the stream to reduce the stream to a single value. It takes an initial value and an accumulator that is a BinaryOperator<T> as arguments. The first time, the accumulator receives the initial value and the first element of the stream as arguments, and returns a value. The second time, the accumulator receives the value returned from its previous call and the second

603

element from the stream. This process continues until all elements of the stream have been passed to the accumulator. The returned value from the last call of the accumulator is returned from the reduce() method. The following snippet of code performs the summation of all integers in the stream:

```
// Sum all integers in the stream
int sum = squaredNumbersStream.reduce(0, (n1, n2) -> n1 + n2);
```

The Integer class contains a static sum() method to perform sum of two integers. You can rewrite the code using a method reference, like so:

```
// Sum all integers in the stream
int sum = squaredNumbersStream.reduce(0, Integer::sum);
```

In this example, I have broken down each operation on the stream in a single statement. Note that you cannot use the returned streams from intermediate operations, except to apply other operations on them. Typically, you care about the result of the terminal operation, not the intermediate streams. Streams have been designed to support method chaining to avoid temporary variables, which you used in this example. You can combine these statements into one statement as follows:

```
// Sum all integers in the numbers list
int sum = numbers.stream()
                .filter(n -> n %2 ==1)
                .map(n -> n * n)
                .reduce(0, Integer::sum);
```

I will chain all method calls on streams to form only one statement in subsequent examples. Listing 13-1 contains the complete program for this example. Note that you are working with only integers in this example. For better performance, you could have used an IntStream in this example. I will show you how to use an IntStream later.

Listing 13-1. Computing the Sum of the Squares of All Odd Integers From 1 to 5

```
// SquaredIntsSum.java
package com.jdojo.streams;

import java.util.Arrays;
import java.util.List;

public class SquaredIntsSum {
        public static void main(String[] args) {
                // Get a list of integers from 1 to 5
                List<Integer> numbers = Arrays.asList(1, 2, 3, 4, 5);

                // Compute the sum of the squares of all odd integers in the list
                int sum = numbers.stream()
                                .filter(n -> n % 2 == 1)
                                .map(n -> n * n)
                                .reduce(0, Integer::sum);

                System.out.println("Sum = " + sum);
        }
}
```

```
Sum = 35
```

I will show many examples of performing aggregate operations on different types of streams. Most of the time, it is will be easier to explain the stream operations using streams of numbers and strings. I will show some real world examples of using streams by using a stream of Person objects. Listing 13-2 contains the declaration for the Person class.

Listing 13-2. A Person Class

```java
// Person.java
package com.jdojo.streams;

import java.time.LocalDate;
import java.time.Month;
import java.util.Arrays;
import java.util.List;

public class Person {
        // An enum to represent the gender of a person
        public static enum Gender {MALE, FEMALE}

        private long id;
        private String name;
        private Gender gender;
        private LocalDate dob;
        private double income;

        public Person(long id, String name, Gender gender,
                LocalDate dob, double income) {
                this.id = id;
                this.name = name;
                this.gender = gender;
                this.dob = dob;
                this.income = income;
        }

        public long getId() {
                return id;
        }

        public void setId(long id) {
                this.id = id;
        }

        public String getName() {
                return name;
        }

        public void setName(String name) {
                this.name = name;
        }
```

```java
    public Gender getGender() {
        return gender;
    }

    public boolean isMale() {
        return this.gender == Gender.MALE;
    }

    public boolean isFemale() {
        return this.gender == Gender.FEMALE;
    }

    public void setGender(Gender gender) {
        this.gender = gender;
    }

    public LocalDate getDob() {
        return dob;
    }

    public void setDob(LocalDate dob) {
        this.dob = dob;
    }

    public double getIncome() {
        return income;
    }

    public void setIncome(double income) {
        this.income = income;
    }

    public static List<Person> persons() {
        Person ken = new Person(1, "Ken", Gender.MALE,
                LocalDate.of(1970, Month.MAY, 4), 6000.0);
        Person jeff = new Person(2, "Jeff", Gender.MALE,
                LocalDate.of(1970, Month.JULY, 15), 7100.0);
        Person donna = new Person(3, "Donna", Gender.FEMALE,
                LocalDate.of(1962, Month.JULY, 29), 8700.0);
        Person chris = new Person(4, "Chris", Gender.MALE,
                LocalDate.of(1993, Month.DECEMBER, 16), 1800.0);
        Person laynie = new Person(5, "Laynie", Gender.FEMALE,
                LocalDate.of(2012, Month.DECEMBER, 13), 0.0);
        Person lee = new Person(6, "Li", Gender.MALE,
                LocalDate.of(2001, Month.MAY, 9), 2400.0);

        // Create a list of persons
        List<Person> persons = Arrays.asList(ken, jeff, donna, chris, laynie, lee);

        return persons;
    }
```

```
        @Override
        public String toString() {
                String str = String.format("(%s, %s, %s, %s, %.2f)",
                        id, name, gender, dob, income);
                return str;
        }
}
```

The Person class contains a static Gender enum to represent the gender of a person. The class declares five instance variables (id, name, gender, dob, and income), getters, and setters. The isMale() and isFemale() methods have been declared to be used as method references in lambda expressions. You will use a list of people frequently, and the class contains a static method persons() to get a list of people.

Creating Streams

There are many ways to create streams. Many existing classes in the Java libraries have received new methods that return a stream. Based on the data source, stream creation can be categorized as follows:

- Streams from values
- Empty streams
- Streams from functions
- Streams from arrays
- Streams from collections
- Streams from files
- Streams from other sources

Streams from Values

The Stream interface contains the following two static of() methods to create a sequential Stream from a single value and multiple values:

- <T> Stream<T> of(T t)
- <T> Stream<T> of(T...values)

The following snippet of code creates two streams:

```
// Creates a stream with one string elements
Stream<String> stream = Stream.of("Hello");

// Creates a stream with four strings
Stream<String> stream = Stream.of("Ken", "Jeff", "Chris", "Ellen");
```

You created a List<Integer> and called its stream() method to get a stream object in Listing 13-1. You can rewrite that example using the Stream.of() method as follows:

```
import java.util.stream.Stream;
...
// Compute the sum of the squares of all odd integers in the list
int sum = Stream.of(1, 2, 3, 4, 5)
                .filter(n -> n % 2 == 1)
                .map(n -> n * n)
                .reduce(0, Integer::sum);

System.out.println("Sum = " + sum);
```

```
Sum = 35
```

Note that the second version of the of() method takes a varargs argument and you can use it to create a stream from an array of objects as well. The following snippet of code creates a stream from a String array.

```
String[] names  = {"Ken", "Jeff", "Chris", "Ellen"};

// Creates a stream of four strings in the names array
Stream<String> stream = Stream.of(names);
```

■ **Tip** The Stream.of() method creates a stream whose elements are of reference type. If you want to create a stream of primitive values from an array of primitive type, you need to use the Arrays.stream() method that will be explained shorty.

The following snippet of code creates a stream of strings from a String array returned from the split() method of the String class:

```
String str  = "Ken,Jeff,Chris,Ellen";

// The stream will contain fur elements: "Ken", "Jeff", "Chris", and "Ellen"
Stream<String> stream = Stream.of(str.split(","));
```

The Stream interface also supports creating a stream using the builder pattern using the Stream.Builder<T> interface whose instance represents a stream builder. The builder() static method of the Stream interface returns a stream builder.

```
// Gets a stream builder
Stream.Builder<String> builder = Stream.builder();
```

The Stream.Builder<T> interface contains the following methods:

- void accept(T t)
- Stream.Builder<T> add(T t)
- Stream<T> build()

The accept() and add() methods add elements to the stream being built. You might wonder about the existence of two methods in the builder to add elements. The Stream.Builder<T> interface inherits from the Consumer<T> interface, and therefore it inherits the accept() method from the Consumer<T> interface. You can pass a builder's instance to a method that accepts a consumer and the method can add elements to the builder using the accept method.

The add() method returns the reference to the builder that makes it suitable for adding multiple elements using method chaining. Once you are done adding elements, call the build() method to create the stream. You cannot add elements to the stream after you call the build() method; doing so results in an IllegalStateException runtime exception. The following snippet of code uses the builder pattern to create a stream of four strings:

```
Stream<String> stream = Stream.<String>builder()
                          .add("Ken")
                          .add("Jeff")
                          .add("Chris")
                          .add("Ellen")
                          .build();
```

Note that the code specifies the type parameter as String when it obtains the builder Stream.**<String>**builder(). The compiler fails to infer the type parameter if you do not specify it. If you obtain the builder separately, the compiler will infer the type as String, as shown:

```
// Obtain a builder
Stream.Builder<String> builder = Stream.builder();

// Add elements and build the stream
Stream<String> stream = builder.add("Ken")
                          .add("Jeff")
                          .add("Chris")
                          .add("Ellen")
                          .build();
```

The IntStream interfaces contain two static methods:

- IntStream range(int start, int end)

- IntStream rangeClosed(int start, int end).

They produce an IntStream that contains ordered integers between the specified start and end. The specified end is exclusive in the range() method whereas it is inclusive in the rangeClosed() method. The following snippet of code uses both methods to create an IntStream having integers 1, 2, 3, 4, and 5 as their elements:

```
// Create an IntStream containing 1, 2, 3, 4, and 5
IntStream oneToFive = IntStream.range(1, 6);

// Create an IntStream containing 1, 2, 3, 4, and 5
IntStream oneToFive = IntStream.rangeClosed(1, 5);
```

Like the IntStream interface, the LongStream class also contains range() 0and rangeClosed() methods that takes arguments of type long and return a LongStream.

Empty Streams

An empty stream is a stream with no elements. The Stream interface contains an empty() static method to create an empty sequential stream.

```
// Creates an empty stream of strings
Stream<String> stream = Stream.empty();
```

The IntStream, LongStream, and DoubleStream interfaces also contain an empty() static method to create an empty stream of primitive types.

```
// Creates an empty stream of integers
IntStream numbers = IntStream.empty();
```

Streams from Functions

An infinite stream is a stream with a data source *capable* of generating infinite number of elements. Note that I am saying that the data source should be "capable of generating" infinite number of elements, rather the data source should have or contain an infinite number of elements. It is impossible to generate and store an infinite number of elements of any kind because of memory and time constraints. However, it is possible to have a function that can generate infinite number of values on demand.

The Stream interface contains the following two static methods to generate an infinite stream:

- `<T> Stream<T> iterate(T seed, UnaryOperator<T> f)`

- `<T> Stream<T> generate(Supplier<T> s)`

The iterator() method creates a sequential ordered stream whereas the generate() method creates a sequential unordered stream. The following sections will show you how to use these methods.

The stream interfaces for primitive values IntStream, LongStream, and DoubleStream also contain iterate() and generate() static methods that take parameters specific to their primitive types. For example, these methods are defined as follows in the IntStream interface:

- `IntStream iterate(int seed, IntUnaryOperator f)`

- `IntStream generate(IntSupplier s)`

Using the Stream.iterate() Method

The iterator() method takes two arguments: a seed and a function. The first argument is a seed that is the first element of the stream. The second element is generated by applying the function to the first element. The third element is generated by applying the function on the second element and so on. Its elements are seed, f(seed), f(f(seed)), f(f(f(seed))), and so on. The following statement creates an infinite stream of natural numbers and an infinite stream of all odd natural numbers:

```
// Creates a stream of natural numbers
Stream<Long> naturalNumbers = Stream.iterate(1L, n -> n + 1);

// Creates a stream of odd natural numbers
Stream<Long> oddNaturalNumbers = Stream.iterate(1L, n -> n + 2);
```

What do you do with an infinite stream? You understand that it is not possible to consume all elements of an infinite stream. This is simply because the stream processing will take forever to complete. Typically, you convert the infinite stream into a fixed-size stream by applying a limit operation that truncates the input stream to be no longer than a specified size. The limit operation is an intermediate operation that produces another stream. You apply the limit operation using the limit(long maxSize) method of the Stream interface. The following snippet of code creates a stream of the first 10 natural numbers:

```
// Creates a stream of the first 10 natural numbers
Stream<Long> tenNaturalNumbers = Stream.iterate(1L, n -> n + 1)
                                       .limit(10);
```

You can apply a forEach operation on a stream using the forEach(Consumer<? super T> action) method of the Stream interface. The method returns void. It is a terminal operation. The following snippet of code prints the first five odd natural numbers on the standard output:

```
Stream.iterate(1L, n -> n + 2)
      .limit(5)
      .forEach(System.out::println);
```

```
1
3
5
7
9
```

Let's take a realistic example of creating an infinite stream of prime numbers. Listing 13-3 contains a utility class called PrimeUtil. The class contains two utility methods. The next() instance method returns the next prime number after the last found prime number. The next(long after) static method returns the prime number after the specified number. The isPrime() static method checks if a number is a prime number.

Listing 13-3. A Utility Class to Work with Prime Numbers

```
// PrimeUtil.java
package com.jdojo.streams;

public class PrimeUtil {
        // Used for a stateful PrimeUtil
        private long lastPrime = 0L;

        // Computes the prime number after the last generated prime
        public long next() {
                lastPrime = next(lastPrime);
                return lastPrime;
        }

        // Computes the prime number after the specified number
        public static long next(long after) {
                long counter = after;

                // Keep looping until you find the next prime number
                while (!isPrime(++counter));

                return counter;
        }
```

```java
        // Checks if the specified nubmer is a prime number
        public static boolean isPrime(long number) {
                // <= 1 is not a prime number
                if (number <= 1) {
                        return false;
                }

                // 2 is a prime number
                if (number == 2) {
                        return true;
                }

                // Even numbers > 2 are not prime numbers
                if (number % 2 == 0) {
                        return false;
                }

                long maxDivisor = (long) Math.sqrt(number);
                for (int counter = 3; counter <= maxDivisor; counter += 2) {
                        if (number % counter == 0) {
                                return false;
                        }
                }

                return true;
        }
}
```

The following snippet of code creates an infinite stream of prime numbers and prints the first five prime numbers on the standard output:

```java
Stream.iterate(2L, PrimeUtil::next)
      .limit(5)
      .forEach(System.out::println);
```

```
2
3
5
7
11
```

There is another way to get the first five prime numbers. You can generate an infinite stream of natural numbers, apply a filter operation to pick only the prime numbers, and limit the filtered stream to five. The following snippet of code shows this logic using the isPrime() method of the PrimeUtil class:

```java
// Print the first 5 prime numbers
Stream.iterate(2L, n -> n + 1)
      .filter(PrimeUtil::isPrime)
      .limit(5)
      .forEach(System.out::println);
```

```
2
3
5
7
11
```

Sometimes you may want to discard some elements of a stream. This is accomplished using the skip operation. The skip(long n) method of the Stream interface discards (or skips) the first n elements of the stream. This is an intermediate operation. The following snippet of code uses this operation to print five prime numbers, skipping the first 100 prime numbers:

```
Stream.iterate(2L, PrimeUtil::next)
      .skip(100)
      .limit(5)
      .forEach(System.out::println);
```

```
547
557
563
569
571
```

Using everything you have learned about streams, can you write a stream pipeline to print five prime numbers that are greater than 3000? This is left as an exercise for the readers.

Using the generate() Method

The generate(Supplier<T> s) method uses the specified Supplier to generate an infinite sequential unordered stream. The following snippet of code prints five random numbers greater than or equal to 0.0 and less than 1.0 using the random() static method of the Math class. You may get a different output.

```
Stream.generate(Math::random)
      .limit(5)
      .forEach(System.out::println);
```

```
0.05958352209327644
0.8122226657626394
0.5073323815997652
0.9327951597282766
0.4314430923877808
```

If you want to use the generate() method to generate an infinite stream in which the next element is generated based on the value of the previous element, you will need to use a Supplier that stores the last generated element. Note that a PrimeUtil object can act as a Supplier whose next() instance method remembers the last generated prime number. The following snippet of code prints five prime numbers after skipping the first 100:

```
Stream.generate(new PrimeUtil()::next)
      .skip(100)
      .limit(5)
      .forEach(System.out::println);
```

```
547
557
563
569
571
```

Java 8 has added many methods to the Random class in the java.util package to work with streams. Methods like ints(), longs(), and doubles() return infinite IntStream, LongStream, and DoubleStream, respectively, which contain random numbers of the int, long, and double types. The following snippet of code prints five random int values from an IntStream returned from the ints() method of the Random class:

```
// Print five random integers
new Random().ints()
            .limit(5)
            .forEach(System.out::println);
```

```
-1147567659
285663603
-412283607
412487893
-22795557
```

You may get a different output every time you run the code. You can use the nextInt() method of the Random class as the Supplier in the generate() method to achieve the same.

```
// Print five random integers
Stream.generate(new Random()::nextInt)
      .limit(5)
      .forEach(System.out::println);
```

If you want to work with only primitive values, you can use the generate() method of the primitive type stream interfaces. For example, the following snippet of code prints five random integers using the generate() static method of the IntStream interface:

```
IntStream.generate(new Random()::nextInt)
         .limit(5)
         .forEach(System.out::println);
```

How would you generate an infinite stream of a repeating value? For example, how would you generate an infinite stream of zeroes? The following snippet of code shows you how to do this:

```
IntStream zeroes = IntStream.generate(() -> 0);
```

Streams from Arrays

The Arrays class in the java.util package contains an overloaded stream() static method to create sequential streams from arrays. You can use it to create an IntStream from an int array, a LongStream from a long array, a DoubleStream from a double array, and a Stream<T> from an array of the reference type T. The following snippet of code creates an IntStream and a Stream<String> from an int array and a String array:

```
// Creates a stream from an int array with elements 1, 2, and 3
IntStream numbers = Arrays.stream(new int[]{1, 2, 3});

// Creates a stream from a String array with elements "Ken", and "Jeff"
Stream<String> names = Arrays.stream(new String[] {"Ken", "Jeff"});
```

■ **Tip** You can create a stream from a reference type array using two methods: Arrays.stream(T[] t) and Stream.of(T...t) method. Providing two methods in the library to accomplish the same thing is intentional.

Streams from Collections

The Collection interface contains the stream() and parallelStream() methods that create sequential and parallel streams from a Collection, respectively. The following snippet of code creates streams from a set of strings:

```
import java.util.HashSet;
import java.util.Set;
import java.util.stream.Stream;
...
// Create and populate a set of strings
Set<String> names = new HashSet<>();
names.add("Ken");
names.add("jeff");

// Create a sequential stream from the set
Stream<String> sequentialStream = names.stream();

// Create a parallel stream from the set
Stream<String> parallelStream = names.parallelStream();
```

Streams from Files

Java 8 has added many methods to the classes in the java.io and java.nio.file packages to support I/O operations using streams. For example,

- You can read text from a file as a stream of strings in which each element represents one line of text from the file.

- You can obtain a stream of JarEntry from a JarFile.

615

You can obtain the list of entries in a directory as a stream of Path.

- You can obtain a stream of Path that is a result of a file search in a specified directory.

- You can obtain a stream of Path that contains the file tree of a specified directory.

I will show some examples of using streams with file I/O in this section. Please refer to the API documentation for the java.nio.file.Files, java.io.BufferedReader, and java.util.jar.JarFile classes for more details on the stream related methods.

The BufferedReader and Files classes contain a lines() method that reads a file lazily and returns the contents as a stream of strings. Each element in the stream represents one line of text from the file. The file needs to be closed when you are done with the stream. Calling the close() method on the stream will close the underlying file. Alternatively, you can create the stream in a try-with-resources statement so the underlying file is closed automatically.

The program in Listing 13-4 shows how to read contents of a file using a stream. It also walks the entire file tree for the current working directory and prints the entries in the directory. The program assumes that you have the luci1.txt file, which is supplied with the source code, in the current working directory. If the file does not exist, an error message with the absolute path of the expected file is printed. You may get a different output when you run the program.

Listing 13-4. Performing File I/O Using Streams

```java
// IOStream.java
package com.jdojo.streams;

import java.io.IOException;
import java.nio.file.Files;
import java.nio.file.Path;
import java.nio.file.Paths;
import java.util.stream.Stream;

public class IOStream {
    public static void main(String[] args) {
        // Read the contents of teh file luci1.txt
        readFileContents("luci1.txt");

        // Print the file tree for the current working directory
        listFileTree();
    }

    public static void readFileContents(String filePath) {
        Path path = Paths.get(filePath);
        if (!Files.exists(path)) {
            System.out.println("The file " +
                    path.toAbsolutePath() + " does not exist.");
            return;
        }

        try(Stream<String> lines = Files.lines(path)) {
            // Read and print all lines
            lines.forEach(System.out::println);
        }
```

```
                catch (IOException e) {
                        e.printStackTrace();
                }
        }

        public static void listFileTree()  {
                Path dir = Paths.get("");
                System.out.printf("%nThe file tree for %s%n", dir.toAbsolutePath());

                try(Stream<Path> fileTree = Files.walk(dir)) {
                        fileTree.forEach(System.out::println);
                }
                catch (IOException e) {
                        e.printStackTrace();
                }
        }
}
```

```
STRANGE fits of passion have I known:
And I will dare to tell,
But in the lover's ear alone,
What once to me befell.

The file tree for C:\book\javabook
build
build\built-jar.properties
...
```

Streams from Other Sources

Java 8 has added methods in many other classes to return the contents they represent in a stream. Two such methods that you may use frequently are explained next.

The chars() method in the CharSequence interface returns an IntStream whose elements are int values representing the characters of the CharSequence. You can use the chars() method on a String, a StringBuilder, and a StringBuffer to obtain a stream of characters of their contents as these classes implement the CharSequence interface.

- The splitAsStream(CharSequence input) method of the java.util.regex.Pattern class returns a stream of String whose elements match the pattern.

Let's look at an example in both categories. The following snippet of code creates a stream of characters from a string, filters out all digits and whitespaces, and prints the remaining characters:

```
String str = "5 apples and 25 oranges";
str.chars()
   .filter(n -> !Character.isDigit((char)n) && !Character.isWhitespace((char)n))
   .forEach(n -> System.out.print((char)n));
```

```
applesandoranges
```

The following snippet of code obtains a stream of strings by splitting a string using a regular expression (","). The matched strings are printed on the standard output.

```
String str = "Ken,Jeff,Lee";
Pattern.compile(",")
       .splitAsStream(str)
       .forEach(System.out::println);
```

```
Ken
Jeff
Lee
```

Representing an Optional Value

In Java, null is used to represent "nothing" or an "empty" result. Most often, a method returns null if it does not have a result to return. This has been a source of frequent NullPointerException in Java programs. Consider printing the year of birth of a person, like so:

```
Person ken = new Person(1, "Ken", Person.Gender.MALE, null, 6000.0);
int year = ken.getDob().getYear(); // Throws a NullPointerException
System.out.println("Ken was born in the year " + year);
```

The code throws a NullPointerException at runtime. The problem is in the return value of the ken.getDob() method that returns null. Calling the getYear() method on a null reference results in the NullPointerException. So, what is the solution? In fact, there is no real solution to this. Java 8 has introduced an Optional<T> class in the java.util package to deal with NullPointerException gracefully. Methods that may return nothing should return an Optional instead of null.

An Optional is a wrapper for a non-null value that may or may not contain a non-null value. Its isPresent() method returns true if it contains a non-null value, false otherwise. Its get() method returns the non-null value if it contains a non-null value, and throws a NoSuchElementException otherwise. This implies that when a method returns an Optional, you must, as a practice, check if it contains a non-null value before asking it for the value. If you use the get() method before making sure it contains a non-null value, you may get a NoSuchElementException instead of getting a NullPointerException. This is why I said in the previous paragraph that there is no real solution to the NullPointerException. However, returning an Optional is certainly a better way to deal with nulls as developers will get used to using the Optional objects in the way they are designed to be used.

How do you create an Optional<T> object? The Optional<T> class provides three static factory methods to create its objects.

- <T> Optional<T> empty(): Returns an empty Optional. That is, the Optional<T> returned from this method does not contain a non-null value.

- <T> Optional<T> of(T value): Returns an Optional containing the specified value as the non-null value. If the specified value is null, it throws a NullPointerException.

- <T> Optional<T> ofNullable(T value): Returns an Optional containing the specified value if the value is non-null. If the specified value is null, it returns an empty Optional.

The following snippet of code shows how to create Optional objects:

```
// Create an empty Optional
Optional<String> empty = Optional.empty();
```

```
// Create an Optional for the string "Hello"
Optional<String> str = Optional.of("Hello");

// Create an Optional with a String that may be null
String nullableString = ""; // get a string that may be null...
Optional<String> str2 = Optional.of(nullableString);
```

The following snippet of code prints the value in an Optional if it contains a non-null value:

```
// Create an Optional for the string "Hello"
Optional<String> str = Optional.of("Hello");

// Print the value in Optional
if (str.isPresent()) {
        String value = str.get();
        System.out.println("Optional contains " + value);
}
else {
        System.out.println("Optional is empty.");
}
```

```
Optional contains Hello
```

You can use the ifPresent(Consumer<? super T> action) method of the Optional class to take an action on the value contained in the Optional. If the Optional is empty, this method does not do anything. You can rewrite the previous code to print the value in an Optional as follows:

```
// Create an Optional for the string "Hello"
Optional<String> str = Optional.of("Hello");

// Print the value in the Optional, if present
str.ifPresent(value -> System.out.println("Optional contains " + value));
```

```
Optional contains Hello
```

Note that if the Optional were empty, the code would not print anything.
The following are four methods to get the value of an Optional:

- T get(): Returns the value contained in the Optional. If the Optional is empty, it throws a NoSuchElementException.

- T orElse(T defaultValue): Returns the value contained in the Optional. If the Optional is empty, it returns the specified defaultValue.

- T orElseGet(Supplier<? extends T> defaultSupplier): Returns the value contained in the Optional. If the Optional is empty, it returns the value returned from the specified defaultSupplier.

- <X extends Throwable> T orElseThrow(Supplier<? extends X> exceptionSupplier) throws X extends Throwable: Returns the value contained in the Optional. If the Optional is empty, it throws the exception returned from the specified exceptionSupplier.

619

The Optional<T> class describes a non-null reference type value or its absence. The java.util package contains three more classes named OptionalInt, OptionalLong, and OptionalDouble to deal with optional primitive values. They contain similarly named methods that apply to primitive data types, except for getting their values. They do not contain a get() method. To return their values, the OptionalInt class contains a getAsInt(), the OptionalLong class contains a getAsLong(), and the OptionalDouble class contains a getAsDouble() method. Like the get() method of the Optional class, the getters for primitive optional classes also throw a NoSuchElementException when they are empty. Unlike the Optional class, they do not contain an ofNullable() factory method because primitive values cannot be null. The following snippet of code shows how to use the OptionalInt class:

```
// Create an empty OptionalInt
OptionalInt empty = OptionalInt.empty();

// Use an OptionaInt to store 287
OptionalInt number = OptionalInt.of(287);

if(number.isPresent()){
        int value = number.getAsInt();
        System.out.println("Number is " + value);
}
else {
        System.out.println("Number is absent.");
}
```

```
Number is 287
```

Several methods in the Streams API return an instance of the Optional, OptionalInt, OptionalLong, and OptionalDouble when they do not have anything to return. For example, all types of streams let you compute the maximum element in the stream. If the stream is empty, there is no maximum element. Note that in a stream pipeline, you may start with a non-empty stream and end up with an empty stream because of filtering or other operations such as limit, skip, etc. For this reason, the max() method in all stream classes returns an optional object. The program in Listing 13-5 shows how to get the maximum integer from IntStream.

Listing 13-5. Working with Optional Values

```
// OptionalTest.java
package com.jdojo.streams;

import java.util.Comparator;
import java.util.Optional;
import java.util.OptionalInt;
import java.util.stream.IntStream;
import java.util.stream.Stream;

public class OptionalTest {
        public static void main(String[] args) {
                // Get the maximum of odd integers from the stream
                OptionalInt maxOdd = IntStream.of(10, 20, 30)
                                                .filter(n -> n % 2 == 1)
                                                .max();
```

```
            if (maxOdd.isPresent()) {
                    int value = maxOdd.getAsInt();
                    System.out.println("Maximum odd integer is " + value);
            }
            else {
                    System.out.println("Stream is empty.");
            }

            // Get the maximum of odd integers from the stream
            OptionalInt numbers = IntStream.of(1, 10, 37, 20, 31)
                                        .filter(n -> n % 2 == 1)
                                        .max();
            if (numbers.isPresent()) {
                    int value = numbers.getAsInt();
                    System.out.println("Maximum odd integer is " + value);
            }
            else {
                    System.out.println("Stream is empty.");
            }

            // Get the longest name
            Optional<String> name = Stream.of("Ken", "Ellen", "Li")
                                        .max(Comparator.comparingInt(String::length));
            if (name.isPresent()) {
                    String longestName = name.get();
                    System.out.println("Longest name is " + longestName);
            }
            else {
                    System.out.println("Stream is empty.");
            }
        }
}
```

```
Stream is empty.
Maximum odd integer is 37
Longest name is Ellen
```

Applying Operations on Streams

Table 13-1 lists some of the commonly used stream operations, their types, and descriptions. You have seen some of these operations in previous sections. Subsequent sections cover them in detail.

Table 13-1. *List of Commonly Used Stream Operations Supported by the Streams API*

Operation	Type	Description
Distinct	Intermediate	Returns a stream consisting of the distinct elements of this stream. Elements e1 and e2 are considered equal if e1.equals(e2) returns true.
filter	Intermediate	Returns a stream consisting of the elements of this stream that match the specified predicate.
flatMap	Intermediate	Returns a stream consisting of the results of applying the specified function to the elements of this stream. The function produces a stream for each input element and the output streams are flattened. Performs one-to-many mapping.
limit	Intermediate	Returns a stream consisting of the elements of this stream, truncated to be no longer than the specified size.
map	Intermediate	Returns a stream consisting of the results of applying the specified function to the elements of this stream. Performs one-to-one mapping.
peek	Intermediate	Returns a stream whose elements consist of this stream. It applies the specified action as it consumes elements of this stream. It is mainly used for debugging purposes.
skip	Intermediate	Discards the first n elements of the stream and returns the remaining stream. If this stream contains fewer than n elements, an empty stream is returned.
sorted	Intermediate	Returns a stream consisting of the elements of this stream, sorted according to natural order or the specified Comparator. For an ordered stream, the sort is stable.
allMatch	Terminal	Returns true if all elements in the stream match the specified predicate, false otherwise. Returns true if the stream is empty.
anyMatch	Terminal	Returns true if any element in the stream matches the specified predicate, false otherwise. Returns false if the stream is empty.
findAny	Terminal	Returns any element from the stream. An empty Optional object is for an empty stream.
findFirst	Terminal	Returns the first element of the stream. For an ordered stream, it returns the first element in the encounter order; for an unordered stream, it returns any element.
noneMatch	Terminal	Returns true if no elements in the stream match the specified predicate, false otherwise. Returns true if the stream is empty.
forEach	Terminal	Applies an action for each element in the stream.
reduce	Terminal	Applies a reduction operation to computes a single value from the stream.

Debugging a Stream Pipeline

You apply a sequence of operations on a stream. Each operation transforms the elements of the input stream either producing another stream or a result. Sometimes you may need to look at the elements of the streams as they pass through the pipeline. You can do so by using the peek(Consumer<? super T> action) method of the Stream<T> interface that is meant only for debugging purposes. It produces a stream after applying an action on each input element. The IntStream, LongStream, and DoubleStream also contain a peek() method that takes a IntConsumer, a LongConsumer, and a DoubleConsumer as an argument. Typically, you use a lambda expression with the peek() method to log messages describing elements being processed.

The following snippet of code uses the peek() method at three places to print the elements passing through the stream pipeline:

```
int sum = Stream.of(1, 2, 3, 4, 5)
               .peek(e -> System.out.println("Taking integer: " + e))
               .filter(n -> n % 2 == 1)
               .peek(e -> System.out.println("Filtered integer: " + e))
               .map(n -> n * n)
               .peek(e -> System.out.println("Mapped integer: " + e))
               .reduce(0, Integer::sum);

System.out.println("Sum = " + sum);
```

```
Taking integer: 1
Filtered integer: 1
Mapped integer: 1
Taking integer: 2
Taking integer: 3
Filtered integer: 3
Mapped integer: 9
Taking integer: 4
Taking integer: 5
Filtered integer: 5
Mapped integer: 25
Sum = 35
```

Notice that the output shows the even numbers being taken from the data source, but not passing the filter operation.

Applying the ForEach Operation

The forEach operation takes an action for each element of the stream. The action may be simply printing each element of the stream on the standard output or increasing the income of every person in a stream by 10%. The Stream<T> interface contains two methods to perform the forEach operation:

- void forEach(Consumer<? super T> action)

- void forEachOrdered(Consumer<? super T> action)

IntStream, LongStream, and DoubleStream also contain the same methods, except that their parameter type is the specialized consumer types for primitives; for example, the parameter type for the forEach() method in the IntStream is IntConsumer.

Why do you have two methods to perform the forEach operation? Sometimes the order in which the action is applied for the elements in a stream is important, and sometimes it is not. The forEach() method does not guarantee the order in which the action for each element in the stream is applied. The forEachOrdered() method performs the action in the encounter order of elements defined by the stream. Use the forEachOrdered() method for a parallel stream only when necessary because it may slow down processing.

The following snippet of code prints the details of females in the person list:

```
Person.persons()
    .stream()
    .filter(Person::isFemale)
    .forEach(System.out::println);
```

```
(3, Donna, FEMALE, 1962-07-29, 8700.00)
(5, Laynie, FEMALE, 2012-12-13, 0.00)
```

The program in Listing 13-6 shows how to use the forEach() method to increase the income of all females by 10%. The output shows that only Donna got an increase because another female named Laynie had 0.0 income before.

Listing 13-6. Applying the ForEach Operation on a List of Persons

```java
// ForEachTest.java
package com.jdojo.streams;

import java.util.List;

public class ForEachTest {
    public static void main(String[] args) {
        // Get the list of persons
        List<Person> persons = Person.persons();

        // Print the list
        System.out.println("Before increasing the income: " + persons);

        // Increase the income of females by 10%
        persons.stream()
                .filter(Person::isFemale)
                .forEach(p -> p.setIncome(p.getIncome() * 1.10));

        // Print the list again
        System.out.println("After increasing the income: " + persons);
    }
}
```

```
Before increasing the income: [(1, Ken, MALE, 1970-05-04, 6000.00), (2, Jeff, MALE, 1970-07-15,
7100.00), (3, Donna, FEMALE, 1962-07-29, 8700.00), (4, Chris, MALE, 1993-12-16, 1800.00),
(5, Laynie, FEMALE, 2012-12-13, 0.00), (6, Li, MALE, 2001-05-09, 2400.00)]
After increasing the income: [(1, Ken, MALE, 1970-05-04, 6000.00), (2, Jeff, MALE, 1970-07-15,
7100.00), (3, Donna, FEMALE, 1962-07-29, 9570.00), (4, Chris, MALE, 1993-12-16, 1800.00),
(5, Laynie, FEMALE, 2012-12-13, 0.00), (6, Li, MALE, 2001-05-09, 2400.00)]
```

Applying the Map Operation

A map operation (also known as mapping) applies a function to each element of the input stream to produce another stream (also called an output stream or a mapped stream). The number of elements in the input and output streams is the same. The operation does not modify the elements of the input stream (at least it is not supposed to).

Figure 13-7 depicts the application of the map operation on a stream. It shows element e1 from the input stream being mapped to element et1 in the mapped stream, element e2 mapped to et2, etc.

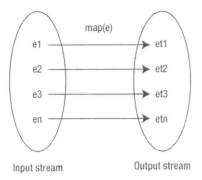

Figure 13-7. *A pictorial view of the map operation*

Mapping a stream to another stream is not limited to any specific type of elements. You can map a stream of T to a stream of type S, where T and S may be the same or different types. For example, you can map a stream of Person to a stream of int where each Person element in the input stream maps to the Person's id in the mapped stream.

You can apply the map operation on a stream using one of the following methods of the Stream<T> interface:

- `<R> Stream<R> map(Function<? super T,? extends R> mapper)`

- `DoubleStream mapToDouble(ToDoubleFunction<? super T> mapper)`

- `IntStream mapToInt(ToIntFunction<? super T> mapper)`

- `LongStream mapToLong(ToLongFunction<? super T> mapper)`

The map operation takes a function as an argument. Each element from the input stream is passed to the function. The returned value from the function is the mapped element in the mapped stream. Use the map() method to perform the mapping to reference type elements. If the mapped stream is of a primitive type, use other methods; for example, use the mapToInt() method to map a stream of a reference type to a stream of int. The IntStream, LongStream, and DoubleStream interfaces contain similar methods to facilitate mapping of one type of stream to another. The methods supporting the map operation on an IntStream are as follows:

- `IntStream map(IntUnaryOperator mapper)`

- `DoubleStream mapToDouble(IntToDoubleFunction mapper)`

- `LongStream mapToLong(IntToLongFunction mapper)`

- `<U> Stream<U> mapToObj(IntFunction<? extends U> mapper)`

The following snippet of code creates an IntStream whose elements are integers from 1 to 5, maps the elements of the stream to their squares, and prints the mapped stream on the standard output. Note that the map() method used in the code is the map() method of the IntStream interface.

```
IntStream.rangeClosed(1, 5)
        .map(n -> n * n)
        .forEach(System.out::println);
```

```
1
4
9
16
25
```

The following snippet of code maps the elements of a stream of people to their names and prints the mapped stream. Note that the map() method used in the code is the map() method of the Stream interface.

```
Person.persons()
    .stream()
    .map(Person::getName)
    .forEach(System.out::println);
```

```
Ken
Jeff
Donna
Chris
Laynie
Li
```

Flattening Streams

In the previous section, you saw the map operation that facilitates a one-to-one mapping. Each element of the input stream is mapped to an element in the output stream. The Streams API also supports one-to-many mapping through the flatMap operation that works as follows:

- It takes an input stream and produces an output stream using a mapping function.

- The mapping function takes an element from the input stream and maps the element to a stream. The type of input element and the elements in the mapped stream may be different. This step produces a stream of streams. Suppose the input stream is a Stream<T> and the mapped stream is Stream<Stream<R>> where T and R may be the same or different.

Finally, it flattens the output stream (that is, a stream of streams) to produce a stream. That is, the Stream<Stream<R>> is flattened to Stream<R>.

It takes some time to understand the flat map operation. Suppose that you have a stream of three numbers: 1, 2, and 3. You want to produce a stream that contains the numbers and the square of the numbers. You want the output stream to contain 1, 1, 2, 4, 3, and 9. The following is the first, incorrect attempt to achieve this:

```
Stream.of(1, 2, 3)
    .map(n -> Stream.of(n, n * n))
    .forEach(System.out::println);
```

```
java.util.stream.ReferencePipeline$Head@372f7a8d
java.util.stream.ReferencePipeline$Head@2f92e0f4
java.util.stream.ReferencePipeline$Head@28a418fc
```

Are you surprised by the output? You do see numbers in the output. The input stream to the map() method contains three integers: 1, 2, and 3. The map() method produces one element for each element in the input stream. In this case, the map() method produces a Stream<Integer> for each integer in the input stream. It produces three Stream<Integer>s. The first stream contains 1 and 1; the second one contains 2 and 4; the third one contains 3 and 9. The forEach() method receives the Stream<Integer> object as its argument and prints the string returned from its toString() method. You can call the forEach() on a stream, so let's nest its call to print the elements of the stream of streams, like so:

```
Stream.of(1, 2, 3)
      .map(n -> Stream.of(n, n * n))
      .forEach(e -> e.forEach(System.out::println));
```

```
1
1
2
4
3
9
```

You were able to print the numbers and their squares. But you have not achieved the goal of getting those numbers in a Stream<Integer>. They are still in the Stream<Stream<Integer>>. The solution is to use the flatMap() method instead of the map() method. The following snippet of code does this:

```
Stream.of(1, 2, 3)
      .flatMap(n -> Stream.of(n, n * n))
      .forEach(System.out::println);
```

```
1
1
2
4
3
9
```

Figure 13-8 shows the pictorial view of how the flatMap() method works in this example. If you still have doubts about the workings of the flatMap operation, you can think of its name in the reverse order. Read it as mapFlat, which means "map the elements of the input stream to streams, and then flatten the mapped streams."

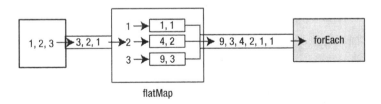

flatMap

Figure 13-8. *Flattening a stream using the flatMap() method*

Let's take another example of the flat map operation. Suppose you have a stream of strings. How will you count the number of the Es in the strings? The following snippet of code shows you how to do it:

```
long count = Stream.of("Ken", "Jeff", "Ellen")
                  .map(name -> name.chars())
                  .flatMap(intStream -> intStream.mapToObj(n -> (char)n))
                  .filter(ch -> ch == 'e' || ch == 'E')
                  .count();

System.out.println("Es count: " + count);
```

```
Es count: 4
```

The code maps the strings to IntStream. Note that the chars() method of the String class returns an IntStream, not a Stream<Character>. The output of the map() method is Stream<IntStream>. The flatMap() method maps the Stream<IntStream> to Stream<Stream<Character>> and finally, flattens it to produce a Stream<Character>. So, the output of the flatMap() method is Stream<Character>. The filter() method filters out any characters that are not an E or e. Finally, the count() method returns the number of elements in the stream. The main logic is to convert the Stream<String> to a Stream<Character>. You can achieve the same using the following code as well:

```
long count = Stream.of("Ken", "Jeff", "Ellen")
                  .flatMap(name -> IntStream.range(0, name.length())
                                           .mapToObj(name::charAt))
                  .filter(ch -> ch == 'e' || ch == 'E')
                  .count();
```

The IntStream.range() method creates an IntStream that contains the indexes of all characters in the input string. The mapToObj() method converts the IntStream into a Stream<Character> whose elements are the characters in the input string.

Applying the Filter Operation

The filter operation is applied on an input stream to produce another stream, which is known as the filtered stream. The filtered stream contains all elements of the input stream for which a predicate evaluates to true. A predicate is a function that accepts an element of the stream and returns a boolean value. Unlike a mapped stream, the filtered stream is of the same type as the input stream.

The filter operation produces a subset of the input stream. If the predicate evaluates to false for all elements of the input stream, the filtered stream is an empty stream. Figure 13-9 shows a pictorial view of applying a filter operation to a stream. The figure shows that two elements (e1 and en) from the input stream made it to the filtered stream and the other two elements (e2 and e3) were filtered out.

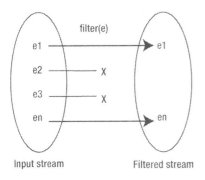

Figure 13-9. *A pictorial view of the filter operation*

You can apply a filter operation to a stream using the `filter()` method of the Stream, IntStream, LongStream, and DoubleStream interfaces. The method accepts an instance of the Predicate interface.

▨ **Tip** In a map operation, the new stream contains the same number of elements with different values from the input stream. In a filter operation, the new stream contains a different number of elements with the same values from the input stream.

The following snippet of code uses a stream of people and filters in only females. It maps the females to their names and prints them on the standard output.

```
Person.persons()
    .stream()
    .filter(Person::isFemale)
    .map(Person::getName)
    .forEach(System.out::println);
```

Donna
Laynie

The following snippet of code applies two filter operations to print the names of all males having income more than 5000.0:

```
Person.persons()
    .stream()
    .filter(Person::isMale)
    .filter(p -> p.getIncome() > 5000.0)
    .map(Person::getName)
    .forEach(System.out::println);
```

Ken
Jeff

You could have accomplished the same using the following statement that uses only one filter operation that includes both predicates for filtering into one predicate:

```
Person.persons()
     .stream()
     .filter(p -> p.isMale() && p.getIncome() > 5000.0)
     .map(Person::getName)
     .forEach(System.out::println);
```

```
Ken
Jeff
```

Applying the Reduce Operation

The reduce operation combines all elements of a stream to produce a single value by applying a combining function repeatedly. It is also called *reduction* operation or a *fold*. Computing the sum, maximum, average, count, etc. of elements of a stream of integers are examples of the reduce operation. Collecting elements of a stream in a List, Set, or Map is also an example of the reduce operation.

The reduce operation takes two parameters called a *seed* (also called an *initial value*) and an *accumulator*. The accumulator is a function. If the stream is empty, the seed is the result. Otherwise, the seed represents a partial result. The partial result and an element are passed to the accumulator, which returns another partial result. This repeats until all elements are passed to the accumulator. The last value returned from the accumulator is the result of the reduce operation. Figure 13-10 shows a pictorial view of the reduce operation.

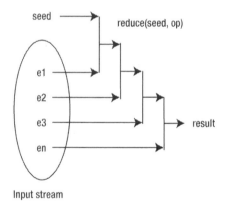

Figure 13-10. A pictorial view of applying the reduce operation

The stream-related interfaces contain two methods called reduce() and collect() to perform generic reduce operations. Methods such as sum(), max(), min(), count(), etc. are also available to perform specialized reduce operations. Note that the specialized methods are not available for all types of streams. For example, having a sum() method in the Stream<T> interface does not make sense because adding reference type elements, such as adding two people, is meaningless. So, you will find methods like sum() only in IntStream, LongStream, and DoubleStream interfaces. Counting the number of elements in a stream makes sense for all types of streams. So, the count() method is available for all types of streams. I will discuss the reduce() method in this section. I will discuss the collect() method in several subsequent sections.

Let's consider the following snippet of code that performs the reduce operation in the imperative programming style. The code computes the sum of all integers in a list.

```
// Create the list of integers
List<Integer> numbers = Arrays.asList(1, 2, 3, 4, 5);

// Declare an accumulator called sum and initialize (or seed) it to zero
int sum = 0;

// Accumulate the partial results in sum
for(int num : numbers) {
        // Accumulate the partial result in sum
        sum = sum + num;
}

// Print the result
System.out.println(sum);
```

15

The code declares a variable named sum and initializes the variable to 0. If there is no element in the list, the initial value of sum becomes the result. The for-each loop traverses the list and keeps storing the partial results in the sum variable, using it as an accumulator. When the for-each loop finishes, the sum variable contains the result. As pointed out in the beginning of this chapter, such a for-loop has no room for parallelization; the entire logic must be executed in a single thread.

Consider another example that computes the sum of incomes of persons in a list:

```
// Declare an accumulator called sum and initialize it to zero
double sum = 0.0;

for(Person person : Person.persons()) {
        // Map the Person to his income double
        double income = person.getIncome();

        // Accumulate the partial result in sum
        sum = sum + income;
}

System.out.println(sum);
```

This time, you had to perform an additional step to map the Person to his income before you could accumulate the partial results in the sum variable.

The Stream<T> interface contains a reduce() method to perform the reduce operation. The method has three overloaded versions:

- T reduce(T identity, BinaryOperator<T> accumulator)

- <U> U reduce(U identity, BiFunction<U,? super T,U> accumulator, BinaryOperator<U> combiner)

- Optional<T> reduce(BinaryOperator<T> accumulator)

The first version of the reduce() method takes an identity and an accumulator as arguments and reduces the stream to a single value of the same type. You can rewrite the example of computing the sum of integers in a list as follows:

```
List<Integer> numbers = Arrays.asList(1, 2, 3, 4, 5);
int sum = numbers.stream()
                .reduce(0, Integer::sum);
System.out.println(sum);
```

15

Let's attempt to do the same with the second example that computes the sum of the incomes.

```
double sum = Person.persons()
               .stream()
               .reduce(0.0, Double::sum);
```

The code generates the following compile-time error. Only the relevant part of the error message is shown.

```
error: no suitable method found for reduce(double,Double::sum)
                   .reduce(0.0, Double::sum);
                   ^
   method Stream.reduce(Person,BinaryOperator<Person>) is not applicable
      (argument mismatch; double cannot be converted to Person) ...
```

The stream() method in Person.persons().stream() returns a Stream<Person>, and therefore, the reduce() method is supposed to perform a reduction on Person object. However, the first argument to the method is 0.0, which implies that the method is attempting to operate on the type Double, not the type Person. This mismatch in the expected argument type Person and the actual argument type Double resulted in the error.

You wanted to compute the sum of the incomes of all people. You need to map the stream of people to a stream of their incomes using the map operation as follows:

```
double sum = Person.persons()
               .stream()
               .map(Person::getIncome)
               .reduce(0.0, Double::sum);
System.out.println(sum);
```

26000.0

Performing a map-reduce operation is typical in functional programming. The second version of the reduce method, shown again for easy reference, lets you perform a map operation, followed by a reduce operation.

- `<U> U reduce(U identity, BiFunction<U,? super T,U> accumulator,` `BinaryOperator<U> combiner)`

Note that the second argument, which is the accumulator, takes an argument whose type may be different from the type of the stream. This is used for the map operation as well as for the accumulating the partial results. The third argument is used for combining the partial results when the reduce operation is performed in parallel, which I will elaborate upon shortly. The following snippet of code prints the sum of the incomes of all people:

```
double sum = Person.persons()
        .stream()
        .reduce(0.0, (partialSum, person) -> partialSum + person.getIncome(), Double::sum);
System.out.println(sum);
```

26000.0

If you examine the code, the second argument to the reduce() method is sufficient to produce the desired result in this case. So, what is the purpose of the third argument, Double::sum, which is the combiner? In fact, the combiner was not used in the reduce() operation at all, even if you specified it. You can verify that the combiner was not used using the following code, which prints a message from the combiner:

```
double sum = Person.persons()
        .stream()
        .reduce(0.0, (partialSum, person) -> partialSum + person.getIncome(),
            (a, b) -> {
                System.out.println("Combiner called: a = " + a + "b = " + b );
                return a + b;
            });

System.out.println(sum);
```

26000.0

The output proves that the combiner was not called. Why do you need to provide the combiner when it is not used? It is used when the reduce operation is performed in parallel. In that case, each thread will accumulate the partial results using the accumulator. At the end, the combiner is used to combine the partial results from all threads to get the result. The following snippet of code shows how the sequential reduce operation works. The code prints a message at several steps along with the current thread name that is performing the operation.

```
double sum = Person.persons()
                .stream()
                .reduce(0.0,
                    (Double partialSum, Person p) -> {
                            double accumulated = partialSum + p.getIncome();
                            System.out.println(Thread.currentThread().getName() +
                            " - Accumulator: partialSum = " +
                            partialSum + ", person = " + p +
                            ", accumulated = " + accumulated);
                        return accumulated;
                    },
```

```
                    (a, b) -> {
                            double combined = a + b;
                            System.out.println(Thread.currentThread().getName() +
                            " - Combiner: a = " + a + ", b = " + b +
                            ", combined = " + combined);
                        return combined;
                    });

System.out.println(sum);
```

```
main - Accumulator: partialSum = 0.0, person = (1, Ken, MALE, 1970-05-04, 6000.00),
accumulated = 6000.0
main - Accumulator: partialSum = 6000.0, person = (2, Jeff, MALE, 1970-07-15, 7100.00),
accumulated = 13100.0
main - Accumulator: partialSum = 13100.0, person = (3, Donna, FEMALE, 1962-07-29, 8700.00),
accumulated = 21800.0
main - Accumulator: partialSum = 21800.0, person = (4, Chris, MALE, 1993-12-16, 1800.00),
accumulated = 23600.0
main - Accumulator: partialSum = 23600.0, person = (5, Laynie, FEMALE, 2012-12-13, 0.00),
accumulated = 23600.0
main - Accumulator: partialSum = 23600.0, person = (6, Li, MALE, 2001-05-09, 2400.00),
accumulated = 26000.0
26000.0
```

The output shows that the accumulator was sufficient to produce the result and the combiner was never called. Notice that there was only one thread named main that processed all people in the stream.

Let's turn the stream into a parallel stream keeping all the debugging messages. The following code uses a parallel stream to get the sum of the incomes of all people. You may get a different output containing a different message, but the sum value would be the same as 26000.0.

```
double sum = Person.persons()
                .parallelStream()
                .reduce(0.0,
                    (Double partialSum, Person p) -> {
                        double accumulated = partialSum + p.getIncome();
                        System.out.println(Thread.currentThread().getName() +
                        " - Accumulator: partialSum = " +
                        partialSum + ", person = " + p +
                        ", accumulated = " + accumulated);
                      return accumulated;
                    },
                    (a, b) -> {
                            double combined = a + b;
                            System.out.println(Thread.currentThread().getName() +
                            " - Combiner: a = " + a + ", b = " + b +
                            ", combined = " + combined);
                          return combined;
                    });
```

```
System.out.println(sum);
```

```
ForkJoinPool.commonPool-worker-4 - Accumulator: partialSum = 0.0, person = (5, Laynie, FEMALE,
2012-12-13, 0.00), accumulated = 0.0
ForkJoinPool.commonPool-worker-2 - Accumulator: partialSum = 0.0, person = (6, Li, MALE,
2001-05-09, 2400.00), accumulated = 2400.0
ForkJoinPool.commonPool-worker-1 - Accumulator: partialSum = 0.0, person = (2, Jeff, MALE,
1970-07-15, 7100.00), accumulated = 7100.0
ForkJoinPool.commonPool-worker-2 - Combiner: a = 0.0, b = 2400.0, combined = 2400.0
ForkJoinPool.commonPool-worker-5 - Accumulator: partialSum = 0.0, person = (3, Donna, FEMALE,
1962-07-29, 8700.00), accumulated = 8700.0
main - Accumulator: partialSum = 0.0, person = (4, Chris, MALE, 1993-12-16, 1800.00),
accumulated = 1800.0
ForkJoinPool.commonPool-worker-3 - Accumulator: partialSum = 0.0, person = (1, Ken, MALE,
1970-05-04, 6000.00), accumulated = 6000.0
main - Combiner: a = 1800.0, b = 2400.0, combined = 4200.0
ForkJoinPool.commonPool-worker-5 - Combiner: a = 7100.0, b = 8700.0, combined = 15800.0
ForkJoinPool.commonPool-worker-5 - Combiner: a = 6000.0, b = 15800.0, combined = 21800.0
ForkJoinPool.commonPool-worker-5 - Combiner: a = 21800.0, b = 4200.0, combined = 26000.0
26000.0
```

The output shows that six threads (five fork/join worker threads and one main thread) performed the parallel reduce operation. They all performed partial reduction using the accumulator to obtain partial results. Finally, the partial results were combined using the combiner to get the result.

Sometimes you cannot specify a default value for a reduce operation. Suppose you want to get maximum integer value from a stream of integers. If the stream is empty, you cannot default the maximum value to 0. In such a case, the result is not defined. The third version of the reduce(BinaryOperator<T> accumulator) method is used to perform such a reduction operation. The method returns an Optional<T> that wraps the result or the absence of a result. If the stream contains only one element, that element is the result. If the stream contains more than one element, the first two elements are passed to the accumulator, and subsequently, the partial result and the remaining elements are passed to the accumulator. The following snippet of code computes the maximum of integers in a stream:

```
Optional<Integer> max = Stream.of(1, 2, 3, 4, 5)
                              .reduce(Integer::max);
if (max.isPresent()) {
        System.out.println("max = " + max.get());
}
else {
        System.out.println("max is not defined.");
}
```

```
max = 5
```

The following snippet of code tries to get the maximum of integers in an empty stream:

```
Optional<Integer> max = Stream.<Integer>empty()
                              .reduce(Integer::max);
if (max.isPresent()) {
        System.out.println("max = " + max.get());
}
```

```
else {
        System.out.println("max is not defined.");
}
```

```
max is not defined.
```

The following snippet of code prints the details of the highest earner in the person's list:

```
Optional<Person> person = Person.persons()
                           .stream()
                           .reduce((p1, p2) -> p1.getIncome() > p2.getIncome()?p1:p2);
if (person.isPresent()) {
        System.out.println("Highest earner: " + person.get());
}
else {
        System.out.println("Could not get the highest earner.");
}
```

```
Highest earner: (3, Donna, FEMALE, 1962-07-29, 8700.00)
```

To compute the sum, max, min, average, etc. of a numeric stream, you do not need to use the reduce() method. You can map the non-numeric stream into one of the three numeric stream types (IntStream, LongStream, or DoubleStream) and use the specialized methods for these purposes. The following snippet of code prints the sum of the incomes of all people. Note the use of the mapToDouble() method that converts a Stream<Person> to a DoubleStream. The sum() method is called on the DoubleStream.

```
double totalIncome = Person.persons()
                        .stream()
                        .mapToDouble(Person::getIncome)
                        .sum();
System.out.println("Total Income: " + totalIncome);
```

```
Total Income : 26000.0
```

To get the minimum and maximum values of a stream, use the min() and max() methods of the specific stream. These methods in the Stream<T> interface take a Comparator as argument and return an Optional<T>. They do not take any arguments in IntStream, LongStream, and DoubleStream interfaces and return OptionalInt, OptionalLong, and OptionalDouble, respectively. The following snippet of code prints the details of the highest earner in a list of people:

```
Optional<Person> person = Person.persons()
                           .stream()
                           .max(Comparator.comparingDouble(Person::getIncome));

if (person.isPresent()) {
        System.out.println("Highest earner: " + person.get());
}
```

```
else {
        System.out.println("Could not get the highest earner.");
}
```

Highest earner: (3, Donna, FEMALE, 1962-07-29, 8700.00)

The following snippet of code prints the income of the highest income in the person list using the max() method of the DoubleStream:

```
OptionalDouble income = Person.persons()
                            .stream()
                            .mapToDouble(Person::getIncome)
                            .max();
if (income.isPresent()) {
        System.out.println("Highest income: " + income.getAsDouble());
}
else {
        System.out.println("Could not get the highest income.");
}
```

Highest income: 8700.0

How will you get the highest earner among males and the highest among females in one stream pipeline? So far, you have learned how to compute a single value using the reduce operation. In this case, you will need to group the people into two groups, males and females, and then compute the person with the highest income in each group. I will show you how to perform grouping and collect multiple values when I discuss the collect() method in the next section.

Streams support a count operation through the count() method that simply returns the number of elements in the stream as a long. The following snippet of code prints the number of elements in the stream of people:

```
long personCount = Person.persons()
                        .stream()
                        .count();
System.out.println("Person count: " + personCount);
```

Person count: 6

The count operation is a specialized reduce operation. Were you thinking of using the map() and reduce() methods to count the number of elements in a stream? The easier way is to map each element in the stream to 1 and compute the sum. This approach does not use the reduce() method. Here is how you do this:

```
long personCount = Person.persons()
                        .stream()
                        .mapToLong(p -> 1L)
                        .sum();
```

The following snippet of code uses the map() and reduce() methods to implement the count operation:

```
long personCount = Person.persons()
                          .stream()
                          .map(p -> 1L)
                          .reduce(0L, Long::sum);
```

The following snippet of code uses only the reduce() method to implement the count operation:

```
long personCount = Person.persons()
                          .stream()
                          .reduce(0L, (partialCount, person) -> partialCount + 1L, Long::sum);
```

■ **Tip** This section showed you many ways to perform the same reduction operation on a stream. Some ways may perform better than others depending on the stream type and the parallelization used. Use primitive type streams whenever possible to avoid the overhead of unboxing; use parallel streams whenever possible to take advantage of the multicores available on the machine.

Collecting Data Using Collectors

So far, you have been applying reduction on a stream to produce a single value (a primitive value or a reference value) or void. For example, you used the reduce() method of the Stream<Integer> interface to compute a long value that is the sum of its elements. There are several cases in which you want to collect the results of executing a stream pipeline into a collection such as a List, a Set, a Map, etc. Sometimes you may want to apply complex logic to summarize the stream's data. For example, you may want to group people by their gender and compute the highest earner in every gender group. This is possible using the collect() method of the Stream<T> interface. The collect() method is overloaded with two versions:

- `<R> R collect(Supplier<R> supplier, BiConsumer<R,? super T> accumulator, BiConsumer<R,R> combiner)`

- `<R,A> R collect(Collector<? super T,A,R> collector)`

The method uses a mutable reduction operation. It uses a mutable container such as a mutable Collection to compute the results from the input stream. The first version of the collect() method takes three arguments:

- A *supplier* that supplies a mutable container to store (or collect) the results.

- An *accumulator* that accumulates the results into the mutable container.

- A *combiner* that combines the partial results when the reduction operation takes place in parallel.

■ **Tip** The container to collect the data using the collect() method need not be a Collection. It can be any mutable object that can accumulate results, such as a StringBuilder.

Suppose you have a steam of people and you want to collect the names of all of the people in an ArrayList<String>. Here are the steps to accomplish this.

First, you need to have a supplier that will return an ArrayList<String> to store the names. You can use either of the following statements to create the supplier:

```
// Using a lambda expression
Supplier<ArrayList<String>> supplier = () -> new ArrayList<>();

// Using a constructor reference
Supplier<ArrayList<String>> supplier = ArrayList::new;
```

Second, you need to create an accumulator that receives two arguments. The first argument is the container returned from the supplier, which is the ArrayList<String> in this case. The second argument is the element of the stream. Your accumulator should simply add the names to the list. You can use either of the following statements to create an accumulator:

```
// Using a lambda expression
BiConsumer<ArrayList<String>, String> accumulator = (list, name) -> list.add(name);

// Using a constructor reference
BiConsumer<ArrayList<String>, String> accumulator = ArrayList::add;
```

Finally, you need a combiner that will combine the results of two ArrayList<String>s into one ArrayList<String>. Note that the combiner is used only when you collect the results using a parallel stream. In a sequential stream, the accumulator is sufficient to collect all results. Your combiner will be simple; it will add all the elements of the second list to the first list using the addAll() method. You can use either of the following statements to create a combiner:

```
// Using a lambda expression
BiConsumer<ArrayList<String>, ArrayList<String>> combiner =
        (list1, list2) -> list1.addAll(list2);

// Using a constructor reference
BiConsumer<ArrayList<String>, ArrayList<String>> combiner = ArrayList::addAll;
```

Now you are ready to use the collect() method to collect the names of all people in a list using the following snippet of code:

```
List<String> names = Person.persons()
                    .stream()
                    .map(Person::getName)
                    .collect(ArrayList::new, ArrayList::add, ArrayList::addAll);
System.out.println(names);
```

```
[Ken, Jeff, Donna, Chris, Laynie, Li]
```

You can use a similar approach to collect data in a Set and a Map. It seems to be a lot of plumbing just to collect data in a simple collection like a list. Another version of the collect() method provides a simpler solution. It takes an instance of the Collector interface as an argument and collects the data for you. The Collector interface is the java.util.stream package and it is declared as follows. Only abstract methods are shown.

```java
public interface Collector<T,A,R> {
        Supplier<A> supplier();
        BiConsumer<A,T> accumulator();
        BinaryOperator<A> combiner();
        Function<A,R> finisher();
        Set<Collector.Characteristics> characteristics();
}
```

The Collector interface takes three type parameters called T, A, and R, where T is the type of input elements, A is the type of the accumulator, and R is the type of the result. The first three methods look familiar; you just used them in the previous example. The finisher is used to transform the intermediate type A to result type R. The characteristics of a Collector describe the properties that are represented by the constants of the Collector.Characteristics enum.

The designers of the Streams API realized that rolling out your own collector is too much work. They provided a utility class called Collectors that provides out-of-box implementations for commonly used collectors. Three of the most commonly used methods of the Collectors class are toList(), toSet(), and toCollection(). The toList() method returns a Collector that collects the data in a List; the toSet() method returns a Collector that collects data in a Set; the toCollecton() takes a Supplier that returns a Collection to be used to collect data. The following snippet of code collects all names of people in a List<String>:

```java
List<String> names = Person.persons()
                        .stream()
                        .map(Person::getName)
                        .collect(Collectors.toList());
System.out.println(names);
```

```
[Ken, Jeff, Donna, Chris, Laynie, Li]
```

Notice that this time you achieved the same result in a much cleaner way.

The following snippet of code collects all names in a Set<String>. Note that a Set keeps only unique elements.

```java
Set<String> uniqueNames = Person.persons()
                        .stream()
                        .map(Person::getName)
                        .collect(Collectors.toSet());
System.out.println(uniqueNames);
```

```
[Donna, Ken, Chris, Jeff, Laynie, Li]
```

The output is not in a particular order because a Set does not impose any ordering on its elements. You can collect names in a sorted set using the toCollection() method as follows:

```java
SortedSet<String> uniqueSortedNames= Person.persons()
                                .stream()
                                .map(Person::getName)
                                .collect(Collectors.toCollection(TreeSet::new));
System.out.println(uniqueSortedNames);
```

```
[Chris, Donna, Jeff, Ken, Laynie, Li]
```

Recall that the toCollection() method takes a Supplier as an argument that is used to collect the data. In this case, you have used the constructor reference TreeSet::new as the Supplier. This has an effect of using a TreeSet, which is a sorted set, to collect the data.

You can also sort the list of names using the sorted operation. The sorted() method of the Stream interface produces another stream containing the same elements on a sorted order. The following snippet of code shows how to collect sorted names in a list:

```
List<String> sortedName = Person.persons()
                                .stream()
                                .map(Person::getName)
                                .sorted()
                                .collect(Collectors.toList());
System.out.println(sortedName);
```

```
[Chris, Donna, Jeff, Ken, Laynie, Li]
```

Note that the code applies the sorting before it collects the names. The collector notices that it is collecting an ordered stream (sorted names) and preserves the ordering during the collection process.

You will find many static methods in the Collectors class that return a Collector meant to be used as a nested collector. One of these methods is the counting() method that returns the number of input elements. Here is an example of counting the number of people in the streams:

```
long count = Person.persons()
                   .stream()
                   .collect(Collectors.counting());
System.out.println("Person count: " + count);
```

```
Person count: 6
```

You may argue that you could have achieved the same result using the count() method of the Stream interface as follows:

```
long count = Person.persons()
                   .stream()
                   .count();
System.out.println("Persons count: " + count);
```

```
Persons count: 6
```

When do you use the Collectors.counting() method instead of the Stream.count() method to count the number of elements in a stream? As mentioned before, collectors can be nested. You will see examples of nested collectors shortly. These methods in the Collectors class are meant to be used as nested collectors, not in this case just to count the number of elements in the stream. Another difference between the two is their type: the Stream.count() method represents an operation on a stream whereas the Collectors.counting() method returns a Collector. Listing 13-7 shows the complete program to collect sorted names in a list.

Listing 13-7. Collecting Results into a Collection

```java
// CollectTest.java
package com.jdojo.streams;

import java.util.List;
import java.util.stream.Collectors;

public class CollectTest {
        public static void main(String[] args) {
                List<String> sortedNames = Person.persons()
                                          .stream()
                                          .map(Person::getName)
                                          .sorted()
                                          .collect(Collectors.toList());
                System.out.println(sortedNames);
        }
}
```

```
[Chris, Donna, Jeff, Ken, Laynie, Li]
```

Collecting Summary Statistics

In a data-centric application, you need to compute the summary statistics on a group of numeric data. For example, you may want to know the maximum, minimum, sum, average, and count of the incomes of all people. The java.util package contains three classes to collect statistics:

- DoubleSummaryStatistics

- LongSummaryStatistics

- IntSummaryStatistics

These classes do not necessarily need to be used with streams. You can use them to compute the summary statistics on any group of numeric data. Using these classes is simple: create an object of the class, keep adding numeric data using the accept() method, and finally, call the getter methods such as getCount(), getSum(), getMin(), getAverage(), and getMax() to get the statistics for the group of data. Listing 13-8 shows how to compute the statistics on a number of double values.

Listing 13-8. Computing Summary Statistics on a Group of Numeric Data

```java
// SummaryStats.java
package com.jdojo.streams;

import java.util.DoubleSummaryStatistics;

public class SummaryStats {
        public static void main(String[] args) {
                DoubleSummaryStatistics stats = new DoubleSummaryStatistics();
                stats.accept(100.0);
                stats.accept(500.0);
                stats.accept(400.0);
```

```
                    // Get stats
                    long count = stats.getCount();
                    double sum = stats.getSum();
                    double min = stats.getMin();
                    double avg = stats.getAverage();
                    double max = stats.getMax();

                    System.out.printf("count=%d, sum=%.2f, min=%.2f, average=%.2f, max=%.2f%n",
                            count, sum, min, max, avg);

        }
}
```

```
count=3, sum=1000.00, min=100.00, average=500.00, max=333.33
```

The summary statistics classes were designed to be used with streams. They contain a combine() method that combines two summary statistics. Can you guess its use? Recall that you need to specify a combiner when you collect data from a stream and this method can act as a combiner for two summary statistics. The following snippet of code computes the summary statistics for incomes of all people:

```
DoubleSummaryStatistics incomeStats =
        Person.persons()
                .stream()
                .map(Person::getIncome)
                .collect(DoubleSummaryStatistics::new,
                        DoubleSummaryStatistics::accept,
                        DoubleSummaryStatistics::combine);

System.out.println(incomeStats);
```

```
DoubleSummaryStatistics{count=6, sum=26000.000000, min=0.000000, average=4333.333333, max=8700.000000}
```

The Collectors class contains methods to obtain a collector to compute the summary statistics of the specific type of numeric data. The methods are named summarizingDouble(), summarizingLong(), and summarizingInt(). They take a function to be applied on the elements of the stream and return a DoubleSummaryStatistics, a LongSummaryStatistics, and an IntSummaryStatistics, respectively. You can rewrite the code for the previous example as follows:

```
DoubleSummaryStatistics incomeStats =
        Person.persons()
                .stream()
                .collect(Collectors.summarizingDouble(Person::getIncome));

System.out.println(incomeStats);
```

```
DoubleSummaryStatistics{count=6, sum=26000.000000, min=0.000000, average=4333.333333, max=8700.000000}
```

The Collectors class contains methods such as counting(), summingXxx(), averagingXxx(), minBy(), and maxBy() that return a collector to perform a specific type of summary computation on a group of numeric data what you get in one shot using the summarizingXxx() method. Here, Xxx can be Double, Long, and Int.

Collecting Data in Maps

You can collect data from a stream into a Map. The toMap() method of the Collectors class returns a collector to collect data in a Map. The method is overloaded and it has three versions:

- toMap(Function<? super T,? extends K> keyMapper, Function<? super T,? extends U> valueMapper)

- toMap(Function<? super T,? extends K> keyMapper, Function<? super T,? extends U> valueMapper, BinaryOperator<U> mergeFunction)

- toMap(Function<? super T,? extends K> keyMapper, Function<? super T,? extends U> valueMapper, BinaryOperator<U> mergeFunction, Supplier<M> mapSupplier)

The first version takes two arguments. Both arguments are a Function. The first argument maps the stream elements to keys in the map. The second argument maps stream elements to values in the map. If duplicate keys are found, an IllegalStateException is thrown. The following snippet of code collects a person's data in a Map<long,String> whose keys are the person's ids and values are person's names:

```
Map<Long,String> idToNameMap = Person.persons()
                                      .stream()
                                      .collect(Collectors.toMap(Person::getId, Person::getName));
System.out.println(idToNameMap);
```

```
{1=Ken, 2=Jeff, 3=Donna, 4=Chris, 5=Laynie, 6=Li}
```

Suppose you want collect a person's name based on gender. Here is the first, incorrect attempt:

```
Map<Person.Gender,String> genderToNamesMap = Person.persons()
        .stream()
        .collect(Collectors.toMap(Person::getGender, Person::getName));
```

The code throws the following runtime exception. Only a partial output is shown.

```
Exception in thread "main" java.lang.IllegalStateException: Duplicate key Ken ...
```

The runtime is complaining about the duplicate keys because Person::getGender will return the gender of the person as the key and you have many males and females.

The solution is to use the second version of the toMap() method to obtain the collection. It lets you specify a merge function as a third argument. The merged function is passed the old and new values for the duplicate key. The function is supposed to merge the two values and return a new value that will be used for the key. In your case, you can concatenate the names of all males and females. The following snippet of code accomplishes this:

```
Map<Person.Gender,String> genderToNamesMap = Person.persons()
        .stream()
        .collect(Collectors.toMap(Person::getGender, Person::getName,
                (oldValue, newValue) -> String.join(", ", oldValue, newValue)));
System.out.println(genderToNamesMap);
```

```
{FEMALE=Donna, Laynie, MALE=Ken, Jeff, Chris, Li}
```

The first two versions of the `toMap()` method create the `Map` object for you. The third version lets you pass a `Supplier` to provide a `Map` object yourself. I will not cover an example of using this version of the `toMap()` method.

Armed with two examples of collecting the data in maps, can you think of the logic for collecting data in a map that summarizes the number of people by gender? Here is how you accomplish this:

```
Map<Person.Gender, Long> countByGender = Person.persons()
        .stream()
        .collect(Collectors.toMap(Person::getGender, p -> 1L,
            (oldCount, newCount) -> oldCount++));

System.out.println(countByGender);
```

```
{MALE=4, FEMALE=2}
```

The key mapper function remains the same. The value mapper function is `p -> 1L`, which means when a person belonging to a gender is encountered the first time, its value is set to 1. In case of a duplicate key, the merge function is called that simply increments the old value by 1.

The last example in this category that collects the highest earner by gender in a `Map` is shown in Listing 13-9.

Listing 13-9. Collecting the Highest Earner by Gender in a Map

```
// CollectIntoMapTest.java
package com.jdojo.streams;

import java.util.Map;
import java.util.function.Function;
import java.util.stream.Collectors;

public class CollectIntoMapTest {
    public static void main(String[] args) {
        Map<Person.Gender, Person> highestEarnerByGender =
            Person.persons()
                .stream()
                .collect(Collectors.toMap(Person::getGender, Function.identity(),
                    (oldPerson, newPerson) ->
                    newPerson.getIncome() > oldPerson.getIncome()?newPerson:oldPerson));

        System.out.println(highestEarnerByGender);
    }
}
```

```
{FEMALE=(3, Donna, FEMALE, 1962-07-29, 8700.00), MALE=(2, Jeff, MALE, 1970-07-15, 7100.00)}
```

The program stores the `Person` object as the value in the map. Note the use of `Function.identity()` as the function to map values. This method returns an identity function that simply returns the value that was passed to it. You could have used a lambda expression of `person -> person` in its place. The merge function compares the income of the person already stored as the value for a key. If the new person has more income than the existing one, it returns the new person.

Collecting data into a map is a very powerful way of summarizing data. You will see maps again when I discuss grouping and partitioning of data shortly.

▒ **Tip** The toMap() method returns a non-concurrent map that has performance overhead when streams are processed in parallel. It has a companion method called toConcurrentMap() that returns a concurrent collector that should be used when streams are processed in parallel.

Joining Strings Using Collectors

The joining() method of the Collectors class returns a collector that concatenates the elements of a stream of CharSequence and returns the result as a String. The concatenation occurs in the encounter order. The joining() method is overloaded and it has three versions:

- joining()
- joining(CharSequence delimiter)
- joining(CharSequence delimiter, CharSequence prefix, CharSequence suffix)

The version with no arguments simply concatenates all elements. The second version uses a delimiter to be used between two elements. The third version uses a delimiter, a prefix and a suffix. The prefix is added to the beginning of the result and the suffix is added to end of the result. Listing 13-10 shows how to use the joining() method.

Listing 13-10. Joining a Stream of CharSequence Using a Collector

```java
// CollectJoiningTest.java
package com.jdojo.streams;

import java.util.List;
import java.util.stream.Collectors;

public class CollectJoiningTest {
        public static void main(String[] args) {
                List<Person> persons = Person.persons();
                String names = persons.stream()
                                    .map(Person::getName)
                                    .collect(Collectors.joining());

                String delimitedNames = persons.stream()
                                        .map(Person::getName)
                                        .collect(Collectors.joining(", "));

                String prefixedNames = persons.stream()
                        .map(Person::getName)
                        .collect(Collectors.joining(", ", "Hello ", ". Goodbye."));

                System.out.println("Joined names: " + names);
                System.out.println("Joined, delimited names: " + delimitedNames);
                System.out.println(prefixedNames);
        }
}
```

```
Joined names: KenJeffDonnaChrisLaynieLi
Joined, delimited names: Ken, Jeff, Donna, Chris, Laynie, Li
Hello Ken, Jeff, Donna, Chris, Laynie, Li. Goodbye.
```

Grouping Data

Grouping data for reporting purposes is common. For example, you may want to know the average income by gender, the youngest person by gender, etc. In previous sections, you used the toMap() method of the Collectors class to get collectors that can be used to group data in maps. The groupingBy() method of the Collectors class returns a collector that groups the data before collecting them in a Map. If you have worked with SQL statements, it is similar to using a "group by" clause. The groupingBy() method is overloaded and it has three versions:

- groupingBy(Function<? super T,? extends K> classifier)

- groupingBy(Function<? super T,? extends K> classifier, Collector<? super T,A,D> downstream)

- groupingBy(Function<? super T,? extends K> classifier, Supplier<M> mapFactory, Collector<? super T,A,D> downstream)

I will discuss the first and second versions. The third version is the same as the second one, except that it lets you specify a Supplier that is used as the factory to get the Map object. In the first two versions, the collector takes care of creating the Map object for you.

■ **Tip**   The groupingBy() method returns a non-concurrent map that has performance overhead when the stream is processed in parallel. It has a companion method called groupingByConcurrent() that returns a concurrent collector that should be used in parallel stream processing for a better performance.

In the most generic version, the groupingBy() method takes two parameters:

- A *classifier* that is a function to generate the keys in the map.

- A *collector* that performs a reduction operation on the values associated with each key.

The first version of the groupingBy() method returns a collector that collects data into a Map<K, List<T>>, where K is the return type of the classifier function and T is the type of elements in the input stream. Note that the value of a grouped key in the map is a list of elements from the stream. The following snippet of code collects the list of people by gender:

```
Map<Person.Gender, List<Person>> personsByGender =
        Person.persons()
             .stream()
             .collect(Collectors.groupingBy(Person::getGender));

System.out.println(personsByGender);
```

```
{FEMALE=[(3, Donna, FEMALE, 1962-07-29, 8700.00), (5, Laynie, FEMALE, 2012-12-13, 0.00)],
MALE=[(1, Ken, MALE, 1970-05-04, 6000.00), (2, Jeff, MALE, 1970-07-15, 7100.00), (4, Chris, MALE,
1993-12-16, 1800.00), (6, Li, MALE, 2001-05-09, 2400.00)]}
```

Suppose you want to get a list of names, grouping them by gender. You need to use the second version of the groupingBy() method that lets you perform a reduction operation on the values of each key. Notice that the type of the second argument is Collector. The Collectors class contains many methods that return a Collector that you will be using as the second argument.

Let's try a simple case where you want to group people by gender and count the number of people in each group. The counting() method of the Collectors class returns a Collector to count the number of elements in a stream. The following snippet of code accomplishes this:

```
Map<Person.Gender, Long> countByGender =
        Person.persons()
                .stream()
                .collect(Collectors.groupingBy(Person::getGender, Collectors.counting()));

System.out.println(countByGender);
```

```
{MALE=4, FEMALE=2}
```

Let's get back to the example of listing a person's name by gender. You need to use the mapping() method of the Collectors class to get a collector that will map the list of people in the value of a key to their names and join them. The signature of the mapping() method is

- mapping(Function<? super T,? extends U> mapper, Collector<? super U,A,R> downstream)

Notice the type of the second argument of the mapping() method. It is another Collector. This is where dealing with grouping data gets complex. You need to nest collectors inside collectors. To simplify the grouping process, you break down the things you want to perform on the data. You have already grouped people by their gender. The value of the each key in the map was a List<Person>. Now you want to reduce the List<Person> to a String that contains a comma-separated list of all people in the list. You need to think about this operation separately to avoid confusion. You can accomplish this reduction as follows:

- Use a function to map each person to his/her name. This function could be as simple as a method reference like Person::getName. Think of the output of this step as a stream of person names in a group.

- What do you want to do with the stream of names generated in the first step? You may want to collect them in a String, a List, a Set, or some other data structure. In this case, you want to join the names of people, so you will use the collector returned from the joining() method of the Collectors class.

The following snippet of code shows how to group the names of person by gender:

```
Map<Person.Gender, String> namesByGender =
        Person.persons()
                .stream()
                .collect(Collectors.groupingBy(Person::getGender,
                    Collectors.mapping(Person::getName, Collectors.joining(", "))));

System.out.println(namesByGender);
```

```
{MALE=Ken, Jeff, Chris, Li, FEMALE=Donna, Laynie}
```

The code collects the names for a group in a comma-separated `String`. Can you think of a way to collect the names in a `List`? It is easy to accomplish this. Use the collector returned by the `toList()` method of the `Collectors` class, like so:

```
Map<Person.Gender, List<String>> namesByGender =
        Person.persons()
                .stream()
                .collect(Collectors.groupingBy(Person::getGender,
                    Collectors.mapping(Person::getName, Collectors.toList())));

System.out.println(namesByGender);
```

```
{FEMALE=[Donna, Laynie], MALE=[Ken, Jeff, Chris, Li]}
```

Groups can be nested. Let's create a report that groups people by gender. Within each gender group, it creates another group based on the month of their births and lists the names of the people born in this group. This is a very simple computation to perform. You already know how to group people by gender. All you need to do is perform another grouping on the values of the keys that is simply another collector obtained using the `groupingBy()` method again. In this case, the value for a key in the map representing the top level grouping (by gender) is a `Map`. Listing 13-11 contains the complete code to accomplish this. The arguments to the `collect()` method are cluttered. You may use static imports to import the static methods from the `Collectors` class to reduce the cluttering a bit. The program assumes that every person has a date of birth.

Listing 13-11. Using Nested Groupings

```java
// NestedGroupings.java
package com.jdojo.streams;

import java.time.Month;
import java.util.Map;
import java.util.stream.Collectors;

public class NestedGroupings {
        public static void main(String[] args) {
                Map<Person.Gender, Map<Month, String>> personsByGenderAndDobMonth
                        = Person.persons()
                                .stream()
                                .collect(Collectors.groupingBy(Person::getGender,
                                    Collectors.groupingBy(p -> p.getDob().getMonth(),
                                    Collectors.mapping(Person::getName,
                                                    Collectors.joining(", ")))));

                System.out.println(personsByGenderAndDobMonth);
        }
}
```

```
{FEMALE={DECEMBER=Laynie, JULY=Donna}, MALE={DECEMBER=Chris, JULY=Jeff, MAY=Ken, Li}}
```

Notice that the output has two top level groups based on gender: Male and Female. With each gender group, there are nested groups based on the month of the person's birth. For each month group, you have a list of those born in that month. For example, Ken and LI were born in the month of May and they are males, so they are listed in the output together.

As the final example in this section, let's summarize the income of people grouped by gender. The program in Listing 13-12 computes the summary statistics of income by gender. I have used static imports to use the method names from the Collectors class to keep the code a bit cleaner. Looking at the output, you can tell the average income of females is 25 dollars more than that of males. You can keep nesting groups inside another group. There is no limit on levels of nesting for groups.

Listing 13-12. Summary Statistics of Income Grouped by Gender

```java
// IncomeStatsByGender.java
package com.jdojo.streams;

import java.util.DoubleSummaryStatistics;
import java.util.Map;
import static java.util.stream.Collectors.groupingBy;
import static java.util.stream.Collectors.summarizingDouble;

public class IncomeStatsByGender {
        public static void main(String[] args) {
                Map<Person.Gender, DoubleSummaryStatistics> incomeStatsByGender =
                        Person.persons()
                                .stream()
                                .collect(groupingBy(Person::getGender,
                                                    summarizingDouble(Person::getIncome)));

                System.out.println(incomeStatsByGender);
        }
}
```

```
{MALE=DoubleSummaryStatistics{count=4, sum=17300.000000, min=1800.000000, average=4325.000000,
max=7100.000000}, FEMALE=DoubleSummaryStatistics{count=2, sum=8700.000000, min=0.000000,
average=4350.000000, max=8700.000000}}
```

Partitioning Data

Partitioning data is a special case of grouping data. Grouping data is based on the keys returned from a function. There are as many groups as the number of distinct keys returned from the function. Partitioning groups data into two groups: for one group a condition is true; for the other, the same condition is false. The partitioning condition is specified using a Predicate. By now, you might have guessed the name of the method in the Collectors class that returns a collector to perform the partitioning. The method is partitioningBy(). It is overloaded and it has two versions:

- partitioningBy(Predicate<? super T> predicate)

- partitioningBy(Predicate<? super T> predicate, Collector<?
  super T,A,D> downstream)

Like the groupingBy() method, the partitioningBy() method also collects data in a Map whose keys are always of the type Boolean. Note that the Map returned from the collector always contains two entries: one with the key value as true and another with the key value as false.

The first version of the partitionedBy() method returns a collector that performs the partitioning based on the specified predicate. The values for a key are stored in a List. If the predicate evaluates to true for an element, the element is added to the list for the key with true value; otherwise, the value is added to the list of values for the key with false value. The following snippet of code partitions people based on whether the person is a male or not:

```
Map<Boolean, List<Person>> partionedByMaleGender =
        Person.persons()
                .stream()
                .collect(Collectors.partitioningBy(Person::isMale));

System.out.println(partionedByMaleGender);
```

```
{false=[(3, Donna, FEMALE, 1962-07-29, 8700.00), (5, Laynie, FEMALE, 2012-12-13, 0.00)],
true=[(1, Ken, MALE, 1970-05-04, 6000.00), (2, Jeff, MALE, 1970-07-15, 7100.00), (4, Chris, MALE,
1993-12-16, 1800.00), (6, Li, MALE, 2001-05-09, 2400.00)]}
```

The second version of the method lets you specify another collector that can perform a reduction operation on the values for each key. You have seen several examples of this kind in the previous section when you grouped data using the groupingBy() method. The following snippet of code partitions people into male and non-male, and collects their names in a comma-separated string:

```
Map<Boolean,String> partionedByMaleGender =
        Person.persons()
                .stream()
                .collect(Collectors.partitioningBy(Person::isMale,
                    Collectors.mapping(Person::getName, Collectors.joining(", "))));

System.out.println(partionedByMaleGender);
```

```
{false=Donna, Laynie, true=Ken, Jeff, Chris, Li}
```

Adapting the Collector Results

So far, you have seen collectors doing great work on their own: you specify what you want and the collector does all the work for you. There is one more type of collector that collects the data, and before returning the result to the caller, lets you modify the result in any way you want. That is, you can adapt the result of the collector to a different type. Such a collector is returned by using the collectingAndThen() method of the Collectors class. The method signature is

- collectingAndThen(Collector<T,A,R> downstream, Function<R,RR> finisher)

The first argument is a collector that collects the data. The second argument is a finisher that is a function. The finisher is passed a result. The finisher is free to modify the result, including its type. The return type of such a collector is the return type of the finisher.

One of the common uses for the finisher is to return an unmodifiable view of the collected data. Here is an example that returns an unmodifiable list of person names:

```
List<String> names = Person.persons()
                      .stream()
                      .map(Person::getName)
                      .collect(Collectors.collectingAndThen(Collectors.toList(),
                              result -> Collections.unmodifiableList(result)));

System.out.println(names);
```

```
[Ken, Jeff, Donna, Chris, Laynie, Li]
```

The collector collects the names in a mutable list and the finisher wraps the mutable list in an unmodifiable list.

Let's take another example of using the finisher. Suppose you want to print a calendar that contains the names of people by the month of their birth. You have already collected the list of names grouped by months of their birth. You may not have any person having a birthday in a specific month. However, you want to print the month's name anyway and just add "None" instead of any names. Here is the first attempt:

```
Map<Month,String> dobCalendar = Person.persons()
        .stream()
        .collect(groupingBy(p -> p.getDob().getMonth(),
                mapping(Person::getName, joining(", "))));

dobCalendar.entrySet().forEach(System.out::println);
```

```
MAY=Ken, Li
DECEMBER=Chris, Laynie
JULY=Jeff, Donna
```

This calendar has three issues:

- It is not sorted by month.

- It does not include all months.

- It is modifiable. The returned Map from the collect() method is modifiable.

You can fix all three issues by using the collector returned from the collectingAndThen() method and specifying a finisher. The finisher will add the missing months in the map, convert the map to a sorted map, and finally, wrap the map in an unmodifiable map. The collect() method returns the map returned from the finisher. Listing 13-13 contains the complete code.

Listing 13-13. Adapting the Collector Result

```
// DobCalendar.java
package com.jdojo.streams;

import java.time.Month;
import java.util.Collections;
import java.util.Map;
import java.util.TreeMap;
```

```java
import static java.util.stream.Collectors.collectingAndThen;
import static java.util.stream.Collectors.groupingBy;
import static java.util.stream.Collectors.joining;
import static java.util.stream.Collectors.mapping;

public class DobCalendar {
        public static void main(String[] args) {
                Map<Month, String> dobCalendar = Person.persons()
                        .stream().collect(collectingAndThen(
                                groupingBy(p -> p.getDob().getMonth(),
                                mapping(Person::getName, joining(", "))),
                        result -> {
                                // Add missing months
                                for (Month m : Month.values()) {

                                        result.putIfAbsent(m, "None");
                                }

                                // Return a sorted, unmodifiable map
                                return Collections.unmodifiableMap(new TreeMap<>(result));
                        }));

                dobCalendar.entrySet().forEach(System.out::println);
        }
}
```

```
JANUARY=None
FEBRUARY=None
MARCH=None
APRIL=None
MAY=Ken, Li
JUNE=None
JULY=Jeff, Donna
AUGUST=None
SEPTEMBER=None
OCTOBER=None
NOVEMBER=None
DECEMBER=Chris, Laynie
```

Finding and Matching in Streams

The Streams API supports different types of find and match operations on stream elements. For example, you can check if any elements in the stream match a predicate, if all elements match a predicate etc. The following methods in the Stream interface are used to perform find and match operations:

- boolean allMatch(Predicate<? super T> predicate)

- boolean anyMatch(Predicate<? super T> predicate)

- boolean noneMatch(Predicate<? super T> predicate)

- `Optional<T> findAny()`

- `Optional<T> findFirst()`

The primitive type streams such as `IntStream`, `LongStream`, and `DoubleStream` also contain the same methods that work with a predicate and an optional one for primitive types. For example, the `allMatch()` method in the `IntStream` takes an `IntPredicate` as an argument and the `findAny()` method returns an `OptionalInt`.

All find and match operations are terminal operations. They are also short-circuiting operations. A short-circuiting operation may not have to process the entire stream to return the result. For example, the `allMatch()` method checks if the specified predicate is true for all elements in the stream. It is sufficient for this method to return false if the predicate evaluates to false for one element. Once the predicate evaluates to false for one element, it stops further processing (short-circuits) of elements and returns the result as false. The same argument goes for all other methods. Note that the return type of the `findAny()` and `findFirst()` methods is `Optional<T>` because these methods may not have a result if the stream is empty.

The program in Listing 13-14 shows how to perform find and match operations on streams. The program uses sequential stream because the stream size is very small. Consider using a parallel stream if the match has to be performed on large streams. In that case, any thread can find a match or not find a match to end the matching operations.

Listing 13-14. Performing Find and Match Operations on Streams

```java
// FindAndMatch.java
package com.jdojo.streams;

import java.util.List;
import java.util.Optional;

public class FindAndMatch {
public static void main(String[] args) {
                // Get the list of persons
                List<Person> persons = Person.persons();

                // Check if all persons are males
                boolean allMales = persons.stream()
                                        .allMatch(Person::isMale);
                System.out.println("All males: " + allMales);

                // Check if any person was born in 1970
                boolean anyoneBornIn1970 =
                        persons.stream()
                                .anyMatch(p -> p.getDob().getYear() == 1970);
                System.out.println("Anyone born in 1970: " + anyoneBornIn1970);

                // Check if any person was born in 1955
                boolean anyoneBornIn1955 =
                        persons.stream()
                                .anyMatch(p -> p.getDob().getYear() == 1955);
                System.out.println("Anyone born in 1955: " +
                                anyoneBornIn1955);

                // Find any male
                Optional<Person> anyMale = persons.stream()
                                        .filter(Person::isMale)
                                        .findAny();
```

```
                if (anyMale.isPresent()) {
                        System.out.println("Any male: " + anyMale.get());
                }
                else {
                        System.out.println("No male found.");
                }

                // Find the first male
                Optional<Person> firstMale = persons.stream()
                                                .filter(Person::isMale)
                                                .findFirst();
                if (firstMale.isPresent()) {
                        System.out.println("First male: " + anyMale.get());
                }
                else {
                        System.out.println("No male found.");
                }
        }
}
```

```
All males: false
Anyone born in 1970: true
Anyone born in 1955: false
Any male: (1, Ken, MALE, 1970-05-04, 6000.00)
First male: (1, Ken, MALE, 1970-05-04, 6000.00)
```

Parallel Streams

Streams can be sequential or parallel. Operations on a sequential stream are processed in serial using one thread. Operations on a parallel stream are processed in parallel using multiple threads. You do not need to take additional steps to process streams because they are sequential or parallel. All you need to do is call the appropriate method that produces sequential or parallel stream. Everything else is taken care of by the Streams API. This is why I stated in the beginning of this chapter that you get parallelism in stream processing "almost" for free.

Most of the methods in the Streams API produce sequential streams by default. To produce a parallel stream from a collection such as a List or a Set, you need to call the parallelStream() method of the Collection interface. Use the parallel() method on a stream to convert a sequential stream into a parallel stream. Conversely, use the sequential() method on a stream to convert a parallel stream into a sequential stream.

The following snippet of code shows serial processing of the stream pipeline because the stream is sequential:

```
String names = Person.persons()          // The data source
                .stream()                // Produces a sequential stream
                .filter(Person::isMale)  // Processed in serial
                .map(Person::getName)    // Processed in serial
                .collect(Collectors.joining(", ")); // Processed in serial
```

The following snippet of code shows parallel processing of the stream pipeline because the stream is parallel:

```
String names = Person.persons()          // The data source
                .parallelStream()        // Produces a parallel stream
                .filter(Person::isMale)  // Processed in parallel
                .map(Person::getName)    // Processed in parallel
                .collect(Collectors.joining(", ")); // Processed in parallel
```

The following snippet of code shows processing of the stream pipeline in mixed mode because the operations in the pipeline produce serial and parallel streams:

```
String names = Person.persons()          // The data source
                .stream()                // Produces a sequential stream
                .filter(Person::isMale)  // Processed in serial
                .parallel()              // Produces a parallel stream
                .map(Person::getName)    // Processed in parallel
                .collect(Collectors.joining(", ")); // Processed in parallel
```

The operations following a serial stream are performed serially and the operations following a parallel stream are performed in parallel. You get parallelism when processing streams for free. So when do you use parallelism in stream processing? Do you get the benefits of parallelism whenever you use it? The answer is no. There are some conditions that must be met before you should use parallel streams. Sometimes using parallel streams may give you worse performance.

The Streams API uses the Fork/Join framework to process parallel streams. The Fork/Join framework uses multiple threads. It divides the stream elements into chunks, each thread processes a chunk of elements to produce partial result, and finally, the partial results are combined to give you the result. Starting up multiple threads, dividing the data into chunks, and combining partial results takes up CPU time. This overhead is justified by the overall time to finish the task. For example, a stream of six people is going to take longer to process in parallel than in serial. The overhead of setting up the threads and coordinating them for such small work is not worth it.

You have seen the use of an Iterator for traversing elements of collections. The Streams API uses a Spliterator (a splittable iterator) to traverse elements of streams. Spliterator is a generalization of Iterator. An iterator provides sequential access to data elements. A Spliterator provides sequential access and decomposition of data elements. When you create a Spliterator, it knows the chunk of data it will process. You can split a Spliterator into two: each will get its own chunk of data to process. The Spliterator is an interface in the java.util package. It is used heavily for splitting stream elements into chunks to be processed by multiple threads. As the user of the Streams API, you will never have to work directly with a Spliterator. The data source of the streams provides a Spliterator. Parallel processing of a stream is faster if the Spliterator can know the size of the streams. Streams can be based on a data source that may have a fixed size or an unknown size. Splitting the stream elements into chunks is not possible if the size of the stream cannot be determined. In such cases, even though you can use a parallel stream, you may not get the benefits of parallelism.

Another consideration in parallel processing is the ordering of elements. If elements are ordered, threads need to keep the ordering at the end of the processing. If ordering is not important for you, you can convert an ordered stream into an unordered stream using the unordered() method.

Spliterators divide the data elements into chunks. It is important that the data source for the stream does not change during stream processing; otherwise the result is not defined. For example, if your stream uses a list/set as the data source, do not add or remove elements from the list/set when stream is being processed.

Stream processing is based on functional programming that does not modify data elements during processing. It creates new data elements rather than modifying them. The same rule holds for stream processing, particularly when it is processed in parallel. The operations in a stream pipeline are specified as lambda expressions that should not modify the mutable states of the elements being processed.

Let's take an example of counting the prime numbers in a big range of natural numbers, say from 2 to 214748364. The number 214748364 is `Integer.MAX_VALUE/10`. The following snippet of code performs the counting in serial:

```
// Process the stream in serial
long count = IntStream.rangeClosed(2, Integer.MAX_VALUE/10)
                        .filter(PrimeUtil::isPrime)
                        .count();
```

The code took 758 seconds to finish. Let's try converting the stream to a parallel stream as follows:

```
// Process the stream in parallel
long count = IntStream.rangeClosed(2, Integer.MAX_VALUE/10)
                        .parallel()
                        .filter(PrimeUtil::isPrime)
                        .count();
```

This time, the code took only 181 seconds, which is roughly only 24% of the time it took when it was processed in serial. This is a significant gain. Both pieces of code were run on a machine with a processor that had eight cores. The code may take different amount of time to complete on your machine.

Summary

A stream is a sequence of data elements supporting sequential and parallel aggregate operations. Collections in Java focus on data storage and access to the data whereas streams focus on computations on data. Streams do not have storage. They get the data from a data source, which is most often a collection. However, a stream can get its data from other sources such as file I/O channel, a function, etc. A stream can also be based on a data source that is capable of generating infinite data elements.

Streams are connected through operations forming a pipeline. Streams support two types of operations: intermediate and terminal operations. An intermediate operation on a stream produces another stream that can serve as an input stream for another intermediate operation. A terminal operation produces a result in the form of a single value. A stream cannot be reused after a terminal operation is invoked on it.

Some operations on streams are called short-circuiting operations. A short-circuiting operation does not necessarily have to process all data in the stream. For example, findAny is a short-circuiting operation that finds any element in the stream for which the specified predicate is true. Once an element is found, the operation discards the remaining elements in the stream.

Streams are inherently lazy. They process data on demand. Data is not processed when intermediate operations are invoked on a stream. Invocation of a terminal operation processes the stream data.

A stream pipeline can be executed in serial or in parallel. By default, streams are serial. You can convert a serial stream into a parallel stream by calling the stream's `parallel()` method. You can convert a parallel stream into a serial stream by calling the stream's `sequential()` method.

The Streams API supports most of the operations supported in the functional programming such as filter, map, forEach, reduce, allMatch, anyMatch, findAny, findFirst, etc. Streams contain a peek() method for debugging purposes that let you take an action on every element passing through stream. The Streams API provides collectors that are used to collect data in collections such as a map, a list, a set, etc. The `Collectors` class is a utility class that provides several implementations of collectors. Mapping, grouping, and partitioning of a stream's data can be easily performed using the collect() method of streams and using a collector provided.

Parallel streams take advantage of multicore processors. They use the Fork/Join framework to process the stream's element in parallel.

Index

■ J, K

Get the eBook for only $10!

Now you can take the weightless companion with you anywhere, anytime. Your purchase of this book entitles you to 3 electronic versions for only $10.

This Apress title will prove so indispensible that you'll want to carry it with you everywhere, which is why we are offering the eBook in 3 formats for only $10 if you have already purchased the print book.

Convenient and fully searchable, the PDF version enables you to easily find and copy code—or perform examples by quickly toggling between instructions and applications. The MOBI format is ideal for your Kindle, while the ePUB can be utilized on a variety of mobile devices.

Go to www.apress.com/promo/tendollars to purchase your companion eBook.

CPSIA information can be obtained at www.ICGtesting.com
Printed in the USA
LVOW09s1228281214

420646LV00017B/465/P